Textbook of Patient Safety and Clinical Risk Management

Liam Donaldson · Walter Ricciardi
Susan Sheridan · Riccardo Tartaglia
Editors

Textbook of Patient Safety and Clinical Risk Management

 Springer

Editors
Liam Donaldson
London School of Hygiene and Tropical
Medicine
London
UK

Susan Sheridan
The Society to Improve
Diagnosis in Medicine
Evanston, IL
USA

Walter Ricciardi
Department of Hygiene
and Public Health
Catholic University of the Sacred Heart
Rome, Italy

Riccardo Tartaglia
Italian Network for Safety in Healthcare
Florence, Italy

This book is an open access publication.
ISBN 978-3-030-59405-3   ISBN 978-3-030-59403-9   (eBook)
https://doi.org/10.1007/978-3-030-59403-9

This Springer imprint is published by the registered company Springer Nature Switzerland AG
The registered company address is: Gewerbestrasse 11, 6330 Cham, Switzerland

Foreword

As a member of the 17th legislature of the Italian Parliament, I was Speaker for the Chamber of Deputies for the establishment of Law 24/2017 on care safety and professional responsibility in health matters. It is a great pleasure for me to present this publication because it is the result of the valuable work of many colleagues all over the world. Together, we have animated the cultural debate and fostered a consolidated and professional network of "clinical risk managers" aimed at improving the quality of care in health services.

With this goal in mind, I founded the "Fondazione Italia in Salute" in 2018, at a time when the sustainability of our Healthcare System seemed to be at risk for various factors, in the face of new health needs. The Foundation chose to promote this book because it is consistent with its mission: to support and strengthen the protection of the right to health and the culture of error prevention through public initiatives, medical-scientific and technical-legal research, national and international networking activities with the aim of establishing a system of recognition and validation of Clinical Practice Guidelines in Italy.

In this book, you will find interesting observations and professional experience provided not only by senior experts but also by medical post-graduates from 30 foreign countries who participated in the First International Meeting "Patient Safety for New Medical Generation" held in Florence on September 3, 2018. The dialogue between senior experts and post-graduates in medicine and nursing sciences is always useful; the surprising participation in this meeting allowed the WHO to present the point of view of the younger generations of doctors on the safety of care. It is no coincidence that "teamwork training" is the cross-cutting theme of all chapters of this book: it is important to overcome the often still too individualistic view of hospital work.

This publication therefore becomes an important educational tool, particularly for young colleagues, to broaden their knowledge of clinical risk and the importance of the human factor in healthcare. In fact, "clinical risk management" has only recently been included as a subject of study in medical degree courses; some years ago, the WHO published some important documents to guide training in care safety.

I believe that having a culture of patient safety is fundamental, and that the change in the professional behaviours becomes effective when knowledge is shared and risk awareness is instilled in all healthcare professionals. To this end, we need to start training new generations of professionals, certainly more open to change, and to promote a culture of care safety.

I would like to thank all the authors of this book because I believe that their excellent work will be very important for the future of international health. Special thanks to Liam Donaldson, Walter Ricciardi, Susan Sheridan and Riccardo Tartaglia for their willingness to produce this book. They represent all the stakeholders in the health security system: Liam, our institutions, Walter, our universities, Susan, our citizens and Riccardo, our health workers.

Enjoy your reading!

Federico Gelli
Fondazione Italia in Salute
Rome, Italy

Preface

Despite the extensive attention and public commitments towards patient safety over the last two decades, levels of avoidable harm in healthcare around the world remain unacceptably high.

By creating a book with broad scope and clear descriptions of the key concepts and thinking in patient safety, we have aimed to connect with a much wider readership than those with a professional or academic interest in the subject.

We have not limited ourselves to theoretical models or risk management methodologies. We have aimed to address safety in various medical specialties. For example there is a discussion of the causation and solutions in conditions such as infantile cerebral palsy; today in many health systems this has a high human and economic cost, some of which are preventable.

We have also dealt with how the structure, culture and leadership of healthcare organizations can determine how many patients suffer avoidable harm and how safe they and their families should feel when putting their trust in local services. Safety problems relating to non-technical skills are also discussed; this is a topic of great importance but under-represented in medical and nursing educational and training curricula.

Any assessment of the prospects for creating much safer healthcare systems and health facilities everywhere will be bound to conclude that it will be a long journey. A clear consequence of this is that it cannot be entirely achieved by the current group of senior patient safety leaders. Their successors need to be grown, mentored and inspired to take up the mantle of future leadership as well as guiding those in day-to-day clinical practice where harm is generated but where it can also be prevented.

That is why this new book has embraced the next generation of health professionals with such warmth and enthusiasm. The idea to write it came as a result of an international meeting on patient safety for young doctors held in Florence, Italy, in 2018. Such doctors came from over 40 countries. Representatives from that meeting have been involved in the chapters in Part III of the book.

The book was conceived and commissioned in a pre-pandemic time, but by the time it was coming near completion COVID-19 was the dominant feature of health and healthcare across the world. This has only served to heighten awareness of patient safety as the pandemic has swept across continents and led to seriously ill patients threatening to overwhelm acute care facilities and care homes in many countries. We have added a chapter that summarizes the safety recommendations developed by the International Society for Quality in Health Care in collaboration with the Italian Network for Safety in Healthcare.

It is encouraging also to see that World Patient Safety Day 2020 had as its theme health worker safety, which, of course, is closely intertwined with patient safety.

We are grateful for the support of the *Fondazione Italia in Salute* (Healthy Italy Foundation) to allow this text to be *open access* in order to be available to the greatest number of interested people. We hope to see it in the hands of young health professionals everywhere, thus giving it a global reach into the next generation of patient safety clinical leaders and practitioners.

We express our deep gratitude to the authors for their work. We also thank those many friends and colleagues who have made themselves available to review the chapters from a technical and linguistic point of view.

We dedicate our work on this book to the memories of all those patients and families who have suffered or died through avoidable harm in their care. It is on the foundation of a safer future for all patients, everywhere in the world, that the goal of universal health coverage should be built.

London, UK   Liam Donaldson
Rome, Italy   Walter Ricciardi
Evanston, USA   Susan Sheridan
Florence, Italy   Riccardo Tartaglia

Acknowledgements

The volume editors wish to thank the following colleagues and friends for the chapters review and for their collaboration to the book preparation:

- Sebastiano Bagnara, Psychologist, Florence, Italy
- Luigi Bertinato, Istituto Superiore di Sanità, Rome, Italy
- Gianni Biancofiore, Intensive care, University of Pisa, Italy
- Stefano Canitano, Radiology, San Camillo de Lellis Rieti, Italy
- Claudio Cricelli, Primary care, Italian Society General Medicine, Italy
- Alessandro Dell'Erba, Forensic Medicine University of Bari, Italy
- Davide Ferorelli, Forensic Medicine University of Bari, Italy
- Alessandra De Palma, Forensic Medicine, IRCS AOU, Bologna
- Enrico Desideri, Public Health, Fondazione Innovazione e Sicurezza delle Cure, Rome, Italy
- Vittorio Fineschi, Forensic Medicine, University La Sapienza, Rome, Italy
- Paola Frati, Forensic Medicine, University La Sapienza, Rome, Italy
- Georgia Libera Finstad, Psychological sciences and techniques, Rome, Italy
- Maurizio Hazan, Lawyer, Milan, Italy
- Roberto Nardi, Internal Medicine, Bologna, Italy
- Patrizia Olmi, Radiotherapist, Florence, Italy
- Maria Pia Ruggeri, Emergency Medicine, Azienda Ospedaliera San Giovanni-Addolorata-Britannico, Rome, Italy
- Anna Maria Marconi, Gynaecologist, University of Milan, Italy
- Chiara Seghieri, Statistic, School of Advanced Study Pisa, Italy
- Andrea Silenzi, General Directorate for Health Prevention, Ministry of Health, Rome

The volume editors also wish to express their thanks for the linguistic revision to:

- Roland Bauman
- Liisa Dollinger
- Lucrezia Romano

Contents

Part I

Introduction

Guidelines and Safety Practices for Improving Patient Safety

Walter Ricciardi and Fidelia Cascini

1.1 Introduction

Actions to improve patient safety have shown widely varying degrees of effectiveness. Usually hospitals are focused on the occurrence of adverse events and the level of adversity to the patient in the contexts of insurance premiums and the costs of malpractice. Furthermore, even risk management units within hospitals focus on these factors, when comparing the performance of departments or wards. However, for the improvement of patient safety in clinical practice, a different approach is required, in which the prevention of patient harm and effectiveness of clinical actions is standardized and assessed on the basis of scientific evidence.

Recommendations that have been translated into guidelines are the best possible evidence-based solutions to clinical practice issues. However, it appears that there are very few clinical guidelines focused on patient safety, particularly in the risk management sector. Furthermore, when using clinical guidelines for quality and safety improvement, practices often seem to diverge. Higher quality and safer clinical practice are consequently difficult to achieve, share, and promote.

Existing knowledge of patient safety essentially covers the nosography of threats and causes of patient harm, as opposed to possible evidence-based solutions that can (a) prevent risks, (b) address healthcare incidents, and (c) which can be compared. This means that etiology, pathogenesis, and observations of safety issues in clinical departments, and, more broadly in healthcare organizations, are often investigated while proven solutions to patient safety issues are rarely discussed. To give an appropriate analogy, it is like saying that there are many papers that have examined perioperative complications, type of surgeries, and patient characteristics. However, no research is available on how the occurrence of these complications have been managed in different settings according to organizational and human factors.

It is essential that healthcare professionals acquire proficiency in producing evidence that can be used for making improvements to patient's safety and managing the risks of adverse events. To successfully achieve this goal, the first step is for them to have a clear idea of what guidelines and practices are. Definitions of these terms will be the content of the first section of this chapter. Once these concepts have been introduced, the second section will show the current picture regarding patient safety and why a greater number of valuable clinical guidelines are needed. The third section will then consider possible solutions, lessons to apply in practice, and will

W. Ricciardi · F. Cascini (✉)
Section of Hygiene and Public Health, Università Cattolica del Sacro Cuore, Rome, Italy
e-mail: walter.ricciardi@unicatt.it;
fidelia.cascini1@unicatt.it

L. Donaldson et al. (eds.), *Textbook of Patient Safety and Clinical Risk Management*,
https://doi.org/10.1007/978-3-030-59403-9_1

explain how to prepare and update a guideline. The challenges we are facing along with the limits of the current guidelines will be considered at the end, which will assist in managing patient safety in future.

1.2 The Need to Understand Guidelines Before Improving Safety

The World Health Organization (WHO) regards guidelines as tools to help people to make decisions and particularly emphasize the concept of choosing from a range of interventions or measures. A WHO guideline is any document developed by the World Health Organization containing recommendations for clinical practice or public health policy. A recommendation tells the intended end-user of the guideline what he or she can or should do in specific situations to achieve the best health outcomes possible, individually or collectively. It offers a choice of different interventions or measures that are intended to have a positive impact on health and explains their implications for the use of resources. Recommendations help the user of the guideline make informed decisions on whether to undertake specific interventions or clinical tests, or if they should implement wider public health measures, as well as where and when to do so. Recommendations also help the user to select and prioritize across a range of potential interventions [1].

With a greater emphasis on clinical practice, the U.S. Institute of Medicine (IOM) defines guidelines as "statements that include recommendations, intended to optimize patient care, that are informed by a systematic review of evidence and an assessment of the benefits and harms of alternative care options" [2]. This definition emphasizes that the foundation of a guideline is a systematic review of the scientific evidence bearing on a clinical issue. The strength of the evidence leads the clinical decision-making process through a set of recommendations. These concern the benefits and harms of alternative care options and address how patients should be managed, everything else being equal.

The U.S. National Guideline Clearinghouse (NGC) of the Agency for Healthcare Research and Quality (AHRQ) also uses the definition of clinical practice guidelines developed by the IOM, stating that "clinical practice guidelines are statements that include recommendations intended to optimize patient care that are informed by a systematic review of evidence and an assessment of the benefits and harms of alternative care options" [3].

The British National Institute for Health and Care Excellence (NICE) stresses scientific evidence as the basis of guidelines. It states: "NICE guidelines make evidence-based recommendations on a wide range of topics, from preventing and managing specific conditions, improving health, and managing medicines in different settings, to providing social care and support to adults and children, safe staffing, and planning broader services and interventions to improve the health of communities" [4].

The Italian National Center for Clinical Excellence (CNEC) that is responsible for the National Guidelines System (SNLG) uses essentially the same definition as NICE, stressing the importance of evidence-based medicine as the foundation of recommendations in guidelines.

The recent report on healthcare quality improvement published by the European Observatory on Health Systems and Policies [5] reiterates that clinical guidelines focus on how to approach patients with defined healthcare problems, either throughout the entire care process or in specific clinical situations. As such, they can be considered as a tool to inform healthcare delivery, with a specific focus on the clinical components, in the context of medical practice as an applied science. Clinical guidelines have the potential to reduce unwarranted practice variation and enhance translation of research into practice; a well-developed guideline which is also well implemented will help improve patient outcomes by optimizing the process of care [6, 7].

From the perspective of international accreditation societies such as Joint Commission International (JCI), guidelines that help healthcare organizations to improve performance and outcomes are part of the foundation of processes aimed at reaching the goal of safe and high-quality care [8]. JCI maintains that clinical practice guidelines are truly major and effective tools in the practice of delivering evidence-based medicine to achieve more effective patient outcomes and safer care. These guidelines, which must be used in all JCI accreditation programs, can achieve their maximum potential when they are both well developed and effectively introduced into clinical practice.

All of the definitions mentioned are consistent. Guidelines are not presented as a substitute for the advice of a physician or other knowledgeable healthcare professionals or providers. They are tools describing recommended courses of intervention whose key elements are the best available scientific evidence and actions according to this evidence. The goal is the promotion of health and consequently, the quality and safety of care. However, it is also desirable for professionals to share within the scientific community the results from using clinical practice guidelines in the context of valuable, real-world experience to inform safety interventions. Professionals are expected to share their current practice to help them apply guidelines to real-life situations and also to improve guidelines in the light of that experience.

Ensuring the quality of healthcare services and making improvements to patient safety require that evidence-based recommendations from guidelines, and their application in the form of practical interventions (best practices), always function as synergetic tools. Nevertheless, there is no consensus on what constitutes practice-based evidence (which is what emerges from routine hospital activities) and what metrics can be used to ensure the quality of this evidence. Healthcare interventions that have been shown to produce desirable outcomes and that are suitable for adaptation to other settings can be called "best practices." A best practice is "*an intervention that has shown evidence of effectiveness in a particular setting and is likely to be replicable to other situations*" [9]. Moreover, a best practice is not a synonym of a good practice or, simply, of a practice: it is an already existing and selected intervention whose effectiveness has already been established. This concept is widely applicable in health care, from patient safety to public health, including the quality of care. In fact, a best practice is based on evidence from up-to-date research and it has the added value of incorporating experience acquired in real-life settings.

A best practice provides tangible solutions as the most effective process or method to achieve a specific objective, with results that are shareable. As a consequence, the practice can then become a model. Some organizations are working on creating best practice models, in particular, on selecting techniques or methodologies that have been proven to be reliable in achieving desired results through consolidated and updated experience and research. The British Medical Journal (BMJ), for example, funds a service (available at https://bestpractice.bmj.com/info/) that collects the latest evidence-based information to support professional decisions and brings together regularly updated research evidence and the knowledge of international experts. According to the BMJ, its best practice tool is "a clinical decision support tool that offers a step-by-step approach to help manage patient diagnosis, prognosis, treatment and prevention."

1.3 The Current Patient Safety Picture and the Demand for Guidelines

In most healthcare settings worldwide, patient safety data is data on the absence of patient safety. On the last patient safety day (September 17, 2019), WHO announced, "Patient safety is a serious global public health concern. It is estimated that there is a 1 in 3 million risk of dying while travelling by airplane. In comparison, the risk of patient death occurring due to a preventable medical accident, while receiving health care, is estimated to be 1 in 300" [10]. WHO's message is based on facts found in studies and statistics. These inform us that one in every 10 patients is harmed while receiving hospital care (amounting to nearly 50% of adverse events considered preventable) [11]. Further, the occurrence of adverse events due to unsafe care is one of the 10 leading causes of death and disability across the world [12]. The report of the WHO continues with the following findings [13]:

- Four out of every 10 patients are harmed in primary and outpatient (ambulatory) health care, with up to 80% of the harm considered to have been preventable.
- Patient harm may account for more than 6% of hospital bed days and more than 7 million admissions.
- The most detrimental errors are related to diagnosis, prescription, and the use of medicines.

Moreover, there are other serious consequences. The WHO report also included the following criticisms concerning the "health status" of patient safety worldwide: the costs from unsafe medication practices or medication errors [14, 15] and from delayed diagnosis [16, 17], the costs of treating the effects of patient harm, the complications from surgery that cause more than 1 million patient deaths every year [18], and the inappropriate or unskilled use of medical radiation leading to health hazards to both patients and staff [19].

Approaches to improve patient safety have already been suggested. Evidence-based care positively affects healthcare practice and patient outcomes. For example, the United States Agency for Healthcare Research and Quality (AHRQ) [20] stated that the chances of a patient receiving safer care when entering a hospital have increased; an estimated 87,000 fewer patients died from hospital-acquired conditions between 2010 and 2014 in the USA. This not only represents a major improvement in patient safety, but also resulted in estimated savings of $19.8 billion. The US Agency reminded noted that hard work to reduce undesired outcomes had been performed by everyone from front-line staff to nurses, physicians, and hospital administrators. Further, theoretical financial savings from safety improvement and patient involvement were identified by WHO [13, 21].

Additional measures to implement safety in practices should be mandatory, such as tools that are mainly evidence-based as well as the education of and outreach to providers and patients, and the widespread use of hospital-based electronic health records. Nevertheless, the practical implementation of evidence-based research to treat unsafe situations remains uncertain. One paradigm case is that of the healthcare-related infections where, although a standardized evidence-based approach to patient safety seems accessible and extremely useful in this field (e.g., hand hygiene guidelines) [22], WHO recently reported [10] that the numbers of healthcare-associated infections remain high, affecting up to 10 out of every 100 hospitalized patients, and that a large proportion were preventable [23–25]. A recent systematic review [26] also observed that 35–55% of healthcare-associated infections were preventable. This suggests that there remains much to be desired in terms of implementation of evidence-based best practices. Further, the levels of reductions in such infections attributable to the implementation of multifaceted, evidence-based interventions are in line with previous estimates [27, 28].

Even in high-income countries where a high level of adherence to current recommendations is expected, and despite the existence of evidence-based strategies, a further reduction in the occurrence of these infections of 30–50% is achievable [26]. In reality, a large discrepancy is emerging between the intention to effect change by employing standard operating procedures and the accurate implementation of such practices in daily practice [29]. Great potential exists to further decrease hospital-acquired infection rates in a variety of settings. Relevant factors in the success of such programs include the study design, baseline infection rates and type of infection [30]. Other factors such as global aging trends and comorbidity are likely to require additional efforts to reduce the risk of infections while medical innovations may also reduce this risk due to the emergence of less invasive techniques (e.g., minimally invasive surgery or noninvasive ventilation).

Suggestions for how to address safety improvement in health care can be derived from a literature review of evaluations of interventions. The negative impact of failing to improve quality and safety in health care is a public health issue [9]. Instead of simply moving onto the next new paradigm, it is worth considering what deficiencies exist in the literature and how these might be rectified [31].

1.4 Implementing the Research on Patient Safety to Improve Clinical Practice

Evidence-based medicine is the use of the best available evidence to inform decisions about the care of individual patients [32]. This means that clinical care choices undergo rigorous evaluation instead of having their effectiveness presumed on the basis of subjective experience or arguments relating to the etiopathogenesis of diseases. Despite this, it has been noticed [31] that implementation efforts typically proceed on the basis of intuition, anecdotal stories of success, or studies that exhibit little of the methodological sophistication seen in the research that established the intervention's benefit, even after multiple rigorously designed and well-conducted clinical trials have established the benefit of a particular care process.

Systematic reviews of the evidence and clinical practice guidelines that synthesize studies addressing important clinical decisions have been underestimated in clinical practice. A variety of factors have prevented clinicians from acquiring evidence in a reliable and timely fashion. Such evidence would include factors that have been the object of only limited study so far. Other elements of implementing evidence-based medicine that have been glossed over include the following: disagreement with the content of guidelines, which could quickly become out of date or have wide variations in methodological quality; the personal characteristics of providers, for example, their resistance to perceived infringements on physician autonomy; and logistical or financial barriers [33].

It has also been noted [31] that research into quality improvement (including patient safety) and the related literature differ from the other biomedical research in two major respects. First, evaluations of specific interventions often fail to meet basic standards for the conduct and reporting of research. Second, and more fundamentally, the choices of particular interventions lack compelling theories that can predict their success or be applied to specific features during their development. Methodological shortcomings in the quality improvement research literature include basic problems with the design and analysis of the interventions as well as poor reporting of the results.

In light of this, a recent review [34] highlighted that delivering improvements in the quality and safety of health care remains an international challenge. In recent years, quality improvement methods such as plan-do-study-act (PDSA) cycles have been used in an attempt to drive such improvements. This method is widely used in healthcare improvement however there are little overarching evaluations of how it is applied. PDSA cycles can be used to structure the process of change iteratively, either as a standalone method or as part of a range of quality improvement approaches, such as the Model for Improvement (MFI), Total Quality Management, Continuous QI, Lean, Six Sigma or Quality Improvement Collaboratives [35–37].

Despite the increased use of quality improvement methods, the evidence base for their effectiveness is poor and unsubstantiated [31, 38, 39]. PDSA cycles are often a central component of quality improvement initiatives; however, few formal objective evaluations of their effectiveness or application have been carried out [40]. Some PDSA approaches have been demonstrated to result in significant improvements in care and patient outcomes [41] while others have demonstrated no improvements at all [42–44]. Thus, evidence of effective quality improvement interventions remains mixed, with literature concluding that quality improvement interventions are only effective in specific settings and are used as "single-bullet" interventions that cannot deliver consistent improvements. Conversely, effective interventions need to be complex and multifaceted [45–47] and developed iteratively to adapt to the local context and respond to unforeseen obstacles and unintended effects [48, 49].

Finding effective quality improvement methods to support iterative development to test and evaluate interventions in clinical care is essential for the delivery of high-quality and high-value care in a financially constrained environment. However, in the field of quality and safety improvement, strategies for implementing evidence-based medicine require an evidence base of their own, unlike in other medical disciplines [50]. Progress in researching quality improvement requires an understanding of the factors driving provider and organizational change. Moreover, possible elements affecting the results of research when implemented in practice, such as organizational factors and human features related to both professionals and patients, have to be considered. Additionally, research into patient safety improvement and its implementation requires looking at the healthcare system as a whole, including professionals, patients, and features of facilities.

Once an intervention to improve safety has been developed, the next step should be a pilot study to confirm that it works or, in other words, a Phase I of clinical studies [51]. The pilot study should start from a study design that includes the formulation of the hypothesis, the method of sampling the population involved in the study, the choice of and correlations between dependent and independent variables, and the analysis and reporting of results. It is important to ensure that the interpretations and explanations of the efficacy and value of interventions adopted to manage specific patient safety issues are shareable.

Researchers and clinicians working on patient safety improvement should take into consideration the following: how to carry out this particular type of research; if it is correct to consider just a sample or the whole population of patients; what techniques to use in data collection and observation processes; and how to describe the data. All of these elements are essential to support the hypothesis of the study, and to give credibility to both the research methodology adopted and the conclusions of the trial. This kind of research is needed to produce informative, reliable, and evidence-based conclusions that ultimately lead to, from a wider point of view, a change of perspective. To be precise, the aim is to switch the focus from the statistics on patient injuries, damages, and claims, to data derived from clinical trials. Ultimately, the purpose of collecting this data is to propose actions and solutions to deal with the lack of safety in healthcare organizations, and medical treatments.

Empirically-derived models are needed to inform decisions to select specific implementation strategies, based on clinical features of the quality target, organizational or social context, and relevant attitudes and beliefs of providers and patients. These models thereby contribute to improvements to quality and the value of the services delivered, and so help to reduce dramatic statistics that can overshadow the vision of a safer healthcare system. It must be noted that although the iterative development of change (PDSA cycle) is the most validated model to improve quality and safety, no single quality improvement tool can absolutely be considered the best. Preferences depend on the skills of professionals and the type of setting which means choosing one method over another for an organization can be difficult.

The choice of the model is an important decision as it can involve serious risks and costly consequences for healthcare organizations. The integration and adaptation of different models to healthcare settings is generally preferable to choosing only one model. However, the problem is that no formal criteria for evaluating the application or reporting of PDSA cycles currently exist. It is only in recent years, through SQUIRE guidelines, that frameworks for publication that explicitly describe PDSA applications have been developed [52, 53]. Such frameworks are necessary to support and assess the effective application of PDSA cycles and to increase their legitimacy as a scientific method for improvement.

1.5 Working Towards Producing Guidelines That Improve Safety Practices

As documents that synthesize current evidence on how to most effectively organize and deliver health services for a given condition [54], guidelines inform healthcare decision-making and can serve as a basis for policy, planning, evaluation, and quality improvement. "Working towards producing guidelines that improve safety practices" means developing structured processes to write, update, and apply guidelines. The most important element to take into account is the methodology. Consequently, it is fundamental to have a plan that is divided into different steps and that can be summarized as a checklist. In fact, a checklist for developing guidelines should contain a comprehensive list of topics and items outlining the practical steps to consider. The checklist is intended for use by guideline developers to plan and track the process of guideline development and to help ensure that no key steps are missed. Following the steps outlined in the checklist ensures that key items are covered and increases the likelihood of the guideline achieving higher scores when evaluated with credibility assessment tools. Checklists for developing guidelines can be combined with guideline credibility assessment tools like AGREE[1] (Appraisal of Guidelines for Research and Evaluation) [55] and other tools that may reflect standards established by the Guidelines International Network[2] (GIN) [56] or Institute of Medicine (IOM).

One easy-to-use and reliable checklist is the GIN-McMaster Guideline Development Checklist, which is available on the internet (https://cebgrade.mcmaster.ca/guidecheck.html). It is divided into 18 steps as follows [57].

1. *Organization, budget, planning, and training.* These involve outlining a detailed plan describing what is feasible, how it will be achieved, and what resources will be required to produce and use the guideline. The plan should define a specific completion date and be expressed in formal, measurable terms.

2. *Priority setting.* This refers to the identification, balancing, and ranking of priorities by stakeholders. Priority setting ensures that resources and attention are devoted to those general areas where healthcare recommendations will provide the greatest benefit to the population, jurisdiction, or country, e.g., chronic obstructive pulmonary disease, diabetes, cardiovascular disease, cancer, and prevention. A priority-setting approach needs to contribute to future plans while responding to existing, potentially difficult circumstances.

3. *Guideline group membership.* This defines who is involved and in what capacity, how the members are selected, and in which steps of the development of the guidelines each of them will participate.

4. *Establishing guideline group processes.* This defines the steps to be followed, how those involved will interact, and how decisions will be made.

5. *Identifying target audience and topic selection.* This involves defining the potential users or beneficiaries of the guidelines and defining the topics to be covered in the guideline (e.g., the diagnosis of chronic obstructive pulmonary disease).

6. *Beneficiary and other stakeholder involvement.* This describes how relevant people or groups who are not necessarily members of the panel (e.g., as the beneficiaries or users) will be affected by the guidelines and involved in their development.

7. *Conflict of interest considerations.* This focuses on defining and managing the potential divergence between an individual's

---

[1]The AGREE (Appraisal of Guidelines for Research and Evaluation) Collaboration developed the most commonly used instrument to assess the quality of a guideline. The instrument comprises 23 criteria grouped in six domains (addressed by the AGREE II): scope and purpose; stakeholder involvement; rigor of development; clarity and presentation; applicability; and editorial independence.

[2]The work of the Guidelines International Network (http://www.g-i-n.net/) promotes the dissemination of guideline-related content and provides an exchange platform for guideline developers and users. Further, the GIN provides reporting guidance for guideline-based performance measurement tools.

interests and his or her professional obligations. These considerations lead to questions about whether actions or decisions are motivated by gain, such as financial, academic advancement, clinical revenue streams, or community standing. Financial, intellectual, or other relationships that may affect an individual's or organization's ability to approach a scientific question with an open mind are included.

8. *Question generation.* This focuses on defining key questions the recommendations should address using the PICO (patient/problem, intervention, comparison, outcome) framework, including the detailed population, intervention (including diagnostic tests and strategies), and outcomes that will be relevant in decision-making (e.g., in chronic obstructive pulmonary disease, should test A or treatments B, C, D, or E be used?).

9. *Considering the importance of outcomes and interventions, values, preferences, and advantages.* This includes integrating how those affected by recommendations should assess the possible consequences into the process of developing guidelines. These considerations can include: (a) patient, caregiver, and healthcare provider knowledge, attitudes, expectations, moral and ethical values, and beliefs; (b) patient goals for life and health; (c) prior experience with the intervention and the condition; (d) symptoms experienced, e.g., breathlessness, pain, dyspnea, weight loss; (e) preferences relating to and importance of desirable and undesirable outcomes; (f) perceived impact of the condition or interventions on quality of life, well-being, or satisfaction; (g) interactions between the work of implementing the intervention, the intervention itself, and patient experiences; (h) preferences for alternative courses of action; and finally, (i) preferences relating to communication content and styles, information and involvement in decision-making and care.

10. *Deciding what evidence to include and searching for evidence.* This focuses on out-
lining inclusion and exclusion criteria based on types of evidence (e.g., rigorous research or anecdotes), study designs, characteristics of the population, interventions, and comparators. It also covers deciding how the evidence will be identified and obtained, which should not be limited to evidence about values and preferences, local data and resources.

11. *Summarizing evidence and considering additional information.* This focuses on presenting evidence in a synthetic format (e.g., tables or brief narratives) to facilitate the development and understanding of recommendations. It also involves identifying and considering additional information relevant to the question under consideration.

12. *Judging quality, strength, or certainty of a body of evidence.* This consists of assessing the confidence one can place in the evidence obtained by transparently evaluating the research (individual- and group studies) and other evidence applying structured approaches. This may include, but is not limited to, evidence about baseline risk or burden of disease, the importance of outcomes and interventions, values, preferences, benefits and drawbacks, use of resources (e.g., finance), estimates of effects, and accuracy of diagnostic tests.

13. *Developing recommendations and determining their strength.* Developing recommendations involves the use of a structured analytical framework and a transparent and systematic process to integrate the factors that influence a recommendation. Determining the strength of the recommendations refers to judgments about how confident a guideline panel is that the implementation of a recommendation will exert a greater number of desirable consequences than undesirable ones.

14. *Wording of recommendations and of considerations about implementation, feasibility, and equity.* This refers to choosing syntax and formulations that facilitate the understanding and implementation of the recommendations, accounting for the views of the guideline panel.

15. *Reporting and peer review.* Reporting refers to how a guideline will be made public (e.g., print, online). Peer review refers to how the guideline document will be reviewed before its publication and how it can be assessed (e.g., for errors), both internally and externally, by stakeholders who were not members of the guideline development group.

16. *Dissemination and implementation.* This focuses on strategies to make relevant groups aware of the guidelines and to enhance their uptake (e.g., publications and tools such as mobile applications).

17. *Evaluation and use.* This refers to formal and informal strategies that allow the evaluation of (a) the guidelines as a process and product; (b) their use or uptake, or both; and (c) their impact and whether or not they will lead to improvements in patient or population health or other consequences.

18. *Updating.* This refers to how and when a guideline will require revision because of changes in the evidence or other factors that influence the recommendations.

All the above-mentioned steps are believed to optimize the development and implementation of guidelines. However, two tough questions on guidelines persist, namely [8]:

(a) Is there enough evidence to make recommendations?
(b) How should we apply recommendations to individual patients?

With respect to the evidence to make recommendations, guideline development tools have, since their inception in 2003, increasingly included the GRADE approach [58–60]. The Grading of Recommendations Assessment, Development and Evaluation (GRADE) approach was created by the eponymous working group (www.gradeworkinggroup.org), which is a collaborative project, consisting mainly of methodologists and clinicians. It provides a framework for assessing the quality (or "certainty") of the evidence supporting, inter alia, guideline recommendations and therefore their resulting strength [61]. Essentially, GRADE classifies recommendations as "strong" when a specific, recommended intervention or management strategy would be chosen, on reasonable grounds, by a majority of patients, clinicians, or policymakers in all care scenarios. In contrast, such recommendations would be classified as "weak" when there is a reasonable range of choices, reflecting the following possible factors: limited evidence quality, uncertain benefit-harm ratios, uncertainty regarding treatment effects, questionable cost-effectiveness, or variability in values and preferences [62]. Further, the GRADE evidence-to-decision framework helps guideline developers to structure their process and evaluation of available evidence [59]. Nonetheless, a trade-off between methodological rigor and pragmatism is required [63, 64].

Concerning the issue of applying recommendations to individual patients, it has been observed that practices from guidelines vary considerably and translating guidelines into practice can fail to close gaps that have been identified, both in the scope and the follow-up of interventions [65]. Education for professionals and/or patients is a good strategy to ensure the implementation of guidelines. Nonetheless, another substantial influence on the ability to implement guidelines is how their implementation has already been built into the guideline development process. The planning of implementation provides a set of concrete, actionable steps to take during the implementation phase [66, 67]. The central elements of successful implementation approaches appear in: their target-oriented dissemination, education and training, social interaction, decision support systems and routine procedures, thereby tailoring implementation strategies to settings and target groups [68]. To assist guideline developers regarding implementation, a tool with context-specific implementability features for the whole guideline process has been developed [69].

Further, clinicians must balance the risks and benefits of any guideline recommendation for an individual patient and consider that patient's preferences. If the patient does not adhere to care recommendations, health benefits will not be maximized or perhaps even realized. Clinical decisions should be based on guideline recommendations, but all decisions must be individualized according to a patient's risk-benefit ratio and incorporate patient preferences through shared decision-making. Clinician leadership in quality improvement efforts and administrative support are key drivers of quality and safety improvement through care-integrated tools and aligned incentives aimed at achieving meaningful guideline implementation.

One of the most prominent developments in the area of guideline implementation in recent years has been the increased utilization of information technologies to facilitate: (a) push mechanisms for guideline adherence, such as decision support components integrated into clinical management software, for example, alerts, reminders, or routine procedures [70]; (b) the use of guidelines at the bedside, available on, for example, mobile guideline apps; (c) the faster and potentially real-time updating of individual guideline recommendations as new evidence emerges, for example, by adding "living guidelines" [71, 72]. Observational data is necessary to describe current health provision and its quality, pinpoint potential patient groups that are adequately covered by guideline recommendations, and identify gaps and issues to be resolved by clinical research. This data is also vital for identifying late onset treatment harms and drug safety issues.

1.6 The Challenges of Improving Safety and the Current Limits of Guidelines

Guidelines are expected to be focused on broad and complex topics, on developing standards to guide healthcare organizations, on providing best practice recommendations for patient care, and on informing the clinical decision-making of health professionals. Successfully incorporating all of these factors into features of guidelines is particularly difficult in today's age of complexity and multimorbidity. This is an age which is also characterized by the desire for personalized medicine and the ambition to push the frontiers of modernization, for example, by introducing artificial intelligence into health care. Thus, beyond the methodological quality of the guideline itself, there are many relevant aspects which represent challenges or limits to take into account regarding guidelines and their applicability.

The first challenge is to improve the effectiveness of a guideline—especially regarding how it improves the safety of care—while also focusing on patient-centeredness; this principle consists of (a) properly taking into account the needs and preferences of patients and of their caregivers and (b) supporting professionals in improving their practice. These dimensions are fundamental to the delivery of care and to patient outcomes as well [73–75]. Patient-centeredness constitutes a more recent focus of the discussion around the development and use of guidelines [76]. Guidelines can facilitate patient education, engagement, and shared decision-making, thus assuring that individual patient values are balanced against the desired outcomes, which are embedded in the trials that form the basis of guideline recommendations. Different modalities of patient involvement exist in different contexts. The two most studied ones are (a) patient group representatives, who are sometimes involved in the guideline development process and (b) guideline documents, which are increasingly produced in different formats for practitioners and patients [77–81].

Another challenge is related to the speed with which medical knowledge progresses and the pace of knowledge production at the primary research level. Guideline recommendations are expected to be kept up to date but a relatively recent, comprehensive review of this issue [82], concluded that 1 in 5 recommendations is out of date 3 years after being launched and that longer updating intervals are potentially too long. Additionally, the development and updating of clinical guidelines represents a challenge because of the speed and resources required for producing and especially updating them. Approaches that can result in efficient and potentially real-time updating of guideline recommendations as new evidence emerges have been discussed, particularly in the form of living systematic reviews and living guidelines [71, 83–85].

With regard to limitations, there are different aspects to consider. Maybe the most restrictive limitation regards the evaluation of the costs of the guideline development process, compared with the effectiveness of guidelines, once they are implemented. This limitation particularly relates to the use (or under-use) of cost-effectiveness analyses as a part of the development process of clinical guidelines and their related challenges or opportunities [86]. A comprehensive cost-effectiveness analysis should cover the costs of the development and of the guideline dissemination/implementation processes, and the change in the effectiveness of health service by putting the guideline into practice. However, data on the costs of guideline development is scarce and, given the vast variability of settings and practices, likely not generalizable [87]. As has been already pointed out [88], only 27% of 200 studies on guideline implementation strategies (of which only 11 were from Europe) had some data on cost and only 4 (2%) provided data on development and implementation. Most of the relevant studies only partially accounted for the costs incurred in the process of guideline production. In some contexts, active implementation seemed to require a substantial upfront investment compared to general dissemination practices. Furthermore, the results regarding optimized processes of care and improved patient outcomes were not sufficient to render them cost-effective [89, 90].

Another relevant limitation is that the concept of a guideline-based quality indicator framework has so far been inadequately elaborated, despite the fact that performance measurement sustains the relationship between clinical guidelines and healthcare data. More and more guideline groups have developed quality indicators along with sets of recommendations [91]. Usually, these indicators are primarily intended as general performance measures. However, a closer look at measurement results can provide insights into the extent to which practice reflects guideline recommendations. In other words, the indicators inform us on the extent of guideline adherence, and consequently feed into how they are shaped. Moreover, an overview of country-specific practices [5] clearly demonstrates how divergent guideline practices can be, especially when viewed as strategies for the improvement of healthcare quality. The context-specific nature of guidelines persists, despite their adaptability to the practices of different countries. In the past, the quality of clinical guidelines was narrowly defined according to how closely recommendations were linked to scientific and clinical evidence [92]; however more recently, researchers have explicitly addressed the question of whether guidelines should be systematically pilot-tested in care delivery settings before being finalized [93].

Switching the focus to how guidelines are implemented, newer studies have shown mixed results regarding the effect of guidelines on outcomes but established a clear link between implementation modalities and patient outcomes [94–97]. Barriers to the adoption of or adherence to guidelines by clinicians have been discussed in the literature. Substantial gaps were found in the evidence on the effectiveness of implementation interventions, especially regarding clinical outcomes, cost-effectiveness, and contributory contextual issues [98]. Barriers included time constraints, limited staffing resources, clinician skepticism, clinician knowledge of guidelines, and the age of the clinician. The characteristics of guidelines, such as format, resources, and end-user involvement, were identified as facilitating factors, along with stakeholder involvement, leadership support, and organizational culture (including multidisciplinary teams and electronic guidelines systems).

Beyond challenges and limits, there is the issue of editorial independence in clinical guideline development. Implementing guideline recommendations that have been created in irregular conditions is not only ethically questionable but may also endanger quality of care, as the content may not actually reflect best available evidence. To give an example of irregular conditions, an international survey of 29 institutions involved in clinical guideline development found variability in the content and accessibility of conflict of interest policies; some institutions did not have publicly available policies and, of the policies available, several did not clearly report critical steps in obtaining, managing, and communicating disclosure of relationships of interest [99]. While financial conflicts of interest seem to have been adequately disclosed in the most rigorously developed guidelines, active management of existing conflicts of interest has lagged behind [100–103]. Beyond measures to address direct financial conflicts of interest, the management of indirect conflicts of interest is also important in guideline development. Such indirect conflicts can include issues related to academic advancement, clinical revenue streams, community standing, and engagement in academic activities that foster an attachment to a specific point of view [104]. Ensuring that guidelines are developed on the basis of robust consensus processes by a multidisciplinary panel can contribute to mitigating the effects of such conflicts [105].

Systematically developed, evidence-based clinical guidelines are in widespread use as a strategy to improve the quality of healthcare services and consequently the safety of care. However, the rigor of their development, their mode of implementation, and the evaluation of their impacts should be improved in many settings to enable their goal of achieving safer healthcare practices. One of the most important knowledge gaps in this respect is the extent to which guidelines affect patient outcomes and how this effect can be enhanced to ensure better care. For that purpose, both quantitatively measured parameters and patient experience should be taken into account. Today, technology and clinical decision support solutions are readily available to help transform research into practice and recommendations. These solutions take clinically approved best practice guidelines and match them with each patient to provide a recommended and customized care pathway for optimal outcomes. They can also be configured to meet the needs of each organization, taking into consideration local needs and practices [8].

1.7 Recommendations

1. The improvement of patient safety should be based on evidence-based recommendations included in well-developed guidelines, which should in turn be rigorously implemented in clinical practice as the best safety practice.
2. More scientific research into healthcare quality and safety improvement is needed, the results and effectiveness of which should be shared across the scientific community worldwide.
3. To face the challenges of a changing healthcare sector in today's age of multi-morbidities, tutors, researchers, caregivers, and patients should work together to address the current limits of clinical guidelines.

References

1. WHO (World Health Organization). WHO handbook for guideline development. 2nd ed. 2014. https://apps.who.int/medicinedocs/documents/s22083en/s22083en.pdf. Accessed 30 Sept 2019.
2. IOM (Institute of Medicine). Clinical practice guidelines we can trust. Washington, DC: The National Academies Press; 2011. http://data.care-statement.org/wp-content/uploads/2016/12/IOMGuidelines-2013-1.pdf. Accessed 30 Sept 2019.
3. AHRQ (Agency for Healthcare Research and Quality). NGC and NQMC inclusion criteria. 2014. https://www.ahrq.gov/gam/summaries/inclusion-criteria/index.html#ast. Accessed 30 Sept 2019.
4. NICE (National Institute for Health and Care Excellence). Developing NICE guidelines: the manual. 2014. https://www.nice.org.uk/media/default/about/what-we-do/our-programmes/developing-nice-guidelines-the-manual.pdf. Accessed 30 Sept 2019.
5. European Observatory on Health Systems and Policies. Improving healthcare quality in Europe. Characteristics, effectiveness and implementation of different strategies. Health Policy Series N° 53. 2019.
6. Qaseem A, et al. Guidelines international network: toward international standards for clinical practice guidelines. Ann Intern Med. 2012;156:525–31.
7. Grimshaw JM, et al. Knowledge translation of research findings. BMC Implement Sci. 2012;7:50.
8. JCI (Joint Commission International). Clinical practice guidelines: closing the gap between theory and practice. 2016.
9. Ng E, de Colombani P. Framework for selecting best practices in public health: a systematic literature review. J Public Health Res. 2015;4:577.
10. WHO (World Health Organization). Patient safety and risk management service delivery and safety. Patient safety fact file. 2019. https://www.who.int/features/factfiles/patient_safety/patient-safety-fact-file.pdf?ua=1. Accessed 30 Sept 2019.

11. de Vries EN, Ramrattan MA, Smorenburg SM, Gouma DJ, Boermeester MA. The incidence and nature of in-hospital adverse events: a systematic review. Qual Saf Health Care. 2008;17(3):216–23. https://doi.org/10.1136/qshc.2007.023622. https://www.ncbi.nlm.nih.gov/pubmed/18519629. Accessed 30 Sept 2019.

12. Jha AK. Presentation at the "Patient Safety—A Grand Challenge for Healthcare Professionals and Policymakers Alike" a roundtable at the grand challenges meeting of the Bill & Melinda Gates Foundation, 18 Oct 2018. https://globalhealth.harvard.edu/qualitypowerpoint. Accessed 30 Sept 2019.

13. Slawomirski L, Auraaen A, Klazinga N. The economics of patient safety in primary and ambulatory care: flying blind. Paris: OECD; 2018. https://doi.org/10.1787/baf425ad-en. Accessed 1 Oct 2019.

14. Aitken M, Gorokhovich L. Advancing the responsible use of medicines: applying levers for change. Parsippany, NJ: IMS Institute for Healthcare Informatics; 2012. http://papers.ssrn.com/sol3/papers.cfm?abstract_id=2222541. Accessed 1 Oct 2019.

15. WHO (World Health Organization). Global patient safety challenge: medication without harm. 2017. http://apps.who.int/iris/bitstream/10665/255263/1/WHO-HIS-SDS-2017.6-eng.pdf?ua=1&ua=1. Accessed 1 Oct 2019.

16. Khoo EM, Lee WK, Sararaks S, Samad AA, Liew SM, Cheong AT, et al. Medical errors in primary care clinics—a cross sectional study. BMC Fam Pract. 2012;13:127. https://doi.org/10.1186/1471-2296-13-127. Accessed 1 Oct 2019.

17. National Academies of Sciences, Engineering, and Medicine. Improving diagnosis in health care. Washington, DC: The National Academies Press; 2015. https://www.ncbi.nlm.nih.gov/books/NBK338596/. Accessed 1 Oct 2019.

18. WHO (World Health Organization). WHO guidelines for safe surgery 2009: safe surgery saves lives. 2009. http://apps.who.int/iris/bitstream/handle/10665/44185/9789241598552_eng.pdf?sequence=1. Accessed 1 Oct 2019.

19. WHO (World Health Organization). Global initiative on radiation safety in healthcare settings. Technical meeting report. 2008. http://www.who.int/ionizing_radiation/about/GI_TM_Report_2008_Dec.pdf. Accessed 1 Oct 2019.

20. AHRQ (Agency for Healthcare Research and Quality). Saving lives and saving money: hospital-acquired conditions update. Washington, DC; 2015.

21. National scorecard on rates of hospital-acquired conditions 2010 to 2015: Interim data from national efforts to make health care safer. In: Quality and patient safety [website]. Rockville, MD: Agency for Healthcare Research and Quality; 2016. https://www.ahrq.gov/professionals/qualitypatient-safety/pfp/2015-interim.html. Accessed 1 Oct 2019.

22. WHO (World Health Organization). WHO guidelines on hand hygiene in health care. 2009. https://apps.who.int/iris/bitstream/handle/10665/44102/9789241597906_eng.pdf;jsessionid=56CB1D55BF9AD7EA4DCDAC163190A671?sequence=1. Accessed 1 Oct 2019.

23. WHO (World Health Organization). Report on the burden of endemic health care-associated infection worldwide. 2011. http://apps.who.int/iris/bitstream/handle/10665/80135/9789241501507_eng.pdf?sequence=1. Accessed 1 Oct 2019.

24. Suetens C, Latour K, Kärki T, Ricchizzi E, Kinross P, Moro ML, et al. Prevalence of healthcare associated infections, estimated incidence and composite antimicrobial resistance index in acute care hospitals and long-term care facilities: results from two European point prevalence surveys, 2016 to 2017. Euro Surveill. 2018;23(46):1800516. https://www.ncbi.nlm.nih.gov/pmc/articles/PMC6247459/. Accessed 1 Oct 2019.

25. WHO (World Health Organization). Fact sheet: antimicrobial resistance. 2018. https://www.who.int/en/news-room/fact-sheets/detail/antimicrobial-resistance. Accessed 1 Oct 2019.

26. Schreiber PW, Sax H, Wolfensberger A, Clack L, Kuster SP, Swissnoso. The preventable proportion of healthcare-associated infections 2005–2016: systematic review and meta-analysis. Infect Control Hosp Epidemiol. 2018;39(11):1277–95. https://www.ncbi.nlm.nih.gov/pubmed/30234463. Accessed 1 Oct 2019.

27. Haley RW, Culver DH, White JW, et al. The efficacy of infection surveillance and control programs in preventing nosocomial infections in US hospitals. Am J Epidemiol. 1985;121:182–205.

28. Umscheid CA, Mitchell MD, Doshi JA, Agarwal R, Williams K, Brennan PJ. Estimating the proportion of healthcare-associated infections that are reasonably preventable and the related mortality and costs. Infect Control Hosp Epidemiol. 2011;32:101–14.

29. Sax H, Clack L, Touveneau S, et al. Implementation of infection control best practice in intensive care units throughout Europe: a mixed-method evaluation study. Implement Sci. 2013;8:24.

30. Harbarth S, Sax H, Gastmeier P. The preventable proportion of nosocomial infections: an overview of published reports. J Hosp Infect. 2003;54:258–66.

31. Shojania KG, Grimshaw JM. Evidence-based quality improvement: the state of the science. Health Affairs (Millwood). 2005;24(1):138–50.

32. Sackett DL, et al. Evidence based medicine: what it is and what it isn't (Editorial). Br Med J. 1996;312(7023):71–2.

33. Cabana MD, et al. Why don't physicians follow clinical practice guidelines? A framework for improvement. J Am Med Assoc. 1999;282(15):1458–65.

34. Taylor MJ, Mc Nicholas C, Nicolay C, Darzi A, Bell D, Reed JE. Systematic review of the application of the plan-do-study-act method to improve quality in healthcare. BMJ Qual Saf. 2014;23:290–8.

35. Nicolay CR, Purkayastha S, Greenhalgh A, et al. Systematic review of the application of

quality improvement methodologies from the manufacturing industry to surgical healthcare. Br J Surg. 2012;99:324–35.

36. Boaden R, Harvey J, Moxham C, et al. Quality improvement: theory and practice in health-care. Coventry: NHS Institute for Innovation and Improvement; 2008.

37. Schouten LMT, Hulscher MEJL, van Everdingen JJE, et al. Evidence for the impact of quality improvement collaboratives: systematic review. BMJ. 2008;336:1491–4.

38. Walshe K. Understanding what works—and why— in quality improvement: the need for theory-driven evaluation. Int J Qual Health Care. 2007;19:57–9.

39. Auerbach AD, Landefeld CS, Shojania KG. The tension between needing to improve care and knowing how to do it. N Engl J Med. 2007;357:608–13.

40. Ting HH, Shojania KG, Montori VM, et al. Quality improvement science and action. Circulation. 2009;119:1962–74.

41. Pronovost P, Needham D, Berenholtz S, et al. An intervention to decrease catheter-related bloodstream infections in the ICU. N Engl J Med. 2006;355:2725–32.

42. Benning A, Ghaleb M, Suokas A, et al. Large scale organisational intervention to improve patient safety in four UK hospitals: mixed method evaluation. BMJ. 2011;342:d195.

43. Landon BE, Wilson IB, McInnes K, et al. Effects of a quality improvement collaborative on the outcome of care of patients with HIV infection: the EQHIV study. Ann Intern Med. 2004;140:887–96.

44. Vos L, Duckers ML, Wagner C, et al. Applying the quality improvement collaborative method to process redesign: a multiple case study. Implement Sci. 2010;5:19.

45. Oxman AD, Thomson MA, Davis DA, et al. No magic bullets: a systematic review of 102 trials of interventions to improve professional practice. CMAJ. 1995;153:1423.

46. Greenhalgh T, Robert G, Macfarlane F, et al. Diffusion of innovations in service organizations: systematic review and recommendations. Milbank Q. 2004;82:581–629.

47. Plsek PE, Wilson T. Complexity science: complexity, leadership, and management in healthcare organisations. BMJ. 2001;323:746.

48. Damschroder LJ, Aron DC, Keith RE, et al. Fostering implementation of health services research findings into practice: a consolidated framework for advancing implementation science. Implement Sci. 2009;4:50.

49. Powell AE, Rushmer RK, Davies HTO. A systematic narrative review of quality improvement models in health care: NHS Quality Improvement Scotland. Report No. 1844045242. 2009.

50. Grol R, Grimshaw J. Evidence-based implementation of evidence-based medicine. Jt Comm J Qual Improv. 1999;25(10):503–13.

51. Hulscheretal ME. Process evaluation on quality improvement interventions. Qual Saf Health Care. 2003;12(1):40–6.

52. Davidoff F, Batalden P, Stevens D, et al. Publication guidelines for quality improvement in health care: evolution of the SQUIRE project. Qual Saf Health Care. 2008;17(Suppl 1):i3–9.

53. Ogrinc G, Mooney S, Estrada C, et al. The SQUIRE (Standards for Quality Improvement Reporting Excellence) guidelines for quality improvement reporting: explanation and elaboration. Qual Saf Health Care. 2008;17(Suppl 1):i13–32.

54. Weisz G, Cambrosio A, Keating P, Knaapen L, Schlich T, Tournay VJ. The emergence of clinical practice guidelines. Milbank Q. 2007;85(4):691–727.

55. Brouwers M, et al. AGREE II: Advancing guideline development, reporting and evaluation in healthcare. Can Med Assoc J. 2010;182:E839–42.

56. Nothacker M, et al. Reporting standards for guideline-based performance measures. Implement Sci. 2016;11:6.

57. Schünemann HJ, Wiercioch W, Etxeandia I, Falavigna M, Santesso N, Mustafa R, Ventresca M, Brignardello-Petersen R, Laisaar KT, Kowalski S, Baldeh T, Zhang Y, Raid U, Neumann I, Norris SL, Thornton J, Harbour R, Treweek S, Guyatt G, Alonso-Coello P, Reinap M, Brožek J, Oxman A, Akl EA. Guidelines 2.0: systematic development of a comprehensive checklist for a successful guideline enterprise. CMAJ. 2014;186:E123–42.

58. Guyatt GH, et al. GRADE guidelines: a new series of articles in the Journal of Clinical Epidemiology. J Clin Epidemiol. 2011;64(4):380–2.

59. Neumann I, et al. The GRADE evidence-to-decision framework: a report of its testing and application in 15 international guideline panels. Implement Sci. 2016;11:93.

60. Khodambashi S, Nytrø Ø. Reviewing clinical guideline development tools: features and characteristics. BMC Med Inform Decis Mak. 2017;17(1):132.

61. GRADE Working Group. Grading quality of evidence and strength of recommendations. BMJ. 2014;328(7454):1490–4.

62. Vandvik PO, et al. Creating clinical practice guidelines we can trust, use, and share: a new era is imminent. Chest. 2013;144(2):381–9.

63. Browman GP, et al. When is good, good enough? Methodological pragmatism for sustainable guideline development. Implement Sci. 2015;10:28.

64. Richter Sundberg L, Garvare R, Nyström ME. Reaching beyond the review of research evidence: a qualitative study of decision making during the development of clinical practice guidelines for disease prevention in healthcare. BMC Health Serv Res. 2017;17(1):344.

65. Gagliardi AR, Alhabib S, Members of Guidelines International Network Implementation Working Group. Trends in guideline implementation: a scoping systematic review. Implement Sci. 2015;10:54.

66. Gagliardi AR, et al. Developing a checklist for guideline implementation planning: review and synthesis of guideline development and implementation advice. Implement Sci. 2015;10:19.

67. Richter-Sundberg L, et al. Addressing implementation challenges during guideline development—a case study of Swedish national guidelines for methods of preventing disease. BMC Health Serv Res. 2015;15:19.

68. Fischer F, et al. Barriers and strategies in guideline implementation—a scoping review. Healthcare (Basel, Switzerland). 2016;4(3):36.

69. Brouwers MC, et al. The Guideline Implementability Decision Excellence Model (GUIDE-M): a mixed methods approach to create an international resource to advance the practice guideline field. Implement Sci. 2015;10:36.

70. Wright A, et al. Best practices in clinical decision support: the case of preventive care reminders. Appl Clin Inform. 2010;1(3):331–45.

71. Akl EA, et al. Living systematic reviews: 4. Living guideline recommendations. J Clin Epidemiol. 2017;91:47–53.

72. Thomas J, et al. Living systematic reviews: 2. Combining human and machine effort. J Clin Epidemiol. 2017;91:31–7.

73. Hewitt-Taylor J. Evidence-based practice, clinical guidelines and care protocols. In: Hewitt-Taylor J, editor. Clinical guidelines and care protocols. Chichester: John Wiley & Sons; 2017. p. 1–16.

74. May C, Montori VM, Mair FS. We need minimally disruptive medicine. BMJ. 2017;339:b2803.

75. Gupta M. Improved health or improved decision making? The ethical goals of EBM. J Eval Clin Pract. 2011;17(5):957–63.

76. van der Weijden T, et al. How can clinical practice guidelines be adapted to facilitate shared decision making? A qualitative key-informant study. BMJ Qual Saf. 2013;22(10):855–63.

77. Elwyn G, et al. Trustworthy guidelines—excellent; customized care tools—even better. BMC Med. 2015;13:199.

78. Fearns N, et al. What do patients and the public know about clinical practice guidelines and what do they want from them? A qualitative study. BMC Health Serv Res. 2016;16:74.

79. Schipper K, et al. Strategies for disseminating recommendations or guidelines to patients: a systematic review. Implement Sci. 2016;11(1):82.

80. Zhang Y, et al. Using patient values and preferences to inform the importance of health outcomes in practice guideline development following the GRADE approach. Health Qual Life Outcomes. 2017;15(1):52.

81. Cronin RM, et al. Adapting medical guidelines to be patient-centered using a patient-driven process for individuals with sickle cell disease and their caregivers. BMC Hematol. 2018;18:12.

82. Martínez García L, et al. The validity of recommendations from clinical guidelines: a survival analysis. Can Med Assoc J. 2014;186(16):1211–9.

83. Elliott JH, et al. Living systematic reviews: an emerging opportunity to narrow the evidence-practice gap. PLoS Med. 2014;11(2):e1001603.

84. Vernooij RW. Guidance for updating clinical practice guidelines: a systematic review of methodological handbooks. Implement Sci. 2014;9:3.

85. Martínez García L, et al. Efficiency of pragmatic search strategies to update clinical guidelines recommendations. BMC Med Res Methodol. 2015;15:57.

86. Drummond M. Clinical guidelines: a NICE way to introduce cost-effectiveness. Considerations? Value Health. 2016;19(5):525–30.

87. Jensen CE, et al. Systematic review of the cost-effectiveness of implementing guidelines on low back pain management in primary care: is transferability to other countries possible? BMJ Open. 2016;6(6):e011042.

88. Vale L, et al. Systematic review of economic evaluations and cost analyses of guideline implementation strategies. Eur J Health Econ. 2017;8(2):111–21.

89. Mortimer D, et al. Economic evaluation of active implementation versus guideline dissemination for evidence-based care of acute low-back pain in a general practice setting. PLoS One. 2013;8(10):e75647.

90. Garrison LP. Cost-effectiveness and clinical practice guidelines: have we reached a tipping point? An overview. Value Health. 2016;19(5):512–5.

91. Blozik E, et al. Simultaneous development of guidelines and quality indicators—how do guideline groups act? A worldwide survey. Int J Health Care Qual Assur. 2012;25(8):712–29.

92. Heffner JE. Does evidence-based medicine help the development of clinical practice guidelines? Chest. 1998;113(3 Suppl):172S–8S.

93. Li H, et al. A new scale for the evaluation of clinical practice guidelines applicability: development and appraisal. Implement Sci. 2018;13(1):61.

94. Roberts ET, et al. Evaluating clinical practice guidelines based on their association with return to work in administrative claims data. Health Serv Res. 2016;51(3):953–80.

95. Cook DA, et al. Practice variation and practice guidelines: attitudes of generalist and specialist physicians, nurse practitioners, and physician assistants. PLoS One. 2018;13(1):e0191943.

96. Kovacs E, et al. Systematic review and meta-analysis of the effectiveness of implementation strategies for non-communicable disease guidelines in primary health care. J Gen Intern Med. 2018;33(7):1142–54.

97. Shanbhag D, et al. Effectiveness of implementation interventions in improving physician adherence to guideline recommendations in heart failure: a systematic review. BMJ Open. 2018;8(3):e017765.

98. Chan WV, et al. ACC/AHA special report: clinical practice guideline implementation strategies: a summary of systematic reviews by the NHLBI implementation science work group: a report of the American College of Cardiology/American Heart Association Task Force on Clinical Practice Guidelines. J Am Coll Cardiol. 2017;69(8):1076–92.

99. Morciano C, et al. Policies on conflicts of interest in health care guideline development: a cross-sectional analysis. PLoS One. 2016;11(11):e0166485.

100. Napierala H, et al. Management of financial conflicts of interests in clinical practice guidelines in Germany: results from the public database guideline watch. BMC Med Ethics. 2018;19(1):65.

101. Campsall P, et al. Financial relationships between organizations that produce clinical practice guidelines and the biomedical industry: a cross-sectional study. PLoS Med. 2016;13(5):e1002029.

102. Shnier A, et al. Reporting of financial conflicts of interest in clinical practice guidelines: a case study analysis of guidelines from the Canadian Medical Association Infobase. BMC Health Serv Res. 2016;16:383.

103. Moynihan R, et al. Undisclosed financial ties between guideline writers and pharmaceutical companies: a cross-sectional study across 10 disease categories. BMJ Open. 2019;9:e025864.

104. Schünemann HJ, et al. Guidelines international network: principles for disclosure of interests and management of conflicts in guidelines. Ann Intern Med. 2015;163(7):548–53.

105. Ioannidis JPA. Professional societies should abstain from authorship of guidelines and disease definition statements. Circ Cardiovasc Qual Outcomes. 2018;11(10):e004889.

Brief Story of a Clinical Risk Manager

Riccardo Tartaglia

2.1 Introduction

This chapter briefly recounts the story of someone who worked as a clinical risk manager of a regional health service for 16 years since his appointment as director of a regional center for clinical risk management and patient safety.

The purpose of this chapter is to provide a testimony of one of the first international experiences of safety management in a public health service. It does not claim to speak to a particular type of profession but aims to relate an experience in which some will recognize themselves, others will be able to find advice, and others will be able to understand the differences with the health reality in which they operate. It may also be useful in order to define the "clinical risk manager," a new professional figure that has now entered the scene in our hospitals.

This story takes place in Italy, a country that, according to international indicators [1] and the World Health Organization (WHO) [2], has a fairly good health service but with very strong variability between the northern and southern regions.

Unfortunately, the economic crisis has worsened the situation and, in terms of quality of care, Italian services no longer occupy the top positions [3].

In the current Italian context, Tuscany is one of the regions with the best indicators of quality of care, along with some northern regions.

Let us briefly describe the context in which the story takes place. Tuscany is located in the center of Italy and covers an area of approximately 23,000 km^2, 67% of which is hilly. It is home to about 3.7 million inhabitants and a health service with 33 acute care hospitals of which three are university hospitals in Florence, Pisa, and Siena. Every year about 550,000 people are admitted to public hospitals in Tuscany. Of them, 1500 patients annually claim compensation for alleged harm resulting from treatment received, but only 40% of these citizens will be awarded compensation, amounting to a total of about 40–50 million euros a year.

Healthcare is mainly public and adopts the tax-financed Beveridge model. The cost of public health service is around 7.4 billion euros a year, with a per capita quota of 1981 euros, compared to a national average of 1888 euros per capita [4].

2.2 The Start

In 1989, Scally and Donaldson [5] promoted clinical risk management in the field of clinical governance and, in 1999, the "To err is human" report was published [6]. At the same time, James

R. Tartaglia (✉)
Italian Network for Safety in Healthcare, Florence, Italy
e-mail: riccardo.tartaglia@bsdesign.eu

© The Author(s) 2021
L. Donaldson et al. (eds.), *Textbook of Patient Safety and Clinical Risk Management*,
https://doi.org/10.1007/978-3-030-59403-9_2

Reason travelled the world making his "Swiss Cheese model" known globally [7], while Charles Vincent published "Clinical risk management: enhancing patient safety" in 2001 [8].

It was precisely in 2001 when the medical director of my hospital brought me the book by Charles Vincent and asked me to take charge of health safety. The reason he proposed this role to me stemmed from my position as manager of a structure that dealt with ergonomics and the human factor in the field of occupational safety, a relevant issue for clinical risk management.

I started working on this topic with some young people from my unit and we grew passionate about it. I was the only doctor, a specialist in occupational health and public health, surrounded by an industrial designer and experts in communication sciences and sociology. The medical director was highly interested in patient safety. We no longer dealt with the latter, except for aspects related to occupational stress and burnout.

We started presenting the Swiss Cheese Model to fellow doctors and nurses, inviting them to promote incident reporting. We stressed the importance of a "no blame" culture to the directors of units, doctors, and nurses, with the support of health management, but our moment of fame came in 2002 when we invited James Reason to Florence. In an auditorium full of doctors and nurses, people began to talk about medical errors, a subject that up until then was untouchable, almost unthinkable. Since forensic medicine was dominant at that time, we wanted to make it clear that our aim was not the pursuit of professional responsibility (i.e., negligence, inexperience, and imprudence), but to learn from error.

Reason concluded his presentation by stating that "we cannot change the human being which by nature is fallible, but we can change working conditions in an attempt to prevent and intercept errors before they cause an adverse event." He also told us that we would still have accidents and that we should learn to manage them, even from the point of view of communication.

A journalist from the most important national television network heard about our Florentine experience and made a report for an important television program in which she showed how doctors discussed their mistakes. In the broadcast, you are presented with a slightly darkened hospital room in which a group of doctors, almost like some secret sect, was discussing adverse events. I believe it was the first significant event audit or confessional meeting filmed for television in Italy.

At that time, the alderman of the Regional Health Service, who participated in the James Reason conference, understood the importance of the subject and launched the establishment of a regional center that would coordinate all the activities for the management of clinical risk and patient safety in Tuscan hospitals. The aim of this center would have been the promotion of a culture of safety, the reporting of adverse events, and learning from adverse events—in a word, our mission. It was announced publicly that one million euros had been raised for the establishment of a regional patient safety center.

2.3   The Evolution of the Patient Safety System

After the James Reason conference, the Tuscany region decided to invest one million euros to organize a center for clinical risk management in an Italian region of 3.7 million inhabitants and 33 acute care hospitals.

I was then in charge of running this center with a budget of only around 600,000 euros for personnel management (the announced investment was therefore somewhat reduced). I of course turned to the operators I already had in my old ergonomic group, 8 young and brilliant technicians chosen on the basis of multidisciplinary skills, and overcame numerous bureaucratic problems that represented the greatest initial operational difficulty—bureaucracy is the greatest enemy of safety.

It is difficult for many to understand the importance of other professional figures in healthcare than traditional doctors, nurses, obstetricians, etc. In Italian healthcare, according to an ancient and outdated conception of professional skills, there is a health area (i.e., traditional health professions) and a technical-administrative area (i.e., statisticians, computer scientists, sociologists, communicators, jurists, engineers). These areas rarely interact and are often separated both physically (e.g., across different buildings) and intellectually. Teamwork is exclusively linked to common interest in a few topics and to the networking skills of individual operators.

In my opinion, the acquisition of knowledge is difficult when people do not work together. This also applies to primary care and hospital professionals. Opportunities and moments for exchange are needed at least weekly.

I must say that in recent years clinical risk management has brought many professionals closer to each other, due to its multidisciplinary approach. For example, IT professionals are now involved in the ergonomics and usability of computerized medical records, which are frequently sources of error, while psychologists and communication experts are involved in the analysis of adverse events. Each of my collaborators had solid training in ergonomics and the human factor, acquired through master degree programs and academic courses, and therefore skills in accident analysis, communication, highly reliable organization, and resilience. If I had immediately opted for a team of doctors and nurses, the budget would probably not have been enough and we would have spent much more time recruiting new staff. Furthermore, for a healthcare organization, a doctor *contractually* costs more than a sociologist or industrial designer.

As a matter of fact, over time the skills available to the team proved both useful and valid for our work. A center that deals with clinical risk and the complexity of the causes of accidents must include professionals that come from various disciplinary areas besides health [9]. With regard to communication problems (which often cause accidents), organizational problems, and problems associated with the interactions with biomedical, ergonomic, and legal equipment, the professionals in our team were much better prepared than other professionals in their own discipline, precisely thanks to the specific training in human factor and risk management.

A scientific committee consisting of the best medical specialists and nurses in the health service had the function of supporting the center in all the more strictly clinical assistance-related aspects which we would encounter during significant events audit, mortality and morbidity meetings, and the promotion of safety practices.

Working in this multidisciplinary context has been culturally enriching for clinicians and nurses as well as other professional figures, resulting in a continual exchange of knowledge that has favored professional growth.

The headquarters were planned to reside in a building of the most important Tuscan hospital.

2.4 The Network of Clinical Risk Manager

After implementing staff training, a network of professionals (one in each hospital) was needed in order to organize the activity, develop a reporting and learning system, and create a risk management system.

We asked the general managers of each hospital to designate a point person for clinical risk and patient safety. In the beginning, we did not expect specifically trained professional figures but professionals from biomedical, psychosocial, and technical fields with good reputation, credibility, and standing among other clinicians and health professionals. Some choices proved to be right and others not, which is normal.

Over time, I noticed a certain vulnerability of this new professional figure. Although safety is the duty of every healthcare worker and cannot be delegated to a single professional, the risk manager often becomes a scapegoat for many problems. For this reason, they are sometimes replaced not on the basis of professional ability and merit but of loyalty to the general manager.

The selected professionals followed a mandatory university course involving over one hundred hours of training and a 1-week internship in a hospital risk management service. Subsequently, in almost all hospitals, the professionals obtained a risk management unit with collaborators.

For each hospital unit, other doctors or nurses, usually one or two, were then identified as facilitators.

The facilitators were expected to be professionals, usually doctors and nurses, who, in addition to performing their daily work, should have had hours dedicated to promoting clinical audits and mortality and morbidity meetings following adverse events, unsafe actions, and missed accidents.

2.5   Training and Instruction

The training of our gladiators, numbering about 30, took place in collaboration with one of the most prestigious Italian universities, the Sant'Anna School of Advanced Studies in Pisa. The course was very hands-on, including lectures by experts on the subject and many exercises on clinical cases of adverse events and the implementation of safety practices. However, the most beautiful experience of this course was the 1-week internship at various international hospitals.

We took our gladiators to numerous hospitals to show them what actions could be taken to improve patient safety. We visited the hospitals of many cities (such as Berlin, London, Boston, Chicago, Copenhagen, Paris, Valencia, and Amsterdam), comparing the different risk management models adopted. This experience was very useful for the planning of our work [10].

What stood out was that, in most of the hospitals we visited, clinical risk management was entrusted to nurses. The doctors were mainly involved in mortality and morbidity meetings and in research projects almost always conducted in multidisciplinary teams.

In our country, risk management is entrusted to medical personnel with the support of senior nurses, albeit with some rare exceptions. I believe that with regard to competences, it is always necessary to evaluate the context of reference and the functions of units, research, or clinical health. The training topics have gradually changed over time, adapting to emerging needs and to the transformation of the role of the professional.

After the risk managers' first year of work, we realized that the professionals coming from the clinical side performed better than those who had worked in health departments. The reason was essentially that the clinical professionals had a closer relationship with the structures we sought to improve.

Furthermore, the managers of quality and accreditation structures and the managers of clinical risk continued to exist as separate entities. The two roles coincided only in rare cases. For this reason, we identified in each hospital a clinical risk manager (CRM) and a patient safety manager (PSM), thus differentiating the functions [11].

In Italy as well as internationally, care safety and quality management and accreditation have had different stories. While clinical risk management was born in more recent times and has attracted the immediate interest of professionals, quality management and accreditation have never fascinated clinicians because of the excessive bureaucracy and the occasional distance of the procedures proposed by clinical practice from real problems.

Regarding our two professional roles, the CRM is a professional who works on the clinical side and is entrusted with risk management in a department, while the PSM is a doctor, nurse, or non-healthcare professional who operates among the health management staff. Figure 2.1 summarizes the differences between these two lines of operation and the professional figures involved.

Today, following specific training and experience, we can provide a professional certification

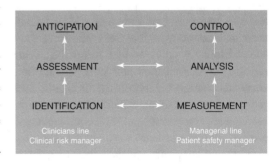

Fig. 2.1 Activities of clinical risk manager and patient safety manager

for this role (clinical risk manager/patient safety manager) in order to enhance their skills and offer more guarantees to insurance system.

The training has substantially contributed to the definition of a risk management model that we have theorized and put into practice over about 15 years.

2.6   Adverse Events

Some of the studies we have conducted in our regional health service [12, 13] did not show higher rates of adverse events compared to other research carried out with similar methodology. Similarly, the claims rate is average compared with other Italian regions.

Our reporting and learning system has clearly lowered the levels of confidentiality thus exposing our health service to the media. Where there is no transparency, it is difficult for serious accidents to emerge as everything is managed confidentially. If significant event audits or mortality and morbidity meetings are organized, news leaks out more easily. Nevertheless, the number of adverse events reported by our operators through our reporting system is always much lower than expected. The expected amount, which is at least 4–5 times higher, was determined from the comparisons we have made with colleagues from other countries where reporting systems have been operating for a longer time.

Under-reporting had been attributable to the fear of judicial consequences until the first of April, 2017, when the law on patient safety and professional liability was instituted. However, in our experience the main cause of under-reporting was the absence of a safety culture (i.e., "I'm not used to reporting, it's just not the way things are done") [14].

The law introduced in 2017 has protected reporting and learning systems from legal action since documents produced within these systems cannot be used for judicial purposes [15]. The development of a clinical risk management system did not completely shelter us from serious accidents but it helped to deepen our understanding of clinical cases with an unexpected outcome.

On February 20, 2007, about 2 years after we started implementing our risk management system, the first important event happened. We had a serious sentinel event that had great media coverage at the national and international levels. It happened in the field of transplant surgery, an area that we mistakenly thought to be fairly safe because it was under the control of national supervisory bodies. Furthermore, it involved an analytical laboratory in which the attention to the procedures of the accreditation and quality system is very high. The case involved the transplantation of two kidneys and a liver from an HIV-positive donor to three patients awaiting transplantation [16].

The event had great resonance but the center, at least in the initial phase, was absolutely not involved in the analysis of what happened. The case was managed by political leaders only and exclusively at a communicative level. It was announced that the cause was human error of an operator who had erroneously transcribed the machine data for serological examinations in the report.

Instead of a culture of learning based on the discussion of organizational problems that can determine the occurrence of significant events, a culture of guilt had prevailed. A culprit was immediately found; the rotten apple was removed from the bunch.

Subsequent analyses conducted by various national and regional committees have shown that in those working conditions any human being could have made mistakes. In this case, that human being was a good and honest biologist, the only one to bear the blame for what had happened. In organizing the task, the human factor had not been taken into account. A "traditional" way of working continued to prevail in which a human being rather than a machine had to perform a monotonous and repetitive job, reporting serological examination results.

It was therefore decided that each of these patients would be rewarded with a very high compensation. It was a decision that served to stop the controversy around the event: the news disappeared from the media in a few days.

As head of clinical risk management, I was determined to resign. After this serious event, I felt it was my duty, even if we had not yet intervened in the transplant system precisely because it was a sector with its own autonomy. I was asked to investigate what had happened. The results of the investigation we conducted brought about many changes, highlighting several critical issues in the transplant system. Donations had increased too quickly compared to the system's ability to meet operational needs.

It was one of the many cases in which I realized that legal truth is not always consistent with "true truth."

With regard to sentinel events, the biggest problem was overcoming the strong desire of politicians and general managers to look for a culprit (culture of guilt) in order to focus their attention on preventing the recurrence of such an event (no-blame culture).

When a serious accident occurs, the citizens want a culprit even if the time taken by justice is much longer than that of the clinical risk manager, whose first goal is to secure the hospital and provide psychological support for the victims of event, both the first victim, the patient, and the second victim, the professional.

2.7   The First Results

We had our first results when we started disseminating all the good safety practices that research had developed in the meantime: introduction of hand hygiene gels, checklists for operating theaters, prevention of postpartum hemorrhage, prevention of thromboembolic complications, bundles for the prevention of CVC infections, etc. Since, more than 30 safety practices have been developed in collaboration with clinicians. The greatest difficulty was the differences in implementation capacity, which depend little on the clinical risk manager. Much depends on the environmental context and on how much importance the general manager gives to safety and quality of care. The best results concerned those hospitals in which management executives gave great importance to the patient safety.

Unfortunately, some general managers were very far removed from the basic principles of clinical risk management. They were only interested in the economic costs and the volume of activity, not value of care.

Obviously, politics has considerable weight and responsibility in imprinting certain behaviors in general managers. Although training has been introduced in management courses, it has never been enough to change the externally ingrained behaviors nor the behaviors guided by the nature of the employees themselves.

Overall, we can affirm that some important successes have been achieved. At an organizational level, we have been equipped for years with a reporting and learning system that is a credit to our organization. There has been a reduction in the number of accidents and falls in the hospital, the latter being the most frequent cause of damage reports. According to third-party data, we are the Italian region with the lowest rate of maternal mortality and mortality in intensive care. Attention to infections has increased even if their rate continues to be high. Much more could and should be done.

2.8   The Relationship with Politics and Managers

Politicians, obviously with some exceptions, have rarely shown interest in the many national and international events we have organized. I realized over time that the topic of patient safety does not excite politicians. The reason is simple: talking about mistakes, the criticalities of a health system, and litigation has no electoral value. It is much more politically profitable to talk about robotic surgery, transplants, technological innovation, and opening up new health services. Even if it is clear from the data that in the last 15 years we have saved money and above all human lives thanks to clinical risk management, politics has always preferred other topics. On the other hand, it is true that patient safety is an electoral campaign theme that can be used to denigrate the political opponent. In fact, whenever elections approached, newspaper headlines about "malpractice" poured in to instrumentally demonstrate the inefficiency of the health service.

One of the critical issues that has arisen in recent years is the lack of autonomy of the center with respect to political apparatus and hospital managers. The regional bodies of clinical government that deal with the safety of care, such as the Tuscan GRC center, must have their own operational and budgetary autonomy. These are technical-scientific bodies that cannot depend directly on the political and administrative government. The model of government agencies should be adopted, guaranteeing these bodies a third-party nature and independence, precisely because of the importance of their role.

Despite the unanimous approval of a specific request by the regional council [17], the regional executive committee has never given autonomy to the center.

As operators, we have always remained administratively dependent on the hospital from which we came. This hospital was one of the structures subjected to evaluation by the regional apparatus and therefore by our center. This obviously led to a clear conflict of interests and consequent management difficulties due to the desire of some managers to influence the activities of the center.

Currently, the Italian law for safety of care foresees in every Italian region the presence of centers for the management of healthcare-associated risk and patient safety. However, the law does not provide precise indications on their administrative location and level of independence. None of these structures has total autonomy,

being administrated by regional apparatuses or managed by personnel employed by hospitals.

Patient safety has never been a topic of pride for politicians even when the results were good. Politicians prefer to maintain an attitude of "understatement" on this issue. There is the awareness that at any time a serious accident can occur and this could be exploited by the opposition against the current administration. It is therefore preferable to promote the "positive" aspects of the health service such as the opening of a new structure, the purchase of new equipment, and the hiring of doctors. Although patient safety is one of the eight domains of healthcare risk management [18], its real importance has not yet been understood (Fig. 2.2).

Another crucial aspect involving the risk manager relates to the culture of guilt facilitated by hindsight bias. Those who do not subscribe to a culture of safety and sometimes even great clinicians often fall into this trap of judging the past based on new knowledge of the facts. In our country, in the event of a serious accident, people immediately want a culprit even when events may have complex causes. In some of the serious accidents in the health service that I investigated, the identification of a culprit and the communication to the public that the cause was due to human error generally reduced the clamor produced by the media. Stating that the problem is the responsibility of a single person and not a structural or organizational problem calms public opinion and is therefore a functional strategy for the system. Even before knowing the facts, we start to attribute the responsibility and the blame most often

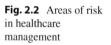

Fig. 2.2 Areas of risk in healthcare management

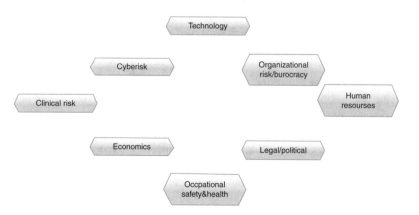

Table 2.1 Differences between human factors and forensic investigations

Type of investigation	Forensic	Human factors/ergonomics
Ownership	Judicial Authority	Clinical Governance Institution
Aim	Ascertain illegal actsFinding criminals	Redesign system interactions to improving safety
Approach	Focus on individual performance (contractual relationship)	Focus on system awareness (organizational context)
Investigation team	Police detectives, coroner, clinicians (team leader with expertise in forensics)	Experts in HF/E: clinicians, psychologists (team leader with expertise in HF/E)
Investigation methods and tools	Police interrogations, recorded interviews, surveillance	Meetings with healthcare professionals based on the systemic analysis
Outcomes	Preliminary investigation report with evidence of individual culpability	Confidential report of contributory factors and recommendation for improving patient safety
Time scale	In keeping with forensic procedures, investigation, debate, and court judgment (years)	In keeping with healthcare organization activities and needs (days/months)
Resulting actions	Judgment in a court of law and sentencing (individual-oriented)	Implementation of improvement actions and learning-focused patient safety measures (system-oriented)

to the individual, rarely to management, and hardly ever to politics.

I have noticed this attitude in numerous cases where even the most evident responsibilities of the political-administrative system were not brought under scrutiny (e.g., lack of personnel, technological criticalities, training criticalities).

Another important aspect is the general managers' understanding of the need to maintain the two lines of action separate in the management of sentinel events. We have repeatedly theorized that the first goal of a risk manager when an accident occurs is to analyze what has happened and quickly introduce prevention measures to secure the system. It is therefore necessary to initiate clinical audits, mortality and morbidity meetings, and root cause analysis.

The search for responsibility is generally the duty of the investigating judiciary or other administrative bodies whose purpose is to identify the judicial and administrative responsibilities.

It is therefore advisable that the risk manager is not involved in investigations aimed at identifying responsibilities. It is also advisable not to make the documentation produced within the reporting and learning systems available to lawyers or judges in order to identify the responsibilities. Exceptions are obviously cases involving malice, that is, intention to cause damage on the part of the professional.

In my experience, I have been in interesting situations in which we, as clinical risk operators, have investigated the same event together with the police. Table 2.1 shows some differences that emerged from a careful analysis of the facts [19].

As I once heard from John Ovretveit in his beautiful lecture in Florence, the successful improvement of patient safety depends only 10% on the clinical risk manager and slightly more (20%) on "safety practices" which must be based in strong scientific evidence. 40% of the success is derived from the cultural landscape in which the practices are disseminated but, above all, 60% is grounded in the climate created by the corporate establishment that favors the achievement of greater safety of care, rewarding and celebrating quality.

2.9 The Italian Law on the Safety of Care

Fourteen years after the birth of the center that I directed, the Italian law on the safety of care was promulgated. Some important international magazines have covered the contents [15, 20].

The law is due to two Italian medical parliamentarians, Federico Gelli and Amedeo Bianco and it is titled "Provisions for care safety and professional responsibility." It has introduced important changes which have provided strength to all those working in the field of clinical risk management.

It has created specific clinical risk management centers in each Italian region with the aim of collecting data on adverse events and promoting best safety practices. It has also protected reporting and learning systems by preventing the use of the internally produced documents for judicial purposes. This law also provides specific training for those who decide to become clinical risk managers in hospitals. The professional certification system implemented in our country is giving further value to this professional role. Finally, it has provided regulation for scientific societies around the generation of guidelines and recommendations for safety of care. It is not yet clear whether hospitals can become "highly reliable organizations" [21] but this law could contribute thanks to the changes it produces.

References

1. Miller LJ, Lu W. These are the world's healthiest nations. www.bloomberg.com/news/articles/2019-02-24/spain-tops-italy-as-world-s-healthiest-nation-while-u-s-slips.
2. World Health Organization. The World Health Report 2000—health systems: improving performance. Geneva: WHO; 2000. www.who.int/whr/2000/en/whr00_en.pdf?ua=1. Accessed 12 May 2014.
3. Corte dei Conti. Referto al Parlamento sulla gestione finanziaria dei servizi sanitari regionali. Esercizio 2017. Deliberazione N. 13/SEZAUT/2019/FRG.
4. Health Consumer Powerhouse. Euro health consumer index 2018. https://healthpowerhouse.com/media/EHCI-2018/EHCI-2018-report.pdf.
5. Scally G, Donaldson LJ. Clinical governance and the drive for quality improvement in the new NHS in England. BMJ. 1998;317(7150):61–5. https://doi.org/10.1136/bmj.317.7150.61.
6. Kohn LT, Corrigan JM, Donaldson MS, Institute of Medicine Committee on Quality of Health Care in America. To err is human: building a safer health system. Washington, DC: National Academic Press; 1999.
7. Reason J. Human error: models and management. BMJ. 2000;320:768–70. https://doi.org/10.1136/bmj.320.7237.768.
8. Vincent C. Clinical risk management: enhancing patient safety. London: BMJ Books; 2001.
9. Vincent C, Bataldan P, Davidoff F. Multidisciplinary centres for safety and quality improvement: learning from climate change science. BMJ Qual Saf. 2011;20(Suppl1):i73–8.
10. Nuti S, Tartaglia R, Niccolai F. Rischio Clinico e Sicurezza del Paziente. Rischio clinico e sicurezza del paziente. Modelli e soluzioni nel contesto internazionale Ed. Bologna: Il Mulino; 2007.
11. Bellandi T, Albolino S, Tartaglia R, Bagnara S. Human factors and ergonomics in patient safety management. In: Human factors and ergonomics in health care and patient safety. 2nd ed. Boca Raton, FL: CRC Press Taylor & Francis Group; 2012. p. 671–90.
12. Tartaglia R, Albolino S, Bellandi T, Bianchini E, Biggeri A, Fabbro G, Bevilacqua L, Dell'Erba A, Privitera G, Sommella L. Adverse events and preventable consequences: retrospective study in five large Italian hospitals. Epidemiol Prev. 2012;35(3–4):151–61.
13. Albolino S, Tartaglia R, Bellandi T, Bianchini E, Fabbro G, Forni S, Cernuschi G, Biggeri A. Variability of adverse events in the public healthcare service of the Tuscany region. Intern Emerg Med. 2017; https://doi.org/10.1007/s11739-017-1698-5.
14. Albolino S, Tartaglia R, Bellandi T, Amicosante AMV, Bianchini E, Biggeri A. Patient safety and incident reporting: the point of view of the Italian healthcare workers. Qual Saf Health Care. 2010;19(Suppl 3):8–12.
15. Bellandi T, Tartaglia R, Sheikh A, Donaldson L. Italy recognises patient safety as a fundamental right A new law takes a bold new step towards enhancing patient safety. BMJ. 2017;357:j2277(Published 22 May 2017). https://doi.org/10.1136/bmj.j2277.
16. Bellandi T, Albolino S, Tartaglia R, Filipponi F. Unintended transplantation of three organs from an HIV-positive donor: report of the analysis of an adverse event in a regional health care service in Italy. Transplant Proc. 2010;42(6):2187–9.
17. Mozione N° 308 del 7 aprile 2016. In merito alla necessità di una revisione dell'attuale sistema del rischio clinico regionale e dell'autonomia del Centro regionale per la gestione del rischio clinico e la sicurezza del paziente.
18. What is risk management in healthcare? https://catalyst.nejm.org/what-is-risk-management-in-healthcare/article. 25 Apr 2018.
19. Tartaglia R, Albolino S, Bellandi T, Biancofiore G, Poli D, Bertolini G, Toccafondi G, Prineas S. Safety analysis on 13 suspicious deaths in intensive care: ergonomics and forensic approach compared. J Patient Saf. 2020; https://doi.org/10.1097/PTS.0000000000000666.
20. Albolino S, Bellandi T, Cappelletti S, Di Paolo M, Fineschi V, Frati P, Offidani C, Tanzini M, Tartaglia R, Turillazzi E. New rules on patient's safety and professional liability for the Italian Health Service. Curr Pharm Biotechnol. 2019;20:615–24. https://doi.org/10.2174/1389201020666190408094016.
21. Bagnara S, Parlangeli O, Tartaglia R. Are hospitals becoming high reliability organizations? Appl Ergon. 2010;41(5):713–8.

Human Error and Patient Safety

3

Helen Higham and Charles Vincent

3.1 Introduction

Making a serious error is one of the most stressful professional experiences for a doctor or for anyone in clinical practice. In other professions, such as architecture or the law, serious mistakes can generally be remedied with an apology and compensation for losses sustained. But in medicine, mistakes can have serious and lifelong consequences for patients and families.

Medical schools rightly encourage the highest standards of professional practice. Doctors are expected to work hard and do their best for their patients and, ideally, not make errors. It is tempting to think that only 'bad' or 'lazy' people make mistakes and that making a serious error implies a flaw in character not worthy of a serious professional. The reality however is that all doctors, indeed all clinicians, will make errors during their career and that some of them will have serious consequences.

We cannot completely avoid errors but we can do much to reduce them, to spot them more quickly and to protect patients from the worst of the consequences. However, in order to do this, we need to understand the nature of error and, in particular, how working conditions strongly influence our behaviour and the likelihood of

error. We also need to understand that while we can make personal efforts to avoid errors, the greatest protection will come from working in a team of people who are willing to recognise errors, speak up, support each other, and protect both patients and colleagues from the consequences of errors.

3.2 What Is an Error?

In everyday life, recognising error seems quite straightforward though admitting it may be harder. Immediate slips, such as making tea when you meant to make coffee, are quickly recognised. Other errors may only be recognised long after they occur. You may only realise you prescribed a drug incorrectly when the patient returns to follow-up clinic a few weeks later with problematic side effects from an overdose. Some errors, such as missing a lung tumour on an X-ray taken to investigate a potential shoulder injury, may only become apparent years later.

An important common theme running through all these examples is that an action is only recognised as an error after the event. Human error is a judgement made in hindsight [1]. There is no special class of things we do or don't do that we can designate as errors; it is just that some of the things we do turn out to have undesirable or unwanted consequences. This does not mean that we cannot study error or examine how our

H. Higham (✉) · C. Vincent
University of Oxford, Oxford, UK
e-mail: helen.higham@ndcn.ox.ac.uk;
charles.vincent@psy.ox.ac.uk

© The Author(s) 2021
L. Donaldson et al. (eds.), *Textbook of Patient Safety and Clinical Risk Management*,
https://doi.org/10.1007/978-3-030-59403-9_3

otherwise efficient brains lead us astray in some circumstances, but it does suggest that there will not be specific cognitive mechanisms to explain error that are different from those that explain other human thinking and behaviour.

Eric Hollnagel [2] points out that the term error has historically been used in three different senses: as a cause of something (wrong site surgery due to human error), as the action or event itself (removing the incorrect kidney) or as the outcome of an action (the death of a patient from renal failure). The distinctions are not absolute in that many uses of the term involve both cause and consequence to different degrees, but they do have a very different emphasis.

The most precise definition of error, and most in accord with everyday usage, is one that ties it to observable behaviours and actions. As a working definition, John Senders [3] proposed that an error means that something has been done which:

- Was not desired by a set of rules or an external observer
- Led the task or system outside acceptable limits
- Was not intended by the actor

This definition of error, and other similar ones [2], imply a set of criteria for defining an error:

- First, there must be a set of rules or standards, either explicitly defined or at least implied and accepted in that environment
- Second, there must be some kind of failure or 'performance shortfall'
- Third, the person involved did not intend this and must, at least potentially, have been able to act in a different way

All three of these criteria can be challenged, or at least prove difficult to pin down in practice. Much clinical medicine is inherently uncertain and there are frequently no easily applicable protocols to guide treatment. In addition, the failure is not necessarily easy to identify; it is certainly not always clear, at least at the time, when a diagnosis is wrong or at what point blood levels of a drug become dangerously high. Finally, the notion of intention, and in theory at least being able to act differently, is challenged by the fact that people's behaviour is often influenced by factors, such as fatigue or peer pressure, which they may not be aware of and have little control over. So, while the working definition is reasonable, we should be aware of the difficulties of applying it in practice.

3.3 Understanding Error

In his analysis of different types of error, James Reason [4] divides them into two broad types of error: slips and lapses, which are errors of action, and mistakes which are, broadly speaking, errors of knowledge or planning. Reason also discusses violations which, as distinct from error, are intentional acts which, for one reason or another, deviate from the usual or expected course of action. These psychological analyses are mainly concerned, with failures at a particular time and probe the underlying mechanisms of error. There is therefore not necessarily a simple correspondence with medical errors which, as discussed above, may refer to events happening over a period of time. However, we will see that this conceptual scheme is very helpful in understanding errors in clinical practice and how they sometimes combine to cause harm to patients.

3.3.1 Slips and Lapses

Slips and lapses occur when a person knows what they want to do, but the action does not turn out as they intended. Slips relate to observable actions and are associated with attentional failures, whereas lapses are internal events and associated with failures of memory. Slips and lapses occur during the largely automatic performance of some routine task, usually in familiar surroundings. They are almost invariably associated with some form of distraction, either from the person's surrounding or their own preoccupation with something in mind.

A trainee doctor working on a surgical ward is prescribing an antibiotic for a patient after a ward round. Just as she opens the patient's drug chart on the computer a nurse interrupts because he is concerned about a patient with very low blood pressure. The doctor goes with the nurse forgetting to complete the prescription. Other tasks follow and there is a substantial delay in delivery of the antibiotic and the patient becomes profoundly septic.

3.3.2   Mistakes

Slips and lapses are errors of action; you intend to do something, but it does not go according to plan. With mistakes, the actions may go entirely as planned but the plan itself deviates from some adequate path towards its intended goal. Here the failure lies at a higher level: with the mental processes involved in planning, formulating intentions, judging, and problem solving [4]. If a doctor treats someone with chest pain as if they have a myocardial infarction, when in fact they have a perforated gastric ulcer, then this is a mistake. The intention is clear, the action corresponds with the intention, but the plan was wrong.

Rule-based mistakes occur when the person already knows some rule or procedure, acquired as the result of training or experience. Rule-based mistakes may occur through applying the wrong rule, such as treating someone for influenza when you should follow the guidelines for meningococcal sepsis. Alternatively, the mistake may occur because the procedure itself is faulty (deficient clinical guidelines for instance).

A swab is inadvertently left in a wound after surgery because the standard operating procedure for counting swabs is not followed properly. (Misapplication of a good rule)
A patient is transferred from one site to another with inadequate medical assistance and monitoring. (Application of a bad rule: the standard operating procedure for the safe transfer of patients is poorly designed and difficult to understand, the patient is inappropriately deemed fit for low dependency transport)

Knowledge-based mistakes occur in novel situations where the solution to a problem has to be worked out on the spot. For instance, a doctor

may simply be unfamiliar with the clinical presentation of a particular disease, or there may be multiple diagnostic possibilities and no clear way of choosing between them; a surgeon may have to guess at the source of the bleeding and make an understandable mistake in their assessment in the face of considerable stress and uncertainty. In none of these cases, does the clinician have a good 'mental model' of what is happening to base their decisions on, still less a specific rule or procedure to follow?

In knowledge-based mistakes, the changes encountered are not recognisable or planned for and rely on the cognitively effortful and error prone processes of reasoning:

A patient deteriorates rapidly after extubation on intensive care and the endotracheal tube cannot be repositioned in the usual way (via the mouth or nose). The team involved has not faced such a challenging situation before and the opportunity to site a surgical airway (tracheostomy) at an early stage is missed. The challenges of making decisions about the choice of airway are compounded by the high levels of stress in this situation.

3.3.3   Violations

Errors are, by definition, unintended in the sense that we do not want to make errors. Violations, in contrast, are deliberate deviations from safe operating practices, procedures, standards, or rules. This is not to say that people intend that there should be a bad outcome, as when someone deliberately sabotages a piece of equipment; usually, people hope that the violation of procedures won't matter on this occasion or will actually help get the job done. Violations differ from errors in several important ways. Whereas errors are primarily due to our human limitations in thinking and remembering, violations are more closely linked with attitudes, motivation, and the work environment. The social context of violations is very important and understanding them, and if necessary curbing them, requires attention to the culture of the wider organisation as well as the attitudes of the people concerned.

Reason distinguishes three types of violations.

- A routine violation is basically cutting corners for one reason or another, perhaps to save time or simply to get on to another more urgent task.
- A necessary violation occurs when a person flouts a rule because it seems the only way to get the job done. For example, a nurse may give a drug which should be double checked by another nurse, but there is no one else available. The nurse will probably give the drug, knowingly violating procedure, but hoping that this is in the patient's interest.
- Optimising violations which are for personal gain, sometimes just to get off work early or, more sinister, to alleviate boredom, 'for kicks'. Think of a trainee surgeon carrying out a difficult operation in the middle of the night, without supervision, when the case could easily wait until morning. The motivation is partly to gain experience, to test oneself out, but there may be a strong element of the excitement of sailing close to the wind in defiance of the senior surgeon's instructions.

In practice, the distinction between slips, mistakes, and violations is not always clear, either to an observer or the person concerned. The relationship between the observed behaviour, which can be easily described, and the psychological mechanism often hard to discern. Giving the wrong drug might be a slip (attention wandered and the doctor picked up the wrong syringe), a mistake (misunderstanding about the drug to be given), or even a violation (deliberate over sedation of a difficult patient). The concepts are not easy to put into practice, except in circumstances where the action, context, and personal characteristics of those involved can be quite carefully explored.

3.4 Understanding the Influence of the Wider System

Human beings have the opportunity to contribute to accidents and clinical incidents at many different points in the process of production and operation. Problems and failures may occur in the design, testing, implementation of a new system, its maintenance and operation. The most obvious errors and failures are usually those that are the immediate causes of an accident, such as a train driver going through a red light or a doctor picking up the wrong syringe and injecting a fatal drug.

The immediate causes described above are the result of actions, or omissions, by people at the scene. However, other factors further back in the causal chain can also play a part in the genesis of an accident or a serious clinical incident. These 'latent conditions' lay the foundations for accidents in the sense that they create the conditions in which errors and failures can occur [5]. This places the operators at the sharp end in an invidious position as James Reason eloquently explains:

> Rather than being the instigators of an accident, operators tend to be the inheritors of system defects ...their part is usually that of adding the final garnish to a lethal brew whose ingredients have already been long in the cooking [4]

The organisational accident model applies this perspective to the study and analysis of accidents in many complex industries [5]. The accident sequence begins (from the left) with the negative consequences of organisational processes, such as planning, scheduling, forecasting, design, maintenance, strategy, and policy. The latent conditions so created are transmitted along various organisational and departmental pathways to the workplace (the operating theatre, the ward, etc.), where they create the local conditions that promote the commission of errors and violations (e.g. high workload or poor human–equipment interfaces). Many unsafe acts are likely to be committed, but very few of them will penetrate the defences to produce damaging outcomes. The fact that engineered safety features, such as alarms or standard procedures, can be deficient due to latent conditions as well as active failures is shown in Fig. 3.1 by the arrow connecting organisational processes directly to defences.

The model presents the people at the sharp end as the inheritors rather than as the instigators of an accident sequence. Reason points out that this may simply seem as if the 'blame' for accidents has been shifted from the sharp end to the system managers. However, managers too are

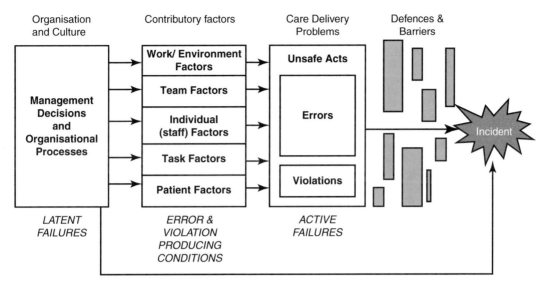

| Organisation and Culture | Contributory factors | Care Delivery Problems | Defences & Barriers |

Fig. 3.1 Organisational accident model from Vincent [6]

operating in a complex environment and the effects of their actions are not always apparent; they are no more, and no less, to blame than those at the sharp end of the clinical environment [7]. Reason also describes the human as the hero in complex work environments where errors are noticed, corrected, and accidents prevented, far more frequently than they are missed [8].

We should emphasise that not every slip, lapse, or mistake needs to be understood in terms of the full organisational framework; some errors are confined to the local context and can be largely explained by individual factors and the characteristics of the particular task at hand. However, major incidents almost always evolve over time, involve a number of people and a considerable number of contributory factors; in these circumstances the organisational model proves very illuminating.

3.5 Contributory Factors: Seven Levels of Safety

Reason's model has been extended and adapted for use in a healthcare setting, classifying the error producing conditions and organisational factors in a single broad framework of factors affecting clinical practice (see Table 3.1).

At the top of the framework are patient factors. In any clinical situation, the patient's condition will have the most direct influence on practice and outcome. Other patient factors such as personality, language, and psychological problems may also be important as they can influence communication with staff. The design of the task, the availability and clarity of protocols and guidelines may influence the care process and affect the quality of care. Individual factors include the knowledge, skills, and experience of each member of staff, which will obviously affect their clinical practice. Each staff member is part of a team within the inpatient or community unit, and part of the wider organisation of the hospital, primary care, or mental health service. The way an individual practises, and their impact on the patient, is constrained and influenced by other members of the team and the way they communicate, support and supervise each other. The team is influenced in turn by management actions and by decisions made at a higher level in the organisation. These include policies for the use of locum or agency staff, continuing education, training, and supervision and the availability of equipment and supplies. The organisation itself is affected by the institutional context, including financial constraints, external regulation, and the broader economic and political climate.

Table 3.1 Framework of contributory factors influencing clinical practice (from Vincent et al. [9])

Factor types	Contributory influencing factor
Patient factors	Condition (complexity and seriousness)
	Language and communication
	Personality and social factors
Task and technology factors	Task design and clarity of structure
	Availability and use of protocols
	Availability and accuracy of test results
	Decision-making aids
Individual (staff) factors	Knowledge and skills
	Competence
	Physical and mental health
Team factors	Verbal communication
	Written communication
	Supervision and seeking help
	Team leadership
Work environmental factors	Staffing levels and skills mix
	Workload and shift patterns
	Design, availability, and maintenance of equipment
	Administrative and managerial support
	Physical environment
Organisational and management factors	Financial resources and constraints
	Organisational structure
	Policy, standards, and goals
	Safety culture and priorities
Institutional context factors	Economic and regulatory context
	National health service executive
	Links with external organisations

3.6 Putting It All Together: Illustration of Two Cases from an Acute Care Setting

Cases and clinical stories have always been used in medical schools and clinical practice as a means of education and reflection on the nature of disease. The presentation of a case of diabetes, for instance, will illuminate understanding of the evolution of the disease, potential complications, and impact on the patient and their family. Cases can also be used to illustrate the process of clinical decision-making, the weighing of treatment options and sometimes, particularly when errors are discussed, the personal impact of incidents and mishaps. Incident analysis, for the purposes of improving the safety of healthcare, may encompass all of these perspectives but critically also includes reflection on the broader healthcare system.

We now take the concepts described above and apply them to clinical practice to show how chains of errors can combine to cause harm to patients. We also examine the role of the wider organisation by considering the various factors that contribute to the likelihood of an error and harm to a patient. We consider two illustrative cases of common presentations in acute hospital settings. The first evolved over several days and the second over a much shorter time frame (hours). In each case, we see a chain of errors and other problems in the process of care which combine to cause harm to the patient. We also, importantly, see how working conditions and wider organisational issues impact on clinical work and how vulnerabilities in the healthcare system pose major risks to patients.

3.6.1 Case 1: An Avoidable Patient Fall

Box 3.1 provides an overview of the events leading up to an avoidable fall on a medical ward. This 88-year-old man had multiple health problems and was admitted in a confused and distressed state. He fell while in hospital with

---

Box 3.1: An Avoidable Patient Fall

Day 1

An 88-year-old man was brought to the emergency department (ED) in the early afternoon by his wife and daughter. He had been becoming increasingly confused at home and was not taking care of himself as he normally would. His past medical history included chronic obstructive pulmonary disease, aortic valve replacement for stenosis, a laminectomy for sciatic nerve decompression, and benign prostatic hypertrophy. His presenting complaint was worsening confusion and hallucinations, disturbed sleep, poor appetite, and increased shortness of breath.

He was clerked in by a trainee doctor at 16:20 and seen by a consultant physician at

17:15 when a provisional diagnosis of sepsis of unknown origin was made. A bed was found on a medical ward (MW) and was transferred from ED at 21:00.

A falls risk assessment was undertaken in ED and he was found to be at high risk, unfortunately no falls action plan was made and the level of risk was not adequately handed over to the staff on MW. The family spoke to members of staff in ED and on MW about their concerns that the patient may fall and injure himself particularly as the bed on MW was in a bay at the end of the ward where the patient would not be easy to observe.

The ward was busy and it was staffed to agreed levels but the dependency of the patients was high. The nurse looking after this patient decided that he was settled and did not need 1:1 care but asked the care support worker (CSW) to review him regularly. The patient was being cared for on a bed with side rails (not recommended in high risk patients as they can become entangled in the rails if they are confused) and not on a low level bed with "crash mattresses" either side as recommended for patients at risk of falling.

At approximately 21:45 the patient was found on the floor by the bed having fallen. He was confused and complaining of pain in the right hip and thigh. He was reviewed by the trainee doctor on call whose note read (sic)

> Asked to see patient as unwitnessed fall, found by nursing staff alert but very confused, admitted with confusion and urinary tract infection. Plan for ECG, review of right hip in the morning for development of swelling/bruising, close observation to prevent further falls, day team to consider if further imaging is required.

The patient was moved to a bay where he could be closely observed, the ECG was reviewed (nothing acute was seen) and the nursing notes recorded an otherwise uneventful night with no obvious pain.

Day 2

The morning ward round was conducted by a different trainee doctor and the speech and language therapists came to review the patient and decided that he was too drowsy and confused to take fluid safely by mouth and so the intravenous infusion should continue. The trainee doctor decided that an X-Ray of the right hip should be done but requested it as a routine investigation and it was not, therefore, prioritised. The handover to the trainee doctor on call that night mentioned that the X-Ray had not been done and that it needed 'chasing'.

Day 3

A different trainee doctor undertook the ward round and notes concerns were raised in the nursing notes about bruising around the right knee but the patient also had a low blood pressure requiring closer monitoring and a fluid challenge. By 13:15, the X-ray had still not been done and the trainee doctor called the radiology department. At 16:00, the trainee doctor was called by the radiologist to report a hip fracture and suggest an urgent referral to the trauma surgeons.

While this patient was successfully treated for his hip fracture and returned home, the fall he sustained led to unnecessary pain, a protracted recovery and added to the concern felt by his family.

long-term consequences for his mobility and quality of life. We could easily see his fall as simply being the consequence of his frail condition and not the fault of healthcare staff. However, whether or not we regard anyone as being at fault, this story exposes some vulnerabilities in the healthcare system.

Following the event outline above, we can identify a series of problems in the care provided and a number of wider contributory factors. Figure 3.2 provides a summary of the key error points during this patient's admission to hospital and includes error types and contributory factors.

The contributory factors in the evolution of this incident were a mixture of problems with systems, organizational, work, and team factors— the kind of issues seen in most healthcare adverse events (these are categorised according to the London Protocol in Table 3.1).

An elderly patient with sepsis is difficult to assess because of their multiple comorbidities and the difficulties of communicating with someone who is confused. The emergency department and ward were also very busy reducing the time available. Nevertheless, we can identify the following problems or 'error points' in the sequence of care:

- Every adult over 65 years admitted to an acute hospital in the NHS should receive a falls risk assessment but it was not done properly. This patient was assessed for falls risk and was categorised (appropriately) as 'high risk' but no plan to reduce the risk was put in place and the information was not clearly handed over by the ED nurse to the nurse on MW.
- Although at high risk of a falls the patient was placed in a bay which was difficult to observe and not kept under close observation. The Care Support Worker allocated to the bay was

busy with someone else while this patient attempted to get of bed and fell.
- The trainee doctor on call on the night of the fall did an appropriate assessment of the patient but did not handover his concerns about the risk of fracture adequately.
- On Day 3 the patient had an additional problem (low blood pressure) another different trainee doctor (without senior assistance) reviewed the patient but was distracted by the low blood pressure and did not prioritise the investigation of the hip.

These are the principle error points (active failures in Reason's terms) in the care of this man that played a part in both the fall and to the delayed diagnosis of fracture. We can also (Table 3.2) look at the wide range of factors that contributed to these problems occurring. These included: the frailty and confusion of the patient made assessment difficult, the inconsistent methods for monitoring and recording falls, the inexperience of the junior doctor, the lack of systematic handover, and the fact that at night the hospital has a lower nurse to patient ratio and that other elderly patients required a high level of support from the nurses on duty.

Fig. 3.2 Error chain describing key error points leading to an avoidable fall and a delay in diagnosis of hip fracture. *Contributory factors (from the London Protocol) are highlighted and colour coded according to type*

Table 3.2 Contributory factors in a case of avoidable fall (from the London Protocol)

Contributory factors	Examples from case of avoidable fall
Patient factors	• The patient was elderly and confused making communication and assessment more challenging (e.g. difficulty communicating pain in the hip after the fall) • Elderly confused patients find strange environments distressing contributing to the risk of wandering and falling • The patient's comorbidities and acute illness (sepsis, poor swallow, low blood pressure) were a distraction to staff contributing to the delay in diagnosing the fracture • The family raised concerns about the risk of falling but these were not acted on
Task/ technology factors	• Protocols for the management of patients at risk of falling were not followed, a busy ED, and lack of adequate training in the use of the protocols contributed to this issue • Records of falls risk were made in different ways between clinical settings—the ED used a computer system and the MW had paper forms
Individual factors	• The trainee doctors did not recognise the risk of fracture after a fall in elderly patients, lack of experience contributed to the delay in prioritising the hip X-ray
Team factors	• Missed opportunities in the handover of care within the nursing and medical teams and the multidisciplinary team overall • Trainee doctors did not provide adequate handovers regarding the fall and requirement for investigation to team members taking over care of the patient • Trainee doctors did not escalate concerns to a senior member of the medical team • No senior medical leadership on ward rounds to support decision-making
Work/ environment factors	• Busy medical ward • Complicated, frail patient requiring extensive assistance with activities of daily living on top of the care required for the acute illness • Providing adequate supervision for a patient at risk of falls is challenging when a ward is busy and when staff numbers are lower (e.g. at night) • The patient was in a bay at the end of the ward making it more difficult to observe him
Organisational factors	• No standardised method of record keeping for falls assessment: electronic records in ED but paper records on MW

3.6.2 Case 2: An Avoidable Emergency Laparotomy in a Case of Ectopic Pregnancy

Box 3.2 provides an overview of events leading up to conversion to emergency laparotomy in a young woman with an ectopic pregnancy. The case resonates with the fall described above in the sense that it would be easy to see the delayed diagnosis and treatment as a result of the patient's youth: her cardiovascular system was able to mask the signs of shock and so medical staff did not suspect haemorrhage. It is only when we take a more holistic view of the incident that we see the latent system and organisational issues which are summarised in Fig. 3.3 along with error types.

Diagnostic challenges are a part of every medical student's training and this case illustrates a well-recognised situation where haemorrhage is masked by the robust response of a healthy car-

Box 3.2: An Avoidable Emergency Laparotomy in a Case of Ectopic Pregnancy
A 28-year-old woman with abdominal pain and lethargy arrived in the busy emergency department (ED) at 16:19 and was seen by a triage nurse who recorded some baseline observations and referred the patient to the ED trainee doctor, stating that she was "not worried" about the patient. The protocol for the investigation and management of early pregnancy in ED was inadequate, and there was a delay in sending the necessary blood samples for diagnosis. The track and trigger score was incorrectly calculated and follow-up observations (for heart rate and blood pressure) were, therefore, not increased in frequency resulting in a delay in calling for an expert opinion from a gynaecologist. The ED trainee doctor did not

recognise the urgency of the situation and when the referral was made to gynaecology the handover did not emphasise the seriousness of the situation adequately. The trainee gynaecologist, therefore, advised that the patient be sent to the gynaecology ward for further assessment without coming to ED to see the patient.

When the patient arrived on the ward, the senior trainee gynaecologist diagnosed an ectopic pregnancy and recognised that the patient's condition was deteriorating (her haemoglobin had dropped significantly to 99 g/L, her blood pressure was falling, and she was now complaining of shoulder tip pain). The decision was made to take the patient to theatre for emergency laparoscopic surgery and because it was now after 18:00, theatres in the main hospital were informed and the case was booked with the on-call anaesthetist. Audits had revealed that very few gynaecological emergencies came to theatre after normal working hours and consequently gynaecological patients were transferred to main theatres out of hours.

When the consultant surgeon was called (there was a 30 min delay in locating him), he agreed to come in and assist with the procedure. The patient arrived in theatre 5 h after the initial presentation with a very low blood pressure and a haemoglobin of 67 g/L. The WHO pre-list briefing was completed without the consultant gynaecologist who did not arrive until the patient was anaesthetised and being prepared for surgery by the senior trainee gynaecologist and after the 'time out' section of the WHO checklist.

At this time, the patient was extremely unwell and there was significantly heightened pressure to get on with the procedure. Tensions were high and when problems arose with the laparoscopy equipment (an accidentally de-sterilised light source and diathermy forceps which were incompatible with the electrical lead) behaviour deteriorated and exacerbated the stress felt by staff in theatre. The delays caused by the equipment problems necessitated a decision to convert to an open procedure which the Consultant made promptly in order to gain control of the bleeding. Once the haemorrhage was controlled and additional blood products were given the operation to remove the fallopian tube was completed uneventfully and the patient was stabilised and transferred to recovery with no further complications.

This case is similar to the one described above in that it contains the same types of contributory factors and errors that led to the eventual adverse event. The patient recovered well but had to stay in hospital longer to recover because the procedure was converted to a more invasive surgical approach.

diovascular system. However, what is not commonly taught in medical school curricula is the risk of missing diagnoses due to distraction and system failures. This young woman's case illustrates those problems very well:

- The nurse in ED was using a poorly designed protocol for early pregnancy which did not stress the importance of urgent blood samples.
- The trainee doctor had limited experience, was busy with other cases, and was influenced by the nurse's lack of concern. He therefore did not request an urgent review of the patient.
- Staffing problems in the hospital meant that emergency gynaecology cases after 18:00 had to be taken to main theatres and transfer time from the gynaecology ward was 20 min. Furthermore, no training was offered to support staff in acclimatising to the different work environment they would be in after hours.
- The WHO checklist was not used adequately which led to a lack of understanding of what type of equipment would be available and no opportunity for a discussion of potential problems and their mitigations.

Fig. 3.3 Error chain describing key error points in a case of emergency laparotomy for ectopic pregnancy. *Contributory factors (from the London Protocol) are highlighted and colour coded according to type*

- The gynaecologists were not used to the scrub staff or the theatre environment and equipment and when the situation became stressful the team did not function effectively and had to perform a more invasive operation to control the bleeding.

These are the principle error points leading to the emergency conversion to laparotomy in what could have been a more straightforward laparoscopic procedure. The heightened stress in this situation further impaired team function but the 'upstream' delays in diagnosis, staff shortages, and the physical location of the ward and theatres along with organisation of the gynaecology service out of hours all contributed to the ultimate crisis (see Table 3.3 for detailed categorisation of contributory factors).

3.7   Conducting Your Own Incident Investigation

There are a number of methods of investigation and analysis available in healthcare, though these tend to be comparatively under-developed in comparison with methods available in industry [10]. In the USA, the most familiar is the root cause analysis approach of the Joint Commission, an intensive process with its origins in Total Quality Management approaches to healthcare improvement [11]. The Veterans Hospital Administration has developed a highly structured system of triage questions which is being disseminated throughout their system. We do not have space to examine all potential methods, which vary in their orientation, theoretical basis, and basic approach. All however, to a greater or lesser extent, uncover factors contributing to the final incident. We will summarise an approach developed at University College London by the Clinical Safety Research Unit known, imaginatively, as the London Protocol [12].

Most other approaches to analysing incidents in healthcare are termed 'root cause analysis'; in contrast, we have described our own approach to the analysis of incidents as a systems analysis as we believe that it is a more accurate and more fruitful description. The term root cause analysis, while widespread, is misleading in a number of respects [13, 14]. Most importantly, it implies that the purpose of an investigation is to identify

Table 3.3 Contributory factors to a gynaecological emergency

Contributory factors	Examples from case of ectopic pregnancy
Patient factors	• The patient's initial presentation was not overtly serious (she was young and so signs of shock were masked) and led to a false sense of security in a less experienced member of the team (the ED trainee doctor) • The patient's rapid deterioration in theatre led to heightened stress amongst the staff in theatre and impaired performance
Task/ technology factors	• The protocol for the management of early pregnancy in ED was not adequate • The WHO briefing should have provided an opportunity to highlight the concerns about equipment but not all team members were present
Individual factors	• The trainee doctor in ED lacked experience in the management of early pregnancy • The scrub staff in theatre knew where the gynaecology equipment was kept but were not using it regularly and did not have regular training to maintain their competencies. When under pressure, the challenge of using unfamiliar equipment was too much • The two gynaecologists were working in an unfamiliar theatre environment • During the most stressful time, the consultant gynaecologist became angry which caused additional stress to the other staff and led to impaired performance
Team factors	• This team did not work together regularly • The WHO briefing was not done with the whole team present • There was no regular programme of simulated emergency training to support the development of teamworking skills in a crisis
Work/ environment factors	• There was a shortage of theatre staff in gynaecology • The gynaecology ward and theatres are on another part of the hospital site, distant from ED and main theatres • It was not possible to staff gynaecology theatres out of hours. This necessitated transfer of gynaecology emergencies to main theatres (which took 20 min) • The theatre environment and equipment in the main suite was very different from gynaecology theatres
Organisational factors	• Recruitment and retention of theatre staff was a problem across all theatre sites • Theatre suites had been designed and built at different times with no standardisation

a single or small number of 'root causes'. If you look back at the two case examples however you will see that there is no 'root cause'. Our analyses have shown a much more fluid and complex picture. Usually, there is a chain of events and a wide variety of contributory factors leading up to the eventual incident. Incident analysis, properly understood, is not a retrospective search for root causes but an attempt to use the incident as a 'window on the system' to reveal the vulnerabilities and hazards that are constant threats to patient care.

Too often the questions asked about an incident focus on "who?" rather than "how?" with the result that individuals rather than systems are targeted and blamed. High reliability organisations have recognised the need to move away from a culture of blame, which leads to reluctance to report incidents, and have developed a

Table 3.4 Critical incident paradigms (adapted from Woods et al. [15])

Old view	New view
Human error is seen as a cause of failure	Human error is seen as the effect of systemic vulnerabilities deeper inside the organisation
Saying what people should have done is a satisfying way to describe failure	Saying what people should have done does not explain why it made sense for them to do what they did
Telling people to be more careful will make the problem go away	Only by constantly seeking out vulnerabilities can organisations enhance safety

just culture where learning from incidents (including near misses) is encouraged and expected. The paradigm shift in these organisations is outlined in Table 3.4 but, unfortunately, is not yet well developed in healthcare [15].

3.8   Systems Analysis of Clinical Incidents

During an investigation, information is gleaned from a variety of sources. Case records, statements, and any other relevant documentation are reviewed. Structured interviews with key members of staff are then undertaken to establish the chronology of events, the main care delivery problems and their respective contributory factors, as perceived by each member of staff. Ideally, the patient, or a member of their family, should also be interviewed though as yet this is not yet common practice in these analyses. The key questions are 'What happened? (the outcome and chronology); How did it happen? (the errors and care delivery problems); and Why did it happen? (the contributory factors)'.

Once the chronology of events is clear there are three main considerations: the errors and other care delivery problems identified within the chronology, the clinical context for each of them, and the factors contributing to the occurrence of the care delivery problems. Any combination of contributory factors might contribute to the occurrence of a single care delivery problem. The investigator needs to differentiate between those contributory factors that are only relevant on that particular occasion and those which are long-standing or permanent features of the unit. For instance, there may be a failure of communication between two midwives which might be an isolated occurrence or might reflect a more general pattern of poor communication on the unit.

While a considerable amount of information can be gleaned from written records, interviews with those involved are the most important method of identifying the contributory factors. This is especially so if the interview systematically explores these factors and so allows the member of staff to collaborate in the investigation. In the interview, the story and 'the facts' are just the first stage. The staff member is also encouraged to identify both the successful aspects of the care provided and the errors and care delivery problems. Both staff members and inter-

viewer can reflect together on the contributory factors, which greatly enriches both the interview and investigation.

Analyses using this method have been conducted in hospitals, primary care settings, and mental health units. The protocol may be used in a variety of formats, by individual clinicians, researchers, risk managers, and by clinical teams. A clinical team may use the method to guide and structure reflection on an incident, to ensure that the analysis is full and comprehensive. For serious incidents, a team of individuals with different skills and backgrounds would be assembled though often only a risk manager or an individual clinician will be needed. The contributory factors that reflect more general problems in a unit are the targets for change and systems improvement. When obvious problems are identified action may be taken after a single incident, but when more substantial changes are being considered other incident analyses and sources of data (routine audits and outcome data) should also be taken into account.

3.8.1   From Analysis to Meaningful Action

When considering the error type in the context of the contributory factors at the time of the error, it becomes clearer how meaningful interventions might be made to prevent similar incidents in future. Sometimes incident investigations point to immediate changes that need to be made, such as replacement of faulty equipment or updating of misleading or inconsistent guidelines. Generally, however, we should not generate plans for major interventions on the basis of a single incident but draw on a wider range of information and check that the findings of the incident are really indicative of more widespread problems. We can nevertheless think about usual intervention that might be made on the basis of our analyses of the two cases.

For example, in the first case there were several rules-based mistakes. The protocol for falls assessment and prevention was not used adequately by the nurses. Some important contributory factors were the inconsistencies in falls risk assessment and recording and also the staffing shortages at critical times. These suggest potential interventions:

- A review of staffing levels and consideration of different working patterns to cover busy times more effectively could help
- Standardising the way falls risk assessments are recorded across all clinical areas (the use of electronic patient records can help here)

The second analysis reveals a rather different range of problems and contributory factors and, correspondingly, different types of potential interventions. Undertaking an emergency laparoscopy is not an unusual occurrence in gynaecology but the knowledge-based mistake leading to conversion to an open procedure can be better understood when we realise that staff were unfamiliar with each other and their equipment and environment, the WHO checklist was done in a hurry and without the consultant surgeon present and that staff had not previously trained as a team to deal with crisis situations. Potential interventions, therefore, might be:

- Scrub staff from gynaecology theatres could work on a rotational basis in the main theatres to ensure they used the environment and equipment and equipment could be standardised across sites
- Training to embed good practice in the use of the WHO checklist for theatre teams
- Regular simulation training to support staff in the management of emergencies

The design and implementation of realistic and sustainable interventions to prevent incidents recurring is a topic outside the scope of this chapter. Suffice it to say that where possible the implementation of a physical rather than a procedural intervention is more likely to succeed (e.g. the design of a device to prevent retention of guidewires after the insertion of a central venous line rather than a change to the procedure requiring additional checks to be made). However, in a financially constrained health service sometimes physical interventions may be prohibitively expensive and well-designed checklists with training to support embedding them in practice may be the best compromise [16].

3.9 Supporting Patients, Families, and Staff

In this chapter, we have focussed on understanding how error and harm occur and offered models of understanding and practical approaches to investigation. We have hopefully persuaded you that understanding the wider psychological and organisational influences on clinical practice will enrich your approach to medicine and provide a foundation for improving the care provided to patients. The chapter would be incomplete however if we did not mention, if only briefly, the need to also consider the aftermath of serious errors and the needs of those affected [17].

The impact of a medical injury differs from most other accidents in two important respects. First, patients have been harmed, unintentionally, by people in whom they placed considerable trust, so their reaction may be especially powerful and hard to cope with. Secondly, and even more important, they are often cared for by the same professions, and perhaps the same people, as those involved in the original injury. They may have been very frightened by what has happened to them, and have a range of conflicting feelings about those involved; this too can be very difficult, even when staff are sympathetic and supportive. Many people harmed by their treatment suffer further trauma through the incident being insensitively and inadequately handled. Conversely when staff come forward, acknowledge the damage, and take the necessary action, the overall impact can be greatly reduced.

In our two examples, the patients eventually recovered although both experienced much unnecessary anxiety and suffering in the process.

However, the long-term consequences some serious incidents can be life changing in terms of pain, disability, and effect on family relationships and the ability to work. Patients and families need support immediately after the serious incident and sometimes over long periods afterwards. The healthcare organisation concerned has a responsibility to provide or arrange for this care. Injured patients need an explanation, an apology, to know that changes have been made to prevent future incidents, and often also need practical and financial help. The absence of any of these factors can be a powerful stimulus to complaint or litigation.

Staff also suffer a variety of consequences when involved in serious incidents. Albert Wu captured the experience of making a serious error in his paper 'the second victim', not implying that the experiences of staff were necessarily comparable to those of injured patients [18]. Surgeons, for instance, can be seriously affected by serious complications that they perceive to have been their fault. Emotional reactions range from guilt and crisis of confidence, to anger and worry about one's career. Even though the intense emotional impact progressively fades, there are certain cases that surgeons recollect many years later. Serious complications often make surgeons more conservative or risk-adverse in the management of patients, which can be detrimental for patient care [19].

3.10 Conclusions and Recommendations

It is an unfortunate truth that the prevailing culture around serious incidents in healthcare remains one of blame. When a serious incident occurs, the first priority is obviously the care of the patient and family. The second priority however should be supporting colleagues and not rushing to blame or condemn people who make serious mistakes. Some types of behaviour deserve blame and sanctions, but even the best people make honest mistakes. When this happens, they need support from both colleagues and their organisation both for their own well-being

and for the sake of all the patients they will be looking after in the future.

High reliability organisations have spent decades developing robust, standardised systems of investigating incidents including the establishment of truly independent expert investigative bodies (such as the UK's Air Accident Investigation Branch, https://www.gov.uk/government/organisations/air-accidents-investigation-branch). Healthcare has learnt from some of these lessons and in April 2017 the Healthcare Safety Investigation Branch was established in the NHS (https://www.hsib.org.uk) with the stated purpose of 'improving patient safety through effective and independent investigations that don't apportion blame or liability'. Their work has only just begun but will draw on existing expertise in the NHS to capture the widely shared ambition of learning from the past to improve the future.

Some branches of medicine, most notably anaesthesia, have been at the forefront of developments in patient safety [20, 21]. Human factors is a core theme throughout the postgraduate curricula for anaesthesia training and quick reference handbooks (much like those in the military or civil aviation) have been developed as cognitive aids for diagnostic challenges particularly in crises (https://anaesthetists.org/Home/Resources-publications/Safety-alerts/Anaesthesia-emergencies/Quick-Reference-Handbook). These developments in postgraduate specialty curricula must be extended to undergraduate teaching in medical and nursing schools. It is only by ensuring that young professionals in healthcare are equipped with the necessary tools to understand the complex, rapidly evolving systems in which they will be working, that they will be able to improve them [22].

References

1. Woods DD, Cook RI. Nine steps to move forward from error. Cogn Technol Work. 2002;4(2):137–44.
2. Hollnagel E. Cognitive reliability and error analysis method: CREAM. Oxford: Elsevier; 1998.
3. Senders JW, Moray N, North Atlantic Treaty Organization. Conference on the nature and source

of human error, 2nd: 1983: Bellagio, I, Human error: cause, prediction, and reduction. Hillsdale, NJ: L. Erlbaum Associates; 1991.

4. Reason JT. Human error. Cambridge: Cambridge University Press; 1990.

5. Reason JT. Managing the risks of organizational accidents. Aldershot: Ashgate; 1997.

6. Vincent C. Patient safety. 2nd ed. Chichester: Wiley-Blackwell Publishing Ltd.; 2010.

7. Reason J. Human error: models and management. BMJ. 2000;320(7237):768–70.

8. Reason JT. The human contribution: unsafe acts, accidents and heroic recoveries. Farnham: Ashgate; 2008.

9. Vincent C, Taylor-Adams S, Stanhope N. Framework for analysing risk and safety in clinical medicine. BMJ. 1998;316(7138):1154–7.

10. Woloshynowych M, Rogers S, Taylor-Adams S, Vincent C. The investigation and analysis of critical incidents and adverse events in healthcare. Health Technol Assess. 2005;9(19):1–143.

11. Spath PL. Error reduction in health care : a systems approach to improving patient safety. San Francisco, CA: Jossey-Bass; 2011.

12. Taylor-Adams S, Vincent C. Systems analysis of clinical incidents: the London protocol. Clin Risk. 2004;10(6):211–20.

13. Macrae C. The problem with incident reporting. BMJ Qual Saf. 2016;25(2):71–5.

14. Peerally MF, Carr S, Waring J, Dixon-Woods M. The problem with root cause analysis. BMJ Qual Saf. 2017;26:417–22.

15. Woods DD, Dekker SWA, Cook R, Johannesen L, Sarter N. Behind human error. Farnham: Ashgate; 2010.

16. Hoffman C, Beard P, Greenall J, David U, White J. Canadian root cause analysis framework. 2006. Available from: http://www.patientsafetyinstitute. ca/en/toolsResources/IncidentAnalysis/Documents/ Canadian Incident Analysis Framework.PDF.

17. Manser T. Managing the aftermath of critical incidents: meeting the needs of health-care providers and patients. Best Pract Res Clin Anaesthesiol. 2011;25(2):169–79.

18. Wu AW. Medical error: the second victim. BMJ. 2000;320(7237):726–7.

19. Pinto A, Faiz O, Bicknell C, Vincent C. Surgical complications and their implications for surgeons' well-being. Br J Surg. 2013;100(13):1748–55.

20. Higham H, Baxendale B. To err is human: use of simulation to enhance training and patient safety in anaesthesia. Br J Anaesth. 2017;119(Suppl_1):i106–14.

21. Gaba DM. Anaesthesiology as a model for patient safety in health care. BMJ. 2000;320(7237):785–8.

22. Vincent C, Amalberti R. Safer healthcare: strategies for the real world. Cham: Springer Open; 2016. Available from: http://www.springer.com/gb/ book/9783319255576.

Looking to the Future

4

Peter Lachman

Learning Objectives
- Understand the future challenges for patient safety
- Describe how psychological safety is essential for safety
- List the social determinants of patient safety
- Comprehend the concepts of co-production of safety
- List facilitators and risks of new technologies for safety

4.1 Introduction

In this chapter, I will explore the issues that we need to address as we proceed on the safety journey. This will include reflections on the beliefs that have resulted in the healthcare system we have created. It is important to consider the real issues of design and whether we need to change all aspects of healthcare delivery if we really want to be safe.

It is clear that the rapid progress in medical science over the past century has resulted in untold benefits for all. Foucault [1] described the emergence as the development of the "*clinical gaze*", whereby the person became a patient with a disease, so was no longer a person, but rather a

P. Lachman (✉)
International Society for Quality in Health Care
(ISQua), Dublin, Ireland

"*clinical diagnosis*" subject to tests and interventions. As a result, the needs of the person were changed, and their narrative was not as important as the medical tests and investigations. There have been many benefits in the development of modern medicine and the science that was created to provide successful interventions. People who became patients were cured or provided longevity. This in turn has resulted in the new challenges of chronic disease and the ageing population [2]. Unfortunately, in many societies, there are both the old problems of infection and late treatment of disease, as well as the new problems of ageing and chronicity. In addition, economic and political decisions have created a vast challenge of poverty-related healthcare with poorer outcomes.

Alongside the technological advance, we also have the loss of the compassionate part of healing which has had a major impact on the psychological safety of healthcare providers and the people who receive care. The improvement in outcomes in terms of disease management has been accompanied by increasing levels of adverse events and harm. The development of the patient safety movement over the past 20 years is a reflection of the advances in healthcare and the realisation that with success came a new problem of inadvertent harm. On reflection, healthcare delivery was not planned to be safe.

As we look to the future, the healthcare industry is at a critical juncture. The rapid develop-

L. Donaldson et al. (eds.), *Textbook of Patient Safety and Clinical Risk Management*,
https://doi.org/10.1007/978-3-030-59403-9_4

ment of theories on how to deliver safe, person-centred care means that we can no longer rely on the excuse that *"healthcare is different"* from other industries, so cannot be reliable and safe. People are now demanding safety and reliability in the care they receive, and they want to be treated as people who happen to be ill, rather than as a number or a disease. Currently, it is by chance rather than by design that one receives highly reliable person-centred and safe care. Yet we continue to build the same type of hospitals, educate future nurses and clinicians as we have always done, and operate in a hierarchical system that disempowers people, rather than enables people to be healthy.

An examination of the patient safety movement provides an understanding of where we need to go as we plan for the future. With some imagination, we can redesign the processes of care to be compassionate and safe. Bates and Singh [3] note that there has been much progress since the publication of *To Err is Human* [4]. We have learnt many methods of quality improvement, and patient safety as a science has numerous theories, methodologies, and tools that, if implemented, can decrease harm: *"Highly effective interventions have since been developed and adopted for hospital-acquired infections and medication safety, although the impact of these interventions varies because of their inconsistent implementation and practice. Progress in addressing other hospital-acquired adverse events has been variable"* [3].

Amalberti and Vincent [5] have taken the view that the healthcare delivery system has inherent risk and that the focus of patient safety should be on the proactive management of that risk. This is true of any complex adaptive system, which makes it difficult to be safe all the time [6]. However, the health system has not been designed with safety as the core function. Given that we know that there is more complexity, perhaps a total redesign of the system is the way we need to go as we move to the future.

Although the provision of healthcare is complex, it is possible to overcome the complexity and provide care that is of the highest standard in

all the domains of quality. To achieve a safe system, we will need to address some fundamental issues that we have accepted as the norm.

4.2 The Vision for the Future

The future vision is often reflected in the concept of *Zero Harm*. There are movements to apply the standards to medicine that we accept in other industries. The argument for and against zero harm is compelling. If we do not aim for zero, what is the number we need to aim for? It may be that we aim for zero in some specific areas while accepting that within the complexity of the healthcare zero, the totality of zero is a mirage, one that we need to aim for but will never reach. It has been argued that the ideal of Zero Harm is unrealistic [7], that we should accept the inherent risk in the delivery of healthcare and therefore actively adopt patient safety initiatives to improve outcomes and minimise risk. Furthermore, we need to accept the stresses healthcare systems face in the delivery of care—be it of demand, finance, or morale.

4.3 The Challenges to Overcome to Facilitate Safety

The pursuit of a healthcare system that is safe will require courage, as the current power base is not conducive to safe care. The power of the medical profession, pharmaceutical industry, and supporting bodies is based on the current model of care, with hierarchies and structures. Hospitals, as a concept, gained their power in the last century and were developed for the illnesses that we have now addressed, so the next stage is to integrate that power with the wider health community. This will result in changing the power imbalance in the system and the recognition that the design of a system with the hospital at the centre can be changed to the hospital as the facilitator of health within a system of care delivery which is focused closer to the home. This will require a reallocation of resources to primary care and a change of healthcare to health. There is a way forward to address these key issues and there is hope that in time healthcare delivery and the promotion of health will be safe with proactive minimisation of risk. People will still be harmed; however, the degree of harm will be different to the current situation. As we redesign services to be safer in the future, we will need a vision that sees beyond the current challenge and plans for an integrated service of care focused on health rather than disease (Box 4.1).

Box 4.1: Changes for the Future

1. **Develop the language and culture of safety**
   - Use the right language about safety
   - Leaders ask the right questions about safety
   - Educate people for safety
2. **Promote psychological safety**
   - Care for both physical and psychological safety of people
   - Nurture providers of care and provide meaning in work
   - Ensure that providers of care have a sense of belonging
   - Listen to and hear person stories
3. **Design for safety**
   - Invest in health rather than healthcare
   - Co-produce safety with people not with patients
   - Place people in charge of their health, not their disease
   - Use human factors to address complexity
4. **Social determinants for Patient Safety**
   - Recognise the importance of social determinants of health and their impact on safety
   - Care is culturally sensitive and promotes safety
5. **Harnessing technology for the future**
   - Digital health for safety
   - Empowering people with technology

4.4 Develop the Language and Culture of Safety

- Use of the language that enhances safety
- Leaders asking the right questions about safety
- Educate people for safety

As healthcare is a complex system, so is the culture which is manifest within any organisation. Culture defines our belief systems and in turn how we behave. Within any organisation this will be complex, with differing safety cultures [8]. The culture we represent is evident in the language we use. *Patient safety* is the current terminology and as we move to a more people-centred approach, the language we use will evolve to being people centred rather than patient focused. Language reflects culture, so if we want to develop a safety culture, then we will need to critically analyse the terminology we use. *Healthcare* is a misnomer as it focuses on disease management, whereas we need to focus on health and the maintenance of both physical and mental well-being. Patients will be protected if we view them as people with a disease, with a life outside the disease, rather than as patients with a disease. This results in a loss of power and control over their own lives and lack of power may be a contributing cause of harm.

Patient Safety is the overall science, *Risk Management* was the first intervention that was developed in the safety journey. In essence, this was not about managing risk but rather about managing incidents that had occurred. While this is essential, it has not resulted in a decrease in harm and the learning from it has not been as great as it should be. The move to learning from investigation has been one of the greatest challenges we have faced. If one considers the integration of resilience engineering into the risk management approach, then the incident investigation will be a study of work as it really is over the pathway and not the incident. We now need to move to the concept of looking at the patient journey and how health is provided, so that the person is protected at all parts of the journey [9]. Management of risk is a proactive activity and is what should happen at all times, not only when there is an incident. It implies the acceptance of risk rather than the desire to eliminate risk, and constant mitigation will decrease the potential for harm.

Another example of language ambiguity is the term, "*near misses*", which is used for when we nearly harm a person but then either due to the action of an individual, or by chance the person is not harmed. This is really a near hit and if it were termed as such, perhaps we would pay more attention to the problem.

Leadership for safety will be the foundation of future work in patient safety. Leaders in healthcare are at all levels in the system, as there needs to be a focus in every microsystem as well in the de facto leadership at executive level. This includes the appreciation of uncertainty, the integration of information from different sources and the setting of the goals that will allow for the development of safe systems. Leadership, therefore, needs to be encouraged at all levels of the organisation, with the development and facilitation of local leadership at the interface with the patient as the key to ensure that there will be a safe environment. Change will require leaders who understand what quality, safe person-centred care really is, with a deep understanding of Systems Theory and Human Factors, as well as knowing how to realign the budget to facilitate change. This requires vision to set the direction, hope to provide succour in trying times, respect for what is being changed and for the work that is done, and courage to make the changes against the resistance that the past ways will present.

At a policy level, the wider implication of a total redesign of the system will require political will to allow the realignment and re-engineering of the healthcare system to one in which all policy is aimed at the long-term health of the community. Politicians need to invest in health while funding healthcare.

All of this change will require courage and imagination, vision, and hope. But more importantly, it will require co-production with all the people involved, particularly people who will be receiving care. The patient safety movement has tended to apply tools and methods to people, rather than designing with them. This implies the

need to be open and transparent with patients and their families.

The healthcare workforce will require an education that enables them to deliver health as well as manage disease safely. This will require an understanding of the theories of Complexity Science, Systems Theory, Patient Safety Science, and Human Factors. Medical curricula must be challenged and changed to educate the clinicians that we require in the future [10].

4.5 Promote Psychological Safety

- Care for both physical and psychological safety of people
- Nurture providers of care and provide meaning in work
- Ensure that providers of care have a sense of belonging
- Address the challenge of clinician burnout

Psychological safety is the foundation for providing safe care for individuals. The work by Edmondson has led the way to understanding that, in order to deliver safe care, we need to engender the "psychological safety" of individuals in the health workplace, so that they in turn are part of the overall culture of safety. Edmondson defines psychological safety as a "*shared belief held by members of a team that the team is safe for interpersonal risk-taking*" [11–13].

The safety movement has called for organisations to facilitate safety culture, in which individuals have responsibilities to be safe and to carry out their work in a manner that will mitigate against harm. Given the complexity of the type of work undertaken in healthcare, this is difficult to achieve within the current hierarchical constructs of most health organisations.

While some hierarchy is essential, the ability to take risks and feel able to challenge in order to promote safe practices is one of the major challenges we will face going forward. Investigations of clinical incidents usually identify communication issues in which hierarchy prevents the communication of potential risk, teamwork being problematic and blame being present. The concept of psychological safety is now central to the development of safe systems, and is therefore as important as the development of tools and methods to facilitate safe care. Much of the concepts of building resilience in healthcare organisations will require attention to how we support all members of staff to be part of teams with a sense of belonging in which the meaning of work includes safety of the individuals, supported to challenge and able to learn in real time.

The concepts of safety need to build the resilience by also learning from what works within the complexity of care delivery to address the well-being of clinicians [14]. Included in the development of a safe environment will be an active programme to prevent burnout of clinical staff as this has a negative impact on both their well-being and the safety of patients. Prevention of burnout has not been part of the traditional patient safety interventions, yet stressed clinicians are unable to deliver safe care. Interventions. As we take a systems and human factors approach to patient safety, part of that approach will be the management of burnout taking into account the multifactorial reasons from education, hierarchies, technology, and overall design of the service [15].

The progress made in development of interventions will now be matched by the concept that the delivery of healthcare requires the concept of patient safety is our core business and all that we do need to be focused on safety. Therefore, all people working in the healthcare setting need to be supported to be safe and to proactively work to their own safety from a psychological and physical perspective. The safety of the people for who they care will then follow.

4.6 Design for Health and for Safety

- Invest in health rather than healthcare
- Co-produce safety with people not with patients
- Place people in charge of their health, not their disease
- Use human factors and ergonomics to address complexity

The patient safety movement has been focused on healthcare which really implies that it is concerned with the negative impacts in the management of disease. The future of the movement will transcend disease and focus on maintaining the health of people, even when they have disease. This approach implies that people with a disease need to have their physical and mental health beyond their disease protected at all times by minimising the risk of harm. To achieve this aim, we need to move to a new paradigm, and change the current design of our healthcare system, which is focused on physiological systems rather than the person as a whole. This implies a change in the systems we have created, which have been medically focused. It does not imply that we destroy all we have, but rather that we examine people flows, human factors, and safety from the eyes of the person receiving care.

The concept of engaging with the people who receive care has become central to the person-centred care movement. The person-centred care approach is more than asking about satisfaction and experience, but rather in sharing responsibility for health and becoming partners in healthcare provision. The realisation that we cannot be safe without the involvement of the people who we care for in the planning and design of services has led to the concept of co-production, in which people are part of the solution rather than part of the problem [16–18]. This approach implies a radical rethink on how we define adverse events, how we look at harm from the viewpoint of the family and person harmed, and how we investigate safety incidents with the inclusion of the patient as a person, not as a patient. It will require a re-evaluation of clinical risk, a change in the power imbalance and real consultation with people about risk and the relative benefit of intervention. Co-production also implies that we co design safety not only with the people we call patients, but also with the providers of care who have to be safe all the time, despite the inherent risk of the clinical processes and especially in trying conditions.

To achieve safety within clinical process will require the integration of safety design as part of the day-to-day operations. Human Factors and Ergonomics (HFE) has been a marginal topic in healthcare, pursued by enthusiasts rather than being core to the programmes that we run. In other chapters, the HFE theories have been presented. HFE will be as integral to medical education as anatomy and physiology, so that it is a seam that runs through all of our thinking [19].

4.7   Social Determinants of Patient Safety

- Define the importance of social determinants of patient safety
- Design care that is culturally sensitive and promotes safety

In recent years, the importance of the determinants of health outcomes has been highlighted with the studies that indicate that people who are less well-off economically, are from ethnic minorities or marginalised groups have worse health outcomes. Poverty, housing, education, literacy, and nutrition are a few of the factors that interplay to cause clinical presentations, as well as the outcome of treatment be it due to poor access, lack of health literacy, or institutionalised prejudice [20]. Health outcomes can be predicted depending on the influences of the social determinants. The poorer one is, the worse is the clinical outcome. Poverty influences life expectancy, the type of diseases to which one will succumb, the access to health, and the quality of healthcare [21]. The patient safety movement has not traditionally researched the impact of the social determinants of health on the risk of harm, either for individuals or for communities [22].

It is logical to expect that people who are poor, have low health literacy, and do not have equal access to the healthcare system, are likely to be at risk of harm due to the immense power differentials and the institutionalised prejudice they experience. If one adds ethnicity, gender, language and status, e.g. refugee or homeless, then the outcome is likely to be even worse. The challenge for the patient safety movement is to acknowledge the inequity and to mitigate against it in the design of programmes. We need to measure this perspective of patient safety in order to allow for

the development of interventions that empower people and address the impact poverty and disadvantage have on safety.

From a global perspective, the work by the Lancet Commission on the increased risk to the people in the poorer nations of the Lower and Middle Income Countries indicates that we will need more than the patient safety methodologies to protect people in those countries from harm [23]. In the future, the Social Determinants of Patient Safety (or SDPS) will be as important in understanding how to prevent harm as are the methods and interventions we use to mitigate against adverse events.

4.8   Harnessing Technology for the Future (Reference Chap. 33)

- Digital health for safety
- Empowering people using technology
- Understand the opportunities and risks of Artificial Intelligence

The challenge we face in the patient safety movement is how we harness the great potential of the digitalisation of health and the introduction of Artificial Intelligence to healthcare delivery. The potential to use new technologies to design out human medical error and resultant harm is great. Nonetheless, it is not necessarily the solution to the challenge of patient safety, but rather an aid towards safer care [24, 25]. The potential of Electronic Health Records, electronic prescribing, and computer ordering systems to address the communication and transcription challenges in patent safety are still to be realised. They have not overcome communication issues, but offer us the opportunity to have better communication and easier pathways, if the implementation is successful. The challenge is to not replace old errors with new ones [26]. As most of the implementation has been in upper income countries, the spread of digital solutions around the globe will need to be carefully considered to ensure that the lessons learnt are applied with the safety of patients at the core.

For people receiving care, the use of smart phone technology can empower them to manage their care with ready access to information, medical records, test results, and control of their own data. This will require careful development, with ceding of power from the professionals to the people receiving care. Co-production of safety solutions will be an essential part of realising the potential of technology.

Artificial Intelligence (AI) has the potential to fundamentally change the way we care for people and to enhance the safety of care. However, the future development and implementation will need to address numerous challenges, such as the reliability of the predictions made from the newly developed machine learning systems. The transferability of the information and how data matches complexity of different health systems and how we as clinicians interact with the new technology [27]. While it is still early in the development of AI solutions that can assist us in our safety journey, we in the patient safety field must join with AI developers to harness the potential of predictive modelling in the future. The safety movement will need to be integral to the development of AI solutions and ensure that there is a safer system in the future [28].

4.9 Conclusion

We have come a long way in the patient safety movement. The standards of care in the past have focused on the processes of care and now need to be redesigned by people who receive care. This will change their focus from measurement of process to a refined assessment of people's experiences and the desired outcomes. Patient safety in the future will not be about the interventions needed, but rather about the people who work in the system, the people who receive care, and how we can design systems to support them in the delivery of reliable and safe care.

If we truly want to aim for Zero Harm as a concept, then we will need to redesign our systems of care through co-production and partnership, and address the challenges of the social determinants, the hierarchical cultures, and the opportunities of technology.

References

Overview

1. Foucault M. The birth of the clinic. An archaeology of medical perception. Paris: Vintage; 1994.
2. Amalberti R, Vincent C, Nicklin W, Braithwaite J. Coping with more people with more illness. Part 1: the nature of the challenge and the implications for safety and quality. Int J Qual Health Care. 2019;31(2):154–8.
3. Bates DW, Singh H. Two decades since to err is human: an assessment of progress and emerging priorities in patient safety. Health Aff. 2018;37(11):1736–43.
4. Donaldson MS, Corrigan JM, Kohn LT. To err is human: building a safer health system. Washington DC: National Academies Press; 2000.
5. Amalberti R, Vincent C. Managing risk in hazardous conditions: improvisation is not enough. BMJ Qual Saf. 2020;29:60–3.
6. The Health Foundation. Research scan: complex adaptive systems. 2010. https://www.health.org.uk/sites/default/files/ComplexAdaptiveSystems.pdf. Accessed 27 Dec 2019.
7. Thomas EJ. The harms of promoting 'Zero Harm'. BMJ Qual Saf. 2020;29:4–6.

Develop the Language and Culture of Safety

8. Mannion R, Davies H. Understanding organisational culture for healthcare quality improvement. BMJ. 2018;363:k4907.
9. Trbovich P, Vincent C. From incident reporting to the analysis of the patient journey. BMJ Qual Saf. 2019;28:169–71.
10. Vosper H, Hignett S, Bowie P. Twelve tips for embedding human factors and ergonomics principles in healthcare education. Med Teach. 2017;40(4):357–63.

Psychological Safety and Well-Being

11. Edmundson AC, Lei Z. Psychological safety: the history, renaissance, and future of an interpersonal construct. Annu Rev Organ Psychol Organ Behav. 2014;1:23–43.
12. Edmondson AC, Higgins M, Singer S, Weiner W. Understanding psychological safety in health care and education organizations: a comparative perspective. Res Hum Dev. 2016;13(1):65–83.
13. Edmondson AC. The fearless organization: creating psychological safety in the workplace for learning, innovation, and growth. New York: Wiley; 2018.
14. Smaggus A. Safety-I, safety-II and burnout: how complexity science can help clinician wellness. BMJ Qual Saf. 2019;28:667–71.

15. National Academies of Sciences, Engineering, and Medicine. Taking action against clinician burnout: a systems approach to professional well-being. Washington, DC: The National Academies Press; 2019. https://doi.org/10.17226/25521.

Design for Safety

16. Batalden M, Batalden P, Margolis P, Seid M, Armstrong G, Opipari-Arrigan L, Hartung H. Coproduction of healthcare service. BMJ Qual Saf. 2016;25:509–17.
17. Batalden P. Getting more health from healthcare: quality improvement must acknowledge patient coproduction—an essay by Paul Batalden. BMJ. 2018;362:k3617.
18. Elwyn G, Nelson E, Hager A, Price A. Coproduction: when users define quality. BMJ Qual Saf. 2019. Published Online First; https://doi.org/10.1136/bmjqs-2019-009830.
19. Hignett S, Lang A, Pickup L, Ives C, Fray M, McKeown C, Tapley S, Woodward M, Bowie B. More holes than cheese. What prevents the delivery of effective, high quality and safe health care in England? Ergonomics. 2018;61(1):5–14.

Social Determinants for Patient Safety

20. Marmot M. Social determinants of health inequalities. Lancet. 2005;365(9464):1099–104.

21. Okoroh JS, Uribe EF, Weingart S. Racial and ethnic disparities in patient safety. J Patient Saf. 2017;13(3):153–61.
22. Boozary AS, Shojania KG. Pathology of poverty: the need for quality improvement efforts to address social determinants of health. BMJ Qual Saf. 2018;27:421–4.
23. Kruk ME, Gage AD, Arsenault C, et al. High-quality health systems in the sustainable development goals era: time for a revolution. Lancet Glob Health. 2018;6(11):e1196–e252.

Digital Health and Patient Safety

24. Agboola SO, Bates DW, Kvedar JC. Digital health and patient safety. JAMA. 2016;315(16):1697–8. https://doi.org/10.1001/jama.2016.2402.
25. Sheikh A. Realising the potential of health information technology to enhance medication safety. BMJ Qual Saf. 2020;29:7–9.
26. Sujan M, Scott P, Cresswell K. Health and patient safety: technology is not a magic wand. Health Informatics J. 2019:1–5. https://doi.org/10.1177/1460458219876183.
27. Macrae C. Governing the safety of artificial intelligence in healthcare. BMJ Qual Saf. 2019;28:495–8.
28. Challen R, Denny J, Pitt M, Gompels L, Edwards T, Tsaneva-Atanasova K. Artificial intelligence, bias and clinical safety. BMJ Qual Saf. 2019;28:231–7.

Safer Care: Shaping the Future

5

Liam Donaldson

5.1 Introduction

Understanding of, and commitment to, patient safety worldwide has grown since the late 1990s. This was prompted by two influential reports: *To Err is Human* [1] produced by the Institute of Medicine (now called the National Academy of Medicine) in the USA and *An Organisation with a Memory* [2] produced by the United Kingdom Government's Chief Medical Adviser. Both reports recognised that error was routine during the delivery of healthcare: affecting something like one in ten of all hospital patients. In a proportion of cases, the outcome produced was serious, even fatal.

The reports also drew attention to the poor performance of healthcare, as a sector, worldwide on safety compared to most other high-risk industries. Notably, aviation has shown remarkable and sustained improvements in the risk to passengers of air travel over four decades. Both reports called for greater focus on, and commitment to, reducing the risks of healthcare.

Since then, the quest to improve the safety of care for patients has become a global movement. Important bodies like the World Health Organization (WHO) [3], the Gulf Cooperation Council (GCC) [4], the Agency for Healthcare Research and Quality (AHRQ) [5], the European Commission [6], and the Organisation for Economic Development (OECD) [7] have produced strategic documents, conducted studies, provided evidence and guidelines, initiated programmes of action, and galvanised the support of political and health leaders worldwide.

This has led to a remarkable transformation in the way that patient safety is viewed. Having been a subject of minority academic interest, it is now a firm priority for most healthcare systems.

Yet, the current state of patient safety worldwide is still a source of deep concern. As data on the scale and nature of errors and adverse events have been more widely gathered, it has become apparent that unsafe actions are a feature of virtually every aspect of healthcare. Furthermore, there is paucity of research on the frequency of errors and their associated burden of harm in areas such as primary care and mental health. Reports of the apparently avoidable deaths of patients regularly feature in media reports in many countries and undermine public confidence in the health services available to citizens. Moreover, many events recur with efforts to prevent them, on a large scale, proving ineffective. Expert commentators have explained this, in part, as being due to a punitive culture of individual blame and retribution holding back an approach that emphasises learning, not judgement as the route to improvement.

L. Donaldson (✉)
London School of Hygiene and Tropical Medicine, London, UK
e-mail: liam.donaldson@lshtm.ac.uk

L. Donaldson et al. (eds.), *Textbook of Patient Safety and Clinical Risk Management*,
https://doi.org/10.1007/978-3-030-59403-9_5

In this chapter, I will reflect on some of perspectives in patient safety that the world of healthcare has adopted. These, and others, are dealt with in-depth in later chapters. I will also set out some of the key developments in the global level journey on patient safety.

5.2 Thinking About Safer Healthcare

By the end of the twentieth century, there was growing interest in avoidable adverse outcomes of healthcare from some clinical groups, researchers, and campaigners as well as victims of healthcare-induced harm and their families. The term used most widely at that time to describe such events was "medical error" [8]. It still is quite a common descriptor but the domain of healthcare that deals with risk of harm to patients and its prevention is now almost universally called "patient safety" [9].

In any complex system like a health service, human error, and mistakes—and hence adverse events—are inevitable. A programme to improve safety for patients cannot be based on eliminating error and mistakes—that would be impossible. A healthcare system, though, can reduce the occurrence of human error, minimise its impact on the patient when it does occur and learn so that actions can be taken to protect future patients.

5.2.1 Accidents and Incidents: The Importance of Systems

In exploring the reasons why things go badly wrong in healthcare, it becomes clear that its situation is not unique. There are many parallels with other sectors. Research and best practice experience outside the healthcare field has shown that safety comes down to appreciating that big improvements are not made by telling people to take care but by understanding the conditions that provoke error.

Extensive study in the non-health field has shown that with most unintended failures there is usually no single explanatory cause for the event.

Rather there is a complex interaction between a varied set of elements, including human behaviour, technological aspects of the system, sociocultural factors, and a range of organisational and procedural weaknesses [10, 11].

Wide scale systematic studies of these issues in healthcare are less common than in other high-risk industries, but available evidence suggests a similarly complex pattern of cause and effect relationship [12, 13].

Understanding the underlying reasons, or root causes, of why things go wrong is critical for success. The deeper causes of adverse patient incidents do, indeed, lie in the management and organisational systems that support the delivery of care. Research has shown that the causes are rooted in factors such as inadequate training, lack of communication, lack of information, faulty equipment, or poor physical environment. Asking staff to work in these conditions will risk causing harm to patients.

Building safety into health services by understanding the sources of risk within systems and eliminating them must be a core priority for all providers of healthcare (Table 5.1).

The key principle in safety generally (not just in healthcare), that unsafe systems provoke human error, is a different way of looking at the world, and requires a different philosophy of practice.

It was the introduction of experts from other fields that changed the way that healthcare looked at its own accidents and errors. No longer would

Table 5.1 Ten practical questions to ask about risk in a clinical service

1	Describe the risks: what could go wrong?
2	What is being done to manage the potential risks?
3	What are the consequences if risks not managed?
4	Are the sources of the risks clinical, organisational, or both?
5	How often will the risks occur?
6	Can you rate the risks' severity?
7	What level of control is there over the occurrence of the risks?
8	What action is necessary to reduce the risks?
9	How will the reduction in risks be sustained?
10	How will you make all relevant staff aware of the risks?

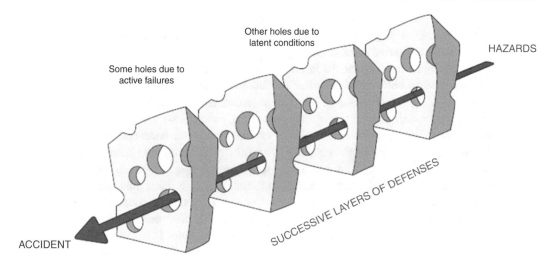

Fig. 5.1 The Swiss Cheese model of accident and incident causation. (*Source*: Professor James Reason by kind permission to the author)

an incident that killed or harmed a patient be seen as an unfortunate one-off local occurrence with no more general lessons to be learned. One of the major figures from outside healthcare to explain this perspective was Professor James Reason from the University of Manchester in England [14]. He put forward a compelling metaphor to encourage more broad-based thinking. He compared the risks of an accident or incident to the holes in slices of a Swiss cheese (Fig. 5.1). The solid pieces of cheese are the system's defences, whilst the holes are the weaknesses. The holes in the slices of James Reason's Swiss cheese—the organisation's system—open, close, and realign constantly. Some of the holes or risks are unsafe actions by individuals: slips, lapses of attention, mistakes, or violations of procedure. Many more are due to what Reason calls "latent conditions". These things like lack of training, weak procedures, and faulty or poorly maintained equipment create preconditions for failure.

Doctors traditionally have not been trained to think systemically. Their concern is the patient in front of them. They realise, of course, that their treatments and decisions can have negative outcomes, but their training puts these in the currency of "complications" or "side effects". The surgeon knows that her patient can develop postoperative bleeding. The physician knows that his

drug can provoke a reaction. The surgeon though probably thinks less about the propensity for the system, through its design, to make it more likely that she will operate on the wrong side of the body. The physician ordering anticoagulants probably thinks more about blood tests and clinical monitoring data than the risk of a patient being given 15,000 units of heparin and killed when the intended dose was 1500 units but the abbreviation for "unit" was interpreted by the administering nurse as a zero.

Every day, around the world, patients die and are harmed because of these and similar circumstances. Human error occurs in weak systems: those that promote error rather than reducing its likelihood. Tomorrow's practitioners must not only think about themselves and their actions. They must also have "systems awareness".

It is also vital for health policymakers, healthcare leaders (not only clinical staff) to understand and embrace systems thinking. Frontline awareness of systemic weaknesses and risks is important but so too is strategic awareness by those responsible for the infrastructure, organisation, and delivery of care for communities and populations.

A system is sometimes a whole healthcare service. It is also a collection of processes of care within a health facility or care setting. In a large hospital, there may be 50 individual service groups all with their own processes and procedures. So, a systems perspective when something goes wrong, for example, can focus on the factors that led to a nurse inadvertently giving an infant a fatal overdose of a drug intravenously. Or, it might take an even broader view if the problem necessitates it. For example, an investigation of high healthcare infection rates might conclude that a group of African hospitals cannot maintain clean care because they do not have a source of clean water. As a result, finding a way to cheaply and locally manufacture an alcohol hand rub could help staff reduce infection rates. That would be aligning a systemic cause of harm with a systemic solution.

There are good examples of large-scale systemic actions led by clinicians. Global clinical networks of specialists and professional bodies are very well placed to identify common high-risk situations and galvanise support for action. The international clinical movement to reduce harm from sepsis [15] has shown how raising awareness and championing the need for action on a systemic patient safety issue can lead to change in attitudes and practice right across the world. Anaesthetic risk has been much reduced by combined research and action driven by organisations in this specialty either nationally, regionally, or globally.

5.2.2 Culture, Blame, and Accountability

The implications of system thinking in patient safety are quite profound. It means that ministries of health, managers of health facilities, the media, and the public must accept this paradigm as an explanation for the harm caused and cannot take a routinely "off with their heads" approach when something serious happens. Blaming individuals is common. It is easy, and generally popular. However, it is unfair, counter to developing a strong patient safety culture where learning benefits future patients. It has led many doctors and nurses who have simply made an honest mistake to end up behind bars. The force of public outrage is often too great for the chief executive officer of a hospital or health minister to withstand. Their principles are sacrificed and they take the easy way out. The damage to their leadership in the eyes of their staff is then incalculable. They did not have the courage to defend the learning culture when the chips were down.

This is one of the most difficult and debated areas of patient safety and is usually referred to as the "blame culture" principle. There are many other dimensions to considering culture in relation to patient safety and the goal of promoting, sustaining, and consistently delivering safer care (Fig. 5.2). Also within the culture of organisa-

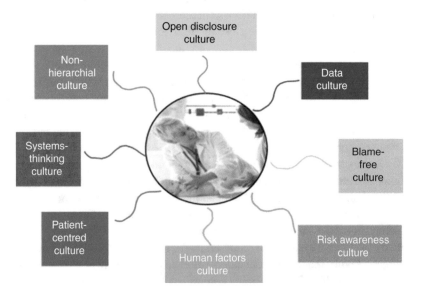

Fig. 5.2 Patient safety culture has many strands (© Sir Liam Donaldson)

tions, there are certain behavioural aspects that will place patients at higher risk, including: for example, an arrogant belief that the organisation is too good to fail, a tendency to avoid dealing with signs that all is not well, hierarchical atti-

> ARROGANCE

> DENIAL

> BLAME

> MESSENGER SHOOTING

> AVERTING GAZE

> HIERARCHIES

> PASSIVE LEARNING

Fig. 5.3 Seven deadly sins: harmful behaviours within health organisations (© Sir Liam Donaldson)

tudes where a junior nurse dare not challenge a senior doctor even if he is behaving unsafely, and ostracising whistle-blowers and others who are trying to highlight dangers (Fig. 5.3).

Modern healthcare is delivered in a complex, fast-moving environment. With the wrong culture, together with staff that are unaware of the potential risks of the care that they are delivering, then unsafe care may burst through and begin to kill and harm patients (Fig. 5.4).

5.2.3 Leadership at the Frontline

There is a caveat to an entirely systemic view of the world. Other high-risk industries do not set aside the need to focus on the individual as well as the system. This is not to blame them but to ensure that they are educated in risk and its importance, skilled, capable, and conscientious.

For example, in the airline industry, the number of times that an airline pilot might be assessed during their career could be as high as a hundred. Rehearsing in a simulator regularly, somebody flying with them in the flight deck, having regular

Fig. 5.4 The bulging triangle: how unsafe care can break out of its boundaries (© Sir Liam Donaldson)

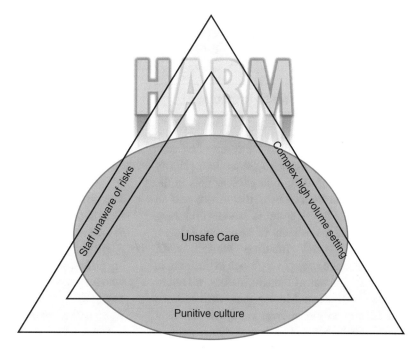

medicals, these are part of the process of ensuring safe air travel. In many parts of the world, once a doctor has finished training, they may not have any regular checks on their performance or challenges to how they would handle emergency situations. Simulation is playing an increasingly important part in healthcare, particularly in education and training. Other industries are much further ahead in simulating unsafe situations and training their staff. It is an exciting idea to develop skills, away from the patient and then bring the practitioner to the patient when they have a higher level of skill. It is not the whole solution to creating "safety-wise" practitioners.

One of the great strategic needs in patient safety is for leadership, and role models in patient safety for young practitioners. There are many wonderful patient safety leaders at global level and within countries. They have been instrumental in making patient safety the priority that it is today within health systems around the world. However, there are far too few of them. Every clinical team in every part of every health system of the world needs skilled committed leadership in patient safety. This is needed because every patient must be protected from the ever-present risk of harm. It is here that we can look to the young generation of doctors, nurses, and other health professionals who are already demonstrating their interest and passion for patient safety.

5.3 Global Action to Improve Safety

Through the early years of the twenty-first century, patient safety began to feature as a priority or programme of work in larger hospitals in the higher income countries of the world, and in some national health systems. It was still a long way from the mainstream of healthcare leaders, policymakers, and frontline clinical staff. Initially, it was a subject very much in the domain of a small number of thought leaders, researchers, and enthusiasts. Moving these deliberations and debates to global level catalysed action in country health systems on a much more extensive basis and served a convening function by bringing health leaders, politicians, experts, researchers, and patient representatives into the same rooms.

5.3.1 Patient Safety on the Global Health Agenda

The World Health Organization (WHO), the United Nations agency responsible for health, first raised the profile of patient safety to global importance. In May 2002, the 55th World Health Assembly (the annual policy-making meeting of all 192 countries of the world) adopted Resolution 55.18. This urged Member States to pay the closest possible attention to the problem of patient safety and to establish and strengthen science-based systems necessary for improving patient safety and the quality of healthcare [16].

Following this, in May 2004, the 57th World Health Assembly supported the creation of an international alliance to facilitate the development of patient safety policy and practice in all member states, to act as a major force for improvement globally. The World Alliance for Patient Safety, a partnership between WHO and external experts, healthcare leaders, and professional bodies, was launched formally in October of 2004.

5.3.2 World Alliance for Patient Safety: Becoming Global

The World Alliance for Patient Safety formulated an initial programme of work framed as a series of six important actions intended to reduce harm caused to patients:

- The first *Global Patient Safety Challenge*, focusing, on the theme of healthcare-associated infection [17]
- A *Patients for Patient Safety* network involving patient organisations and led by individuals who had suffered avoidable harm from healthcare [18]
- A *Taxonomy for Patient Safety*, ensuring consistency in the concepts, principles, norms, and terminology used in patient safety work [19]

- A *Research for Patient Safety* initiative to identify priorities for patient safety-related research in high-income, middle-income, and low-income countries as well as projects and capacity building particularly aimed at low-income countries [20]
- A *Solutions for Patient Safety* programme to identify, develop, and promote worldwide interventions to improve patient safety
- A set of *Reporting and Learning* best practice guidelines to aid in the design and development of existing and new reporting systems [21].

The overall aims of this global partnership for patient safety were: to promote the development of evidence-based norms for the delivery of safer patient care, to create global classifications for medical errors, and to support knowledge sharing in patient safety between member states. There was also a strong advocacy role to raise awareness of the risks of unsafe care and generate a better understanding of the reasons why harm occurs, to draw attention to the most effective preventive measures, as well as establishing the means to evaluate them.

At the outset, there were three core principles that underpinned the initial focus for action at global level:

- A commitment to placing patients at the centre of efforts to improve patient safety worldwide
- A focus on improving ways to detect and learn from information about patient safety problems within and across countries (with a particular emphasis on methods and tools for detecting patient safety problems in low-income countries)
- A need to build up the knowledge base of interventions which have been shown to help solve patient safety problems, together with a more rapid and systematic dissemination of information worldwide on successful strategies.

The World Alliance for Patient Safety, in its publications, its events, and when its members spoke at conferences, always sought to educate and inform about the concepts and philosophy that should underlie a modern approach to safety in healthcare.

5.3.3 The Global Patient Safety Challenges

As each of the foundation strands of the global patient safety initiative began to be implemented, they attracted a great deal of interest, involvement, and began to shape change in healthcare systems around the world.

At the beginning, it had been important to choose a major aspect of patient safety that affected all countries of the world and was big enough to warrant intensive action on a global scale. Healthcare infection fitted these criteria immediately. It was endemic within every healthcare system. In high-income countries, there was great concern, not just about the persistence of the problem, but the emergence of life-threatening antimicrobial-resistant strains such as methicillin-resistant *Staphylococcus aureus* (MRSA). In low-income and middle-income countries, the problem was even more serious especially where the infrastructure of care was weak.

The first Global Patient Safety Challenge, aimed to engage the world's health systems in a movement to reduce healthcare infection. It began by convening all the leading experts to formulate ground breaking new evidence-based guidelines on hand hygiene. In addition, a major study was mounted to assess the burden of healthcare infection (particularly in low- and middle-income countries). This first Challenge *Clean Care is Safe Care* [17] invited health ministers to personally, and publicly, sign a pledge to address healthcare infection in their countries.

The first Global Patient Safety Challenge was the flagship element of the World Alliance for Patient Safety's initiative. It was highly visible and easily understood by politicians, health professionals, and the public. It was relevant to all countries: rich, poor, and emerging economies. Everyone had a vested interest in its success because anyone could need treatment in a health facility and could therefore become the victim of harm by acquiring an infection.

In driving forward *Clean Care is Safer Care*, a wide range of supporting activities and campaigns was implemented. The idea of this Challenge generated huge interest and enthusiasm across all six WHO regions. As ministers signed their pledges in country and regional launches and events, from a small start, eventually, the commitments covered 85% of the world's population.

The WHO hand hygiene global campaign (*SAVE LIVES: Clean Your Hands*) [22] launched in 2009 has been particularly successful. Before the Challenge, alcohol-based hand rubs (hand sanitisers) were not commonplace in hospitals around the world. The core message was that the lack of consistent, immediate, access to a sink equipped with soap and single-use towels (high-income countries) and/or the unavailability of clean water (many low-income countries) put patients at risk. The evidence of higher efficacy, effectiveness, and skin tolerability of alcohol-based hand rubs made them the method of choice to assure hand hygiene. The Challenge made alcohol hand rubs more affordable to the poorest hospitals of the world by ensuring that the University Hospital of Geneva formulation

became available with no patent restriction for local manufacture.

A further key step in achieving the global reach of the hand hygiene programme was the development of the *Five Moments* for hand hygiene model [23]. This emphasised the points in the process of patient care when the risks of transmission of an infection by a caregiver's hands were highest. The *Five Moments*' visual image (Fig. 5.5) is striking and easily remembered by frontline staff; therefore, it has acted as a technical educational tool that succeeded in standardising practice worldwide but also it has become a brand of safety with global spread.

Overall, the first Global Patient Safety Challenge represented a proven change model that mobilised the world around infection prevention through: (a) awareness raising about the burden of the problem to engage stakeholders; (b) an approach to engage nations through demonstrable commitment; (c) the availability of evidence-based guidance and implementation tools to drive improvement.

The original concept of such a Challenge was of a 2-year start-up period, after which responsibility for its continuance would pass to WHO member states and their healthcare systems. However, *Clean Care is Safer Care* generated so

Fig. 5.5 Five moments for hand hygiene. (*Source*: World Health Organization—reproduced with permission)

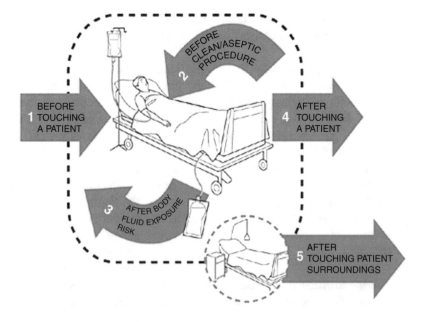

much momentum, passion, and so great a sense of solidarity across the world that the WHO's team in Geneva was continuing to play a strong leadership role 10 years after the launch. This success and the perception of the need for supporting infection prevention and control improvement in many countries, led the WHO to institute a new, formalised infection prevention and control global unit.

Other important achievements of the first Challenge and associated global infection prevention and control work included:

- An assessment of the burden of healthcare infection in low- and middle-income countries
- WHO guidelines and 100s of associated publications
- Fifty-five hospital departments across six countries demonstrated scientifically successfully implemented a hand hygiene multimodal improvement strategy
- Over 30 countries established WHO-guided local production of alcohol-based hand rub
- Over 50 countries ran successful hand hygiene national campaigns
- Almost 20,000 health facilities in 177 countries joined the *WHO SAVE LIVES: Clean Your Hands* campaign
- Global initiatives and engagement of thousands of health workers around hand hygiene every year on 5th May
- Patient engagement/information tools issued
- Reports from seven global surveys, on hand hygiene and a range of infection prevention and control and antimicrobial resistance priorities
- Hand hygiene and infection prevention and control messages embedded in key programmes of work including antimicrobial resistance, *WASH* and maternal and child health
- Alcohol-based hand rub featured in the WHO List of Essential Medicines
- Guidance produced on infection prevention and control during the 2014–15 Ebola virus disease outbreak (through the leadership of the team)

- New evidence-based guidelines on injection safety and ongoing testing of an implementation campaign in three countries supported by more than 20 new tools
- New evidence-based guidelines for the prevention of surgical site infections based on 27 systematic literature reviews and including 29 recommendations
- New evidence-based guidelines on the core components of effective infection prevention and control programmes to reduce harm from health care-associated infections and antimicrobial resistance

A second Global Patient Safety Challenge recognised the relatively high burden of disease arising from unsafe surgical care. *Safe Surgery, Saves Lives* [24] created a surgical checklist that was piloted, evaluated, and promoted for use globally. Initial evaluations showed that the checklist reduced morbidity and mortality associated with surgery in early studies of its use. Major professional bodies across the world endorsed it. It is in widespread use in hospitals in many countries and, increasingly, it is seen as essential if the key risks of surgery are to be avoided. However, the original checklist has been widely adapted whilst the experience of the surgical checklist's use worldwide has not been formally revisited since its launch.

The checklist concept was developed further with the creation of the *WHO Safe Childbirth Checklist* [25], which focuses on reducing risk and adverse outcomes related to childbirth for both mothers and babies. Of the more than 130 million births occurring each year, an estimated 303,000 result in the mother's death, 2.6 million in stillbirth, and another 2.7 million in a newborn death within the first 28 days of birth. The majority of these deaths occur in low-resource settings and most could be prevented. The *WHO Safe Childbirth Checklist* supports the delivery of essential maternal and perinatal care practices and addresses the major causes of maternal death, intra-partum-related stillbirths, and neonatal deaths. The *Safe Childbirth Checklist Collaboration* has already made significant strides to improving maternal and neonatal health. It is hoped that the Checklist can become an effective life-saving tool that can be used in a wide range of settings.

5.3.4 Patients and Families: Championing Change

In addition to the expert reports that had drawn the attention of policymakers to problem of unsafe care, a powerful driving force for change was the visibility of tragic and harrowing situations in which patients had suffered serious harm or died. Some of the victims of this unsafe care, or often surviving family members, had risen above their personal tragedy to tell their stories very publicly and call for the world's healthcare systems to take action.

The World Alliance for Patient Safety established the *Patients for Patient Safety Programme* as one of its first actions. Susan Sheridan (a contributor to this book), whose son suffered brain damage, and whose husband died, both associated with medical error, was the first external lead of this programme. Over time, a global network of patient champions was established. Many were themselves victims of avoidable harm or they were a parent of a child who had died or had been harmed.

With the expanding ageing population, the rise in non-communicable diseases and ever-rising healthcare costs, there is more willingness than ever by healthcare providers to engage with patients, families, and communities. Recognising these challenges and opportunities, the *Patients for Patient Safety Programme* has restructured its approach to emphasise four key strategic objectives:

- Advocacy and awareness raising
- Capacity development and strengthening

- Partnerships with healthcare providers and policymakers
- Influencing and contributing to policy and research priorities

The *Patients for Patient Safety* network now has over 500 advocates, also known as *Patients for Patient Safety* champions, in 54 countries. Newsletters are produced quarterly to promote the sharing of knowledge and experiences.

The champions involved in the *Patients for Patient Safety Programme* have: acted as advocates for the importance of tackling unsafe care in the healthcare systems of their countries; participated in education and training programmes for healthcare professional staff; supported other victims of harm who have contacted them; and, served on boards and advised hospitals on the design of their services.

The role of patients and family members in the quest for safer healthcare worldwide has been of incalculable benefit to the advancing the case of patient safety globally in the last decade (Table 5.2). Their experience, wisdom, and courage has fuelled a journey whose eventual endpoint will be a coalescence of compassion and learning to eradicate serious harm from every healthcare system in the world.

5.3.5 African Partnerships for Patient Safety

African Partnerships for Patient Safety (APPS) [26] was launched in 2009. It was designed to fill a perceived gap in patient safety in Africa. It was part of a WHO response to the commitment to strengthen patient safety articulated by 46 ministries of health at the 58th session of WHO's Regional Committee for Africa in 2008.

Table 5.2 Value of involvement of patients and families who have suffered harm

Role	Benefit
Educator	Reinforces professional values of caring, compassion, and respect
Storyteller	Wins hearts and minds of leaders and frontline staff; stays in the memory
Advocate	Gains commitment at wider political, public, and professional levels; initiates campaigns for specific actions (e.g. for sepsis, for in-patient suicide)
Partner	Strengthens design and delivery of future care pathways and patient safety programmes
Reporter	Highlights new risks and improvement opportunities

African Partnerships for Patient Safety developed a multi-country, hospital-to-hospital partnership programme. Initial support came from the United Kingdom Department of Health. Subsequently, the Government of France funded expansion of the programme beyond English speaking countries. During the period 2009–2014, *African Partnerships for Patient Safety* oversaw the implementation of 17 hospital-to-hospital partnerships. The partnerships comprised European hospitals from three countries (France, Switzerland, and the United Kingdom) and hospitals in 17 different countries in the WHO African Region (Benin, Burkina Faso, Burundi, Cameroon, Côte d'Ivoire, Ethiopia, Ghana, Malawi, Mali, Niger, Rwanda, Senegal, Togo, Uganda, the United Republic of Tanzania, Zambia, and Zimbabwe). Linguistic diversity was maintained through the involvement of English, French, and Portuguese speaking countries.

As *African Partnerships for Patient Safety* evolved, south–south patient safety partnerships were established between hospitals in Zimbabwe and between Morocco and its partnership hospital further south. In addition, a partnership was established involving the Johns Hopkins University Armstrong Institute for Patient Safety & Quality and institutions in three African countries (Liberia, South Sudan, and Uganda).

African Partnerships for Patient Safety received widespread international attention and recognition. It illustrated how teams skilled in infection prevention and control and patient safety can act as a bridge between disease-specific programmes and health systems. This strengthens interaction at the health facility level. It provided a very tangible entry point for broader improvement in service delivery. Evaluation of the programme showed gains in hand hygiene compliance by health workers, implementation of the WHO Surgical Safety Checklist, training and education of healthcare workers, medication safety, healthcare waste management, clinical audit, teamwork, and leadership.

A defining feature of the *African Partnerships for Patient Safety* approach is that it presented an alternative to traditional vertical, expert-driven, technical assistance improvement models. It used frontline expertise from across both arms of the partnership hospitals with a focus on co-development and relationship building. The tools developed by the programme are now being utilised across the world, notably through the United Kingdom's Department for International Development Health Partnerships Scheme, hospital partnership initiatives led by Expertise France, partnerships supported by the Ministry of Foreign Affairs of Japan, partnerships supported by the Tuscany region of Italy and a recent major initiative focused on hospital partnerships initiated by the Ministry of Health in Germany.

African Partnerships for Patient Safety illustrated how frontline passion and energy has driven implementation of patient safety initiatives through strong human interaction and solidarity across continents. The work has informed national policy direction in multiple countries in the WHO Region of Africa. Importantly, *African Partnerships for Patient Safety* has shone the light on the potential for high-income countries to learn from low-income countries, the so-called reverse innovation.

The work of *African Partnerships for Patient Safety* has provided a strong foundation for the development of a wider international effort on "twinning partnerships for improvement". This is particularly relevant given the increasing importance placed on quality as part of the fabric of Universal Health Coverage-driven reform processes across the world, and in particular in low-income countries.

5.3.6 Third Global Patient Safety Challenge: *Medication Without Harm*

The World Health Organization (WHO) launched its third Global Patient Safety Challenge in 2016 [27]. Its aim is to reduce the global burden of iatrogenic medication-related harm by 50% within 5 years. The intention is to match the global reach and impact of the WHO's two earlier Global Patient Safety Challenges, *Clean Care is Safer Care* and *Safe Surgery Saves Lives*. The third Challenge,

Medication Without Harm, invites health ministers to initiate national plans addressing four domains of medication safety, namely: engaging patients and the public; medicines as products; education, training, and monitoring of healthcare professionals; and systems and the practices of medication management (Fig. 5.6). It also commits the WHO to use its convening and coordinating powers to drive forward a range of global actions. A tool to empower patients is already available.

Three key areas of medication safety have been identified as early priorities. They will be the most visible and public-facing aspects of this latest Challenge, just as hand hygiene and the surgical checklist were the flagship elements of the first two Global Patient Safety Challenges. They are: high-risk medicine situations; polypharmacy; and transitions of care. Each is associated with a substantial burden of harm and, if appropriately managed, could reduce the risk of harm to large numbers of patients in health systems across the world.

5.3.7 The 2019 WHA Resolution and World Patient Safety Day

Further impetus and fresh momentum was injected into the global patient safety movement in 2019 when the World Health Assembly again considered patient safety. This came at a time when, despite efforts of the previous decade, harm due to unsafe care was recognised as one of the 10 leading causes of morbidity and mortality globally, exceeding malaria and tuberculosis and level with HIV.

In May 2019, the 72nd World Health Assembly designated patient safety as a global health priority; adopted resolution WHA72.6 [28] and established an annual World Patient Safety Day. WHA72.6 requests the WHO's Director General: "To emphasize patient safety as a key strategic priority in WHO's work across Universal Health Coverage agenda", and: "To formulate a global patient safety action plan in consultation with Member States, regional economic integration

Fig. 5.6 Third Global Patient Safety Challenge: strategic framework (© World Health Organization 2018. Some rights reserved. This work is available under the CC BY-NC-SA 3.0 IGO licence)

organisations and all relevant stakeholders, including in the private sector".

This major commitment and the delivery of a comprehensive action plan will drive the shape of patient safety programmes across the world for the next decade.

5.4   Conclusions

In an era when the human genome has been mapped, when air travel is safer than ever before, and when information flows across the globe in seconds, patients cannot be reassured that they will not die because of weaknesses in the way that their care is organised and delivered.

Despite the extensive work that has been put in at global level and in health systems around the world, a sustainable model for safe healthcare is not in place.

Firstly, the scale of the problem is so great that it can no longer just be left to special interest and to advocacy. The ownership of the problem of patient safety needs to be everybody's business. The action to tackle it needs to be everybody's business.

Secondly, this has been going on for just too long. There can be no other high-risk industry with such a poor record in improving known areas of risk.

Thirdly, the WHO and other global agencies and leaders are calling on the 194 countries of the world to implement a policy of Universal Health Coverage. It is essential that health systems are built with patient safety and quality of care as their organising principle. Almost everyone who accesses healthcare will at some point be treated. That treatment needs to be safe. What stronger connection could there be between patient safety and universal health coverage?

References

1. Kohn K, Corrigan J, Donaldson M. To err is human. Washington, DC: National Academy Press; 2000.
2. Chief Medical Officer. An organisation with a memory: a report on learning from adverse events in the NHS. London: The Stationery Office; 2000.
3. Donaldson LJ, Fletcher MG. The WHO world alliance for patient safety: towards the years of living less dangerously. Med J Aust. 2006;184(10):S69–72.
4. Siddiqi S, Elasady R, Khorshid I, Fortune T, Leotsakos A, Letaief M, et al. Patient Safety Friendly Hospital Initiative: from evidence to action in seven developing country hospitals. Int J Qual Health Care. 2012;24(2):144–5.
5. Agency for Healthcare Research and Quality (AHRQ). Advances in patient safety: from research to implementation. 05-0021. CD ROM. Bethesda: AHRQ; 2005.
6. European Commission (EC). Report on the member states' implementation of council recommendations on patient safety. Brussels: EC; 2012.
7. Organisation for Economic Development and Cooperation (OECD). Measuring patient safety: opening the black box. Paris: OECD; 2018.
8. Leape LL. Error in medicine. J Am Med Assoc. 1994;272:1851–7.
9. Lilford R, Stirling S, Maillard N. Citation classics in patient safety research: an invitation to contribute to an online bibliography. Qual Saf Health Care. 2006;15(5):311–3.
10. Macrae C. Close calls: managing risk and resilience in airline flight safety. Basingstoke: Palgrave Macmillan; 2014.
11. Strauch B. Investigating human error: incidents, accidents, and complex systems. Burlington, VT: Ashgate; 2002.
12. Smetzer JL, Cohen MR. Lessons from the Denver medication error/criminal negligence case: look beyond blaming individuals. Hosp Pharm. 1998;33:640–57.
13. Toft B. External inquiry into the adverse incident that occurred at Queen's Medical Centre, Nottingham 4th January 2001. London: Department of Health; 2001.
14. Reason J. Managing the risks of organisational accidents. Aldershot: Ashgate; 1997.
15. Reinhart C, Daniels R, Kissoon N, Machad FR, et al. Recognising sepsis as a global health priority: a WHO resolution. N Engl J Med. 2017;377:414–7.
16. World Health Organization (WHO). World Health Assembly resolution WHA 55.18. Geneva: WHO; 2002.
17. Pittet D, Donaldson L. Challenging the world: patient safety and health care-associated infection. Int J Qual Health Care. 2006;18(1):4–8.
18. World Health Organization (WHO). Patients for patient safety: the London declaration. Geneva: WHO; 2006.
19. World Health Organization (WHO). The final technical report for the conceptual framework for the international classification for patient safety. Geneva: WHO; 2009.
20. Bates DW, Larizgoitia I, Prasopa-Plaizier N, Jha AK, Research Priority Setting Working Group of the WHO World Alliance for Patient Safety. Global priorities for patient safety research. BMJ. 2009;338:b1775.

21. World Alliance for Patient Safety. WHO draft guidelines for adverse event report and learning systems: from information to action. Geneva: WHO; 2005.
22. Allegranzi B, Storr J, Dziekan G, et al. The first global patient safety challenge "Clean care is safer care": from launch to current progress and achievements. J Hosp Infect. 2007;65(Suppl. 2):115–23.
23. Pittet D, Allegranzi B, Sax H, Dharan S, Pessoa-Silva CL, Donaldson LJ, et al. Evidence-based model for hand transmission during patient care and the role of improved practices. Lancet Infect Dis. 2006;6(10):641–52.
24. World Alliance for Patient Safety. The second global patient safety challenge: safe surgery saves lives. Geneva: World Health Organization; 2008.
25. World Health Organization (WHO). Safe childbirth checklist collaboration: improving the health of mothers and neonates. Geneva: WHO; 2014.
26. Syed SB, Gooden R, Storr J, et al. African partnerships for patient safety: a vehicle for enhancing patient safety across two continents. World Hosp Health Serv. 2009;45:24–7.
27. Donaldson LJ, Kelley ET, Dhingra-Kumar N, Kieny M-P, Sheikh A. Medication without harm: WHO's third global patient safety challenge. Lancet. 2017;389(10080):1680.
28. World Health Organization (WHO). Resolution WHA 72.6: global action on patient safety. Geneva: WHO; 2019.

Patients for Patient Safety

Susan Sheridan, Heather Sherman,
Allison Kooijman, Evangelina Vazquez,
Katrine Kirk, Nagwa Metwally, and Flavia Cardinali

6.1 Introduction

The people have a right and duty to participate individually and collectively in the planning and implementation of their own health care—WHO Alma Ata Declaration (1978) [1]

Unsafe care results in approximately 2.6 million deaths per year. It is one of the top 10 causes of death worldwide [2]. Recognizing unsafe care as a growing global burden, in 2019 the 72nd World Health Assembly (WHA) [3], the policy setting body for the World Health Organization (WHO), ratified the Global Action on Patient Safety [4]. Through this document, the WHA urged Member States to "work in collaboration with other Member States, civil society organizations, patients' organizations, professional bodies, academic and research institutions, industry and other relevant stakeholders to promote, prioritize and embed patient safety in all health policies and strategies" [4]. The WHA further urged Member States to "put in place systems for the engagement and empowerment of patients, families and communities (especially those who have been affected by adverse events) in the delivery of safer health care, including capacity building initiatives, networks and associations; and to work with them and civil society, to use their experience of safe and unsafe care positively in order to build safety and harm minimization strategies as well as compensation mechanisms and schemes, into all aspects of the provision of health care, as appropriate" [4].

Simply stated, the WHA, through The Global Action on Patient Safety, called for Member States to democratize healthcare by engaging with the very users of the healthcare system—patients, families, and community members—along with other partners—in the "co-production" of safer healthcare.

In this chapter, I share how preventable harm to my son, Cal, from neonatal jaundice, and the

S. Sheridan (✉)
The Society to Improve Diagnosis in Medicine, Evanston, IL, USA
e-mail: Sue.sheridan@Improvediagnosis.org

H. Sherman
Patient Safety and Quality Improvement Specialists, LLC, Chicago, IL, USA

A. Kooijman
Patients for Patient Safety Canada, Vancouver, BC, Canada

E. Vazquez
Patients for Patient Safety Mexico/Pan American Network for PFPS, Mexico City, Mexico

K. Kirk
The Danish Patients for Patient Safety, Copenhagen, Denmark

N. Metwally
Patients for Patient Safety Champion—Egypt, Member of the Supreme Council, The Egyptian Red Crescent, Cairo, Egypt

F. Cardinali
Quality Department, National Agency for Regional Healthcare Services (AGENAS), Rome, Italy
e-mail: cardinali@agenas.it

© The Author(s) 2021
L. Donaldson et al. (eds.), *Textbook of Patient Safety and Clinical Risk Management*,
https://doi.org/10.1007/978-3-030-59403-9_6

death of my late husband, Pat, from the failure to communicate a malignant pathology, catapulted me into a global movement of patients, family members, communities, and civil society advocating for safer care that became known as the WHO's Patients for Patient Safety (PFPS) Programme (mentioned in the previous chapter). I along with others around the world who have experienced harm from unsafe care have harnessed our wisdom, our grief, and our anger to courageously partner with passionate thought leaders in healthcare including clinicians, researchers, policy makers, medical educators, and quality improvement experts to co-produce patient safety initiatives to ensure that our healthcare systems "learn" from our adverse events and implement systematic strategies to reduce risk of harm. The real-world examples of co-production within this chapter demonstrate the important role of civil society as well as how patients, families, and communities "that have experienced adverse events can use their experience of safe and unsafe care positively in order to build safety and harm reduction strategies" in developing and developed countries [4].

6.2 What is Co-production in Healthcare?

Co-production is the "interdependent work of users and professionals to design, create, develop, deliver, assess and improve the relationships and actions that contribute to the health of individuals and populations through mutual respect and partnership that notices and invites each participant's unique strengths and expertise" [5]. Co-produced patient safety initiatives are "mutually beneficial…at every level and in every health-related endeavor, from designing educational curricula to setting research priorities to hiring faculty and leadership to operating health organizations" [5]. Patients are not viewed as "'users and choosers' but as 'makers and shapers' [which] allows for planning and implementing new policies that can potentially lead to better health outcomes and patient experiences" [6].

6.3 Background: The Genesis of a Global Movement for Co-production for Safer Care

In 2002, the 55th WHA passed Resolution WHA55.18 which established "the need to promote patient safety as a fundamental principle of all health systems" and resulted in WHO launching the World Alliance for Patient Safety (now known as the WHO Patient Safety Programme) [7, 8]. The World Alliance for Patient Safety consisted of six action programmes, one of which was the Patients for Patient Safety Programme (the PFPS Programme), where I served as the External Lead for 7 years. The PFPS Programme is a global network of committed patients, families, healthcare professionals, and policy makers who are connected by the common objective of promoting safer care through patient involvement. They bravely advocate for and collaborate in patient safety efforts at the local, national, and international levels [9]. These individuals, known as PFPS Champions, teach, offer hope and provide inspiration. They have organized as individuals, networks, patient associations/organizations and in discrete patient programs within established public and civil society structures. Their dedication to co-producing safer healthcare is guided by the seminal document, the London Declaration, which was authored by representatives from 21 countries who had experienced harm directly or indirectly as a result of unsafe care. The London Declaration calls for partnership and the democratization of healthcare to improve patient safety:

> **The London Declaration**
> *We, Patients for Patient Safety, envision a different world in which healthcare errors are not harming people. We are partners in the effort to prevent all avoidable harm in healthcare. Risk and uncertainty are constant companions. So, we come together in dialogue, participating in care with providers. We unite our strength as advocates for care without harm in the developing as well as the developed world.*
> *We are committed to spread the word from person to person, town to town, country to country. There is a right to safe healthcare and we will not let the current culture of error and denial, continue. We*

call for honesty, openness, and transparency. We will make the reduction of healthcare errors as a basic human right that preserves life around the world.

We, Patients for Patient Safety, will be the voice for all people, but especially those who are now unheard. Together as partners, we will collaborate in:

- *Devising and promoting programs for patient safety and patient empowerment.*
- *Developing and driving a constructive dialogue with all partners concerned with patient safety.*
- *Establishing systems for reporting and dealing with healthcare harm on a worldwide basis.*
- *Defining best practices in dealing with healthcare harm of all kinds and promoting those practices throughout the world.*

In honor of those who have died, those left disabled, our loved ones today and the world's children yet to be born, we will strive for excellence, so that all involved in healthcare are as safe as possible as soon as possible. This is our pledge of partnership [10].

By co-producing patient safety initiatives, the PFPS Programme, PFPS Champions, and Member States democratize patient safety and fulfill the promise and potential of the directives stated in both the London Declaration and the WHA Global Action on Patient Safety.

6.4 Co-Production in Research

There is growing awareness that patient engagement in health research is not only ethically important, but leads to evidence for developing the most effective interventions, policy and practice recommendations, and planning for ongoing research [11].

6.4.1 Example: United States

6.4.1.1 Mothers Donating Data: Going from Research to Policy to Practice

My son, Cal, and other newborn babies suffered from preventable brain damage in the United States as a result of the failure to test and treat neonatal jaundice (hyperbilirubinemia), known as kernicterus. After determining that a pre-discharge bilirubin test would have helped prevent our newborns from suffering, mothers of children with kernicterus formed a nonprofit organization (civil society), Parents of Infants and Children with Kernicterus (PICK) [12]. The PICK Board of Directors, comprised of the mothers, had two specific goals: (1) co-design a safer healthcare system for newborns to include a universal, pre-discharge bilirubin test; and (2) co-design materials to empower parents with information. While the healthcare providers were sympathetic to these mothers, healthcare leaders stated clearly that changes to care or educational materials could not be made based solely on anecdotes; evidence-based research was necessary. PICK partnered with leading published researchers on neonatal jaundice, treating clinicians and patient safety experts to engage in developing the evidence necessary to revise clinical guidelines to include a universal newborn bilirubin test and revised parent education materials to empower parents to help prevent future harm to newborns from elevated bilirubin levels. Through the collaboration with the researchers, the PICK mothers helped to collect and donate clinical data of 125 newborns who were discharged as healthy from the place of birth but subsequently sustained kernicterus. The collection of data became known as the Pilot USA Registry of Kernicterus [13]. PICK formed the Kernicterus Prevention Partnership Coalition that included various governmental agencies, academic institutions, and other stakeholders. These organizations were unified by a nonbinding memorandum of understanding. PICK and the researchers partnered with a leading public health agency to fund and analyze the data, the results of which indicated that kernicterus was an emerging public health issue and that implementation of a universal bilirubin (jaundice) test would help identify newborns at risk of hyperbilirubinemia and reduce the number of cases of kernicterus. PICK also partnered with a leading healthcare system with a large data set of clinical information on newborns. Analysis of their data also supported the implementation of a universal bilirubin test. A separate governmental health agency also partnered with PICK to fund the co-production, testing and the usability of parent education materials in different populations about the risks of newborn jaundice and included proactive steps they could take to identify and prevent harm to their newborns [14].

The outcome of PICK's co-production in research contributed to the revision of clinical practice guidelines to include a universal pre-discharge bilirubin test [15] and the dissemination of a "Sentinel Event Alert" by a national hospital accreditor with recommendations on newborn jaundice management [16], established kernicterus as a "Never Event" per a national quality measures organization, developed a national parent education campaign [14] and materials and co-developed and co-delivered curricula for continuing medical education courses.

There were many factors that contributed to PICK's achievements. One of the key factors was that a major national government agency invited stakeholders, including patients, to publicly comment at a National Summit on Medical Errors and Patient Safety. The organizers of this summit offered guidance to those unfamiliar with public comment how to best craft their testimony. At that summit, I, testified about the preventable harm that my son had suffered from undiagnosed and untreated neonatal jaundice and advocated for collaboration amongst all stakeholders to prevent future cases. Another success factor was the determination, persistence, and relentless call for action from the community of mothers with children with kernicterus who formed a respected, independent, nonprofit organization with by-laws and objectives to prevent harm to future newborns through a model of partnership. Further these mothers served as a "living repository" of clinical data for research regarding kernicterus unavailable through traditional data collection methods and were the conduit to collecting additional data from mothers across the world with children with kernicterus. This enabled the researchers to actively collaborate with the mothers as subject matter experts. As a result of these factors, deep, trusting, mutually beneficial relationships formed with patient safety experts, cli-

nicians, and leadership in government agencies, research institutions, medical education, and healthcare systems who willingly partnered with the mothers, despite criticism from peers. The healthcare leaders voluntarily helped the mothers gain capacity to be effective advocates for changes in jaundice management protocols. They helped educate the mothers about the structure of the healthcare system, the responsibilities of the various decision-making bodies, the current science and evidence base for management of newborn jaundice and gaps in the literature. They provided guidance and tips on successful storytelling and public speaking skills, partnered as presenters at national conferences and in interviews with media and provided resources, infrastructure and credibility that facilitated the development of the necessary evidence for successful implementation of a systems-based approach to the prevention of kernicterus.

6.4.1.2 Civil Society: Driving Patient-Centered Research to Prevent Diagnostic Errors

Researchers estimate that up to 80,000 deaths per year in US hospitals can be attributed to some form of diagnostic error. Misdiagnosis affects 12 million Americans in ambulatory care settings annually. The National Academy of Medicine's 2015 report, Improving Diagnosis in Health Care, highlights the urgent need for a research agenda on the diagnostic process and diagnostic errors and states that "patients are central to the solution" and there is a need to "establish partnerships with patients and families to improve diagnosis [17]. The Society to Improve Diagnosis in Medicine (SIDM), where I serve as the Director of Patient Engagement, is a US-based nonprofit organization (civil society) dedicated to reducing diagnostic errors. We believed that if researchers joined forces with trained patients and family members with lived experience in diagnostic error to co-produce diagnostic safety research projects, the research questions and outcomes would be more relevant, effective, and patient centered. SIDM pursued funding from the Patient-Centered Outcomes Research Institute (PCORI) to (1) recruit patients and family members who had experienced diagnostic error and diagnostic safety researchers to co-develop a curriculum that provides patients and family members with the knowledge, skills, and tools to effectively partner in the design, execution, and dissemination of diagnostic research; and (2) collectively co-produce patient-centered research topics and questions to pursue to improve diagnosis [18].

SIDM collaborated with Project Patient Care, an independent nonprofit organization of patients, family members, and patient advocates and the Medstar Institute for Quality and Safety to help recruit the patient and family participants and to develop the curriculum. I led the project that included patients and family members from key disease-related organizations and representatives from Patient and Family Advisory Councils (PFACs) at major healthcare institutions—all who had experienced diagnostic error. Prominent diagnostic researchers from academic medical centers also participated in the project. Together with the project team, the patients and researchers co-produced an innovative, patient-centered curriculum. This curriculum was continuously evaluated and refined to ensure patient engagement in diagnostic research. Applying the knowledge and methods developed in the curriculum, patients and researchers co-produced a list of patient-centered diagnostic research topics and questions for future research. One of these resultant research questions focused on disparities in diagnosis due to visible factors of age, sex, and race/ethnicity. This project was awarded funding for a 2-year research project to be led by SIDM and a major academic institute.

The promising results of SIDM's project are due to several factors. SIDM is an established nonprofit organization (i.e., a civil society organization) that has embedded patient and family engagement as a strategic priority in its mission and dedicated resources to employ a PFPS Champion as a full-time Director of Patient Engagement. Having SIDM develop and lead this project provided the credibility to secure funding from a large national research institute to support staff, the patients, family members, researchers, leadership, as well as an infrastructure designed

to support sustainability. Patients and family members from national disease groups who have firsthand experiences with diagnostic error were invaluable in identifying research questions and topic suggestions that often went unrecognized or unconsidered. The project developed and delivered an innovative, patient-centered training curriculum that enabled patients and family members to effectively distill their personal stories of diagnostic error and participate as true partners in the development of research questions. Because of its success, the curriculum has been replicated in other training efforts in acute care settings and methods and tools from the curriculum have been shared nationally and internationally as an approach to engage patients, family members, and other stakeholders in diagnostic improvement efforts [19].

6.5 Co-production in Medical Professions Education Courses

Patient engagement is a promising avenue in the area of healthcare education. Having real patients articulate their experiences and viewpoints helps those taking part in training to appreciate the patient perspective and the importance of preserving trust between clinicians and patients. These core values are essential to care that is compassionate, quality assured and, above all, safe. Exposure to patient stories during training is valuable and helps to motivate practitioners to improve safety [20].

There is evidence that teaching by patients has a lasting impact in the areas of technical skills interpersonal skills, empathic understanding, and developing an individualized approach to the patient [21].

6.5.1 Example: Mexico

6.5.1.1 Leveraging a Regional Network of PFPS Champions to Enhance Medical Education

According to a study on patient safety in Latin America (IBEAS), "on any given day, 10% of the patients admitted to the hospitals… had experienced some kind of harm due to health care" [22]. Evangelina Vazquez Curiel [23], a PFPS champion and single mother in Mexico whose newborn son experienced harm soon after birth, along with other patients, family members and healthcare professionals in Latin America, identified the lack of patient safety education for healthcare professionals in Latin America as a major contributing factor to unsafe care. She actively collaborated with academic institutions in Mexico, the local Ministry of Health and the Pan American Network of PFPS champions to co-produce an online patient safety course for healthcare professionals in Latin America that would bring patient safety experts, patients, and healthcare professionals from various healthcare systems together. Course co-developers, educators, patients, speakers, and learners are from eight countries—Mexico, Costa Rica, Peru, Paraguay, Uruguay, Ecuador, Chile, and Columbia. The objectives of the course are to (1) continuously train healthcare workers from remote and low-resource settings about patient safety and quality; (2) bring patient safety experts from across the Latin American region together to serve as educators and discussion leaders; (3) raise awareness of health literacy and highlight the role it plays in preventing adverse events; and (4) encourage dialogue between patients, family members, civil society, and healthcare providers/ treating professionals to reduce power imbalances. The curriculum is comprised of 11 modules, three of which focus on the WHO Global Challenges (Clean Care is Safer Care [24], Safe Surgery [25], and Medication without Harm [26]). The remaining eight focus on the fundamentals of improving patient safety and quality of care. At the end of the patient safety course, participants receive a certificate from The University of New Mexico of Tula.

Over 2000 healthcare professionals from a myriad of socio-economic backgrounds, practicing in rural public hospitals to small and large private hospitals have participated in the online course. The course was launched in 2016 and continues to be offered in 2020.

The success of the online patient safety course was primarily due to Ms. Vazquez Curiel's per-

sonal devotion, fervor, and effective networking in advocating for safer care. Because of her capacity to understand and appreciate the challenges of healthcare, and with the credibility of being a PFPS champion, Ms. Vazquez Curiel developed trusting relationships with healthcare leaders in Mexico, the Pan American Health Organization (PAHO), and other patient leaders and advocates in the Americas. Another contributing factor in the co-production and popularity of the online course was the Pan American Network of PFPS which is an informal group of like-minded, patients, family members, healthcare professionals, and policy makers with similar goals and experiences in patient safety that spans 10 countries in the Americas. This network was formed as a result of PAHO/WHO sponsored PFPS workshops. Its goals are to promote patient participation in efforts to improve quality and safety in healthcare and to improve patient skills for dialogue with healthcare planners and policy makers. The formation of the regional network has resulted in a vibrant, connected, multi-stakeholder regional community that shares best practices and risk mitigation strategies [27]. Finally, this course would not have succeeded without the volunteer healthcare professionals', academic institution leaders', and educators' willingness to collaborate with the PFPS community to co-produce a novel curriculum on patient safety that fosters a transparent, safe environment for dialogue about learning from unsafe care.

6.5.2 Example: Denmark

6.5.2.1 Patients as Educators
Communication breakdowns at crucial moments in the provision of healthcare were leading to serious adverse events, including death, in Danish hospitals. The Danish Society for Patient Safety, a civil society organization and member of the WHO PFPS Programme [28], organized The Danish Patients for Patient Safety (The Danish PFPS), a network of volunteer patients and/or family members who had experienced severe medical harm as a result of communication failures, to actively address this issue. The Danish

PFPS group believed that (1) effective communication between patients, family members, and healthcare providers was desperately lacking at crucial moments in the provision of care and that this failure to communicate lead to the serious medical errors; and (2) patients and/or family members who had been affected by adverse events sharing their real-world learning through storytelling would be an impactful method of teaching residents communications skills. Danish PFPS champions collaborated with medical leaders and educators in different regions of Denmark to co-produce and fully implement a live storytelling session as part of the compulsory three-day communication skills course [29]. During the storytelling sessions, a patient or family member from the Danish PFPS described his/her experience with medical error in a manner that highlighted the points in care where the doctor's communication skills, both good and poor, were especially important to the outcome of the care. Immediately after the Danish PFPS champion completed his/her story, the storyteller and communication course instructor guided the medical residents through a structured reflection process. The medical residents were then asked to think about what they could learn from the story and how they might incorporate these lessons into their clinical work.

To date, approximately 2500–2800 medical residents have completed the workshop. Medical residents consistently share that they have a greater appreciation of what the patient or family member experienced and have a better understanding of why truly listening to patients and family members is essential to provide safe and appropriate care. This feedback validated that live storytelling by patients and/or family members is an effective method to explore the human experience of care. As a result, the session has been permanently integrated into the regional standard curriculum for the medical resident communications training course since 2012.

The successful integration of the live storytelling session into the residents' communication course is due to the resolve and determination of Ms. Katrine Kirk, who experienced an adverse event herself, and the Danish PFPS network to transform their personal stories of unsafe care into learning opportunities coupled with the receptiveness of the Head of Training and the Curriculum Coordinator for residents in the capital region of Denmark who valued the inclusion of patient storytellers as viable "teachers" for medical residents. Together they thoughtfully structured the storytelling session to optimize resident learning while reducing concerns of those instructors trained in traditional, evidence-based teaching methods. Another factor of the success of the adoption of the storytelling course was the ongoing support and capacity building for the PFPS Champions that included presentations skills training offered by the Danish Society for Patient Safety. It was critical for the PFPS Champions to learn how to constructively craft and share their stories in a way that would result in meaningful learning for the residents without being perceived as adversarial. The Danish PFPS Network hopes to spread the idea of patient storytelling in communications training to the rest of Denmark and to systematically analyze the long-term impact and effectiveness.

6.6 Co-production in Healthcare Organization Quality Improvement

Hospitals are increasingly recognizing the crucial role of patients' perspectives in establishing a culture of safety. Many institutions have prioritized engaging patient representatives in the design and nurturing of safety efforts and emphasize transparency in reporting errors and care problems [30].

6.6.1 Example: Egypt

6.6.1.1 Improving Disparities in Care for New Mothers: The Power of Partnership Between a Civil Society Leader and a Public Teaching Hospital

There were significant disparities between the level of care provided to women delivering babies in Cairo at the public maternity teaching hospital versus the private hospital. An Egyptian member of The Red Crescent, a civil society organization, Nagwa Metwally, now a PFPS champion, along with other concerned community members believed that by integrating local volunteer citizens into the hospital system to observe and document quality and safety issues would help improve the quality of care and experiences of mothers at the public maternity teaching hospital [31]. Ms. Metwally met with the Dean of the medical schools and described the mission of the proposed quality improvement project. She later met with the Director of the public teaching maternity hospital. During this meeting, she thoughtfully and strategically described the envisioned quality improvement project and positioned the project as an "offer to help" and an opportunity for collaboration. This resulted in a partnership at the public maternity teaching hospital that embedded citizen volunteers in the hospital to help improve quality hospital services through observation. The goals of the project included (1) change the culture to be more patient centered; (2) ensure dignity and proper treatment for mothers; (3) create a safe environment in which mothers felt they could share their preferences and request and receive parent education; and (4) provide capacity building to the healthcare team, especially nurses, for the provision of safer and more compassionate care for the new mothers. Ms. Metwally and citizen volunteers joined the hospital team as observers to serve as an "extra set of eyes" to identify and record issues related to the WHO's Global Patient Safety Challenges [24–26] and the WHO's patient safety curriculum, which included hospital cleanliness, safe surgery, healthcare provider behavior, glove use, hand hygiene practices, staff and patient interaction, and other safety issues. Over 50 citizen volunteers and some residents served as observers conducting walking "tours" within the hospital noting and documenting safety and care concerns which they would later share with the Director of the hospital for consideration for improvement efforts.

Successes of the quality improvement project included the acceptance of these citizen observers as part of the hospital team as well as meaningful hospital-level policy changes. For example, policy change affected the hospital's promotion policy for nurses. The criteria for promotion are now based on efficiency, skill, and education rather than seniority only. The hospital also implemented a new evaluation criterion for medical residents to advance to medical doctors. The medical school adopted a doctor/patient relationship skills evaluation as part of the clinical skills final examination that medical residents must take to become doctors. In addition, there was an overall increase in awareness of patient safety issues, improved hospital cleanliness, as well as a greater use of gloves and hand hygiene practices [32]. The success of the quality improvement in the maternity hospital enabled Ms. Metwally to co-produce similar quality improvement projects in geriatrics and emergency hospitals.

Numerous factors contributed to the success of this co-produced quality improvement effort at the public maternity teaching hospital. The resolve and profound humanitarian commitment by Ms. Metwally and the Red Crescent of which she was a member, was crucial to highlighting the need to improve the equity, patient centeredness, and patient safety for new mothers in the community. Having the backing of a credible, trustworthy civil society organization helped facilitate the connection with the leaders of the medical schools and the hospital. Furthermore, framing the quality improvement project as a "way to help out" as well as demonstrating empathy by acknowledging the challenges that the public hospital faced was key to developing a trusting, respectful collaborative relationship. The willingness of the Dean of the medical schools and the Director of the maternity hospital to partner with Ms. Metwally, the Red Crescent and citizen volunteers to implement an innovative approach to quality improvement demonstrated the courage, humility, integrity, and open-mindedness needed from strong leadership to realize the benefits of this type of collaboration. Despite the fact that none of the partners in this active collaboration had previous training in implementing a co-produced quality improvement project such as this, they were resourceful and successful because of their trust in each other and in the belief that their mutual goal was in the best interest of all in involved, was patient centered and improved safety and quality.

6.6.2 Italy

6.6.2.1 Democratizing Healthcare: A Government-Driven/Citizen Partnership to Improve Patient Centeredness

The Italian National Agency for Regional Health (AGENAS) launched a government-driven healthcare organization quality improvement project co-produced with civil society organizations and citizens. The national program was aimed at evaluating and improving the level of patient centeredness in public and private hospitals throughout the country. AGENAS developed an innovative participatory evaluation methodology. The methodology was coordinated by AGENAS and carried out in cooperation with the Active Citizenship Network and the Italian Regions. AGENAS trained teams of healthcare professionals and citizens to go on site visits in public and private hospitals. During the site visits, these teams completed a checklist comprised of 142 items exploring four areas of interest: person-oriented processes, physical accessibility and comfort, access to information and transparency, and patient–professional relationships. Following the site visits, the data was collected and sent to a National Database where it was analyzed and sent back to the regions, hospitals, and teams for local public dissemination. Improvement plans were jointly identified and carried out by hospital professionals and citizens. A Plan-Do-Check-Act process was then carried out by local teams. Over 400 accredited public and private hospitals participated in this national evaluation. Site visits were made by the trained teams comprised of approximately 600 health professionals, 300 citizen associations, and 700 citizens. The overall results of the project indicate a moderately high level of person centered-

ness, especially in the larger hospitals [33]. Where new assessments have been carried out in 2019, there have been significant reports of improvements in all four areas of interest. This Italian national program has shown the effectiveness of co-production of a quality improvement initiative that actively engaged organizations, professionals, and citizens to promote patient centeredness.

A major component of success of the national program to improve person centeredness was the strong leadership at AGENAS that was dedicated to and valued the inclusion of citizens as partners in the quality improvement initiative. Examples of this included actively engaging citizens in all phases of the assessment and improvement cycle, as well as providing feedback and publicly disseminating project results. Another component of success was the strategic partnerships that AGENAS developed to maximize outreach to the citizen community. They formed strong alliances with the regional governments and health agencies and partnered with Active Citizenship Network, the association with the widest expertise in the civic evaluation of quality of health. A further component of success was the national program's commitment to providing training and capacity building to the citizens and other participants to optimize engagement by developing joint training on materials and tools of the participatory assessment of person centeredness. The participatory evaluation methods and tools were then applied to assess patient safety. The success of the national program has led to further implementations of this type of active collaboration between government, healthcare professionals, civil society organizations, and citizens to co-produce healthcare organization quality improvement projects.

6.7 Co-Production in Policy

Patient and family engagement in policy development has gained increasing recognition. For example, patients can be engaged in the development and dissemination of tools, information and educational materials [20].

6.7.1 Example: Canada

6.7.1.1 Working from Within: Co-producing National Policy as an Insider

In Canada, unintended patient harm occurs every 1 min and 18 s throughout the healthcare system, with a death resulting every 13 min and 14 s. To address this growing concern, Patients for Patient Safety Canada (PFPSC) [34], a patient program under the Canadian Patient Safety Institute (CPSI) [35], a publicly funded, not for profit corporation and designated WHO Collaborating Centre in Patient Safety and Patient Engagement, has co-produced seminal documents that influence policy at the national level on patient safety. These include the Canadian Disclosure Guidelines [36], Canadian Incident Analysis Framework [37], Engaging Patients in Patient Safety—a Canadian Guide [38], and Five Questions to Ask About Your Medications [39].

More recently, PFPSC was engaged in the co-production of the Canadian Quality and Patient Safety (CQPS) Framework, a joint initiative between CPSI and the Health Standards Organization (HSO) [40]. The framework was designed by a multi-stakeholder Advisory Committee, including patient and family members of PFPSC, with the specific aim to "establish consensus on quality and patient safety goals for health and social services to focus action and resources that improve patient experience and outcomes and reduce care variation" [41].

Members of PFPSC have been active participants in the development and socialization of the CQPS Framework from the outset, as equal players, and regarded as experts through their lived experience and patient advocacy. PFPSC Co-Chairs served on the governance Steering Committee and Evaluation Working Group. An independent public affairs firm was commissioned to provide public consultation; an opportunity for all stakeholder groups to provide input into the CQPS Framework. This independent evaluation demonstrated that collective impact initiatives, co-designed and co-led by patients as authentic partners, can be transformational. This collaborative work will continue as the Framework is implemented, adopted by health systems, and as its impact is evaluated.

The success of PFPSC and CPSI and the co-production of patient safety policy improvement efforts is largely due to the integration PFPSC into the organizational structure of CPSI as well as the trust and respect that has been developed by having a shared commitment to patient safety and healthcare system improvement.

CPSI made patient engagement a strategic priority and supported the development of a Canadian network of patients and family members which resulted in the formation of PFPSC. CPSI assigned a budget and staff to support PFPSC and patient engagement. CPSI partners with PFPSC in all of its programs, committees, and corporate initiatives, including executive recruitment and strategic planning. This structure is mutually beneficial in that it allows PFPSC to leverage CPSI resources, corporate functions and staff expertise and time, and it provides PFPSC credibility, increasing their opportunities to integrate the perspective of the patient community into national patient safety improvement efforts. Alternatively, CPSI, benefits from PFPSC participation as subject matter experts with lived experience of harm from unsafe care on which to base patient safety policy.

The leadership and patient-centered culture of CPSI were fundamental building blocks for successful partnership and integration of patients into the work of the Institute. Equally, the tenacity of the PFPSC patients and family members in advocating for patient needs and the willingness to adapt within a structured environment were necessary for sustainability and co-production of seminal documents and policy projects.

6.8 Conclusion

Patient safety is a growing global concern. Parents, daughters, sons, siblings, other family members, community members, and our dear friends are harmed unnecessarily from unsafe care. It is essential that all stakeholders, especially those who have suffered from adverse events, have the opportunity to actively collaborate in co-producing patient safety solutions. Those who have experienced adverse events identify gaps in safety and quality and offer wisdom, data, and stories unavailable through traditional sources. Each of these case studies illustrates the power and potential of co-production with patients, families, and communities in research, medical professions education, healthcare quality improvement and policy. Each is different in scope, structure, and purpose and engage different stakeholders at different levels yet they all highlight the necessary building blocks for co-production of patient safety initiatives and each responds to the call made in the London Declaration, the WHO PFPS Programme, and the WHA to place patients at the center of efforts to improve patient safety.

The building blocks include:

1. **Dedicated, resilient patient, family, and community members** who have directly or indirectly experienced unsafe care yet are willing to partner with healthcare decision-makers and learn how to navigate the complexities, structures and limitations of different healthcare systems. They have become accomplished storytellers, networkers and connectors and have gained appreciation of the many challenges that healthcare providers and leaders face while remaining unwilling to accept the status quo.
2. **Courageous, passionate healthcare leaders** with the moral imperative to integrate the patient/citizen community into patient safety improvement efforts. These leaders are visionaries who visibly demonstrate their commitment to listen and learn from others. They value the input from others as highly as their own and integrate what they learn into governance, missions and strategies that promote patient involvement. They hard-wire the necessary resources to overcome political, cultural and financial barriers into budgets and infrastructures that support patient participation.
3. **Capacity building opportunities**

- **for patients, families and communities** to help them develop the skills to effectively share their personal stories of unsafe care that captures the hearts and minds, builds trust and prompts action from the audiences and to have productive dialogue with healthcare leaders including policy makers, researchers, medical educators and quality improvement experts,
- **for healthcare professionals and leaders** to learn how to utilize effective patient-centered methods to collaborate, communicate with, listen to and engage with patients, families and community members in a democratic way.

4. **Structure** that establishes how patients, families and communities operate to obtain their goals. There is no one structure that is considered the gold standard for the organization of patients, families and communities. Structures may be formal or informal. Informal structures tend to be loosely organized, autonomous, volunteer patient networks that collaborate with healthcare professionals, leaders and organizations. More formal structures tend to be established patient organizations and associations which operate independently from the healthcare system or government such as civil society organizations. Finally, there are publicly funded structures that embed patients, family and community members into their strategic plans, budgets and activities necessary to achieve organizational goals. Whether formal or informal, it is essential that the structure preserves the values, preferences and outcomes that matter most to patients, families and communities and that these serve as overarching principles that guide the actions and priorities of the safety initiatives. It is also important that the structure facilitates access for patients, families and community members to healthcare decision-makers as well as financial and human resources to systematically analyze the outcomes of co-produced safety initiatives to improve, scale and spread, or disseminate the benefits of implementation and to ensure sustainability.

All stakeholders must accept, value, and support meaningful patient engagement in the co-production of our efforts to improve patient safety including in the design of research, medical education, policy making, and healthcare organization quality improvement.

We must continue to strive to democratize our healthcare. We "must have a powerful voice and role in the decisions and systems that affect… [our] health, and…[be given the] tools that help…[us] to become far more actively engaged…health professionals and institutions must value social equity and the individual in the context of community" [42]. I know this because I have lived it and witnessed the successes.

References

1. Declaration of Alma-Ata International Conference on Primary Health Care, Alma-Ata, USSR, 6–12 Sept 1978.
2. Flott K, Fontana G, Darzi A. The global state of patient safety. London: Imperial College London; 2019.
3. The World Health Assembly. Available at: https://www.who.int/about/governance/world-health-assembly. Accessed 18 Dec 2019.
4. World Health Organisation (WHO). Resolution WHA 72.6: global action on patient safety. Geneva: WHO; 2019.
5. Ihi.org. About this IHI virtual expedition. 2019. Available at: http://www.ihi.org/education/WebTraining/Expeditions/coproduction/Pages/default.aspx. Accessed 17 Dec 2019.
6. Turakhia P, Combs B. Using principles of co-production to improve patient care and enhance value. AMA J Ethics. 2017;19(11):1125–31.
7. World Health Organisation (WHO). World Health Assembly resolution WHA 55.18. Geneva: WHO; 2002.
8. World Alliance for Patient Safety. https://www.who.int/patientsafety/worldalliance/en/. Accessed 18 Dec 2019.
9. World Alliance for Patient Safety. Patients for Patient Safety. https://www.who.int/patientsafety/patients_for_patient/regional_champions/en/. Accessed 18 Dec 2019.
10. World Health Organisation (WHO). Patients for Patient Safety: the London declaration. Geneva: WHO; 2006.
11. Woodgate RL, Zurba M, Tennent P. Advancing patient engagement: youth and family participation in health research communities of practice. Res Invol Engage. 2018;4:9.
12. pic-K. pic-K. Available at: https://pic-k.org/. Accessed 20 Dec 2019.
13. Johnson L, Bhutani V, Karp K, et al. Clinical report from the pilot USA Kernicterus Registry (1992 to 2004). J Perinatol. 2009;29:S25–45.
14. Centers for Disease Control and Prevention. Jaundice and Kernicterus|CDC. Available at: https://www.cdc.gov/ncbddd/jaundice/index.html. Accessed 20 Dec 2019.
15. Maisels M, Bhutani V, Bogen D, Newman T, Stark A, Watchko J. Hyperbilirubinemia in the newborn infant >=35 weeks' gestation: an update with clarifications. Pediatrics. 2009;124(4):1193–8.
16. Reliasmedia.com. JCAHO issues warning on kernicterus danger|2001-07-01|AHC Media: Continuing Medical Education Publishing. Available at: https://www.reliasmedia.com/articles/71202-jcaho-issues-warning-on-kernicterus-danger. Accessed 20 Dec 2019.
17. National Academies of Sciences, Engineering, and Medicine. Improving diagnosis in health care. Washington, DC: The National Academies Press; 2015.
18. Society to Improve Diagnosis in Medicine. Available at: https://www.improvediagnosis.org/news_posts/sidm-approved-for-a-250000-engagement-award-from-the-patient-centered-outcomes-research-institute/. Accessed 20 Dec 2019.
19. Society to Improve Diagnosis in Medicine. Disparities—society to improve diagnosis in medicine. Available at: https://www.improvediagnosis.org/disparities/. Accessed 20 Dec 2019.
20. World Health Organisation (WHO). Patient engagement: technical series on safer primary care. Geneva: WHO; 2016.
21. Spencer J, Godolphin W, Karpenko N, Towle A. Can patients be teachers? Involving patients and service users in healthcare professionals' education. Newcastle: The Health Foundation; 2011.
22. World Health Organisation (WHO). IBEAS: a pioneer study on patient safety in Latin America: towards safer hospital care. Geneva: WHO; 2011.
23. Vazquez Curiel E. WHO News Archive. Who.int. Available at: https://www.who.int/gpsc/news/Evangelina-Vazquez-Curiel.pdf. Accessed 20 Dec 2019.
24. Allegranzi B, Storr J, Dziekan G, et al. The first global patient safety challenge "Clean care is safer care": from launch to current progress and achievements. J Hosp Infect. 2007;65(Suppl. 2):115–23.
25. World Alliance for Patient Safety. The second global patient safety challenge: safe surgery saves lives. Geneva: World Health Organization; 2008.
26. Donaldson LJ, Kelley ET, Dhingra-Kumar N, Kieny M-P, Sheikh A. Medication without harm: WHO's third global patient safety challenge. Lancet. 2017;389(10080):1680.
27. Gomez A. PAHO/WHO|PAHO Today, December 2008 Edition—Patient Champions Launch New Advocacy Network. Pan

American Health Organization/World Health Organization. 2019. Available at: https://www.paho.org/hq/index.php?option=com_content&view=article&id=585:2009-patient-champions-launch-new-advocacy-network&Itemid=40623&lang=en. Accessed 18 Dec 2019.

28. Patientsikkerhed. The Danish Society for Patient Safety. Available at: https://patientsikkerhed.dk/om-os/. Accessed 20 Dec 2019.

29. Patientsikkerhed. Danish presentations and experience days: A8: The Danish Way: teaching doctors to listen. Live patient storytelling in communication skills courses. Available at: https://patientsikkerhed.dk/internationalforum2020/danske-oplaeg/. Accessed 20 Dec 2019.

30. Psnet.ahrq.gov. Patient Engagement and Safety|PSNet. Available at: https://psnet.ahrq.gov/primer/patient-engagement-and-safety. Accessed 18 Dec 2019.

31. Metwally, N. Towards building capacity in patients and empowering patient voices in Egypt. 2018.

32. Event.icebergevents.com.au. Nagwa Metwally, Egypt—Speakers|World Hospital Congress. Available at: https://event.icebergevents.com.au/whc2018/speakers/nagwa-metwally-egypt. Accessed 20 Dec 2019.

33. Carinci F, Labella B, Cardinali F, Carzaniga S, Cerilli M, Duranti G, Lamanna A, Raho V, Caracci G. A National Program to improve person centeredness in hospital through a partnership with citizens. Eur J Pub Health. 2018;28(4) https://doi.org/10.1093/eurpub/cky214.178. Accessed 20 Dec 2019.

34. Patientsafetyinstitute.ca. Patients for Patient Safety Canada. Available at: https://www.patientsafetyinstitute.ca/en/About/Programs/ppsc/Pages/default.aspx. Accessed 18 Dec 2019.

35. Patientsafetyinstitute.ca. About CPSI. Available at: https://www.patientsafetyinstitute.ca/en/About/Pages/default.aspx. Accessed 18 Dec 2019.

36. Patientsafetyinstitute.ca. Canadian Disclosure Guidelines: being open with patients and families. 2011. Available at: https://www.patientsafetyinstitute.ca/en/toolsresources/disclosure/pages/default.aspx. Accessed 20 Dec 2019.

37. Patientsafetyinstitute.ca. Canadian incident analysis framework. 2012. Available at: https://www.patientsafetyinstitute.ca/en/toolsResources/IncidentAnalysis/Documents/Canadian Incident Analysis Framework.PDF. Accessed 20 Dec 2019.

38. Patientsafetyinstitute.ca. The engaging patients in patient safety—a Canadian Guide. 2018. Available at: https://www.patientsafetyinstitute.ca/en/toolsResources/Patient-Engagement-in-Patient-Safety-Guide/Documents/Engaging Patients in Patient Safety.pdf. Accessed 20 Dec 2019.

39. Patientsafetyinstitute.ca. Five questions to ask about your medications. Available at: http://www.patientsafetyinstitute.ca/en/toolsResources/5-Questions-to-Ask-about-your-Medications/Pages/default.aspx. Accessed 20 Dec 2019.

40. Patientsafetyinstitute.ca. Canadian quality and patient safety framework for health and social services. 2019. Available at: https://www.patientsafetyinstitute.ca/en/toolsResources/Canadian-Quality-and-Patient-Safety-Framework-for-Health-and-Social-Services/Pages/default.aspx. Accessed 18 Dec 2019.

41. Girard-Griffith F. CPSI-HSO quality and patient safety framework for health and social services public online focus group consultation interview with the Patient Partner Network by conducted by Compass Rose. 2019.

42. Tang PC, Smith MD, Adler-Milstein J, Delbanco T, Downs SJ, Mallya GG, Ness DL, Parker RM, Sands DZ. The democratization of health care: a vital direction for health and health care. NAM perspectives. Discussion paper. Washington, DC: National Academy of Medicine; 2016.

Human Factors and Ergonomics in Health Care and Patient Safety from the Perspective of Medical Residents

7

Pascale Carayon, Peter Kleinschmidt, Bat-Zion Hose, and Megan Salwei

7.1 Introduction

Health care is about people with various roles (e.g., patient, caregiver, clinician) who interact and collaborate in connected care processes of diagnosis, treatment, monitoring, and management. Ensuring that these processes produce "good" outcomes for patients (e.g., quality of care, patient safety, positive patient experience) as well as for clinicians involved in their care (e.g., quality of working life of clinicians) remains a major challenge around the world. The US National Academies' report on Crossing the Global Quality Chasm [1] indicates that inappropriate and unsafe care remain widespread around the world. In particular, "between 5.7 and 8.4 million deaths occur annually from poor quality of care in LMICs for … selected set of conditions …, which represents between 10% and 15% of the total deaths in LMICs … in 2015" (page S-2).

P. Carayon (✉)
Department of Industrial and Systems Engineering, Wisconsin Institute of Healthcare Systems Engineering, University of Wisconsin-Madison, Madison, WI, USA
e-mail: pcarayon@wisc.edu

P. Kleinschmidt
UW Health, Madison, WI, USA
e-mail: PKleinschmidt@uwhealth.org

B.-Z. Hose · M. Salwei
University of Wisconsin-Madison, Madison, WI, USA
e-mail: bhose@wisc.edu; msalwei@wisc.edu

Two other reports also published in 2018 draw attention to patient safety challenges and gaps in health care quality around the world [2]. Systems approaches have been recommended to address these complex health care quality and patient safety problems [1, 3], as well as to improve work systems and working conditions for clinicians [4].

The discipline of human factors (or ergonomics) (HFE) provides systems concepts and methods to improve care processes and outcomes for patients, caregivers, and clinicians. According to the International Ergonomics Association, HFE is "the scientific discipline concerned with the understanding of interactions among humans and other elements of a system, and the profession that applies theory, principles, data and methods to design in order to optimize human well-being and overall system performance" [5]. According to this definition of HFE by the IEA, people are at the center of (work) systems; systems and their elements and interactions should be designed to support performance and enhance well-being of people. HFE emphasizes the physical, cognitive, and organizational dimensions of work systems. Medical residents are key stakeholders in delivery of high-quality, safe care; they are often at the center of work systems that deliver care to patients in hospitals, primary care or specialty care facilities, emergency departments, and other care settings. Therefore, it is important to design the work system of medical residents to improve

© The Author(s) 2021
L. Donaldson et al. (eds.), *Textbook of Patient Safety and Clinical Risk Management*,
https://doi.org/10.1007/978-3-030-59403-9_7

quality and safety of care. The discipline, approaches, and methods of HFE can help to achieve this goal.

7.2 Application of SEIPS Model to Medical Residents

The SEIPS (Systems Engineering Initiative for Patient Safety) model [6, 7] is an HFE systems model that can be used to describe the work of medical residents and its impact on patient safety and resident outcomes, such as well-being, safety, and learning. According to the SEIPS model, medical residents perform a range of tasks (e.g., clinical tasks, learning activities) using various tools and technologies; this occurs in a physical and organizational environment (see Fig. 7.1). The design of the work system, i.e., its individual elements and their interactions, influences care processes and educational processes, which in turn produce outcomes for patients (e.g., patient safety) and for residents (e.g., well-being, learning).

Medical residents perform a range of tasks that have been documented and described in multiple studies. For instance, Carayon et al. [8]

described the work of residents in intensive care units (ICUs), including adult, pediatric, medical, and surgical units. Prior to conducting observations, researchers developed a list of 17 tasks (e.g., direct patient interaction). Four human factors engineers observed residents in multiple ICUs for a total of 242 h. Observers recorded time spent by residents in the following categories: (1) direct patient care (e.g., clinical review and documentation), (2) care coordination (e.g., conversation with team physician), (3) indirect patient care (e.g., administrative review and documentation), and (4) non-patient care (e.g., non-clinical conversation). Other studies of medical residents have also shown that significant proportion of their time is spent on tasks that are indirectly related to patient care [9] and that medical residents are often interrupted while performing tasks [10].

Residents perform tasks using various technologies, in particular health information technologies such as EHR (electronic health record) and CPOE (computerized provider order entry). Those technologies have significant impact on tasks performed by residents, including time spent on various tasks and the sequence or flow

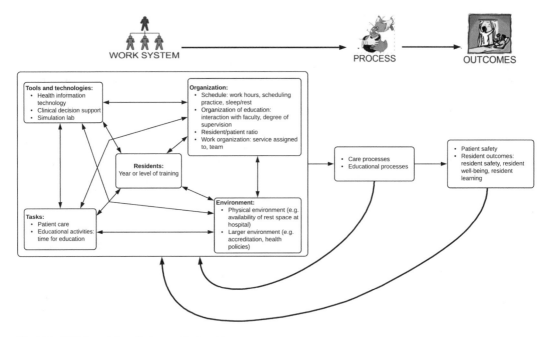

Fig. 7.1 SEIPS model applied to medical residents

of tasks. For instance, after the implementation of EHR technology in intensive care units, residents spent significantly more time on clinical documentation and review: from 18% to 31%, respectively, before and after EHR implementation [11]. They also performed a higher frequency of activities per hour after EHR implementation: from 117 to 154 activities per hour. This may reflect increased intensification of work around the use of EHR technology.

Eden et al. [12] described several work system factors in graduate medical education that interact and influence residents' educational process and resident learning; these work system interactions impact the extent to which the resident workforce is able to provide high-quality, patient-centered, and affordable health care. For instance, the payment structures (*organization*), availability of accredited residency positions (*environment*), as well as lifestyle and demographic factors (*person*) affect the residency pipeline and the number of physicians in specialty and subspecialty fields. Other work system factors, such as telehealth (*technology*) and an increased presence of physician assistants (*organization*) are changing the roles, responsibilities, and work demands of physicians. The graduate medical education work system should be designed so that the educational processes produce physicians that can support the health needs and goals of populations around the world.

A recent report by the National Academies of Sciences, Engineering, and Medicine demonstrates the influence of work system factors on resident well-being. Forty-five to sixty percent of medical residents' experience symptoms of burnout, which is characterized by high emotional exhaustion, high depersonalization, and a low sense of accomplishment from work [13]. In particular, the electronic health record (*technology*) is recognized as a source of burnout among physicians. For instance, in a study of residents and teaching physicians, 37% reported at least 1 symptom of burnout with 75% associating burnout with the use of the EHR. Additionally, physicians who used the EHR after work for more than 6 h per week were 3 times more likely to report symptoms of burnout compared to physicians

who spent 6 h or less per week [14]. The negative impact of the EHR on resident well-being is in part due to the increased clerical (*tasks*) and documentation (*organization*) burden. The SEIPS model can be used to understand how work system factors interact and influence resident outcomes such as burnout and learning).

We adapted a scenario from the AHRQ (Agency for Healthcare Research and Quality) WebM&M website (https://psnet.ahrq.gov/) to demonstrate how work system elements can interact and influence patient care.

> A 70-year-old healthy man (*person*) went to a routine follow-up appointment (*task*) with his primary care doctor (*person*). His doctor (*person*) was a third-year internal medicine resident in his final month of training and would soon leave the institution to begin his fellowship. After a discussion with the patient, the resident decided to screen him for prostate cancer with the prostate-specific antigen (PSA) test (*person* and *task*). In the past, the patient's PSA tests had always been normal. This time, the patient's PSA test returned and was elevated at a level where cancer is almost certain (83 ng/ml). However, the resident had completed his training before receiving an electronic alert (*technology*) about the patient's PSA test. The electronic alert remained unread (*technology, task, organization*) as there was no system in place that supported smooth handoffs to oncoming residents (*organization, task, person*). Several months later, the patient (*person*) presented with low back pain. His new physician, another internal medicine resident (*person*), ordered imaging tests (*task*) that confirmed metastatic prostate cancer. While the new resident (*person*) reviewed the patient's chart (*task and technology*), he uncovered the missed follow-up for the patient's elevated PSA.

This scenario includes several interacting work system elements (e.g., technology and organization) that resulted in a patient's delayed diagnosis of prostate cancer.

7.3 Linkage of Work System to Patient Safety and Medical Resident Well-Being

One of the primary drivers of workplace reform as it relates to resident well-being and health is through the institution of duty hour limitations.

This reform is largely attributed to the death of Libby Zion, an 18-year-old woman who was under the care of residents in a hospital emergency department in New York City in 1984 [15]. Publicity from this case spurred conversations about fatigue and patient safety issues connected to unrestricted hours worked by residents, and many countries began to impose work hour limitations in the 1990s as a result. The European Working Time Directive became law in 1998 and included limiting physicians working hours to 48 h per week and limiting hours for physicians in training [16]. Training hours in the United States limited work hours first in 2003 [17], then further in 2011 to a cap of 80 h per week, with the aim of improving both patient safety and trainee safety [18].

Measuring the impact of duty hour restrictions has been controversial. A systematic review in 2015 on work hour restrictions found inconsistent results, often with studies in direct contradiction with expectations regarding patient safety and resident well-being [19]. Since then two large randomized controlled trials have evaluated outcomes more extensively, randomizing trainees to restrictive conditions under the 2011 limits vs more flexible schedules. The FIRST trial randomized 118 surgical programs and first published results in 2015. This was followed by the iCOMPARE trial, which randomized 63 internal medicine residency programs. In both studies, primary outcomes included no difference in patient safety events between groups [20, 21] and no significant difference in educational outcomes between groups [22]. Residents in the iCOMPARE trial were more satisfied with their educational experience in the work hour restricted arm of the study though this effect was not seen in the FIRST trial, while program directors were more satisfied in the flexible schedule study arm.

The exact degree of duty hour restriction necessary to impact patient safety remains controversial [23]. Critics of studies showing minimal impact argue that work hour restrictions are inconsistently applied or may not be carefully implemented [24]. For example, limiting time at work on duty may just shift to more work at home when off duty, or compressing work to a nar-rower window and leading to increased stress [25]. Despite results of the FIRST and iCOM-PARE trials, significant data exist to show that extended shifts in the hospital setting can have adverse effects on technical and cognitive performance and lead to impairment outside the workplace [26–28].

Work hour limitations in the EU are generally more restrictive than in the United States yet have led to similarly controversial results. A systematic review by Rodriguez-Jareño and colleagues [23] found that long working hours, defined by the European Working Time Directive as more than 48 h per week, to be associated with an increased incidence of physician needle-stick injuries and motor vehicle accidents. Additionally, a study by Zahrai et al. [29] found a significant relationship between resident hours spent in the hospital and poor general health and physical function. However, another study found no improvements in resident self-reported physical health by reducing working hours [30].

Despite these controversies, efforts should be made to mitigate fatigue and burnout. Burnout has been demonstrated to increase cognitive failures and difficulties with attention [31]. A systematic review demonstrated a strong connection between poor well-being and negative patient safety outcomes such as medical errors. This was particularly closely linked with depression, anxiety, poor quality of life, and stress, along with moderate to high levels of burnout [32]. Growing data on the impact of burnout on both clinical outcomes and physician safety has led to repeated calls for greater emphasis on addressing this issue [33]. This is critical as it relates to training environments for residents along with the broader systems in which health care professionals work; it is becoming more apparent that fatigue and burnout is a significant safety issue for both patients and physicians, including physicians-in-training. Outside of duty hours, several other work system factors can contribute to poor resident well-being, fatigue, and burnout including training, work schedule flexibility, autonomy, clinical experience, and supervisor behavior [34, 35]. As there are multiple, sometimes conflicting goals, regulations on working hours as well as other work system factors (e.g., flexibility of schedules, technology design, training environment) should be carefully considered in order to mitigate negative effects on residents and patient safety.

7.4   Challenges and Trade-Offs in Improving Residents' Work System

Medical residents work and learn in various care settings and in interaction with other clinicians. The challenge is how to optimize the work system of medical residents, as well as the work systems of others that are involved in patient care. In a previous section, we discussed the challenge of designing safe and healthy work schedules for medical residents. Some interventions aimed at reducing work hours of medical residents have unfortunately had negative impact on the attending physicians who supervise them: work gets passed on from medical residents to attending physicians who are then experiencing overload and stress. Therefore, any intervention aimed at improving the work system of medical residents needs to prevent or mitigate negative consequences for other health care professionals involved in patient care.

Improving residents' work system can be challenging as it may lead to improvement in some outcomes, but deterioration in other outcomes. Myers et al. [36] assessed internal medicine and general surgical residents' attitudes about the effects of the Accreditation Council for General Medical Education duty hours regulations effective July 1, 2003 [37]. They surveyed 111 internal medicine residents and 48 general surgical residents from six geographically diverse programs in the United States. The sample was limited to residents who had experienced residency before and after implementation of the duty hours regulations. The survey included questions on residents' opinions of [1] quality of patient care and safety and [2] residency education. Both medical and surgical residents reported that the quality of care decreased with continuity of care decreasing a lot. Medical resi-

dents reported a greater decrease in available opportunities for bedside learning and teaching than surgical residents. The authors of the study noted that duty hours reform may lead to teaching hospitals caring for the same patient volume with fewer resident physician-hours; therefore, intensifying the work of residents. Thus, there is a need to optimize and improve the resident work system to consider all outcomes, including continuity of patient care and educational opportunities.

7.5   Role of Residents in Improving Their Work System

There is a long tradition in the HFE literature and practice of involving "workers" in work system redesign; this is known as participatory ergonomics [38]. In participatory ergonomics projects, the "workers" participate in providing input and ideas about how to improve tasks, technologies, environments, organizations, and processes. Sometimes workers are actively engaged in making decisions about how to redesign the work system. Participatory ergonomics projects vary with regard to content (e.g., improving the design of EHR technology), decision making (e.g., providing input or making decisions on process improvement), and stage (e.g., initial analysis of work system or implementation of redesign) [39]. In a project aimed at enhancing family engagement in bedside rounding in a pediatric hospital, researchers implemented a participatory ergonomics process in which residents along with attending physicians, nurses, and parent proposed and helped to implement a bundle of interventions [40]. The interventions consisted of a checklist of best practices for engaging families during bedside rounding (e.g., introducing health care team members) and training of residents in the new rounding process. Specific elements of the checklist (e.g., asking the family for questions, reading back orders) were related to improvement in perceived quality and safety of care by parents [41]. Involving residents in this work system and process redesign was critical to the successful implementation of the interventions as key stakeholders. In addition to involving residents in specific improvement projects, health care organizations have created dedicated structures to involve residents more systematically, such as involvement of residents in safety/quality councils [42].

The Institute of Medicine report "Resident Duty Hours: Enhancing Sleep, Supervision, and Safety" [43] spurred a significant change in resident work structure. It also prompted greater emphasis on both training and direct resident involvement in quality improvement and patient safety initiatives. Out of this movement, the Accreditation Council for Graduate Medical Education in the United States (ACGME) drafted its Clinical Learning Environment Review (CLER) guidelines in 2014 [44]. Included in the guidelines are requirements that training programs integrate quality improvement and patient safety training into resident curricula and that residents should have direct involvement in organizational quality improvement projects. Hospitals and health systems have taken a variety of strategies to fulfill this requirement while also integrating residents into quality improvement initiatives and work system redesigns.

A systematic review in 2010 identified components for a resident quality curriculum, which should include concepts of continuous quality improvement, root cause analysis, and systems thinking [45]. Implementation of quality curricula was well accepted and effective in improving knowledge. Further, 32% of studied curricula (13/41) resulted in local changes in care delivery and 17% (13/41) significantly improved target processes of care, indicating that direct training itself of trainees can improve the quality environment of an organization.

Several organizations have heeded the call for resident involvement in improving their work systems by establishing quality councils and safety officer positions for residents and other trainees [4]. This is a critical component to boosting resident involvement in safety and quality improvement their institutions. In the following paragraph, we lay out a model for a resident safety council drawing on experiences published by several institutions in the United States and Canada [42, 46]. Similar councils have since demonstrated measurable improvements in improvements in patient safety goals [47, 48].

The following should be considered when designing and implementing a resident safety council:

- The council should be resident led.
- Appoint a resident chair who works directly along system administrators and other hospital groups to direct quality improvement projects.
- Relevant subcommittees, for example, Quality, Safety, Research, Education, each chaired by council members can further direct the focus of the group.
- Agendas and meeting topics are both chosen by and presented by residents to this helps assure that meetings remain interactive and productive, rather than becoming a series of lectures.
- The safety council should remain voluntary though with an effort to establish representation from all training programs at an institution.
- Encourage a multidisciplinary presence at council meetings. Graduate medical education staff, hospital administrators, representatives from organizational QI and patient safety departments, and patient–family representatives should all be involved in meetings.
- The safety council should serve as a tool to draw residents directly onto institutional QI committees, such as Event Evaluation Teams, Root Cause Analysis, Medical Records committees, and Interdisciplinary Model of Care Committees.

Implementing a robust quality improvement and safety curriculum supported by a resident-led council can empower residents to implement large-scale quality work, to engage their peers, and help foster growth of the next generation of leaders in patient safety.

7.6 Conclusion

In many health care organizations, especially academic medical centers, residents are the primary clinicians providing patient care. Recognizing the unique needs of medical residents both in their role of delivering safe and effective care and also in meeting their educational objectives requires a robust approach to understand the work systems in which residents operate. Human factors and ergonomics principles, and specifically the Systems Engineering Initiative for Patient Safety (SEIPS) model, can inform decisions when working to evaluate and improve resident work systems. This is particularly important when addressing patient safety and resident well-being. As health care becomes increasingly interconnected and reliant on multidisciplinary teams, it is important to consider unanticipated consequences of changes in work systems, particularly on how they may affect processes and outcomes for residents, but also for all other team members.

Acknowledgments This chapter was supported by the Clinical and Translational Science Award (CTSA) program, through the NIH National Center for Advancing Translational Sciences (NCATS), Grant Number: 1UL1TR002373. The content is solely the responsibility of the authors and does not necessarily represent the official views of the NIH.

References

1. NASEM (National Academies of Sciences E, and Medicine). Crossing the global quality chasm. Washington, DC: The National Academies Press; 2018.
2. Berwick DM, Kelley E, Kruk ME, Nishtar S, Pate MA. Three global health-care quality reports in 2018. Lancet. 2018;392(10143):194–5.
3. Kaplan GS, Bo-Linn G, Carayon P, Pronovost P, Rouse W, Reid P, et al. Bringing a systems approach to health. Washington, DC: Institute of Medicine and National Academy of Engineering; 2013.
4. NASEM (National Academies of Sciences E, and Medicine). Taking action against clinician burnout: a systems approach to professional well-being. Washington, DC: National Academies Press; 2019.
5. International Ergonomics Association (IEA). The discipline of ergonomics. 2000. http://www.iea.cc/ergonomics/.
6. Carayon P, Hundt AS, Karsh B-T, Gurses AP, Alvarado CJ, Smith M, et al. Work system design for patient safety: the SEIPS model. Qual Saf Health Care. 2006;15(Suppl I):i50–8.
7. Carayon P, Wetterneck TB, Rivera-Rodriguez AJ, Hundt AS, Hoonakker P, Holden R, et al. Human factors systems approach to healthcare quality and patient safety. Appl Ergon. 2014;45(1):14–25.
8. Carayon P, Weinger MB, Brown R, Cartmill R, Slagle J, Van Roy KS, et al. How do residents spend their time in the intensive care unit? Am J Med Sci. 2015;350(5):403–8.
9. Hollingsworth JC, Chisholm CD, Giles BK, Cordell WH, Nelson DR. How do physicians and nurses spend their time in the emergency department? Ann Emerg Med. 1998;31(1):87–91.
10. Gabow PAMD, Karkhanis AMS, Knight ARN, Dixon PP, Eisert SP, Albert RKMD. Observations of residents' work activities for 24 consecutive hours: Implications for workflow redesign. Acad Med. 2006;81(8):766–75.
11. Carayon P, Wetterneck TB, Alyousef B, Brown RL, Cartmill RS, McGuire K, et al. Impact of electronic health record technology on the work and workflow of physicians in the intensive care unit. Int J Med Inf. 2015;84(8):578–94.
12. Eden J, Berwick D, Wilensky G. Graduate medical education that meets the nation's health needs. ERIC; 2014.
13. National Academies of Sciences E, and Medicine. Taking action against clinician burnout: a systems approach to professional well-being. Washington, DC: National Academies Press; 2020.
14. Robertson SL, Robinson MD, Reid A. Electronic health record effects on work-life balance and burnout within the I(3) population collaborative. J Grad Med Educ. 2017;9(4):479–84.
15. Brensilver JM, Smith L, Lyttle CS. Impact of the Libby Zion case on graduate medical education in internal medicine. Mt Sinai J Med (NY). 1998;65(4):296–300.
16. BMA—What is the European Working Time Directive? 31 Dec 2019. Available from: https://www.bma.org.uk/advice/employment/working-hours/ewtd.
17. Ulmer C. Committee on Optimizing Graduate Medical Trainee (Resident) Hours and Work Schedules to Improve Patient Safety for the Institute of Medicine. Resident duty hours: enhancing sleep, supervision, and safety. 2008.
18. Nasca TJ, Day SH, Amis ES Jr. The new recommendations on duty hours from the ACGME Task Force. N Engl J Med. 2010;363:e3(1)–e3(6).
19. Bolster L, Rourke L. The effect of restricting residents' duty hours on patient safety, resident well-being, and resident education: an updated systematic review. J Grad Med Educ. 2015;7(3):349–63.
20. Bilimoria KY, Chung JW, Hedges LV, Dahlke AR, Love R, Cohen ME, et al. National cluster-randomized trial of duty-hour flexibility in surgical training. N Engl J Med. 2016;374(8):713–27.

21. Silber JH, Bellini LM, Shea JA, Desai SV, Dinges DF, Basner M, et al. Patient safety outcomes under flexible and standard resident duty-hour rules. N Engl J Med. 2019;380(10):905–14.

22. Desai SV, Asch DA, Bellini LM, Chaiyachati KH, Liu M, Sternberg AL, et al. Education outcomes in a duty-hour flexibility trial in internal medicine. N Engl J Med. 2018;378(16):1494–508.

23. Rodriguez-Jareño MC, Demou E, Vargas-Prada S, Sanati KA, Škerjanc A, Reis PG, et al. European Working Time Directive and doctors' health: a systematic review of the available epidemiological evidence. BMJ Open. 2014;4(7):e004916.

24. McMahon GT. Managing the most precious resource in medicine. N Engl J Med. 2018;378(16):1552–4.

25. Auger KA, Landrigan CP, Gonzalez del Rey JA, Sieplinga KR, Sucharew HJ, Simmons JM. Better rested, but more stressed? Evidence of the effects of resident work hour restrictions. Acad Pediatr. 2012;12(4):335–43.

26. Barger LK, Cade BE, Ayas NT, Cronin JW, Rosner B, Speizer FE, et al. Extended work shifts and the risk of motor vehicle crashes among interns. N Engl J Med. 2005;352(2):125–34.

27. Ayas NT, Barger LK, Cade BE, Hashimoto DM, Rosner B, Cronin JW, et al. Extended work duration and the risk of self-reported percutaneous injuries in interns. JAMA. 2006;296(9):1055–62.

28. Ware JC, Risser MR, Manser T, Karlson JKH. Medical resident driving simulator performance following a night on call. Behav Sleep Med. 2006;4(1):1–12.

29. Zahrai A, Chahal J, Stojimirovic D, Schemitsch EH, Yee A, Kraemer W. Quality of life and educational benefit among orthopedic surgery residents: a prospective, multicentre comparison of the night float and the standard call systems. Can J Surg. 2011;54(1):25.

30. Stamp T, Termuhlen P, Miller S, Nolan D, Hutzel P, Gilchrist J, et al. Before and after resident work hour limitations: an objective assessment of the well-being of surgical residents. Curr Surg. 2005;62(1):117–21.

31. Linden DVD, Keijsers GPJ, Eling P, Schaijk RV. Work stress and attentional difficulties: an initial study on burnout and cognitive failures. Work Stress. 2005;19(1):23–36.

32. Hall LH, Johnson J, Watt I, Tsipa A, O'Connor DB. Healthcare staff wellbeing, burnout, and patient safety: a systematic review. PLoS One. 2016;11(7):e0159015.

33. Dyrbye LN, Shanafelt TD, Sinsky CA, Cipriano PF, Bhatt J, Ommaya A, et al. Burnout among health care professionals: a call to explore and address this underrecognized threat to safe, high-quality care. Washington, DC: National Academy of Medicine; 2017.

34. Dyrbye L, Shanafelt T. A narrative review on burnout experienced by medical students and residents. Med Educ. 2016;50(1):132–49.

35. Eckleberry-Hunt J, Lick D, Boura J, Hunt R, Balasubramaniam M, Mulhem E, et al. An exploratory study of resident burnout and wellness. Acad Med. 2009;84(2):269–77.

36. Myers JS, Bellini LM, Morris JB, Graham D, Katz J, Potts JR, et al. Internal medicine and general surgery residents' attitudes about the ACGME duty hours regulations: a multicenter study. Acad Med. 2006;81(12):1052–8.

37. Philibert I, Friedmann P, Williams WT, Hours ftmotAWGoRD. New requirements for resident duty hours. JAMA. 2002;288(9):1112–4.

38. Noro K, Imada A. Participatory ergonomics. London: Taylor & Francis; 1991.

39. Haines H, Wilson JR, Vink P, Koningsveld E. Validating a framework for participatory ergonomics (the PEF). Ergonomics. 2002;45(4):309–27.

40. Xie A, Carayon P, Cox ED, Cartmill R, Li Y, Wetterneck TB, et al. Application of participatory ergonomics to the redesign of the family-centred rounds process. Ergonomics. 2015;58:1726–44.

41. Cox ED, Jacobson GC, Rajamanickam VP, Carayon P, Kelly MM, Wetterneck TB, et al. A family-centered rounds checklist, family engagement, and patient safety: a randomized trial. Pediatrics. 2017;139(5):e1688.

42. Tevis SE, Ravi S, Buel L, Clough B, Goelzer S. Blueprint for a successful resident quality and safety council. J Grad Med Educ. 2016;8(3):328–31.

43. Ulmer C, Wolman DW, Johns ME, editors. Resident duty hours: enhancing sleep, supervision, and safety. Washington, DC: The National Academies Press; 2008.

44. Weiss KB, Bagian JP, Wagner R. CLER pathways to excellence: expectations for an optimal clinical learning environment (executive summary). J Grad Med Educ. 2014;6(3):610–1.

45. Wong BM, Etchells EE, Kuper A, Levinson W, Shojania KG. Teaching quality improvement and patient safety to trainees: a systematic review. Acad Med. 2010;85(9):1425–39.

46. Liao JM, Co JP, Kachalia A. Providing educational content and context for training the next generation of physicians in quality improvement. Acad Med. 2015;90(9):1241–5.

47. Dueker JM, Luty J, Perry DA, Izumi S, Fromme EK, DiVeronica M. A resident-led initiative to increase documentation of surrogate decision makers for hospitalized patients. J Grad Med Educ. 2019;11(3):295–300.

48. Cohen SP, Pelletier JH, Ladd JM, Feeney C, Parente V, Shaikh SK. Success of a resident-led safety council: a model for satisfying CLER pathways to excellence patient Safety goals. J Grad Med Educ. 2019;11(2):226–30.

Part II
Background

Patient Safety in the World

8

Neelam Dhingra-Kumar, Silvio Brusaferro, and Luca Arnoldo

8.1 Introduction

"First, do no harm," the principle of non-maleficence, is the fundamental principle to ensuring safety and quality of care. Patient safety is defined as the prevention of errors and adverse effects associated with healthcare.

The global movement for patient safety was first encouraged in 1999 by the report of the Institute of Medicine (IOM) "To err is human." Although some progress has been made, patient harm is still a daily problem in healthcare systems around the world. While long-standing problems remain unresolved, new, serious threats are emerging. Patients are getting older, have more complex needs and are often affected by multiple chronic diseases; moreover, the new treatments, technologies and care practices, while having enormous potential, also offer new challenges. To guarantee the safety of care in this context, the involvement of all stakeholders, including both healthcare professionals and patients, is needed together with strong commitment from healthcare leadership at every level.

8.2 Epidemiology of Adverse Events

Available evidence suggests hospitalizations in low- and middle-income countries lead annually to 134 million adverse events, contributing to 2.6 million deaths. About 134 million adverse events worldwide give rise to 2.6 million deaths every year. Estimates indicate that in high-income countries, about 1 in 10 patients is harmed while receiving hospital care. Many medical practices and care-associated risks are becoming major challenges for patient safety and contribute significantly to the burden of harm due to unsafe care.

About one patient in ten is harmed while receiving acute care and about 30–50% of these events are preventable. This issue is not only related to hospitals, in fact it is estimated that four patients out of ten are harmed in primary care and outpatient settings and, in these contexts, about 80% of events are preventable. Moreover, this problem affects both high-income and low- and middle-income countries.

N. Dhingra-Kumar
WHO Patient Safety Flagship: A Decade of Patient Safety 2020–2030, Geneva, Switzerland
e-mail: dhingran@who.int

S. Brusaferro
University of Udine, DAME, Udine, Italy

Italian National Institute of Health, Rome, Italy
e-mail: silvio.brusaferro@uniud.it

L. Arnoldo (✉)
University of Udine, DAME, Udine, Italy
e-mail: luca.arnoldo@uniud.it

© The Author(s) 2021
L. Donaldson et al. (eds.), *Textbook of Patient Safety and Clinical Risk Management*,
https://doi.org/10.1007/978-3-030-59403-9_8

The burden of this issue also affects economic resources. The Organisation of Economic Co-operation and Development (OECD) has estimated that adverse events engender 15% of hospital expenditures and activities. For all these reasons, investments in patient safety are necessary to improve patient outcomes and to obtain financial savings which could be reinvested in healthcare. Prevention expenditures are lower than treatment ones and they add important value to the national healthcare systems.

8.3 Most Frequent Adverse Events

Adverse events affect patients in all the various steps of care, in both acute and outpatient settings, and they are transversal globally. Although priorities differ according to the characteristics of each country and its healthcare system, it is essential to support the management of clinical risks to ensure safety of care.

Below are brief descriptions of the main patient safety issues and the burden each represents worldwide, as identified by the World Health Organization.

8.3.1 Medication Errors

A medication error is an unintended failure in the drug treatment procedure which could harm the patient. Medication errors can affect all steps of the medication process and can cause adverse events most often relating to prescribing, dispensing, storage, preparation, and administration. The annual combined cost of these events is one of the highest, an estimated 42 billion USD.

8.3.2 Healthcare-Associated Infections

Healthcare-associated infections are the infections that occur in patients under care, in hospitals or in another healthcare facilities, and that were not present or were incubating at the time

of admission. They can affect patients in any type of care setting and can also first appear after discharge. They also include occupational infections of the healthcare staff. The most common types of healthcare-associated infections are pneumonia, surgical site infections, urinary tract infections, gastro-intestinal infections, and bloodstream infections. In acute care settings, the prevalence of patients having at least one healthcare-associated infection is estimated to be around 7% in high-income countries and 10% in low- and middle-income countries, while prevalence in long-term care facilities in the European Union is about 3%. Intensive care units (ICU) have the highest prevalence of healthcare-associated infections worldwide, ICU-associated risk is 2–3 times higher in low- and middle-income countries than in high-income ones; this difference also concerns the risk for newborns which is 3–20 times higher in low- and middle-income countries.

8.3.3 Unsafe Surgical Procedures

Unsafe surgical procedures cause complications for up to 25% of patients. Each year almost 7 million surgical patients are affected by a complication and about 1 million die. Safety improvements in the past few years have led to a decrease in deaths related to complications from surgery. However, differences still remain between low- and middle-income countries and high-income countries; in fact, the frequency of adverse events is three times higher in low- and middle-income countries.

8.3.4 Unsafe Injections

Unsafe injections can transmit infections such as HIV and hepatitis B and C, endangering both patients and healthcare workers. The global impact is very pronounced, especially in low- and middle-income countries where it is estimated that about 9.2 million disability-adjusted life years (DALYs) were lost in the 2000s.

8.3.5   Diagnostic Errors

A diagnostic error is the failure to identify the nature of an illness in an accurate and timely manner and occurs in about 5% of adult outpatients. About half of these errors can cause severe harm. Most of the relevant data concern high-income countries but diagnostic errors are also a problem for low- and middle-income countries, mainly related to limited access to care and diagnostic testing resources.

8.3.6   Venous Thromboembolism

Venous thromboembolism is one of the most common and preventable causes of patient harm and represents about one third of the complications attributed to hospitalization. This issue has a significant impact both in the high-income countries, where 3.9 million cases are estimated to occur yearly, and in low- and middle-income countries, which see about 6 million cases each year.

8.3.7   Radiation Errors

Radiation errors include cases of overexposure to radiation and cases of wrong-patient and wrong-site identification. Each year, more than 3.6 billion X-ray examinations are performed worldwide, of which 10% are performed on children. Additionally, other types of examinations involving radiation are frequently performed, such as nuclear medicine (37 million each year) and radiotherapy procedures (7.5 million each year). Adverse events occur in about 15 cases per 10,000 treatments.

8.3.8   Unsafe Transfusion

Unsafe transfusion practices expose patients to the risk of adverse transfusion reactions and transmission of infections. Data on adverse transfusion reactions from a group of 21 countries show an average incidence of 8.7 serious reactions per 100 000 distributed blood components.

8.4   Implementation Strategy

Through the years, some progress has been made in raising awareness of practices that support patient safety. For example, in 2009 the European Union issued the "Council recommendation on patient safety, including the prevention and control of healthcare-associated infections (2009/C 151/01)" and in 2012 it launched the "European Union Network for Patient Safety and Quality of Care, PaSQ" a network that aims to improve safety of care through the sharing of information and experience, and the implementation of good practices.

In many countries, support of patient safety practices has developed through the establishment of national plans, networks, and organizations; moreover, some countries, such as the United States, Australia, and Italy, have also enacted national laws on the topic.

In 2019, an important landmark resolution (WHA72.6) 'Global action on patient safety' was adopted by the 194 countries that participated in the 72nd World Health Assembly held in Geneva. Based on the common agreement that this matter is a major global health priority, a whole day was dedicated to its discussion. As a result, the 17th of September 2019 became the first "World Patient Safety Day." Every year, this day will be dedicated to promoting public awareness and engagement, enhancing global understanding, and spurring global solidarity and action. The aim is to engage all the categories of people involved in providing care: patients, healthcare workers, policymakers, academics, and researchers, as well as professional networks and healthcare industries.

8.5   Recommendations and Future Challenges

Some progress has been made in addressing patient safety issues since 1999, but in order to overcome this challenge it is important to implement a system that guarantees daily safety measures in all care settings and that involves all stakeholders, including both healthcare professionals and patients.

First of all, it is important to promote transparency around events that have led to harm and open disclosure with the patient, their family, caregivers, and other support persons. At the same time, it is necessary to encourage public awareness of the measures taken by healthcare organizations for the prevention of adverse events. This need is underlined by the result of a Eurobarometer survey that found that European citizens perceive the risk of being harmed during care to be higher than in reality, both in hospitals and in non-acute settings—in fact more than half of the respondents believed that they could be harmed while receiving care. The model of patient care should switch from a "patient-centered" approach to a "patient-as-partner" approach that establishes direct and active participation in ensuring one's own safety in care: the patient should become a member of the healthcare team.

It is necessary to reaffirm the idea that patient safety is not in the hands of one professional in particular, but in the hands of each healthcare worker. All healthcare organizations have the unavoidable duty to introduce and support the training of all healthcare workers in specific matters of safety.

The probability of making mistakes decreases when the environment is designed with error prevention in mind, incorporating well-structured tasks, processes, and systems. For the continuous improvement, healthcare systems must have immediate access to information that supports learning from experience in order to identify and implement measures that prevent error. Therefore, healthcare systems must dispense with the "blame and shame" culture which prevents acknowledgment of errors and hampers learning and must promote a "safety culture" which allows insight to be gained from past errors. A safety culture can only be established in an open and transparent environment and only if all levels of the organization are involved. In this context, an efficient reporting system should be a cornerstone for healthcare organizations, collecting experiences and data (e.g., of adverse events and near misses) and providing feedback from professionals. In addition, it is essential to guarantee support for professionals involved in adverse events; the "second victims" of an adverse event are healthcare workers who might have been emotionally traumatized. Without adequate support, a second victim experience can harm the emotional and physical health of the involved professional, generate self-doubt regarding their clinical skills and knowledge, reduce job satisfaction to the point of wanting to leave the healthcare profession, and, as a result of all these issues, can affect patient safety.

Another area for improvement is the synergy between patient safety, safety allied programs, health and clinical program and healthcare activities such as accreditation and management of quality of care. Therefore, regardless of the way such functions are structured within countries and healthcare organizations, the branches of patient safety, safety allied programs and quality of care must collaborate to identify common priorities, tools, actions, and indicators to align efforts and enhance outcomes.

The needs brought about by the international movement of people and the differences in safety priorities across the globe have focused the attention on the importance of an international, common strategy for patient safety. To this end, strong commitment is needed from the major international healthcare organizations for the creation of international networks and the sharing of knowledge, programs, tools, good practices, and benchmarking according to standardized indicators. Thus, the global strategy for patient safety must involve three distinct steps. The first step is to secure strong international commitment, including both high-income and low- and middle-income countries, with particular emphasis on those which have not yet been involved, especially in the low- and middle-income group. The second step is to focus on specific patient safety issues that depend on local context and require tailored solutions. The third step is to coordinate between all stakeholders to optimize impacts, avoid the duplication of efforts, and pool programs, strategies, and tools. It is also essential to identify trends and recurring issues and evaluate shared indicators. This strategy should form part of a "glocal" approach adopted by all countries, regions, and healthcare organizations: the selection of specific actions tailored on the particularity of each context, while benefitting from the new level of collaboration, knowledge, and opportunities afforded by globalization.

Bibliography

1. Institute of Medicine (US) Committee on Quality of Health Care in America, Kohn LT, Corrigan JM, Donaldson MS. To err is human: building a safer health system. Washington, DC: National Academy Press (US); 2000.
2. Global priorities for patient safety research. Geneva: World Health Organization; 2009. Available from: http://apps.who.int/iris/bitstream/handle/10665/44205/9789241598620_eng.pdf;jsessionid=86A5928D299B2CC2B9EBAA241F34663D?sequence=1. Accessed 10 Feb 2020.
3. Quality of care: patient safety. Report by the Secretariat (A55/13), Geneva: World Health Organization; 2002. Available from: https://www.who.int/patientsafety/worldalliance/ea5513.pdf?ua=1&ua=1. Accessed 10 Feb 2020.
4. Slawomirski L, Auraaen A, Klazinga N. The economics of patient safety: strengthening a value-based approach to reducing patient harm at national level. Paris: OECD; 2017. Available from: http://www.oecd.org/els/health-systems/The-economics-of-patient-safety-March-2017.pdf. Accessed 14 Feb 2020.
5. Patient safety-global action on patient safety. Report by the Director-General. Geneva: World Health Organization; 2019. Available from: https://apps.who.int/gb/ebwha/pdf_files/WHA72/A72_26-en.pdf. Accessed 13 Feb 2020.
6. Patient safety in developing and transitional countries. New insights from Africa and the Eastern Mediterranean. Geneva: World Health Organization; 2011. Available from: http://www.who.int/patientsafety/research/emro_afro_report.pdf?ua=1. Accessed 12 Feb 2020.
7. Wilson RM, Michel P, Olsen S, Gibberd RW, Vincent C, El-Assady R, et al. Patient safety in developing countries: retrospective estimation of scale and nature of harm to patients in hospital. BMJ. 2012;344:832.
8. Slawomirski L, Auraaen A, Klazinga N. The economics of patient safety in primary and ambulatory care: flying blind. Paris: OECD; 2018. https://doi.org/10.1787/baf425ad-en. Accessed 10 Feb 2020.
9. Atken M, Gorokhovich L. Advancing the responsible use of medicines: applying levers for change. Parsippany, NJ: IMS Institute for Healthcare Informatics; 2012. Available from: http://papers.ssrn.com/sol3/papers.cfm?abstract_id=2222541. Accessed 13 Feb 2020.
10. WHO global patient safety challenge: medication without harm. Geneva: World Health Organization; 2017. Available from: http://apps.who.int/iris/bitstream/10665/255263/1/WHO-HIS-SDS-2017.6-eng.pdf?ua=1&ua=1. Accessed 11 Feb 2020.
11. Report on the burden of endemic health care-associated infection worldwide. Geneva: World Health Organization; 2011. Available from: http://apps.who.int/iris/bitstream/handle/10665/80135/9789241501507_eng.pdf?sequence=1. Accessed 14 Feb 2020.
12. Suetens C, Latour K, Kärki T, Ricchizzi E, Kinross P, Moro ML, et al. Prevalence of healthcare-associated infections, estimated incidence and composite antimicrobial resistance index in acute care hospitals and long-term care facilities: results from two European point prevalence surveys, 2016 to 2017. Euro Surveill. 2018;23(46):1800516.
13. WHO guidelines for safe surgery 2009: safe surgery saves lives. Geneva: World Health Organization; 2009. Available from: http://apps.who.int/iris/bitstream/handle/10665/44185/9789241598552_eng.pdf?sequence=1. Accessed 10 Feb 2020.
14. Bainbridge D, Martin J, Arango M, Cheng D. Perioperative and anaesthetic-related mortality in developed and developing countries: a systematic review and meta-analysis. Lancet. 2012;380(9847):1075–81.
15. Hauri AM, Armstrong GL, Hutin YJ. The global burden of disease attributable to contaminated injections given in healthcare settings. Int J STD AIDS. 2004;15(1):7–16.
16. Singh H, Meyer AN, Thomas EJ. The frequency of diagnostic errors in outpatient care: estimations from three large observational studies involving US adult populations. BMJ Qual Saf. 2014;23(9):727–31.
17. Khoo EM, Lee WK, Sararaks S, Samad AA, Liew SM, Cheong AT, et al. Medical errors in primary care clinics—a cross sectional study. BMC Fam Pract. 2012;26(13):127.
18. National Academies of Sciences, Engineering, and Medicine. Improving diagnosis in health care. Washington, DC: National Academies Press; 2015. Available from: https://www.ncbi.nlm.nih.gov/books/NBK338596/pdf/Bookshelf_NBK338596.pdf. Accessed 10 Feb 2020.
19. Singh H, Graber ML, Onakpoya I, Schiff G, Thompson MJ. The global burden of diagnostic errors in primary care. BMJ Qual Saf. 2017;26(6):484–94.
20. Clinical transfusion process and patient safety: aide-mémoire for national health authorities and hospital management. Geneva: World Health Organization; 2010. Available from: http://www.who.int/bloodsafety/clinical_use/who_eht_10_05_en.pdf?ua=1. Accessed 14 Feb 2020.
21. Janssen MP, Rautmann G. The collection, testing and use of blood and blood components in Europe. Strasbourg: European Directorate for the Quality of Medicines and HealthCare (EDQM) of the Council of Europe; 2014. Available from: https://www.edqm.

eu/sites/default/files/report-blood-and-blood-compo-nents-2014.pdf. Accessed 10 Feb 2020.

22. Boadu M, Rehani MM. Unintended exposure in radio-therapy: identification of prominent causes. Radiother Oncol. 2009;93:609–17.

23. Global initiative on radiation safety in healthcare set-tings. Technical meeting report. Geneva: World Health Organization; 2008. Available from: http://www.who.int/ionizing_radiation/about/GI_TM_Report_2008_Dec.pdf. Accessed 10 Feb 2020.

24. Shafiq J, Barton M, Noble D, Lemer C, Donaldson LJ. An international review of patient safety mea-sures in radiotherapy practice. Radiother Oncol. 2009;92:15–21.

25. Fleischmann C, Scherag A, Adhikari NK, Hartog CS, Tsaganos T, Schlattmann P, et al. Assessment of global incidence and mortality of hospital-treated sepsis. Current estimates and limitations. Am J Respir Crit Care Med. 2016;193(3):259–72.

26. Leape L. Testimony before the President's Advisory Commission on consumer production and quality in the health care industry, 19 Nov 1997.

27. Workplace Health and Safety Queensland. Understanding safety culture. Brisbane: The State of Queensland; 2013. Available from: https://www.work-safe.qld.gov.au/__data/assets/pdf_file/0004/82705/understanding-safety-culture.pdf. Accessed 13 Feb 2020.

28. Yu A, Flott K, Chainani N, Fontana G, Darzi A. Patient safety 2030. London: NIHR Imperial Patient Safety Translational Research Centre; 2016.

29. Special Eurobarometer 411 "Patient safety and quality of care". Available from: https://ec.europa.eu/commfrontoffice/publicopinion/archives/ebs/ebs_411_en.pdf. Accessed 13 Feb 2020.

30. Karazivan P, Dumez V, Flora L, et al. The patient-as-partner approach in health care: a conceptual framework for a necessary transition. Acad Med. 2015;90(4):437–41.

31. Donabedian A. Explorations in quality assess-ment and monitoring, The definition of quality and approaches to its assessment, vol. 1. Ann Arbor, MI: Health Administration Press; 1980.

32. Council Recommendation of 9 June 2009 on patient safety, including the prevention and control of healthcare associated infections. Official Journal of the European Union, C 151, 3 July 2009. Available from: https://eur-lex.europa.eu/legal-content/EN/TXT/?uri=uriserv:OJ.C_.2009.151.01.0001.01.ENG&toc=OJ:C:2009:151:TOC. Accessed 11 Feb 2020.

33. European Union Network for Patient Safety and Quality of Care, PaSQ Joint Action. Available from: http://pasq.eu/Home.aspx. Accessed 11 Feb 2020.

34. Patient safety and quality improvement act of 2005. Available from: https://www.govinfo.gov/content/pkg/PLAW-109publ41/pdf/PLAW-109publ41.pdf. Accessed 14 Feb 2020.

35. National Health Reform Act 2011. Available from: https://www.legislation.gov.au/Details/C2016C01050. Accessed 14 Feb 2020.

36. Legge 8 marzo 2017 n.24. GU Serie Generale n.64 del 17-03-2017. Available from: https://www.gazzettauf-ficiale.it/eli/id/2017/03/17/17G00041/sg. Accessed 14 Feb 2020.

Infection Prevention and Control

9

Anna L. Costa, Gaetano Pierpaolo Privitera,
Giorgio Tulli, and Giulio Toccafondi

9.1   Introduction

A healthcare-associated infection (HAI) is defined as: "An infection occurring in a patient during the process of care in a hospital or other health-care facility which was not present or incubating at the time of admission. This includes infections acquired in the hospital, but appearing after discharge, and also occupational infections among staff of the facility" [1]. The term "healthcare associated" has replaced the former ones used to refer to such infections (i.e., "nosocomial" or "hospital"), as evidence has shown that HAIs can occur as a result of the provision of healthcare in any setting. While the specific risks may differ, the basic principles of infection prevention and control apply regardless of the setting [2].

HAIs are one of the most common adverse events in care delivery and pose a major public health problem impacting morbidity, mortality, and quality of life. At any one time, up to 7% of patients in developed countries and 10% of patients in developing countries will be affected by at least one HAI [3]. These infections also represent a significant economic burden at the societal level, accounting for a considerable proportion of costs; for example, in 2006, the mean excess cost of HAIs in Belgium was close to 6% of public hospital spending, while in the UK it was 2.6% [4]. The estimated cumulative burden in disability-adjusted lost years (DALY) of the six top HAIs is twice the collective burden of 32 other communicable diseases (501 DALYs versus 260 DALYs) [5].

9.2   Main Healthcare-Associated Infection

The main HAIs are generally distributed anatomically as follows: 35% involve the urinary tract, 25% the surgical site, 10% the lungs, 10% the bloodstream. The remaining 10% involve other sites [6].

9.2.1   Urinary Tract Infections (UTIs)

Urinary tract infections are the most common HAIs and most patients with healthcare-

A. L. Costa
Medical Direction, Presidio Ospedaliero del Levante Ligure, ASL5 La Spezia, La Spezia, Italy

G. P. Privitera
Department of Translational Research in Medicine, University of Pisa and Pisa University Hospital, Pisa, Italy

G. Tulli
Tuscan Health Agency, Florence, Italy

G. Toccafondi (✉)
Clinical Risk Management and Patient Safety Center, Tuscany Region, Florence, Italy
e-mail: toccafondig@aou-careggi.toscana.it

© The Author(s) 2021
L. Donaldson et al. (eds.), *Textbook of Patient Safety and Clinical Risk Management*,
https://doi.org/10.1007/978-3-030-59403-9_9

associated UTIs have either undergone genitourinary or urological manipulation (10–20%) or permanent urethral catheterization (around 80%), or both. Infections are usually defined by microbiological criteria: positive quantitative urine culture ($\geq 10^5$ microorganisms/ml, with a maximum of two isolated microbial species). Morbidity and mortality from UTIs are low compared to other HAIs, but they can sometimes lead to bacteremia and death [1]. The high prevalence of urinary catheter use—between 15% and 25% of hospitalized patients may receive short-term indwelling urinary catheters—leads to a large cumulative number of infections and resulting complications and deaths. The source of microorganisms causing UTIs can be endogenous (as in most cases) or exogenous, such as via contaminated equipment or via the hands of healthcare staff. Microbial pathogens can enter the urinary tract of catheterized patient either via migration along the outside of the catheter in the periurethral mucous sheath or via movement along the internal lumen of the catheter from a contaminated collection bag or catheter-drainage tube junction. The most frequently associated pathogens are *Escherichia coli*, *Pseudomonas*, *Enterococcus*, *Klebsiella*, *Enterobacter*, and *Proteus*. Multivariate analyses have underlined that the duration of catheterization is the most important risk factor in the development of catheter-associated bacteriuria. Other risk factors include colonization of the drainage bag, diabetes mellitus, female gender, poor quality of catheter care [7].

Antimicrobial resistance of urinary pathogens is an increasing problem; in Europe, *Escherichia coli* is reported to be resistant to fluoroquinolones in 8–48% of the isolates and to third-generation cephalosporins in 3–82%, and *Klebsiella pneumoniae* is reported to be resistant to third-generation cephalosporins in 2–82% of the isolates and to carbapenems in 0–68% [8].

9.2.2   Bloodstream Infections (BSIs)

Bloodstream infections represent a smaller proportion of HAIs, but the associated case fatality rate is high [1]: 25–30% of patients with healthcare-associated bloodstream infections die, and the attributable mortality is at least 15% [6]. They also influence the length of stay and costs [9]. The incidence is increasing, particularly for certain organisms such as multiresistant coagulase-negative *Staphylococcus*, *Enterobacteriales*, and *Candida* spp.

The Surveillance and Control of Pathogens of Epidemiologic Importance (SCOPE) project surveillance system showed that 70% of all healthcare-associated bloodstream infections are associated with a central venous catheter [6]. Infections may occur at the skin entry site of the intravascular device or in the subcutaneous path of the catheter. Organisms colonizing the catheter within the vessel may produce bacteremia without visible external infection. The cutaneous flora, whether resident or transient, is the source of infection. The main risk factors are length of catheterization, level of asepsis at insertion, and continuing catheter care [1]. The leading causes of healthcare-associated bloodstream infections are coagulase-negative staphylococci, *Staphylococcus aureus*, enterococci, and Candida species. More than 90% of coagulase-negative staphylococci and 60% of *S. aureus* isolates are resistant to methicillin, more than 30% of enterococci to vancomycin, and more than 10% of Candida organisms to first-generation triazoles [6]. Large and sustained reduction (up to 66%) in rates of catheter-related bloodstream infections has been obtained by implementing procedures recommended to reduce BSIs, such as hand washing, using full-barrier precautions during the insertion of central venous catheters, cleaning the skin with chlorhexidine, avoiding the femoral site if possible, and removing unnecessary catheters [10].

9.2.3   Surgical Site Infections

Surgical site infections (SSI) are infections occurring in the incision site or in deep tissues where surgery has been performed, within 30 days of surgery or longer if a prosthetic device has been implanted. SSIs are one of the most frequent healthcare-associated infections, accounting for about 20–25% of all HAIs and about 38% of the HAIs in surgical patients, with an incidence up to 19%, depending on the kind of surgery [11–13]. SSIs may involve the superficial or deep layers of the incision (in two thirds of cases), or the organ or area manipulated or traumatized (in one third of cases) [14]. SSIs can range from wound discharge to a life-threatening condition and they are associated with considerable morbidity. SSIs lead to an increase in the length of hospital stay by 3.3–32.5 days and patients are twice as likely to die, twice as likely to spend time in intensive care, and five times more likely to be re-admitted after discharge. Healthcare costs increase substantially for patients with SSI [15–20].

Factors influencing the potential for infection include endogenous (patient-related) and exogenous (process/procedural-related) variables. Related patient characteristics include extremes of age, poor nutritional status, obesity (i.e., more than 20% above the ideal body weight), coincident remote site infections or colonization, diabetes, and cigarette smoking. Process/procedural-related variables include surgical procedure classification (e.g., "contaminated" or "dirty"), length of surgery, and type of postoperative incision care [14, 21].

An independent risk factor for some postoperative infections is failure in the administration of perioperative antibiotic prophylaxis when indicated. Incorrect timing of surgical prophylaxis is associated with increases by a factor of 2–6 in the rates of surgical site infection for operative procedures in which prophylaxis is generally recommended [11].

Practices to prevent SSIs aim to minimize the number of microorganisms introduced into the operative site or enhance the patient's defenses against infection.

9.2.4 Healthcare-Associated Pneumonia

Healthcare-associated pneumonia occurs in various patient groups. The most important group is that of patients on ventilators in intensive care

units (ICU) [1], where the rate of pneumonia, the main type of infection, is a quality and safety indicator of care [22]. There is a high case fatality rate related to ventilator-associated pneumonia (VAP) although the attributable risk is difficult to determine because of the high patient comorbidity. The microorganisms involved are often endogenous (e.g., from the digestive system or upper respiratory tract), but may be exogenous, often from contaminated respiratory equipment. Known risk factors for infection include type and duration of ventilation, quality of respiratory care, severity of patient's condition (e.g., organ failure), and any previous use of antibiotics [1].

A recent meta-analysis of randomized and non-randomized studies published before June 2017 employed VAP prevention bundles and reported on their effect on mortality; the meta-analysis found that "simple interventions in common clinical practice applied in a coordinated way as a part of a bundle care are effective in reducing mortality in ventilated ICU patients" [23].

9.3 Antimicrobial Resistance

While there has been progress in the struggle against HAIs over time, antimicrobial resistance has become one of the greatest challenges of the twenty-first century and a cause for global concern due to its current and potential impact on global health and the costs to healthcare systems. Recent reports suggest that absolute numbers of infections due to resistant microbes are increasing globally [24].

Multidrug-resistant organisms (MDRO), which are predominantly bacteria, are resistant to multiple classes of antimicrobial agents. Antimicrobial resistance increases the morbidity and mortality associated with infections and increases costs of care because of prolonged hospitalization and other factors such as a need for more expensive drugs. A major cause of antimicrobial resistance is the exposure of a high-density, high-acuity patient population in frequent contact with healthcare workers to extensive antimicrobial use, along with the related risk of cross-infection.

The main MDROs are methicillin-resistant *Staphylococcus aureus* (MRSA), which are responsible for up to a third of healthcare-associated bloodstream infections, vancomycin-resistant enterococci (VREs) with mobile resistance determinants (e.g., VanA and VanB), and a range of Gram-bacteria (MDRGNs) with multiple classes of drug resistance to or resistant mechanisms against critically important antimicrobials. Highly transmissible resistance is a particular feature of Gram-bacteria, especially Enterobacteriaceae; several strains of Gram-bacteria (e.g., *Pseudomonas aeruginosa* and *Acinetobacter baumannii*) have now been identified that exhibit resistance to essentially all commonly used antimicrobials. These organisms are associated with treatment failure and increased morbidity [2].

While bacteria develop resistance to commonly used antibiotics, the number of new antibiotics introduced into the market is small as this class of medicine is not as profitable for pharmaceutical industries as medications for chronic disease. Moreover, the bacteria's capacity to develop resistance makes new antibiotics obsolete early after marketing and consequently causes their development to be even less profitable [25].

With the increase in antimicrobial resistance, progress in modern medicine, which relies on the availability of effective antibacterial drugs, is now at risk, and the expectation is that medicine will be increasingly unable to treat infections currently considered to be routine.

9.4 Healthcare-Associated Infection Prevention

Traditionally, healthcare-associated infections have been considered a "stand-alone" problem and specific professional profiles have been developed as well as legislation and policies aimed at infection prevention and control (ICP).

Core competencies (i.e., competencies that should be a minimum prerequisite for all profes-

sionals in this field) have been defined by the European Centre for Disease Prevention and Control (ECDC) for infection control and hospital hygiene professionals [26] matching the profile of a medical doctor (an ICP practitioner) or a nurse (an ICP nurse) working in Europe. Competencies are grouped into domains which are in turn grouped into four areas: program management, quality improvement, surveillance and investigation of healthcare-associated infections, and infection control activities.

In Italy, central regulation about infection control has for years been based on just two documents issued by the Ministry of Health, one in 1985 (*Fighting against Hospital Infection*) [27] and the other in 1988 (*Fighting against Hospital Infection: the surveillance*) [28]; so, at the local level, policies have varied.

In all the European Region, decisions about infection prevention and control have often been made at the institutional level, with or without national or continental recommendations in mind, with available resources and dominant clinical cultures playing a pivotal role [29].

The large number of international guidelines targeting specific healthcare-associated infections that have been proposed over time by different agencies has resulted in varying applications and outcomes.

In particular, the WHO has provided "WHO Guidelines on Hand Hygiene in Health Care" [30], "Global Guidelines for the Prevention of Surgical Site Infection" [31], and "Guidelines for the prevention and control of carbapenem-resistant Enterobacteriaceae, *Acinetobacter baumannii* and *Pseudomonas aeruginosa* in health care facilities" [32].

In the EU, things changed with the "Council Recommendation of 9 June 2009 on patient safety, including the prevention and control of healthcare associated infections" [33] in which HAIs were covered as a safety problem. The recommendation provides guidance on patient empowerment and promotes a culture of patient safety. In terms of HAI-related actions, it states that member states should use case definitions agreed upon at the EU level to allow consistent reporting; European case definitions for reporting communicable diseases were updated in 2012 [34]. The council recommendation triggered the development of national strategies and reporting and learning systems in many member states. The ECDC network for the surveillance of healthcare-associated infections (HAI-Net) supports member states in establishing or strengthening active surveillance systems. Decisions made at the level of the EU contributed to the improvement of HAI surveillance systems through the adoption of a common, specific case definition for HAI and a framework for national surveillance.

The 2011 Cross-border Patients' Rights Directive [35] highlights the importance of transparency and provides guidelines for setting up national contact points for the diffusion of information about care standards, taking into account advances in medical science and good medical practices.

In fact, HAIs are recognized as part of the safety problems for patients and thus they should be addressed.

The ECRI Institute's "Top 10 Patient Safety Concerns" is a list released in 2019 identifying top-priority safety concerns such as newly identified risks, existing concerns that have changed due to developments in technology or new care delivery models, and persistent issues that need focused attention or present new opportunities for intervention. Unsurprisingly, the list includes three infection-related issues: "Antimicrobial Stewardship in Physician Practices and Aging Services," "Early Recognition of Sepsis across the Continuum," and "Infections from Peripherally Inserted IV Lines" [36].

In 2016, the WHO issued international, evidence-based guidelines regarding the core components of IPC programs [3]. The guidelines were developed by international experts to prevent HAIs and combat antimicrobial resistance, while taking into account the strength of available scientific evidence, the impact on cost and resources, as well as patient values and preferences. The guidelines provide a framework for implementing or developing IPC programs, applicable to any country and adaptable to local context, available resources, and public health needs.

9.4.1 The Prevention and Control of Healthcare-Associated Infection: A Challenge for Clinical Risk Management

Guidelines for tackling HAIs uniformly address the issue with a systemic approach. A systemic approach reframes IPC endeavors as components of a wider and more complex system which manages patient safety and quality of care [37].

Individually reliable components may generate unsafe outcomes when interacting within the system as a whole, even if they are functioning appropriately. A proper surgical intervention or evidence-based antiblastic therapy may be undermined by IPC that is not effective throughout the care continuum.

Consequently, safety is an emergent property of the system, not dependent on the reliability of the individual components but on the management of the interactions between every part of the system, including people, devices, processes, and administrative control [38].

Multiple studies indicate that the most common types of adverse events affecting hospitalized patients are adverse drug events, HAIs, and surgical complications [39].

HAIs are unintended, unwelcome consequences of healthcare that, if serious, can have dreadful effects, and are often similar to other adverse events, in that they can prolong the length of stay, cause harm to the patient, and are preventable to a large extent.

Notwithstanding the fact that HAIs are injuries related to management of care processes rather than complications of disease [40], healthcare workers perceive HAIs differently from adverse events. When not discussed further or brought under a higher level of scrutiny—even if they are reported to the patient and the family—HAIs will be probably presented as complications of care and not as preventable events.

It has been proposed that this difference in approach toward HAIs originates from factors such as the widespread belief that antibiotics can solve infection-related problems, the weakness of evidence supporting HAI-preventing interventions, the sense of responsibility felt by healthcare staff, and the perceived intractability of the problem [25].

With this mindset, HAIs pose a significant challenge to the way in which clinical risk management is deployed in healthcare systems.

The International Classification for Patient Safety taxonomy (ICPS) [41] aids in the detection of failures, contributing factors, and near misses within an incident analysis framework. Learning and reporting systems are based on "lagging" indicators [41] as they refer to the post hoc detection of critical occurrences and aim to enhance incident detection capability and the potential to learn from failures. Consequently, these systems are very unlikely to detect the risks posed to patient safety by HAIs. Since they are designed to be event-focused rather than hazard-based, learning and reporting systems are fed with only events that have already occurred for subsequent identification and analysis. Moreover, the preconditions for HAIs to occur are products of a silent behavior occurring most of the time when the patients are not "on-board" of healthcare processes. While both the active failure (i.e., the point of error) and the latent failure (i.e., the origin of error) are often easy to identify, in the case of an adverse event, the scene changes completely when an HAI is involved. Even with an understanding of bacterial spread, it is most often difficult to identify the source of a particular HAI within a healthcare organization, and so healthcare professionals have the tendency to view the problem as ineluctable. However, HAIs and other types of adverse events often happen due to the recurrence of similar circumstances. Therefore, in order to improve safety, clinicians and managers need to look more carefully at the context, and apply the lessons learnt.

Risk management is about reducing the probability of negative patient outcomes or adverse events by systematically assessing, reviewing, and then seeking ways to prevent, occurrence. Fundamentally, risk management involves clinicians, managers, and healthcare providers in identifying the conditions surrounding practice that put patients at risk of harm and in acting to prevent and control these circumstances to manage and reduce risks [42].

Successful approaches for preventing and reducing HAIs involve applying a risk management framework to manage both the human and systemic factors associated with the transmission of infectious agents. This approach ensures that infectious agents, whether common (e.g., gastrointestinal viruses) or evolving (e.g., influenza or multiresistant organisms), can be managed effectively [2].

Involving patients and their carers is essential for the successful prevention of infection and control in clinical care. Patients need to be sufficiently informed to be able to participate in reducing the risk of transmission of infectious agents.

Although infection prevention specialists (IPs) have long assessed risks related to populations served, services provided, surveillance data, and outbreaks, and lapses in desired practices, new accreditation standards, and rules require that risk assessment and goal-setting should be systematic for an effective approach to infection prevention and control.

Risk assessment and goal-setting need to form a more structured, formal process to enhance a well-designed and thoughtful approach to infection prevention. In the case of HAIs, it may be misleading to place the emphasis solely on the reporting of adverse events and the detection of near misses. In order to fruitfully integrate clinical risk management and IPC, surveillance must be merged with an epidemiological approach within a risk assessment framework.

Risk is defined as the combination of the probability of occurrence of a hazard generating harm in a given scenario and the severity of that harm. Risk is therefore contextual and can only be assessed with respect to a given scenario. Pragmatically, risk is the interaction between a hazard and present vulnerabilities.

Over the years, healthcare organizations and government agencies have developed numerous strategies and guidelines to combat infection. But before organizations can draw up an effective prevention plan, they must consider the existing risks; organizations need a comprehensive and structured approach to assess hazards and vulnerabilities related to HAIs within a healthcare system.

The Joint Commission for Accreditation of Healthcare Organizations (JCAHO) and Joint Commission International (JCI) standards require accredited organizations to perform an assessment to evaluate their infection risks and set goals and objectives based on the results of the assessment [43].

An Infection Prevention and Control (IPC) Risk Assessment (RA) describes the infection risk which is unique to that particular institution. This Infection Control Risk Assessment (ICRA) will help the institution assess the complexity of the identified risk and define actions that can possibly reduce the effects [44]. In a healthcare organization, infection risks can originate from a variety of areas, such as lack of hand hygiene, unsafe injection practices, poor cleaning, disinfection, sterilization of instruments and scopes, and inadequate environmental cleaning. To understand which risks are the most threatening, the current situation needs to be analyzed.

Operationally, the risk scoring will help determine the severity and the prioritization of each hazard and vulnerability identified: a risk can be categorized as high, medium, or low depending on the estimated severity of harm. Risk assessment is an ongoing process as infection risk changes over time and often rapidly. An infection control risk assessment must consider different elements before establishing IPC policies and procedures, goals, and objectives. A comprehensive, hospital-wide risk assessment plan documenting how the healthcare facility is prioritizing patient and healthcare worker safety is essential in any healthcare organization. It is the first step in a systematic process to raise awareness and to create and implement a PCI Plan [44].

The important issues are whether a known or potential risk is likely to occur, its significance should it occur, and whether the organization is adequately prepared to handle it so that the negative effects are eliminated or minimized. The hospital identifies risks for acquiring and transmitting infections through thoughtful examination of what could cause harm to patients, staff, families, and visitors.

Ideally, RA in IPC is best performed by an experienced IPC practitioner, maybe with input from staff in the clinical area concerned. The IPC practitioner may need assistance from clinicians, laboratory staff, or data managers, depending on the location and type of hazard being investigated.

Risk assessment should be performed when:

- a new IPC service is established, in particular standard precautions, transmission-based precautions, infection surveillance, cleaning, laundry and waste management, reprocessing of reusable instruments, and renovation projects
- a new piece of clinical equipment or an instrument is procured
- a new procedure or diagnostic test is implemented
- a problem in IPC practice or policy, or a related issue is identified
- at least annually to re-evaluate the IPC program priorities

Conducting a risk assessment is a crucial task for healthcare organizations. The point of the process is not to identify and compile risks, but to serve as the basis for developing actionable goals and measurable objectives for the infection control program. In other words, assessment should form the foundation of the organization's infection prevention plan.

Once the most menacing risks have been identified in a healthcare facility and understood, goals and measurable objectives can be developed to combat these threats.

The Joint Commission's Infection Prevention and Control standards require organizations to use the risk assessment process to set goals for a comprehensive infection control plan. Specifically, Standard IC.01.04.01 states that "based on the identified risks, [the organization] sets goals to minimize the possibility of transmitting infections" [43]. The standard includes the following elements of performance:

- The organization's written infection prevention and control goals include the following:
  - Addressing prioritized risks.
  - Limiting unprotected exposure to pathogens.
  - Limiting the transmission of infections associated with procedures.
  - Limiting the transmission of infections associated with the use of medical equipment, devices, and supplies.
  - Improving compliance with hand hygiene guidelines.
- A goal is a broad statement indicating the change we want to make. It identifies a main issue and it is not measurable. For example, goals may include:
  - Improving hand hygiene.
  - Implementing disaster preparedness kits.
  - Reducing the risk of surgical site infections.
- A measurable objective specifies quantifiable results in a specific length of time. It defines the who, what, when, where, and how of our strategy.
- Successful risk management in IPC needs the following key elements that will help to produce effective projects:
  - An active IPC committee that assists with risk assessment and implementation of IPC measures.
  - Robust policies and procedures that lay the foundation for good institutional IPC practice.
  - Committed leadership supporting IPC.
  - A safety culture.

9.4.2 Risk Management Tools

Risk management tools are applicable in infection risk assessment including both reactive and proactive methods. The first, based on the information of internal reporting, will analyze the causes of adverse events (AEs) already occurred, as epidemics or serious infections, in order to propose some corrective actions. They include the following.

9.4.2.1 Root Cause Analysis

Root cause analysis (RCA) is a process for identifying the basic or causal factor(s) underlying variation in performance that can produce unexpected and undesirable adverse outcomes. A root cause analysis focuses primarily on systems and processes, not individual performance. The objective of an RCA must not be to assign individual blame; rather, through RCA, a team works together to understand a process and the causes or potential causes of variation that can lead to error, identifying process changes that would make such variation less likely to recur.

A root cause is the most fundamental reason (or one of several fundamental reasons) a failure or underperformance has occurred. In contrast with the usual use of the word, "cause" does not carry an assignment of blame or responsibility in the context of RCA. Here, the focus is on a positive, preventative approach to changes in a system and its processes following a sentinel event, a near-miss sentinel event, or a cluster of less serious yet potentially harmful incidents. Although root cause analysis is associated more frequently with the investigation of a single event, the methodology can also be used to determine the cause of multiple occurrences of low-harm events. When analyzing events as a cluster, RCA can result in the identification of common error causes.

Root cause analysis is designed to answer the following three questions: (1) What happened? (2) Why did it happen? (3) What can be done to prevent it from happening again? [45].

9.4.2.2 Significant Event Audit

A significant event audit (SEA) is a process in which individual episodes, whether beneficial or deleterious, are analyzed in a systematic and detailed way to ascertain what can be learnt about the overall quality of care and to indicate any changes that might lead to future improvements. Put simply, an SEA is a *qualitative* method of clinical audit. In this respect, it differs from traditional audits that tend to deal with larger scale, *quantifiable* patient data sets and involve criteria and standards which can be measured and compared against. However, SEA should still involve a systematic attempt to investigate, review, and learn from a single event that is deemed to be significant by the healthcare team.

The seconds are performed before the occurrence of AEs and aim to reduce their frequency and/or severity. The seconds should be applied above all in risky environments such as in the ICU. The following subsections provide further detail.

9.4.2.3 Process Analysis

A process is defined as a sequence of successive steps in the service of a goal. Each step is a producer of a specific contribution that needs to be identified in terms of issues, content, and quality-security. The analysis can involve either an existing, high-stakes practice that generates actual or potential dysfunctions or a new practice to be verified before it is implemented.

The steps of analysis are:

- describing a process from start to finish: its objectives, successive steps, actors, etc.
- identifying and analyzing the critical points
- proposing improvements to management for the organization, especially in terms of interfaces between services

This analysis is carried out by all the stakeholders involved and can be completed using the method presented in the nest subsection [46].

9.4.2.4 Failure Modes and Effects Analysis

Failure Modes and Effects Analysis (FMEA) is a systematic, proactive method for evaluating a process to identify where and how it might fail and to assess the relative impact of different failures in order to recognize the parts of the process that need change. FMEA includes the following steps: failure modes (i.e., What could go wrong?), failure causes (i.e., Why would the failure happen?), failure effects (i.e., What would be the consequences of each failure?). Teams use FMEA to evaluate processes for possible failures and to prevent such failures by correcting the processes proactively instead of reacting to adverse events after failures have occurred. This emphasis on

prevention may reduce risk of harm to both patients and staff. FMEA is particularly useful in evaluating a new process before its implementation and in assessing the impact of a proposed change to an existing process.

9.4.3   The Best Practices Approach

The United Nations Population Fund's (UNFPA) "Glossary of Monitoring and Evaluation Terms" defines "best practices" as planning or operational practices that have been proven successful in particular circumstances and which are "used to demonstrate what works and what does not and to accumulate and apply knowledge about how and why they work in different situations and contexts."

UNESCO describes best practices as having four common characteristics: being innovative; making a difference; having a sustainable effect; having the potential to be replicated and to serve as a model for generating initiatives elsewhere.

Even if there is not a universally accepted definition, a best practice is a practice that, upon rigorous evaluation, has demonstrated success, has had an impact, and can be replicated. Some best practices in the ICP field are presented in the following subsections.

9.4.3.1 Hand Hygiene

Hand hygiene has long been recognized as the single most effective way to prevent the spread of infections.

The most common cause of HAIs is transient flora acquired and spread by direct contact with patients or with environmental surfaces. If transferred to susceptible sites such as invasive devices (e.g., central venous and urinary catheters) or wounds, these organisms can cause life-threatening infections.

Several studies have demonstrated the effect of hand cleansing on HAIs rates and on the reduction in cross-transmission of antimicrobial-resistant pathogens.

Ease of access to hand washing facilities (e.g., soap and water) and alcohol-based hand rubs can influence the transmission of HAIs.

In 2009, the World Health Organization produced guidelines on hand hygiene in healthcare in which are outlined the "five moments" to perform hand hygiene:

- before touching a patient
- before a clean or aseptic procedure
- after risk of body fluid exposure
- after touching a patient
- after touching a patient's surroundings

Hand hygiene must also be performed before putting on gloves and after their removal.

Evidence suggests that compliance with proper hand hygiene after contact with a patient's surroundings is generally very poor in hospitals, as healthcare workers underestimate the role of environmental surfaces in the transmission of HAIs.

Effective hand hygiene relies on appropriate technique as much as on selection of the correct product. Inappropriate technique may only partially remove or kill microorganisms on hands, despite the superficial appearance of having complied with hand hygiene requirements.

To wash hands correctly, both hands and wrists need to be fully exposed to the product and therefore should be free from jewellery and long-sleeved clothing—in other words, they should be bare below the elbow. Each healthcare facility should develop policies regarding jewellery, artificial fingernails, or nail polish worn by healthcare workers.

Alcohol-based hand rubs are recommended because of their ease of use and availability at the point of care. They are suitable for use except when hands are visibly soiled or potentially contaminated with body fluids, or when caring for patients with vomiting or diarrheal illness. Soap and water should be used in these instances, as well as after contact with patients with *C. difficile* infection or their environment, as alcohol hand rubs are not effective in reducing spore contamination.

When using alcohol gel, hands should be free of dirt and organic material and the solution must come into contact with all the surfaces of the hand; hands should be rubbed vigorously until the solution has evaporated. When washing hands with a liquid soap, the solution should come into contact with all the surfaces of the hands and hands should be rubbed together for a minimum of 10–15 s. Particular attention should be paid to the tips of the fingers, the thumbs, and the areas between the fingers. Hands should be thoroughly rinsed and then dried with a good-quality paper towel [30].

Each year, the "WHO SAVE LIVES: Clean Your Hands" campaign aims to progress the goal of maintaining a global profile on the importance of hand hygiene in healthcare and to bring people together in support of hand hygiene improvement around the world.

9.4.3.2 Antimicrobial Stewardship

Antibiotics, like all medication, may have side effects, including adverse drug reactions and *Clostridioides difficile* infection (CDI). Nevertheless, the misuse of antibiotics has also contributed to the growing problem of antibiotic resistance. Unlike other medications, the potential for the spread of resistant organisms means that the misuse of antibiotics can adversely influence the health of patients who are not even exposed to them.

The relationship between the unrestrained use of antimicrobials in all human health settings as well as agriculture and animal husbandry and the emergence of bacterial resistance is well documented [47].

Infection prevention and control practices are recognized as a key part of an effective response to antimicrobial resistance, as they reduce the need for antimicrobials and the opportunity for organisms to develop resistance. Vaccination can also reduce antimicrobial resistance by preventing infectious diseases, even primary viral infections, often inappropriately treated with antibiotics [2].

Programs dedicated to improving antibiotic use, commonly referred to as "Antibiotic Stewardship Programs" (ASP), can both optimize the treatment of infections and reduce adverse events associated with antibiotic use, thus improving not only the quality of patient care but also patient safety by increasing the frequency of correct prescriptions for both therapy and prophylaxis.

Successful antimicrobial stewardship programs have been associated with reduced facility resistance rates as well as reduced morbidity, mortality, and costs.

Antibiotic stewardship consists of the implementation of policies that support optimal antibiotic use through interventions which are tailored and prioritized depending on the needs of the hospital, the organizational context, and factors such as size of the facility, staffing, and resources.

A systemic integration of antimicrobial, infection prevention, and diagnostic stewardship (AID) has been proposed in order to reduce the need for antimicrobials and the opportunity for organisms to develop resistance [48]. It is necessary for cross-disciplinary borders and approach infection management in an integrated, multidisciplinary manner. Microbiology laboratories and clinical microbiologists can provide significant contributions to ASPs, including the dissemination of antimicrobial susceptibility reports and enhanced culture by means of fast microbiology [49] and diagnostic stewardship [50]. Participating in ASPs is mainly seen as a task for clinical microbiologists and/or infectious disease specialists, together with (hospital) pharmacists. However, such an endeavor deeply involves bedside doctors and nurses, boards of directors, and diagnostic laboratories since patients commonly transition between different healthcare settings. Antimicrobial stewardship programs require multidisciplinary efforts which depend also on the support of the hospital's administration, the allocation of adequate resources, and the cooperation and engagement of prescribers.

Only a comprehensive healthcare network using an integrated approach may contain the spread of antimicrobial resistance. From this perspective, infection management is thus a responsibility for all stakeholders involved in such a network.

It is vital that infection control and prevention measures are integrated into a unified AID program to improve overall infection management. Without the proper infection prevention mea-

sures, other interventions such as ASPs and Diagnostic Stewardship Programs (DSP) will not achieve the optimal effect.

Stewardship interventions can be listed in three categories: broad, pharmacy-driven, and infection and syndrome specific. Broad interventions include:

- Antibiotic timeouts accompanied by a reassessment of the continuing need for and choice of antibiotics when more information is available.
- Prior authorization, restricting the use of certain antibiotics bound to preventative evaluation performed by an antibiotic expert.
- Prospective auditing and feedback, with reviews of antibiotic therapy by an expert in antibiotic use not involved in the treatment (e.g., a day-2 bundle with face-to-face case audits performed by the antimicrobial stewardship team) [51].

Pharmacy-driven interventions include:

- Automatic changes from intravenous to oral antibiotic therapy in appropriate situations.
- Dose adjustments in cases of organ dysfunction (e.g., renal adjustment).
- Dose optimization including dose adjustments based on therapeutic drug monitoring.
- Automatic alerts in situations where therapy might be unnecessarily duplicative.
- Time-sensitive automatic stop orders for specified antibiotic prescriptions.
- Detection and prevention of antibiotic-related drug interactions.

Infection and syndrome-specific interventions are intended to improve prescribing for specific syndromes and situations such as community-acquired pneumonia and urinary tract infections, skin and soft tissue infections, empiric coverage of methicillin-resistant *Staphylococcus aureus* (MRSA) infections, *Clostridioides difficile* infections, and treatment of culture proven invasive infections; however, prompt and effective treatment for severe infection or sepsis should be provided in any case [52].

Antimicrobial stewardship programs need to be monitored both at the process level (i.e., Are policies being followed as expected?) and at the outcome level (i.e., Have antibiotic use and patient outcomes improved?) [2, 52].

9.4.3.3 Care Bundles

"Care bundling" is an approach developed by the United States Institute of Healthcare Improvement [53] to help healthcare workers consistently deliver the safest possible care for patients undergoing treatments known to increase patients' risk of healthcare-associated infections. A bundle is a set of evidence-based practices (generally three to five) that improve patient outcomes when performed collectively and reliably.

The elements of a bundle are well-established practices, combined into a structured protocol that is agreed upon and is the responsibility of the whole clinical team. Characteristics of a bundle include the following:

- All elements are necessary and make up a cohesive unit of steps that must be completed in their entirety to succeed; while getting some of them right may be an improvement, it is not as good as getting them all right. The more reliably all the bundle elements are delivered, the better the outcomes [54].
- Each element is based on randomized and controlled trial evidence.
- The bundle involves an all-or-nothing measure which makes implementation clear-cut.

Existing care bundles can be used as tools and developed further by each facility to meet its needs.

Two examples of bundles are described below.

CAUTI Maintenance Bundle

One example of a bundle procedure for the maintenance of urinary catheters includes the following steps:

- Perform a daily review of the need for the urinary catheter.
- Check the catheter has been continuously connected to the drainage system.

- Ensure patients are aware of their role in preventing urinary tract infection, or if the patient is unable to be made aware, perform routine daily meatal hygiene.
- Empty urinary drainage bags frequently enough to maintain urine flow and prevent reflux, using a separate urine collection container for each patient and avoiding contact between drainage bags and the container.
- Perform hand hygiene and put on gloves and apron before each catheter care procedure; on procedure completion, remove gloves and apron and perform hand hygiene again.

Ventilator Bundle

Ventilated patients are at high risk for several serious complications: ventilator-associated pneumonia (VAP), venous thromboembolism (VTE), and stress-induced gastrointestinal bleeding. Five elements of care have been identified for the prevention of these events in ventilated patients and are supported by solid level-one trials:

- elevation of the head of the bed (HOB) to between 30° and 45°
- daily sedative interruption and daily assessment of readiness to extubate
- peptic ulcer disease (PUD) prophylaxis
- deep venous thrombosis (DVT) prophylaxis (unless contraindicated)
- daily oral care with chlorhexidine [55]

9.5 Engaging Patients and Families in Infection Prevention

Engaging patients and families in improving healthcare safety means creating effective partnerships between those who provide care and those who receive it—at every level, including individual clinical encounters, safety committees, executive suites, boardrooms, research teams, and national policy-setting bodies. An effective partnership can generate benefits, both in the form of improved health and outcomes for patients and in safer and more productive work environments for healthcare professionals [56].

In healthcare facilities, patients and visitors should be informed about what they can do to prevent the spread of infection and keep themselves infection-free.

Healthcare workers should, where possible:

- explain the processes of infection prevention and control to patients and their caregivers
- engage patients and their caregivers in the decision-making process regarding their care and how it is delivered
- be sure that patients and their caregivers are aware that they can ask questions to healthcare professionals

Written material such as brochures and posters can be used to reinforce verbal discussions with patients as part of their care.

Engagement in hand hygiene can be encouraged by sharing hand hygiene videos with patients and families, asking them to demonstrate proper technique, providing family members and visitors access to hand washing stations and hand hygiene supplies, and asking patients to speak up if they observe staff not following safe practices.

With regard to personal protective equipment (PPE), patients and family members can be provided information at admission about why PPE is being used along with a demonstration of how to don and doff it. It is useful to explain what the hospital is doing to prevent the spread of infections, answering questions with clear and straightforward explanations.

Engagement in antibiotic stewardship involves educating patients on the risks related to the inappropriate use of antibiotics and on what the hospital is doing to monitor the use of antibiotics and to implement good stewardship practices. Patient advocates should be part of the antibiotic stewardship team and data on efforts to reduce inappropriate antibiotic use should be shared, soliciting patient feedback on how best to be included in the efforts [57].

9.6 Identification and Rapid Management of Sepsis: A Test Bed for the Integration of Risk Management and IPC

9.6.1 Sepsis and Septic Shock Today

Sepsis was recently defined as a life-threatening organ dysfunction caused by dysregulated host response to infection [58]. If not recognized early and managed promptly, it can lead to septic shock, multiple organ failure, and death. Any type of infectious pathogen can potentially cause sepsis. Sepsis and septic shock are time-critical, evolving syndromes. The guidelines of the 2017 Surviving Sepsis Campaign [59] identify the crucial components of treatment: resuscitation with fluids, administration of antibiotics, administration of vasopressors, and surgical control of the infectious source.

In the case of suspicion of sepsis and septic shock, it is necessary to act immediately by carrying out the actions of the "sepsis six" [60] bundle complemented by the surgical source control of infection.

For patients with suspected sepsis, the goal is to start antibiotic therapy immediately but with the commitment of all operators to reduce the therapy's duration while maintaining all safety margins and the greatest possible benefits. In 2018, the American society of Infectious Diseases took a critical position with respect to the 2017 Surviving Sepsis Campaign guidelines because they appeared to be excessively inclined to propose standardized indications on the administration of antibiotic therapy, including the clinical management of patients in whom the diagnosis of infection is uncertain. Patients with uncertain diagnosis of infection need to be placed on a clinical path that allows the acquisition of more information by means of appropriate diagnostics and the consequent re-evaluation of their level of risk, as they would not benefit from a standardized and prolonged antibiotic therapy. The benefits of treating patients who are infected need to be weighed against the dangers of treating patients who are not but at first appear to be. Antimicrobial resistance is a major factor in determining clinical unresponsiveness to treatment and a rapid evolution to sepsis and septic shock. Sepsis patients with resistant pathogens have been found to have a higher risk of hospital mortality.

Septic shock is defined as a sub-type of severe sepsis with lactate greater than or equal to 4 mmol/L or hypotension (i.e., mean arterial pressure (MAP) <65 mm Hg and systolic blood pressure <90 mm Hg) not responsive to fluid bolus [61].

Sepsis is a severe complication of an infection. Anyone affected by an infection can progress to sepsis conditions but some vulnerable populations are at a higher risk, including elderly people, pregnant women, neonates, hospitalized patients, and people with HIV/AIDS, liver cirrhosis, cancer, kidney disease, autoimmune diseases, or no spleen [62].

By this new definition, sepsis is a medical emergency. However, as an evolving, syndromic condition with multiple causative organisms, sepsis can present in patients various signs and symptoms at different times. Warning signs and symptoms include fever or low temperature and shivering, altered mental status, difficulty breathing or rapid breathing, increased heart rate, weak pulse or low blood pressure, low urine output, cyanotic or mottled skin, cold extremities, and extreme body pain or discomfort.

Suspecting sepsis is a first major step toward early recognition and diagnosis [63–65].

There are two main steps to prevent sepsis:

1. prevention of microbial transmission and infection
2. prevention of the development of an infection into sepsis conditions

In both community and healthcare facilities, the prevention of the development of sepsis requires appropriate antibiotic treatment of infections, including reassessment for optimization, seeking medical care promptly, and early detection of sepsis signs and symptoms. Scientific evidence has clearly demonstrated the effectiveness of infection prevention. For instance, improved hand hygiene practice in healthcare can reduce infection by as much as 50% [66].

Identifying and not underestimating signs and symptoms along with detecting biomarkers such as procalcitonin are crucial elements for the early diagnosis of sepsis and the timely establishment of appropriate clinical management. After early recognition, diagnostics that help identify the causal pathogen of infection leading to sepsis are also important to guide targeted antimicrobial treatment. Antimicrobial resistance (AMR) can jeopardize clinical management of sepsis because empirical antibiotic treatment is often required. Therefore, it is important to understand the epidemiology of AMR in the local setting. Once the source of infection is determined, source control such as drainage of an abscess is also critical. Early fluid resuscitation to improve volume status is important in the initial phase of sepsis management. In addition, vasopressors may be required to improve and maintain tissue perfusion. The appropriate management of sepsis over time should be guided by repeated exams and diagnostics, including vital signs monitoring.

9.6.2 Sepsis as an Adverse Event: Failures in Identification and Management

In a recent paper, Rhee et al. [67] reported the findings of a retrospective review of hospital deaths and discharges to hospice in three large academic medical centers and three affiliated community hospitals.

Detailed medical record reviews were performed on 568 in-hospital deaths and discharges to hospice to determine if sepsis was present during the hospitalization and if it was a cause of death. For patients who died with or due to sepsis, investigators identified potential signs of suboptimal sepsis care, including delays in initiating antibiotic therapy or source control, and inadequate fluid resuscitation, and made an overall assessment of the preventability of sepsis-associated death. 264 of the 300 deaths from sepsis (88.0%; 95%CI, 83.8–91.5%) were considered unpreventable (4–6 rating on the Likert scale) and only 36 deaths (12.0%; 95%CI, 8.6–16.2%) were considered potentially preventable, of which 11 (3.7%) were definitely or moderately likely preventable and 25 (8.3%) were possibly preventable. There were no identifiable suboptimal aspects of care in 232 sepsis-associated deaths (77.3%). Of the 68 cases with suboptimal care (22.7%), the most common problems were:

1. delays in antibiotics, in 33 cases (48.5%)
2. delays in source control, in 19 cases (27.9%)
3. inappropriate empirical antibiotic therapy, in 16 cases (23.5%)

Of these 68 cases, 32 deaths (47.1%) were judged to be definitely, moderately likely, or possibly preventable. Generally, the non-preventable, sepsis-associated deaths occurred in patients with major underlying comorbidities, severe, acute, concurrent illnesses, and/or florid sepsis that progressed despite optimal care. A total of 42 major errors were identified in the 36 sepsis-associated deaths that were potentially preventable. Most of the errors were related to:

1. delays in recognition and treatment of sepsis ($n = 16$)
2. inappropriate antibiotic therapy administered after recognition of sepsis ($n = 10$)
3. delays in source control ($n = 7$)

Two patients had potentially preventable hospital-acquired infections, while three had procedural complications (i.e., bleeding and ischemia) and three had medication-related adverse events (i.e., bleeding from excessive oral anticoagulation) that triggered a cascade of events leading to sepsis and death. One patient was inadequately monitored in a hospital ward after admission and there was delayed recognition of an unstable arrhythmia. Of the 36 potentially preventable deaths, only 1 patient met criteria for hospice on admission (i.e., due to end-stage liver disease). This patient's death was still considered possibly preventable as he did not receive Gram-negative antibiotic coverage for pneumonia

caused by *Escherichia coli*. The authors concluded that only a minority of sepsis-associated deaths in this cohort were preventable through better hospital-based care. Conclusions about the prevention of sepsis-associated deaths through better hospital-based care must be contextualized based on the care that is delivered. This study cohort was assembled from patients of three highly regarded academic medical centers and three affiliated community hospitals. The rate of suboptimal sepsis care reported in this cohort—just under 23%—is substantially lower than in other studies. For comparison, in a recent publication from New York State's sepsis improvement efforts, adherence to a 3-h sepsis bundle increased from 53.4% to 64.7% in 183 acute care hospitals during the 27-month study period [68]. An international point prevalence study found only a 19% completion rate of all elements of a 3-h sepsis bundle [69]. The lower rate of suboptimal care reported by Rhee and colleagues suggests that sepsis care in the hospitals included in this study may have been substantially better than that in many other hospitals, with correspondingly less room for improvement and fewer sepsis-associated deaths deemed to be preventable through better hospital care; in hospitals with more deficiencies in sepsis care, more deaths from sepsis may be preventable. Despite the challenge of identifying which sepsis-associated deaths may be potentially preventable, Rhee's study does reflect the reality that some sepsis-associated deaths are not preventable with the tools currently available for the recognition and management of sepsis. This finding should serve as a call to action to advance the sepsis research agenda [70]. Early recognition and prompt management of sepsis have been associated in numerous studies with improved patient outcomes, and current clinical practice guidelines emphasize this concept [59].

9.7 Conclusions

Successful approaches for preventing and reducing HAIs involve implementing a risk management framework to manage both human and systemic factors associated with the transmission of infectious agents.

Infection prevention in healthcare facilities mainly relies on properly functioning infection prevention and control programs and teams, effective hygiene practices and precautions, including hand hygiene, along with clean, well-functioning environments and equipment.

The implementation of best practices and the replication of improvement actions deserve a context-focused approach that targets the specific risks and hazards appearing in given scenarios. In the future, infection prevention needs to become adaptive by embodying an array of techniques and methods to assess risks and design targeted solutions that rely on the fostering of multidisciplinary healthcare teams.

References

1. World Health Organization Department of Communicable Disease, Surveillance and Response. Prevention of hospital-acquired infections: a practical guide. 2nd ed. WHO/CDS/CSR/EPH/2002.12.
2. Australian Guidelines for the Prevention and Control of Infection in Healthcare. Guidelines on core components of infection prevention. Canberra: National Health and Medical Research Council; 2019.
3. Guidelines on core components of infection prevention and control (IPC) programmes at the national and acute health care facility level. Geneva: World Health Organization; 2016.
4. Slawomirski L, Auraaen A, Klazinga N. The economics of patient safety. Strengthening a value-based approach to reducing patient harm at national level. Paris: OECD; 2017.
5. Cassini A, Plachouras D, Eckmanns T, Abu Sin M, Blank HP, Ducomble T, Haller S, Harder T, Klingeberg A, Sixtensson M, Velasco E, Weiß B, Kramarz P, Monnet DL, Kretzschmar ME, Suetens C. Burden of six healthcare-associated infections on European population health: estimating incidence-based disability-adjusted life years through a population prevalence-based modelling study. PLoS Med. 2016;13(10):e1002150.
6. Wenzel RP. Health care-associated infections: major issues in the early years of the 21st century. Clin Infect Dis. 2007;15(45 Suppl 1):S85–8.
7. Iacovelli V, Gaziev G, Topazio L, Bove P, Vespasiani G, Finazzi AE. Nosocomial urinary tract infections: a review. Urologia. 2014;81(4):222–7.
8. Antimicrobial resistance global report on surveillance. Geneva: World Health Organization; 2014.
9. Kaye KS, Marchaim D, Chen TY, Baures T, Anderson DJ, Choi D, Sloane R, Schmader KE. The impact of nosocomial bloodstream infections on mortality, length of stay and hospital costs in older adults. J Am Geriatr Soc. 2014;62(2):306–11.
10. Pronovost P, Needham D, Berenholtz S, Sinopoli D, Chu H, Cosgrove S, Sexton B, Hyzy R, Welsh R, Roth G, Bander J, Kepros J, Goeschel C. An intervention to decrease catheter-related bloodstream infections in the ICU. N Engl J Med. 2006;355(26):2725–32.
11. Burke JP. Infection control— a problem for patient safety. N Engl J Med. 2003;348(7):651–6.
12. Horan TC, Culver DH, Gaynes RP, Jarvis WR, Edwards JR, Reid CR. Nosocomial infections in surgical patients in the United States, January 1986–June 1992. National Nosocomial Infections Surveillance (NNIS) system. Infect Control Hosp Epidemiol. 1993;14(2):73–80.
13. Petrosillo N, Drapeau CM, Nicastri E, Martini L, Ippolito G, Moro ML, ANIPIO. Surgical site infections in Italian Hospitals: a prospective multicenter study. BMC Infect Dis. 2008;8:34.
14. Mangram AJ, Horan TC, Pearson ML, Silver LC, Jarvis WR. Guideline for prevention of surgical site infection, 1999. The Hospital Infection Control Practices Advisory Committee. Infect Control Hosp Epidemiol. 1999;20(4):250–78.
15. De Lissovoy G, Fraeman K, Hutchins V, Murphy D, Song D, Vaughn BB. Surgical site infection: incidence and impact on hospital utilization and treatment costs. Am J Infect Control. 2009;37(5):387–97.
16. Monge Jodra V, Sainz de Los Terreros Soler L, Diaz-Agero Perez C, Saa Requejo CM, Plana Farras N. Excess length of stay attributable to surgical site infection following hip replacement: a nested case-control study. Infect Control Hosp Epidemiol. 2006;27(12):1299–303.
17. Kirkland KB, Briggs JP, Trivette SL, Wilkinson WE, Sexton DJ. The impact of surgical—site infections in the 1990s: attributable mortality, excess length of hospitalization, and extra costs. Infect Control Hosp Epidemiol. 1999;20(11):725–30.
18. Jenney AW, Harrington GA, Russo PL, Spelman DW. Cost of surgical site infections following coronary artery bypass surgery. ANZ J Surg. 2001;71(11):662–4.
19. Whitehouse JD, Friedman ND, Kirkland KB, Richardson WJ, Sexton DJ. The impact of surgical-site infections following orthopedic surgery at a community hospital and a university hospital: adverse quality of life, excess length of stay, and extra cost. Infect Control Hosp Epidemiol. 2002;23(4):183–9.
20. Coello R, Charlett A, Wilson J, Ward V, Pearson A, Borriello P. Adverse impact of surgical site infections in English hospitals. J Hosp Infect. 2005;60(2):93–103.
21. Lee KY, Coleman K, Paech D, Norris S, Tan JT. The epidemiology and cost of surgical site infections in Korea: a systematic review. J Korean Surg Soc. 2011;81(5):295–307.

22. Álvarez-Lerma F, Sánchez García M, Task Force of Experts for Project "Zero VAP" in Spain. The multimodal approach for ventilator-associated pneumonia prevention-requirements for nationwide implementation. Ann Transl Med. 2018;6(21):420.

23. Pileggi C, Mascaro V, Bianco A, Nobile CGA, Pavia M. Ventilator bundle and its effects on mortality among ICU patients: a meta-analysis. Crit Care Med. 2018;46(7):1167–74.

24. Tacconelli E, Pezzani MD. Public health burden of antimicrobial resistance in Europe. Lancet Infect Dis. 2019;19(1):4–6.

25. Gardam MA, Lemieux C, Reason P, Van Dijk M, Goel V. Healthcare associated infection as patient safety indicators. Healthcare Papers, vol. 9(3).

26. European Centre for Disease Prevention and Control. Core competencies for infection control and hospital hygiene professionals in the European Union. Stockholm: ECDC; 2013.

27. Circolare Ministero Sanità N. 52/1985. Lotta Contro le Infezioni Ospedaliere.

28. Circolare Ministero della Sanità N. 8/1988. Lotta Contro le Infezioni Ospedaliere: la Sorveglianza.

29. Marschang S, Bernardo G. Prevention and control of healthcare-associated infection in Europe: a review of patients' perspectives and existing differences. J Hosp Infect. 2015;89(4):357–62.

30. WHO guidelines on hand hygiene in health care. First global patient safety challenge clean care is safer care. Geneva: World Health Organization; 2009.

31. Global guidelines for the prevention of surgical site infection. Geneva: World Health Organization; 2016.

32. Guidelines for the prevention and control of carbapenem-resistant Enterobacteriaceae, *Acinetobacter baumannii* and *Pseudomonas aeruginosa* in health care facilities. Geneva: World Health Organization; 2017.

33. European Council's "Recommendation of 9 June 2009 on patient safety, including prevention and control of healthcare-associated infection".

34. Commission Implementing Decision 2012/506/EU amending decision 2002/253/EC laying down case definitions for reporting communicable diseases to the community network under decision no. 2119/98/EC of the European Parliament and of the Council.

35. Directive 2011/24/EU of the European Parliament and of the Council of 9 March 2011 on the application of patients' rights in cross-border healthcare.

36. 2019 Top 10 patient safety concerns. Executive Brief. Plymouth Meeting, PA: ECRI Institute; 2019.

37. Storr J, Wigglesworth N, Kilpatrick C. Integrating human factors with infection prevention and control. London Health Found. Thought paper May 2013.

38. Leveson N. A systems approach to risk management through leading safety indicators. Reliab Eng Syst Saf. 2015;136:17–34.

39. Vincent C. The essentials of patient safety. Chichester: BMJ Books; 2011.

40. World Health Organization. WHO draft guidelines for adverse event reporting and learning systems. Geneva: World Health Organization; 2005. p. 78.

41. Vincent C, Carthey J, Macrae C, Amalberti R. Safety analysis over time: seven major changes to adverse event investigation. Implement Sci. 2017;12(1):151.

42. Managing the risk of healthcare associated infection in NHSScotland. Report of a Joint Scottish Executive Health Department and NHSScotland Working Group. 2001.

43. Using the risk assessment to set goals and develop the infection prevention and control plan. In: Risk assessment for infection prevention and control. Oakbrook Terrace, IL: The Joint Commission; 2010.

44. Nazeer ZB. J Infect Dis Ther. 2017;5(7): (Suppl). https://doi.org/10.4172/2332-0877-C1-035.

45. Root cause analysis in health care: tools and techniques. Oakbrook Terrace, IL: The Joint Commission; 2015.

46. La gestion du risqué infecteux dans un établissement de santé. Conception CClin Ouest—juin 2014.

47. Wielinga PR, Schlundt J. Food safety: at the center of a one health approach for combating zoonoses. In: Mackenzie JS, Jeggo M, Daszak P, Richt JA, editors. One health: the human-animal-environment interfaces in emerging infectious diseases: food safety and security, and international and national plans for implementation of one health activities. Berlin: Springer; 2013. p. 3–17.

48. Dik JWH, Poelman R, Friedrich AW, Panday PN, Lo-Ten-Foe JR, Van Assen S, et al. An integrated stewardship model: antimicrobial, infection prevention and diagnostic (AID). Future Microbiol. 2016;11(1):93–102.

49. Mangioni D, Viaggi B, Giani T, Arena F, Arienzo SD, Forni S, Tulli G, Rossolini GM. Diagnostic stewardship for sepsis: the need for risk stratification to triage patients for fast microbiology workflows. Future Microbiol. 2019;14:169–74.

50. Messacar K, Parker SK, Todd JK, Dominguez SR. Implementation of rapid molecular infectious disease diagnostics: the role of diagnostic and antimicrobial stewardship. J Clin Microbiol. 2017;55(3):715–23.

51. Dik JWH, Hendrix R, Friedrich AW, Luttjeboer J, Panday PN, Wilting KR, et al. Cost-minimization model of a multidisciplinary antibiotic stewardship team based on a successful implementation on a urology ward of an academic hospital. PLoS One. 2015;10(5):1–12.

52. CDC. Core elements of Hospital Antibiotic Stewardship Programs. Atlanta, GA: US Department of Health and Human Services, CDC; 2014. Available at http://www.cdc.gov.

53. Resar R, Griffin FA, Haraden C, Nolan TW. Using care bundles to improve health care quality. IHI Innovation Series white paper. Cambridge, MA: Institute for Healthcare Improvement; 2012. http://www.ihi.org/resources/Pages/IHIWhitePapers/UsingCareBundles.aspx. Accessed 27 Oct 2019.

54. Understanding bundles: an IHI faculty conversation. http://www.ihi.org/resources/Pages/ImprovementStories/UnderstandingBundlesIHIFacultyConversation.aspx. Accessed 27 Oct 2019.

55. How-to guide: prevent ventilator-associated pneumonia. Cambridge, MA: Institute for Healthcare Improvement; 2012. http://www.ihi.org/resources/Pages/Tools/HowtoGuidePreventVAP.aspx. Accessed 27 Oct 2019.

56. Safety is personal. Partnering with patients and families for the safest care. Report of the roundtable on consumer engagement in patient safety. Boston, MA: National Patient Safety Foundation; 2014.

57. Engaging patients and families in infection prevention. https://www.cdc.gov/infectioncontrol/pdf/strive/PFE101-508.pdf.

58. Singer M, Deutschman CS, Seymour CW, et al. The third international consensus definitions for sepsis and septic shock (sepsis-3). JAMA. 2016;315(8):801–10.

59. Rhodes A, et al. Surviving sepsis campaign international guidelines for management of sepsis and septic shock: 2016. Crit Care Med. 2017;45(3):486–552.

60. Daniels R, Nutbeam T, McNamara G, Galvin C. The sepsis six and the severe sepsis resuscitation bundle: a prospective observational cohort study. Emerg Med J. 2011;28(6):507–12.

61. Rhodes A, et al. Surviving sepsis campaign: international guidelines for management of sepsis and septic shock: 2016. Intensive Care Med. 2017;43:304–77.

62. Gotts JE, Matthay MA. Sepsis: pathophysiology and clinical management. BMJ. 2016;353:i1585.

63. United States Centers for Disease Control and Prevention. Healthcare professional (HCP) resources: sepsis. 2018-02-01T06:23:15Z. https://www.cdc.gov/sepsis/get-ahead-of-sepsis/hcp-resources.html.

64. Global Sepsis Alliance. Toolkits. https://www.worldsepsisday.org/toolkits/.

65. UK Sepsis Trust. Education. 2018. https://sepsistrust.org/education/.

66. Luangasanatip N, Hongsuwan M, Limmathurotsakul D, et al. Comparative efficacy of interventions to promote hand hygiene in hospital: systematic review and network meta-analysis. Br Med J. 2015;351:h3728.

67. Rhee C, et al. Prevalence, underlying causes and preventability of sepsis associated mortality in US acute care hospital. JAMA Network Open. 2019;2(2):e-187571.

68. Levy MM, Gesten FC, Phillips GS, et al. Mortality changes associated with mandated public reporting for sepsis: the results of the New York state initiative. Am J Respir Crit Care Med. 2018;198(11):1406–12.

69. Rhodes A, Phillips G, Beale R, et al. The surviving sepsis campaign bundles and outcome: results from the International Multicentre Prevalence Study on Sepsis (the IMPreSS study). Intensive Care Med. 2015;41(9):1620–8.

70. Coopersmith CM, De Backer D, Deutschman CS, et al. Surviving sepsis campaign: research priorities for sepsis and septic shock. Crit Care Med. 2018;46(8):1334–56.

The Patient Journey

Elena Beleffi, Paola Mosconi, and Susan Sheridan

10.1 Introduction

Almost 20 years after publication "To Err is Human: Building a Better Health System" (Kohn et al. 1999), patient safety is still not widely implemented. This report from the Institute of Medicine is the milestone that constituted a turning point for improving quality of care and patient safety identifying the need to rethink healthcare delivery to provide safe, effective, and efficient care.

The barriers of implementing patient safety as a driving force for change towards more effective healthcare include multiple factors: insufficient involvement of all stakeholders contributing to the care process, lack of willingness of organizations and individuals to learn from errors and scarce investments in patient safety improvement and research.

There is a growing need to promote systems approaches to finding solutions in healthcare to improve the safety of care, the quality of healthcare delivery, patients' health and citizens' well-being.

The discussion paper "Bringing a Systems Approach to Health" defines the systems approach as one "that applies scientific insights to understand the elements that influence health outcomes; models the relationships between those elements; and alters design, processes, or policies based on the resultant knowledge in order to produce better health at lower cost" [1].

A multidisciplinary approach must include the involvement of citizens and patients as fundamental contributors to the design, implementation, delivery, and evaluation of health services.

This means that citizen participation plays an essential role, bringing the unique point of view of patients and family members into the debate on patient safety and quality of care.

Patients and more generally citizens, when actively and systematically engaged, bring ideas and experiences which can support a collaborative and reciprocal learning process among the healthcare stakeholders. This produces knowledge that leads to improved practices, a real knowledge creation process where the dynamic participation of all actors in healthcare systems contribute to an active learning environment where the identification, the investigation, and the planning of solu-

E. Beleffi (✉)
Centre for Clinical Risk Management and Patient Safety, Tuscany Region—WHO Collaborating Centre in Human Factors and Communication for the Delivery of Safe and Quality Care, Florence, Italy
e-mail: beleffie@aou-careggi.toscana.it

P. Mosconi
Laboratory for Medical Research and Consumers Involvement, Public Health Department, Istituto di Ricerche Farmacologiche Mario Negri IRCCS, Milan, Italy
e-mail: paola.mosconi@marionegri.it

S. Sheridan
The Society to Improve Diagnosis in Medicine, Evanston, IL, USA
e-mail: Sue.sheridan@Improvediagnosis.org

© The Author(s) 2021
L. Donaldson et al. (eds.), *Textbook of Patient Safety and Clinical Risk Management*,
https://doi.org/10.1007/978-3-030-59403-9_10

tions related to health incidents is a cyclic process enabling healthcare knowledge creation.

The added value of involving patients in healthcare is, respect to other more complex interventions, a low cost opportunity to take into consideration unconventional points of view creating and building knowledge and providing original insights and ideas that otherwise would not be considered.

Health professionals and patients' skills and knowledge are acquired through individual experience or education and transferred to the health organizations in a perspective of co-production of healthcare. It is a merging of the efforts of those who produce and those who use the solutions to address health problems. It serves to establish a strengthened and long-term relationship in terms of trust and effectiveness and to distribute the responsibilities among all stakeholders [2].

In light of these arguments, the systems approach—inspired by the fundamentals of ergonomics and human factors (HFE)—creates new alliances between healthcare and engineering, of which patient journey is a challenging example [3].

Applying the systems approach to patient safety allows the analysis of the factors that characterize the encounters and the interactions between healthcare professionals and patients during the entire course of care. The observation of possible critical issues to the individual and specific encounter between clinician and patient is crucial in widening the scope of observation and research of the entire "journey" of the patient, taking into consideration the complexity of patient, their values and needs, their preferences, the economic and social context in which they live, and language and communication issues.

These observations and research should be carried out considering the interconnections and interactions together with the components of the processes; importance should be given to the context, and to manage the complexity, the value of a holistic approach.

10.2   The Patient Journey

A modern health system looks to the future in the context of the challenges imposed by the real world. It must manage the gap between guide-lines and health protocols and what effectively happens and how reality is perceived by patients and family members.

It is more and more necessary to bring the patient's point of view in the analysis of the care process, in the incident reporting and analysis, in the design and implementation of solutions and guidelines in healthcare.

Vincent and Amalberti in "Safer Healthcare" (2016) [4] stated that the incident analysis should broaden the class of events having consequences on patient safety. Incidents reported from the patient's point of view should be included in addition to those suggested by health professionals. Additionally, when analyzing an incident, it should be done in the context of the patient journey rather than a single episode.

Instead of focusing on the individual encounter, it is necessary to extend the observation timeframe by applying the examination of contributing factors to each of the encounters that compose the patient journey (temporal series of encounters with healthcare facilities, a hospital unit, a specialist visit, a primary care clinic, a home health agency), considering both the negative and positive events and the points for improvement that were revealed (Fig. 10.1).

The adoption of this wider approach is unique in that it incorporates the patient's perspective of safety and includes new features in the incident analysis such as asking patients to recount the episode of care, including patient and family in the investigation team when possible, asking patients the contributory factors from their point of observation and perception and involving patients and families in the reflections and comments on the disclosure process [4].

The episodes patients and families can highlight are often different from those that professionals are more accustomed to reporting. However, patients could be involved in further ways in incident reporting and assessment, and today patient-derived information constitutes a free and little used resource.

As per McCarthy's definition, "patient journey mapping describes the patient experience, including tasks within encounters, the emotional journey, the physical journey, and the various touch points" [5]. Carayon and Woldridge define "patient journey as the spatio-temporal

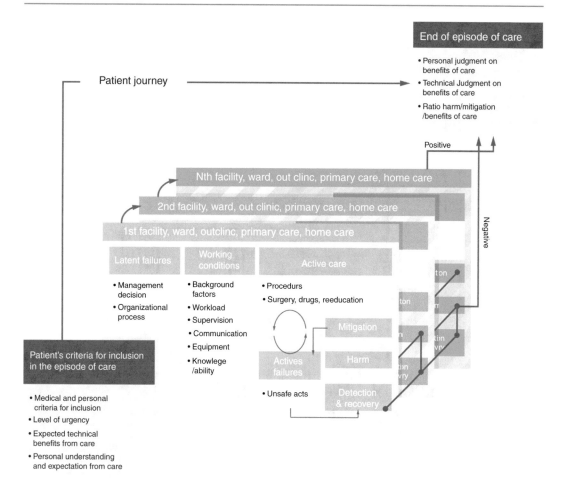

Fig. 10.1   Analysis of safety along the patient journey

distribution of patients' interactions with multiple care settings over time" [3], where at each point of touch with each healthcare service along the patient journey, the patient interacts with several system elements (task interaction, physical environment, interaction with tools and technologies, organization interaction, interaction with other organizations and other people, interaction with other people and teams within the organization) (Fig. 10.2).

The patient journey represents the time sequence of what happens to the patient, especially during transitions of care, in particular considering that the health professional who takes care of the patient only sees the portion of care for which he is responsible and in which he has an active role. Conversely, the patient is the only

person who has a continuously active and first-hand role during their health journey. They alone are in possession of information that characterizes the entire care experience.

Moreover, when patients navigate their journey, they contact and interface with multiple work systems at several time points, where the sequence of interactions in the work systems determine the outcome experienced by patients and families, healthcare professionals, and health organizations. (Fig. 10.3). Each local work system is influenced by a wider socio-organizational context, which can be formal healthcare organization (such as hospital, primary care facility, nursing home) or informal (home).

Every point of the patient journey offers data on health outcomes and patient experience out-

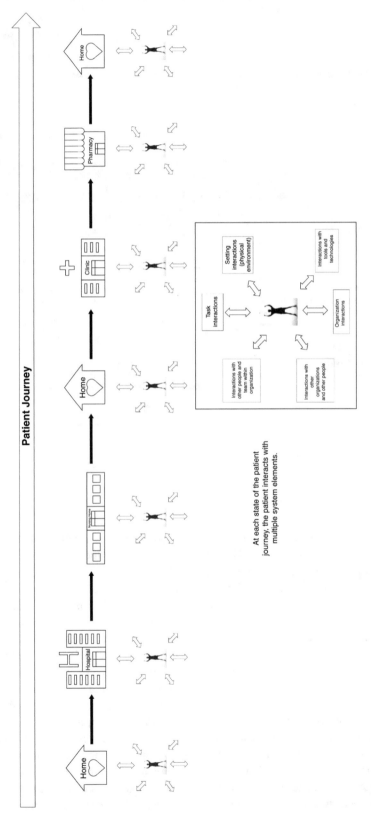

Fig. 10.2 The patient journey as a set of interactions and transitions

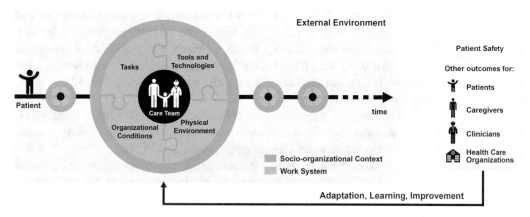

Fig. 10.3 SEIPS 3.0 model: sociotechnical systems approach to patient journey and patient safety

comes that should be used as feedback to redesign healthcare work systems in terms of adaptation, learning, improvement.

Patient's experience represents an important resource in participatory collaborative design, especially in the patient journey where this experience is the result of multiple interactions across space and time.

10.3 Contextualizing Patient Safety in the Patient Journey

Many of the incidents or near-misses during healthcare are not due to serious errors, but to the combination of small failures, such as limited experience of a recently qualified doctor, use of obsolete equipment, an infection difficult to diagnose or inadequate communication within a team.

We know that the analysis of an incident requires looking back to the succession of events that have occurred and that led to the problematic episode, considering both active and latent errors, and all the aspects connected directly or indirectly. It is fundamental to examine the safety of the entire patient journey, all the encounters that make up the entire care process, to study the whole medical history of the patient in an attempt to reconstruct all the elements that characterize the "health journey", not only from the viewpoint of the health professionals, but also from that of the patient and family.

In light of these arguments, new concepts, tools, models, and methods need to be embraced to support patient safety in the patient journey.

A significant contribution in terms of concepts, frameworks, and models is offered by Industrial and Systems Engineering, and often human factors and systems engineering (HF/SE) have an approach to include the preferences and the needs of stakeholders when designing solutions to address the critical aspects of a health process.

Human factors and ergonomics are described as "the scientific discipline concerned with the understanding of interactions among humans and other elements of a system, and the profession that applies theory, principles, data and methods to design in order to optimize human well-being and overall system performance. Practitioners of ergonomics and ergonomists contribute to the design and evaluation of tasks, jobs, products, environments and systems in order to make them compatible with the needs, abilities and limitations of people. Ergonomics helps harmonize things that interact with people in terms of people's needs, abilities and limitations" [6].

Process models have found widespread use in drug management, visit planning, care transition, to name a few, and can offer tools and methods to investigate interprofessional and physician–patient communication, interruptions and health information handover.

Drawing from the finding of Carayon's studies [3], the Systems Engineering Initiative for

Patient Safety (SEIPS) model gives a description of five work system elements which when applied to a definite patient journey model should outline who (person) is doing what (tasks) with tool and technologies, taking into consideration the physical and organizational environment where all these activities take place. All these factors have to be examined for both patients and workers and the process analysis and modelling have to consider what patients and families/caregivers, healthcare professionals and workers actually do (*work-as-done* versus *work-as-imagined*).

Patients, families, and caregivers are deeply involved in the healthcare process due to the tasks they carry out in the intermediate sectors of care between encounters. Away from direct interactions with professionals, they have to perform multiple actions requiring understanding of what behaviour to adopt, which instructions to follow, how to administer a medication and how to communicate with hospital doctors, general practitioner, and home healthcare professionals [3].

Taking into account what has been highlighted so far, one of the leading and most challenging keys to success in improving patient safety is to adopt a systems approach to patient safety which includes the patient's perspective about their health journey throughout the time of care and across all the care settings.

This assumption highlights that patients and their families are valuable resources and can play an important role in patient safety improvement efforts. Viewing health systems as "co-producing systems", patients can engage as partners in co-producing patient safety improvement activities individually, in groups and collectively. Individual patient and family member participation/co-production of safer care is fundamental. Equally as important is the co-management and co-governance of healthcare services, in addition to the engagement of communities in policy definition and designing activities.

In fact, patient engagement directs the design of healthcare systems towards the preferences, the values, the real-life experiences, and—not less important—the skills of the people to enhance patient safety in the patient journey.

Such a change of perspective involves multiple dimensions of interactions and relationship between patients and professionals, encompassing cooperation, dialogue and listening, trust, reciprocity and peer-to-peer work [2].

It follows that on the one hand the healthcare organizations have to demonstrate the willingness to support health professionals to effectively engage patients in the patient journey to achieve the common goal of reducing the risk of patient harm or incidents as well as the willingness to integrate patients and family members as partners into quality and safety improvement efforts. On the other hand, it is necessary to motivate and encourage patients and families/caregivers to actively participate during the individual care process for safer care as well as partner in organizational patient safety improvement efforts to ensure safer care for others.

The working group *Patient and Family Involvement for the delivery of Safe and Quality Care* [7] stated that the utmost priority to realize the patient involvement is the training of patients, followed by the promotion of interdisciplinary training programmes for healthcare professionals to promote patient and family engagement, the implementation of multilevel structures that allow for participatory processes by patients and smarter allocation of resources in healthcare that supports involving citizens in patient safety improvement efforts for better healthcare.

This working group was part of the activities of the "1st International Meeting about Patient safety for new generations—Florence, 31st August and 1st September 2018" organized by the Centre for Clinical Risk Management and Patient Safety, Tuscany Region—WHO Collaborating Centre for in Human Factors and Communication for the Delivery of Safe and Quality care [7].

Therefore, training for both patients/families/advocates and health professionals is a pillar on which to build active engagement of patients and consequently an effective and efficient patient journey. From this perspective, the participation of patients (i.e. representatives of patients' associations and organizations, patient and citizen advocates) in training courses—specifically designed for this target audience of trainees and aimed to encourage co-production of care—is an essential and effective activity to co-produce a better healthcare system in terms of quality and safety of care.

Sharing a common language, promoting citizens' and patients' awareness of importance of co-production of care, teaching the key role that patients can play in making treatments safer (investments in health literacy), learning to work together and within a network (locally, regionally, and nationally/internationally) on priority safety and quality of care issues: these are some of the main strengths of training courses aimed to be at the basis of active engagement of patients and citizens.

Examples of successful training courses include "PartecipaSalute" and "Accademia del Cittadino" organized in Italy by Laboratory for Medical Research and Consumers Involvement of the Istituto di Ricerche Farmacologiche Mario Negri IRCCS and the Centre for Clinical Risk Management and Patient Safety, Tuscany Region. The following paragraph describes this educational experience which is specifically designed for citizens and patients to improve their knowledge and skills in patient safety and quality of care, with the aim of co-producing better healthcare services.

10.4   From PartecipaSalute to the Accademia del Cittadino: The Importance of Training Courses to Empower Patients

Over the last few years in the field of health and research and with regard to participation and involvement of citizens and patients, we have witnessed the transition from a paternalist to a partnership model. Individual citizens and those citizens involved in patients' associations or groups have acquired a new role: no longer passive but actively involved in decision-making regarding health, healthcare, and research in the health field [8, 9].

This is a progressive step-by-step process based on the recognition and implementation of the key concepts such as health literacy and empowerment. Health literacy, more properly used at individual level is defined as the capacity to obtain, read, understand, and use healthcare information in order to make appropriate health decisions and follow instructions for treatment [10]. Empowerment, more used at the community level, is a process that, starting from the acquisition of accurate knowledge and skills, enables groups to express their needs and more actively participate to request better assistance, care, and research. At this level, the availability of organized independent and evidence-based training courses is essential to allow people to be able to critically appraise and use information about the effects of healthcare interventions. Consequently, they will have the skills to participate in the multidisciplinary working groups (composed of researchers, health professionals, patient and citizen advocates, institutional representatives).

In the late 1990s, the Istituto di Ricerche Farmacologiche Mario Negri IRCCS held the first training courses of this kind focused at breast cancer associations. Some years later, within the project PartecipaSalute—a not-for-profit research project designed to foster a strategic alliance among healthcare professionals, patients, and their organizations—an ad hoc training programme for representatives of citizens' and patients' organizations was defined with a multimodule format [11, 12]. This was an innovative approach, at least in the Italian setting in that period.

PartecipaSalute training programme has combined different experiences: the Mario Negri Institute IRCCS experience in collaborative research activities with patients' associations, the Italian Cochrane Centre with the activities aimed at promoting the principles of evidence-based medicine, and Zadig long-term experience in health communication. The above promoters jointly developed the PartecipaSalute training programme on the belief that data are more important than opinions, and that every decision should be supported by well-conducted research data.

The spread of this belief to patients and citizens with the purpose of stronger involvement was a key point of PartecipaSalute training courses.

Therefore, patient, family, and community knowledge of the principles of how evidence is developed through clinical research is essential to make or support decisions in the health debate, to promote better clinical research, or to convey correct information. The strength of the PartecipaSalute programme was based on the exchange of experiences in an interactive way aimed at creating opportunities for discussion, overcoming the teacher–learner model. Each session started with an interactive discussion of a real situation—such as a screening, vaccination, therapy—and after sharing data, opinions or articles from media, evidence was presented and discussed, underlining significant methodological aspects. The programme offered the opportunity to debate the value and significance of the methodology offering critical appraisal tools. Each participant was invited to take an active part, starting from direct personal or associative experience. Table 10.1 presents the topics considered in the first three editions of the training programme. The participation was free, and different types of materials were provided including an ad hoc manual published by PartecipaSalute, copies of the PowerPoint presentation and articles.

Considering the characteristics of the programme and its modular structure, the PartecipaSalute training programme could be adapted to specific contexts. In fact, the experience of PartecipaSalute was adopted at the regional level by Regione Toscana (Centre for Clinical Risk Management and Patient Safety and the Quality of healthcare and Clinical pathways of Health Department, Tuscany Region) developing a more specific training programme called PartecipaSalute-Accademia del Cittadino (Academy of Citizen), focused on patient safety and risk management. In particular, after some modules on methods related to evidence-based medicine, uncertainties in medicine and information and communication in health, the training was mainly dedicated to regional and local activities on clinical risk management, the role of

Table 10.1 Topics considered in PartecipaSalute [4, 5] and PartecipaSalute-Accademia del Cittadino training courses

ABCs of clinical research
Aimed to offer conceptual and practical bases and technical tools to critically appraise the methodology of epidemiological/clinical research; to know and discuss relationships between ethics and clinical research, including participation on Ethics Committees.

Uncertainties in medicine
Aimed to discuss the probabilistic nature of the medical knowledge; to understand the intrinsic variability of the clinical practice; to deepen the relevance of values and preferences in medical decisions.

Conflicts of interest in medicine
Aimed to encourage critical awareness about conflicts of interest in medicine, in clinical research, and among citizens' and patients' associations; to discuss the impact of conflicts of interest on clinical practice and clinical research.

Health information
Aimed to present the strategies and methods behind the communication, in particular, related to marketing of drugs and devices; to coach a critical reading of medical and scientific literature, lay people articles, and mass media health campaigns.

Credibility and strength of consumers'/patients' associations
Aimed to discuss the requirements needed to raise the credibility of patients' associations; to identify the possible role of advocacy of patients' associations in healthcare.

Participate equally in multidisciplinary groups
Aimed to discuss the model, role, and activities of representatives of consumers and patients within the working groups evaluating feedback and results obtained.

patients' associations to improve patient safety and to support the implementation of best practices, the analysis and data of adverse events and risk assessment in terms of quality and safety in the care processes (Table 10.2).

The PartecipaSalute-Accademia del Cittadino joint training programme has been implemented in three editions over the last decade and has trained about 100 members of patient and citizen advocates representing 38 patients' associations. The courses ranged from 5 to 3 modules of 2 days each in residential mode to allow participants to get to know each other and create a network of associations committed to be engaged in clinical research, quality, and healthcare safety issues.

Table 10.2 Topic integration in the PartecipaSalute-Accademia del Cittadino joint courses

Adverse events and safety of care
Aimed to explain what are the adverse events in healthcare, how they arise, and how it can become an opportunity for improvement; methods to analyze incidents and near-miss events with the multidisciplinary approach of ergonomics and human factors; and what reporting and learning systems are and the role of patients in reporting medical error.
The new role of patients and citizens in the evaluation of quality and safety in the health system
Aimed to help participants learn the best practices for patient safety and the accreditation system for quality and safety of care, to enable active participation in the co-design of the practices, the implementation, the evaluation, and the diffusion of safety solutions to make patient safety a reality.
The interpretation of health quality and safety data, the participation tools to empower patients and citizens in the healthcare experience
Aimed to enable trainees how to identify complete and reliable data on the quality and patient safety, how to interpret them and what they are for. Which are the tools that patient and citizen associations can use to participate in the planning and assessment of healthcare.

The entire educational experience was characterized by the use of participatory training methods, based on working groups, practical exercises, lectures from experts with opportunities for discussions. As a result of this training course model, the participants were recognized as "expert patients" and were regularly involved in basic activities for promoting patient safety as auditors on significant events and helping to define policies on patient safety at the Tuscany regional level. In addition, they have participated in patient safety walkarounds in hospitals and in developing eight cartoons intended to promote the education of citizens for the prevention of the most diffused risks (such as prevention of infections, prevention of falls and handovers).

Feedback on the satisfaction on tutors, topics discussed and knowledge gained was regularly requested from participants through questionnaires distributed before and after the programme. In general, positive feedback was received; participants appreciated the interactive methods of work, the clarity of the language, and the effort to make difficult problems easy to understand. An ad hoc questionnaire was provided to the participants regarding the methodology of clinical research, always showing an improvement in the self-evaluated knowledge before and after the course. Feedback of the results of the evaluation was also shared with each participant. Most of participants reported their experience to other members of the organization. In particular, in the case of the Regione Toscana training, the possibility of immediately transferring what was learned in the course in all the activities in collaboration with the health institutions, policy makers, and health professionals—such as working groups on patient safety best practices, participation to audits, development of tools to improve health literacy—was appreciated.

Some limitations emerged from these experiences. The selection of participants is the first issue, not only because the training course is accessible to a small number of participants (in general no more than 30 participants), but also because the groups comprised of middle-aged and retired participants, with few younger ones. Additionally, there were few individual patient or family member representatives from patient associations. The majority of those representing patient associations were in managerial or leadership positions. Furthermore, it is difficult to choose between small, local, or bigger regional associations. Residential training courses also restricted the participation for geographical reasons.

The PartecipaSalute and ParteciaSalute-Accademia del Cittadino training experiences show that patients and citizens are willing to get actively involved in healthcare and the research debate. There is a real desire to improve their knowledge and skills on health and research issues and allow some general considerations regarding the active engagement of citizens representing associations and advocacy groups.

In conclusion, it is very important to invest in a process of empowerment aimed to have well-trained activists involved vigorously and constructively in the debate, design, and assessment of health and research. Switching from tokenism to active participation is necessary to effectively partner with patients and the general population to design, plan, and co-produce safer more effective healthcare, while also supporting better more patient-centred research [13, 14].

Also, the training courses are feasible and useful, as has recently been discovered also by pharma or other groups that organize courses mainly focused on drugs and drug development, thus directing the participation of the groups more to market needs than to public health.

Furthermore, this training initiative facilitates the networking among associations in part overcoming the difficulties that derive from personalization and division among the associations representing citizens and patients.

Finally, this illustrates the importance of the design and promotion of training courses with institutions, such as the Regione Toscana, in order to be able to implement projects of real collaboration between institutions, healthcare professionals, and consumers' and patients' representatives.

healthcare systems, universities, and policy makers).

However, little has been done to overcome some healthcare systems barriers: the power imbalance between the doctor and patient, language differences, the lack of diffusion of non-technical skills and, last but not least, the lack of evidence about the value of patient involvement.

To be widely implemented, patient engagement in the patient journey requires courageous leadership, organizational efforts, a wider culture of safety of care, the implementation of multi-level structures for the engagement of patients and resources from smarter spending in healthcare.

Education is the landmark to integrate meaningful patient and citizen engagement in healthcare. Training of patients is the fundamental starting point to develop shared knowledge, co-produce projects, and implement an active multi-level participation of patients and families for the improvement of quality and safety of care.

10.5 Recommendations

A systemic approach to health can provide valuable models for wider implementation of patient safety. A multidisciplinary approach includes the involvement of citizens and patients as unique stakeholders in the design, implementation, delivery, and assessment of health services.

Involving patients in healthcare is an opportunity to bring uncommon points of view into policy making and to create shared knowledge between healthcare professionals and patients.

The implementation of patients' and families'/caregivers' perspectives in the patient journey is the golden opportunity to leverage crucial input, such as experiential knowledge, safer care, patient motivation, and trust and social cohesion into the co-production of safety solutions in healthcare. This represents a way to get closer to person-centred care, to create opportunities for patients to meet and share information and knowledge, to develop structures and policies for patient involvement at different levels (with

References

1. Kaplan G, Bo-Linn G, Carayon P, Pronovost P, Rouse W, Reid P, Saunders R. Bringing a systems approach to health, Discussion Paper. Institute of Medicine and National Academy Engineering. 2013.
2. Palumbo R. Contextualizing co-production of health care: a systematic literature review. Int J Public Sect Manag. 2016;29(1):72–90. https://doi.org/10.1108/IJPSM-07-2015-0125.
3. Carayon P, Wooldridge AR. Improving patient safety in the patient journey: contributions from human factors engineering. In: Smith AE, editor. Women in industrial and systems engineering. Key advances and perspective in emerging topics, Women in engineering and science, vol. 12. Cham: Springer; 2019. p. 275–99.
4. Vincent C, Amalberti R. Safer healthcare-strategies for the real world, vol. 5. Cham: Springer Open; 2016. p. 47–57.
5. McCarthy S, O'Raghallaigh P, Woodworth S, Lim YL, Kenny LC, Adam F. An integrated patient journey mapping tool for embedding quality in healthcare service reform. J Decis Syst. 2016;25(Suppl 1):354–68. https://doi.org/10.1080/12460125.2016.1187394.
6. International Ergonomics Association (IEA). Definition and domains of ergonomics. https://www.iea.cc/whats/. Accessed 23 Dec 2019.

7. International Meeting about Patient safety for new medical generations—Florence, 31 Aug and 1 Sept 2018. http://iea2018.org/?page_id=4373. Accessed 23 Dec 2019.

8. Castro EM, Van Regenmortel T, Vanhaecht K, Sermeus W, Van Hecke A. Patient empowerment, patient participation and patient-centeredness in hospital care: a concept analysis based on a literature review. Patient Educ Couns. 2016;99(12):1923–39. https://doi.org/10.1016/j.pec.2016.07.026. Epub 2016 Jul 18.

9. Coulter A, Ellins J. Effectiveness of strategies for informing, educating, and involving patients. Br Med J. 2007;335:24–7.

10. IOM. Health literacy: a prescription to end confusion. Washington DC: National Academies Press, 2004; Am J Prev Med. 2009;36(5):446–51.

11. Mosconi P, Colombo C, Satolli R, Liberati A. PartecipaSalute, an Italian project to involve lay people, patients' associations and scientific-medical representatives on the health debate. Health Expect. 2007;10:194–204.

12. Mosconi P, Satolli R, Colombo C, Villani W. Does a consumer training work? A follow-up survey of the PartecipaSalute training programs. Health Res Policy Syst. 2012;10:27. https://doi.org/10.1186/1478-4505-10-27.

13. Ocloo J, Matthews R. From tokenism to empowerment: progressing patient and public involvement in healthcare improvement. BMJ Qual Saf. 2016;25:626–32. https://doi.org/10.1136/bmjqs-2015-004839.

14. Chalmers I, Bracken MB, Djulbegovic B, Garattini S, Grant J, Gülmezoglu AM, Howells DW, Ioannidis JP, Oliver S. How to increase value and reduce waste when research priorities are set. Lancet. 2014;383:156–65. https://doi.org/10.1016/S0140-6736(13)62229-1.

Adverse Event Investigation and Risk Assessment

Tommaso Bellandi, Adriana Romani-Vidal, Paulo Sousa, and Michela Tanzini

11.1 Risk Management in Complex Human Systems and Organizations

11.1.1 Living with Uncertainty

Risk is an integral part of human activities, both in living and working environments. Every day, an individual performs a considerable number of actions, which, in most cases, are "inter-actions" with other people or tools or work environments. Interactions are more complex than elementary actions because the people, objects, or contexts with which we interact and offer opportunities for (affordance) and constraints on action [1–3]. Interactions have consequences that can change the status of objects or people. In the worst sce-narios, an object used in an unexpected way can break or even cause fatal damage; inappropriate communication with another person may offend or provoke violent reactions.

The consequences of an interaction are not always predictable. For this reason, in the development of humanity, organizations have progressively emerged, places and structures in which, more or less formally, legitimate and illegitimate behaviors are distinguishable [4], in order to contain the risk associated with the intrinsic unpredictability of interactions. Organizations are socially regulated contexts, in which more or less explicit norms influence the choices and behavior of individuals. The rules, however, can be sometimes fallacious or deficient, consequently favoring the wrong choices or inhibiting the correct actions. Rules are the bureaucratic expression of power and can therefore benefit some subjects to the detriment of others, sometimes fostering environments that, in hindsight (the "historical truth") are recognized as harmful for the organization itself or for the individuals who belong to it [5].

In today's world, practically all human activities take place within organizations, subject to rules, involving the use of tools and interpersonal relationships. It is these interactions that determine the development of an environment of greater or lesser safety for the subjects who are a part of it or who, for some reason or another, are involved in its dynamics. It is exactly starting

T. Bellandi (✉)
Patient Safety Unit , Northwest Trust, Regional Health Service of Tuscany, Lucca, Italy
e-mail: tommaso.bellandi@uslnordovest.toscana.it

A. Romani-Vidal
Hospital Universitario Ramón y Cajal, Preventive Medicine, Madrid, Spain

P. Sousa
National School of Public Health, Lisbon, Portugal
e-mail: paulo.sousa@ensp.unl.pt

M. Tanzini
Centro Gestione Rischio Clinico e Sicurezza del Paziente, Florence, Italy
e-mail: tanzinim@aou-careggi.toscana.it

L. Donaldson et al. (eds.), *Textbook of Patient Safety and Clinical Risk Management*,
https://doi.org/10.1007/978-3-030-59403-9_11

from these interactions that people attribute meaning to their being and to the world around us, in the constant attempt to find reasons for the activities we find ourselves performing. The activities are to be considered as aggregates of tasks more or less driven by objectives along with the material conditions in which they are carried out.

11.1.2 Two Levels of Risk Management in Healthcare Systems

First of all, it is necessary to embed the two activities of "risk assessment" and "investigation of adverse events" in the organizational processes of health systems. Both activities may provide reasons for study and research, or be linked to organizational objectives such as patient safety, cost containment or, compliance with regulatory obligations. Setting aside the dynamics of research, from an operational point of view the assessment of risk as an organizational function should permeate both the choices of clinicians and managers, if we accept that patient safety is an essential goal of health organizations. On the other hand, the analysis of adverse events could be an activity entrusted to specialists in the investigation of accidents, or shared between both the frontline and the bottom end as an integral part of the risk assessment process, if it is meant and used for organizational development.

Highly reliable organizations [6] manage to effectively reduce risk, thanks to a constant commitment to safety from top management, which establishes high-level objectives and provides a source of inspiration and vision for the operational lines which, on their end, have the responsibility of planning and control over operations, thanks to a true distribution of the decision-making process. In practice, these organizations work because they are structured to deal with risk, anticipating situations in which a problem is more likely to occur and knowing how to mitigate the possible consequences. Of course, this

organizational competence emerges from the knowledge of its members who, at various levels, are trained to detect errors promptly, analyze them and understand their causes, quantify the probability of system failure, and take action to reduce their reoccurrence according to a priority scale. If we adopt the systemic perspective, then safety culture, which influences the knowledge and decisions of individuals, must be based on the values of participation and transparency to empower everyone to report an error, to understand processes and procedures, and to enable the development and modification of rules, tools, environments, and relationships between people. In other words, the organizational development has to be understood as a systematic monitoring and adjustment of critical interactions between system components.

Even in healthcare organizations therefore, risk management should involve both management and frontline operators. Starting with the integration of patient safety into the strategic objectives of the institution, risk management must become an integral part of health practices as well as technical and administrative support operations. At the board level, patient safety management can be established, responsible for planning and linking operational and support functions to involve risk assessment in decision-making processes at all levels. Acting as a true knowledge broker, this management would be able to uphold the strategic objective of patient safety in the various communities of practices that make up an organization [4]. At the level of the operating units, clinical risk management is established, responsible for analyzing adverse events, understanding the incidents from the systemic perspective and, subsequently, guiding learning from errors in anticipation of risk in real time.

In order to effectively and efficiently assess risks in hevalthcare, it is necessary to use theories and methods consistent with the level of complexity of health activities. The systemic approach [7] provides a lens capable of visualizing health activities by tracking the dynamics of the interactions between the subjects involved, the tools, and the environments in which they take place. It also takes into consideration the reasons and interpretations that underlie the choices and behaviors of individuals and community practices.

Ergonomics, or human factors engineering (HFE), as "interaction science" has its focus on systems' dynamics and design of interfaces. Therefore, HFE provides a valid and robust theoretical and methodological knowledge base to address health risks within an integrated framework, encompassing patient safety and clinical risk management [8, 9] (Fig. 11.1).

11.2 Patient Safety Management

The patient safety function must first of all contribute to organizing the data relating to the possible risks present in the health system, so that they can be accessed systematically and whenever necessary. There are both data generated specifically for patient safety, and data produced routinely for other purposes, but which may be useful for risk assessment. Both types of data refer to a range of activities of healthcare organizations, as shown in Table 11.1.

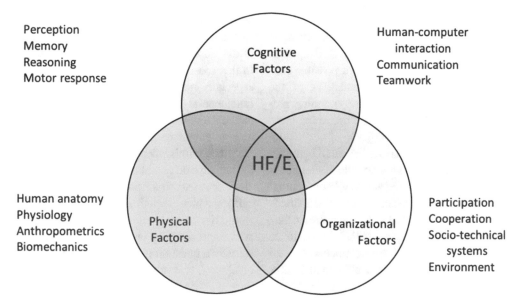

Fig. 11.1 Ergonomics and human factors (HFE), the science of interactions. *Source:* https://iea.cc/what-is-ergonomics/

Table 11.1 Data integration for patient safety

	Data for patient safety	Nonspecific data
Delivery of clinical and care processes	Incident reports and analysis	Administrative data (i.e., discharge records, emergency admissions, drug prescriptions)
	Structured record reviews	Digital archives of clinical tests (i.e., Radiology and Laboratory Information Systems)
Quality management	Reliability analysis Registry of non-conformities	Process indicators
	Reports of safety walkarounds Self-evaluations of accreditation/ certification requirements	Reports of accreditation/certification surveys
Patient reported measures	Patient reported experiences and outcomes including safety events	Claims and complaints Public enquiries

Data integration is certainly the best way to have the widest representation of possible risks [10] even if, as mentioned, it is necessary for the Patient Safety Manager to help define the method of collection and the structure of specific data, possibly also intervening in information flows of nonspecific data to obtain ad hoc or periodic reports of relevant information, such as the indication of a possible sentinel event included in a claim and not previously reported. In other words, the corporate patient safety function must transform large masses of qualitative and quantitative data into information useful for assessing the current risk and for producing organizational knowledge [11] relating to the appropriate response to mitigate future risk.

In risk assessment, in addition to the classical criteria of frequency with which dangerous events occur and of the severity of possible consequences, the criteria of imputability of the event to patient care and of corresponding preventability of adverse events are becoming more relevant. Thanks to the emergence of novel studies and research in various clinical contexts, some events considered historically as complications or "accidents" have actually been demonstrated to be preventable and therefore attributable to the treatment provided or omitted rather than to the patient's underlying pathology or to an acceptable side effect of the treatments. A clear example of a type of complication that is now considered an adverse event is an infection related to the central venous catheter. Evidence demonstrated that in many situations [12, 13] this type of infections have been cleared, thanks to good practices. In the category of "accidents," we can consider patient's falls, where adequate evidence is available: to evaluate risk factors and classify patients at risk; to apply preventive actions so to reduce their frequency and contain their consequences [14, 15].

Studies and records of performance evaluation and healthcare outcomes are also possible sources of risk assessment data although they should be appropriately investigated in the context of clinical audits to reconcile the variations that may appear due to the quality of the data essentially coming from administrative flows, affected by, as an example, the limited validity of hospital mortality data [16].

11.3 Clinical Risk Management

The clinical risk management function exists to anticipate adverse events and to mitigate the possible consequences when they occur. It is a matter of implementing the Hippocratic principle "primum non nocere" in clinical and care practice, using the technological and organizational resources available at a given time and in a specific operating context. At this level, risk management takes place in real time, in front of and with patients, following good practices for safe care and continually re-evaluating the correctness of diagnoses and the effectiveness of treatments. In this sense, the analysis of adverse events and especially near-misses can and must become a fundamental activity in the management of patients and departments because, if carried out as a systematic review of clinical cases, almost in real time, within operating structures, it can limit the negative effects of adverse events on patients, clinicians, and organizations. Beyond the technicalities which sometimes intimidate those who would like to apply an instrument such as significant event auditing or root cause analysis, it is actually a question of integrating the two phases of clinical reasoning. It includes diagnosis and therapy, with almost real-time reflection on the effects of diagnostic and therapeutic decisions and actions, starting from the cases that give rise to doubts, which for one reason or another cause surprise or concern and interfere with the ordinary flow of activities, and which, therefore, demand an analysis and an explanation, drawing the attention of the operator in charge of that patient.

The process just described is the aforementioned "Sensemaking" [17], i.e., the need to find a valid explanation in the face of a problematic situation. The specific knowledge of risk management can help healthcare workers to take into consideration the complex interactions between human, technical, and organizational factors underlying the problematic situation, restoring to the classical "clinical picture" the colors and shapes that constitute the substance, and the frame that is the reference context. Table 11.2 lists the operational phases for the analysis of the adverse event, which we will see in detail in the next paragraph.

The level of formalization and depth of the analysis may vary in consideration of health systems' policies and available resources; however, all the methods of systemic analysis of adverse events have in common the five activities described in Table 11.2.

The activity of analyzing adverse events and near-misses can therefore become the third pillar of clinical competence to complement diagnostic and therapeutic activities, keeping the focus on patient safety. The risk of a drift to bureaucratize Significant Event Audit (SEA) and Root Cause Analysis (RCA), or, even worse, the risk of the exploitation of formally non-punitive analysis to identify a scapegoat, are still present. The true measure of cultural change and organizational development towards patient safety lies precisely in the effective integration of the analysis of adverse events into clinical and care practices. These are activities that can be made professional certification requirements for healthcare workers, to be evaluated both through

retrospective review of cases subjected to systemic analysis and through prospective checks in which the same clinical case becomes the object of simulation in which the decisions and actions of clinicians are evaluated using behavioral markers related to technical and non-technical skills. Both methods require the establishment of teams of investigators composed of clinicians from the specialist branch and experts in ergonomics and the human factor, possibly but not necessarily external to the structure. Examples of systemic efficacy evaluations can be traced both in the Netherlands [18] and in the United States Veteran Health Administration [19], while in France the participation in the reporting and learning system is a real professional certification requirement defined by the Haute Autorité de Santé. The evaluation of technical and non-technical competences in simulated scenarios taken from clinical cases of adverse events is found in many works, now also the subject of in-depth reviews [20, 21].

11.4 Systemic Analysis of Adverse Events

11.4.1 The Dynamics of an Incident

For the purpose of this chapter, we take the definition of a "patient safety incident" to include near-misses, adverse events, and sentinel events, usually distinguished by the severity of the consequences. Also, we do not differentiate between the terms "accident" and "incident," where the former is generally used in high-risk industry referring to an event that affects quite a large number of victims, while the latter usually refers to individual harm.

Incidents in healthcare should be studied according to the systemic perspective, in order to be able to fully understand them and to foster organizational learning. The actions and failures of the individual play a central role, but the individual's way of thinking and acting is strongly conditioned by the clinical context and by the broader organizational dynamics. Incubation of an incident begins with defects in high-level

Table 11.2 Steps for adverse events investigation

Activity	Description
Selection of the incident	Spontaneous reporting, clinical record review, informal discussion of clinical cases
Data collection about the incident and its circumstances	Analysis of clinical records; interviews with operators and with the patient/family members; collection of procedures, protocols, guidelines, or reference literature
Analysis of the incident	Timeline, checklist, or diagram of contributing factors; peer review
Report	Summary description of the event, of the criticalities detected, and of the improvement actions
Follow-up	Sharing report, selection, and adoption of improvement actions; evaluation of results

organizational processes, such as the planning and programming of production of services, the forecasting of activity volume, the planning and maintenance of environments and technologies, the development strategies and personnel policies. Failures at this level create latent conditions of danger that penetrate and spread in operational contexts such as the operating room or the emergency room. There they can cause local conditions, such as excessive workload or poor interaction with the equipment, which contribute to errors or violations. Many unsafe actions may be performed at the frontline, but few are able to penetrate the defenses of the system and generate the adverse patient outcome. The fact that the safety barriers engineered in the system, such as alarms and procedures, have deficiencies due not only to latent errors but also to active errors is illustrated in Fig. 11.2 by an arrow that pierces the barriers defense system generating the accident. Figure 11.2 is an adapted version of the

famous Swiss-cheese model of accident dynamics, in which clinicians who work on the frontline are represented as the last barrier before the accident and as the inheritors of the system's failures rather than those responsible for the unsafe actions that cause incidents. However, the model should not be understood as an invitation to shift the assignment of responsibility from frontline professionals to managers at the organizational level, given that managers also work in a complex environment, in which the ramifications of decisions and actions are not immediately obvious. Therefore, according to Reason [22] managers are neither more nor less to blame than the operators of the frontline, since, as human beings, they can also make mistakes in planning and execution. It is therefore appropriate for the safety culture to be shared at all levels so that managers and designers take into account the dangerous conditions that may arise from their decisions or actions. Sometimes the perception of risk is

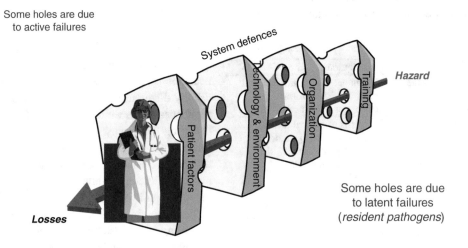

Fig. 11.2 Swiss-cheese model of accident dynamic adapted to healthcare

lower in those who work at a great distance from the frontline because the lack of direct contact with production processes and the context of operations pushes *blunt end* managers and designers to underestimate the dynamics of performance safety. To blame is the attitude of managers and designers who decide and act without a constant confrontation with the reality of the frontline and without involving in the strategic decisions those who are in direct contact with the production process.

In healthcare, the distance between the blunt end and the sharp end is in some cases accentuated by the fact that some political and organizational choices take place outside healthcare facilities and are based on risk and benefit assessments that are not always consistent with the mission of health facilities. There are therefore problems of an inter-organizational type that go beyond the boundaries of health facilities and which, sometimes, can be decisive for the quality and safety of care. As observed in the aviation context [23], the pharmaceutical and biomedical equipment industry, the government, and related agencies, professional associations and scientific societies make a substantial contribution to the design of the structures and of the processes of diagnosis and treatment, introducing a further level of complexity in the system that is lacking in the representation depicted in Fig. 11.2.

The problem of hyper-regulation in healthcare is particularly critical because, if it is true that this is a sector in which the autonomy of professionals of the first line is so accentuated that any attempt to standardize the practices may clash with established professional traditions, and in which the personalization of care is an important part of the clinical touch, then a blind standardization of the procedures can have a negative impact on patient safety [24].

11.4.2 A Practical Approach: The London Protocol Revisited

Vincent and colleagues [25, 26] extended the Reason model to apply to the analysis of patient

safety incidents, classifying the conditions of the clinical context that favor errors and the characteristics of the organizational system in a single frame of factors that influence clinical practices. The model originally included seven factors of which the environmental and technological factor was then split into two different classes, given the increasing relevance of devices and digital applications (Table 11.3). At the forefront of clinician–patient interactions are factors relating to the patient's condition. In all clinical situations, a patient's condition directly affects practices and outcomes of health services. Other factors, such as a patient's personality, communication style, and any psychosocial problems, can be very important because they affect communication with healthcare professionals. The design of activities and tasks, the availability and usefulness of protocols, and the results of diagnostic tests can also influence the care process and the quality of the results. Individual human factors include the knowledge, skills, and experience of each health professional, and also affect the quality and safety of services. Each staff member is part of a group within an operating unit, as part of a large hospital or out-patient facility which is in turn embedded in a healthcare system. The way in which an individual works and their impact on the patient is bound and influenced by the other members of the group, by the way they communicate, support, and supervise each other.

The group is influenced by the organizational actions and decisions of the management of the unit and of the healthcare system. These include allocation of human and technological resources, staff training, objectives and periodic management verifications, and so on. Management of the health system is in turn influenced by the property and the institutional contexts, including economic constraints, current legislations, and the broader political and economic climate.

The framework of eight factors is a useful scheme for the analysis of patient safety incidents, which include both clinical factors and high-level organizational conditions. It represents therefore a useful guide for the analysis of adverse events as it invites clinicians and risk managers to take into consideration a wide range

Table 11.3 Scheme of contributory factors

Contributory factor	Description
Patient characteristics	Conditions (complexity and seriousness) Language and communication Personality and social factors
Task/activity	Design and structural clarity of the task/activity Availability and use of procedures Availability and accuracy of diagnostic test results Support in decision-making
Human factors of the healthcare workers	Knowledge and skills Competence Physical and mental health
Team	Verbal communication Written communication Supervision and help opportunities Team structure (compatibility, consistency, leadership, etc.)
Technologies	Involvement in selection and design Equipment availability Usability and reliability Ordinary and extraordinary maintenance
Work environment	Staffing and skills mix Workloads and shift organization Administrative and management support Physical environment
Management and work organization	Financial resources and constraints Organizational structure Policies, standards, and objectives Safety culture and priorities
Institutional context	Economic and regulatory context Health policy Links with external organizations

of factors that at different levels determine the results of health services. When applied in a systematic way to the analysis of incidents, it allows for a ranking of the factors that highlights those with a greater bearing on patients' outcomes and for the prioritization of interventions to prevent system failures in the future.

A clinical case can be examined from many perspectives, each of which can highlight facets of the care process. Cases have always been used to train health professionals and to reflect on the nature of diseases. They also serve to illustrate the dynamics of decision-making, the evaluation of clinical practices, and above all, when errors are discussed, the impact of accidents or failures on people. The analysis of accidents, for the purposes of clinical risk management, covers all these aspects and includes broader considerations regarding the reliability of the health system.

There are different techniques for analyzing cases in healthcare. In the United States, the most common technique is root cause analysis (RCA). This approach to case analysis, employed by the Joint Commission, is very thorough and intensive, requires time and resources, and originated from the "Total Quality Management" approach to health safety. RCA is promoted and has been adopted in many countries, with results that do not always correspond to investment in time and resources [27].

For a wide range of reasons, the so-called London protocol [26] approach to system analysis seems more convincing and, in fact, it has been translated into many languages and is widely used in health systems all around the world. The term "Root Cause Analysis,", an analysis of the root cause, even if widespread, is misleading because it implies the possibility of tracing the incident back to a single cause. Given the complexity of the healthcare world, this is very difficult because clinical practices are determined by many factors that interact at various levels. The performance outcome is therefore the result of a chain of failures instead of the evident consequence of a single root cause. An even more important objection to the use of the term "Root Cause Analysis" concerns the purpose of the investigation. The analysis of adverse events does not aim, in fact, to search for the cause but for the overall improvement of a system that has not been able to prevent the accident. Of course, it is necessary to understand what happened and why, if only to explain it to the patient and their family. If the purpose is to improve the safety of the system, we must go beyond the cause and reflect on what the accident reveals about the holes and inadequacies of the system in which it occurred.

The incident is a window into the system, a breakdown [28] that allows us to grasp the dynamics which are impalpable when everything is going well: we speak therefore of "System analysis," that is the analysis of interactions within the system in which the events took place. In this sense, the study of cases is not a retrospective search for the root cause, but an attempt to look to the future to prevent risks to patient safety. The root cause is not important because it concerns the past, not the future and risk prevention activities. The shortcomings of the system revealed by the incident remain present until action is taken to remove them, after a careful analysis of the factors that contributed to them.

The London protocol is the model we have adopted for the analysis of cases of adverse events in the context of peer reviews, i.e., audits and mortality and morbidity reviews. The sources of information used to reconstruct the case are the spontaneous reports of the operators, the review of the clinical documentation, or the observations made in the field. The main questions that guide the analysis are:

1. When did it happen? (timeline of events and consequences)
2. What happened? (type of problem and clinical conditions)
3. Why did it happen? (contributory and latent factors)

Although clinical documentation is an excellent source for reconstructing the dynamics of accidents, interviews with the subjects involved in the management of the case under analysis are very important to piece together the reality of the situation because in official documents one sometimes tends to report only non-compromising information. In some cases, on-site observation can help to understand patient flows within the clinical context and critical interactions between professionals and technologies in the real environment.

Once the timeline of events has been reconstructed, through the analysis of clinical docu-

mentations, interviews of people involved in the case and eventual on-site visits, we proceed to the identification of the type of care delivery problems and to the description of the factors that contributed to it.

Care delivery problems are actions, omissions, or deviations in the diagnostic-therapeutic process that have direct or indirect effects on the quality of care. Some problems concern the monitoring of the patient's condition, the timing of the diagnosis, errors in the treatment, etc. Clinical conditions concern basic patient health status and the intrinsic risks of the treatments that contributed to the accident.

Factors that contribute to the event are the conditions in which the accident occurred, inherited from previous decisions by the professionals who were acting in the place and at the time of the adverse event. Any combination of determinants can contribute to a problem in care. Analysts must distinguish the factors relevant only to the particular instance from those that consistently appear in the operational context or throughout the entire organization. For example, there may be a communication problem between two doctors that contributes to an adverse event. If this problem is not usual, it may not require further consideration, but the fact that it has been found indicates shortcomings in the system, which must be explored in order to find a solution and prevent the problem from invalidating the quality of communication in critical situations.

The factors that have contributed to the adverse event are the target of improvement actions, which in some cases are instituted after a single accident, especially when the consequences are very serious. To implement more extensive and costly interventions, it is necessary to collect a series of incidents to detect latent factors that require priority prevention measures. It is advisable to always provide indicators to assess over time the impact of the improvement actions undertaken.

In the Tuscan model, unlike the one proposed by Vincent and colleagues, the analysis of problem type and latent factors [27] takes place in the context of peer meetings with all the actors who have managed the case. In fact, the London protocol requires one or more external analysts to reconstruct the case and analyze it with reference to clinical documentation, interviews with operators, and any observations made in the field. In the Tuscan model, on the other hand, the clinicians, with the help of an internal facilitator prepared for this role, analyze the incidents in their own operational reality. This favors the development of a shared perspective on problems and a commitment to promote and implement improvement initiatives that arise from the analysis, in a more informal atmosphere and focused on individual behaviors through the review of morbidity and mortality, a more profound and detailed way when conducting a significant event audit. Table 11.4 describes the different techniques of incident analysis included in the Tuscan model for patient safety management.

Table 11.4 Tuscan technical standard for patient safety incident analysis

SEA = Significant event audit

SEA is an interdisciplinary and interprofessional peer review method for the in-depth analysis of a single patient safety incident with the aim of identifying improvement actions that concern the different aspects of the system: technology, people, and organization. SEA is inspired by the London Protocol, which provides for the reconstruction of what happened and the circumstances in which the events occurred, the analysis of possible care delivery problems and contributing factors compared with the standards of good practice, the definition and implementation of possible improvement actions. The reconstruction of the chronology of the facts takes place through an individual or group structured dialogue with the operators of the service concerned, the revision of the clinical documentation, and the possible observation in the field of welfare practices. The analysis of the contributing factors and the proposal for possible improvement actions is the product of the group work generally coordinated by an expert facilitator, with the possible support of the staff from the trust patient safety unit.

SEA concludes with the preparation of an Alert Report, which includes:

    1. The summary description of the case examined

    2. The classification of the type of accident

    3. The classification of contributing factors and mitigating factors

    4. The standards and reference bibliography

    5. Any immediate corrective action to take care of patients and family members

    6. Any immediate corrective actions at organizational level to prevent the repetition of the event

    7. Any improvement actions, including quantitative or qualitative monitoring indicators

At SEA can participate external experts to support the analysis of the case and the definition of improvement actions. It is desirable to consider the involvement of patient, family members or representatives of patient associations in the discussion phase of the case and the presentation of the results, as required by the Ministry's Guideline for the Management and Communication of Adverse Events and the Recommendation of the European Council on patient safety. The SEA is part of the continuous training plan and participation is part of the training obligations of health and social-health workers.

M&M = Review of mortality and morbidity

M&M is an interdisciplinary and interprofessional peer review method aimed at periodic analysis of critical clinical cases with the aim of identifying behaviors and practices that can improve criticality management and decrease risk levels. The M&M can be configured as a Review for Security, in which are faced problems of organizational type inside the service that can have repercussions on the safety of the patients, in particular in the structures that do not have functions of type clinical care. Cases or problems are selected by the FQS, taking into account the reports of the operators. The FQS prepares the review meeting by collecting the available documentation and company or literature standards related to the topics to be discussed in a group. At the end of the M&M, a summary report is prepared in which this information is traced: the title of the cases addressed, the brief description of what was analyzed, the reference bibliography, the number, names, profile, and organizational unit to which the participants. M&M is part of the continuous training plan and participation is part of the training obligations of health and social-health workers.

RCA = Root cause analysis

RCA is the structured method for in-depth analysis of sentinel events envisaged by the Ministry of Health under the SIMES protocol. The analysis modality foresees the same phases of the SEA, with the addition of the compilation of a standard questionnaire for the identification of at least one cause or contributing factor, from which must necessarily result a subsequent risk prevention action, subjected to monitoring by the Regional Center for Patient Safety and by the Ministry of Health. RCA is generally conducted by experts in risk management.

11.5 Analysis of Systems and Processes Reliability

The analysis of the cases of adverse events can be illuminating, permitting the detection of deficiencies of the system and the creation of improvement plans following a bottom-up approach. Once the systemic perspective is learned, we can also proceed by adopting a diametrically opposed approach to patient risk analysis. In other words, one can start from the analysis of diagnostic-therapeutic processes instead of one or more cases of accidents that actually occurred, systematically examining the possibilities of failure, following the approach of Human and System Reliability Analysis—HRA [29].

HRA was defined as the application of relevant information to the behavioral characteristics of human beings and of systems to the design of objects, infrastructures, equipment, and environments used in places of life and work. HRA techniques are used both in accident analysis and more generally in the analysis of organizational processes and have been used for over 50 years in high-risk industries and in the military sector. Of these, the most famous is Failure Modes and Effects Analysis (FMEA), which we will discuss later.

HRA techniques are applicable at all stages of the life cycle of a production process. The techniques developed to predict in advance the possible failures of a system and the prevention and containment measures of damages have been associated in particular with the growth of the nuclear power industry [30]. To obtain the consent of populations for the installation of nuclear power plants, the results of risk assessments made with HRA have been widely disseminated, in order to demonstrate the designers' ability to anticipate risks and to reassure the inhabitants of areas near plants. This type of analysis involves the detailed specification of the characteristics of the processes, the quantification of probability and failure modes, the measurements of the possibility of different types of human error, and finally consideration of the effects resulting from all possible combinations of error and system failure, in order to obtain an overall assessment of system security.

Reality has shown on several occasions that this risk assessment method is not sufficient to guarantee the safety of high-risk production processes and even less the safety of workers and inhabitants of areas near plants [31]. The complexity of many safety-critical systems makes an a priori analysis of possible system failures and human errors impossible and unreliable. Despite this, it is considered useful to apply this type of healthcare technique to promote reflection among frontline operators before introducing technical or organizational innovation. For example, before introducing a new procedure, it is useful to reflect on the possible, critical aspects of the different phases of the procedure, or, in the case of technological innovation, back-up solutions can be prepared to deal with any malfunctions of the instrument. Given the tendency towards improvization rather than planning in health practices, the use of HRA techniques can foster the development of systemic thinking aimed at anticipating risk situations and preparing operators to manage them to protect patients.

There are numerous risk prediction techniques that have been developed in the industry, in many cases for commercial purposes, without scientific validation or supporting publications. For those confronting this type of technique, difficulty arises from the use of various acronyms to name instruments that are often similar but originating in different environments, such as FMEA, PSA, PRA, SLIM, HEART, THERP, HAZOP, and other acronyms that in some cases are proprietary variants of the HRA approach [32].

Some techniques are primarily aimed towards the detailed description of a task or a sequence of technical actions. For example, in "hierarchical task analysis," the activity is broken down into a series of tasks, sub-tasks, and operations, down to a considerable level of detail that can be useful to detect the risks of each individual operation, quantify and classify them, and to determine the security measures to be adopted to avoid failure of the task, while also taking into account situational and systemic factors.

The purpose of quantifying the risks is to develop probabilistic models that should allow us to predict errors and to estimate the probability of system failure. Quantification is the most controversial aspect of the HRA because assigning numerical values to uncertain events caused by multiple factors, i.e., the expected probability that an operator makes a mistake, is an enormous challenge from the scientific and the practical point of view. Quantification is often entrusted to the judgment of a group of experts and is not the fruit of rigorous observation of operational practices and of recording the frequency of actual errors. These techniques have a normative character in and of themselves, that is, they tend to describe activities as they should be and errors as can be expected on the basis of "a priori" knowledge of the problems.

They are descriptions of synthetic and nonanalytical things, which therefore cannot take into account the complexity of the operations and the dynamic trend of practices at the sharp end. In healthcare, they have been successfully applied, especially in areas such as the blood transfusion sector that, due to the nature of the activities performed, allow a detailed synthetic description and a precise guide to the application of procedures.

The technique of greatest interest to the health field is the "old" Failure Modes and Effects Analysis (FMEA). Many organizations that promote clinical risk management have proposed its use to assess the risks linked with the various steps of a diagnostic-therapeutic process both proactively and reactively. The FMEA is a methodology that guides security officers in analyzing the criticality of a work-related process and identifying possible improvement actions to reduce the risk of accidents. It is a prevention tool that identifies the weak areas of a process and develops improvement actions based on subjective judgments provided by the process stakeholders. The purpose of the analysis is to understand the risks of a process, i.e., what could go wrong (failure mode) and what the possible consequences could be (failure effects), in order to make the process safer and more efficient.

Created in 1949 by the US military to determine the effects of system and equipment failures, it has been used by NASA since 1960 to predict bankruptcies, and to plan preventive measures and back-up systems for the Apollo space program [29]. Since then, the FMEA has been used in many safety-critical sectors such as the aerospace industry, industrial chemical processes, nuclear and automotive.

FMEA is a particularly flexible and rather simple tool; for this reason, it is sometimes used, in reactive mode, in the analysis of cases together with the systemic model. It is predominantly used in a proactive manner, which requires accredited facilities to perform at least one analysis with FMEA each year.

The application of FMEA in proactive mode involves the description of the steps in a process, failure modes (what could go wrong?), contributory factors (why should failure happen?), and effects of each failure (what could be the consequences of any failure?).

The application of FMEA is divided into seven steps:

1. Select a process to be evaluated with FMEA, bearing in mind that this technique works best for the analysis of linear processes that do not have many sub-processes. In the case of many sub-processes, it is advisable to apply the technique to each individual sub-process.
2. Organize a multidisciplinary group with all the actors who have been involved in the process being analyzed, some of whom may be included only for the part of the analysis that concerns them.
3. Set a meeting to analyze the process starting with the description of steps in the process, trying to describe each phase in a detailed manner and without any bias.
4. For each step of the process, list all the possible failure modes (FM), that is all that could go wrong, including rare and minor problems. Then proceed to identify the possible contributory factors and consequences of each failure mode.
5. For each failure mode identified, have the group assign a numerical value on a scale from 1 to 10 for the frequency of the FM (where 1 represents a very low frequency and 10 a very high one), the severity of the possi-

ble consequences (where 1 represents a low severity and 10 a very high one) and the probability of identifying FM on the part of the operators (where 1 represents a high probability of identification and 10 a low one).

6. Calculate the Risk Priority Index (RPI) for each FM, taking the product of the frequency score (F), the severity score (S), and the probability of identifying the failure by the operators (I). The possible calculation results range from an RPI equal to 1 to an RPI equal to 1000.

7. Define improvement plans, starting from the FM that have accumulated a higher RPI score and therefore require priority interventions.

While defining the improvement plan, it is useful to keep in mind that if the FM has a high frequency it would be advisable to eliminate the contributory factors, or to add technological or organizational constraints, such as a procedure that envisages an independent double control, so as to change the process and reduce the probability of failure. If, on the other hand, the failure mode is difficult to identify by the operators, it is necessary to increase its visibility, for example by an appropriate use of alarms or other warning systems, or by including a passage in a procedure that anticipates the event. Finally, if the failure mode can generate very serious consequences, it is necessary to draw up emergency plans to counteract a decay towards disaster or a repetition of the event at a short, temporal, and spatial distance in the same healthcare facility or in others of the same healthcare system.

11.6 An Integrated Vision of Patient Safety

Due to the limitation of resources available for health systems, in high-income as well as in low- and middle-income countries, risk assessment and the analysis of adverse events can ultimately contribute substantially to the reduction of waste and to the better use of human and technological resources. Many industries have learnt to renew their systems in the crisis, starting from the reduc-

tion of waste and the improvement of the reliability of processes and products. Healthcare systems, in the same way, could emerge from any crisis disseminating the analysis and prevention of risks on the operational lines, with the active involvement of all health professionals and, at the same time, by centralizing patient safety management to embed risk prevention in corporate strategies.

The connection between clinical risks and financial risks related to the direct and indirect costs of adverse events is an indispensable reason for top management to act on patient safety, as highlighted by those institutions and insurance companies that reward health systems that do well and sanction those that fall short, with respect to value for patients as well as accountability of management and health professionals.

In conclusion, patient safety departments or units, clinicians, and citizens must make a common commitment to rethink and reorganize health services, to have the courage to change consolidated habits, and to finally replace the paternalism that has determined for centuries the doctor–patient relationship so that, under a banner of open and transparent communication around the risks and opportunities of every health service, they may walk together through the realm of uncertainty.

References

1. Reason J. Human error. Cambridge: Cambridge University Press; 1990.
2. Reason J. The human contribution: unsafe acts, accidents and heroic recoveries. Farnham Surrey: Ashgate; 2008.
3. Norman D. The psychology of everyday things. New York: Basic Books; 1988.
4. Wenger E. Communities of practice: learning, meaning and Identity. Cambridge: Cambridge University Press; 1998.
5. Beck U. Risikogesellschaft. Auf dem weg in eine andere moderne. Frankfurt a.M.: Suhrkamp; 1986.
6. Hines S, Luna K, Lofthus J, Marquardt M, Stelmokas D. Becoming a high reliability organization: operational advice for hospital leaders. Rockville, MD: Agency for Healthcare Research and Quality; 2008.
7. Carayon P, Hundt AS, Karsh BT, Gurses AP, Alvarado CJ, Smith M, Brennan PF. Work system design for patient safety: the SEIPS model. BMJ Qual Saf. 2006;15(Suppl 1):i50–8.

8. Carayon P, editor. Handbook of human factors and ergonomics in health care and patient safety. 2nd ed. Boca Raton, FL: CRC Press; 2011.

9. Albolino S, Bagnara S, Bellandi T, Llaneza J, Rosal-Lopez G, Tartaglia R, editors. Healthcare systems ergonomics and patient safety 2011. Boca Raton, FL: CRC press; 2011.

10. Vincent C. Patient safety. Chichester: BMJ Books; 2011.

11. Nonaka I, Takeuchi H. The knowledge-creating company: how Japanese companies create the dynamics of innovation. Oxford: Oxford University Press; 1995.

12. Lipitz-Snyderman A, Steinwachs D, Needham DM, Colantuoni E, Morlock LL, Pronovost PJ. Impact of a statewide intensive care unit quality improvement initiative on hospital mortality and length of stay: retrospective comparative analysis. BMJ. 2011;342:d219.

13. Palomar Martínez M, Alvarez Lerma F, Riera Badía MA, León Gil C, López Pueyo MJ, Díaz Tobajas C, Sierra Camerino R, Benítez Ruiz L, Agra Varela Y. Grupo de Trabajo del Estudio Piloto "Bacteriemia Zero". Med Intensiva. 2010;34(9):581–9.

14. Oliver D, Healey F, Haines TP. Preventing falls and fall-related injuries in hospitals. Clin Geriatr Med. 2010;4:645–92.

15. Bellandi T e gruppo di lavoro regionale per la prevenzione delle cadute. La prevenzione delle cadute in ospedale. Pisa: ETS; 2011.

16. Girling AJ, Hofer TP, Wu J, Chilton PJ, Nicholl JP, Mohammed MA, Lilford RJ. Case-mix adjusted hospital mortality is a poor proxy for preventable mortality: a modelling study. BMJ Qual Saf. 2012;12:1052–6.

17. Weick K, Sutcliffe C. Managing the unexpected: assuring high performance in an age of complexity. San Francisco, CA: Jossey-Bass; 2001.

18. Smits M, Janssen J, de Vet R, Zwaan L, Timmermans D, Groenewegen P, Wagner C. Analysis of unintended events in hospitals: inter-rater reliability of constructing causal trees and classifying root causes. Int J Qual Health Care. 2009;4:292–300.

19. Bagian J, King B, Mills P, McKnight S. Improving RCA performance: the Cornerstone Award and the power of positive reinforcement. BMJ Qual Saf. 2011;20:974–82.

20. Yule S, Flin R, Paterson-Brown S, Maran N. Non-technical skills for surgeons in the operating room: a review of the literature. Surgery. 2006;139(2):140–9.

21. Hull L, Arora S, Aggarwal R, Darzi A, Vincent C, Sevdalis N. The impact of nontechnical skills on technical performance in surgery: a systematic review. J Am Coll Surg. 2012;214(2):214–30.

22. Reason J. Human error: models and management. BMJ. 2000;320(7237):768–70.

23. Shappell SA, Wiegmann DA. A human error approach to accident investigation: the taxonomy of unsafe operations. Int J Aviat Psychol. 1997;7(4):269–91.

24. Bellandi T, Albolino S. Human factors and ergonomics for a safe transition to digital health. Stud Health Technol Inform. 2019;265:12–21.

25. Vincent C, Taylor-Adams S, Stanhope N. Framework for analysing risk and safety in clinical medicine. BMJ. 1998;316(7138):1154–7.

26. Taylor-Adams S, Vincent C. Systems analysis of clinical incidents: the London protocol. Clin Risk. 2004;10(6):211–20.

27. Bellandi T, Tartaglia R, Albolino S. The Tuscany's model for clinical risk management. In: Tartagllia R, editor. Healthcare systems ergonomics and patient safety. London: Taylor and Francis; 2005. p. 94–100.

28. Winograd T, Flores F. Understanding computers and cognition: a new foundation for design. Norwood, NJ: Intellect Books; 1986.

29. Kirwan B. A guide to practical human reliability assessment. London: CRC Press; 2017.

30. Slovic P. The perception of risk. London: Routledge; 2016.

31. Perrow C. Normal accidents: Living with high-risk technologies. Updated ed. Princeton University Press: Princeton, NJ; 2011.

32. Lyons M, Adams S, Woloshynowych M, Vincent C. Human reliability analysis in healthcare: a review of techniques. Int J Risk Saf Med. 2004;16(4):223–37.

From Theory to Real-World Integration: Implementation Science and Beyond

12

Giulia Dagliana, Sara Albolino, Zewdie Mulissa, Jonathan Davy, and Andrew Todd

12.1 Introduction

12.1.1 Characteristics of Healthcare and Its Complexity

The increasing complexity and dynamicity of our society (and world of work) have meant that healthcare systems have and continue to change and consequently the state of healthcare systems continues to assume different characteristics. The causes of mortality are an excellent example of this rapid transformation: non-communicable diseases have become the leading cause of death, according to World Health Organization (WHO) data, but at the same time there are new problems emerging such as infectious diseases, like Ebola or some forms of influenza, which occur unexpectedly or without advanced warning. Many of these new diseases diffuse rapidly through the different parts of the globe due to the increasingly interconnected nature of the world. Another example of the healthcare transformation is the innovation associated with the introduction and development of advanced communication and technology systems (such as minimally invasive surgery and robotics, transplantation, automated antiblastic preparation) at all levels of care. Consequently, the social and technical dimensions of healthcare are becoming more and more complex and provide a significant challenge for all the stakeholders in the system to make sense of and ensure high quality healthcare. These stakeholders include but are not limited to patients and their families, caregivers, clinicians, managers, policymakers, regulators, and politicians. It is an inescapable truth that Humans are always going to be part of the healthcare systems, and it is these human, who by their very nature introduce variability and complexity to the system (we do not necessarily view this as a negative and this chapter will illustrate). A microlevel a central relationship in focus is that between the clinician and the patient, two human beings, making the health system a very peculiar organization compared to similarly high-risk organizations such as aviation or nuclear energy. This double human being system [1] requires significant effort (good design) in managing unpredictability through the development of personal and organization skills, such as the ability to react positively and rapidly to unexpected events and to adopt a resilient strategy for survival and advancement. In contrast to other

G. Dagliana (✉) · S. Albolino
Centre for Clinical Risk Management and Patient Safety, Tuscany Region—WHO Collaborating Centre in Human Factors and Communication for the Delivery of Safe and Quality Care, Florence, Italy
e-mail: daglianag@aou-careggi.toscana.it

Z. Mulissa
Institute for Healthcare Improvement,
Addis Ababa, Ethiopia

J. Davy · A. Todd
Human Kinetics and Ergonomics, Rhodes University, Makhanda, South Africa

© The Author(s) 2021
L. Donaldson et al. (eds.), *Textbook of Patient Safety and Clinical Risk Management*,
https://doi.org/10.1007/978-3-030-59403-9_12

similar industries, in terms of level of risk and system safety, healthcare settings are still plagued by numerous errors and negative events involving humans (and other elements) at various levels within the system. The emotional involvement is very high due to the exposure to social relationships daily and results in significant challenges to address both technical and non-technical issues simultaneously.

The context becomes a key element for understanding how to find a balance in this continuous struggle to manage the social and technical aspects of the healthcare system, to standardize the evidence-based clinical process and personalization of the care related to the diversity of the patients. The analysis of the situational characteristics is vital to understanding how to apply solutions that consider the peculiar dynamicity of healthcare settings. It is also important to underline that, among the general acknowledged diversity, there are some settings which have similar patients and common practices, different risks and a different way to look at safety [2]. The implications are that each context in which care is provided presents with its own unique challenges, practices, risks, and approaches to promote safety. Thus, risk identification and analysis, quality and safety strategies should also be different according to the contextual nuances. For example, a trauma center cannot have the same strategy to improve safety as a blood transfusion service: the trauma center is based on managing the unexpected due to emergency situations while the blood transfusion process is more a planned standardized process. In the trauma center to stay safe, you have to adapt and develop team-based skills, in a blood service you need to make sure the blood is not contaminated and is administered to the right person, and this work that you can easily standardize. This complexity and diversity of healthcare is the main characteristic to keep in mind when trying to understand healthcare systems, and it should be included in any design of the system and in any research intervention project and thus to be able to define effective actions for improvement. Therefore, the purpose of this chapter is to firstly highlight some of the key issues in healthcare relating to adverse events and

medical errors. Secondly, to discuss the approaches adopted to ensure quality and safety in healthcare, including some of the new approaches being advocated in the human factors and ergonomics community. Lastly, we will provide some suggests for opening a discussion on the way forward through the integration of various approaches into a coherent transdisciplinary view of healthcare.

12.1.2 Epidemiology of Adverse Events and Medical Errors

According to the last Consensus Study Report released by The National Academies of Sciences, Engineering and Medicine "*Crossing the Global Quality Chasm Improving Health Care Worldwide*" healthcare in all global settings today suffers from high levels of deficiencies in quality across many domains, causing ongoing harm to human health [3]. According to WHO global estimates, at least five patients die every minute because of unsafe care. In High Income Countries (HICs), the incidence of adverse events is approximately 9%, of which around 60% could be prevented [4]. A recent Organization for Economic Co-operation and Development (OECD) analysis found that 15% of all hospital costs in OECD nations are due to patient harm from adverse events [5].

In countries with limited resources, every year there are 134 million adverse events related to unsafe care, causing more than 2.6 million deaths annually. Many of these adverse events are largely preventable as they result from unsafe treatment systems, and not patient pathology. In a study on frequency and preventability of adverse events, across 26 low- and middle-income countries, the rate of adverse events was around 8%, of which 83% could have been prevented and most alarmingly 30% led to death [6].

In low- and middle-income countries, a combination of unfavorable factors such as understaffing, inadequate structures and overcrowding, lack of healthcare infrastructure/resources, a shortage of basic equipment, and poor hygiene and sanitation are common place, all of which can be attributed to limited financial resources, contribute to unsafe patient care. A weak safety and quality culture, flawed processes of care and disinterested leadership teams further weaken the ability of healthcare systems and organizations to ensure the provision of safe and effective healthcare [7].

Errors can be classified according to their outcome, the setting where they take place (e.g., inpatient versus outpatient), the kind of procedure involved (medication, surgery, etc.) or the probability of occurrence (high versus low). Error categories are analyzed by taking into consideration their prevalence, avoidance, and associated factors as well as the different strategies for detecting medical errors [8]. Among the problems that commonly occur in healthcare provision are adverse drug events, improper transfusions, misdiagnoses, under and over treatment, unsafe injection practices, surgical injuries and wrong-site surgery, radiation errors involving overexposure to radiation and cases of wrong-patient and wrong-site identification, sepsis, venous thromboembolism, unsafe care in mental health settings including use of restraint, suicide, absconding and reduced capacity for self-advocacy; falls, pressure ulcers, and mistaken patient identities. High error rates with serious consequences are most likely to occur in intensive care units, operating rooms and emergency departments. Medical errors are also associated with extremes of age, new procedures, urgency and severity of medical condition being treated [9–12]. Medical errors occur right across the spectrum of the assistance process, from prescription to administration and can be attributed to both the social and technical components of the system. In spite of the high prevalence of medical errors and the very evident harm to patients, in many contexts, fear around the reporting of these errors is commonplace, which in turn impedes progress and learning for improvement and error prevention [13].

12.1.2.1 Barriers to Safe Practice in Healthcare Settings

The experience of countries that are heavily engaged in national efforts to reduce error and increase safe provision of healthcare services, clearly demonstrate that, although health systems differ from country to country, many threats to patient safety have similar causes and often similar solutions. Zecevic (2017) and Farokhzadian (2018) identified the following barriers to safe care provision: heavy workloads, lack of time, lack of resources and poor communication, inadequate organizational infrastructure, insufficient leadership effectiveness, inadequate efforts to keep pace with national and international standards and overshadowed values of team participation [14, 15]. Leape and Berwick (2005) argue that the barriers to the reduction of errors in the context of healthcare remain rooted in the nature and the culture of medicine. Regarding the context of healthcare, the shear complexity of the system, given the many different specialties and parts of the system that are involved in the care process, increases the likelihood of poor interactions and risk of failure [16]. Linked to this, with respect to the culture of medicine, continued professional fragmentation and a lack of teamwork, characterized by different medical specialists or parts of the care process continuing to work in silos, further contribute to the risk of errors in the healthcare system, as found by Hignett et al. (2018) in their study of barriers to the provision of effective healthcare in England. This status quo is perpetuated by a very strong hierarchical, authoritarian structure and the perceived threat that enhanced collaboration and communication may undermine or threaten professional independence and autonomy [16]. Poor or disturbed communication (due to fragmented work structure and poor design of the physical environment, respectively) also present additional barriers to effective and safe practice [17].

Aligned to this is the continued culture of fear around reporting of mistakes or errors made, given the person-centered blame culture that Leape and Berwick (2005) and more recently, Holden (2009) maintains still very much a part of most industries, including aviation and healthcare. In response to this, there is still a need for the development of effective and appropriate reporting and learning systems [18, 19], which, if introduced alongside a just culture, may play an important role in identifying systemic weaknesses, which Woods and Cook

(2002) argue is a more effective method of recovering from errors than identifying problematic or "flawed humans" (p. 140). However, in their small study, Mitchell et al. (2016) report that poor reporting processing, a lack of engagement on the part of medical staff to report, poor or no feedback and inaction on events reported, a lack of institution level support and funding and inadequate integration and leveraging of ever-changing health information technology remain as barriers to effective reporting and learning system development and integration.

12.1.3 Error and Barriers to Safety: The Human or the System?

In 1999, the Institute of Medicine (IOM) released a landmark report—to Err is Human, which many authors argue was a turning point for patient safety in the United States and more globally [20]. Amongst many important recommendations, significant points outlined in the report included the fact that errors, although common and costly, can be prevented to improve patient safety, provided that the systems-related contributory factors to these errors become the focus of addressing safety issues in healthcare (IOM 1999). While many commentators argue that there is an increased appreciation of the systemic nature of errors in the healthcare setting [16, 18–20] some still assert that, unfortunately, there is a very prevalent person-centered blame culture in high reliability organizations such as aviation and healthcare, which to some extent is a "psychological tendency and an industry norm" [21]. This way of thinking and error assignment is referred to by Reason (2000) and Dekker (2002) as person approach, which holds that errors occur because of unwanted human variability and fallibility that happens in safe system. This view of error stresses that people working at the sharp end perform unsafe acts, characterized by various errors and violations that arise from abnormal cognitive processes such as forgetfulness and inattention, which can only be rectified by reducing human variability, setting better boundaries through training and discipline and possibly even naming and shaming [22, 23].

In contrast, as highlighted by the IOM and other authors [22, 23] errors can be better understood by taking a systems approach or view. This holds that safety is an emergent property of the way in which a system is designed and not a product of the action of its individual components [21, 24]. From this perspective, errors which occur at the sharp end, are the result of a host of latent systemic conditions or design flaws, or what Reason refers to as "resident pathogens" (2000; p. 769) and active failures of people while performing their work. Therefore, it is not necessarily the human who causes the error (no matter the context) but rather the human's interactions with the broader system (the tools, tasks, environment, other people in a certain organizational framework and context) which, if the system has latent failures, result in the occurrence of error. Woods and Cook (2002) stress that in order to recover from error there is a need to search for systemic vulnerabilities, while understanding work as it is performed at the sharp end. This enables the detection of latent failures within the design of the system by those who operate within in it, a critical step to informing decision-makers on what needs to be prioritized to improve safety and reduce the likelihood of the same thing happening again.

Effectively, it is critical to understand whether there is compatibility between the social side of work (humans, their beliefs and cultures) and the technical side of work (how it is designed organized and actually executed). This requires an appreciation of sociotechnical systems theory, which is expanded below. Additionally, as articulated in the seminal paper by Rasmussen (1997), to effectively manage risk associated with work, no matter the context, there is a need to consider the various levels of stakeholders involved in the control, regulation, and execution of work. This is captured in Rasmussen's Hierarchical Risk Management Framework, which stresses the importance of the vertical integration of knowledge and decisions across all stakeholders (which, in this model include Government, Regulators, Company executives, and management and staff at the sharp end) [25]. In other words, knowledge and actions of how work is done and its associated challenges at the sharp end should be communicated up the hierarchy to inform decisions made higher up. Equally, decisions at higher levels should also influence the decisions and action at lower levels [25, 26]. This repeated assertion of the need for vertical integration between different levels of stakeholders within systems, support calls from other authors [16, 18–20] who all argue for more national and institutional support for programs aimed at enhancing patient safety, combined with a continued need for multidisciplinary scientific research and management teams. This research, as asserted by Bindman et al. (2018) and Bates and Singh (2018), should be embedded within the context of specific healthcare systems and contribute to the better understanding of problems within specific systems, solutions for which can be developed through learning laboratories and pilot interventions *in situ*. In order to become more responsive to the calls to understand error from a systemic perspective in the context of healthcare (rather than just as the fault of the human), while fostering better cross-field and cross-hierarchy collaboration amongst relevant stakeholders, the application of different methods, such as implementation science, ethnography, and Human Factors and Ergonomics, may provide a more holistic overview of the challenges within different context. This knowledge can then be leveraged to develop context-specific and culturally sensitive interventions. Following sections therefore highlight these important approaches for ensuring quality and safety in healthcare systems.

12.2 Approaches to Ensuring Quality and Safety

12.2.1 The Role of Implementation Science and Ethnography in the Implementation of Patient Safety Initiatives

Treating and caring for people in a safe environment and protecting them from healthcare-related avoidable harm should be national and interna-

tional priorities, calling for concerted international efforts [13]. Achieving a culture of safety requires an understanding of the values, attitudes, beliefs, and norms that are important to healthcare organizations and what attitudes and behaviors are appropriate and expected for patient safety [27]. Differences between contexts (e.g., policies, culture, and healthcare organization characteristics) may explain variations in the effects of patient safety solutions implementation. Problematically, knowledge of which contextual features are important determinants of patient safety solutions is limited. The lack of understanding could in part be due to the complex nature of unpacking context. As Øvretveit and colleagues have reported (2011), few studies assessed the effect of context on the implementation of safety and quality interventions. In the field of patient safety research, there is little evidence or consensus around which contexts are the most salient for patient safety practice implementation and which contextual factors impact improvement interventions [28]. At the same time, it is hard to identify a unique model for designing and implementing safety interventions that can build a sufficient understanding of highly complex systems such healthcare. Implementation science is one of the most recognized frameworks for transferring evidence-based solutions from the theory of the research to the everyday life of the real world at the frontline. Implementation research is indeed defined in the literature as "the scientific study of methods to promote the systematic uptake of research findings and other evidence-based practices into routine practice, and, hence, to improve the quality and effectiveness of health services. It includes the study of influences on healthcare professional and organizational behavior" [29].

The aim of implementation research is broader than traditional clinical research as it proposes a systemic analysis not limited solely to assessing the effect of the introduction of a new variable, but rather to verify how this variable impacts on operators, the organization, the physical environment, and up to the highest level of health policies [30]. Implementation-research studies and ethnographic methods of investigation, applied for research in patient safety and clinical risk management, have stressed the importance of organizational and cultural characteristics of the context in the implementation process of intervention. At the core of implementation research lies the idea that every improvement solution has to be oriented to bring an organizational and behavioral improvement triggering virtuous processes toward safety that over time become part of the heritage of the system [31]. Therefore, interventions to improve patient safety would be most effective when developed by those with local "expertise" and local knowledge, while taking into account evidence-based solutions from other contexts [32]. Local expertise and knowledge are indeed critical resources for understanding of what is culturally appropriate, the different priorities and capacities to answer the needs of the populations (resources and infrastructures), and the characteristics and relationships of different health system stakeholders.

According to this approach, the analysis tends to be more holistic, system oriented and amenable to adaptation rather than simply assessing the impact of change factors on the individual components of the system [33]. Here the complexity is not explained in terms of the sum of the individual parts, but in terms of the relationships between the software (non-physical resources such as organizational policies and procedures), hardware (physical resources as workplace, equipment, tools), environment (such as climate, temperature, socioeconomic factors), and liveware (human-related elements as teamwork, leadership, communication, stress, culture), the so-called SHELL model [34].

Implementation science provides research designs that combine methods of quantitative analysis and qualitative investigation. Both qualitative and quantitative methods are essential during the development phase of the intervention and during the evaluation. They combine epidemiological data with an ethnographic analysis [35]. The relevance of ethnographic studies has been highlighted in patient safety since the publication of several reports during the 1970s in the United States [36]. These qualitative studies enable the analysis of the traditional structures and cultural aspects by using methods such as interviews (semi-structured, structured), observation (direct or video), and focus groups [37]. The added value of the ethnographic method lies in its ability to analyze what actually happens in the care settings, to understand how the work is actually done rather than the work as imagined and prescribed [38]. This helps to identify factors and variables that can influence the process at different stakeholder levels, namely patient, caregiver, department, structure, organization, community, and political decision-makers [30].

Several models for translating the implementation science approach into practice have been defined by international agencies and organizations working in the field of safety and quality of care. Some focused on how to build bidirectional collaboration for improvement between stakeholders in different geographical areas and in particular between HICs and LMICs—with one such example being the World Health Organization (WHO) Twinning partnership for improvement (TPI) model [39]. Other approaches focused more on the process to be followed in order to propose safety solutions that are suitable for the specific context, respondent to multidisciplinarity, scalable, sustainable, and adaptable to context and user-needs changes—for example, the Institute for Healthcare Improvement (IHI)'s Collaborative Breakthrough [40] model, while the International Ergonomics Association (IEA) General Framework Model [41] is oriented to understanding the interactions among humans and other elements of a system in order to optimize human well-being and overall system performance. The following sections provide a brief outline of each of these approaches.

12.2.1.1 WHO Twinning Partnership for Improvement (TPI) Model

The hospital-to-hospital model developed in the WHO African Partnership for Patient Safety (APPS) program provides the foundation on which the "Twinning partnership for improvement" was developed. APPS aimed to build sustainable patient safety partnerships between hospitals in countries of the WHO African Region and hospitals in other regions. TPI takes the learning and experience from across the African region and moves the role of partnership working into new and critical areas to support the development of quality, resilient, and universal health services [39]. At the heart of this model is the fact that partnerships provide a vehicle for dialogue that generates ideas and opportunities to address the multiple barriers to improvement. The focus on solution generation co-developed by hospital partnerships support improvement and generates mutual benefits to all parties involved. The TPI approach to improvement is based on a six-step cycle and facilitates the development of partnerships, the systematic identification of patient safety gaps, and the development of an action plan and evaluation cycle according to the following steps:

1. Partnership development that supports the establishment of fully functioning, communicative twinning relations between two or more health institutions.
2. Needs assessment that allows the baseline situation to be captured, so priority technical areas can be identified to form the basis for an evaluation of the implemented activities.
3. Gap analysis that allows for the identification of key priority areas for focused improvement efforts.
4. Action planning that provides twinning partnerships with the opportunity to jointly agree and develop targeted action plans.
5. Action is the stage of the implementation of the agreed plan of activity with focused action on both arms of the twinning partnership to help deliver effective health services.
6. Evaluation and review enables twinning partnerships to assess, against their baseline, the impact of both their technical improvement work.

12.2.1.2 Institute for Healthcare Improvement Breakthrough Collaborative

A reference model widely used for the implementation of improvement interventions is the Collaborative Breakthrough model proposed by the Institute for Healthcare Improvement [40].

The principle that underlies the use of this model is that for every intervention to be successful it must be adapted to the context, taking into account the organizational and cultural specifics and the available human and economic resources. Once the area that needs improvement has been identified, actions must be based on evidence in literature, solutions promoted by international actors or experiences already made in other contexts and that have already produced evidence of effectiveness. Multidisciplinary groups of experts evaluate the hypothesized solutions with respect to the available literature, reference standards, and characteristics of the context of application. Social, organizational, anthropological, economic, human factors, and ergonomics knowledge, combined with the clinical knowledge can facilitate a better understanding of the emergent characteristics of the system, which in turn can develop interventions that try to take into account the complexity of the system. According to the model, each intervention—which could be an organizational change, the implementation of a new cognitive support tool or a tool for decision-making—become the object of a pilot project in the specific context and evaluated in terms of usability, feasibility, and impact on quality and safety. In this phase, the Plan-Do-Study-Act model (reference) allows the improvement hypothesis to be periodically reassessed and reformulated in relation to what emerges from the study phase. In the evaluation phase, qualitative and quantitative methods of analysis can be used: questionnaires, interviews, field observations along with pre-post intervention prospective analysis. The results of the tests and the analysis of the data are the basis for a possible redesign of the solution to make it more appropriate for the context of application.

12.2.1.3 Case Study: Kenya

The Centre for Clinical Risk Management and Patient Safety—WHO Collaborating Centre in Human Factors and Communication of the Delivery of Safe and Quality Care (Italy), in collaboration with the Centre for Global Health of the Tuscany Region and the University Hospital of Siena in 2015 promoted a partnership with a hospital in Kenya with focus on patient safety and quality improvement. The operative approach promoted for introducing improvement solutions and strategies in the hospital combined the WHO African Partnership for patient safety approach with the Institute of Healthcare Improvement Collaborative Breakthrough model. Following the six-step cycle approach of the APPS, on the ground quantitative self-assessment, a gap analyses and need assessment were conducted, from which it emerged that there was a need to work on the safety and quality of maternal and neonatal care. Partners thus decided to focus on building a collaborative project for the implementation of the Safe Childbirth Checklist and to evaluate the locally adapted version of the tool in terms of impact on safety and quality, its usability, and feasibility.

The process of implementation has combined the Collaborative Breakthrough model and the Twinning Partnership for Improvement and has foreseen the following steps:

1. Evaluation of the specific characteristics of the context in terms of: safety culture, resources and technology available, organization of the work, work flows, characteristics of the workers, their relations and needs, cognitive workload.
2. Administration of a questionnaire to assess the level of maturity of the safety culture (Surveys on Patient Safety Culture™ (SOPS™) Hospital Survey released by the Agency for Healthcare Research and Quality (AHRQ) [42].
3. Creation of a multidisciplinary group for the personalization of the SCC: gynecologists, midwives, and nurses form the maternal and child department, safety and quality team of the hospital, quality and safety, and HFEs experts from partner institution.
4. Coaching of the frontline workers on the use of the SCC tool.
5. Six-month piloting of the SCC.
6. Evaluation of the impact of the SCC on some selected process indicators related to the care delivered to the mother and the new-born.
7. Administration of a questionnaire to evaluate the usability and feasibility of the tool.
8. Application of the PDSA for re-evaluating the first version of the SCC and re-customization of the tool according to the results of clinical record review and the usability questionnaire.

The analyses of the AHRQ Hospital Survey on Patient Safety administrated to a group of 50 hospital workers to measure their perception about patient safety issues, medical errors, and reporting showed that workers felt that top management was committed to improving patient safety and that this represented a positive platform for developing quality and safety interventions. Additionally, about 50% of the staff associate the occurrence of an adverse event to potentially being blamed rather than the event being used as a learning opportunity. Linked to this, most of the health workers reported that there is a limited culture of reporting events related to near-misses and that when a few adverse events have been reported and discussed, this produces positive change. Lastly, staff indicated that they wanted to be part of a positive environment for teamwork and collaboration with top management.

The second source of evaluation of the introduction of the SCC was a questionnaire administrated to users aiming at understanding whether the checklist was usable, coherent with the workflow and work organization, whether it overloaded workers or it facilitate communication, teamwork, and adherence to best clinical practices. The result of the questionnaire showed that: 70% of the midwives considers the checklist easy or very easy to us; 56% said that the tool had significantly improved their practice around childbirth, and 50% reported that it had significantly improved communication and teamwork.

Finally, the evaluation of the impact of the SCC on quality and safety of care was conducted through a prospective pre- and post-intervention clinical records review on a randomly selected sample of clinical records. The analyses shown that the introduction of tool had led to a significant increase in the evaluation of heart rate during pre-partum, the administration of the antibiotic therapy in case of mother's temperature >38° or in case of membranes' rupture >24 h, the administration of antihypertensive treatment in case of diastolic blood pressure >120 [43].

12.2.2 Challenges and Lessons Learned from the Field Experience and the Need for More Extensive Collaboration and Integration of Different Approaches

The implementation of the Safe Childbirth Checklist in Kenya represented one of the first attempts to merge internationally validated models for quality and safety improvement in healthcare. The positive results obtained in terms of clinical and organizational outcomes demonstrated that the integration of the two models can give significant support for understanding and identifying *what* should be done to promote improvement, what kind of interventions are the most suitable and effective for a specific context. Following the TPI six-step cycle and the QI approach, it is possible to describe the level of maturity of a system in terms of safety culture and safety "logistics" (needs assessment); to identify possible gaps in the care process and the clinical areas where an intervention is necessary; to plan actions according to the gap analyses and act according to the characteristics of the environment while testing hypotheses aimed at improvement and possible prototypes. However, the understanding of the key technical and social aspects that required changing for effective implementation were not always made explicit by these approached. Therefore, what needs to be further investigate and discussed is how HFE can become a driving component of safety and quality improvement programs. A more HFE-oriented approach aimed at promoting behavioral changes toward safer healthcare systems, could promote a deeper understanding of technical, socioeconomic, political and environmental sub-systems when trying to build an understanding of the work system characteristics. Moreover, a more comprehensive understanding of the relation between all the component of the systems, different stakeholders that act in the context at different levels, their relation and needs could help to scale-up solution from the local to the national level keeping a bottom-up approach for the design of the solution. In other words, HFE could make it explicit *how* to make changes toward safety of care happen, how to fit theory into the real world, in the specific context, taking into account peculiarities of the system and promoting multidisciplinary collaboration for facing, in an holistic manner, multidimensional issues such as those that arise from a high-complexity systems as the healthcare.

12.2.3 Human Factors and Ergonomics

According to the International Ergonomics association "Ergonomics (or human factors) is the scientific discipline concerned with the understanding of interactions among humans and other elements of a system, and the profession that applies theory, principles, data and methods to design in order to optimize human well-being and overall system performance." Wilson (2014) further argues that HFE has six fundamental notions that define the approach that should be adopted by practitioners and researchers: (1) Systems approach; (2) Context; (3) Interactions; (4) Holism; (5) Emergence; (6) Embedding. In other words, HFE takes a systems approach that acknowledges the importance of context, emergence and holism in elucidating interactions between various system elements and developing this understanding requires being embedded in the system. This suggests that HFE should always be embedded in the practice of healthcare for effective patient safety and therefore HFE (and consequently those responsible for implementation) should be viewed as part of the organization and not as outside consultants. At the heart of the embedded approach to HFE is the participation of all key stakeholders and subject matter experts [44]. In fact, participatory ergonomics is well established, for example, almost 20 years ago

Haines et al. (2002) proposed and validated a participatory ergonomics framework. The participatory ergonomics approach focuses on the involvement of people in both the planning and controlling a significant amount of their own work activities. This is coupled ensuring that they have sufficient knowledge and power to have an influence on processes and outcomes [45]. Due to the focus on and acknowledgment of stakeholders at all levels in the system HFE also promotes a micro, meso, and macro view of the system. At a micro level, the focus would be on the individual and their interactions with their task (e.g., between a nurse and their patient), while the meso level takes a slightly broader view at a group or team level and their interaction with work. Lastly, at the macro level the characteristics of the whole system is taken into account and organizational factors need to be considered. Important models at this level of analysis would be those developed by Rasmussen (1997), the specifics of which are discussed elsewhere in this chapter as they promote both a top-down and bottom-up approach.

Human factors and ergonomics has its focus on the interactions between humans, technologies, and organizations within a physical and cultural environment. Fundamental notions of HFE mean that the tools and methods that support the implementation of patient safety interventions can be adapted to the context needs of local stakeholders. Further the approach considers the interaction with healthcare operators, acknowledging several dimensions of the implementation site at the different level of the system: micro, meso, and macro (i.e., it promotes a systemic view of the implementation process). The main interactions are those that are derived from the complexity of the system and in particular hospital organization (design of clinical pathways, healthcare operator workloads and shifts, protocols, procedures, tasks, and activities), environment/physical organization (facilities, furniture and device design; technical and economic resources) and human aspects influencing care delivery (religion, customs, social behaviors, social organization, social hierarchies).

From a healthcare perspective the dual outcomes of HFE could be reoriented as patient outcomes (quality of care and patient safety) and employee and organization outcomes [46]. Importantly, HFE acknowledges the interdependence of these two outcomes. That is, in order to promote patient safety outcomes it is necessary to promote organizational outcomes (including the well-being of those working within these organizations). The ability of HFE to support these two outcomes is dependent on its understanding of sociotechnical systems theory and its values. Considering the clear social and technical characteristics of healthcare highlighted earlier in this chapter, an understanding of sociotechnical systems theory is of obvious benefit here. Clegg (2000) argued that sociotechnical systems theory "has at is core the notion that the design and performance of new systems can be improved, and indeed can only work satisfactorily, if the social and the technical are bought together and treated as interdependent aspects of a work system." Human factors and ergonomics practitioners therefore take the technical (processes, tasks and technology used to transform inputs to outputs), social (attributes of people (such as skills, attitudes, values), relationships among people, reward systems) and environmental sub-systems (outside influences such as stakeholders) into account when trying to build an understanding of the work system characteristics. Sociotechnical systems principles were first proposed by Cherns in 1976 and have subsequently been developed by several authors including Clegg (2000). Recently, Read et al. proposed a set of values for HFE and sociotechnical systems theory based on these principles:

1. Humans as assets
2. Technology as a tool to assist humans
3. Promotion of quality of life
4. Respect for individual differences
5. Responsibility to all stakeholders

HFE therefore places an emphasis on seeing the humans within the system (patients, caregivers, etc.) as assets rather than "problems" or potential for introducing error. These principles and values are again consistent both with the participatory ergonomics principles and with recent calls for transdisciplinary teams focused on engaging with all relevant stakeholders. It is therefore clear that HFE is a salient discipline for the problems faced by the healthcare system relating to patient safety.

The application of the HFE participatory approach within healthcare has been extensively researched with Hignett et al. (2005) illustrating the numerous benefits associated with such an approach. Within the context of this book chapter, the ability of participatory ergonomics tactics to promote transdisciplinarity in team characteristics [47], is also an important consideration [46]. This is vital as earlier aspects of this chapter highlight the increasing need for transdisciplinary team collaboration for solving complex healthcare and patient safety issues. Unfortunately, currently HFE is only well established in the West and has little traction in many countries in the Global South (see Thatcher and Todd 2019 for further details [46]). Furthermore, when there are multinational transdisciplinary teams working in healthcare in emerging economies, the nature of the collaboration is typically poor; this is in spite of good practice frameworks existing. Schneider and Maleka (2018) and Hedt-Gauthier et al. (2018) have both illustrated the problematic nature of these relationships in healthcare. These problems are not isolated to healthcare settings, with Thatcher and Todd (2019) that it is necessary to foster respectful progress through a program of action that acknowledges the lessons that the people of the Global South can teach the North.

12.3 Way Forward

12.3.1 International Ergonomics Association General Framework Model

International Ergonomics Association in response the problems identified above has developed a General Framework Model that is focused on using the values of HFE to guide their interactions and collaborative development efforts in LMICs. Evidence of patient safety interventions have been mainly based on high cost projects in HICs. This evidence needs translation and adaptation when developed for LMICs. Human Factors and Ergonomics (HFE) and in particular the IEA General Framework Model are the suggested research approaches to adapt tools to the context within which they will be applied. Indeed Thatcher and Todd (2019) recently argued that training and implementation models must focus on up skilling local capacity allowing LIC and LMIC countries to solve their own problems, thus recognizing the emergent characteristics of patient safety issues and the emergent nature of organizational culture. The IEA approach is consistent with this and is underpinned by several philosophical standpoints published in the international development standing committee of the IEA triennial report from 2018. These focus on:

1 An engagement with, and understanding of, how knowledge and technology are effectively diffused across countries. That is, diffusion occurs within sociotechnical systems and as such should be negotiated, enabled, and diffused (Greenhalgh et al. 2004)

2 Using the relationship between stakeholders, emergence and networks as promoted by Wheatley and Frieze to promote the development of communities of good practice and then translate these into systems of influence

3 Closer alignment and integration of science and practice

The IEA general framework model was developed based on the aforementioned principles and focused on the provision of a participatory framework to facilitate the systematic design of HFE-related projects. The GFM outlined in Fig. 12.1 although presented in an eight step model is in fact a highly iterative process, as the characteristics at one step are made explicit they may require the reexamination of previous steps. For example as the understanding of who stakeholders are (step 4) and what the relationships are between stakeholders (step 5) is devel-

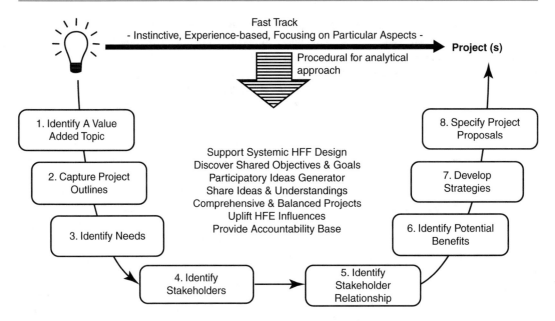

Fig. 12.1 International Ergonomics Association model for the promotion of collaboration across multiple stakeholders within a system

oped so the understanding of what a value-added topic is (step 1) and what the actual needs are (step 3) may need to be refined. Through this iterative process, the various stakeholders within the system are able to discover shared objectives and goals, and consequently collaborate in the generation of ideas on the solutions to be implemented within the constraints of system they are attempting to shape. The framework therefore promotes an interrogation of the social characteristics of the system (through a detailed examination of the various stakeholders and their relationships to each other) and how the technical aspects of the system can be aligned with the strengths and weaknesses of various stakeholders through the development of benefits and implementation strategies. The framework also promotes the use of contextually appropriate tools and methods at each step that meet the requirements of elucidating the necessary information. For example, in more advanced systems the initial steps (1–3) can be facilitated through the use of existing HFE tools such as cognitive work analysis, while in less mature systems alternative tools may be more appropriate.

As mentioned in Sect. 12.2.2 and as emerged from the overview on barriers and facilitating factors that can influence the positive results of an improvement project, context, and its actors (stakeholders) represent the main elements to take into account when designing and implementing solutions. This requires an appreciation of both the social and technical components of the system within which the improvement project is to take place. Therefore, just understanding the context is not sufficient for the success of interventions that aim at creating a long-lasting behavioral change that become part of the cultural heritage of a specific system and a shared and recognized attitude. In order to make this cultural change lasting over time, it has to be embedded in the system, it need to be thought of, designed, and implemented by actors that participate in the system, that are part of the system and that are recognized as to be parts of that systems. Furthermore, the emerging characteristics of safety and culture need to be taken into account, and those that remain within the system once the improvement project is complete need to be empowered to understand the system and to respond appropriately to new emergent problems.

Considering the case study on the introduction of the SCC in one hospital of Kenya, we argue that the application of the GFM model would have possibly represented for the implementers a fundamental step before the start of the collaborative to better understand the sociotechnical characteristics of the setting and thus reduce possible challenges and improve the sustainability of improvement made. At the beginning of the project, no HFE experts where available within the hospital nor experts in safety and quality of care. External experts with little knowledge about the particular characteristics of and the level of maturity of the systems in terms of safety culture and safety "logistic" would have been facilitated in the understanding *how* to make the new improvement solution working in the everyday local way of working at the frontline by the application of the GFM. This would be an initial step in ensuring that all local stakeholders are identified, valued, empowered, and included in problem identification and solution finding. As such an important first step in the process of making HFE knowledge and principles (and for that matter safety and quality healthcare) available on the ground through transfer of knowledge and coaching would have taken place.

For sure the bottom-up approach followed in the introduction of the SCC has been made possible to have a direct participation of hospitals stakeholders from the very beginning of the project but to date it has not be sufficient in order to turning it into a large-scale project and to involve also macro-systems level actors such as institutional bodies.

As we continue to seek to improve the provision of healthcare across the globe, a deeper integration between quality and safety improvement models and the HFE models would be an important and useful departure point. Implementation science and HFE promote a systemic view of patient safety and advocate for a movement aware from disciplinarily to multi- and transdisciplinary approaches to solution finding. It is our contention that integrating our models to foster

such an approach coupled with an acknowledgment of local knowledge and skills in LMICs are vital for future improvement projects. In such an integrated manner would it be possible to take implementation of both quality and safety improvement and human factors and ergonomics projects beyond their current scope.

References

1. Bagnara S, Parlangeli O, Tartaglia R. Are hospitals becoming high reliability organizations. Appl Ergon. 2010;41(5):713–8. https://doi.org/10.1016/j.apergo.2009.12.009. Epub 2010 Jan 27.
2. Vincent C, Amalberti R. Safer healthcare. Strategies for the real world. Cham: Springer Open; 2016. https://doi.org/10.1007/978-3-319-25559-0.
3. National Academies of Sciences, Engineering, and Medicine. Crossing the global quality chasm: improving health care worldwide. Washington, DC: The National Academies Press; 2018. https://doi.org/10.17226/25152.
4. Tartaglia R, Albolino S, Bellandi T, Bianchini E, Biggeri A, Fabbro G, Bevilacqua L, Dell'erba A, Privitera G, Sommella L. Adverse events and preventable consequences: retrospective study in five large Italian hospitals. Epidemiol Prev. 2012;36(3–4):151–61.
5. Slawomirski L, Auraaen A, Klazinga N. The economics of patient safety. Strengthening a value-based approach to reducing patient harm at national level. Paris: OECD; 2017.
6. Wilson RM, Michel P, Olsen S, Gibberd RW, Vincent C, et al. Patient safety in developing countries: retrospective estimation of scale and nature of harm in patient and hospital. BMJ. 2012;344:e832.
7. Hignett S, Lang A, Pickup L. More holes than cheese. What prevents the delivery of effective, high quality and safe health care in England? Ergonomics. 2018;61(1):5–14. https://doi.org/10.1080/00140139.2016.1245446.
8. La Pietra L, Calligaris L, Molendini L, Quattrin R, Brusaferro S. Medical errors and clinical risk management: state of the art. Acta Otorhinolaryngol Ital. 2005;25(6):339–46.
9. Brennan TA, Leape LL, Laird NM, Hebert L, Localio AR, Lawthers AG, et al. Incidence of adverse events and negligence in hospitalized patients. 2010 [cited 2019 Oct 18]. https://doi.org/10.1056/NEJM199102073240604. Available from: https://www.nejm.org/doi/10.1056/NEJM199102073240604?url_ver=Z39.88-2003&rfr_id=ori%3Arid%3Acrossref.org&rfr_dat=cr_pub%3Dwww.ncbi.nlm.nih.gov.
10. A WHO, Safe childbirth checklist programme: an overview. Geneva: WHO; 2013.

11. Jha AK, Larizgoitia I, Audera-Lopez C, Prasopa-Plaizier N, Waters H, Bates DW. The global burden of unsafe medical care: analytic modelling of observational studies. BMJ Qual Saf. 2013;22(10):809–15.

12. Boadu M, Rehani MM. Unintended exposure in radiotherapy: Identification of prominent causes. Radiother Oncol. 2009;93(3):609–17.

13. World Health Organization. Patient safety: making health care safer. 2017 [cited 2019 Oct 16]. Available from: https://apps.who.int/iris/handle/10665/255507.

14. Zecevic AA, Li AH-T, Ngo C, Halligan M, Kothari A. Improving safety culture in hospitals: facilitators and barriers to implementation of systemic falls investigative method (SFIM). Int J Qual Health Care. 2017;29(3):371–7.

15. Farokhzadian J, Dehghan Nayeri N, Borhani F. The long way ahead to achieve an effective patient safety culture: challenges perceived by nurses. BMC Health Serv Res. 2018;18(1):654.

16. Leape LL, Berwick DM. Five years after to err is human: what have we learned? JAMA. 2005;293(19):2384–90.

17. Hignett S, Lang A, Pickup L, Ives C, Fray M, McKeown C, et al. More holes than cheese. What prevents the delivery of effective, high quality and safe health care in England? Ergonomics. 2018;61(1):5–14.

18. Clancy CM. Ten years after to err is human. Am J Med Qual. 2009;24(6):525–8.

19. Mitchell I, Schuster A, Smith K, Pronovost P, Wu A. Patient safety incident reporting: a qualitative study of thoughts and perceptions of experts 15 years after 'To Err is Human'. BMJ Qual Saf. 2016;25(2):92–9.

20. Bates DW, Singh H. Two decades since to err is human: an assessment of progress and emerging priorities in patient safety. Health Aff. 2018;37(11):1736–43.

21. Holden RJ. People or systems? To blame is human. The fix is to engineer. Prof Saf. 2009;54(12):34.

22. Reason J. Human error: models and management. BMJ. 2000;320(7237):768–70.

23. Dekker SW. The re-invention of human error. Hum Factors Aerospace Saf. 2001;1(3):247–65.

24. Woods DD, Cook RI. Nine steps to move forward from error. Cogn Tech Work. 2002;4(2):137–44.

25. Rasmussen J. Risk management in a dynamic society: a modelling problem. Saf Sci. 1997;27(2–3):183–213.

26. Cassano-Piche AL, Vicente KJ, Jamieson GA. A test of Rasmussen's risk management framework in the food safety domain: BSE in the UK. Theor Issues Ergon Sci. 2009;10(4):283–304.

27. Ghobashi MM, El-Ragehy HAG, Ibrahim HM, Al-Doseri FA. Assessment of patient safety culture in primary health care settings in Kuwait. Epidemiol Biostat Public Health. 2014;11(3) [cited 2019 Oct 21]. Available from: https://ebph.it/article/view/9101.

28. Taylor SL, Dy S, Foy R, Hempel S, McDonald KM, Øvretveit J, Pronovost PJ, Rubenstein LV, Wachter RM, Shekelle PG. What context features might be important determinants of the effectiveness of patient safety practice interventions? BMJ Qual Saf. 2011;20:611–7. https://doi.org/10.1136/bmjqs.2010.049379.

29. Eccles MP, Mittman BS. Welcome to implementation science. Implement Sci. 2006;1(1):1–3.

30. Bauer MS, Damschroder L, Hagedorn H, Smith J, Kilbourne AM. An introduction to implementation science for the non-specialist. BMC Psychol. 2015;3(1):1–12.

31. Hawe P, Shiell A, Riley T, Gold L. Methods for exploring implementation variation and local context within a cluster randomised community intervention trial. J Epidemiol Community Health. 2004;58:788–93.

32. Øvretveit JC, Shekelle PG, Dy SM, et al. How does context affect interventions to improve patient safety? An assessment of evidence from studies of five patient safety practices and proposals for research. BMJ Qual Saf. 2011. Published Online First: 13 Apr 2011; https://doi.org/10.1136/bmjqs.2010.047035.

33. Cristofalo MA. Implementation of health and mental health evidence-based practices in safety net settings. Soc Work Health Care. 2013;52(8):728–40.

34. Hawkins FH, Orlady, H.W. (Ed.). Human factors in flight, vol. 1993. Aldershot: Avebury Technical; 1993.

35. Cupit C, Mackintosh N, Armstrong N. Using ethnography to study improving healthcare: reflections on the "ethnographic" label. BMJ Qual Saf. 2018;27(4):258–60.

36. Dixon-Woods M. Why is patient safety so hard? A selective review of ethnographic studies. J Heal Serv Res. 2010;15(Suppl 1):11–6.

37. Magazi B, Stadler J, Delany-Moretlwe S, Montgomery E, Mathebula F, Hartmann M, et al. Influences on visit retention in clinical trials: Insights from qualitative research during the VOICE trial in Johannesburg, South Africa. BMC Womens Health. 2014;14(1):1–8.

38. Hollnagel E, Wears R, Braithwaite J. From safety-I to safety-II: a white paper. 2015. p. 1–32.

39. Recovery Partnership Preparation Package. Twinning partnerships for improvement. Geneva: World Health Organization; 2016. p. 20.

40. Institute for Healthcare Improvement. The breakthrough series: IHI's collaborative model for achieving breakthrough improvement (IHI innovation series white paper). Cambridge: Institute for Healthcare Improvement; 2003.

41. International Ergonomic Association. https://www.iea.cc/.

42. https://www.ahrq.gov/sops/surveys/hospital/index.html.

43. Dagliana G, Tommasini B, Zani S, Esposito S, Akamu M, Chege F, Ranzani F, Caldes MJ, Albolino S. WHO safe childbirth checklist: the experience of Kenya according to the WHO African Partnership for Patient Safety. In: Proceedings of the 20th congress of the International Ergonomics Association (IEA 2018), Healthcare ergonomics, vol. I. Cham: Springer; 2018.

44. Wilson J. Fundamentals of systems ergonomics/ human factors. Appl Ergon. 2014;45:5–13.
45. Hignett S, Carayon P, Buckle P, Catchpole K. State of science: human factors and ergonomics in healthcare. Ergonomics. 2013;56(10):1491–503.
46. Thatcher A, Todd A. HFE in underdeveloped countries. How do we facilitate equitable, egalitarian, and respectful progress. In: Roscoe R, Chiou E, Wooldridge A, editors. Advancing diversity, inclusion, and social justice through human systems engineering. Boca Raton, FL: CRC Press; 2020.
47. Naweed A, Ward D, Gourlay C, Dawson D. Can participatory ergonomics process tactics improve simulator fidelity and give rise to transdisciplinarity in stakeholders? A before-after case study. Int J Ind Ergon. 2018;65:139–52.

Part III

Patient Safety in the Main Clinical Specialties

Intensive Care and Anesthesiology

13

S. Damiani, M. Bendinelli, and Stefano Romagnoli

Learning Objectives/Questions Covered in the Chapter

- Most frequent errors and adverse events in anesthesiology and the intensive care unit (ICU).
- Strategies to reduce the occurrence of medication errors both in the operating room and in the ICU.
- Basic principles for the provision of safe anesthesia care: monitoring, knowing, and taking care of the equipment, planning, non-technical skills.
- Application of cognitive aids to improve the safety of surgical patients. Cognitive aids have been developed for intra- and perioperative crises.
- Proposals of models aimed at implementing safety solutions.

S. Damiani
Department of Anesthesia and Critical Care, Azienda Ospedaliero-Universitaria Careggi, Florence, Italy
e-mail: damianisa@aou-careggi.toscana.it

M. Bendinelli
Section of Anesthesia and Critical Care, Department of Health Science, University of Florence, Florence, Italy
e-mail: matteo.bendinelli@unifi.it

S. Romagnoli (✉)
Department of Anesthesia and Critical Care, Azienda Ospedaliero-Universitaria Careggi, Florence, Italy

School of Anesthesia and Critical Care, University of Florence, Florence, Italy
e-mail: stefano.romagnoli@unifi.it

- Implications of the psychological status of staff for patient safety and possible interventions.
- Typical building issues when designing ORs and ICUs.

13.1 Introduction

Given the wide range of medical disciplines afferent to anesthesiology (anesthesia, perioperative care, intensive care medicine, pain therapy, and emergency medicine), anesthesiologists have always had a great, cross-specialty opportunity to influence safety and quality of patients' care. In recent decades, several efforts have been made to establish a model of safety and different risk-reduction strategies have been engaged: for example, the establishment of the American Society of Anesthesiologists (ASA) Committee on Patient Safety and Risk Management in 1984 and the birth of the Anesthesia Patient Safety Foundation in the subsequent year, which were significant moments for the improvement of patients' healthcare quality and for the history of anesthesiology at large.

Indeed, quality and safety in this field have improved, thanks to upgrades of the anesthesia delivery equipment, better monitoring, improved airway management and emergency devices, availability of recovery rooms, and better training; pharmacological advances have led to the

development of new receptor antagonists of opioids and hypnotics, and new anesthetic drugs,
characterized by shorter and more predictable
onset and offset times and fewer side effects. The
development of simulation training has changed
the approach to crises and contributes to the
development of a safety culture beginning in the
residency period.

Nevertheless, operating rooms (ORs) and
intensive care units (ICUs) remain settings burdened by an extremely high risk of error. Surgery
increasingly involves older and sicker patients
undergoing more complex interventions; in the
meantime, anesthesiologists have been requested
to become rapidly competent at using new drugs,
devices, and monitoring systems. The situation is
not different in the ICUs, where physicians and
nurses are expected to provide high-quality care
to critically ill patients, often making life-
threatening decisions very quickly in a stressful
environment while managing high-tech equipment and applying complex procedures.

13.2 Epidemiology of Adverse Events

A study of reported adverse events under anesthesia [1] estimated that about 1.5% of surgical
interventions are complicated by critical events,
but the true incidence is likely underestimated;
moreover, a systematic review [2] found that surgical and anesthetic adverse events, many of
them deemed preventable, contribute to 12.8–
52.2% of unplanned ICU admissions. In industri-
alized countries, major complications are
reported [3] to occur in 3–16% of impatient surgical procedures, with permanent disability or
death rates of approximately 0.4–0.8%; the
anesthesia-specific mortality is estimated [4] to
be about 1/100,000 cases. Hence, even if the
overall anesthetic risk is estimated to be a small
proportion of the total risk of the surgical procedures, with an estimated [5] 312.9 million operations in 2012, anesthesia-related perioperative
mortality represents a small but relevant proportion of cases and, given the ubiquity of surgery,
the implementation of strategies aimed at improv-

ing safety of surgical care has significant implications for public health [3].

Across medical specialties, preventable
patient harm is more prevalent in the ICU [6].
ICUs are complex environments where the severity of illnesses, the high levels of stress, the variety of therapies and routes of administration
make medical errors and deaths due to preventable harm more common [7]. In the Critical Care
Safety Study [8], Rothschild et al. found a daily
rate of 0.8 adverse events and 1.5 serious errors
for 10 ICU beds, with a rate for serious errors of
149.7 per 1000 patient-days. Notably, 45% of all
adverse events were judged preventable.

13.3 Most Frequent Errors

A recent review [9] suggests that cognitive errors
(Table 13.1) are the most important contributors
to patient harm in anesthesiology: growing evidence shows that mere technical errors or errors
caused by a lack of knowledge account for only a
small part of incorrect diagnosis and treatment in
this setting. The role of non-technical skills for
patient safety has progressively become more
evident through the years and, on this topic, one
of the most striking moments of reflection for the
healthcare community was Martin Bromiley's
report [10] on the death of his wife in 2005.
Fixation errors, absence of planification, teamwork breakdown, poor communication, unclear
leadership, lack of situational awareness, and
other non-technical aspects of performance in
anesthesiology and critical care medicine can
negatively impact patient outcome. This could be
even more relevant during intraoperative crises
and emergencies, where failure of adherence to
best practices can be common [11].

Another important source of patient harm is
represented by medication errors, which can
occur at four steps of the drug treatment process:
prescription, transcription, dispensation, and
administration. As reported by the Anesthesia
Quality Institute [12], 44% of medication error
claims involve incorrect dosing, 30% substitution
of an unintended drug for the correct one, 10%
administration of a contraindicated drug, and 8%

Table 13.1 Cognitive error catalogue (from Stiegler et al. [9])

Cognitive error	Definition	Illustration
Anchoring	Focusing on one issue at the expense of understanding the whole situation	While troubleshooting an alarm on an infusion pump, you are unaware of sudden surgical bleeding and hypotension
Availability bias	Choosing a diagnosis because it is in the forefront of your mind due to an emotionally charged memory of a bad experience	Diagnosing simple bronchospasm as anaphylaxis because you once had a case of anaphylaxis that had a very poor outcome
Premature closure	Accepting a diagnosis prematurely, failure to consider reasonable differential of possibilities	Assuming that hypotension in a trauma patient is due to bleeding, and missing the pneumothorax
Feedback bias	Misinterpretation of no feedback as "positive" feedback	Belief that you have never had a case of unintentional awareness because you have never received a complaint about it
Confirmation bias	Seeking or acknowledging only information that confirms the desired or suspected diagnosis	Repeatedly cycling an arterial pressure cuff, changing cuff sizes, and locations because you "do not believe" the low reading
Framing effect	Subsequent thinking is swayed by leading aspects of initial presentation	After being told by a colleague, "this patient was extremely anxious preoperatively", you attribute postoperative agitation to her personality rather thon low blood sugar
Commission bias	Tendency toward action rather than inaction. Performing unindicated maneuvres, deviating from protocol. May be due to overconfidence, desperation, or pressure from others	"Better safe than sorry" insertion of additional unnecessary invasive monitors or access; potentially resulting in a complication
Overconfidence bias	Inappropriate boldness, not recognizing the need for help, tendency to believe we are infallible	Delay in calling for help when you have trouble intubating because you are sure you will eventually succeed
Omission bias	Hesitation to start emergency maneuvres for fear of being wrong or causing harm, tendency toward inaction	Delay in calling for chest tube placements when you suspect a pneumothorax because you may be wrong and you will be responsible for that procedure
Sunk costs	Unwillingness to let go of a failing diagnosis or decision, especially if much time/resources have already been allocated. Ego may play a role	Having decided that a patient needs an awake fiber optic intubation, refusing to consider alternative plans despite multiple unsuccessful attempts
Visceral bias	Countertransference; our negative or positive feelings about a patient influencing our decisions	Not troubleshooting an epidural for a laboring patient because she is "high maintenance" or a "complainer"
Zebra retreat	Rare diagnosis figures prominently among possibilities, but physician is hesitant to pursue it	Try to "explain away" hypercarbia when malignant hyperthermia should be considered
Unpacking principle	Failure to elicit all relevant information, especially during transfer of care	Omission of key test results, medical history, or surgical event
Psych-out error	Medical causes for behavioral problems are missed in favor of psychological diagnosis	Elderly patient in post-anesthesia care unit (PACU) is combative—prescribing restraints instead of considering hypoxia

timing errors. Factors most frequently leading to medication errors or near-misses [13] are distraction (16.7%), haste, stress, or pressure to proceed (production pressure, 12.5%), and the misreading of labels on medication vials or ampoules (12.5%).

Poor design and lack of familiarity with equipment and monitoring devices are likely sources of error and have been identified as major determinants in many adverse events; in this context, the anesthetic delivery equipment is the most common source of problems. Remarkably, equipment misuse is far more common than pure equipment failure, highlighting the fact that human error is responsible for equipment-related mishaps in as high as 90% of cases [14].

Physician burnout and the psychological status of staff are significant concerns for both quality of care and patient safety in critical care. Burnout syndrome has been identified in all categories of healthcare professionals and several studies have shown a high prevalence in ICU staff [15], up to 40%. Risk factors include [16] continuous or long shifts, night shifts, work overload, and poor workplace organization. Healthcare staff who are burned out, depressed, or anxious are unable to fully engage in patient care and are more likely to make errors, increasing the risk to the safety of patients; moreover, burnout personnel may be more reluctant to report medical errors [17]. Depression symptoms were shown to be an independent risk factor for medical error in a prospective observational study [15] involving 31 ICUs.

13.4 Safety Practices and Implementation Strategies

13.4.1 Medication Errors

Errors in medication are defined [18] as the mistakes that occur in the drug treatment process and that lead to, or have the potential to lead to, harm to the patient; such errors typically occur when a drug is prescribed, dispensed, prepared, or administered. In a review of more than 10,000 case forms, Cooper et al. [13] reported an incidence of one in 113–450 patients; in ICU, they are reported in a large proportion of incidents, accounting for up to 78% of serious errors [8].

The high-stress, time-sensitive nature of work in the operating room may explain the high risk of medication errors in this setting; consistently, it has been demonstrated [19] that their rate of occurrence for ICU patients is greater than that for patients admitted to general medical wards. In both environments, the high number of drugs and the IV route of administration, which often requires multiple infusion pump setups or calculations of infusion rate, create more opportunities

for error. Moreover, the potency of many drugs utilized in these settings (vasopressors and inotropes, strong opioids, general anesthetics) even at small doses increases the risk of harm to critical patients, which typically have little physiological reserve.

Being a substantial, potentially lethal, source of patient harm, several institutions have hence targeted this issue. For example, recently, the European Board of Anaesthesiology has produced recommendations for safe medication practice [20] (Table 13.2).

Chartaceous prescriptions have a high risk of errors due to misinterpretation of handwriting; the use of informatized prescription can surely bring down the number of medication errors due to failure in interpretation. Also, electronic medical records can alert physicians and nurses to potential mistakes (e.g., contraindications, double prescriptions, drug interactions, dilution incompatibilities) and allow a timely documentation of drug administration, granting trackability of every phase of the pharmacological treatment process.

Errors which involve administration of the wrong medication or giving medication to the wrong patient can be reduced by 40% with the implementation of bar-code medication administration technology [21] which matches each and every patient's electronic order with patient identifiers (wristbands), thus enhancing the adherence to the "five rights of medication administration" (right patient, medication, time, dose, and route).

A critical point in the process is the admission of a patient from the emergency department or the OR to the ICU, and from the ICU to the OR: clinicians should investigate the types of drugs and the lines to which they are infusing. Before the discharge, extreme attention must be paid to vasoactive medications, ensuring that they do not run out during transport. Drug concentrations must be clearly reported and known both precisely and accurately to the ICU personnel, that often has its own dilution protocols, so that pumps can be programmed correctly; in this

Table 13.2 Main principles for the correct preparation and administration of drugs

- All the drugs prepared for use in anesthesia, intensive care, emergency medicine, and pain medicine should be clearly labelled by the use of pre-printed labels for syringes, including peel-off flag labels on ampoules and vials, whenever possible; in their absence, handwritten labels or permanent marker pens may be used.
- Similarly, all drug infusion bags, catheters, and infusion lines should be labelled.
- Each syringe should be labelled immediately after that a drug has been drawn into, and anyway before it leaves the operator's hand.
- The medication name on the user-applied label should be matched with the drug name on the ampoule.
- Prepare one medication and one syringe at a time.
- Never put labels on empty syringes.
- Avoid distraction or interrupting others during the preparation and administration of patients' medications.
- In the preparation of high-risk medications (e.g., potassium chloride, heparin, adrenaline), it is recommended a double-check at any stage.
- The anesthetic work surface should be standardized for drawing up, arranging and holding syringes; for example, emergency drugs separated from agents for the induction of general anesthesia.
- Cannulae should be flushed after administration of drugs (e.g., at the end of general anesthesia) to reduce the risk of inadvertent administration of drugs in the recovery room or on the ward.
- Any medicine or fluid that cannot be identified at any time during a procedure (e.g., an unlabelled syringe) should be considered unsafe and immediately discarded.
- Drugs should be stored in ways designed to facilitate their easy identification and minimize the risk of error or misidentification and ALERT labels on look-alike, sound-alike medications should be used.
- Vials and ampoules should be stored in their original packaging until just before they are drawn up.
- To minimize the risk of cross-infection, the content of any one ampoule should be administered to only one patient.

phase, communication is crucial: a proper sign-out should occur directly between the OR anesthetist and nurses and the ICU physicians and nurses. In the ICU, the adoption of shared dilution protocols could be of help, creating a standard for clinical practice.

13.4.2 Monitoring

Monitoring is the cornerstone for the provision of a safe anesthesia and a fundamental prerequisite for the effective care of critical patients. In a scientometric analysis, Vlassakov et al. [22] found that the rapid development of anesthesia monitoring may be one possible explanation for the increased safety of anesthesia over the past 40 years.

Standards for basic monitoring during anesthesia have been well established and several guidelines exist. Firstly, ASA [23] highlights that qualified anesthesia personnel shall be present in the room throughout the conduct of all general or regional anesthetics and monitored anesthesia care, mainly because of the rapid changes that may occur in patient status during anesthesia. In the case of a known hazard (e.g., radiation), remote observation is allowed, under the condition that some provision for monitoring the patient is made. Remote observation is also fundamental during radiologic investigations for critical patients.

Basic anesthesia monitoring implies the continuous evaluation of the patient's oxygenation, ventilation (including capnography), circulation, and temperature during all anesthetics [23]. Nevertheless, technological advancements over the past few years have provided advanced monitoring systems that should be adapted to the different settings and levels of care, mainly depending on a patient's history and the procedure planned (Fig. 13.1).

Hemodynamic monitoring has evolved considerably, shifting from invasive techniques to less invasive hemodynamic monitoring for the estimation of cardiac output and other measures of circulatory function, both in anesthesia and in the ICU. For example, the use of pulse contour analysis avoids the complications related to a pulmonary artery catheter, while still providing valuable information for effective therapeutic changes.

Noticeably, a useful and quite recent tool that helps anesthesiologists optimize anesthetic admin-

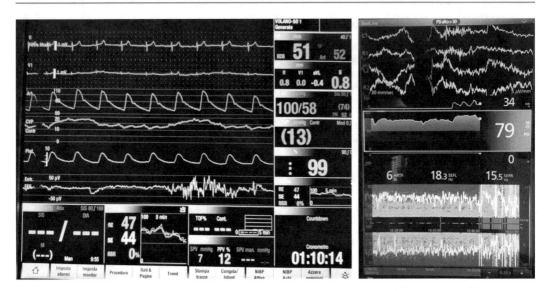

Fig. 13.1 In the image to the left an example of monitoring for the operating room; to the right monitoring of the depth of sedation in ICU

istration, both in the OR and in the ICU, is the processed EEG of the frontal lobes (i.e., BIS™—Medtronic, Boulder, CO, USA; Entropy®—GE Healthcare, Helsinki, Finland; SedLine™—SEDline, Masimo Corp., Irvine, CA, USA). Tracking the depth of sedation was highly effective in reducing the risk of intraoperative awareness in 7,761 high-risk patients when compared with guiding the dose based on clinical signs [24]; at the same time, it improves anesthetic delivery, preventing the risk for oversedation and reducing recovery times [25]. This could also be of utmost importance to the ICU, where oversedation is associated with higher rates of ventilator-associated pneumonia and longer ICU stays [26]. In the recent ENGAGES study [27], EEG-guided anesthesia using BIS in elderly patients undergoing major surgery was associated with a significantly lower 30-day mortality and lower intraoperative use of phenylephrine, even though these were investigated as secondary endpoints.

Whenever muscle relaxants are given during anesthesia, the use of a peripheral, neuromuscular transmission monitor (nerve stimulator) is recommended [28] to allow for a rational administration of neuromuscular blocking and reversal agents, and to reduce the risk of residual curarization and its associated complications, as clinical tests alone cannot reliably exclude the presence of residual curarization [29].

Transesophageal echocardiography is mainly a diagnostic tool, but it can provide important information about a patient's hemodynamic status (preload, cardiac contractility, calculation of cardiac output) and it is estimated [30] that its use in critical patients, together with transthoracic echocardiography, can lead to relevant therapeutic changes in about 25% of cases.

Finally, the efficacy of monitoring for safety may be impaired by poor design and inactivated or inappropriate alarms. Default settings for ventilators, monitors, and alarms should always be checked to determine if they are appropriate [31]. Monitors should clearly display readings and ASA states [23] that alarms should be audible to the anesthesiologist and the anesthesia care personnel. Nevertheless, alarm fatigue is a well-known problem, especially in the critical care setting: excessive false alarms occur frequently and can interfere with clinical activity, contribute to work stress, and desensitize the personnel, leading to a delayed or inadequate response [32]. Several solutions have been proposed (smart alarms taking into account multiple parameters, adaptive time delays, noise reduction strategies, setting of sensible and targeted thresholds) but need to be further investigated.

13.4.3 Equipment

The care of critically ill patients and patients under general anesthesia is dependent on the use of complex medical equipment; monitoring devices, ventilators, renal replacement therapy machines, extracorporeal circulation technologies, infusion pumps, point-of-care diagnostic tools, each with different designs and characteristics, are increasingly populating the market, adding complexity to the intra- and perioperative settings. Unfortunately, this equipment has the potential to develop faults, to be used incorrectly, or to fail: in the ICU, it is estimated that context equipment and supply issues account for 15.8% of total adverse events [33]; similarly, equipment is involved in approximately 14–30% of all intraoperative problems and the anesthetic delivery equipment is the most common source of problems [14].

Besides the wide range of products available in the market, each anesthesia and critical care provider must be familiar with the products available in the provider's own setting, including not only their correct use, but also their indications and limits. Anesthesia providers should be aware of the common causes of equipment malfunction and should be trained in the recognition and management of these events. Study and training sessions and on-site training can be useful for this purpose; simulation programs can further reinforce practitioner competency in the use of new equipment and provide experience in the management of common equipment failure in both straightforward and crisis situations, anticipating its occurrence in the real clinical setting [14].

In 2008, ASA updated pre-anesthesia checkout guidelines (PAC) and provided general principles for all anesthesia delivery systems, summarizing checkout tasks to be completed daily and prior to each procedure. Any anesthesia or ICU department should adapt them to their own anesthesia machine design and practice setting [31]. When correctly implemented, PAC can prevent equipment failure and subsequent patient injury; furthermore, it ensures that backup equipment is ready to use in case of intraoperative failures. For example, it is fundamental that a backup machine, an alternative oxygen supply, and manual ventilation devices (Ambu Bag) are always ready to use. In order to meet these requirements and as the responsible party for the proper functioning of all the equipment used to provide anesthesia care [31], anesthesiologists should be competent in performing all the tasks of the PAC.

13.4.4 Cognitive Aids

It has been demonstrated that cognitive function is compromised as stress and fatigue levels increase, as often happens in the operating room and in intensive care settings, during intraoperative crises and emergencies for example. Here, the complexity of medical conditions and therapies available, the multiple layers of professional roles involved, and the high workload can easily lead to increased errors, decreased compliance with recommended practices, and decreased proficiency in the delivery of care. In this setting, the development of checklists and other cognitive aids has recently risen to prominence and certain procedures or critical events that have been targeted with the use of checklists have shown significant improvements in outcome [34].

Apart from the famous study [35] conducted by Pronovost and collaborators (see the "Building a safety culture" paragraph), another successful application of checklists for the improvement of patient outcomes has been the Surgical Safety Checklist, presented by the WHO in 2008 within the *Safe Surgery Saves Lives* initiative and developed after a comprehensive consultation with experts in surgery, anesthesia, and other related specialties from across all WHO regions. This checklist was developed with the aim of reducing the occurrence of patient harm [3] in the form of errors and adverse events, and increasing teamwork and communication among surgical team members; it targets a routine sequence of events at three cardinal points of the surgical process: preoperative patient evaluation, surgical intervention, and preparation for postoperative care [3]. The use of surgical safety checklists during routine operative care has been associated with significant reductions in both complications and mortality and has rapidly become a standard of care in the vast majority of countries [36].

The experience of their use in ordinary care has triggered investigations of the potential benefits deriving from cognitive aids in emergency situations; here, time and cognitive resources are limited and it has been demonstrated that the ability to rapidly put in place the right therapeutic interventions is crucial, as outcomes are often time dependent. Moreover, evidence suggests that, during emergencies, failure to adhere to best practices and to recall previously learned protocol is common [11]; in Advanced Cardiac Life Support (ACLS) scenarios, for example, it is known [37] that there is a significant decay in clinicians' knowledge retention over time after the completion of certification and it has been demonstrated [38] that errors and omissions of indicated steps are associated with decreased survival odds. These premises formed the basis for the development of crisis checklists for the operating room (Fig. 13.2), a type of cognitive aid designed to help the surgical team remember critical steps *during* intraoperative crises [11]. Some examples are the Anaesthetic Crisis Manual, the Operating Room Crisis Checklists developed at Brigham and Women's Hospital of Boston, the Stanford Emergency Manual, and the Crisis Management Handbook from the Australian Patient Safety Foundation. Arriaga et al. [36] found that the use of surgical crisis checklists was associated with a nearly 75% reduction in failure to adhere to critical steps in management during operating-room crises in a high-fidelity simulated operating room [11]; these data are consistent with that of Ziewacz et al. [39].

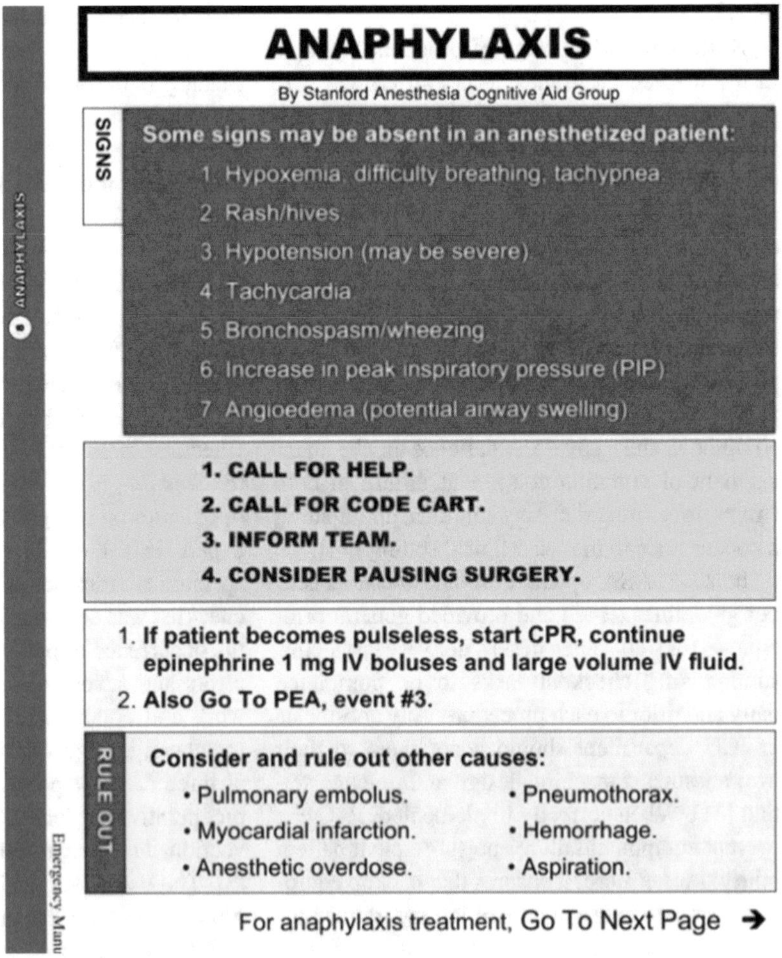

Fig. 13.2 A checklist from the Emergency Stanford Manual

ANAPHYLAXIS

By Stanford Anesthesia Cognitive Aid Group

SIGNS

Some signs may be absent in an anesthetized patient:

1. Hypoxemia, difficulty breathing, tachypnea.
2. Rash/hives.
3. Hypotension (may be severe).
4. Tachycardia.
5. Bronchospasm/wheezing.
6. Increase in peak inspiratory pressure (PIP).
7. Angioedema (potential airway swelling).

1. **CALL FOR HELP.**
2. **CALL FOR CODE CART.**
3. **INFORM TEAM.**
4. **CONSIDER PAUSING SURGERY.**

1. **If patient becomes pulseless, start CPR, continue epinephrine 1 mg IV boluses and large volume IV fluid.**
2. **Also Go To PEA, event #3.**

RULE OUT

Consider and rule out other causes:

- Pulmonary embolus.
- Myocardial infarction.
- Anesthetic overdose.
- Pneumothorax.
- Hemorrhage.
- Aspiration.

For anaphylaxis treatment, Go To Next Page →

There are also numerous other cognitive aids that have been developed for the perioperative and critical care settings, including ACLS algorithms and anesthesia adaptations for the perioperative setting, Malignant Hyperthermia Association of the United States protocols, a checklist for the treatment of local anesthetic systemic toxicity (LAST) from the American Society of Regional Anesthesia and Pain Medicine, pediatric critical events checklists from the Society for Pediatric Anesthesia, Emergency Neurological Life Support checklists by the Neurocritical Care Society, checklists for the preparation of the operating room, for anesthesia in traumatic patients, and for general emergency protocols, as well as other resources [11].

Globally, many major anesthesia societies support and have adopted cognitive aids [11]: among them the Anesthesia Patient Safety Foundation, the American Society of Anesthesiologists, and the European Society of Anesthesiology. Interestingly, the American Society of Regional Anesthesia and Pain Medicine published in 2010 a practice advisory on local anesthetic systemic toxicity, which included a checklist on the treatment of LAST, and recommended keeping the LAST checklist available in any area where high doses of local anesthetics are used. In 2014, the Society for Obstetric Anesthesia and Perinatology developed a consensus statement on the management of cardiac arrest in pregnancy, recommending that a checklist emphasizing key tasks be immediately available; the American Heart Association encourages institutions to create point-of-care checklists to be used during obstetric crises including maternal cardiac arrest.

13.4.5 Communication and Teamwork

The connection between safety and communication has been known for a long time. Given the complexity of ICUs and the multiple team handovers required during patient care, critical care units are areas where patients are more vulnerable to communication breakdowns.

The quality of the relationships between nurses, doctors, and other staff working in perioperative settings affects patient outcomes: good *teamwork,* when team members communicate efficiently and respect each other while working toward a common goal, allows the team to reduce complications and mortality [7]. Conversely, communication failures and bad relationships can lead to increased risk of error, length of stay, resource use, caregiver dissatisfaction, and turnover. In the ICU, the implementation of a daily-goals form can help to set and share tasks and care plans and to improve communication among caregivers [40].

Insight can also be gained from Crisis Resource Management, a well-known approach that refers to all the non-technical skills that have been demonstrated to optimize teamwork and make the teamwork more effective during an emergency. It holds effective communication as one of its key principles [41], underlining the importance of a climate of open information exchange among all personnel.

Simulation training could be a good way to improve relationships and trust within teams and is rapidly becoming part of resident education, even if the relationship between simulation training in anesthesiology and improved outcomes still needs to be clearly defined. In fact, besides helping with technical skills training, simulation can reinforce the non-technical skills needed to work as a team, such as communication behaviors, leadership skills, collaboration, task management, situation awareness, and decision-making [42].

13.4.6 Building a Safety Culture

The success of many interventions that aim to improve patient safety depends not only on the application of evidence-based practices, but also on changes in workplace culture and on group implemented strategies. Many efforts have been made toward the development of a culture of safety in this discipline, in order to improve patient safety and care quality. Safety culture is the collection of beliefs, values, and norms relating to patient safety and shared among the members of an organization, unit, or team [43]. It influences behavior, attitude, cognition, and one's perception of one's own work, promoting safe practices and the prioritization of patient safety over other goals (e.g., efficiency).

The implementation of a safety culture requires sustained involvement across multiple levels of an organization, through a series of steps including the engagement of frontline providers, the selection and creation of team-based projects, the development of safety education programs (including communication and teamwork skills), and the implementation and evaluation of strategies [7]. Despite the fact that its implementation may be a difficult and challenging process (Table 13.3), current evidence [7] supports the

efficacy of a strong safety culture in the reduction of adverse events and lower mortality.

One of the clearest examples of successful implementation of safety culture in critical care was the milestone study conducted by Pronovost et al. [35], which reported a large and sustained reduction in rates of catheter-related bloodstream infection in 103 ICUs across Michigan through a quality improvement framework that included:

- a daily-goals sheet to improve clinician-to-clinician communication
- training of team leaders across medical and nursing staff
- a checklist to ensure adherence to evidence-based infection-control practices for central line insertion (Fig 13.3)
- empowerment of all ICU staff to intervene in case of non-adherence to any of the aforementioned practices
- periodic feedback reports
- tracking and sharing of collected data

Table 13.3 Barriers to the implementation of a safety culture in anesthesia and critical care medicine

- Environmental and organizational complexity: multiple professional layers are involved in the care of patients, each with divergent occupational responsibilities and expertise.
- Necessity of bundling multiple interventions at several time points throughout the process of care.
- Cultural barriers: for example, clinicians may think that the use of cognitive aids to manage emergencies reflects a lack in knowledge or in decision-making skills.
- Punitive responses to errors and the fear of legal consequences are obstacles to the creation of a reporting culture and reduce the opportunity to learn from errors.
- Patient safety in high-stakes sectors requires training and education, thus time and resources: this may discourage some clinicians and cause conflict with the economic interests and staffing policies of healthcare institutions.
- Production pressure (e.g., tight operating room schedules, need for high patient turnover in post-surgical ICUs) threatens the implementation of safe patient care and might negatively influence the operator's perception of safety practices.
- Lack of communication between frontline workers and senior management regarding their perspective on patient safety culture and their respective professional expectations.
- Communication failure between different professional backgrounds, for example, between surgeons and anesthesiologists and between physicians and nurses.

Other means of implementation could be interdisciplinary rounding, encouragement of error reporting, and team training; importantly, this includes simulation training. Engaging patients and families in safety culture is deemed important too, since patients can be a relevant source of information in the reporting of adverse events [7].

It should be further considered that financial pressures may lead administrators to limit investments in patient safety improvements, with the additional risk of spreading safety culture problems among the staff. Many aspects of the financial performance of a hospital may lead to hazardous changes in staffing, quality control, physician education, investment in up-to-date equipment, monitoring of adverse events, and may cause other safety issues which eventually may affect patient outcomes. Several pieces of evidence [44, 45] show that there can be a trade-off between financial objectives and patient safety, and that this should be taken into account by a hospital's administration.

| Catheter-related Blood Stream Infection |
| Care Team Checklist |

Purpose: To work as a team to decrease patient harm from catheter-related blood stream infection
When: During **all** central venous or central arterial line insertions or re-wires
By whom: Bedside nurse

1. Today's date   _____ / _____ / _____
                                                                month   day   year

2. Procedure   ☐ New line   ☐ Rewire

3. Procedure regimen   ☐ Elective   ☐ Emergent

4.   Yes   No   Don't know
   Before the procedure, did the housestaff:
   Wash hands (Chlorhexidine) immediately prior   ☐   ☐   ☐
   Sterilize procedure site   ☐   ☐   ☐
   Drap the entire PATIENT in a sterile fashion   ☐   ☐   ☐

   During the procedure, did the housestaff:
   Use sterile GLOVES   ☐   ☐   ☐
   Use hat, mask and sterile gown   ☐   ☐   ☐
   Maintain a sterile field   ☐   ☐   ☐

   Did all personnel assisting with procedure follow
   the above precautions   ☐   ☐   ☐

   After the procedure:
   Was a sterile dressing applied to the site   ☐   ☐   ☐

Please return completed form to the designated location in your ICU

Fig. 13.3 Example of central line insertion checklist

13.4.7 Psychological Status of Staff and Staffing Policies

Human factors and well-being at work are relevant issues when discussing patient safety. Regarding this topic, burnout syndrome has recently gained popularity: it is a complex, work-related, psychological status, resulting from chronic workplace stress that has not been successfully managed. It is defined in ICD-11 as the combination of:

- high exhaustion
- increased mental distance from one's job or feelings of negativism or cynicism related to one's job
- reduced professional efficacy

A variety of interventions have been proposed to address the psychological status of staff and can be divided into two categories [47]: (1) interventions focused on improving the ICU environment; (2) interventions focused on the individual's ability to cope with the working environment. Multidimensional interventions are more likely than single interventions to succeed in preventing and treating psychological disorders among the staff.

Since 2005, the American Association of Critical Care Nurses has defined [46] six standards to establish and sustain a healthy work environment: (1) skilled communication; (2) true collaboration; (3) effective decision-making; (4) appropriate staffing; (5) meaningful recognition; (6) authentic leadership. Other levels of intervention that have been proposed [47] for a healthy ICU environment are the improvement of end-of-life care and of ethical team deliberations, the utilization of team debriefing, structured communication, the employment of time and stress management skills, interdisciplinary discussions, and the sharing of critical decisions with team members. Family conferencing to discuss prognosis and treatment goals could mitigate moral distress in ICU clinicians.

Intensivist- and nurse-to-patient ratios can also impact patient care and staff well-being, and are associated with improved safety and better outcomes for patients [16]. In 2013, the Society of Critical Care Medicine addressed this issue and published a statement [16] to aid hospitals in determining their intensivist staffing, recognizing that proper ICU staffing impacts patient safety and staff well-being. Assessments of staff satisfaction, burnout, and stress should be part of institution policies. Moreover, staffing policies should factor in surge capacity and non-direct patient care duties (family meetings, consultations, teaching).

Finally, the presence of acute or chronic psychological disorders among healthcare providers, due to private or work-related stress, as well as addiction or substance abuse, sleep disorders, mood disturbance, and overall well-being should be investigated in the context of occupational medicine examinations and should never be underestimated. Critical care providers should be taught how to recognize the risk factors and symptoms for burnout and should be encouraged to seek assistance when needed [47].

13.4.8 The Building Factor

The environment of operating rooms and ICUs is perceived as static by architects and engineers. Consequently, workplaces are often designed smaller than they actually need to be. For instance, the aisles of the operating rooms should be at least 2 m large to allow the easy and safe transfer of stretchers, but this space is often narrowed by drug carts, echo machines, and other empty stretchers. Similarly, it should be taken into account that the new technologies and devices continuously introduced in clinical practice are usually cumbersome, running the risk of making poorly designed workplaces very uncomfortable [48]. Small ICU rooms may slow down the process of care and hamper the management of critical situations, especially when more clinicians are required.

Relaxation areas or other environments in which the staff may take a break should be considered when planning operating rooms and ICUs, and natural lighting should be guaranteed when feasible [49]. Indeed, breaks should be regularly planned in order to reduce the risk of fatigue and consequently improve the well-being of workers and patient safety. Shifts longer than 8 h should be avoided, and, when this is not possible, adequate recovery time between the shifts should be ensured [50, 51]. For instance, in Italy the employment contract of NHS hospitals includes rules on shift and work breaks, but they are often disregarded in practice.

The regular use of assessment tools [52], such as the Health and Safety Executive's Fatigue and Risk Index Tool, is paramount to identify workers that are at risk of injury.

13.5   Recommendations

One of the main duties of anesthesia and critical care providers is to provide patient safety.

Medication error is a substantial source of patient harm in anesthesiology. Recommendations for safe medication practices exist and must be respected. The use of electronic medical records should be favored over chartaceous prescriptions, eventually coupling with bar-code medication administration technology.

A proper sign-out that also addresses medication infusions should occur during the admission to or the discharge from the ICU.

Standards for monitoring have been well established by ASA and are fundamental requisites for the provision of safe anesthesia care since they can detect physiologic perturbations and acute events allowing for intervention before the patient suffers harm. Nevertheless, anesthetist and perioperative physicians should be familiar with advanced monitoring techniques, such as pulse contour analysis, depth of general anesthesia monitoring, neuromuscular monitoring, and transesophageal echocardiography; their use could have important implications for a clinical practice, for example, allowing the rational administration of anesthetic drugs and fluids. As highlighted by ASA, qualified anesthesia personnel shall be present in the room throughout the conduct of all general or regional anesthetics and monitored anesthesia care.

Anesthesia providers must be familiar with the equipment available in their own settings, including not only the equipment's correct use, but also its indications and limits. Every anesthesia provider should know and be competent in the performance of all the items of the ASA preanesthesia machine checklist. Competency in early recognition and management of common equipment failure is a requisite for patient safety.

The WHO surgical safety checklist improves compliance with safety practices and has been demonstrated to have an impact on surgical patient outcome; it is able to prevent patient harm and perioperative complications. The use of cognitive aids during intraoperative crises and emergencies should be encouraged; their use may contribute to better patient outcomes, reducing failure of adherence to the best evidence-based practices and mitigating the effect of stress and ineffective teamwork on performance. Checklists should be integrated into clinical practice through effective training and implementation strategies. Institutions should encourage the creation of adapted point-of-care checklists at critical points

of a patient's treatment in the hospital (e.g., operating room, ICU, obstetrics).

Simulation training of critical events need to be incorporated into the education of all clinicians who work in the operating room and in the ICU. Anesthetists should receive this type of formation since residency. Simulation training should include the use of crisis checklists and emergency manuals, and the simulation of equipment failure.

Efforts should be made to establish a culture of safety in critical care, as safety culture could promote effective improvements in patient safety and sustain them over time. Efforts should be conducted at a multidisciplinary level including administrations, while engaging patients and families in this process is also deemed important. Reporting of errors and adverse events should be encouraged and collected data should be tracked and shared among the personnel. Hospitals' financial plans should include investments in patient safety since overlooking this aspect may increase the probability of adverse patient safety events.

Institutions should regularly assess the appropriateness of their ICU staffing models via objective data. Critical care providers should be taught how to recognize the risk factors and symptoms for burnout and should be encouraged to seek assistance when needed. Policies of routine screening of ICU staff members for symptoms of depression, burnout, and anxiety should be implemented.

The size, layout, and organization of the workplace impacts staff well-being and patient safety. It is crucial that administrators, architects, and engineers involve lead clinicians and focus on input from clinical staff when designing operating rooms and ICUs.

References

1. Charuluxananan S, Punjasawadwong Y, Suraseranivongse S, et al. The Thai anesthesia incidents study of anesthetic outcomes II. Anesthetic profiles and adverse events. J Med Assoc Thail. 2005;88:S14–29.

2. Vlayen A, Verelst S, Bekkering GE, et al. Incidence and preventability of adverse events requiring intensive care admission: a systematic review. J Eval Clin Pract. 2012;18(2):485–97.

3. World Health Organization. World alliance for patient safety—safe surgery saves lives. Geneva: WHO; 2008. https://www.who.int/patientsafety/safesurgery/knowledge_base/SSSL_Brochure_finalJun08.pdf.

4. Staender SE, Mahajan RP. Anesthesia and patient safety: have we reached our limits? Curr Opin Anaesthesiol. 2011;24(3):349–53.

5. Weiser TC, Haynes AB, Molina G, et al. Estimate of the global volume of surgery in 2012: an assessment supporting improved health outcomes. Lancet. 2015;385:S11.

6. Panagioti M, Khan K, Keers RN, et al. Prevalence, severity, and nature of preventable patient harm across medical care settings: systematic review and meta-analysis. BMJ. 2019;366:I4185.

7. Thornton KC, Schwarz JJ, Gross AK, et al. Preventing harm in the ICU—building a culture of safety and engaging patients and families. Crit Care Med. 2017;45(9):1531–7.

8. Rothschild JM, Landrigan CP, Cronin JW, et al. The critical care safety study: the incidence and nature of adverse events and serious medical errors in intensive care. Crit Care Med. 2005;33(8):1694–700.

9. Stiegler MP, Neelankavil JP, Canales C, et al. Cognitive errors detected in anaesthesiology: a literature review and pilot study. Br J Anaesth. 2012;108(2):229–35.

10. Bromiley M. The case of Elaine Bromiley: Clinical Human Factors Group; 2005. p. 1–18.

11. Hepner DL, Arriaga AF, Cooper JB, et al. Operating room crisis checklists and emergency manuals. Anesthesiology. 2017;127(2):384–92.

12. Sandnes DL, Stephens LS, Posner KL, et al. Liability associated with medication errors in anesthesia: closed claims analysis. Anesthesiology. 2008;109:A770.

13. Cooper L, DiGiovanni N, Schultz L, et al. Influences observed on incidence and reporting of medication errors in anesthesia. Can J Anaesth. 2012;59(6):562–70.

14. Dalley P, Robinson B, Weller J, et al. The use of high-fidelity human patient simulation and the introduction of new anesthesia delivery systems. Anesth Analg. 2004;99(6):1737–41.

15. Garrouste-Orgeas M, Perrin M, Soufir L. The Iatroref study: medical errors are associated with symptoms of depression in ICU staff, but not burnout or safety culture. Intensive Care Med. 2015;41(2):273–84.

16. Ward NS, Afessa B, Kleinpell R, et al. Intensivist/patient ratios in closed ICUs: a statement from the Society of Critical Care Medicine Taskforce on ICU staffing. Crit Care Med. 2013;41(2):638–45.

17. Halbesleben JR, Rathert C. Linking physician burnout and patient outcomes: exploring the dyadic relationship between physicians and patients. Health Care Manag Rev. 2008;33(1):29–39.

18. Pharmacovigilance Risk Assessment Committee. Good practice guide on recording, coding, reporting and assessment of medication errors (EMA/762563/2014). European Medicines Agency. 2015.

19. Wilmer A, Louie K, Dodek P, et al. Incidence of medication errors and adverse drug events in the ICU: a systematic review. Qual Saf Health Care. 2010;19(5):e7.

20. Whitaker D, Brattebø G, Trenkler S, et al. The European Board of Anaesthesiology recommendations for safe medication practice. Eur J Anaesthesiol. 2017;34(1):4–7.

21. Thompson KM, Swanson KM, Cox DL, et al. Implementation of bar-code medication administration to reduce patient harm. Mayo Clin Proc Innov Qual Outcomes. 2018;2(4):342–51.

22. Vlassakov KV, Kissin I. A quest to increase safety of anesthetics by advancements in anesthesia monitoring: scientometric analysis. Drug Des Devel Ther. 2015;9:2599–608.

23. American Society of Anesthesiologists. Standards and Practice Parameters Committee. Standards for basic anesthetic monitoring. 2011. https://www.asahq.org/standards-and-guidelines/standards-for-basic-anesthetic-monitoring.

24. Punjasawadwong Y, Phongchiewboon A, Bunchungmongkol N. Bispectral index for improving anaesthetic delivery and postoperative recovery. Cochrane Database Syst Rev. 2014;6:CD003843.

25. Chhabra A, Subramaniam R, Srivastava A, et al. Spectral entropy monitoring for adults and children undergoing general anaesthesia. Cochrane Database Syst Rev. 2016;3:CD010135.

26. Hajat Z, Ahmad N, Andrzejowski J. The role and limitations of EEG-based depth of anaesthesia monitoring in theatres and intensive care. Anaesthesia. 2017;72:38–47.

27. Wildes TS, Mickle AM, Abdallah AB, et al. Effect of electroencephalography-guided anesthetic administration on postoperative delirium among older adults undergoing major surgery: the ENGAGES randomized clinical trial. JAMA. 2019;321(5):473–83.

28. Gelb AW, Morriss WW, Johnson W, et al. World Health Organization-World Federation of Societies of Anaesthesiologists (WHO-WFSA) international standards for a safe practice of anesthesia. Can J Anaesth. 2018;65(6):698–708.

29. Lien CA, Kopman AF. Current recommendations for monitoring depth of neuromuscular blockade. Curr Opin Anaesthesiol. 2014;27(6):616–22.

30. Vignon P, Mentec H, Terre S, et al. Diagnostic accuracy and therapeutic impact of transthoracic and transesophageal echocardiography in mechanically ventilated patients in the ICU. Chest. 1994;106(6):1829–34.

31. Sub-Committee of ASA Committee on Equipment and Facilities. Recommendations for pre-anesthesia checkout procedures. 2008. http://asahq.org/standards-and-guidelines/2008-asa-recommendations-for-pre-anesthesia-checkout.

32. Ruskin KJ, Hueske-Kraus D. Alarm fatigue: impacts on patient safety. Curr Opin Anaesthesiol. 2015;28(6):685–90.

33. Corwin GS, Mills PD, Shanawani H, et al. Root cause analysis of ICU adverse events in the veterans health administration. Jt Comm J Qual Patient Saf. 2017;43(11):580–90.

34. Hales BM, Pronovost PJ. The checklist—a tool for error management and performance improvement. J Crit Care. 2006;21(3):231–5.

35. Pronovost P, Needham D, Bernholtz S, et al. An intervention to decrease catheter-related bloodstream infections in the ICU. N Engl J Med. 2006;355(26):2725–32.

36. Arriaga AF, Bader AM, Wong JM, et al. Simulation-based trial of surgical-crisis checklists. N Engl J Med. 2013;368(3):246–53.

37. Semeraro F, Signore L, Cerchiari EL. Retention of CPR performance in anaesthetists. Resuscitation. 2006;68(1):101–8.

38. McEvoy MD, Field LC, Moore HE, et al. The effect of adherence to ACLS protocols on survival of event in the setting of in-hospital cardiac arrest. Resuscitation. 2014;85(1):82–7.

39. Ziewacz JE, Arriaga AF, Bader AM, et al. Crisis checklists for the operating room: development and pilot testing. J Am Coll Surg. 2011;213(2):212–7.

40. Pronovost P, Berenholtz S, Dorman T, et al. Improving communication in the ICU using daily goals. J Crit Care. 2003;18(2):71–5.

41. Goldhaber-Fiebert SN, Howard SK. Implementing emergency manuals: can cognitive aids help translate best practices for patient care during acute events? Anesth Analg. 2013;117(5):1149–61.

42. Green M, Tariq R, Green P. Improving patient safety through simulation training in anesthesiology: where are we? Anesthesiol Res Pract. 2016;2016:1.

43. Weaver SJ, Lubomsky LH, Wilson RF, et al. Promoting a culture of safety as a patient safety strategy: a systematic review. Ann Intern Med. 2013;158(5 Pt 2):369–74.

44. Encinosa WE, Bae J. Health information technology and its effects on hospital costs, outcomes, and patient safety. Inquiry. 2011;48(4):288–303.

45. Bazzoli GJ, Chen HF, Zhao M, et al. Hospital financial condition and the quality of patient care. Health Econ. 2008;17(8):977–95.

46. American Association of Critical-Care Nurses. AACN standards for establishing and sustaining healthy work environments: a journey to excellence. Am J Crit Care. 2005;14(3):187–97.

47. Moss M, Good WS, Gozal D, et al. A critical care societies collaborative statement: burnout syndrome in critical care health-care professionals. A call for action. Am J Respir Crit Care Med. 2016;194(1):106–13.

48. Ibrahim AM, Dimick JB, Joseph A. Building a better operating room: views from surgery and architecture. Ann Surg. 2017;265(1):34–6.

49. Berry K. Operating room architecture and design and the effects on staff morale. ACORN J. 2008;21(2):6–16.

50. Banakar M. The impact of 12-hour shifts on nurses' health, wellbeing, and job satisfaction: a systematic review. J Nurs Educ Pract. 2017;7(11):69–83.

51. Ferri P, Guadi M, Marcheselli L, et al. The impact of shift work on the psychological and physical health of nurses in a general hospital: a comparison between rotating night shifts and day shifts. Risk Manag Healthc Policy. 2016;9:203.

52. Noone P, Waclawski E. Fatigue risk management systems needed in healthcare. Occup Med. 2018;68(8):496–8.

Safe Surgery Saves Lives

Francesco Venneri, Lawrence B. Brown,
Francesca Cammelli, and Elliott R. Haut

The World Health Organization (WHO) Safe Surgery Saves Lives campaign aimed to implement safe surgical procedures and patient safety best practices to reduce the incidence of adverse events both in the operating room and in the ward. For decades, the main objectives of safe surgery were mainly focused on the technical procedure. More recently, the implementation of non-technical skills and interpersonal communication have been found to play a significant role in preventing harm in surgical care settings.

A surgeon is educated with the focus on clinical care, decision-making, and technical skills required to perform surgical procedures techniques that yield the best outcome. Surgery requires skill, adaptation, accuracy, and knowing when it is appropriate to operate. Despite these factors, mistakes still occur in the pre-operative clinic, operating theater, intensive care unit, and surgical ward. Surgeons (and all physicians) should be willing to discuss unsuccessful cases and learn from mistakes throughout their career. These issues should be shared with surgical trainees at all levels including students, residents, and fellows at teaching hospitals, as they are essential for their clinical development. They also provide a context for lifelong learning and personal growth throughout every successful career.

14.1 Safety Best Practices in Surgery

Best practices in medicine have become a must and many health care institutions and systems have embedded safety practices in their goals and quality achievement policies. Patient safety itself has become an "institution" on its own and since the 1999 Institute of Medicine publication "To Err is Human," risk management programs in health care facilities worldwide have been leading the trends in reducing patient harm and implementing quality assurance in health care so as to contribute to a solid reduction in costs and expenses.

Evidence-based medicine and evidence-based health care data prove that when best practices are well applied in health care procedures, the return in terms of adverse event reduction and

F. Venneri
Florence Healthcare Trust, Patient Safety,
Florence, Italy
e-mail: francesco.venneri@uslcentro.toscana.it

L. B. Brown
Department of Surgery, The Johns Hopkins University School of Medicine, Baltimore, MD, USA
e-mail: lbrow191@jhmi.edu

F. Cammelli
General Surgery Department, Careggi University Hospital, Florence, Italy

E. R. Haut (✉)
Division of Acute Care Surgery, Department of Surgery, The Johns Hopkins University School of Medicine, Baltimore, MD, USA
e-mail: ehaut1@jhmi.edu

© The Author(s) 2021
L. Donaldson et al. (eds.), *Textbook of Patient Safety and Clinical Risk Management*,
https://doi.org/10.1007/978-3-030-59403-9_14

patient well-being are assured and are measurable according to standards of health care models recognized worldwide. Physicians, nurses, other health care professionals, policy makers, and stakeholders in medicine rely on a teamwork basis and this must encourage managers and politicians to enhance among professionals the urge to apply best practices, measure them on an appropriateness, efficacy, and efficiency basis and implement all to let them be compliant among health care workers.

This is particularly true and peculiar in the field of surgery. Surgery on its own is considered a craftsman attitude discipline, where individuality and self-appraisal are the most reliable factors for quality assurance; but this is not reliable in terms of outcomes and evidence-based medicine or nursing principals. In other words, surgery relies on evidence-based best practices and surgeons must have this evidence of their success and compliance; otherwise, all may be reluctant of their application and implementation.

14.2   Factors Which Influence Patient Safety in Surgery

Despite its complexity, health care institutions are widely considered to be reliable systems, with the primary intent of "doing no harm." However, compared to true high reliably organizations such as airlines or nuclear power industries, health care is nowhere close to the safety patients expect. In order to understand the real meaning of safety in surgery, we must first understand the numerous steps required in every surgical setting and the pathway of the surgical patient.

All physicians require strong cognitive skills for decision-making in order to optimize patient outcomes. In addition to these competencies, a surgeon is a specialist in the field of the "manual arts." In other words, an artisan who uses their hands as a means of cure. The surgical profession throughout the years has radically changed as techniques, procedures, instrumentation, gender, training, costs, risks, and infection control are concerned. Each of these factors play a significant role in patient safety and should be considered with respect to field of surgery.

14.3   Techniques and Procedures

In the last two decades, surgical procedures have radically changed a surgeon's approach to patients presenting with surgical pathologies. Additionally, less severe pathologies, such as inguinal hernia or varicose veins, have led to changes from inpatient hospitalizations to outpatient in settings for surgical management. In the 1970s and 1980s, inguinal hernia repair was frequently treated with an overnight hospital stay. Now, this procedure is routinely performed on an outpatient basis. This new way of approaching many surgical diseases has inclined hospitals to place emphasis on outpatient surgery cases. These changes have affected every aspect of surgical care, including the focus on patient safety.

These changes in setting also require higher levels of patient empowerment and improved communications. Patients now must understand the setting in which their surgery will occur and the resulting decreased length of stay be educated on the potential complications that might arise, especially as they may occur at home, rather than in a hospital setting. Changes in techniques and procedures also require that surgical trainees should be compliant to best practices to lower the incidence of adverse events occurring in settings where human factors play a major role. Prosthetics, biological stitches, antibiotic prophylaxis, and prevention of deep venous thrombosis have also radically changed and modified protocols, requiring adjustments and implementation. Patient safety is not static, changes occur frequently and the entire health care community must keep up with them in these ever-changing times. The importance of updating guidelines, searching for evidence-based standards and redesigning the process of surgery were challenges that hospitals, private clinics, and other major surgical settings have had to grapple with. Additionally, attending surgeons have had to rethink how to train residents and fellows in a manner that optimized efficiency without comprising patient outcomes.

14.4 Surgical Equipment and Instruments

Industries manufacturing surgical instruments have gradually updated their knowledge and dedicated all efforts to design and usability of surgical equipment. Many surgeons assist with usability trials before companies introduce new products, equipment, and/or instruments. These steps in human factors engineering (or ergonomics) are important to undertake to maximize patient safety in the operating theater and surgical/procedural suites. Ease of use with minimal training and intuitive designs allows surgeons to rapidly learn how to use the technology and minimize any safety risks to patients due to a long, steep learning curve.

In the field of inguinal hernia repair, prosthetic mesh options have improved over the years. The improved ergonomics of these materials have made them particularly attractive to surgeons performing these procedures. This means that patient may not only stand up a few hours following surgery, but it is a "must" to go home and perform simple maneuvers as walking, driving, and therefore a much faster return to work or other day activities. The aim therefore is a faster recovery from disability and/or discomfort. The concept of minor surgery has been introduced yet it must not be considered less important, but instead as a quicker return to ordinary life. This is also true for less or minor invasive procedures, such as laparoscopic surgery. Laparoscopy radically changed not only the approach to certain pathologies but changed surgeons minds and behaviors.

14.5 Pathways and Practice Management Guidelines

In recent years, the surgical community has implemented guidelines for Enhanced Recovery After Surgery (ERAS) procedures. This type of protocol has been shown to improve patient outcomes and provide safer care. Standardized guidelines can ensure optimal care to all patients, decrease variation, cut costs, and reduce disparities in care.

Other pathways allow patients to leave the hospital settings following minor surgical procedures such as breast, orthopedic, anorectal, and urologic procedures.

These factors all influence patient safety issues because changes in hospital settings, instrument implementation, training, and health care policies may affect health care professionals, patients, and institutions.

14.6 Gender

Surgery was once considered a "masculine" discipline, with the stereotype of a hard-working man with a great deal of self-confidence and self-esteem. Since the early 1990s, medical schools have enrolled fewer male students and increased the proportion of women. In the United States, approximately 50% of medical school graduates are now women. This trend has also had an effect on resident trainees in surgery. While this ratio has changed in some surgical fields (i.e., general surgery), it has not changed as much in others (i.e., neurosurgery, urology). The field of surgery has noted many successful female surgeons both in the hospital and in academic domains.

This change in gender population of a specialty, historically linked to male figures, has had an effect on patients' awareness and way of thinking, yielding a change in behaviors and outcomes. Gender diversity must not only be considered in the surgical field but all across medicine and medical specialties, as it relevant to patient safety and trust. Studies have shown that this gender diversity is associated with improved patient outcomes. Teamwork studies have shown that having even a single woman on the team (as opposed to a team of all men) improves team dynamics, decision-making, and patient safety.

14.7 Training

The relationship between surgical safety and training on the use of emerging technologies is important to consider. This issue has been most hotly debated since the development of minimally invasive, laparoscopic, and robotic surgery. While these new technologies may provide less invasive, less painful procedures, the risks compared to open surgery may be the same, or possibly higher. Residents in surgery must follow an accurate training log and acquire not only skills, but also consider the appropriateness and benefits of operating with these approaches. These factors are critically linked to patient safety and risk management. A surgeon never reaches a 100% safe and sure learning curve, but is constantly exposing patients to risks and uncertainty. Teaching hospitals and scientific associations worldwide are focused on reducing learning gaps in the way care is delivered around the globe.

Training must include all aspects of care including decision-making and problem-solving, as well as the manual, technical skills required to physically perform complex surgical procedures. Laparoscopy and robotic surgery have dramatically changed training steps and protocols; many residents are well acquainted with these highly technological approaches. However, open approaches to certain surgery has become less commonly performed; this may represent a gap in problem-solving among young trainees or newly assessed surgeons on their first rounds in hospitals or in operating theaters. A highly trained efficient surgeon in laparoscopic approaches or robotics may find difficulty in approaching an open surgery in case of an emergency situation. This may become a patient safety issue, and patients should be informed of their surgeons' abilities and case-history if rapid conversion to open surgery is required.

14.8 Costs and Risks

Surgery has true financial costs, and it is expensive as it relates to patient safety and outcomes. These should be issues of main concern not only to hospital managers, but to patients, politicians, and health care policy makers worldwide. Quality indicators and plans for surgical safety should be a point of discussion when a Chief Executive Office (CEO) examines a hospital budget in terms of efficacy and efficiency. Costs and risks influence patient safety in terms of appropriateness; accurate patient selection contributes to limiting not only adverse events, but also implementing quality assurance among health care professionals for their patients. It has been suggested that spending money upfront for quality care and ensuring patient safety will save cost in the long run as outcomes improve. These improved outcomes are also often associated with shorter length of stays, fewer diagnostics tests, and less overall care to mitigate the effects of complications after surgery.

14.9 Infection Control

Hospital acquired infections are a major cause of patient morbidity and mortality and represent an important area of concern as it relates to patient safety overall. One area of concern within the realm of surgery is that of surgical site infections. Many approaches have been undertaken to prevent these infections. Some are exceedingly data driven such as the use of pre-operative prophylactic antibiotics before surgical incision. Others, however, are promulgated without strong evidence. Many hospitals are increasingly restricting the use of fabric surgical scrub caps in the operating room, instead favoring disposable bouffants. In 1973, very scant literature demonstrated that providers who carry Staphylococcus aureus in their hair could spread those bacteria to patients. However, more recent data demonstrates that there is no difference in surgical site infections between physicians who wear fabric versus disposable scrub caps. It has also been suggested that personalized fabric scrub caps (identifying name and position) as popularized with the #TheatreCapChallenge hashtag on social media improve closed loop communication within the operating room, which may have implications on improving patient safety. The final decision has not yet been made between the competing goals of improved communication vs. decreasing infections although the authors of this chapter do favor the cloth caps with clinicians' names.

14.10 Surgical Safety Checklist

The checklist approach to improving medical care has been promoted by many physicians, most notably; Dr. Peter Pronovost in his seminal work on checklists to prevent central line-associated bloodstream infections (CLABSI) in the intensive care unit. The concept was introduced into surgery by Dr. Atul Gawande, a surgeon at Harvard Medical School, and who studied the application of a safety instrument in the operating theater. In 2008, The World Health Organization (WHO) promoted a campaign to encourage all health care institutions performing surgery globally to apply the Surgical Safety Checklist in their settings. Studies have demonstrated a 33% reduction of potentially lethal adverse events when this simple surgical checklist is applied. It is based on a simple list of discrete actions to be performed when the patient is admitted to the operating room, before surgical incision, and after the procedure (before returning to the ward). The aim of this instrument is to ensure appropriate equipment is available, reduce wrong-site surgery, confirm patient identity, correct management of the surgical site, avoid or reduce surgical site infection, reduce incidence of DVT (deep venous thrombosis) or pulmonary embolism (PE), prevent the risk of unintentionally retained foreign objects, and assure the appropriate postoperative setting for the patient.

The items included in the checklist are simple to detect and the time required to apply this best practice is estimated to be only 3–4 min. The checklist is divided into actions to be performed before and after the procedure and are named as follows: sign-in, time-out, sign-out. These three phases refer to main issues controlled as correct site, correct procedure, correct patient, equipment control and assessment, antibiotic administration, consolidation of central venous access, sponge count, surgical specimen control and identification, blood availability, and correct postoperative assignment. Surgeons, anesthetists, nurses, and other health care workers in the operating theater, and moreover also in the ward, must believe in this checklist, as it is a cognitive artifact to improve safety and reduce errors.

The above best safety practices may be mentioned all together being an integrated part of the WHO Safe Surgery Saves Lives Campaign manual which enhances safe surgery policies among professionals and institutions to reduce adverse events and prevent harm to patients undergoing surgery. Most of these best practices are promoted on a national basis according to each country's health care policies and strategies.

14.11 Overlap Between Surgical and Other Safety Initiatives

While some safety issues are unique to surgery (i.e., wrong-site surgery, unintentionally retained foreign objects), other safety issues overlap with other areas of medicine, although they may be found in surgical patients as well (i.e., prevention of venous thromboembolism, risk of blood transfusion). Surgeons, anesthetists, and nurses must consider all risks to patient safety, not only those unique to surgery. We all need to ensure best practices for every decision in the care of surgical patients. This may include optimal blood pressure, anticoagulation, blood sugar, and other comorbidity management to prevent preoperative complications including myocardial infarction, stroke, venous thromboembolism, hypoglycemia, delirium, and many others.

Most of the best practices above are a peculiarity of the clinical risk management and patient safety organization within health care facilities. Clinical audit, morbidity and mortality rounds, incident reporting and learning system, sentinel and never event analysis are tools used to diffuse the culture of risk assessment and management in health care and are majorly based on a human factor and cognitive approach promoting a no blame culture and systemic approach method. Global trigger tool assessment is considered to be a best practice because through some error indicators traced within clinical records and other items may easily outline mishaps and errors within the health care system and allow professionals to identify criticalities and promote implementation strategies. These are trigger items identified on a major occurrence basis which prove to surely favor the onset of mistakes or mishaps within a clinical pathway. Sentinel and never events are those which cause either severe harm to patients or death; these are considered to be lethal events that compromise trustworthiness in health care services and professionals. Informed consent, communications errors, and patient empowerment are all best practices on the same threshold; in other words, they are all aligned to assure clear communication to patients, acquire a satisfactory informed consent for procedures and pathways using a simple language and explanations which are understood by all levels of individuals undergoing medical treatment.

14.12 Technical and Non-technical Skills

Health care is considered to be a complex system, accounting a high reliability level of care and ultrasafe practices to assure no harm to patients as well as to professionals. This may not be true for some realties worldwide. The health care environment is not only complex, but dealing with human beings and events correlated to behavior and disease may lead to harmful outcomes. Due to potentially dangerous nature of medicine, a systems approach is necessary to understanding what went wrong and in what manner may surely help to build safer hospitals, health care settings, equipment and training.

Approaches to improve patient safety include both technical and adaptive work. The technical component has a relatively clear, "right" answer to solve a problem or prevent a safety occurrence in the future. More commonly, the problem requires an adaptive solution. These solutions rely on a change in attitudes, beliefs, and/or behaviors. Cognitive psychology helps us understand why humans make errors and how the human mind manages to deal with them–sometimes detecting unsafe actions before causing harm. This is one of the most important goals of clinical risk management. In order to understand the onset of human errors in health care, we must first understand human factors and their interactions in systems.

Non-technical skills are the cognitive and social skills of experienced professionals. The importance of these skills and their application to surgical safety are largely diffused within the medical institutions since the 1990s when researchers started to observe teamwork, communication, situational awareness, and leadership among surgical teams and their influence on the team itself and on patient outcome. The research performed yielded extraordinary results and since then, many medical institutions began to focus their improvement work on human factors rather than working to improve only technical skills. We know from accident analysis and other psychological research that they contribute to enhance technical performance, reduce error, and improve safety. Therefore, we may summarize these aspects as behavioral aspects of performance necessary to enhance good clinical practice. These behaviors are not directly related to the use of clinical expertise, drugs, or surgical equipment. The most frequent non-technical skills known in research are the following:

- communication
- teamwork
- leadership
- situation awareness
- decision-making
- problem-solving
- managing fatigue and stress
- task analysis

The interactions among persons, settings, relationships, attributions, and behavior rely on the way human factors across these situations and how they may improve safety in health care settings.

In a surgical setting, failures to communicate (both speaking up, or listening), to be assertive, lack of decision-making, and problems related to leadership and low situational awareness often contribute to adverse events. These mishaps account for performance failures and bad outcomes. It is very important to detect failures in communication early, but this capability requires training on human factors and human interactions.

14.13 Simulation

A training method often used in health care settings is simulation. Simulation allows trainees to practice both technical and non-technical skills in a safe, educational environment. They can be taught new skills by using either low fidelity or high-fidelity simulation equipment. For example, laparoscopy can be practiced using a simple cardboard box-based training system. Or robotic surgery can be practices on the equivalent machine that the surgeons would use in the operating theater. Experts can walk trainees through uncommon scenarios, situations, or experiences and coach trainees to adjust behaviors, adapt a model, use techniques, be resilient to undesired situations, communicate effectively, and/or manage to deal with stress and fatigue.

Effective simulation requires experienced personal dedicated to training both technical non-technical skills, such as crew management teams in aviation settings where pilots and crew members are trained to face unexpected situations and apply rescue procedures. While surgeons will clearly be the experts on the technical side, many other types of clinicians (or non-clinicians) can be effective for the non-technical portions. This pursues safety and quality improvement in a complex setting such as a cabin crew emergency plan for an airline cockpit team. The same occurs in health care and emergency medicine and surgery offer many of these unexpected situations where professionals sometimes make errors due to the lack in teamwork and communication among members of the same team. A surgical setting is complex and human interactions among persons, equipment, status, organization, and other factors may lead to either a successful result or a failure; this failure might be patient death, disability, or other negative outcome.

Trainees at every level (medical students, interns, residents, registrars, etc.) should all train on non-technical skills interaction on a regular basis. In addition, faculty, or consultants, can also benefit from this type of training and practice even after their formal surgical training is compete. Many other non-health care organizations train their employees (i.e., airline pilots) or other technical professionals on teamwork behavior and communications; these are human factors which help to reduce errors, increase performance status, and improve safety.

14.14 Training Future Leaders in Patient Safety

The Accreditation Council for Graduate Medical Education (ACGME) has mandated that all affiliated United States teaching hospitals, medical centers, health systems, and other clinical settings receive feedback through the Clinical Learning Environment Review (CLER) Program. The CLER program was established in 2012 to provide educational leaders and health care executives formative feedback to improve patient care. The six focus areas of this program are patient safety, health care quality, care transitions, supervision, well-being, and professionalism.

In regard to patient safety, the CLER program has been designed to assess whether clinical sites have processes in place to identify and implement sustainable, systems-based improvements to address patient safety vulnerabilities. The following seven patient safety pathways are assessed through the CLER program:

- Pathway 1: Education on patient safety
- Pathway 2: Culture of safety
- Pathway 3: Reporting of adverse events, near-misses/close calls, and unsafe conditions

- Pathway 4: Experience in patient safety event investigations and follow-up
- Pathway 5: Clinical site monitoring of resident, fellow, and faculty member engagement in patient safety
- Pathway 6: Resident and fellow education and experience in disclosure of events
- Pathway 7: Resident, fellow, and faculty member engagement in care transitions

Significant work remains on how to ensure the highest level of care for patients. Resident and fellow trainee physicians are a critical part of this process. The Institute of Medicine has recommended that health professional training includes quality improvement (QI) education in an effort to promote safe, high-quality, and patient-centered care.

Some major efforts to engage physicians in training are also underway. For example, the inaugural "Patient safety for the new medical generation: Promoting human factors culture in young medical doctors" meeting was held in Florence, Italy, in the summer of 2018. This meeting invigorated international collaborations (including getting three of this chapter's authors to meet for the first time.)

Local institutional efforts to train junior doctors in the field of patient safety abound throughout the world as well. Locally, at The Armstrong Institute at Johns Hopkins there is ongoing dedication to improving patient safety through quality improvement education for its trainees. The graduate medical education leadership at Johns Hopkins recognized a need to increased training for residents in fellows in both QI leaders. Consequently, the Armstrong Institute Resident/Fellow Scholars (AIRS) program was developed. Although the program has changed over the years in scope and specifics, the overall goal to give a combination of didactic and hands on education opportunities remain. The program includes didactics such as a 2-day worship in Lean Six Sigma methodology, frequent interactive group lectures, and practice-based components to observe frontline QI efforts in the health care setting. In addition, participants undertake a mentored QI project to put their newly learned skills to use in a real-world setting. Ultimately, this intensive curriculum creates physicians who are well versed in QI methodology and whom can lead these efforts in the future. With the implementation of such a curricula, resident and fellow physicians are empowered to design and execute QI projects based on deficiencies they have noted within the clinical environment.

In addition to this intensive in-person training, there exist many online longitudinal courses that allows for anyone to study patient safety topics remotely. This is currently a free massive open online course (MOOC) offered by Johns Hopkins University through Coursera (https://www.coursera.org/specializations/patient-safety). In the course, you will learn to identify core aspects of a strong patient safety culture, analyze safety and quality measures, describe the attributes of systems processes that support a strong safety culture, and develop a patient safety plan or QI strategic plan. Many other online and in-person educational materials are available in numerous languages and from many organizations around the world.

14.15　Clinical Cases

In this section, we share clinical cases of adverse events that occur more than they should at major surgical departments and teaching hospitals around the globe. While the cases may sound familiar, they are not actual patients, but are conglomerations of scenarios that we have heard of and have been studied by local patient safety teams. The approach to these events was to understand, on a systemic basis, what went wrong and as Gawande mentions in his book "The Checklist Manifesto," how to make things go right. These clinical cases represent an educational basis towards patient safety issues in surgical settings. Situational awareness, communication failures, and other non-technical skills are leading issues in these cases and are often the leading causes of errors occurring in surgery patients.

14.15.1 "I was rather sure that they were here!!!" The Case of the Missing Forceps

14.15.1.1 Case Analysis According to Risk Management Approach

- **Setting**: A major teaching hospital. A 72-year-old male patient undergoing general surgery for right-sided colon cancer.
- **Procedure**: Open right hemicolectomy under general anesthesia.
- **Team**: Performing surgeon, assistant surgeon (trainee), scrub nurse, anesthetist, assistant nurse.
- **Procedure time**: 3 hours without any delay.

A 72-year-old male patient was submitted to general surgery for a right-sided colon cancer. The surgeon performing the procedure clearly informed the patient that the procedure was a right colon resection by an open laparotomy approach. The patient was admitted to ward; prepared for surgery according to recent protocols applied in the hospital and surgery began at 9:45 a.m. The day of surgery was Thursday; no apparent organizational mishaps; the performing surgeon had 20 years of experience and the assistant surgeon (a trainee) has 4 years of experience. Both had performed a sufficient number of bowel surgeries to be comfortable. The scrub nurse has 15 years experience in abdominal surgery procedures and has been recently trained on laparoscopic procedures. The anesthetist is a 20-year veteran, experienced specialist and chief of the intensive care staff. The assistant nurse has 7 years of experience in the operating theater. No particular concerns are noted until at nearly 1 h from beginning the performing surgeon came across massive bleeding due to an incidental lesion of a mesenteric vein branching form an unusual site. This event caused some confusion amongst the team, and many sponges were used to pack the bleeding site and surgically ligate and repair the damaged vessel. The vessel damage also required an extension of bowel resection—due to involvement of the remaining bowel so as not to cause severe hypoxia to the remaining

organ tract. This accident caused the surgical team to apparently "lose control" of the setting and situation, having been concentrated on avoiding massive bleeding and shock. The procedure resumed after 1 h and finished 1 h later. Much confusion was perceived in the theater and the anesthetist urged to finish as quickly as possible because patient had several critical low blood pressure episodes.

The performing surgeon left the operating theater and asked the assistant to suture and close the laparotomy incision. The assistant nurse was occupied with another patient and called another nurse to attend the sponge and instrument counting procedure. The assistant surgeon left the operating theater without confirming the sponge or instrument count. The patient was accompanied to the ward and discharged after 10 days from the hospital.

The patient returned for surgical and oncological follow-up and a first visit was scheduled 1 month from surgery. The surgeon visits the patient and asks him several questions regarding his health status after surgery. The patient states that no particular symptom or situation occurred after surgery except for recurrent episodes of lower right back pain responding to common analgesia medications. The patient was sent to ambulatory for blood sampling and then addressed on the same day for a plain X-ray of the abdomen. Blood test values were normal in range but the X-ray demonstrated a metal foreign body in the lower right abdominal quadrant which clearly represented a 12 cm surgical forceps.

This case was submitted to the clinical risk management and patient safety team of the hospital and a root cause analysis approach was proposed to investigate the unintentionally retained foreign object (URFO). The entire surgical staff was invited, the case was discussed, and an improvement plan was agreed upon. Since then, no member of the surgical team leaves the operating room without assuring sponge and instrument count is correct and all parties agree. A surgical safety checklist was implemented that explicitly tasks individual team members with certain steps based on their roles. For example, the surgeons re-inspect the surgical wound while the circulating nurse calls early for X-ray to rule out a retained object. Quality assurance controls performed every 6 months to assess compliance to safe surgery issues.

The importance of a clinical risk management and patient safety policy is a fundamental managerial aspect of safe health care and these principles must be embedded into all levels of leadership governing hospitals and health care institutions. Patient safety awareness must be a convincing issue to deal with when quality performance indicators are discussed and monitored to achieve best levels of safety and safe care. Teamwork, communication, and a shared sense of responsibility are useful practices to encourage a culture of safety in the surgical setting.

14.15.2 "I used to move my left arm before surgery" A Case of Patient Positioning on the Operating Table

14.15.2.1 Case Analysis According to Risk Management Approach

- **Setting**: A regional hospital. 54–year-old female patient undergoing breast surgery
- **Procedure**: Left external quadrantectomy for a suspected breast cancer and sentinel lymph node detection
- **Team**: Performing surgeon, assistant surgeon, scrub nurse, anesthetist, assistant nurse
- **Procedure time**: 3 hours without any delay

A 54-year-old female patient was admitted to a general surgery ward in a regional hospital. The patient presented with a suspected breast cancer nodule located in her left breast in the upper left quadrant. The surgery was posted for an upper left quadrantectomy and sentinel lymph node biopsy. She was placed on the operating table according to usual and routine position indications by the surgeon prior to surgery. Two assistant nurses positioned the patient and extended her left arm and positioned it according to sur-

geon's directions. The operation was performed and lasted 3 h.

Upon awakening, the patient was unable to move her left arm and had sensation of paralysis. This symptom was investigated further and a partial temporary paralysis of the brachial plexus was revealed by electromyography examination. A root cause analysis revealed a series of mishaps and pitfalls that were discussed in a morbidity and mortality conference with all surgeons and operating room personal.

Improvement suggestions were to provide the operating room with diagrams and/or pictures or any other visual means of patient positions on the operating table in relationship to the specific surgical procedure. Each performing surgeon and anesthetist must control patient position before surgery and nurses must be trained on safe maneuvers. Specific risks based on the patient positioning should be understood by all team members to ensure appropriate prevention techniques are undertaken. Peripheral nerve injury is a common potentially preventable complication of poor patient positioning. Nerves can be injured by either of two mechanisms: stretch or compression. Common nerve injuries from patient positioning during surgery to consider are to the brachial plexus and its branches (commonly seen during breast surgery) or peroneal nerve injury during surgery performed in lithotomy position. Pressure injury is another common risk from ineffective postponing or padding and can be seen in numerous areas including the sacral region for supine cases or the face in prone cases.

14.15.3 "My clinic note said to remove the left lung nodule" A Case of Wrong Site Surgery

- **Setting**: A major teaching hospital. 65-year-old male undergoing video-assisted thoracoscopic (VATS) wedge resection.
- **Procedure**: Right Video-Assisted Thoracoscopic Surgery (VATS) Wedge Resection.

- **Team:** Surgical Attending, Surgical Resident, Scrub Nurse, anesthetist, circulating nurse, pre-op nurse.
- **Procedure time**: 1.5 h.

The patient is a 65-year-old male a history of pancreatic adenocarcinoma s/p pancreaticoduodenectomy in 2015 who presented to clinic with bilateral pulmonary nodules. Recent CT imaging demonstrated a 1 cm nodule on the right side in the lower lobe and a 7 mm nodule in the left lower lobe. Both nodules were peripherally located within the lower lobes. CT guided biopsy revealed a metastatic nodule on the right and benign disease of the left lower lobe nodule. He was referred to the thoracic surgery clinic for evaluation and surgical management for tissue diagnosis. The consulting surgeon planned for a VATS wedge resection of the right lower lung nodule and documented the existence of both nodules in his assessment and plan. He was posted on the surgery schedule for a right VATS lower lobe wedge resection. However, the plan on the most recent clinic note indicated that the patient would undergo a left lower lobe wedge resection.

On the day of surgery, the patient presented to the pre-op area and was consented by the surgical team for a left lower lobe wedge resection after the plan on the clinic note was reviewed. The patient was marked on the left side, which was confirmed by the nurse in the pre-op area. In the operating theater, during the "operative time out" the left side was again noted to be the correct side and all the parties in the operating theater agreed. The patient underwent a left VATS wedge resection. This nodule was sent to pathology as a frozen specimen and was noted to be benign. At this point, the surgeon broke scrub to review all the previous documentation, pathology notes and CT imaging. He realized that he had performed a wedge resection of the incorrect site—a "wrong site procedure." The team proceeded with the VATS resection on the correct side, and the patient recovered uneventfully.

When discussed, numerous points of failure were noted and the team realized there were les-

sons to be learned. First, they all realized that the discrepancy between the posting (Right VATS) and the procedure they agreed to perform (Left VATS) should have raised suspicion and led to a more thorough double check. Second, they did not include the patient in the discussion. When asked in retrospect, he stated that he did not want to speak up since he just assumed "the doctors and nurses knew what they were doing." Third, they agreed that the imaging should have been displayed (which would have shown two nodules) and then, the pathology should have been double checked to ensure the correct side was operated on. Other contributing factors included the fact that the team felt pressure to proceed quickly to get all the multiple cases for the day completed in a timely fashion.

Bibliography

1. Reason J. In: Vincent CA, editor. Clinical risk management. London: BMJ; 1995. p. 31–4.
2. Vincent CA. Risk, safety and the dark side of quality. Br Med J. 1997;314:1775–6.
3. Kohn LT, Corrigan JM, Donaldson MS. To err is human: building a safer health system. Washington, DC: Institute of Medicine, National Academy Press; 1999.
4. Reason J. Human error: models and management. BMJ. 2000;320:768–70.
5. Helmreich RL. On error management: lessons from aviation. BMJ. 2000;320:781–5.
6. Sexton JB, Thomas EJ, Helmreich RL. Error, stress, and teamwork in medicine and aviation: cross sectional surveys. BMJ. 2000;320:745.
7. Reason J. Understanding adverse events: human factors. In: Vincent CA, editor. Clinical risk management: enhancing patient safety. London: BMJ; 2001. p. 9–30.
8. Joint Commission on Accreditation of Healthcare Organization. Patient safety program. 2001. http://www.jcaho.org/index.html.
9. Leape L. Human factors meets health care: the ultimate challenge. Ergon Des. 2004;12:612.
10. Gawande A. Checklist manifesto—how to get things right. New York: H. Holt & Co.; 2009.
11. Lin F, Yule Y. Enhancing surgical performance—a primer in non technical skills. Palm Bay, FL: Apple Academic Press Inc.; 2015.
12. Van Der Veer GC, Bagnara S, Kempen GAM. Cognitive ergonomics. Amsterdam: North Holland; 1992.

13. Rinke ML, Mock CK, Persing NM, Sawyer M, Haut ER, Neufeld NJ, Nagy P. The Armstrong Institute Resident/Fellow Scholars: a multispecialty curriculum to train future leaders in patient safety and quality improvement. Am J Med Qual. 2016;31(3):224–32.

14. Co JPT, Weiss KB, CLER Evaluation Committee. CLER pathways to excellence, version 2.0: executive summary. J Grad Med Educ. 2019;11(6):739–41.

15. Duncan KC, Haut ER. Competing patient safety concerns about surgical scrub caps—infection control vs. breakdowns in communication. J Patient Saf Risk Manag. 2019;24(6):224–6.

Emergency Department Clinical Risk

15

Riccardo Pini, Maria Luisa Ralli,
and Saravanakumar Shanmugam

Learning Objectives
- The epidemiology of adverse events in emergency department.
- The importance of measuring quality of performance (quality indicators).
- The necessity of providing safety practices and implementation strategy.
- The necessity of finding tools to avoid or reducing adverse events in emergency medicine.
- The importance of implementation infrastructure requirements.

15.1 Background of Emergency Departments

The emergency department (ED) of any institution is an entry point for a significant number of patients to any health care organization. It has to

R. Pini (✉) · M. L. Ralli
Department of Clinical and Experimental Medicine, University of Florence and Emergency Medicie Department, Careggi University Hospital, Florence, Italy
e-mail: riccardo.pini@unifi.it

S. Shanmugam
Dr. Mehta's Hospital, Chennai, India

Society for Emergency Medicine India, Hyderabad, India

Emergency Medicine, Chennai, India

be conveniently located on the ground floor with direct access to the patients and ambulance. The entrance of the emergency department is always separate from the outpatient department (OPD) entrance. The department caters to various trauma and medical emergencies in both adults and in children round the clock and is adequately staffed with emergency physicians, and nursing staff to handle such emergencies at all times and days.

The common medical emergencies handled in the emergency department includes neurological emergencies like seizures or stroke, respiratory like asthma or any breathing difficulty, cardiac emergencies like myocardial infarction or cardiac arrest or any acute arrhythmia, varied abdominal and gastrointestinal emergencies and trauma emergencies that may include head injury, facial and oromaxillary injuries, chest injury, abdominal injury, musculoskeletal injuries and fractures. Apart from this, the department also caters to patients with poisoning, drowning, hanging, acute allergy, and anaphylaxis and also handles any mass or multiple casualty events and medico legal cases. During non-outpatient hours, the department also handles outpatient-based complaints and nonemergency cases who generally are triage out to OPD during OPD hours.

Unlike wards or ICU, the beds in the emergency department are utilized on a continuous basis for different patients on a given day for initial stabilization and are eventually transferred to appropriate inpatient care areas of the Health

Care Organization for continuity of care under different specialties (or) discharged from ED after initial treatment with follow-up advice. There are no recommendations or scope for providing continuity of care in the emergency department/beds. The department also oversees operations of the prehospital emergency medical services (ambulance) and coordinates their services.

Maintaining quality and developing error-free systems have been the focus of engineering over the last few decades. The "non-health care" system quality assurance program summarizes their quality assurance in two practical headings, namely paying attention to detail and handling uncertainties.

More recently, quality issues have received much attention in the medical field, and there has been some wisdom from the airline industry, replicated to health care in error prevention by introduction of safety checklists. There are however some fundamental differences between the medical and engineering field (man and machine).

The first aspect is dealing with uncertainties. One of the primary differences between man and machine is the degree of variability. Unlike machines that can be "cloned," every individual human being is different and each responds and reacts differently to illness and treatment. While there is a general pattern of presentation and response to illness, the uncertainties that one need to be prepared and deal with is more in the medical domain than in the engineering domain.

In emergency medicine, the uncertainties are particularly enormous as mostly the presenting illness is not well defined by the patients and he/she is not fully coherent or conscious to give his symptoms, signs not obviously evident, no support documents or prior medical history available, short therapeutic window, delayed or denied consent and affordability to emergency medical care.

The second aspect is paying attention to detail. Although on the surface this appears to be similar between the medical and engineering field, there is a fundamental difference. Domain experts in the engineering field have made a remarkable difference for machines.

However, the domain experts in medicine need to start understanding the key performance metrics and measure for ensuring better outcomes but still need to have a holistic approach and expertise in order to be successful and have a low margin for error. There is also a lack of adequate expertise in emergency medicine available all over the world.

In light of the above, how do we approach quality issues in the emergency departments?

Prerequisites of a good quality assurance program are:

(a) It should be reasonably simple
(b) It should be locally relevant
(c) Easily implementable
(d) Should not be resource intense
(e) Should have tangible outcomes which can be measured

15.2   Epidemiology of Adverse Events in Emergency Department

The emergency department (ED) is considered particularly high risk for adverse events (AE): 60% of ED patients experienced Medication Error [1].

An AE is defined as "an injury caused by medical management rather than by the underlying disease or condition of the patient" [2]. It represent a significant threat to patient safety and public health.

From a systematically review about AE related to emergency department care [3], appears that many studies conducted in multiple countries have reported a prevalence of AE among hospitalized patients ranging from 2.9% to 16.6%, with 36.9% to 51% of events considered preventable [4–8].

Some studies indicate that adverse events related to medical conditions as myocardial infarction, asthma exacerbation, and joint dislocation reach up to 37% [9]. They have shown also that 33% of the near-misses were intercepted.

For what concern chief complain, "alert fatigue" is one of the significant reasons for errors when there is an EMR/HIT [10].

The 29% doctors reported adverse event or near-miss of their ER patients due to poor hand off [11].

The 12% of ED revisits within 7 days is due to adverse events [12].

15.3 Most Frequent Errors Depends on: Patient, Provider, and System

Reasons because the ED is considered particularly high risk for AE include:

- First of all, **patient complexity**, it depends on many issues: age estreme, communication barrier, vague complaints, undifferentiated presentation, mental status changes, cognitive impairment, complex medical condition, delayed presentation, myths and traditional beliefs, and lack of awareness/education or knowledge of a disease.
- Secondly, **care workers**, they could risk making mistakes due to the lack of knowledge and experience on diseases and procedural skills, fatigue (they disrupt sleep cycles for health care), prejudice, and risk-taking behavior (not use personal protective equipment during procedures).
- Thirdly, **the relationship patient–doctor**. Many AE depends on bad communication: at average discharge, the verbal exchange between doctor and patient lasts 76 s. So the incomplete information during an average discharge is 65% [13]. Only 76% of the ED patients get a written diagnosis at discharge and only 34% of the ED patients get instructions on when and how to return to ER/Hospital [14].
- Fourthly, **the work environment** is characterized by time constraints, staff inadequacy, staff's lack of experience, team/communication problems, overcrowding, equipment lack or failures.

- Lastly, there are **other emerging factors**: multicultural/multilingual patient, relocation/migration of doctors to various countries and health care systems, multi-electronic health recorder (EHR) systems with poor integration for seamless flow.

15.4 Safety Practices and Implementation Strategy

To guarantee the safety practices and avoid AE, we have to do implementation strategy in many settings [15–25]:

1. Infrastructure requirements
2. Basic clinical management process and protocols for quality emergency care
3. Establishing a unit quality department
4. Measuring quality of performance (quality indicators)
5. Sharing best practices
6. Adapting to changing realities

15.4.1 Infrastructure Requirement

The factors which influence the emergency department size and design include a general scope of clinical services provided in the Health Care Organizations (HCO), average volume of ER visits, total number of beds in the HCO, availability of other support services like Radiology & Lab, total floor space, geographical location, demography of the patients who will be handled in the ER (pediatric vs geriatric), or (medical emergencies vs trauma) maximum number of possible users in a given time.

The emergency department design includes:

- **Entrance with:**
  1. Direct access from the road for ambulance and vehicles—clearly marked and with temporary vehicle parking space for cars and other means of patient transport.
  2. Ramp for wheel chair/stretcher.

3. Stretcher and wheelchair placing area.

4. Well lit entrance with wide doors which can open both ways or one way opening into the ER.

5. The doors should be wide enough to move a patient in an emergency trolleys comfortably in and out. The ideal width would be minimum 6 ft when both the door are wide open.

- **Waiting area** can be of a total size that includes seating, telephones, display for literature, public toilets, and circulation space.

- **Triage area** should be able to accommodate patients in wheel chair/emergency stretcher/ walking in. The ideal space would depend on the volume of patients received in the department. There is a close operational relationship between triage and reception where registration counter is located.

- **Resuscitation room (priority 1)**

  1. Should be at least one resuscitation room with a single dedicated bed in the ER.

  2. Ideally there should be an individual closed space with provision for emergency stretcher bed, multi-paramonitor, defibrillator, crash cart, ventilator in each room.

  3. The room should accommodate 4–5 staffs including doctors comfortably and to be able to move around the patient.

- **Urgent care (priority 2, 3)**

  1. Minimum recommended space between centers of two adjoining beds is 2 m.

  2. Each bed can be separated by a screen on all three sides for providing privacy.

- **Consultation room (priority 4)** for examination and treatment of priority 4 patients.

- **Emergency short stay unit (if applicable)**

  1. This facility may be provided either within or adjacent to the emergency unit for the prolonged observation and ongoing treatment of patients who are planned for subsequent discharge (directly from the ED). Mostly applicable to high volume ED.

  2. The types of patients planned to be admitted to this unit will determine the number and type of beds provided, and the design of associated monitoring and equipment however 8 beds is considered to be the minimum functional size.

3. The configuration of the short stay unit should be a minimum of 1 bed per 4000 attendances per year.

- **Nursing station**: a staff room/utility storage room/security room/toilets/pharmacy substores.

The design described below is important to manage patient flow:

The emergency department can have two types of patient input-throughput and output flow based on the volume and space available in the health care institution.

- *For a large volume department*, the entry and exit point of the emergency department are separate. The triage room and registration can be done at the entry, and there is also facility for registering the patient at the entry point. After triage, the patients are moved to the appropriate pre-identified bed space/area for further care. All priority 1 patients are moved to the resuscitation room. Priority 2 and 3 are treated in the urgency care areas which can also be the observation area. Priority 4 patients are triaged out to outpatient department (OPD) or can be handled in emergency room in a pre-designated fast track room or doctor consultation room (especially in non-OPD hours) in the emergency department, and an emergency bed is not necessary for these category of patients. On disposition, the patients are moved into the hospital or discharged through an exit, away from the entry area. Billing counters can be situated at the exit. Bed side billing can also be done.

- *For low volume emergency departments* and HCOs with limited space, the entry and exit is through the same point and the registration and billing counter is essentially located at the entry/exit point. No separate triage room or space is provided and all the patients visiting ER are allotted a bed straight away and a bed side triaging is done. All priority 1 patients are either moved to the bed identified for resuscitation purpose or resuscitation can happen in the same bed. Priority 2, 3, and 4 are treated in emergency beds (Priority 4 can also be treated in ER doctor consultation room (if available). On disposition, the patients are moved into the hospital or discharged through the same entry/exit point. Billing counters can be situated here and bed side billing can also be done.

15.4.2 Basic Clinical Management Process and Protocols for Quality Emergency Care

Each emergency department is unique as the patient profile varies with locality of the hospital infrastructure within the same city and level of acuity which that particular hospital can handle. Also the disease profiles and health care systems vary across the globe.

Clinical management protocols are based on evidence-based recommendations and best practice recommendation where a clinical evidence is not possible.

Clinical protocols have to be region based applicable to the population demography of the hospital and their health needs.

For example, a trauma center hospital may look into how efficiently they can manage a patient of poly trauma and process to better clinical outcome, like initiating a massive transfusion vs a peripheral pediatric hospital where the nature of emergencies tend to be more medical in nature than surgical.

Irrespective of the locality—the protocols need to be tested and constantly upgraded based on recent updates.

Appropriate mock assessments periodically and audits are a must to ensure the policies and processes and implemented at the ground level.

15.4.3 Establishing a Unit Quality Department

Establishment of quality department is essential in order to examine the association between the scope of quality improvement (QI) implementation in hospitals and hospital performance on selected indicators of quality. Various key performance indicators (KPI) may be set by an identified champion from the emergency department who may be certified through various national or international training programs for being an internal auditor program or quality implementation in hospital and with help from external accrediting agencies.

Reviews on various aspects of improving KPI must be taken up as a continuous process in order to reduce errors. Coordinate care among settings and practitioners and ensure relevant, accurate information is available when needed as critical elements in providing high level of care.

- **It is extremely important in achieving quality control of the highest standard in medical equipment**: Periodic checks at least once a year is essential in achieving this goal. Can be done for a range of equipment including defibrillators, ventilators, pulse oxymeters, infusion pumps, patient monitors, etc. This may be done as part as set of national and international standards by trained engineers with the help of specialized testing and calibrating equipment as per manufacturer recommendations. It should be concluded by documenting test results and issuing a calibration report. Any measuring equipment or device needs to be tested and checked for its accuracy and calibrated whenever need arises. Testing is done as per domestic standards which implies in accordance with manufacturer specifications, for both safety and performance tests. The results need to be formally documented.
- **Key parameters for testing and calibrating in emergency department may include**
  1. Defibrillators: Electrical safety tests, biphasic energy measurements, ECG, performance and arrhythmia simulation, wave form simulation
  2. Pulse oxymeter: Electrical safety, O_2 saturation, heart rate, pulse amplitude, selectable pigmentation, and ambient light condition
  3. Infusion pumps: Flow rates, occlusion alarm tests, pressure
  4. Ventilators: Modes, lung parameters, etc.
- The entire activity must be subjected to appropriate methods of internal control and inspection.

15.4.4 Measuring Quality of Performance (Quality Indicators)

However, institutions need to adapt appropriate quality indicators, and the following quality indicators can represent the quality of emergency departments:

- Door-to-triage time
- Door-to-doctor time
- Door-to-needle time in stroke thrombolysis
- Pain score assessment
- Investigation return time
- Nurse/patient ratio
- Patient satisfaction level
- Time taken for discharge
- Mortality (Adjusted)
- Length of stay
- Left without been seen by a doctor
- Pain assessment/reassessment
- Safety—patient falls, medication error, failed intubation rate
- Incident reporting and RCA
- Infections—hand-hygiene compliance

- **Door-to-triage time**
  - Description: Time interval of patient arrival to nurse triage
  - Type of parameter: Outcome
  - Formula: Time from patient arrival to time when triage is completed for a particular category of patients
  - Benchmark: Does not exist
  - Action plan: Ensures quality in design, conformance
- **Door-to-doctor time**
  - Description: In case of emergency the time shall begin from the time the patient's arrival at the emergency till the time that the initial assessment is completed
  - Type of parameter: Outcome
  - Formula: Sum of the time taken for assessment/total number of patients in emergency
  - Benchmark: Does not exist
  - Action plan: Ensures quality in design, conformance

- **Door-to-needle time in stroke thrombolysis**
  - Description: In case of acute onset ischemic stroke in window period
  - Type of parameter: Morbidity in stroke
  - Formula: Number of stroke patients thrombolyzed/number of eligible stroke patients for thrombolysis
  - Benchmark: Does not exist
  - Action plan: Ensures quality in design, conformance
- **Mortality parameter**
  - Description: Standardized mortality rate (SMR)
  - Type of parameter: Outcome
  - Formula: Number of deaths/number of discharges and deaths $\times$ 100
  - Benchmark: None
  - Action plan: Ensures quality in design and conformance
- **Patient satisfaction (effective communication)**
  - Description: Efficacy of communication
  - Type of parameter: Process
  - Formula: Quarterly average score/Max score possible $\times$ 100
  - Benchmark: Not known
  - Action plan: Through patient satisfaction
- **Patient fall rates**
  - Description: Patient fall rate
  - Type of parameter: Safety; morbidity
  - Formula: Number of falls/number of bed days
  - Benchmark: 8.46/1000 bed days
  - Action plan: Ensures quality in design (beds) and conformance (sedation)
- **Medication errors**
  - Description: Medication error
  - Type of parameter: Safety
  - Formula: (Number of errors/number of bed days) $\times$ 1000
  - Benchmark: 1.2 to 947/1000 bed days (reported)
  - Action plan: Clinical pharmacists; process (2-people check)
- **Compliance to hand-hygiene protocols**
  - Description: Compliance to hand hygiene
  - Type of parameter: Infection; outcome; safety

- Formula: (Number adhered/total number of procedures) × 100
- Benchmark: 90% adherence
- Action plan: Surveillance; health education
- **Investigation return time**
  - Description: Radiology CT investigation report
  - Type of parameter: Adherence to protocol
  - Formula: Time of order to time of reporting
  - Benchmark: 60 min
  - Action plan: Clinical audit
- **Length of stay in ER**
  - Description: Average length of stay
  - Type of parameter: Adherence to protocol, safety
  - Formula: Total length of stay of all patients in hours/total number of patients
  - Benchmark: 240 min
  - Action plan: Audit
- **Nurse patient ration in ER**
  - Description: Nurse per bed per shift
  - Type of parameter: Safety, mortality, morbidity
  - Formula: Number of nurse/number of beds in each shift
  - Benchmark: Does not exists
  - Action plan: Audit
- **Pain management in ER**
  - Description: Proportion of patients presenting with pain in whom validated pain score is documented
  - Type of parameter: Key performance indicator
  - Formula: Patients with pain assessment using validated score/total number of patients presented with pain × 100
  - Benchmark: Does not exists
  - Action plan: Audit
- **Time taken for discharge**
  - Description: Discharge is the process by which a patient is shifted out from the ED with all concerned medical summaries after ensuring stability
  - Type of parameter: Safety
  - Formula: Sum of time taken for discharge/number of patients discharged

- Benchmark: Does not exists
- Action plan: Audit
- **Left against medical advice**
  - Description: Percent of patients who leave the ED before examination
  - Type of parameter: Safety
  - Formula: Total number of patients who leave ER before seen by doctor/total number presented to ER during the time of study × 100
  - Benchmark: Does not exists
  - Action plan: Audit
- **Non-conformance control and management**
  - Any non-conformance observed should be properly reported through incident reporting system which will be reviewed by a multidisciplinary committee and quality department of the hospital.
  - The non-conformances could be
    (a) Near-miss
    (b) Medical error
    (c) Sentinel event
- **Configuration control and management under quality of design**
  - Any process change in hospital flow system or physical layout or functions related to assignment pattern of doctors/staff need to be reported and discussed in the leadership team meet of the institution along with the justification of such a change and approval.

15.4.5 Sharing Best Practices

A "Best Practice" can be defined as a technique or methodology that has proven reliably to lead to a desired result.

At a minimum, a best practice should:

- Demonstrate evidence of success
- Affect something important (e.g., safety, wait time)
- Have the potential to be replicated to other settings
- Evidence-based protocols/guidelines must be incorporated to deliver care

- Guidelines can improve patient safety, streamline methods of care, lower costs and increase efficiency
- Communication and academic discussions among Clinicians and Department staff may ensure a smooth process for implementation of guidelines, e.g., hand washing practices/reducing rates of central venous catheter-related infection
- Ensure guidelines are updated regularly
- Institutional support from leadership and making evidence-based guidelines a habit among all levels of staff

15.4.6 Adapting to Changing Realities

15.4.6.1 Digitization

Opportunities for using data to improve the health system are partially driven by technological advances. New analytical methods, more efficient processing, and automation of routine analyses and analytics, for example, make it easier to draw insights from health data and to present the resulting information in an actionable format.

In the clinical setting, secondary use of health data can improve quality initiatives and the effectiveness of frontline care. For health system management, health data can be used to manage and improve the effectiveness and efficiency of the health system by informing program, policy, and funding decisions. For example, costs can be reduced by identifying ineffective interventions, missed opportunities, and duplication of services.

To facilitate health research, health data can be used to support research that informs clinical programs, health system management, and population and public health. Such research spans multiple fields.

15.4.6.2 Measuring Patient Feedback

Patient feedback systems are used to know their experiences when visiting the hospital, understanding of the services hospitals offer and opinions on changes you may have recently introduced or plan to make.

With a good feedback system, one can increase your understanding of what patients think about a hospital, understand areas of concern and take action to transform the experience for patients. One can make changes and use the system to monitor patient reaction, gradually improving the practice based on accurate feedback.

Patient experience measures:

- should be developed with patient input to ensure that they are representative of their needs, values, and preferences
- reveal critical information about the extent to which care is truly patient centered
- provide a rigorous, validated alternative to the subjective reviews that are posted on a large number of review sites

Service Excellency

Other than the time lines mentioned at the 4 priority levels, other measures that may be undertaken to reduce times:

- Gather prior information about arrival of patient
- Delegate documentation to other trained staff
- Create appropriate policies in order to reduce time
- Use telecommunication systems to deliver relevant information about patient from the time of first paramedic contact

Clinical Audit

- The review of clinical performance against agreed standards, and the refining of clinical practice as a result—a cyclical process of quality improvement in clinical care.
- The systematic critical analysis of the quality of health care, including the procedures used for diagnosis, treatment and care, the use of resources, and the resulting outcome and quality of life for patients.
- Monitor the use of particular interventions, or the care received by patients, against agreed standards. Any deviation from "best practices" can then be examined in order to understand and act upon the causes.

There are different modalities with which we can do a clinical audit:

- **Standards-based audit (criteria-based audit)**

  This is the recommended process. Current practice is compared against defined criteria, standards, or best practices, through the "audit cycle"

- **Peer review audit**

  With the benefit of hindsight, the quality of services provided is assessed by a team, reviewing case notes and seeking ways to improve clinical care. This is especially applicable in "interesting" or "unusual" cases.

- **Significant event audit**

  Adverse occurrences, critical incidents, unexpected outcomes, and problematic cases causing concern are reviewed systematically and solutions implemented. Surveys targets for opinions or suggestions may include patients or special focus groups. Information gathered is then analyzed and change implemented as appropriate.

Stages of an audit

1. Prepare and plan for the project
2. Select an area to audit
3. Defining criteria and setting up standards
4. Collection of data
5. Analyze results
6. Identify solutions for improvement and implement changes
7. Re audit to monitor the impact of changes (close audit loop)

This must be led by senior clinicians in the department and must be reported to the audit review boards and discussed with higher stakeholders for implementation and continuous improvement.

15.4.6.3 Test Optimization

In the emergency department, accurate diagnosis in a minimum of time is critical to ensure the best patient outcomes. Every minute is essential.

High-risk patients with potentially life-threatening conditions must be identified quickly and appropriate treatment initiated. At the same time, cost containment and optimized patient flow management are also essential.

Use of protocols play an important role, for example, the latest guidelines for diagnostic management of acute venous thromboembolism, which recommend using algorithms that combine clinical probability assessment with a quantitative D-Dimer test. This limits the number of required imaging tests, offering cost saving and prevention of patient harm or Troponin I may safely rule-out and accurately rule-in acute Myocardial infarction (non-ST elevation myocardial infarction) in 70% of suspected chest pain patients when sent at an appropriate time.

Patient-centered outcomes research as applied to optimization in tests such as those mentioned above or diagnostic imaging includes the engagement of patients in the decision-making process to order imaging, deliver the results to patients and caregivers, and follow-up incidental findings from the diagnostic test. One aspect of patient-centered care is the process of shared decision-making, which allows patients and their providers to make health care decisions together, taking into account the best scientific evidence available, as well as the patient's values and preferences.

Clinical decision rules (CDRs) are evidence-based algorithms derived from original research and are used to provide guidance for clinical decision-making. They can either be "directive" (suggesting a course of action) or "assistive" (providing evidence to enhance clinical judgment).

Well-validated CDRs can potentially reduce the use of diagnostic tests and empower clinicians with risk assessments for a given constellation of clinical symptoms and signs. They can also serve to reduce inappropriate variation in practice by offering evidence to assist the clinician at the point of care.

15.4.6.4   Work Culture

Safety
Various factors compromise the security of working doctors in the emergency rooms. Few of these include:

1. 24 h accessability of the emergency department
2. Lack of adequately trained armed or security guards
3. Patient pain and discomfort
4. Family member stress due to patient's condition and fear of the unknown
5. Family member anger related to hospital policies and the health care system in general or cramped space
6. Long wait times

At a minimum, workplace violence prevention programs should:

1. Create and disseminate a clear policy of zero tolerance for workplace violence, verbal and nonverbal threats and related actions.
2. Ensure that managers, supervisors, coworkers, clients, patients, and visitors know about this policy.
3. Ensure that no employee who reports or experiences workplace violence faces reprisals.
4. Encourage employees to promptly report incidents and suggest ways to reduce or eliminate risks.
5. Require records of incidents to assess risk and measure progress.
6. Outline a comprehensive plan for maintaining security in the workplace. This includes establishing a liaison with law enforcement representatives and others who can help identify ways to prevent and mitigate workplace violence.
7. Assign responsibility and authority for the program to individuals or teams with appropriate training and skills.
8. Ensure that adequate resources are available for this effort and that the team or responsible individuals develop expertise on workplace violence prevention in health care and social services.

9. Affirm management commitment to a worker-supportive environment that places as much importance on employee safety and health as on serving the patient or client.

Reference to Standards
Developing benchmarks to incorporate best practices is absolutely essential to maintain quality in health care. Quality governing bodies such as QCI and accreditation boards like the NABH work in collaboration with hospitals across the country to achieve the same. Benchmarking of a particular standard may be derived from the best evidences in clinical practice or standards set by external agencies such as the WHO. Further, continuous audits and statistical analysis by existing quality departments across hospitals may ensure implementation and impact of implementation as a prerequisite to continuous quality improvement. Potential key performance indicators may also be identified. Also benchmarks can be internal based on the measured performances of the department.

Communication Best Practice
All emergency departments have to ensure that the patients, relatives, the primary physician are well informed about the clinical status of the patient through a structured communication protocol. A communication checklist to ensure adequate communication has taken before disposition needs to be implemented in all emergency departments.

Culture of Safety
Culture of safety with promotion of reporting errors, teamwork, communication openness, transparency with feedback, learning from errors, and administrative collaboration. Identify champions of quality and patient safety in ER.

Standardize
- Communication
- Crucial information
- Verifying comprehension
- Discharge process
- Hand off
- Measures (e.g., kgs vs lbs)
- Documentation

- Time shifts
- Checklists
- Transparency
- Public posting/reporting of quality data
- Patient satisfaction and experience scores
- Feedback reviews
- Communication and Resolution Programs (CRP)

Regulation
- Professional self-regulation
- Maintenance of certification
- External accreditation
- Leadership program for emerging units

Financial Incentive
- Incentive for performance
- "No pay" for preventable complications
- Accountable care organization—Group incentive to deliver coordinated care and outcome

Liability Reform
- Enterprise liability
- Safe harbors
- Administrative compensation systems or health courts

15.5 Clinical Cases About Worse Practices That Didn't Consider the Importance of Non-Technical Skills/Technical Skills

15.5.1 Non-Technical Skills Case

A 50-year-old white man with a history of hypertension, hyperlipidemia, obesity (body mass index, 34.9 kg/m^2), and chronic tobacco use presented with presyncope symptoms.

Severe pressure-like chest pain had started 24 h previously and had completely resolved spontaneously 12 h before the current presentation. An electrocardiogram (ECG) showed persistent ST-segment elevation in the anterior leads. He was hemodynamically well compensated. Initial laboratory reports showed cardiac troponin I elevation to a level above 50 ng/mL. After 15 min he came into the hospital, the patient experienced sustained ventricular tachycardia and then lost consciousness. He had no spontaneous respirations, and neither the carotid nor femoral pulses could be palpated. So the resuscitation team came into the patient room. The team members are good staff who came from different hospitals and they had not ever worked together, so they were able to perform the functions of their role but they did not understand how they have to interface with the other members of the team.

The team leader did not know the team members and tried to ensure that the resuscitation effort flows smoothly and that each task is completed properly, but he failed.

He did not organize the team because he did not know the abilities of each of the team members. He did not monitor the performance of each role. He did not clearly define each task and verify that assignments are understood.

The team member did not let the team leader know if a task was beyond one's own skill level and did not inform the leader that the task was understood completed.

They did not speak clearly, nobody kept the time of the drugs, the shock time, neither revaluation's time, and the resuscitation was getting worse.

The team was out of control.

Fortunately, a nurse draws attention to changes in the patient's status and she notes that the patient had ROSC.

This is an example that what happens to team members and the leader when each one did not meet the expectations of own role in the team, there was not clear, property, closed-loop communication; there was no knowledge sharing.

Below you could find ACLS' team dynamics guidelines [26]. One of the new features in the 2015 guidelines is an emphasis on team dynamics. In order to provide optimal outcomes, each team member must be able to perform the functions of his role and must understand how his role interfaces with other roles on the team. Usually, a resuscitation team will have one team leader. This leader is responsible for ensuring that the resuscitation effort flows smoothly and that each task is completed properly. This role is often filled by a physician but can be done by anyone who can:

- Organize the team
- Monitor the performance of each role
- Perform any skills if necessary
- Model appropriate behaviors
- Coach other members of the team as necessary
- Focus on provision of exceptional care
- Mentor the group by providing a critique of team and individual performance when the resuscitation is over

Team members should be assigned to roles based on their scope of practice and training for the assigned tasks. A team member must be able to:

- Understand his role in this resuscitation
- Perform the tasks assigned
- Understand the ACLS protocols and algorithms
- Promote and contribute to the success of the team

Expectation	Team leader actions	Team member actions
Roles	Knows the abilities of each of the team members	Team member will let the team leader know if a task is beyond his skill level; asks for help if unable to complete a task
Communication	Clearly defines each task and verifies that assignments are understood; confirms performance of task	Informs the leader that task is understood; informs the leader when each task is completed
Messages	Speaks clearly and in a normal tone of voice when giving assignments and orders	Speaks clearly and in a normal tone of voice when acknowledging assignments and orders, and feels comfortable questioning unclear orders

Expectation	Team leader actions	Team member actions
Knowledge sharing	Asks for suggestions from team members for alternative actions when needed	Shares information with team and helps to identify actions that may be inhibiting the resuscitation effort
Intervention	Intervenes quickly but gently if a team member is about to perform an incorrect action or if a task is taking too long	Asks the leader to repeat an order if the member thinks an error will occur and feels comfortable suggesting alternative courses of action
Evaluation and summary	Asks for suggestions for alternative actions from team members; is constantly aware of patient's responses; keeps team members informed of patient's current status and plans for change in actions; provides positive and corrective feedback as needed	Draws attention to changes in the patient's status or response to treatments

15.5.2 Technical Skills: Central Venous Line

A 77-year-old man presented to the emergency department with abdominal pain. His medical history included treated hypertension and hyper-cholesterolemia, previous heavy alcohol intake, and mild cognitive impairment. He was drowsy and confused when roused and was peripherally cold with cyanosis. The systemic arterial blood pressure was 75/50 mm Hg, and the heart rate was 125 beats/min. The abdomen was tense and distended. After the administration of 20 mL/kg of intravenous crystalloid, the blood pressure was not restored, so the EM physician decided to start vasopressor infusion to support blood pressure.

In order to avoid phlebitis or sclerosis, the doctor decided to place a central venous line in the right internal jugular vein. Considering the urgent clinical scenario, he did the procedure without ultrasound using anatomical landmarks.

He was very scared about the patient's vital parameters that were getting worse, so he settled on to not prepare the site in a sterile fashion neither wear sterile dressing nor place the patient in the appropriate position for the site selected (IJV).

He did not infiltrate the skin with 1% lidocaine for local anesthesia around the site of the needle insertion.

Using anatomical landmarks, he inserted the introducer needle with negative pressure, but suddenly the patient turned his head due to pain and he misplaced the needle in the carotid artery. So he went out with the needle and squeezed the punctured site to avoid hematoma. He tried again but he did pneumothorax and he had to put a chest tube to decompress it.

Finally, he placed the CVC line; a computed tomographic scan of the abdomen showed extraluminal gas and suspected extraluminal feces consistent with a perforated sigmoid colon. He was treated with intravenous antibiotics and taken to the operating room for laparotomy and was admitted to ICU.

This is an example of what happens if you do not follow procedures, do not use guidelines and checklist, and do not do it again and again over a fake patient in simulation laboratory. Following procedures, guidelines, checklist, and simulation's experience, it could be possible avoiding CVC's complications that include pain at cannulation site, local hematoma, infection (both at the site and bacteremia), misplacement into another vessel (possibly causing arterial puncture or cannulation), vessel laceration or dissection, air embolism, thrombosis, and pneumothorax requiring a possible chest tube.

What was the doctor supposed to do?

1. Prepare the equipment, syringe and needle for local anesthetic, small vial of 1% lidocaine, syringe and introducer needle, scalpel, guidewire, tissue dilator, sterile dressing, suture and needle, central line catheter. If it is difficult to remind everything, it is possible to use a checklist with all the equipments and you have to put a tick near the material you bring.

2. Place the patient in the appropriate position for the site selected, then prepare the site in a sterile fashion using the sterile solution, sterile gauze, and sterile drapes. For the internal jugular and subclavian approach, place the patient in reverse Trendelenburg with the head turned to the opposite side of the site.

3. Infiltrate the skin with 1% lidocaine for local anesthesia around the site of the needle insertion.

4. Use the bedside ultrasound to identify the target vein, if anatomical landmarks are not clear.

5. Insert the introducer needle with negative pressure until venous blood is aspirated. Whenever possible, the introducer needle should be advanced under ultrasound guidance to ensure the tip does not enter the incorrect vessel or puncture through the distal edge of the vein.

6. Once venous blood is aspirated, stop advancing the needle. Carefully remove the syringe and thread the guidewire through the introducer needle hub.

7. While still holding the guidewire in place, remove the introducer needle hub.

8. If possible, use the ultrasound to confirm the guidewire is in the target vessel in two different views.

9. Next, use the scalpel tip to make a small stab in the skin against the wire just large enough to accommodate the dilator (and eventually, the central venous catheter). Insert the dilator with a twisting motion.

10. Advance the CVL over the guidewire. Make sure the distal lumen of the central line is

uncapped to facilitate passage of the guidewire.

11. Once the CVL is in place, remove the guidewire. Next, flush and aspirate all ports with the sterile saline.

12. Secure the CVL in place with the suture and place a sterile dressing over the site.

15.6 Recommendation

Research on AE in multiple care settings has identified that the emergency department (ED) is considered particularly high risk for adverse events (AE).

To guarantee the safety practices and avoid AE, we have to do implementation strategy in many settings: infrastructure requirements, basic clinical management process and protocols for quality emergency care, establishing a unit quality department, measuring quality of performance (quality indicators), sharing best practices, adapting to changing realities and create and disseminate a clear policy of zero tolerance for workplace violence, verbal and nonverbal threats and related actions.

Developing benchmarks to incorporate best practices is absolutely essential to maintain quality in health care is very important too. Further, continuous audits and statistical analysis by existing quality departments across hospitals may ensure implementation and impact of implementation as a prerequisite to continuous quality improvement. Potential key performance indicators may also be identified.

Structured communication protocol allows the patients, relatives, the primary physician are well informed about the clinical status of the patient. A communication checklist to ensure adequate communication has taken before disposition needs to be implemented in all emergency departments.

Furthering the promotion of reporting errors, teamwork, communication openness, transparency with feedback, learning from errors, and administrative collaboration.

Identify champions of quality and patient safety in ER.

Furthering standardize communication, time shifts, checklists, patient satisfaction and experience scores, feedback reviews.

In the clinical practice, it is important doing alias clinical audit to examine any deviation from "best practices" to understand and act upon the causes.

The simulation also has to become a way to avoid AE in emergency department improving care workers' technical and no-technical skills.

References

1. Patanwala AE, Warholak TL, Sanders AB, Erstad BL. A prospective observational study of medication errors in a tertiary care emergency department. Ann Emerg Med. 2010;55(6):522–6.
2. Kohn LT, Corrigan JM, Donaldson MS, editors. To err is human: building a safer health system. Washington, DC: National Academy Press; 2000.
3. Stang AS, Wingert AS, Hartling L, Plint AC. Adverse events related to emergency department care: a systematic review. PLoS One. 2013;8(9):e74214. https://doi.org/10.1371/journal.pone.0074214.
4. Baker GR, Norton PG, Flintoft V, Blais R, Brown A, et al. The Canadian Adverse Events Study: the incidence of adverse events among hospital patients in Canada. CMAJ. 2004;170:1678–86.
5. Thomas EJ, Studdert DM, Burstin HR, Orav EJ, Zeena T, et al. Incidence and types of adverse events and negligent care in Utah and Colorado. Med Care. 2000;38:261–71.
6. Wilson RM, Runciman WB, Gibberd RW, Harrison BT, Newby L, et al. The quality in Australian health care study. Med J Aust. 1995;163:458–71.
7. Brennan TA, Leape LL, Laird NM, Hebert L, Localio AR, et al. Incidence of adverse events and negligence in hospitalized patients. Results of the Harvard Medical Practice Study I. N Engl J Med. 1991;324:370–6.
8. Leape LL, Brennan TA, Laird N, Lawthers AG, Localio AR, et al. The nature of adverse events in hospitalized patients. Results of the Harvard Medical Practice Study II. N Engl J Med. 1991;324:377–84.
9. Camargo CA Jr, Tsai CL, Sullivan AF, et al. Safety climate and medical errors in 62 US emergency departments. Ann Emerg Med. 2012;60(5):555–563.e20.
10. Farley HL, Baumlin KM, Hamedani AG, et al. Quality and safety implications of emergency department information systems. Ann Emerg Med. 2013;62(4):399–407.
11. Horowitz LI, Meredith T, Schuur JD, Shah NR, Kulkarni RG, Jeng GY. Dropping the baton: a quali-

tative analysis of failures during the transition from emergency department to inpatient care. Ann Emerg Med. 2009;53(6):701–710.e4.

12. Calder L, Pozgay A, Riff S, et al. Adverse events in patients with return emergency department visits. BMJ Qual Saf. 2015;24(2):142–8.

13. Rhodes KV, Vieth T, He T, et al. Resuscitating the physician-patient relationship: emergency department communication in an academic medical center. Ann Emerg Med. 2004;44(3):262–7.

14. Vashi A, Rhodes KV. Sign right here and you're good to go: a content analysis of audiotaped emergency department discharge instructions. Ann Emerg Med. 2011;57(4):315–322.e1.

15. Crossing the Quality Chasm: A New Health System for the 21st CenturyInstitute of Medicine (US) Committee on Quality of Health Care in America Washington (DC): National Academies Press (US). 2001. https://doi.org/10.17226/10027.

16. WHO guidelines for essential trauma care. 2004. https://www.who.int/violence_injury_prevention/publications/services/guidelines_traumacare/en/.

17. Pre hospital trauma care systems. 2005. https://www.who.int/violence_injury_prevention/publications/services/39162_oms_new.pdf.

18. Mass casualty management system. 2007. https://www.who.int/hac/techguidance/tools/mcm_guidelines_en.pdf.

19. WHO surgical safety checklist. 2008. https://www.who.int/patientsafety/safesurgery/checklist/en/.

20. WHO guidelines for trauma quality improvement programs. 2009. https://www.who.int/emergencycare/trauma/essential-care/guidelines/en/.

21. Prang K-H, Canaway R, Bismark M, Dunt D, Kelaher M. The impact of Australian healthcare reforms on emergency department time-based process outcomes: An interrupted time series study. PLoS One. 2018;13(12):e0209043. https://doi.org/10.1371/journal.pone.0209043.

22. WHO trauma care checklist. 2016. WHO trauma care checklist. 2016 https://www.who.int/publications/i/item/trauma-care-checklist.

23. Shanmugam S. ISRO—SEMI—AHPI Health quality upgrade enabling space technology in ER. 2017. https://www.caho.in/sites/default/files/ER-QUEST.pdf.

24. NABH—guidelines for ER accreditation. 2017 https://www.nabh.co/Emergency_Documents.aspx.

25. IFEM quality frame work update. 2018. https://www.ifem.cc/wp-content/uploads/2019/05/An-Updated-Framework-on-Quality-and-Safety-in-Emergency-Medicine-January-2019.pdf.

26. ACLS provider manual. 2015. https://shopcpr.heart.org/courses/acls.

Obstetric Safety Patient

16

Antonio Ragusa, Shin Ushiro, Alessandro Svelato, Noemi Strambi, and Mariarosaria Di Tommaso

16.1 Introduction

In healthcare, the patient safety system which has been developed following the study of the various phases necessary for its determination, supplies strategies to avoid the repetition of circumstances that originally has led an individual to make mistakes. In fact, the culture of risk management, starting from the consideration that the errors are not eliminable, is based on the belief that they need to be properly analyzed, implementing intervention strategies that avoid its repetition, in order to become good learning opportunities.

The risk is the condition or potential event, intrinsic or extrinsic to the process, which can modify the expected outcome. It is measured in terms of probability and consequences, as a product of the probability that a specific event can occur and the seriousness of the damage that can follow this. In the calculation of risk, human ability to identify and contain the consequences of the potentially harmful event is also considered [1].

In obstetrics, there is cultural confusion regarding the concept of risk, as a measurement of the probability of damage in a given population, and the concept of risk as the presence of danger for an individual.

That is, the approach which considers all women to be at risk, without systematically defining the degree of probability with which a complication can occur in a specifically assisted obstetric condition, is not functional, nor positive regarding assistance for several reasons:

- **Cultural**: the culture of risk increases the anxiety of operators and women. While scientific investigation of uncertainty promises to increase safety; in actual fact, it increases our insecurity, distorting the emphasis on the prevention of impending risks, and transforming the majority of healthy pregnant women into pre-sick people.
- **Organizational**: no healthcare system can always guarantee maximum efficiency. It is useful that the organization is optimized for a significant event, while it is reasonable to apply low intensity assistance in the normal course of activity.

A. Ragusa (✉) · A. Svelato
Obstetrics and Gynecology Department, Fatebenefratelli Hospital, San Giovanni Calibita, Rome, Italy

S. Ushiro
Division of Patient Safety, Kyushu University Hospital, Fukuoka, Japan
e-mail: ushiro@surg2.med.kyushu-u.ac.jp

N. Strambi · M. Di Tommaso
Department of Health Sciences, Obstetrics and Gynecology, University of Florence, Careggi Hospital Florence, Florence, Italy

Fetal Maternal Department, AOU Careggi Hospital, Florence, Italy
e-mail: mariarosaria.ditommaso@unifi.it

© The Author(s) 2021
L. Donaldson et al. (eds.), *Textbook of Patient Safety and Clinical Risk Management*,
https://doi.org/10.1007/978-3-030-59403-9_16

- **Pragmatic**: in a healthcare system, operators cannot be kept on continuous alert so as not to let down their guard precisely in the circumstances in which they should be fully present.
- **Epidemiological**: the value of a diagnostic test useful to highlight the presence of a maternal or fetal pathology depends on the knowledge of the *a priori* probability that pathology occurs in the population under investigation.

For Bayes' theorem, the positive predictive value of a diagnostic test is directly related to the prevalence of the negative outcome, to be avoided in the population under investigation [2]. In other words, the presence of a pathological test is really indicative of pathology, the greater the *a priori* prevalence of the same in the subject undergoing the test. *Vice versa*, the percentage of false positives of the test is greater the lower the probability of the appearance of pathology in the subject undergoing the test.

If the prevalence is not taken into account, there will be a much more frequent alarm than necessary. For example, in a physiological population with low probability (<1%) of having a fetal acidosis, the presence of a pathological cardiotocographic tracing implies an effective presence of acidosis in 16% of cases. *Vice versa*, in a pre-eclamptic patient, who has a high probability of an acidosis risk (about 30%), due to placental hypoperfusion and the consequently reduced reserves in the underdeveloped fetus, the same tracing implies the presence of acidosis in 89% of cases. From these considerations it follows that it is appropriate to have a greater or lesser diligence or interventionism in the presence of pathological traces in physiology and risk.

A rational attitude is therefore that of getting used to mentally cataloging the *a priori* probability of possible pathologies, which the woman or fetus that is seen during pregnancy or in labor could present. Although it is not possible to foresee everything, it is necessary to be aware that a pathology is not equally distributed in all pregnancies, but will depend on specific variables that we must take into account every time we take care of a woman, to optimize assistance in a personalized way [3]. In conclusion, it is not possible to define a woman at risk without defining the type of risk and the probability that this risk can develop.

A further problem directly related to the safety of the obstetric patient derives from the fact that in obstetrics, perhaps more than in other medical disciplines, we can witness a rapid transition from a situation of well-being to an acute pathology, moreover in a context such as birth that is usually accompanied by positive, celebratory emotions. This immediately leads both operators and families to think that something has not been done as it should have been [4].

But it is a fact that adverse events are ubiquitous in today's clinical practices despite the best intentions to improve patient health. If complications related to the course of a certain disease or specific treatment have been accepted for centuries as part of the care process; another matter is the question of error. It is only since the end of the last century that we have started talking about the prevention of adverse events or claims for damages related to an error. Human and systemic errors are intrinsic to the complex care system and we are well aware of their weight in medicine. So this is why all possible strategies must be put in place to avoid a foreseeable error through risk management. Getting and making things right when things go wrong defines a successful safety program [5].

16.2 Patient Safety

Risk management identifies a set of actions which improve the quality of health services in order to guarantee patient safety. Risk management tools are represented by four processes: **identification**, **analysis**, **control**, and **financial coverage of risk**.

Risk investigation is the process by which situations, the user and the procedure are identified, which can lead, or have led, to a loss. The approach is based on the assumption that any error is the consequence of problems that precede it and that such problems could become manifest even before the adverse event occurs.

The map of critical areas identifies various criticalities in different ways; it presupposes the presence of a surveillance epidemiological observatory and can be carried out according to the needs of the research, the time, the concentration of adverse events in a given sector, the severity of the adverse events, etc. Its interpretation must always be very cautious as a starting point for a critical analysis and not used as the conclusive outcome of an investigation.

Risk control consists of the implementation of prevention procedures and strategies that lead to the creation of a specific risk prevention/mitigation plan. The control focuses on the training of employees in terms of information, consent, accurate compilation of a medical record, hospital discharge sheets, and reporting of unwanted events. It should also concentrate on the development of protocols, procedures, and/or control measures that can improve the safety of the assisted person and on the efficiency of the risk management units understood as monitoring capacity, interpretation of the causes of unwanted events, and identification of clinical corrective factors.

In the context of control measures, particular importance is given to the audit which is a formal process of clinical verification that controls the effectiveness of the interventions while evaluating the assistance in its various components. It aims to improve the quality and outcomes of patient care through a structured review conducted by groups of colleagues, that is with peer reviews, which after examining the clinical practice used and its results, based on the standards adopted and the elements that emerge from the verification, provide any necessary indications to modify it. The audit must give answers to questions concerning the service provided to the patient by all the professionals involved. Financial risk coverage must identify the funds necessary to cover the risk management plan and must necessarily also include insurance coverage of the settings most exposed to financial risk.

Integrated management must involve changes in clinical practice aimed at promoting a culture of safety that is more attentive and closer to the dual patient mother/fetus and infant, as well as to

operators. Therefore, in the first instance it is useful to identify the training, organizational and technological criticalities encountered in the maternal–infant clinical path with reference to pregnancy, childbirth, and assistance to the newborn. The training criticalities are also to be considered in relation to the reduced volume of activities, while the organizational ones are mostly linked to a lack of continuity in the territory/hospital care and due to the lack of neonatal intensive care beds. A recent review also suggests that educational interventions aimed at improving the quality of care and training health workers may improve the safety of women and their infants during childbirth [6]. In the second instance, all risk management actions must be reported through the prevention of their realization, so as to constitute a sort of "risk control plan in the maternal and child area" [7].

In the **maternal and child** care area, risk management must involve all sectors in which an error can materialize in various phases of the mother and the newborn to be effective. In terms of obstetrics, attention to the three types of criticality: training, organization, and technology must focus on prevention in the **preconception** phase, during **pregnancy** and during **childbirth** assistance.

The clinical assistance to pregnancy and labor begins **in the preconception period** because it is an important time concerning the prevention of some risks, which should be identified and corrected before the concretization of these risks. The main risks are malformations, genetic, teratogenic caused by physical and toxic agents, infectious, deficiency, coming from maternal–fetal incompatibility and prematurity. In this phase, the anamnesis plays an important role in the identification of the risk, and criticalities that can emerge are of exclusive pertinence training. Folic acid supplementation, the abolition of incorrect lifestyle habits (e.g., drugs and alcohol use, smoking), close glycemic control of diabetic women, lengthening the interval between pregnancies, are just some of the examples of malformation and prematurity risk containment already in the preconception phase.

Risks associated with pregravidical anamnestic factors involved right from the start of pregnancy, especially if they have not already been carried out in the preconception period, must be identified, along with a timely diagnosis of extrauterine pregnancy. The speed here avoids, first of all, the need to intervene in emergency situations due to serious hypovolemic maternal shock related to hemopertoneal as a consequence of extrauterine pregnancy rupture, and secondly, it allows for more conservative treatments and less invasive interventions, such as medical treatment with methotrexate and video laparoscopy of the tubes. In this context, the critical points that can be detected often concern training aspects. The use of a sort of checklist aimed at identifying anamnestic risk factors important for pregnancy management right from the beginning of a pregnancy can be of great help, and it is the first step of the obstetric triage whose task is to highlight specific care pathways for the assessment of the risk profile which is a dynamic concept in continuous evolution during pregnancy. The minimal number of maternal screening tests to be carried out in the antenatal period which must be guaranteed to every woman are identified by the Maternity Clinical Risk Management Standards (CNST) [8]. The fetal screening involves fetal anomalies and Down Syndrome, the maternal screening involves infection in pregnancy such as rubella, hepatitis B, HIV, syphilis, and hemoglobinopathies such as sickle cell anemia and thalassemia [9].

During pregnancy, the correct surveillance of pregravidic diseases such as heart disease, respiratory failure, and hypertension is essential in order to monitor their possible deterioration, for the protection of maternal health and life. To safeguard the health of the future newborn, the timely diagnosis of fetal growth restriction and the realization of the risk of spontaneous premature birth allows optimization of the survival and quality of life of "small" infants both by optimizing the timing of birth in the case of fetal growth restriction, and by centralizing pregnant women (transport in utero) to hospitals equipped with neonatal intensive care whenever a premature baby is expected to be born.

Childbirth labor remains, however, the most critical phase for the safeguarding of the health and life of women. Obstetric emergencies such as postpartum hemorrhage, eclampsia, sepsis, thromboembolism, and anesthetic intervention are clinical aspects that must be monitored to prevent maternal death or serious disease related to labor and delivery.

During labor, cord prolapse, uterine rupture, uterine inversion, and shoulder dystocia are among obstetric emergencies that require timely and adequate treatments that not only require specific protocols, but also a pre-ordered and routinely monitored organizational support network using checklists, simulations, "mnemonic" and "reminder" posters.

Even vaginal delivery after a cesarean section, operative delivery and the so-called cardiotocographic emergencies are clinical pathway events that deviate from physiology, but since they are part of obstetric pathology they must, in any case, be foreseen. For each of these occurrences the risk factors must be identified a priori, as they are often, but not always present, for their realization and the treatment plans to be implemented [10].

In the clinical path, the analysis of errors represents an effective tool for prevention through the construction of barriers that prevent the realization of the damage that can result. In the obstetric area, as well, efforts have been and are still being made in order to identify errors and causes of mortality and morbidity in advance in order to offer safety indicators [11].

16.3 Most Frequent Errors and Adverse Events

The creation of these barriers is facilitated by the identification of missed missions, the so-called **near-misses**, defined as unscheduled events caused by errors that, however, do not determine the damage that they were potentially able to achieve. Through identification and analysis of a system of errors that create damage and near-miss events in the labor and delivery room, it is possible to identify interventions to reduce potential damage. The first systematic review of near-miss events in obstetrics is recent and reports an incidence of 0.69%, but refers to a context with a careful multi-year organization on patient safety and, as such, the data cannot be generalized. In that context, the analysis of unexpected events, including near-misses, in the labor-delivery room was 3959 cases in 2010 out of a total of 203,708 births, with an incidence of 1.9%. For each near-miss event, the hazard score is reported based on four parameters: (a) the worst possible outcome; (b) the identification method; (c) the number of barriers encountered; and (d) the quality of the barriers. Through the hazard score, it is possible to outline four classes of events: (1) high-risk frequency and low hazard score; (2) high frequency and high hazard score; (3) low-risk frequency and high hazard score; (4) low-risk frequency and low hazard score [12].

Since interventions based on the use of checklists integrated into clinical practice have proven to be effective in reducing death and complications both in the area of intensive care and surgery, the World Health Organization for Developing Countries has developed a checklist, the **WHO Safe Childbirth Checklist**, which focuses on the major causes of morbidity and mortality in the mother and newborn during delivery [13]. In fact, patient safety has a measurable economic effect, saves lives, and reduces morbidity. The reduction in mortality associated with birth is a priority of global health and low quality care is recognized to be the factor that most contributes to birth-related harm.

A systematic analysis describes global levels and trends in maternal mortality between 1990 and 2015. The global maternal mortality ratio (MMR) has a relative decline of 43.9% (34.0–48.7) from 1990 to 2015. The MMR reduced 385 deaths *per* 100,000 live births (80% uncertainty interval ranges from 359 to 427) in 1990 to 216 deaths (207–249) in 2015 with 303,000 (291,000–349,000) maternal deaths globally. Even though there is a global decrease of maternal mortality, this progress should be accelerated and immediate action is necessary to substantially reduce preventable maternal deaths [14]. The percentage of maternal deaths that can be foreseen and there-

fore preventable varies from 28% to 50% [15–17].

In order to introduce the patient safety concept to those making decisions especially in poor resources settings, the WHO Safe Childbirth Checklist guides the selection of patient safety policy points to ensure that the national policy is comprehensive and adequately detailed.

The items on this document identify the major causes of maternal and neonatal death in developing countries. Examples include postpartum hemorrhage, dystocic labur, hypertensive disorders, intrapartum events such as suboptimal assistance to the mother, neonatal infections, and prematurity. The items are grouped to be used in four critical and crucial moments: (a) on admission of the woman to the hospital; (b) at the beginning of the expulsion period or before the cesarean section; (c) 1 h after birth and (d) before discharge [18].

The pilot study of implementation of the checklist showed a clear improvement in terms of maternal–fetal neonatal health which makes it very promising. For the preparation of checklists, the priority identification of recurrent errors is useful, as only by recognizing them can they be avoided. Table 16.1 shows in descending order, the most common and frequent errors for some obstetric emergencies, highlighted during simulations [19].

Another risk control tool in obstetrics is that of the **MEOWS** (Modified Early Obstetric Warning System), an early alarm system for the timely recognition and treatment of all acute pathological situations, developed on the basis of the Confidential Enquiry into Maternal and Child Health report of 2003–2005, the validation of which has proved to be a useful aid to be used at the patient's bedside to predict morbidity, whose diagnostic criteria and alarm threshold parameters, and "trigger points," are well defined [20, 21] and reported in Table 16.2 [22].

Furthermore, this system can be easily learned, implemented, and interpreted. Available evidence suggests that MEOWS should enhance surveillance programs and action plans in order to reduce severe maternal morbidity and mortality

Table 16.1 Common and Recurrent Errors Detected by Simulation

Scenario	Error
Eclamptic seizure	Inappropriate ventilation technique
	Incorrect treatment of $MgSO_4$ intoxication
	Underdetection of $MgSO_4$ intoxication
	No ventilation performed in an apneic patient
	Essential blood tests (liver and renal function, coagulation) not carried out
	Unfamiliarity with hydralazine dosage
	Incorrect dosage or dilution of $MgSO_4$
	Foley catheter not inserted
Postpartum hemorrhage	Underestimation of blood loss
	Unfamiliarity with prostaglandin administration to achieve myometrial contraction
	Late transition to the operating room
	Delayed administration of blood products
	Unfamiliarity with ergot myometrial stimulators dosage
	Essentials blood test (fibrinogen, PT, PTT, cross and match) not carried out
	Under detection of consumption coagulopathy
	Source of bleeding (episiotomy wound exploration, uterine cavity revision, etc.) not explored
	Urinary bladder not drained
Shoulder dystocia drill	Inadequate documentation of the event
	Delayed episiotomy
	Ineffective suprapubic pressure
	Incorrect McRoberts technique
	No episiotomy performed
	Incorrect order of actions and maneuvers
Breech delivery	Incorrect fixation of the limbs
	Hasty attempt to deliver the arms
	Inappropriate Mauriceau and Bracht maneuvers
	No episiotomy performed

Table 16.2 Limits of trigger thresholds for MEOWS parameters

	Yellow trigger	Red trigger
Temperature (°C)	35–36	<35 or >38
Systolic BP (mmHg)	150–160 or 90–100	<90 or >160
Diastolic BP (mmHg)	90–100	>100
Heart rate (beat/min)	100–120 or 40–50	<40 or >120
Respiratory rate (breaths/min)	21–30	<10 or >30
Oxygen saturation (%)	–	<95
Pain score	2–3	–
Neurological response	Voice	Unresponsive, pain

In 2005, the Royal College of Obstetricians and Gynaecologists declared: "Essential elements of providing a good standard of practice and care are professional competence, good relationships and communication with patients and colleagues and observance of professional ethical obligations" [24]. Clear **communication** is synonymous with resolutive and cognitive skills, it also implies an accurate transcription of the event in the medical record and can mitigate the fallout of negative outcomes [25].

When an adverse event occurs, closing the circle with the patient is an essential component in doing things correctly. Many times, it is difficult to admit the incident, but the establishment of a relationship of trust at the basis of the doctor–patient relationship allows a better outcome also in medico-legal terms. Given the difficulty in communicating bad news, many different strategies have been develop regarding the disclosure method. For example, a real protocol has been developed at Yale University where communication with the patient is structured like all the various care processes [4, 26–28].

by identifying, managing, and possibly avoiding preventable maternal adverse events [23].

A further element on which to base prevention is communication both between operators and with women and their relatives, focusing on information useful for current assistance.

16.4 Recommendation

The cornerstones on which control and risk management in obstetrics is based are:

(a) obstetric triage for the identification of protocols and specific care paths.

(b) the application of guidelines and protocols for different clinical situations related to the birth path.

(c) the use of checklists to analyze the most vulnerable points of the process accurately.

(d) simulations.

(e) the collection of data in delivery rooms must be precise and systematic, if the data collected will not be truthful or will be collected and described incorrectly, all the conclusions and consequent corrective measures will be wrong [26].

Additional elements on which accident prevention is based are: optimization of internal and external communication, communication with the patient, organization of the team and clinical documentation. However, intervening in these areas does not represent a specificity of the maternal infantile path but that of the prevention of adverse events in all medical-surgical disciplines.

In conclusion, the resulting safety system, developed following the study of the various phases of error determinism in three areas (training, organizational and technological), allows the implementation of risk control strategies that avoid the repetition of circumstances that lead to mistakes. The set of actions identified constitute a sort of risk control plan in the maternal and child area which, by improving the quality of the services provided to the mother and the newborn, should guarantee their safety [27].

Safeguarding the health and life of the mother and the future baby are the main objectives of a correct clinical course of pregnancy [28].

References

1. Leape LL. Reporting of adverse events. N Engl J Med. 2002;347(20):1633–8.

2. Godlee F. Are we at risk of being at risk? BMJ. 2010;341:c4766.

3. NHS National Reporting and Learning System Feedback Report. Safety first: a report for patients, clinicians and healthcare managers. 2006.

4. Pettker CM. Systematic approaches to adverse events in obstetrics, part II: event analysis and response. Semin Perinatol. 2017;41(3):156–60.

5. Pettker CM. Systematic approaches to adverse events in obstetrics, part I: event identification and classification. Semin Perinatol. 2017;41:151–5.

6. Antony J, Zarin W, Pham B, et al. Patient safety initiatives in obstetrics: a rapid review. BMJ Open. 2018;8:e020170.

7. RCOG, RCM, RCA, RCPCH. Safer childbirth. Minimum standards for the organisation and delivery of care in labour. London: RCOG Press; 2007. p. 1–80.

8. https://resolution.nhs.uk/services/claims-management/clinical-schemes/clinical-negligence-scheme-for-trusts/maternity-incentive-scheme/.

9. NHS Litigation Authority. Clinical negligence scheme for trusts maternity clinical risk management standards 2012-13. Managing risk DNV. 2012.

10. ACOG Committee Opinion. Patient safety in obstetrics and gynecology, no. 447. 2009, reaffirmed 2019.

11. Pronovost PJ, Holzmuller CG, Ennen CS, Fox HE. Overview of progress in patient safety. Am J Obstet Gynecol. 2011;204:5–10.

12. Clark SL, Meyers RN, Frye DR, et al. A systematic approach to the identification and classification of near-miss events on labor and delivery in a large national health care system. Am J Obstet Gynecol. 2012;207:441–5.

13. WHO Safe Childbirth Checklist: implementation guide improving the quality of facility-based delivery for mothers and newborns. WHO Library Cataloguing. 2015.

14. Alkema L, ChouD, HoganD, etal. Global, regional, and national levels and trends in maternal mortality between 1990 and 2015, with scenario-based projections to 2030: a systematic analysis by the UN Maternal Mortality Estimation Inter-Agency Group. Lancet. 2016;387(10017):462–474.

15. Berg CJ, Harper MA, Atkinson SM, et al. Preventability of pregnancy-related deaths: results of a state-wide review. Obstet Gynecol. 2005;106:1228–34.

16. Clark SL, Belfort M, Dildy GA et al Maternal death in the 21st century: causes, prevention and relationship to cesarean delivery. Am J Obstet Gynecol. 2008;199(1):36e1–36e5.

17. Spector JM, Agrawal P, Kodkany B, et al. Improving quality of care for maternal and newborn health: prospective pilot study of the WHO Safe Childbirth Checklist Program. PLoS One. 2012;7(5):e35151.

18. Philip Banfield P, Roberts C. The early detection of maternal deterioration in pregnancy. London: The Health Foundation; 2015.

19. Maslovitz S, Barkai G, Lessing JB, et al. Recurrent obstetric management mistakes identified by simulation. Obstet Gynecol. 2007;109:1295–300.

20. Zuckerwise LC, Lipkind HS. Maternal early warning systems—towards reducing preventable maternal mortality and severe maternal morbidity through

improved clinical surveillance and responsiveness. Semin Perinatol. 2017;41(3):161–5.

21. Wu AW, Steckelberg RC. Medical error, incident investigation and the second victim: doing better but feeling worse? BMJ Qual Saf. 2012;21(4):267–70.

22. Singh S, McGlennan A, England A, Simons R. A validation study of the CEMACH recommended modified early obstetric warning system (MEOWS). Anaesthesia. 2012;67:12–8.

23. Mackintosh N, Watson K, Rance S, Sandall J. Value of a modified early obstetric warning system (MEOWS) in managing maternal complications in the peripartum period: an ethnographic study. BMJ Qual Saf. 2014;23(1):26–34.

24. RCOG, Clinical Governance Advice. Improving patient safety: Risk management for maternity and gynaecology, no. 2. 2005.

25. Ragusa A, Crescini C. Emergenze Urgenze in sala parto, Piccin. 2015.

26. Svelato A, Ragusa A, Manfredi P. General methods for measuring and comparing medical interventions in childbirth: a framework. BMC Pregn Childbirth. 2020 (in press).

27. Pettker CM, Thung SF, Lipkind HS, et al. A comprehensive obstetric patient safety program reduces liability claims and payments. Am J Obstet Gynecol. 2014;211:319–25.

28. Gazzetta Ufficiale 131 del 7 giugno 2000. Decreto Ministeriale del 24.4.2000. Piano Sanitario Nazionale 1998-2000. Progetto Obiettivo Materno Infantile (POMI).

Patient Safety in Internal Medicine

17

Micaela La Regina, Alessandra Vecchié,
Aldo Bonaventura, and Domenico Prisco

Learning Objectives/Questions Covered in the Chapter

- How many are the adverse events (AEs) in Internal Medicine (IM)?
- What are the most frequent errors?
- How to prevent medication or identification errors?
- How to prevent AEs in invasive procedures in IM?
- How to prevent clinical reasoning errors?
- How to improve team working and communication among health operators in IM?
- What are the safety practices to be implemented in IM?

M. L. Regina (✉)
S.S. Risk Management, ASL5 Liguria,
La Spezia, Italy
e-mail: micaela.laregina@asl5.liguria.it

A. Vecchié
Pauley Heart Center, Division of Cardiology,
Department of Internal Medicine, Virginia
Commonwealth University, Richmond, VA, USA

A. Bonaventura
Pauley Heart Center, Division of Cardiology,
Department of Internal Medicine, Virginia
Commonwealth University, Richmond, VA, USA

First Clinic of Internal Medicine, Department of
Internal Medicine, University of Genoa, Genoa, Italy

D. Prisco
Department of Experimental and Clinical Medicine,
University of Florence, Florence, Italy
e-mail: domenico.prisco@unifi.it

17.1 Epidemiology of Adverse Events

There are few specific studies on epidemiology of AEs in IM. Most of them are focused on particular events, such as medication, interventional procedures, or diagnostic reasoning errors.

The first historical study conducted in IM was that by Schimmel in 1960 [1]. He found that 20% of patients admitted to a university medical service in USA experienced one or more untoward "iatrogenic" episodes. Anyway, such pioneering study was not based on the current definition of AE and reported only drug reactions and untoward effects of diagnostic and therapeutic procedures — the so-called diseases of medical progresses, the price to pay for modern medical care [2, 3]. Twenty years later, Steel et al. [4] reported a rate of 36% AEs in the medical service of a teaching hospital. Then, the Harvard Medical Practice Study I [5] found a rate of AEs of $3.6 \pm 0.3\%$ ($30.9 \pm 4.4\%$ of them due to negligence) in IM and $7 \pm 0.5\%$ ($28 \pm 3.4\%$ of them due to negligence) in general surgery, and the Quality in Australian Healthcare Study (QAHCS) displayed an incidence of 6.6% in IM versus 13.8% in general surgery [6]. More recently, studies from the UK [7], the USA [8], Portugal [9], and Spain [10] reported an incidence ranging from 10% to 23.2%. Fatality ranges from 2% [2] to 20% [6] in the various studies. Such large variability of incidence and severity can depend on differences in AEs definition, settings (only IM wards or all medical wards), study design, and severity threshold of investigators in the adjudication of events.

Medical errors — compared to surgical ones — are more preventable (73% vs 53% [6]; 75% vs 41% [7]), and often less overt because diagnosis and time of occurrence can be less clear and multiple providers are involved [11]. They are also associated to longer hospitalizations being directly related to the time spent in hospital [1, 12]. Indeed, they have been defined "the hazards of hospitalization" [1]. They are more common and severe in the elderly [10, 12, 13], and more events can occur in the same patient [1]. Lower educational level, transfer from other institutions, associated chronic conditions, severe prognosis on admission, general functional status on admission, level of awareness on admission and at discharge, associated kidney/liver failure or impaired function on admission and at discharge, number of drugs taken (on admission, during hospital stay, and at

discharge), patients' knowledge about disease, medications, and their side effects [9] are other known risk factors for AEs in IM.

17.2 Most Common Errors

In IM, errors can occur in any step of inpatient journey from admission to discharge, and in any clinical process from clinical history collection to diagnostic work-up, drug therapy, invasive procedures, and so on. Further, they can occur before admission to IM and be recognized later, on the ward.

The words "error" and "AE" do not have the same meaning. AEs are "injuries caused by medical management rather than by the underlying disease or condition of the patient". Medical errors can result or not in patient harm, but not all of them lead to AEs. Generally, only preventable AEs imply medical errors [14]. Table 17.1 displays the most frequent AEs occurring in IM, according to hospitalization phase and process.

Table 17.1 List of the most frequent AEs in internal medicine according to hospitalization phase and process

Phase	Process	Adverse event	Contributing factors
Pre-admission	Initial assessment and treatment	Incorrect/incomplete diagnosis Incorrect/incomplete/delayed treatment Reactions to drugs or transfusions Inappropriate admission Admission to inappropriate ward	Lack of patient information Incorrect clinical reasoning Busy and noisy environment Fatigue, distraction Bed unavailability Lack, inadequacy, or violation of policies on admission appropriateness and hospital patient flow
Admission	Patient identification	Tests and treatment to the wrong patient	Identity documents not available Patient cognitive impairment Poor social support Busy and noisy environment Misunderstanding Typing error Inadequate or lacking information technology Lack, inadequacy, or violation of policies
	Clinical history collection	Diagnostic omission or delay Drug–disease interaction	Inadequate skills Physician knowledge deficit
	Medication recognition	Preventable adverse drug reactions, including withdrawal reactions Unintentional drug discrepancies Administration delay	Distraction, fatigue Busy and noisy environment Outlier status Patient cognitive impairment Poor social support Lack of policy Inadequate or lacking information technology

Phase	Process	Adverse event	Contributing factors
	Physical examination	Diagnostic omission or delay Drug–disease interaction	Inadequate skills Superficial examination Knowledge deficit Distraction, fatigue Busy and noisy environment Outlier status
	Initial diagnosis and therapy	Wrong, delayed, or omitted diagnosis or treatment Hurry, external pressure Premature closure	Inadequate skills Knowledge deficit Missed diagnostic clues Distraction, fatigue Busy and noisy environment Inadequate or lacking computerized order entry
Hospital stay	Clinical monitoring; response to pathological findings	Unexpected death or clinical worsening Unexpected intensive care transfer Diagnostic or therapeutic omission or delay	Unexperienced team High workload Patient unable to ask for help Lack, inadequacy, or violation of policies
	Medication process	Adverse drug reactions due to: ordering/storing errors, inappropriate, or wrong prescription, wrong administration Drug–drug and drug–disease interactions	Wrong identification or transcription Knowledge deficit Medical record not available, illegible, not informative Allergy or contraindications not assessed Inadequate or lacking computerized order entry Lack of supervision Poor teamwork Lack, inadequacy, or violation of policies Distraction, fatigue Busy and noisy environment
	Diagnostic work-up	Wrong, delayed, or omitted diagnosis or treatment Hurry, external pressure Premature closure	Inadequate skills knowledge deficit Missed diagnostic clues Medical record not available, illegible, not informative Missed request Allergy or contraindications not assessed Poor planning Poor teamwork Lack of supervision Inadequate or lacking computerized order entry Distraction, fatigue Busy and noisy environment

(continued)

Table 17.1 (continued)

Phase	Process	Adverse event	Contributing factors
	Consultations	Identification errors Wrong, delayed, or omitted diagnosis or treatment	See identification errors Planning deficit Medical record not available, illegible, not informative Inadequate skills knowledge deficit Missed diagnostic clues Inadequate or lacking computerized order entry Missed request Poor teamwork Distraction, fatigue Busy and noisy environment
	Invasive procedures	Wrong procedure, wrong patient, or wrong site Omitted or delayed procedure Preventable complications (i.e., pneumothorax during thoracentesis)	See identification errors Inadequate skills Inappropriate timing or indication Patient not informed and informed consent not signed Uncooperative patient Medical record not available, illegible, not informative or updated Poor planning Allergy or contraindications not assessed Missed request Unexperienced operator Lack of supervision Lack or inadequacy of devices Inadequate or lacking computerized order entry Distraction, fatigue Busy and noisy environment Lack, inadequacy, or violation of policies
	General care	Falls, delirium, healthcare-related infections (HAI), suicide, entrapment, wandering, healthcare-related venous thromboembolism, etc.	Unsuitable footwear Wet floor Busy and noisy environment Inappropriate or omitted basic care Gloves, soap, water, or alcohol hand-rub unavailable or underused Inadequate skills knowledge deficit Lack, inadequacy, or omission of risk stratification Medical record not updated, illegible, or not informative Poor teamwork Lack of supervision Poor vigilance Poor or omitted patient education Fragile patient Patient cognitive impairment Lack, inadequacy, or violation of policies

Table 17.1 (continued)

Phase	Process	Adverse event	Contributing factors
	Handover	Diagnostic or therapeutic omission or delay Unexpected death or clinical worsening	Unexperienced team Inadequate skills Lack of structured handover Busy and noisy environment Distraction, fatigue Poor teamwork Lack, inadequacy, or violation of policy
	Communication to patient and/or caregiver	Privacy failure Communications provided to people not authorized by the patient Diagnostic or therapeutic omission or delay due to poor or absent compliance with care team indications or missed information Patient/caregiver dissatisfaction	Inadequate non-technical skills Lack or non-compliance with ad hoc protocols High workload Lack of time Poor teamwork Misunderstanding Patient cognitive impairment Poor social support Organizational failure (lack of reference operators)
Last day	Discharge planning	Canceled or delayed discharge Lack of planning controls and follow-up Early readmission for the same reason	Poor teamwork Poor decision-making Patient/caregiver not engaged Poor patient/caregiver education Pressure to discharge Poor social support No anticipatory prescribing Lack, inadequacy, or violation of policy
	Discharge	Discharge letter to the wrong patient Incomplete discharge letter Wrong or inappropriate discharge destination Unintentional drug discrepancies Adverse drug reactions Omitted or delayed diagnosis communication Omitted or delayed treatment	See identification errors Medical record not available, illegible, not informative or updated Pending tests results Busy and noisy environment Distraction, fatigue Pressure to discharge Poor teamwork and communication Poor multidisciplinary assessment Poor medication reconciliation Medications not available Medical devices not available or malfunctioning No patient recall ongoing results Poor patient/caregiver education Lack, inadequacy, or violation of policies

AEs in IM have been classified variously, e.g. according to the clinical process or the nature of disorder caused by AEs [7, 9] (see Tables 17.2 and 17.3). It is disappointing how the frequency of certain AEs has worsened in decades: healthcare-associated infections (HAIs) passed from 9.5% in 1960 [1] to 21.4% in 2008 [10].

When you think about the potential most frequent errors in IM, you probably think mainly about medication and diagnostic errors since

Table 17.2 Types and preventability of AEs in IM [9]

Categories	Rate (%)	Preventability (%)
General care	16.4	47.8
Medication process	37.8	34
Healthcare-related infections	21.4	16.7
Invasive procedures	21.4	40
Diagnostic process	2.8	100

Table 17.3 Types of AEs, classified according to the nature of resulting disorder [11]

Disorders	Rate (%)
Infectious	24
Electrolytic	18
Metabolic/endocrine	12
Hematological/coagulation	9
Gastrointestinal	8
Neurological	4
Cardiovascular	2.5
Skin/allergic	2

medical diagnosis and therapy are its core business. Diagnostic errors —more appropriately defined as "decision-making errors"— account for 10–15% in complex disciplines, such as IM, compared to 2–5% of perceptive ones (dermatology or radiology) [15]. Medication errors are highly prevalent among older patients or patients with multiple comorbidities and polypharmacy [16], all patients typically admitted to IM. Moreover, healthcare-acquired infections are likely to be another common AE in IM, favored by intravascular catheters and immunosuppressant treatments [17].

17.2.1 Patient Identification Errors

Identification errors (IEs) are commonly associated with surgery, but they can occur in every setting. Many other medical errors, included in this review, such as medication or blood transfusion errors, can result from patient misidentification at the point of care as well as at registration. IEs usually affect more people. When a patient receives a medication intended for another patient, the harm is done to the patient receiving the wrong medica-

tion and to that who fails to receive the correct treatment [18]. A recent review from ECRI institute disclosed that 72% of IEs occur at the point of care and 12.6% at registration. Diagnostic and therapeutic procedures are involved in 36% and 22% of cases respectively, and consequences may be fatal [18]. Information technology amplified the problem, as IEs can generate duplicate medical records or mistaken identity. There are no specific studies on IEs in IM, but increasing staff workload and patients cognitive impairment make them a non-negligible problem.

The main barrier to IEs is cultural: the awareness of the correct identification and of misidentification consequences must be improved, so that health operators spontaneously abandon incorrect practice. Figure 17.1 summarizes what to do and not to do to prevent IEs. Technology (patient's palm scan, bar-code wristband, radiofrequency identification system, etc.) can help but cannot substitute the role of humans. One can scan the bar-code wristband of the right patient, but administrate the drugs to another one. Patients' education and empowerment are equally important [18].

17.2.2 Clinical Reasoning Errors

Errors in diagnostic and management process can be considered together as clinical reasoning errors (CREs) [19] or decision-making errors, as diagnostic and management reasoning can be similarly conceptualized.

According to the American National Academy of Medicine (previous Institute of Medicine), a diagnostic error is a failure to: (a) establish an accurate and timely explanation of the patient's health problem(s) or (b) communicate that explanation to the patient. This definition includes: wrong, delayed, or omitted diagnosis [20]. The incidence of diagnostic errors varies according to definition, discipline, and research approach. For instance, 1 in 10 diagnoses are wrong (according to "secret shoppers" approach that uses "secret patients" to provide detailed, unbiased insights, and feedback on healthcare processes), 1 in 10–20 autopsies identifies major diagnostic dis-

Fig. 17.1 What healthcare operators have to do and not to do to avoid patient identification errors

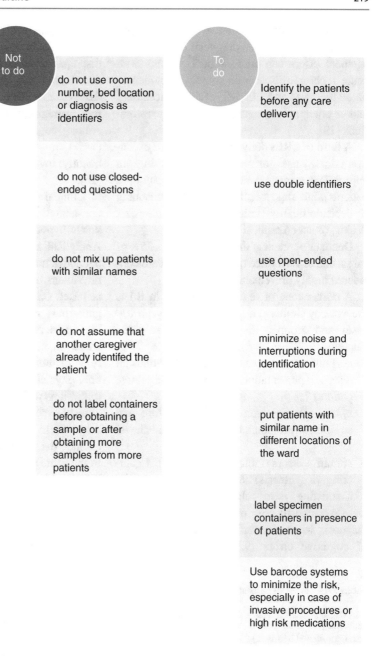

Not to do

do not use room number, bed location or diagnosis as identifiers

do not use closed-ended questions

do not mix up patients with similar names

do not assume that another caregiver already identifed the patient

do not label containers before obtaining a sample or after obtaining more samples from more patients

To do

Identify the patients before any care delivery

use double identifiers

use open-ended questions

minimize noise and interruptions during identification

put patients with similar name in different locations of the ward

label specimen containers in presence of patients

Use barcode systems to minimize the risk, especially in case of invasive procedures or high risk medications

crepancies, 1 in 3 patients have experienced a diagnostic error (according to patients' survey), 1 in 20 patients will experience a diagnostic error every year (according to chart review). They are the most common cause for malpractice claims [21], and about half of physicians admit at least a diagnostic error per month and perceive diagnostic errors as the most dangerous (according to physicians' survey) [22].

The most commonly missed or delayed diseases are: pulmonary embolism and drug reaction or overdose (2.5%), lung cancer (3.9%), colorectal cancer (3.6%), acute coronary syndrome (3.1%), breast cancer (2.9%), and stroke (2.6%) [23]. Physicians overestimate their diagnostic ability: only 10% of clinicians admit they performed any error in diagnosis over the past year, but up to 40% of diagnoses about which clinicians were certain resulted wrong at autopsy [24]. Further, even when diagnosis is right, management errors can arise: 1 in 2 patients with acute or chronic diseases do not receive evidence-based therapies and 1 in 3–5 receive unnecessary and/or potentially dangerous drugs or investigations [19].

A third of CREs derive from deficits of execution (slips, lapses, or oversights in carrying out appropriate management in correctly diagnosed patients), but almost half are errors of reasoning or decision quality (failure to elicit, synthesize, decide, or act on clinical information).

Death or permanent disability result in 25% of cases, and at least three quarters of them are considered highly preventable [22].

A cornerstone of research on CREs in IM is the work by Graber et al. [25]. They analyzed 100 cases and grouped diagnostic errors in three categories:

- no-fault errors (in case of masked or unusual disease presentation or non-collaborative patient) 7%
- system-related errors (technical failure and equipment problems or organizational flaws) 19%
- cognitive errors (faulty knowledge, data gathering, or synthesis) 28%.

Coexisting system-related and cognitive errors were reported in 46% of cases. Further, wrong diagnosis was characterized by a predominance of cognitive errors (92% vs 50%), whereas delayed diagnosis by the predominance of system-related ones (89% vs 36%). Cases where discrepancy resulted from autopsy were mainly due to cognitive factors (90% vs 10%). Overall, 228 system-related factors and 320 cognitive factors, averaging 5.9 per case, were identified [26]. Among cognitive factors, faulty data gathering (14%) or synthesis (83%) resulted more frequently involved than faulty knowledge (3%) [26].

Clinical reasoning can proceed analytically or non-analytically (Table 17.4) to generate diagnostic hypotheses, investigations, and treatment. Analytical reasoning (also called "hypothetic-deductive model") is commonly used by younger physicians or in unfamiliar or unusual cases and is based on lists of differential diagnoses and gathering of information to validate such diagnoses. Non-analytical reasoning is faster and based on mental heuristics (maxims, shortcuts, rules of thumb) or pattern recognition. In practice, physician compare current patient's symptoms/signs with previous cases, collected through clinical experience and/or study and get the right diagnosis in few seconds [27]. One type does not exclude the other and they can be mutually used in the same patient. None of them is error-proof. If mental heuristics and pattern recognition are efficient and accurate in many situations, they can also predispose to errors, as patient's picture does not always fit the expected pattern, because of an atypical presentation, comorbidities, or

Table 17.4 Types of clinical reasoning: a comparison [27]

Non-analytical (system 1)	Characteristics	Analytical (system 2)
Intuitive (based on pattern recognition and heuristic)	Modality	Hypothetic-deductive
Developed through clinical experience and study	Development	Generation of list of diagnoses to be validated
Commonly used by expert/senior physicians	Application	Commonly used by not expert/ younger physicians Commonly used in atypical or unfamilial cases
Minor cognitive load Automatic, unconscious	Awareness	Major cognitive load Conscious
Faster Diagnosis in 10 s	Time	Slower Diagnosis in minutes/hours
More efficient	Efficiency	Less efficient (based on memory work)

evolving diseases [28]. Another Achille's heel of non-analytical reasoning (N-AR) are biases, constructs founded on perceptions, prejudices or ideologies, outside of critical thinking. Bias can be distinguished in internal or external to the clinicians [19] either in cognitive or affective bias [27] (see Table 17.5). Breakdowns in analytical reasoning most often derive from not following appropriate diagnostic "rules" and include: missing key data, inadequate review of existing data, deficits in medical knowledge, lacking skills in evidence-based practice and decision-making,

Table 17.5 Bias and heuristics in clinical reasoning: examples and corrective strategies [19]

Bias	Description	Example	Corrective strategy
Anchoring	Tendency to fixate on first impression and not to consider further information available	The physician diagnosed a viral meningitis instead of cervical osteomyelitis on the basis of high fever and neck pain, ignoring neck pain worsened not only on flexion, but also on palpation and previous fore-harm wound	Think beyond your favorite diagnosis or first impression Reconsider initial diagnosis when new data or unexpected clinical course
Availability	Tendency to accept the diagnosis that more easily comes to mind because of recent observation rather than to consider prevalence and incidence of such diagnosis	The physician diagnosed a viral meningitis instead of cervical osteomyelitis, as he had just seen a case of viral meningitis	Consider always disease prevalence and incidence
Confirmation	To look only for signs and symptoms that confirm your favorite hypothesis or to interpret clinical findings only to support such hypothesis, without looking for or even disregarding opposite evidences	The physician diagnosed a skin rash under the axilla of a diabetic patient as intertrigo missing a diagnose of erythema migrans due to Lyme disease	Utilize an objective tool, such as a differential diagnosis checklist, to verify if diagnosis correlates with technical findings
Diagnosis momentum bias	To consider definite a diagnosis without evidence, but due to a label applied to the first contact and transmitted by all the people who took care of the patient	The physician attributed to alcohol withdrawal syndrome the psychomotor agitation of a patient with a sticky label of alcoholic, missing a life-threatening sepsis	Critically review diagnoses of others and look for evidence to support them
Framing[a]	To decide on options based on whether the options are presented with positive or negative connotations or to be influenced by the context	The physician may decide to request a cranial CT scan in the same patient more often if it has been presented as associated with 90% of true positives than 10% of false negatives The physician may diagnose more easily a ruptured abdominal aneurysm in ER than in outpatient clinic	Change perspective
Gambler's fallacy	To believe a diagnosis less probable, if it occurred in several previous patients	The physician missed a diagnosis of pulmonary embolism as he diagnosed four cases of pulmonary embolism in the last week	Consider always pre-test probability

(continued)

Table 17.5 (continued)

Bias	Description	Example	Corrective strategy
Multiple alternative bias	To reduce differential diagnosis to few more familial hypotheses, when multiple options are available	The physician missed a rare diagnosis of familial Mediterranean fever and submitted the patient to surgery for appendicitis	Utilize an objective tool, such as a differential diagnosis checklist Verify if diagnosis correlates with technical findings
Outcome bias	To opt for the diagnosis associated with the best outcome, valuing more physician hope than clinical data	The physician interpreted as benign a lung nodule, instead to order further investigations	
Frequency gambling bias and worst-case bias	In ambiguous clinical picture, to opt for a benign diagnosis, assuming benign diseases are more common. It is opposite to the worst-case bias	The physician interpreted the poly-globulia as reactive rather than as a proliferative disorder in a heavy smoker	Broaden the history to search for other causes or associations
Posterior probability error	To assume that a patient presenting with the same symptoms has always the same disease	The physician diagnosed heart failure instead of pulmonary embolism in a patient presenting with dyspnea and a repeated hospital admissions for heart failure	Use a differential diagnosis checklist and rule out worst-case scenario Consider prevalence and incidence of any hypothesis
Search satisfying bias	In presence of a main diagnosis, to stop to look for secondary ones. In this way, the physician will miss comorbidities, complications, and additional diagnoses	To attribute to hypertensive heart disease the atrial fibrillation occurred in a patient with essential hypertension, missing hyperthyroidism	
Sunk cost bias[a]	The tendency to pursue a course of action, even after it has proved to be suboptimal, because resources have been invested in that course of action	The physician continued to look for a cancer in a patient with fatigue, even if investigations are repeatedly negative "Do not cling to a mistake just because you spent a lot of time in making it" Aubrey De Graf	
Visceral bias	To opt for a diagnosis being influenced by emotions	The physician attributed iron-deficiency anemia to hypermenorrhea in a patient her age without looking for bowel diseases	
Commission bias	Tendency to do something even if it is not supported by robust evidence and may in fact do harm	The physician complied with the request for lumbar puncture of the parents of an 18-year-old girl with fever and headache to rule out meningococcal meningitis although the neutrophil count was normal. The girl then developed a severe post-puncture headache and was admitted to hospital	Consider always evidence and balance benefits and risks

Table 17.5   (continued)

Bias	Description	Example	Corrective strategy
Premature closure	To stop seeking other information after reaching a diagnostic conclusion	The radiologist did not see a second fracture, after the first has been identified	Review the case, seek other opinions (e.g., radiology backup), and consult objective resources (e.g., an orthopedic review that might include mention of a common concomitant fracture)
Representativeness bias	To make a diagnosis considering only typical manifestations of a disease	The physician missed a diagnosis of myocardial infarction presenting with nausea and vomiting	Consider atypical manifestations, especially in women
Extrapolation bias[a]	To generalize experiences and clinical trial results to groups of patients in whom intended actions have not been properly evaluated	The physician ordered a CT scan to exclude an acute coronary syndrome in a patient with previous coronary artery bypass grafting (CABG)	Use tests for evidence-based indications

[a]These biases can affect not only diagnostic process but also treatment decisions

erroneous consideration of tests value, poor supervision of N-AR [28]. At the end, also noisy environment, interruptions, high workload, fatigue, and time pressure can impair reasoning [27].

Health Research & Educational Trust (HRET), Hospital Improvement Innovation Network (HIIN) team, and Society to Improve Diagnosis in Medicine (SIDM) [29] published "Diagnostic error—Change Package," a document including a menu of strategies and concepts that any hospital should implement (improving teamwork effectiveness and diagnostic process reliability, engaging patients and caregivers, reinforcing learning system, and optimizing cognitive performances of clinicians) [29]. For this last aim, several tools are available: (a) checklists for diagnostic process such as CATCH (Comprehensive history and physical exam, Alternate explanations, Take a diagnostic timeout to be certain, Consider critical diagnoses not be missed, Help if needed) [30]; (b) mnemonic decision support tools like VITAMIN CC & D checklist (Vascular, Infection & Intoxication, Trauma & Toxins, Autoimmune, Metabolic, Idiopathic & Iatrogenic, Neoplastic, Congenital, Conversion, Degenerative); (c) lists of Red Flags; (d) electronic decision support systems like *Isabel*, associated with the highest

accurate diagnosis retrieval rates [31]; (e) debiasing questions (Table 17.6) [32]; (f) reflective practice by the following options:

– The *crystal ball experience* [29]: stop and ask: "if my diagnosis was wrong, which alternatives should I consider?"

– The *ROWS (Rule Out Worst case Scenario)* [29]: exclude first the most severe possible diagnoses.

– The *Blue and Red Team Challenge* [33], borrowed from military sector, is a safe method to improve clinical decision-making in complex clinical situations. Staff is divided into two teams: the Blue Team takes clinical history, makes the synthesis and generates diagnostic hypotheses; the Red Team acts as an independent reviewer by thinking critically about the clinical picture and identifying alternative diagnoses to those presented.

– *Take 2—think, do* [32] is designed to improve awareness and recognition of potential errors and reduce morbidity and mortality of wrong, missed, or delayed diagnosis. Literally, it means "Take 2 minutes to deliberate diagnosis" to verify if there are situations that need a closer look or diagnosis re-evaluation (Think moment) and act (Do moment). A closer look is necessary if physician is Hungry, Angry,

Table 17.6 "Debiasing questions" to avoid cognitive errors in high-risk situations: what should I ask myself [33]

High-risk situations	Questions
Handoff	Is this patient handed off to me from another shift?
External influence Excessive confidencein collaborators or colleague	Did the patient, a nurse, or another doctor suggest to me this diagnosis, directly or indirectly?
Excessive self-confidence	Did I choose the first diagnosis that came to my mind?
Premature closure	Did I consider any organ and apparatus?
Prejudice or identification	Do not I like that patient for some reason? Do I have something in common with that patient?
Noisy and/or busy environment	Was there any interruption or distraction during the evaluation of that patient?
Personal fatigue	Was I sleepy or tired during that patient evaluation?
Cognitive overload	Am I overloaded or over-extended from a cognitive point of view?
Stereotyped situation	Am I stereotyping that patient?
Time pressure, high workload	Am I neglecting some "must not miss" diagnosis?

Late, or Tired (HALT), at risk of cognitive biases (e.g., context, framing bias) or in case of difficult patient engagement, knowledge deficit, time pressure, high-risk presentations; diagnosis re-evaluation if things are not going as planned, patient is deteriorating, response to treatment is not as expected, at shift change or discharge or in case of patient's/caregiver's concern. Strategies to review and challenge the diagnosis are individual strategies, i.e., Diagnostic Timeout; Team-based strategies, e.g., Red Team Blue Team Challenge; second opinion from specialist services or senior medical officer. Such approach helps to rule out the worst-case scenario, identify atypical or rare presentations, re-evaluate patients who do not improve, acknowledge patient and caregivers' concerns, recognize high-risk patient groups, favor discussion or appropriate referral and

escalation for diagnostic dilemmas, effective communication in case of care transfer.

At the end, appropriate and effective clinical reasoning should be trained. The "twelve tips for teaching avoidance of diagnostic errors" and "ten commandments to reduce cognitive errors" can be helpful to this scope [32].

17.2.3 Medication Errors

Medication errors (MEs) are unintended, preventable events that can cause or lead to inappropriate medication use or patient harm [34]. You make MEs if you give the right medication to a wrong patient or the wrong medication/dose to the right patient, if you prescribe a medication to the wrong patient or without indication or when you forget to give a medication that was due. MEs are one of the most common medical errors occurring in every setting: 41.7% happen in care homes, 38.3% in primary care, and 20% in secondary care settings. It has been estimated that less than 1% cause harm to patients [35]. Associated harm is moderate in 26% of cases and severe in 2% [35]. They are also costly in terms of lives and resources [36].

MEs fall in the broadest category of adverse drug events (ADEs) that represent 5% of all AEs in high-income countries and 2.9% in low-middle income ones, according to WHO estimation [37]. ADEs are untoward, preventable or not, outcomes due to medications. If a patient has a skin rash due to an antibiotic, it is an ADE; if allergy was known, it is a preventable ADE. Preventable ADEs are formally MEs. Lastly, potential ADEs (pADEs) are MEs with the potential to cause an injury [38].

Given the well-known problem of under-reporting of ADEs, MEs affect about 4.8–5.3% of hospitalized patients with a significant variability by setting: intensive care is the most affected, whereas obstetrics the least as many drugs are prohibited [36, 39–41]. MEs may occur at any stage of medication process from ordering to transcription, dispensing, administering, and monitoring. About 80% happen during prescribing (39%) or nurse administration (38%), the remaining 20% during transcription and verification (12%) or pharmacy dispensing (11%) [42]. Any type of error can result from different proximal causes and a single proximal cause can lead to a variety of errors. For example, lack of drug knowledge can cause wrong choice, dose, frequency, route, or technique of administration. Wrong dose can result from lack of drug or patient knowledge, slip or memory lapses, transcription errors, and so on. Behind proximal causes there are latent causes or system failures. Leape et al. counted 16 different system failures, but the first seven have in common an impaired access to information and accounted for 78% of all MEs, whereas work and staff assignment have been associated to a broad range of errors such as slips, dose- and identity-checking, breakdown of allergy barriers [41].

Frequency of MEs/ADEs in IM has been poorly investigated. An 8-month prospective, cross-sectional study found that 89% of the patients experienced at least one ME during hospitalization, with a mean of 2.6 errors per patient or 0.2 errors per ordered medication. More than 70% of MEs happened during prescription. The most prevalent prescription MEs were inappropriate drug selection, prescription of unauthorized drugs or for untreated indications. The most involved drugs were cardiovascular agents followed by antibiotics, vitamins, minerals, and electrolytes [43].

MEs are more frequent and severe in the so-called high-risk situations due to high-risk patients and/or providers, medications, or settings. High-risk patients are younger or older, multi-morbid or chronic patients (with liver and/or renal impairment), on polypharmacy [44–47]. High-risk providers are younger or not expert providers [48, 49]. High-risk systems are hospitals delivering acute care (e.g. error rates are likely higher for drugs administered intravenously compared with other routes [50]) and high-risk medications are the so-called high-alert medications (HAMs) and look-alike, sound-alike medications (LASA). HAMs have a heightened risk of causing significant patient harm when used erroneously. They include drugs with a low therapeutic index and drugs at a high risk of harm when administered by the wrong route or at wrong dosage or when other system errors occur. The acronym A-PINCH serves as a reminder of them, it stays for **A**nti-infective, **P**otassium and other electrolytes, **I**nsulin, **N**arcotics and other analgesics, **C**hemotherapeutic agents, **H**eparin and other anticoagulants. LASA are drugs with similar names or boxes [50].

Although there is no standard definition, polypharmacy is generally defined as the concurrent use of five or more medications [51], over-the-counter and complementary medicines included. It increases MEs because it reduces compliance and favors timing and/or dosing errors, duplications, or omissions. Drug–drug and drug–disease interactions, instead, increase ADEs [51]. It is particularly risky in IM as it cares for poly-pathological patients, even if internists could be more aware and cautious, as supposed by a French study [52].

Care transition is a key moment of care for several reasons, medication safety included. It occurs when a patient moves to, or returns from, home, hospital, residential care setting or simply outpatient clinics, general practitioners' office or consultation. In care transition unintentional (changes not supported by clinical reason) and/or undocumented (motivated but not documented changes) medication discrepancies can occur [53]. They are MEs that can lead to ADEs. A mean of 1.72 unintentional discrepancies per patient have been reported at hospital admission (0.16 per patient potentially harmful) and 2.05 per patient (0.3 potentially harmful) at discharge from hospital [54].

Causes of MEs are numerous, so multiple simultaneous interventions are needed to reduce their rate and impact [36]. In recent years, information technology has been established as a cornerstone for MEs reduction. Recent meta-analysis highlighted that in hospital computerized physician's order entry is associated with a greater than 50% decline in pADEs [55], and the use of barcode assisted medication administration substantially reduced the rate of MEs and pADEs [56].

Medication reconciliation (MR) is recommended to avoid unintentional discrepancies between patients' medications across transitions in care. At a minimum, medication reconciliation refers to the completion of a "Best Possible Medication History" (BPMH) and the act of correcting any unintended discrepancies between a patient's previous medication regimen and the proposed medication orders at admission (from home or a healthcare facility, such as a nursing home), inpatient transfer (to or from other services or units, such as the intensive care unit), or discharge (to home or a healthcare facility). More advanced medication reconciliation involves inter-professional collaboration (e.g. a physician and nurse or pharmacist conducting medication reconciliation as a team), integration into discharge summaries and prescriptions, and provision of medication counseling to patients [23]. Medication reconciliation has also been bundled with other interventions to improve the quality of transitions in care, such as patient counseling about discharge care plans, coordination of follow-up appointments, and post-discharge telephone calls [24–26].

It refers to the completion of the BPMH and the correction of any unintended discrepancies between patient's previous therapy and that prescribed on admission to hospital or other healthcare facility, at discharge from them or in case or transfer to other wards or settings. More advanced system of MR include inter-professional collaboration (physician, nurse, pharmacist as a team), integration of MR in discharge letters and prescriptions, medication counseling to patients. It seems that MR alone cannot reduce postdischarge hospital utilization within 30 days, but it requires to be associated with other interventions such as coordinated discharge plan, counseling about discharge plan to patients, follow-up appointments and post-discharge phone calls. Evidence shows that pharmacist involvement increase intervention's success [57]. Beyond that there are several strategies that any operator can use to prevent MEs (Table 17.7).

17.2.3.1 Special Focus: Oxygen and Noninvasive Ventilation

Oxygen is actually a drug and, moreover, the most prescribed drug in hospitals. Oxygen is indicated in many critical conditions and is a life-

Table 17.7 Individual behavioral strategies to avoid medication errors

1. Write orders legibly
2. Limit verbal orders, especially in case of high alert or look—alike, sound-alike medications
3. Have always an independent double check for "high-alert drugs"
4. Eliminate the need for calculations through use of tables
5. Use pumps if indicated and available
6. Avoid dangerous abbreviations such as those in the ISMP list
7. Avoid the "trailing zero" and put always a zero before decimals
8. Take a complete medication review at any patient encounter
9. Know any drug you prescribe, dispense, or administer
10. Adjust doses to liver and/or renal function
11. Check allergies and interactions before prescription and/or administration
12. Check patient identity, drug, dosage, dose, route, and rate before prescribe, dispense, or administer
13. Ask if you are in doubt or you do not know
14. Explain the purpose of any medication introduction or withdrawal to patients, caregivers, and other team members
15. Put safety ahead of timeliness and exercise caution when you are out of the normal safety zone of practice

saving drug, as it prevents severe hypoxemia. However, it can potentially cause serious damage or even death if it is not properly administered and managed. The National Patient Safety Agency (NPSA) published in 2009 a report of 281 incidents in which an inappropriate prescription and management of oxygen caused 9 deaths and contributed to other 35 [58]. The analysis of these events highlighted various error modes: (1) failed or incorrect prescription; (2) oxygen administration without a written prescription; (3) failure to monitor or to act in the event of altered oxygen saturation levels; (4) confusion between oxygen and compressed air or other gases, erroneous flows, inadvertent disconnection of the flow; (5) empty cylinder equipment, missing equipment. Therefore, NPSA has issued a series of recommendations to improve the safety of oxygen therapy (Table 17.8).

Noninvasive mechanical ventilation, thanks to its potential for use outside intensive care, for example in IM, has been shown to significantly

Table 17.8 Recommendations to improve safety in oxygen therapy and noninvasive ventilation [60–63]

Oxygen therapy	Noninvasive ventilation

1. Always ask yourself if the patient needs oxygen. Routine use of oxygen in patients with myocardial infarction, stroke, or dyspnea without respiratory failure is not supported by the evidence
2. Prescribe oxygen indicating the target of peripheral saturation (SpO$_2$) to be achieved: 94–98% for critically hypoxemic patients and 88–92% in patients at risk of hypercapnia (obese, kyphoscoliotic and affected by other restrictive syndromes, patients with neuromuscular diseases) or with manifest hypercapnic respiratory failure
3. Use the appropriate device. Nasal cannulas are adequate for most patients; the mask with reservoir must be reserved to limited cases of critically ill patients. Use a 28% ventimask for high-risk patients with COPD or who require low-dose oxygen
4. A correct oxygen prescription includes target, device, and dose (flow in l/min and fiO$_2$%)
5. Report in medical records the results when you check blood gases during oxygen therapy
5. Before start oxygen, have blood gas analysis in all critical patients and, in particular, if you suspect acidosis or hypercapnia. Peripheral saturimetry does not provide information on pH and pCO$_2$
6. Monitor patients in oxygen therapy using systems for the early identification of clinical deterioration (e.g., NEWS)
7. In an emergency, do not delay the administration of oxygen, to make the written prescription
8. Educate patients, caregivers, and support staff (social and health workers) to correctly manage oxygen in hospital and at home
	Organizational level
	Short-term actions:
	   1. Write down, share, and update a local policy
	   2. Provide a checklist for each model of ventilator available in the department, in particular about circuit assembly, definition of controls and alarms)
	   3. Perform and document staff training and periodic retraining
	Long-term actions:
	   1. Check staff competences annually
	   2. Make available the material used for the training
	   3. Create a multidisciplinary team with clear roles and criteria for intervention
	Operational level
	   1. Offer continuous monitoring of oxygen peripheral saturation to patients on noninvasive mechanical ventilation
	   2. Perform intermittent controls of pH and pCO$_2$ by blood gas analysis
	   3. Provide continuous electrocardiographic monitoring in case of heart rate >120/min or arrhythmias or possible associated heart defects.

reduce mortality, the use of intubation and mechanical ventilation, especially in patients with COPD exacerbation.

A recent review [59] of AEs reported during noninvasive ventilation has shown some high-risk situations: (1) inadequate monitoring of patients unable to ask for help; (2) alarms deactivated by the staff; (3) staff not familiar with the ventilators and their proper use (e.g. if they require a CO$_2$ valve or not; when patients bring home appliances to the hospital); (4) implementation of a new ventilator or a new interface without training. In Table 17.8, Joint Commission International [60]/British Thoracic Society/Intensive Care Society [61] recommendations to improve the safety of noninvasive ventilation are listed.

17.2.4 Interventional Procedure-Related Errors

The National Institute for Health and Care Excellence (NICE) defines an "interventional

procedure" as a procedure used for diagnosis and/or treatment that involves [62]:

- making a cut or a hole to gain access to the inside of a patient's body—for example, when carrying out an operation or inserting a tube into a blood vessel
- gaining access to a body cavity (such as the digestive system, lungs, womb, or bladder) without cutting into the body — for example, examining or carrying out treatment on the inside of the stomach using an instrument inserted via the mouth
- using electromagnetic radiation (which includes X-rays, lasers, gamma-rays, and ultraviolet light) — for example, using a laser to treat eye problems.

Interventional procedures most frequently carried out autonomously by the internists at bedside are: thoracentesis, paracentesis, rachicentesis, osteo-medullary biopsy, central venous accesses, joint aspirations, but literature does not provide data on their frequency. Errors during interventional procedures can cause various AEs of different severity, but apart from complication rates there substantially no data about other quality measures. For example, we know that the most common AE of thoracentesis is pneumothorax occurring in up to 39% of patients [63] (10–50% of them requiring tube thoracostomy), but we know very few about success rate, adequacy of the diagnostic specimens obtained, wait time, accuracy and completeness of clinical documentation, and patient satisfaction of thoracentesis and other procedures performed bedside on IM inpatients. On such premises, at General Hospital of Toronto an audit on procedural quality of interventional procedures was conducted in General Internal Medicine [64].

Over a 2-week period, 19 procedures (4 thoracenteses, 6 paracenteses, 8 lumbar punctures, and 1 arthrocentesis) were attempted, of which 14 at the bedside and 5 by interventional radiology. Only 7 (50%) of the bedside procedures were successful. The most common reason for failure was inability to aspirate fluid. Less than 25% of bedside procedures were done on ultrasound guidance. The majority were carried out by students and residents, but only 7 (50%) were documented as supervised. None of the operators used procedural timeouts or checklists. Over 50% of the bedside procedures were performed on evenings or weekends with less success (44% vs 60%), suggesting that procedures should be done during the daytime, when there is more availability of support and supervision. The quality of documentation was also suboptimal. Less than 50% of the procedures documented that the specific risks of the procedure were explained to the patient, how much local anesthetic was used, or what was the side (i.e., left or right). Communication with general practitioner was poor as well: only 66% of the discharge summaries included the date of the procedure and only 75% the results of the procedure [64]. Another study on lumbar puncture investigating for headache on an acute medical admission unit reported that documentation of position and cerebrospinal fluid (CSF) opening pressure was poor (42% and 32%, respectively) even if essential, and only 32% had paired serum glucose measured [65].

Procedure-related errors are due to procedural and system factors [66], such as lack of clinician comfort with performing the procedure, inadequate supplies, insufficient time, or patient factors such as body habitus or characteristics of the fluid collection such as loculation. Once more, there is good evidence that clinicians are performing fewer bedside procedures and are less confident in their bedside procedural skills [67, 68]. So, interventions able to improve safety turn out to be: ultrasound guidance, use of a procedure-specific checklist, patient identification policy and pre-procedural briefing about patient characteristics and risk factors, routine review of physician-specific procedural outcomes, periodic evaluation of operators' competences, training through simulation, supervision until competence is consistently demonstrated and creation of dedicated teams [69–71], periodic assessment of procedural quality including informed consent obtained, waiting time, use of procedural timeout and sonography if needed, number of attempts, success and complication rate, diagnostic sampling quality, completeness of diagnostic tests, avoidance of waste, documentation completeness, legibility (for handwritten notes) and accuracy, wrong side errors, need for repeat procedure and patient satisfaction [64].

17.2.5 Communication Errors

Inter-professional communication in IM wards is complex, owing to the variety of patients' population with changing clinical conditions and constant turnover, and multiple providers' alternation [72]. A lot of information is exchanged every day among care providers in IM, through face-to-face (ward rounds, handover, briefing), synchronous (telephone or page), or asynchronous ways (clinical chart, text messages, emails, written handoff). Anyway, there are only few empirical studies that explore inter-professional communication in IM [73], even if effective inter-professional communication in such information-intensive environment is critical to achieve a safe and timely care.

The most common communication strategies in IM include: handover, ward rounds, clinical chart, briefing, and debriefing. In addition, there are other informal communication ways such as corridor conversation or chance hallway encounters.

17.2.5.1 Handoff

Up to 70% of sentinel events stem at least in part from miscommunications, often occurring during shift changes [74]. The transfer and acceptance of patient-care responsibility achieved through effective communication is technically called "handoff." It is a real-time process of passing patient-specific information from one caregiver/team to another for the purpose of ensuring continuity and safety of care [75]. US International Joint Commission recommendations for handover are reported in Table 17.9 [75]. The most relevant is to refer to standardized handoff tools and methods (forms, templates, checklists, protocols, mnemonics, etc.). A recent review reported at least 24 different handoff mnemonics [76]. The minimum critical content to communicate to the receiver should include: (1) sender contact information; (2) illness assessment, including severity; (3) patient summary, including events leading up to illness or admission, hospital course, ongoing assessment, and plan of care; (4) to-do action list; (5) contingency plans; (6) allergy list; (7) code status; (8) medication list; (9) dated laboratory tests; (10) dated vital signs [75].

The most commonly used mnemonics are SBAR and its variants (I-SBARR, ISOBAR) and I-PASS. The former, developed in military setting to quickly pass information in command

chain [77], has been adopted in healthcare with evidence for improved patient safety. Anyway, it is more suitable for emergency calls [77]. I-PASS Handoff Bundle was developed at the Boston Children Hospital and includes team training, verbal mnemonic, and structured printed tool. Medical errors fell by 40%—from 32% of admissions at baseline to 19% of admissions 3 months during the pilot study [78]. Currently, the I-PASS Mentored Implementation Program is a collaboration with the Society for Hospital Medicine funded by AHRQ, to facilitate implementation of the I-PASS Handoff Bundle in IM [79], as it is more suitable for complex patients.

17.2.5.2 Ward Round

According to the Royal College of Physicians (RCP) and the Royal College of Nurses (RCN), ward round (WR) is "a complex clinical process during which the clinical care of inpatients is reviewed" [80]. It is also considered "a ritual of hospital life" [81] and "the cornerstone of hospital care" [82]. Undoubtedly, it is the main moment of information exchange in IM [83], critical to ensure high-quality, safe, and timely care. However, modern hospital organization is threatening effective WR, in particular because of staff shortage. In order to "save the ward round," RCP and RCN recently purposed to structure WR, as its standardization could warrant effectiveness and efficiency. A structured multidisciplinary WR includes four steps: (1) preparation; (2) pre-round briefing; (3) round; (4) post-round briefing. WR scheduling is not a negligible aspect to avoid overlapping with other activities (i.e. drug rounds, mealtimes, or visiting hours) or other team rounds in case of outliers. Inadequate scheduling can generate resources and efficiency issues but also safety problems, e.g. lack of the nurse responsible for the patient during WR and time wasted commuting to wards [80]. Preparation and pre-round briefing are critical to save time and resources for WR, post-round briefing to clearly delegate any task. A debrief should be conducted at the end of WR. Briefing and debriefing are practices borrowed from military world where they are used to assign mission tasks and verify them at the end. Briefing should be

Table 17.9 Recommendations to increase handover safety [77]

Recommendations of International Joint Commission
1. Have a standardized approach to handoff communication
2. Prefer communications face to face, otherwise by telephone or video conference
3. Avoid only electronic or paper communications
4. Choose locations free from interruptions and noise
5. Include multidisciplinary team and also patient and family if appropriate
6. Do not rely on the patient and/or caregiver for the transfer of important information
7. Be traceable in case of need

well-structured, concise, focused, shared, and reported in medical chart. For bedside round, RCP and RCN purpose a structure with precise roles and responsibilities for doctors, nurses, other professionals, and patients, listing the activities that should be carried out by any of them. In this way, everyone brings his/her competencies and opinions, decisions are taken collegially, anyone is simultaneously informed, patients and/or caregiver actively participate and are timely informed about care plan [80]. That

means no essential information is missed, breakdown in communication among team members and with patient or family is prevented, time and resources utilization is optimized, quality, and safety are warranted. Figure 17.2 includes a checklist for bedside round.

Other subsidiary rounds are board rounds (BRs) and intentional rounds (IRs). BRs are held away from bedside, next to a white board. They should be used to facilitate patient review but cannot replace bedside round. They can be used

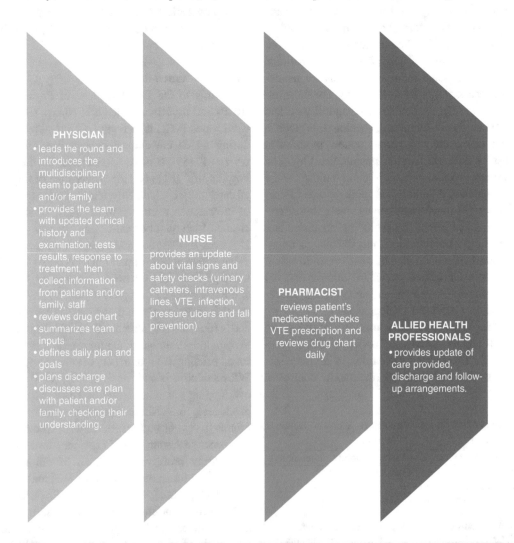

PHYSICIAN
• leads the round and introduces the multidisciplinary team to patient and/or family
• provides the team with updated clinical history and examination, tests results, response to treatment, then collect information from patients and/or family, staff
• reviews drug chart
• summarizes team inputs
• defines daily plan and goals
• plans discharge
• discusses care plan with patient and/or family, checking their understanding.

NURSE
provides an update about vital signs and safety checks (urinary catheters, intravenous lines, VTE, infection, pressure ulcers and fall prevention)

PHARMACIST
reviews patient's medications, checks VTE prescription and reviews drug chart daily

ALLIED HEALTH PROFESSIONALS
• provides update of care provided, discharge and follow-up arrangements.

PATIENT AND/OR CAREGIVE
express their feeling or concerns, ask questions about care plan or discharge and provide any additional information.

Fig. 17.2 Roles and responsibilities of the different health professionals during bedside round

also for post-round briefing to summarize all issues, identify and prioritize tasks, and delegate responsibilities appropriately [80]. IRs are proactive nurse rounds to check patients at set intervals. During IRs, nurses assess patient's experience and essential care needs (4 P: positioning, pain, personal needs, and placement). In terms of patient safety, positioning check helps to prevent pressure ulcers, personal needs (i.e., toilet) and placement of personal items checks reduce falls. Nevertheless, IRs facilitate team to organize workload [80].

17.2.5.3 Clinical Records

Keeping clinical records (CRs) is an integral component in good professional practice and the delivery of high-quality care. Regardless of the type of documentation (electronic or paper), a good and updated CRs allow continuity and coordination of care, aid informed decision-making, avoid repetition of tests or other investigations, improve communication between the various health professionals and improve time management. Bad CRS misinform healthcare professionals and patients, prolong hospitalization, jeopardize patient care leads to serious incidents and increase medical-legal risk [84]. Figure 17.3 summarizes what to do and not to do to keep good medical records.

17.3 Safety Practices and Implementation Strategy

According to the Agency for Healthcare Research and Quality and the National Quality Forum "*a Patient Safety Practice is a type of process or structure whose application reduces the probability of adverse events resulting from exposure to the healthcare system across a range of diseases and procedures*" [85].

In 2001 [86] and 2013 [85], an international panel conducted an evidence-based assessment of patient safety strategies (PSSs). The PSSs were categorized according to the following aspects: frequency and severity of the problem addressed, strength of evidence of the effectiveness of the safety strategy, the evidence or potential harmful consequence of the safety strategy, an estimation of implementation difficulties and costs. It categorizes each PSS according to the following: the scope of the underlying problem that the PSS addresses (its frequency and severity); the strength of evidence about the effectiveness of the safety strategy; the evidence or potential for harmful consequences of the strategy; a rough estimate of the cost of implementing the strategy (low, medium, or high); and an assessment of the difficulty of implementing the strategy. As a result of this process, 10 PSSs were identified as "strongly encouraged" and other 12 as "encouraged" for adoption [85].

Here, we report some safety practices relevant to IM, most of them included in the list of strongly encouraged or encouraged for adoption [87].

17.3.1 Prevention of Age and Frailty-Related Adverse Events

Falls. The rate of falls in acute care hospitals varies from 1 to 9 per 1000 bed-days. The first effective strategy relies on the timely recognition of patients with risk factors for falls (Table 17.10) [88]. The National Institute for Health and Care Excellence (NICE) recommends to regard as the population at risk all inpatients older than 65 and those between 50 and 64 who are identified as being at high risk of falling [89]. Actually, some tools are available to discriminate between high- and low-risk patients, but they may show limitations in specific populations. Morse Falls Score (MFS) and STRATIFY Score are the two most widely validated tools. However, they were not judged to be diffusely adopted and generate greater benefits than nursing staff clinical judgment [90]. NICE guidelines do not recommend any predictive score [89]. Besides, various assessments and interventions should take place (Table 17.11): (1) all aspects of the inpatient environment —including flooring, lighting, and furniture— must be identified and addressed; (2) high-risk patients should be considered for multifactorial evaluation in order to timely identify cognitive impairment, incontinence, fall history,

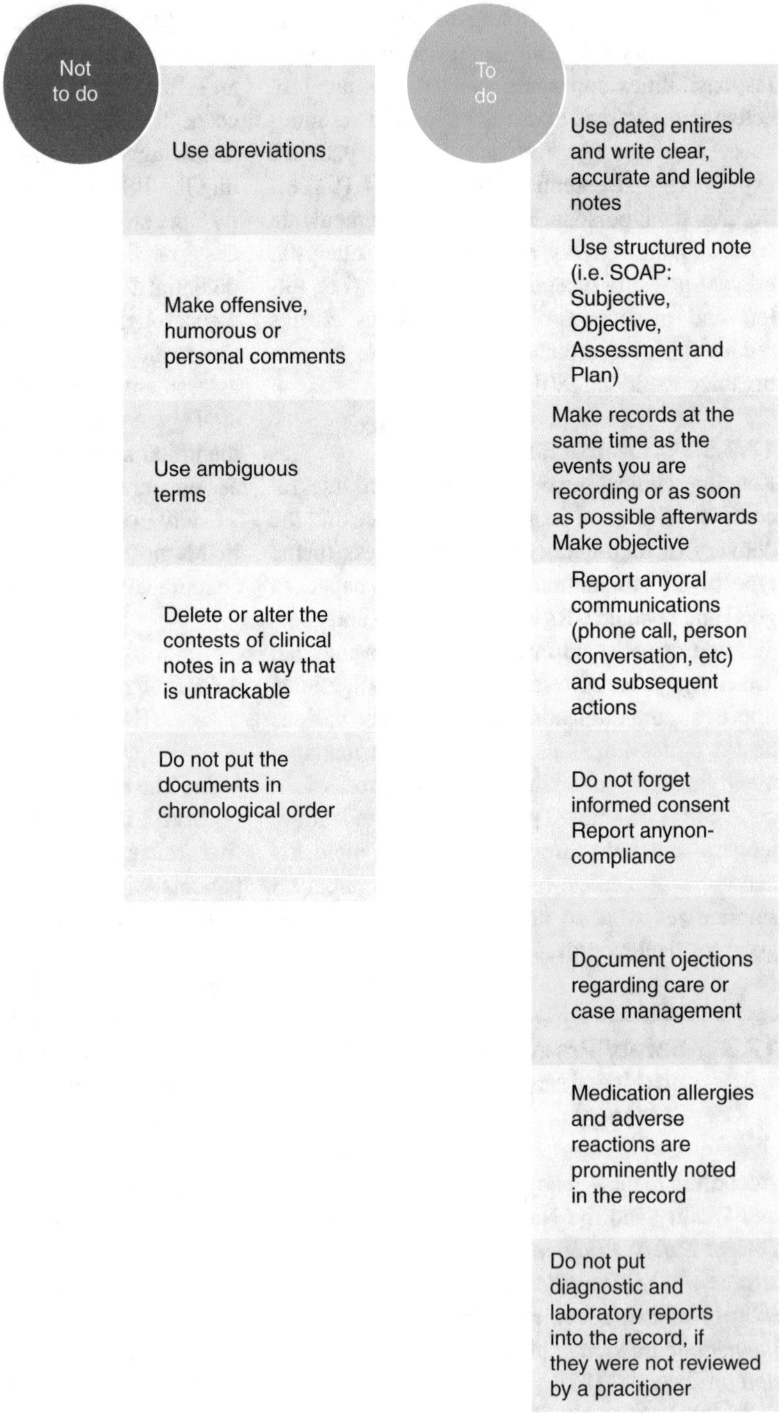

Fig. 17.3 What healthcare operators have to do and not to do to keep good clinical records

Not to do

Use abreviations

Make offensive, humorous or personal comments

Use ambiguous terms

Delete or alter the contests of clinical notes in a way that is untrackable

Do not put the documents in chronological order

To do

Use dated entires and write clear, accurate and legible notes

Use structured note (i.e. SOAP: Subjective, Objective, Assessment and Plan)

Make records at the same time as the events you are recording or as soon as possible afterwards Make objective

Report anyoral communications (phone call, person conversation, etc) and subsequent actions

Do not forget informed consent Report anynon-compliance

Document ojections regarding care or case management

Medication allergies and adverse reactions are prominently noted in the record

Do not put diagnostic and laboratory reports into the record, if they were not reviewed by a pracitioner

Table 17.10 Risk factors for falls in hospitalized patients [90]

Age >85 years
Male sex
Recent fall
Gait instability
Agitation and/or confusion
New urinary incontinence or frequency
Adverse drug reactions (especially with psychotropic drugs)
Neurocardiovascular instability (usually orthostatic hypotension)

Table 17.11 External and internal factors associated with falls [182]

External factors	Internal factors
Prior falls	Physical restraint
Visual impairment	Unsuitable footwear
Stroke	Unsuitable ambulation aids
Joint diseases (i.e., arthritis/arthrosis)	Environmental factors (stairs, bathtub with no support, poor lighting, etc.)
Orthostatic hypotension	
Acute diseases needing hospitalization	
Gait instability	
Cognitive impairment	
Urinary incontinence	
Drugs (impacting on blood pressure, glycemia, and gait)	

medications (Table 17.12) or health problems increasing the risk of falls, unsuitable footwear, and visual impairment. There is a high-quality evidence that multicomponent interventions can reduce risk for in-hospital falls by as much as 30% [91]. The optimal bundle is not clearly defined but relevant components are: patients risk assessment, patient and staff education, bedside signs and wristband alerts, footwear advice, scheduled and supervised toileting, and medication review [91]. In particular, patients' education should include exhaustive oral and written information to patients/caregivers —taking into consideration the patient's ability to understand and retain this information— about (1) patient's risk factors for falls; (2) how to call the nurse as well as when to ask for help before moving from or around the bed; (3) when and how to raise bed rails; (4) other interventions aimed at addressing individual risk factors.

Harms due to interventions have not been studied systematically, but they may include an increased use of restraints and sedatives and decreased patients' mobilization [91].

Key factors for a successful implementation of such multicomponent interventions include: leadership support, engagement of frontline in the design of the intervention, multidisciplinary committee, pilot-testing the intervention, and changing nihilistic opinions about falls [91].

Wandering. It refers to two different, sometimes associated, behaviors: (1) the tendency of nursing home residents or hospital inpatients to persistently walk, spatial disorientation, or a combination of both [92]; (2) a situation in which a subject with dementia has become lost in the community. Although not all subjects with cognitive impairment exhibit wandering behavior, all are at risk for wandering away from the care setting and becoming lost [93].

The first measure to prevent wandering consists of an accurate assessment of patient's diseases impairing cognition such as Alzheimer's disease, fronto-temporal dementia, Lewy body disease, multi-infarct dementia, and delirium, on admission. In such cases, supervision is pivotal to reduce wandering-related problems [94] and should allow an immediate identification of patients at risk (e.g. through colored wristbands, armbands, or gowns), strategies providing an intensive surveillance (i.e. rooms close to the nursing station so that can be easily controlled by nurses and patients cannot go out without passing through it), and engagement of family members. This latter can play an important role during hospitalization as a familiar voice or face can decrease fear and agitation of the patients, thus reducing the patient's willing of wandering. Other strategies may include the avoidance of rooms near elevators, stairs, or exit doors as patients with cognitive impairment tend to respond to what they see around them. Placing clothes, shoes, and suitcases out of the patient's view can help as well. Finally, electronic monitoring could represent a big help, installed in the

Table 17.12 Drugs increasing the risk of falls [182]

Drugs with sedative effect on the CNS	Drugs acting on the CV system	Laxatives	Drugs causing hypoglycemia
Barbiturates	Diuretics	All types	Sulfonylureas
Sleep-inducing/sedative drugs	Antiarrhythmic drugs		Insulin
Tricyclic antidepressants	Vasodilators		
Antipsychotics/neuroleptics	Cardiac glycosides		
Antiparkinsonian agents			
Analgesics			
Anxiolitics			
Seizure medications			

CNS central nervous system, *CV* cardiovascular

division of a hospital or a nursing home and potentially linked to local law enforcement agency, such as in the Project Lifesaver technology (https://projectlifesaver.org/).

On the other end, inappropriate building organization, overworked and under-resourced system, and limited staff knowledge of these problems may represent risk factors for patients' wandering [95, 96].

Bed entrapment occurs when a patient is being caught, trapped, or entangled in the bed rails, mattress, or bed frame of a hospital bed [97]. Many health conditions can favor this event, such as cognitive and communication impairments, frailty, agitation, uncontrolled pain, uncontrolled body movements, and bladder and/or bowel dysfunction. Healthcare professionals should perform a patient's evaluation to identify those at risk and monitor them by concentrating on the following elements: mental status, disease-related reasons for a reduced mobility capacity (obesity, neuromotor deficits), prior long bedridden period, risk of fall and fall-related injuries, urine/fecal incontinence, and the paradox effect of certain drugs.

In order to prevent this event, it is very important for all medical staff to familiarize with the areas of the bed where patients are most often entrapped (Fig. 17.4 and Table 17.13) [97]. These areas account for 80% of entrapment accidents occurring in the hospital. The US Food and Drug Administration (FDA) provided some precise indications for the sizes of the different parts of the bed aimed at reducing as much as possible these accidents. For instance, in order to avoid

trunk, head, and neck to be blocked in the bottom part of the bed, mattresses should cover completely this area and resist to patient's movements and weight. Similarly, entrapment risks in the empty spaces between rails should be avoided. In Table 17.13, requirements for the size of the different bed areas are provided [98].

Aspiration pneumonia is considered as a continuum including community- and hospital-acquired pneumonias. However, data of in-hospital aspiration pneumonias are lacking as solid diagnostic criteria are not available [99, 100].

An important step to face this dangerous complication is represented by the recognition of risk factors (Table 17.14). Indeed, patients presenting with many risk factors have a 9- to 13-fold increased risk of death and adverse outcomes [101]. Compared to patients with community-acquired pneumonia, those at risk for aspiration experienced a 70% increased risk for 1-year mortality, a 3-fold risk for recurrent pneumonia, and a 1.5-fold risk for re-hospitalization [101].

Since most of the elderly patients admitted to IM are assuming a long list of drugs, a great effort should be done to avoid sedatives, hypnotics, antipsychotic agents, and anti-histamines, if possible [102]. Additionally, patients with dysphagia, especially those affected by a previous stroke or a neurodegenerative disease, can benefit from speech and swallowing evaluation, before allowing feeding [103]. Oral feeding should always be preferred to enteral tube feeding using a mechanical soft diet with thickened liquids, avoiding pureed food and thin liquids.

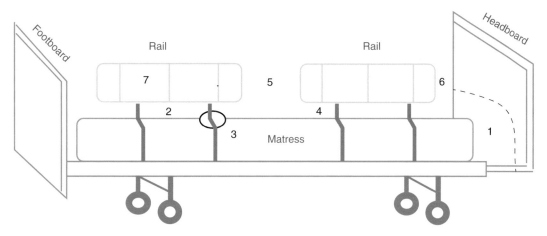

Fig. 17.4 Areas where patients are most often entrapped. Zone 1: between the headboard or footboard and the mattress; zone 2: under the rails; zone 3: between the rail and the mattress; zone 4: under the ends of the rail; zone 5: between the 2 bed rails; zone 6: between the end of the rail and the edge of the headboard or footboard; zone 7: within the rails [100]

Table 17.13 Areas of the bed at risk for entrapment and recommendations from the US Food and Drug Administration (FDA) [99]

Zones	Definition	Recommendations
Zone 1	Any open space within the perimeter of the rail	A loosened bar or rail can modify the size of the space. The recommended space is <120 mm (i.e., head breadth)
Zone 2	The space under the rail between a mattress compressed by the weight of a patient's head and the bottom edge of the rail at a location between the rail supports or next to a single rail support	Consider all factors modifying the mattress compressibility The recommended space should be small enough to avoid head entrapment, i.e., <120 mm
Zone 3	The space between the inner surface of the rail and the mattress compressed by the weight of the patient's head	This space should be small enough to avoid head entrapment considering the mattress compressibility and any lateral shift of the mattress or rail, i.e., recommended space <120 mm
Zone 4	The space growing between the mattress compressed by the patient and the lower part of the rail, at its end	Consider mattress compressibility, lateral shift of the mattress or rail, and degree of play from loosened rails to avoid entrapment of the patient's neck, i.e., recommended space <60 mm
Zone 5	This area is occupied when partial length head and foot side rails are used on the same side of the bed	FDA recognizes these parts as at risk for entrapment encouraging manufacturers to report entrapment events at this area
Zone 6	The space between the end of the rail and the side edge of the headboard or footboard	

However, when enteral feeding is unavoidable, patients should be positioned in a semi-recumbent and anti-Trendelenburg position to reduce the chance of gastric aspiration/regurgitation. In patients with dysphagia, it is helpful to consider a nutritional rehabilitation, during which swallowing exercises and early mobilization may reduce risks of aspiration and/or recurrences [104, 105]. While the effectiveness of the nasogastric tube and the post-pyloric feeding is controversial, the use of angiotensin-converting enzyme inhibitors (as anti-hypertensive drug) and cilostazol (as an anti-platelet drug) acting on substance P and bradykinin and improving cough

Table 17.14 Risk factors for aspiration pneumonia [103–105]

Impaired swallowing	Esophageal disease, including dysphagia, head/neck cancer, stricture, achalasia, scleroderma, polymyositis
	Chronic obstructive pulmonary disease
	Neurologic diseases, including seizures, multiple sclerosis, Parkinson's disease and parkinsonism, stroke, dementia
	Extubation from mechanical ventilation
Impaired consciousness	Stroke or intracerebral hemorrhage
	Cardiac arrest
	Drug overdose and medications, such as narcotic agents, general anesthetic agents, and some antidepressant agents
	Alcohol abuse
Increased amount of gastric content reaching the lungs	Percutaneous enteral tube feeding, especially when associated with gastric dysmotility and cognitive impairment
	Gastro-esophageal reflux
	Gastroparesis
Conditions impairing the cough reflex	Stroke
	Medications
	Alcohol
	Degenerative neurologic diseases
Others	Male sex
	Smoking
	Diabetes mellitus

and swallowing reflexes showed more consisting results [106–108].

Oral hygiene may represent an important preventive action in non-ventilated patients: it has been demonstrated that chlorhexidine or mechanical oral cleaning reduce up to 60% risk of aspiration pneumonia [109]. However, it is important to remember that chlorhexidine can be toxic if aspirated into the lungs, especially by ventilated patients. The association of oral care to supplemental nutrition also demonstrated to lower aspiration pneumonia [110]. Anyway, a comprehensive oral care program (manual tooth, gum brushing, chlorhexidine mouthwashes, and upright positioning during feeding) evaluated in a cluster-randomized controlled trial conducted among nursing home residents showed a higher number of pneumonias/lower respiratory tract infections in the intervention group [111]. On the other hand, a short course ($\leq$24 h) of prophylactic β-lactam antibiotics was shown to reduce the risk of aspiration around the time of endotracheal intubation [112].

Delirium is a neuropsychiatric syndrome characterized by altered consciousness and attention with cognitive, emotional, and behavioral symptoms. It occurs among hospitalized patients—mainly in elderly frail people—at a rate from 14% to 56% and increases morbidity and mortality [113]. In this condition, multiple risk factors have been identified so that suggested intervention is obviously multicomponent. Evidence shows that they are effective in preventing delirium onset in at-risk patients in a hospital setting, without significant associated harms but it is insufficient to identify which multicomponent interventions are the most beneficial, and which components within a program provide the most benefit [114, 115]. The aim of primary prevention is to prevent physiological derangements by early mobilization, good hydration, sleep enhancement, family and caregiver involvement, in addition to physiotherapy and rehabilitation, as summarized in Table 17.15.

Since it is usually triggered by different factors, prevention strategies need to be reassessed during hospital stay [114].

Approaches including the education of nursing aides and caregivers, music therapy and psychotherapy gave no definitive results [114].

The main recently published studies on pharmacological approach are summarized in a review by Oh et al. [114]. In general, antipsychotic drugs did not demonstrate any clear benefit in preventing delirium [116], similarly to cholinesterase inhibitors, ketamine, melatonin, and melatonin-receptor agonist (ramelteon) [117, 118]. Hence, there is a lack of support in using drugs for prevention or treatment of delirium, especially when considered as a unique entity.

Table 17.15 Multicomponent non-pharmacologic approaches to prevent delirium (adapted from [116])

Type of approach	Description
Orientation and therapeutic activities	• Provide adequate lighting, calendars, and clocks in order to help the patient orienting in the space • The patient should be oriented in the space and in the role of the healthcare providers • Stimulate the patient with activities, such reminiscing, and favor the visits of family members
Fluid consumption	• Patients should be encouraged to drink, eventually consider parenteral fluids • It is helpful for the monitoring of fluid balance by personnel in patients with heart failure or renal disease
Early mobilization	• Early postoperative mobilization should be encouraged as well as regular ambulation through specific programs • Patients should be involved in active exercises based on their capacities • Walking aids (canes, walkers) must be always nearby
Feeding assistance	• General nutrition guidelines should be followed. If needed, an advice from a dietician can be asked • A proper fit of dentures must be provided
Vision and hearing	• Reversible cause of the impairment should be fixed • Working hearing and visual aids must be available and used when needed
Sleep enhancement	• All medical or nursing procedures must be limited or avoided during sleep times • Noise at night time must be avoided
Infection prevention	• Infections must be early recognized and treated • Unnecessary catheterization must be avoided • Infection-control procedures must be taken into consideration
Pain management	• It is always important to assess the pain, especially among those patients with communication difficulties • Pain must be monitored and managed in patients with known or suspected pain
Hypoxia	• Hypoxia and oxygen saturation must always be monitored
Psychoactive medication protocol	• The list of medications, including class and number, must always be checked and modified, if needed

At the end, if non-pharmacological strategies were proved to be effective on delirium onset, no convincing impact was provided for hospital mortality, 6-month mortality, or institutionalization. As well, frailty, as a key predictor of outcomes, was not taken into consideration [119].

17.3.2 Prevention of Healthcare-Associated Infections

Healthcare-associated infections (HAIs) represent a relevant problem for hospitalized patients all over the world. Some 3.2 million patients in Europe suffer every year from HAIs, of which nearly one third is considered preventable [120].

Many preventive strategies may help in reducing the spreading of HAIs [121]. For instance, patients coming from the intensive care unit to IM should be screened if they present with neutropenia, diarrhea, skin rashes, known communicable disease, or if they are known carriers of an epidemic bacterial strain. The recognition of risk factors, listed in Table 17.16 may help in reducing HAIs, too.

As hands are the most common vehicle for transmission of infections, hand hygiene is the single most effective measure to prevent the horizontal transmission of infections among hospitalized patients and healthcare personnel. In 2003, World Health Organization promoted a world challenge on this topic, introducing the five moments for hand hygiene, two before and three after approaching the patient: (1) before touching the patient in order to protect him/her from germs carried on healthcare personnel's hands; (2) before aseptic procedures to protect the patient against germs, including the patient's own ones;

Table 17.16 Common risk factors increasing the risk of HAIs [122, 123]

Patient-related	Age >70 years
	Shock
	Major trauma
	Acute renal failure
	Coma
Treatment-related	Prior and/or prolonged antibiotic therapy
	Mechanical ventilation
	Drugs affecting the immune system (steroids, chemotherapy)
	Indwelling catheters
Environment-related	Prolonged intensive care unit stay (>3 days)

(3) after body fluid exposure; (4) after touching the patient; and (5) after touching the patient's surrounding (these three latter moments are intended to protect the personnel and the environment from the patient's germs) and two methods, with water and soap or alcohol-based solutions [122].

In addition, standard precautions include preventive measures that should always be used, irrespective of a patient's infection status. Sterile gloves should be worn after hand hygiene in case of sterile procedures or exposition to body fluids. It is important not to wear the same gloves when caring for more patients, remove them and wash hands after caring for a single patient. Wearing gown, mask, and eye protection/face shield is very important to avoid soiling clothing and skin during procedures potentially delivering body fluids [122].

In patients known or suspected to have airborne, contact or droplet infections (*M. tuberculosis*, *H. influenzae*, varicella zoster virus, herpes virus among others), additional precautions should be followed.

For airborne infections, isolation with negative-pressure ventilation is preferable. Additionally, all people entering the room, including visitors, must wear respiratory protections (such as the disposable N-95 respirator mask).

For contact infections, single use patient-care equipment is recommended. If unavoidable, adequate cleaning and disinfection before using to another patient is mandatory. As well, the movements of the patients across different wards should be limited.

In droplet infections, the patient should be isolated and his/her movements limited, while respiratory protections must be worn when entering the isolation room. Additional specific strategies to prevent specific nosocomial infections have been reported by Mehta et al. [123].

Finally, environmental factors cannot be neglected. Adequate cleaning and disinfection are important, especially when considering the patient's closest surfaces, such as bedrails, bedside tables, doorknobs, and equipment. The frequency of cleaning should be as follows: surface cleaning twice weekly, floor cleaning 2–3 times/day, and terminal cleaning after discharge or death. Central air-conditioning systems should ensure that air recirculates through appropriate filters (air should be filtered to 99% efficiency down to 5 μm). Isolation facility should include both negative- and positive-pressure ventilations. Alcohol gel dispensers should be positioned at the entry of every rooms and near entrance/exit for health operators, patients, and visitors.

17.3.3 Prevention of Venous Thromboembolism

The hospitalization for an acute condition is responsible for an eight-fold increase in the thrombotic risk and accounts for nearly 25% of all thromboembolic events [124]. However, risk stratification of patients admitted to IM is often complicated by their high heterogeneity [125, 126]. For this purpose, the Padua Prediction Score has been implemented and validated by Prandoni et al. [126]. It includes 11 thrombotic risk factors and identifies patients at high or low risk for venous thromboembolism (VTE) (Table 17.17). Patients with a score <4 (nearly 60% of the patients) are at low risk, while those with a risk score ≥4 (nearly 40%) have a high risk. Indeed, in the 3-month follow-up period, the incidence of VTE without any prophylaxis in the low-risk group was 0.3%, while the incidence in the high-

Table 17.17 The Padua Prediction Score [127]

Baseline characteristics	Score
Active cancer[a]	3
Previous venous thromboembolism (excluding superficial vein thrombosis)	3
Reduced mobility[b]	3
Already known thrombophilic condition[c]	3
Recent (≤1 month) trauma and/or surgery	2
Elderly age (≥70 years)	1
Heart and/or respiratory failure	1
Acute myocardial infarction or ischemic stroke	1
Acute infection and/or rheumatologic disorder	1
Obesity (BMI ≥30)	1
Ongoing hormonal treatment	1

[a]Patients with local or distant metastases and/or in whom chemotherapy or radiotherapy had been performed in the previous 6 months
[b]Bedrest with bathroom privileges (either due to patient's limitations or on physicians order) for at least 3 days
[c]Defects of anti-thrombin, protein C or S, factor V Leiden, G20210A prothrombin mutation, and antiphospholipid syndrome

risk group was 11% (hazard ratio HR 32.0, 95% confidence interval 4.1–251.0). Based on these findings, the Padua Prediction Score was recommended as a tool for the identification of high-risk patients requiring thromboprophylaxis [125]. Anyway, the hemorrhagic risk should also be considered. In the study by Prandoni et al., major or clinically relevant bleeding complications were found in 1.6% of high-risk patients receiving pharmacological prophylaxis although all bleeding complications were non-fatal [126]. In another study, active gastroduodenal ulcer, prior bleeding within 3 months, and low platelet count (<50,000/mm³) were recognized as the strongest independent risk factors for bleeding [127]. Other bleeding risk factors included age >85 years, male sex, hepatic or renal failure, intensive care unit stay, central venous catheter, rheumatic disease, and cancer. All these factors have been integrated in a score for bleeding risk stratification (IMPROVE score), highlighting that more than a half of the major bleeding events were experienced by patients with a score ≥7 [127].

Combining thrombotic and hemorrhagic risk assessments, pharmacological and non-pharmacological measures can be adopted to safely reduce in-hospital VTE [128].

Current evidence is concordant in recognizing a similar efficacy of low-molecular-weight heparin (LMWH) and low-dose unfractionated heparin (LDUH) in patients hospitalized in the medical setting although LMWH is more likely to be associated with a lower risk of bleeding. Fondaparinux, the only selective inhibitor of factor Xa approved for the treatment and prevention of thrombosis, showed a similar performance compared to heparin both in terms of thromboprophylaxis and risk of bleeding [125]. For patients with an increased risk of bleeding, alternative treatments, such as graduated compression stockings, intermittent pneumatic compression, and venous foot pumps, all aiming at reducing venous stasis by inducing the movement of blood from superficial to deep veins through the perforator veins are recommended [125].

Since IM usually receives a great number of patients often showing particular features (elderly, obese or underweight people, impaired kidney function, cancer), these specific populations need different managements [129].

Elderly patients present differences in terms of pharmacokinetics and an increased risk of bleeding, compared to the general population [130]. Further, older patients (>80 years) show a ten-fold risk increased risk for VTE compared to younger ones. Indeed, in the MEDENOX study, enoxaparin was greatly effective in reducing the risk of VTE in patients >80 years hospitalized in medical wards [131].

Obesity and overweight are recognized risk factors for VTE. The main concern is to modify or not the dosages to get the same efficacy in such conditions. A study conducted in a medical ward in the USA tested the 0.5 mg/kg/day enoxaparin dosage in obese patients showing its feasibility and efficacy and, at the same time, the absence of any bleeding event, symptomatic VTE, or dangerous thrombocytopenia [132]. Some differences arose in a study among patients undergoing bariatric surgery [133] underlining potential differences in terms of absorption among the different formulations of LMWH. For this reason, for obese patients, dosages may need to be modified according to the drug used.

In patients with kidney disease, LMWH and fondaparinux clearance is reduced and a modification of the dosage is required. Usually, LMWH can be used at the dosage indicated for thromboprophylaxis with a limited risk of bioaccumulation in patients with kidney disease treated for a limited period of time [134]. LDUH can be a valid alternative in patients with advanced kidney disease. Prophylactic doses of fondaparinux must be reduced when kidney function is severely impaired: 1.5 mg/day when estimated glomerular filtration rate (eGFR) is 20–50 mL/min/1.73 m². Fondaparinux is not recommended when eGFR is below 20 mL/min/1.73 m² [135].

Patients with active cancer are known to be at increased risk of arterial embolism and VTE as well as bleeding events. Although treated for a long time with LMWH, recently direct oral anticoagulants have been found to be effective in reducing the risk of VTE and arterial embolism in many large randomized clinical trials. With this regard, an exhaustive report on these therapeutic strategies can be found in a recent review by Mosarla et al. [136]. Direct oral anticoagulants, however, are not yet approved for the prophylaxis of venous thromboembolism in these patients, but only in secondary prevention.

17.3.4 Prevention of Pressure Ulcers

Complications from hospital-acquired pressure ulcers cause about 60,000 deaths and relevant morbidity and resources consumption every year in the USA. Diabetes, obesity, and older age are known risk factors [137].

Moderate-strength evidence suggests that implementing multicomponent initiatives for pressure ulcer prevention in acute and long-term care settings can improve processes of care and reduce pressure ulcer rates [137].

Interventions usually address impaired mobility and/or nutrition and/or skin health. Using support surfaces, regularly repositioning the patient, optimizing nutritional status, and moisturizing sacral skin help to prevent pressure ulcers, along with initial and periodic risk stratification and personalized care for high-risk individuals. Many

different pressure ulcer risk assessment tools are used in clinical practice (i.e. Braden, Norton, Exton-Smith, Waterlow, Knoll, …), but a recent Cochrane review was unable to suggest that the use of one tool over the others because of low or very low certainty of available evidence [138]. Multicomponent interventions typically include 3–5 evidence-based practices that "when performed collectively and reliably, have been proven to improve patient outcomes" [139]. Further, experts recommend to pay attention to organizational and care coordination components [140, 141]. Organizational components include selecting lead team membership, establishing policies and procedures, evaluating quality processes, educating staff, using skin champions, and communicating written care plans. Care coordination components include creating a culture of change and establishing regular meetings to facilitate communication, collegiality, and learning [137].

Key components of successful implementation efforts include: simplification and standardization of pressure ulcer-specific interventions and documentation, involvement of multidisciplinary teams and leadership, designated skin champions, ongoing staff education, and sustained audit and feedback [137].

17.3.5 Clinical Monitoring by Early Warning Scores

Many hospitalized patients experience vital signs deterioration before cardiac arrest, unanticipated intensive care unit admission or unexpected death [142, 143]. Indeed, one or more aberrant vital signs can be detected by nurses or physicians in 60% of cases before the adverse event [144]. A rapid recognition of these antecedents and an appropriate treatment can prevent further deterioration so avoiding the development of the adverse outcomes. Several studies suggest that the triad of (1) early detection, (2) timeliness of response, and (3) competency of the response is crucial for patient's outcomes [145–147]. According to these considerations, the use of the so-called early warning scores (EWS) has been widely implemented by hospitals to efficiently identify and treat patients who present with or develop acute illness [147, 148]. Although different and heterogeneous EWS exist, they are characterized by few key features. First, they require a systematic method to measure simple vital signs at the right intervals in all patients to recognize those with clinical deterioration. The assessment of vital signs need to be simple and usable by all healthcare professionals after an appropriate training. Second, clear definitions of the urgency and of the appropriate clinical response are necessary. The trigger for the clinical response should not be too sensitive in order to avoid alerts but it also should not be so insensitive that it never leads to system response activation [149]. In the EWS, the points for the final score are allocated for each physiologic parameter according to how much it deviates from a predefined normal range, so that a higher score corresponds to greater patient's deterioration. So, clinical response can be adapted in terms of urgency and provider's level of expertise, ranging from the increase of vital signs monitoring to the activation of rapid response team. The vital signs considered in each EWS typically include pulse rate, breathing rate, blood pressure, level of consciousness and temperature [150]. There is, however, variability in other parameters included (e.g. pain, level of respiratory support, urine, age), in weights assigned, and in thresholds for triggering the response. In Table 17.18, the chart of National Early Warning Score (NEWS) used in the UK is reported, as an example [151]. Another important issue to consider is the frequency of vital signs monitoring.

Ideally, it should be done frequently enough to identify patient's deterioration at a time that allows interventions to improve outcomes. There is no evidence that continuous surveillance has a positive effect on mortality [152, 153]. Moreover, although an increase in monitoring frequency leads to a higher detection of events, it is also associated with a rise in expense and workload [149]. Thus, it is necessary to find a balance between patient's safety and available resources. According to evidence, patients at low risk should be monitored at least twice daily, whereas an increase in assessment frequency is required when EWS raise [154]. The appropriate responses to EWS can be described with an escalation protocol, in which at every threshold corresponds an action (see Table 17.19). Providers at every level of the chain have to operate according to their competences and skills. They have also to call medical emergency team (MET) when it is indicated by the protocol. Several studies, however, reported omission to call MET in 25–42% of cases in which patients presented calling criteria [155, 156]. Reasons for non-adherence to protocol include negative attitude toward MET, staffs' confidence in their own ability, fear to appear incompetent or of criticism by the MET [155–158]. Ongoing education and training in the use of EWS is essential for all healthcare staff involved in the assessment and monitoring of acutely ill patients. A standardized system, jointly to a diffuse knowledge of it, is essential to achieve the aim of a rapid recognition of patient's deterioration, an appropriate clinical response and a favorable outcome.

Table 17.18 National Early Warning Score (NEWS), adapted from [153]

Physiological parameters	3	2	1	0	1	2	3
Respiration rate	≤8		9–11	12–20		21–24	≥25
Oxygen saturation	≤91	92–93	94–95	≥96			
Any supplemental oxygen		Yes		No			
Temperature	≤35.0		35.1–36.0	36.1–38.0	38.1–39.0	≥39.1	
Systolic blood pressure	≤90	91–100	101–110	111–219			≥220
Heart rate	≤40		41–50	51–90	91–110	111–130	≥131
Level of consciousness				A			V, P or U

Table 17.19 Clinical response to NEWS trigger, adapted from [153]

NEWS	Frequency of monitoring	Clinical response
0	Minimum 12 hourly	Continue NEWS monitoring
1–4 Low risk	Minimum 6 hourly	Registered nurse to decide if increased frequency of monitoring and/or escalation of clinical care is required
5–6 or 3 in 1 parameter Medium risk	Minimum 1 hourly	• Registered nurse to urgently inform the medical team caring for the patient • Urgent assessment by a clinician with core competencies to assess acutely ill patients • Clinical care in an environment with monitoring facilities
7 or more High risk	Continuous monitoring	• Registered nurse to immediately inform the medical team caring for the patient • Emergency assessment by a clinical team with critical care competencies, which also includes a practitioner/s with advanced airways skills • Consider transfer to Intensive Unit Care

17.3.6 Sepsis Bundles

The mortality rate for severe sepsis and septic shock remains a major concern in clinical practice [159]. The Surviving Sepsis Campaign (SSC) is a joint collaboration of the Society of Critical Care Medicine and the European Society of Intensive Care Medicine created in 2002 to increase sepsis awareness, improve early diagnosis, increase the use of appropriate timely care, develop guidelines and spread them, in order to reduce morbidity and mortality for sepsis. Sepsis bundles were presented for the first time in the SSC Guideline for the management of severe sepsis and septic shock in 2004 [160]. They were created to bring guidelines key elements to clinicians' daily practice [161]. Indeed, a bundle is a small and straightforward set of evidence-based practices that, when performed altogether, have been proven to improve outcomes [162]. Hospitals that have successfully implemented sepsis bundles have consistently shown improved outcomes and reductions in healthcare spending [163]. Over the years, sepsis bundles have been revised according to most recent scientific evidence [164, 165]. The most recent version is the hour-1 bundle, published in June 2018 [166]. Sepsis is a medical emergency. Early recognition and prompt management in the first hours after its development improve the survival [167]. Accordingly, the aim of hour-1 bundle is to begin sepsis management and resuscitation immediately although some of the actions require more than 1 h to be completed.

The hour-1 bundle includes five key steps:

1. Measure lactate levels and re-measure if initial lactate is >2 mmol/L. Lactate is a surrogate for tissue perfusion measurement [168]. Lactate-guide resuscitation has been shown to reduce mortality in randomized control trials [169, 170]. So that, if initial lactate is elevated (>2 mmol/L), the measure should be repeated within 2–4 h and the treatment should be based on its values with the aim of normalizing lactate.

2. Obtain blood cultures prior to antibiotics administration (at least two sets, aerobic and anaerobic). If obtaining blood cultures is difficult, however, do not delay antibiotic treatment beginning. The identification of pathogens improve outcomes, but can be difficult to obtain after antimicrobial treatment for the rapid sterilization of cultures [171].

3. Administer broad-spectrum antibiotics. The antimicrobial treatment should be started empirically with one or more intravenous broad-spectrum antibiotics. Therapy should be narrowed once pathogen is identified.

4. Begin rapid administration of 30 mL/kg of crystalloid fluids in case of hypotension or lactate ≥4 mmol/L. Fluid resuscitation should be started immediately after the recognition of sepsis signs. The use of colloids did not show any clear benefit and it is, therefore, not recommended by guidelines.

5. Administer vasopressor for hypotension during or after fluid resuscitation, in order to achieve a mean arterial pressure ≥65 mmHg.

All these actions must be initiated within 1 h from "Time Zero," defined as the time of triage in the Emergency Department or, in case of sepsis presenting in another care location, from the earliest chart annotation consistent with elements of sepsis or septic shock.

A successful treatment of sepsis and septic shock require the collaboration of all healthcare professionals. The role of nurses is particularly important because they interact constantly with patients and they can provide early recognition of sepsis and implement a rapid clinical response [172]. Education programs on sepsis screening and hour-1 bundle should be strongly recommended for the entire medical staff. The website survivingsepsis.org provides resources and tools to improve sepsis knowledge.

17.3.7 Safe Management of Outlier Patients

"Outlier" or "out-lying hospital in-patient" is a patient who, is admitted wherever an unoccupied bed is, because of unavailability of hospital beds in his/her clinically appropriate ward [173, 174]. In such case, clinical management is on charge of physicians of the clinically appropriate ward (generally IM ward), but care is delivered by nursing staff of the hosting ward (often a surgical ward). Outliers phenomenon involve commonly medical patients in countries with a public health system that faced hospital beds cuts, over the last decades. Outliers represent about 7–8% of all admissions every year [173]. They are the other neglected face of hospital overcrowding. From a patient safety point of view, they have been defined, according to Reason's Swiss cheese model, "a latent condition which may underpin adverse events." Identification errors, missed or delayed diagnosis and treatment, HAIs, delirium and falls could be amplified by outlier status, due to delay between admission and medical evaluation, discontinuity of care, errors or delay in tests request/execution, inadequate communication

between ward-teams, less familiarity with monitoring and treatment by hosting team [174]. Despite their compelling nature, they have been poorly studied. Available evidence shows a trend to increase in-hospital mortality and hospital readmission, but presents many serious limitations [174]. Also evidence-based guidelines to safely manage outliers clinical risks are still lacking. Only some bed management policies, formulated mainly by NHS Trusts across the UK [175, 176] contain some indications to ensure safety, dignity, and duty of care for both patients and staff involved in the care of outliers. As an example, that from Portsmouth Hospitals NHS trust recognizes that the best choice is not to admit to off-service units, but when unavoidable, the risk for patients and staff need to be minimized. It recommends not to admit to off-service units directly from emergency department or acute medicine, except in rare cases. It prescribes to rate patients' suitability to be moved to other units, with a score (RAG) based on clinical and mental health needs, level of acuity and dependency and clinical capability of the receiving area. RAG must be assessed within 24 h from admission and reviewed every day. Further, outliers must be placed in the same level of care and treatment that they would receive if cared in their appropriate unit. They must be reviewed by medical and/or nursing teams from their clinically appropriate unit daily. Patient treatment plans must be updated including pending investigations and discharge plans carefully documented in the patient's health records. The number of bed moves during each patient's stay must be minimized. Relatives must be informed of every movement and patients must be involved in decision by signing an informed consent [177].

17.4 Case Studies

17.4.1 Case Study 1

Female, 36 y-o, immigrant, unemployed, living with her husband and a 6 y-o daughter. Access to Emergency Room (ER) at 5.30 p.m. for left flank pain and hematuria. Previous history of kidney stones. Giordano's test positive. Her general practitioner suggests hospital admission for alcohol withdrawal. Blood tests reveal increased neutrophils, c-reactive protein and transaminases; abdominal US scan shows left hydro-nephrosis but not signs of liver damage. After 5 h, she is discharged with a diagnosis of hypertransaminasemia in chronic alcohol abuse. Left renal colic. ER physician says she preferred go back home to fix her daughter tonight and will come back tomorrow. Twelve hours later, she is back to ER. ER physicians writes: "the patient comes back for left flank pain". Her general practitioner contacted social and psychiatric services. She remains in the ER until 5.00 p.m. without clinical nor laboratorial re-evaluation. Then she is admitted to a medical ward for bilateral renal colic and alcohol abuse. At 9 p.m. onset of worsening psychomotor agitation, treated by diazepam, gabapentin, vitamin B6, and fluids. At 8 a.m., she receives the first dose of antibiotics (i.v. piperacillin/tazobactam). At 9 a.m., nurse reports hypotension (90/60 mmHg) and low peripheral oxygen saturation (92% room air); instead physician writes in medical record "inappropriate admission," withdrawal syndrome in chronic alcohol abuse. At 2 p.m., morning shift physician hands off the patient saying she is going home because she rejects treatment. During the afternoon, psychomotor agitation worsens so that the treatment with fluids and oxygen is compromised and relatives are asked to provide assistance to her. She receives multiple administration of i.v. midazolam. At 8 p.m., she has cardiorespiratory arrest. She is resuscitated and transferred to intensive care unit. A diagnosis of post-anoxic coma and septic shock by Escherichia coli is made and the patient dies after 20 days without ever regaining consciousness.

17.4.2 Case Study 2

A 78-year-old man, previous gastric ulcer and depression, affected by metastatic colon cancer in home palliative care, was admitted to IM ward on December 27th at 1.00 a.m., after rejecting hospice admission to die at home, just the day before. He was on transdermal and sublingual (breakthrough cancer pain) opioids, intravenous opioids, haloperidol, and hyoscine (elastomeric pump). He died about 20 h later. Ten days after, his wife and son made a claim for bad assistance. They complained that their relative was removed from sedation, so he was awake in the grip of its devastating pains; his pain was not asked or evaluated; no painkillers were given. They were told by the nurses: "We can't do more than that. Sedation is a matter of anesthesia." On the contrary, electronic medical record reported that patient was unresponsive to any stimulus since admission; sedation was not interrupted; intravenous opioids dose was progressively increased; pain evaluation was frequent and pain control was achieved in few time. Health operators declared also that his relatives were allowed to stay with him until the end and any their desire such as music listening was satisfied. Why so different perceptions?

Despite of technical expertise and some human compassion, audit disclosed communication failure, and inappropriate setting (acute care ward). First of all, ward team missed medication and care plan recognition with palliative doctors, and, most of all, it did not effectively take care of family concerns and expectations. Health operators did not explore family feelings, did not provide frequent and punctual information about what was done and reassurance about their beloved clinical condition, in particular unconsciousness.

17.4.3 Epicrisis and Recommendations

17.4.3.1 Clinical Case 1
1. Be aware of *Medical mimics* or secondary psychoses, medical conditions mimicking psychiatric disorders, especially in patients with previous psychiatric history.
2. Remember that infections, trauma, autoimmune, metabolic, neurological diseases, and pharmacological withdrawal can present with psychiatric symptoms, from psychomotor agitation to anxiety, depression, dementia, or apathy.

3. Think about medical mimics in case of: patient over 40 years and no previous psychiatric history, no history of similar symptoms or worsening of previous symptoms, family concern, chronic comorbidities, history of head injury, change in headache pattern, worsening after antipsychotics or anxiolytics, history of changing psychiatric diagnoses over time, difficult or unlikable patient, polypharmacy, abnormal autonomic signs, visual disturbance, visual, olfactory or tactile hallucinations, nystagmus, illusions, speech deficit, abnormal body movement [178].

4. Have a complete medical and psychiatric history, an exhaustive review of systems to identify symptoms/signs suggestive of medical diseases, review of any drug prescription, over-the-counter and alternative medications included, a careful mental status examination, diagnostic tests for diseases known to mimic psychiatric disorders (look for head trauma, syphilis or hypothyroidism, glucose or electrolyte or blood gases alterations, sepsis, etc.)

5. Avoid incorrect assumptions (patient triaged as psychiatric, is psychiatric; patient with psychiatric history, has only psychiatric disease; young patients suffer from functional disorders; abnormal vital signs are due to mental/emotional state) and pitfalls (cursory history from limited sources, incomplete review of system, incomplete physical and neuropsychiatric exam, failure to review medications) [179].

17.4.3.2 Clinical Case 2

- In end-of-life care, ensure skillful communication with patients and families.
- Define and share with patient and/or family realistic goals of care.
- Pay attention to understanding the patient's and family's concerns besides competent symptom management [180].

Acknowledgments The authors gratefully thank Roberto Nardi, MD for his very helpful and accurate review and Julia Bashore, BS for the language check of this chapter.

References

1. Schimmel EM. The hazards of hospitalization. Ann Intern Med. 1964;60:100–10. https://doi.org/10.7326/0003-4819-60-1-100.
2. Barr DP. Hazards of modern diagnosis and therapy: the price we pay. J Am Med Assoc. 1955;159(15):1452–6.
3. Moser RH. Diseases of medical progress. N Engl J Med. 1956;255(13):606–14. https://doi.org/10.1056/NEJM195609272551306.
4. Steel K, Gertman PM, Crescenzi C, Anderson J. Iatrogenic illness on a general medical service at a university hospital. N Engl J Med. 1981;304(11):638–42. https://doi.org/10.1056/NEJM198103123041104.
5. Brennan TA, Leape LL, Laird NM, Hebert L, Localio AR, Lawthers AG, et al. Incidence of adverse events and negligence in hospitalized patients. Results of the Harvard Medical Practice Study I. N Engl J Med. 1991;324(6):370–6. https://doi.org/10.1056/NEJM199102073240604.
6. Wilson RM, Runciman WB, Gibberd RW, Harrison BT, Newby L, Hamilton JD. The quality in Australian health care study. Med J Aust. 1995;163(9):458–71.
7. Vincent C, Neale G, Woloshynowych M. Adverse events in British hospitals: preliminary retrospective record review. BMJ. 2001;322(7285):517–9. https://doi.org/10.1136/bmj.322.7285.517.
8. Thomas EJ, Studdert DM, Burstin HR, Orav EJ, Zeena T, Williams EJ, et al. Incidence and types of adverse events and negligent care in Utah and Colorado. Med Care. 2000;38(3):261–71. https://doi.org/10.1097/00005650-200003000-00003.
9. Madeira S, Melo M, Porto J, Monteiro S, Pereira de Moura JM, Alexandrino MB, et al. The diseases we cause: iatrogenic illness in a department of internal medicine. Eur J Intern Med. 2007;18(5):391–9. https://doi.org/10.1016/j.ejim.2006.12.009.
10. Bellido D, Leon A, Manas MD, Marchan E, Esquinas G, Ros J. Adverse events in an internal medicine: a prospective study. Rev Calid Asist. 2017;32(5):296–8. https://doi.org/10.1016/j.cali.2017.02.003.
11. Collopy BT. Adverse events in the 'medical' ward. J Qual Clin Pract. 2001;21(3):49.
12. Baker GR, Norton PG, Flintoft V, Blais R, Brown A, Cox J, et al. The Canadian adverse events study: the incidence of adverse events among hospital patients in Canada. CMAJ. 2004;170(11):1678–86.
13. Zegers M, de Bruijne MC, Wagner C, Hoonhout LH, Waaijman R, Smits M, et al. Adverse events and potentially preventable deaths in Dutch hospitals: results of a retrospective patient record review study. Qual Saf Health Care. 2009;18(4):297–302. https://doi.org/10.1136/qshc.2007.025924.
14. Grober ED, Bohnen JM. Defining medical error. Can J Surg. 2005;48(1):39–44.
15. Nendaz M, Perrier A. Diagnostic errors and flaws in clinical reasoning: mechanisms and prevention

in practice. Swiss Med Wkly. 2012;142:w13706. https://doi.org/10.4414/smw.2012.13706.

16. Boostani K, Noshad H, Farnood F, Rezaee H, Teimouri S, Entezari-Maleki T, et al. Detection and management of common medication errors in internal medicine wards: impact on medication costs and patient care. Adv Pharm Bull. 2019;9(1):174–9. https://doi.org/10.15171/apb.2019.020.

17. Haque M, Sartelli M, McKimm J, Abu Bakar M. Health care-associated infections—an overview. Infect Drug Resist. 2018;11:2321–33. https://doi.org/10.2147/IDR.S177247.

18. ECRI. Institute Patient Safety Organization's deep dive: patient identification executive summary. 2016. https://www.ecri.org/Resources/Whitepapers_and_reports/PSO%20Deep%20Dives/Deep%20Dive_PT_ID_2016_exec%20summary.pdf. Last accessed 25 Oct 2019.

19. Scott IA. Errors in clinical reasoning: causes and remedial strategies. BMJ. 2009;338:b1860. https://doi.org/10.1136/bmj.b1860.

20. Committee on Diagnostic Error in Health Care, Board on Health Care Services, Institute of Medicine, The National Academies of Sciences E, Medicine. Overview of diagnostic error in health care. 2015.

21. Wilson RM, Harrison BT, Gibberd RW, Hamilton JD. An analysis of the causes of adverse events from the quality in Australian health care study. Med J Aust. 1999;170(9):411–5.

22. Schiff GD, Hasan O, Kim S, Abrams R, Cosby K, Lambert BL, et al. Diagnostic error in medicine: analysis of 583 physician-reported errors. Arch Intern Med. 2009;169(20):1881–7. https://doi.org/10.1001/archinternmed.2009.333.

23. Ely JW, Levinson W, Elder NC, Mainous AG 3rd, Vinson DC. Perceived causes of family physicians' errors. J Fam Pract. 1995;40(4):337–44.

24. Podbregar M, Voga G, Krivec B, Skale R, Pareznik R, Gabrscek L. Should we confirm our clinical diagnostic certainty by autopsies? Intensive Care Med. 2001;27(11):1750–5. https://doi.org/10.1007/s00134-001-1129-x.

25. Graber ML, Franklin N, Gordon R. Diagnostic error in internal medicine. Arch Intern Med. 2005;165(13):1493–9. https://doi.org/10.1001/archinte.165.13.1493.

26. Phua DH, Tan NC. Cognitive aspect of diagnostic errors. Ann Acad Med Singap. 2013;42(1):33–41.

27. Clinical Excellence Commission. Diagnostic error: learning resource for clinicians. 2015. http://www.cec.health.nsw.gov.au/__data/assets/pdf_file/0005/305843/6.Diagnostic-Error-Learning-resource-for-clinicians.pdf. Last accessed 25 Oct 2019.

28. Health Research & Educational Trust. Improving diagnosis in medicine change package. 2018. http://www.hret-hiin.org/. Last accessed 25 Oct 2019.

29. Graber ML. Educational strategies to reduce diagnostic error: can you teach this stuff? Adv Health Sci Educ Theory Pract. 2009;14(Suppl 1):63–9. https://doi.org/10.1007/s10459-009-9178-y.

30. Riches N, Panagioti M, Alam R, Cheraghi-Sohi S, Campbell S, Esmail A, et al. The effectiveness of electronic differential diagnoses (DDX) generators: a systematic review and meta-analysis. PLoS One. 2016;11(3):e0148991. https://doi.org/10.1371/journal.pone.0148991.

31. Croskerry P, Singhal G, Mamede S. Cognitive debiasing 1: origins of bias and theory of debiasing. BMJ Qual Saf. 2013;22(Suppl 2):ii58–64. https://doi.org/10.1136/bmjqs-2012-001712.

32. Clinical Excellence Commission. Take 2—think, do Project. 2015. http://www.cec.health.nsw.gov.au/__data/assets/pdf_file/0008/305846/3.Take-2-Think-Do-Information-for-Clinicians.pdf. Last accessed 28 Oct 2019.

33. Graber ML, Kissam S, Payne VL, Meyer AN, Sorensen A, Lenfestey N, et al. Cognitive interventions to reduce diagnostic error: a narrative review. BMJ Qual Saf. 2012;21(7):535–57. https://doi.org/10.1136/bmjqs-2011-000149.

34. National Coordinating Council for Medication Error Reporting and Prevention (NCC MERP). Taxonomy of medication errors. 1998. https://www.nccmerp.org/sites/default/files/taxonomy2001-07-31.pdf. Last accessed 25 Oct 2019.

35. Wittich CM, Burkle CM, Lanier WL. Medication errors: an overview for clinicians. Mayo Clin Proc. 2014;89(8):1116–25. https://doi.org/10.1016/j.mayocp.2014.05.007.

36. Elliott R, Camacho E, Campbell F, Jankovic D, Martyn St James M, Kaltenthaler E, Wong R, Sculpher M, Faria R. Prevalence and economic burden of medication errors in the NHS in England. Rapid evidence synthesis and economic analysis of the prevalence and burden of medication error in the UK. Policy Research Unit in Economic Evaluation of Health and Care Interventions. Universities of Sheffield and York; 2018.

37. Jha AK, Larizgoitia I, Audera-Lopez C, Prasopa-Plaizier N, Waters H, Bates DW. The global burden of unsafe medical care: analytic modelling of observational studies. BMJ Qual Saf. 2013;22(10):809–15. https://doi.org/10.1136/bmjqs-2012-001748.

38. Bates DW, Boyle DL, Vander Vliet MB, Schneider J, Leape L. Relationship between medication errors and adverse drug events. J Gen Intern Med. 1995;10(4):199–205. https://doi.org/10.1007/bf02600255.

39. Cullen DJ, Sweitzer BJ, Bates DW, Burdick E, Edmondson A, Leape LL. Preventable adverse drug events in hospitalized patients: a comparative study of intensive care and general care units. Crit Care Med. 1997;25(8):1289–97. https://doi.org/10.1097/00003246-199708000-00014.

40. Jimenez Munioz AB, Muino Miguez A, Rodriguez Perez MP, Escribano MD, Duran Garcia ME, Sanjurjo SM. Medication error prevalence. Int J Health Care Qual Assur. 2010;23(3):328–38. https://doi.org/10.1108/09526861011029389.

41. Leape LL, Bates DW, Cullen DJ, Cooper J, Demonaco HJ, Gallivan T, et al. Systems analysis of

adverse drug events. ADE Prevention Study Group. JAMA. 1995;274(1):35–43.

42. Kohn LT, Corrigan J, Donaldson MS, editors. To err is human: building a safer health system. Washington, DC: National Academy Press; 2000.

43. Bedell SE, Jabbour S, Goldberg R, Glaser H, Gobble S, Young-Xu Y, et al. Discrepancies in the use of medications: their extent and predictors in an outpatient practice. Arch Intern Med. 2000;160(14):2129–34. https://doi.org/10.1001/archinte.160.14.2129.

44. Bell CM, Brener SS, Gunraj N, Huo C, Bierman AS, Scales DC, et al. Association of ICU or hospital admission with unintentional discontinuation of medications for chronic diseases. JAMA. 2011;306(8):840–7. https://doi.org/10.1001/jama.2011.1206.

45. Coleman EA, Smith JD, Raha D, Min SJ. Posthospital medication discrepancies: prevalence and contributing factors. Arch Intern Med. 2005;165(16):1842–7. https://doi.org/10.1001/archinte.165.16.1842.

46. Salanitro AH, Osborn CY, Schnipper JL, Roumie CL, Labonville S, Johnson DC, et al. Effect of patient- and medication-related factors on inpatient medication reconciliation errors. J Gen Intern Med. 2012;27(8):924–32. https://doi.org/10.1007/s11606-012-2003-y.

47. Dornan T et al. An in-depth investigation into causes of prescribing errors by foundation trainees in relation to their medical education: EQUIP study. http://www.gmcuk.org/FINAL_Report_prevalence_and_causes_of_prescribing_errors.pdf_28935150.pdf. Last accessed 25 Oct 2019.

48. Ryan C, Ross S, Davey P, Duncan EM, Francis JJ, Fielding S, et al. Prevalence and causes of prescribing errors: the PRescribing Outcomes for Trainee Doctors Engaged in Clinical Training (PROTECT) study. PLoS One. 2014;9(1):e79802. https://doi.org/10.1371/journal.pone.0079802.

49. Aspden P, Wolcott J, Bootman JL, Cronenwett LR, editors. Preventing medication errors: quality chasm series. Washington, DC: Institute of Medicine of the National Academies; 2007. https://www.nap.edu/read/11623/chapter/1. Last accessed 25 Oct 2019.

50. Medication safety in high-risk situations. Geneva: World Health Organization; 2019 (WHO/UHC/SDS/2019.10). Licence: CC BY-NC-SA 3.0 IGO.

51. Masnoon N, Shakib S, Kalisch-Ellett L, Caughey GE. What is polypharmacy? A systematic review of definitions. BMC Geriatr. 2017;17(1):230. https://doi.org/10.1186/s12877-017-0621-2.

52. Dupouy J, Moulis G, Tubery M, Ecoiffier M, Sommet A, Poutrain JC, et al. Which adverse events are related to health care during hospitalization in elderly inpatients? Int J Med Sci. 2013;10(9):1224–30. https://doi.org/10.7150/ijms.6640.

53. Medication safety in transitions of care. Geneva: World Health Organization; 2019 (WHO/UHC/SDS/2019.9). Licence: CC BY-NC-SA 3.0 IGO.

54. Salanitro AH, Kripalani S, Resnic J, Mueller SK, Wetterneck TB, Haynes KT, et al. Rationale and design of the multicenter medication reconcili-

ation quality improvement study (MARQUIS). BMC Health Serv Res. 2013;13:230. https://doi.org/10.1186/1472-6963-13-230.

55. Nuckols TK, Smith-Spangler C, Morton SC, Asch SM, Patel VM, Anderson LJ, et al. The effectiveness of computerized order entry at reducing preventable adverse drug events and medication errors in hospital settings: a systematic review and meta-analysis. Syst Rev. 2014;3:56. https://doi.org/10.1186/2046-4053-3-56.

56. Poon EG, Keohane CA, Yoon CS, Ditmore M, Bane A, Levtzion-Korach O, et al. Effect of bar-code technology on the safety of medication administration. N Engl J Med. 2010;362(18):1698–707. https://doi.org/10.1056/NEJMsa0907115.

57. Kwan JL, Lo L, Sampson M, Shojania KG. Medication reconciliation during transitions of care as a patient safety strategy: a systematic review. Ann Intern Med. 2013;158(5 Pt 2):397–403. https://doi.org/10.7326/0003-4819-158-5-201303051-00006.

58. Lamont T, Luettel D, Scarpello J, O'Driscoll BR, Connew S. Improving the safety of oxygen therapy in hospitals: summary of a safety report from the National Patient Safety Agency. BMJ. 2010;340:c187. https://doi.org/10.1136/bmj.c187.

59. Risk of severe harm and death from unintentional interruption of non-invasive ventilation. https://www.england.nhs.uk/wp-content/uploads/2015/02/psa-niv.pdf. Last accessed 28 Oct 2019.

60. Safety in respiratory care: a guide to JCAHO requirements. http://hcpro.com/content/32186.pdf. Last accessed 28 Oct 2019.

61. Davidson AC, Banham S, Elliott M, Kennedy D, Gelder C, Glossop A, et al. BTS/ICS guideline for the ventilatory management of acute hypercapnic respiratory failure in adults. Thorax. 2016;71(Suppl 2):ii1–35. https://doi.org/10.1136/thoraxjnl-2015-208209.

62. National Safety Standards for Invasive Procedures (NatSSIPS). https://improvement.nhs.uk/documents/923/natssips-safety-standards.pdf. Last accessed 28 Oct 2019.

63. Gordon CE, Feller-Kopman D, Balk EM, Smetana GW. Pneumothorax following thoracentesis: a systematic review and meta-analysis. Arch Intern Med. 2010;170(4):332–9. https://doi.org/10.1001/archinternmed.2009.548.

64. MacMillan TE, Wu RC, Morra D. Quality of bedside procedures performed on general medical inpatients: can we do better? Can J Gen Intern Med. 2014;9(1):17–20.

65. Hewett R, Counsell C. Documentation of cerebrospinal fluid opening pressure and other important aspects of lumbar puncture in acute headache. Int J Clin Pract. 2010;64(7):930–5. https://doi.org/10.1111/j.1742-1241.2010.02415.x.

66. Daniels CE, Ryu JH. Improving the safety of thoracentesis. Curr Opin Pulm Med. 2011;17(4):232–6. https://doi.org/10.1097/MCP.0b013e328345160b.

67. Wigton RS, Alguire P, American College of Physicians. The declining number and variety of

procedures done by general internists: a resurvey of members of the American College of Physicians. Ann Intern Med. 2007;146(5):355–60. https://doi.org/10.7326/0003-4819-146-5-200703060-00007.

68. Wickstrom GC, Kolar MM, Keyserling TC, Kelley DK, Xie SX, Bognar BA, et al. Confidence of graduating internal medicine residents to perform ambulatory procedures. J Gen Intern Med. 2000;15(6):361–5. https://doi.org/10.1046/j.1525-1497.2000.04118.x.

69. Sevdalis N, Arora S. Safety standards for invasive procedures. BMJ. 2016;352:i1121. https://doi.org/10.1136/bmj.i1121.

70. DeBiasi EM, Puchalski J. Thoracentesis: state-of-the-art in procedural safety, patient outcomes, and physiologic impact. PLEURA. 2016;3:2373997516646554. https://doi.org/10.1177/2373997516646554.

71. La Regina M. Strumenti per una gestione sicura delle procedure invasive. Ital J Med. 2019;7(6):121–2.

72. Gotlib Conn L, Reeves S, Dainty K, Kenaszchuk C, Zwarenstein M. Interprofessional communication with hospitalist and consultant physicians in general internal medicine: a qualitative study. BMC Health Serv Res. 2012;12:437. https://doi.org/10.1186/1472-6963-12-437.

73. Conn LG, Lingard L, Reeves S, Miller KL, Russell A, Zwarenstein M. Communication channels in general internal medicine: a description of baseline patterns for improved interprofessional collaboration. Qual Health Res. 2009;19(7):943–53. https://doi.org/10.1177/1049732309338282.

74. The Joint Commission. Sentinel event alert. 2017. https://www.jointcommission.org/assets/1/18/SEA_58_Hand_off_Comms_9_6_17_FINAL_(1).pdf. Last accessed 25 Oct 2019.

75. Joint Commission Center for Transforming Healthcare. Improving transitions of care: hand-off communications. 2014. https://psnet.ahrq.gov/issue/improving-transitions-care-hand-communications. Last accessed 25 Oct 2019.

76. Riesenberg LA, Leitzsch J, Little BW. Systematic review of handoff mnemonics literature. Am J Med Qual. 2009;24(3):196–204. https://doi.org/10.1177/1062860609332512.

77. Haig KM, Sutton S, Whittington J. SBAR: a shared mental model for improving communication between clinicians. Jt Comm J Qual Patient Saf. 2006;32(3):167–75.

78. Starmer AJ, Spector ND, Srivastava R, West DC, Rosenbluth G, Allen AD, et al. Changes in medical errors after implementation of a handoff program. N Engl J Med. 2014;371(19):1803–12. https://doi.org/10.1056/NEJMsa1405556.

79. O'Toole JK, Starmer AJ, Calaman S, Campos ML, Hepps J, Lopreiato JO, et al. I-PASS mentored implementation handoff curriculum: champion training materials. MedEdPORTAL. 2019;15:10794. https://doi.org/10.15766/mep_2374-8265.10794.

80. Royal College of Physicians, Royal College of Nursing. Ward rounds in medicine: principles for best practice. 2012. https://www.rcplondon.ac.uk/projects/outputs/ward-rounds-medicine-principles-best-practice. Last accessed 25 Oct 2019.

81. Iedema R, Sorensen R, Braithwaite J, Flabouris A, Turnbull L. The teleo-affective limits of end-of-life care in the intensive care unit. Soc Sci Med. 2005;60(4):845–57. https://doi.org/10.1016/j.socscimed.2004.06.024.

82. Triggle N. Call to make ward rounds 'cornerstone of hospital care'. 2012. https://www.bbc.com/news/health-19816017. Last accessed 25 Oct 2019.

83. Weber H, Stockli M, Nubling M, Langewitz WA. Communication during ward rounds in internal medicine. An analysis of patient-nurse-physician interactions using RIAS. Patient Educ Couns. 2007;67(3):343–8. https://doi.org/10.1016/j.pec.2007.04.011.

84. Mathioudakis A, Rousalova I, Gagnat AA, Saad N, Hardavella G. How to keep good clinical records. Breathe (Sheff). 2016;12(4):369–73. https://doi.org/10.1183/20734735.018016.

85. Shekelle PG, Pronovost PJ, Wachter RM, McDonald KM, Schoelles K, Dy SM, et al. The top patient safety strategies that can be encouraged for adoption now. Ann Intern Med. 2013;158(5 Pt 2):365–8. https://doi.org/10.7326/0003-4819-158-5-201303051-00001.

86. Shojania KG, Duncan BW, McDonald JM, Wachter RM. Making health care safer: a critical analysis of patient safety practices. 2001. http://citeseerx.ist.psu.edu/viewdoc/download?doi=10.1.1.125.2605&rep=rep1&type=pdf. 25 Oct 2019.

87. Nardi R., Tirotta D., Pinna G., Pirin G. Prevenzione dei rischi in Medicina Interna, casi particolari: atti autolesivi, vagabondaggio, intrappolamento nel paziente ospedalizzato, in: Rischio clinico in sanità e prevenzione dei rischi del paziente ricoverato in ospedale. Quad Int J Med. 2019.

88. Oliver D, Daly F, Martin FC, McMurdo ME. Risk factors and risk assessment tools for falls in hospital in-patients: a systematic review. Age Ageing. 2004;33(2):122–30. https://doi.org/10.1093/ageing/afh017.

89. Falls: assessment and prevention of falls in older people. National Institute for Health and Care Excellence: clinical guidelines. London; 2013.

90. Haines TP, Hill K, Walsh W, Osborne R. Design-related bias in hospital fall risk screening tool predictive accuracy evaluations: systematic review and meta-analysis. J Gerontol A Biol Sci Med Sci. 2007;62(6):664–72. https://doi.org/10.1093/gerona/62.6.664.

91. Miake-Lye IM, Hempel S, Ganz DA, Shekelle PG. Inpatient fall prevention programs as a patient safety strategy: a systematic review. Ann Intern Med. 2013;158(5 Pt 2):390–6. https://doi.org/10.7326/0003-4819-158-5-201303051-00005.

92. Rowe MA, Glover JC. Antecedents, descriptions and consequences of wandering in cognitively-impaired adults and the Safe Return (SR) program. Am J Alzheimers Dis Other Dement. 2001;16(6):344–52. https://doi.org/10.1177/153331750101600610.

93. Cipriani G, Lucetti C, Nuti A, Danti S. Wandering and dementia. Psychogeriatrics. 2014;14(2):135–42. https://doi.org/10.1111/psyg.12044.

94. Rowe M. Wandering in hospitalized older adults: identifying risk is the first step in this approach to preventing wandering in patients with dementia. Am J Nurs. 2008;108(10):62–70; quiz 1. https://doi.org/10.1097/01.NAJ.0000336968.32462.c9.

95. Borbasi S, Jones J, Lockwood C, Emden C. Health professionals' perspectives of providing care to people with dementia in the acute setting: toward better practice. Geriatr Nurs. 2006;27(5):300–8. https://doi.org/10.1016/j.gerinurse.2006.08.013.

96. Sheth HS, Krueger D, Bourdon S, Palmer RM. A new tool to assess risk of wandering in hospitalized patients. J Gerontol Nurs. 2014;40(3):28–33; quiz 4–5. https://doi.org/10.3928/00989134-20140128-06.

97. Hospital beds—risk of patient entrapment. 2017. https://healthycanadians.gc.ca/recall-alert-rappel-avis/hc-sc/2017/62960a-eng.php. Last accessed 16 Aug 2019.

98. Todd JF. Waking up to hospital bed entrapment risks. Nursing. 2008;38(1):14–5. https://doi.org/10.1097/01.NURSE.0000305896.81298.69.

99. DiBardino DM, Wunderink RG. Aspiration pneumonia: a review of modern trends. J Crit Care. 2015;30(1):40–8. https://doi.org/10.1016/j.jcrc.2014.07.011.

100. Mandell LA, Niederman MS. Aspiration pneumonia. N Engl J Med. 2019;380(7):651–63. https://doi.org/10.1056/NEJMra1714562.

101. Son YG, Shin J, Ryu HG. Pneumonitis and pneumonia after aspiration. J Dent Anesth Pain Med. 2017;17(1):1–12. https://doi.org/10.17245/jdapm.2017.17.1.1.

102. Herzig SJ, LaSalvia MT, Naidus E, Rothberg MB, Zhou W, Gurwitz JH, et al. Antipsychotics and the risk of aspiration pneumonia in individuals hospitalized for nonpsychiatric conditions: a cohort study. J Am Geriatr Soc. 2017;65(12):2580–6. https://doi.org/10.1111/jgs.15066.

103. Hannawi Y, Hannawi B, Rao CP, Suarez JI, Bershad EM. Stroke-associated pneumonia: major advances and obstacles. Cerebrovasc Dis. 2013;35(5):430–43. https://doi.org/10.1159/000350199.

104. Taylor JK, Fleming GB, Singanayagam A, Hill AT, Chalmers JD. Risk factors for aspiration in community-acquired pneumonia: analysis of a hospitalized UK cohort. Am J Med. 2013;126(11):995–1001. https://doi.org/10.1016/j.amjmed.2013.07.012.

105. van der Maarel-Wierink CD, Vanobbergen JN, Bronkhorst EM, Schols JM, de Baat C. Meta-analysis of dysphagia and aspiration pneumonia in frail elders. J Dent Res. 2011;90(12):1398–404. https://doi.org/10.1177/0022034511422909.

106. Momosaki R. Rehabilitative management for aspiration pneumonia in elderly patients. J Gen Fam Med. 2017;18(1):12–5. https://doi.org/10.1002/jgf2.25.

107. Ohkubo T, Chapman N, Neal B, Woodward M, Omae T, Chalmers J, et al. Effects of an angiotensin-converting enzyme inhibitor-based regimen on pneumonia risk. Am J Respir Crit Care Med. 2004;169(9):1041–5. https://doi.org/10.1164/rccm.200309-1219OC.

108. Passaro L, Harbarth S, Landelle C. Prevention of hospital-acquired pneumonia in non-ventilated adult patients: a narrative review. Antimicrob Resist Infect Control. 2016;5:43. https://doi.org/10.1186/s13756-016-0150-3.

109. Kaneoka A, Pisegna JM, Miloro KV, Lo M, Saito H, Riquelme LF, et al. Prevention of healthcare-associated pneumonia with oral care in individuals without mechanical ventilation: a systematic review and meta-analysis of randomized controlled trials. Infect Control Hosp Epidemiol. 2015;36(8):899–906. https://doi.org/10.1017/ice.2015.77.

110. Higashiguchi T, Ohara H, Kamakura Y, Kikutani T, Kuzuya M, Enoki H, et al. Efficacy of a new post-mouthwash intervention (wiping plus oral nutritional supplements) for preventing aspiration pneumonia in elderly people: a multicenter, randomized, comparative trial. Ann Nutr Metab. 2017;71(3–4):253–60. https://doi.org/10.1159/000485044.

111. Juthani-Mehta M, Van Ness PH, McGloin J, Argraves S, Chen S, Charpentier P, et al. A cluster-randomized controlled trial of a multicomponent intervention protocol for pneumonia prevention among nursing home elders. Clin Infect Dis. 2015;60(6):849–57. https://doi.org/10.1093/cid/ciu935.

112. Valles J, Peredo R, Burgueno MJ, Rodrigues de Freitas AP, Millan S, Espasa M, et al. Efficacy of single-dose antibiotic against early-onset pneumonia in comatose patients who are ventilated. Chest. 2013;143(5):1219–25. https://doi.org/10.1378/chest.12-1361.

113. Reston JT, Schoelles KM. In-facility delirium prevention programs as a patient safety strategy: a systematic review. Ann Intern Med. 2013;158(5 Pt 2):375–80. https://doi.org/10.7326/0003-4819-158-5-201303051-00003.

114. Oh ES, Fong TG, Hshieh TT, Inouye SK. Delirium in older persons: advances in diagnosis and treatment. JAMA. 2017;318(12):1161–74. https://doi.org/10.1001/jama.2017.12067.

115. Hshieh TT, Yue J, Oh E, Puelle M, Dowal S, Travison T, et al. Effectiveness of multicomponent nonpharmacological delirium interventions: a meta-analysis. JAMA Intern Med. 2015;175(4):512–20. https://doi.org/10.1001/jamainternmed.2014.7779.

116. Neufeld KJ, Yue J, Robinson TN, Inouye SK, Needham DM. Antipsychotic medication for prevention and treatment of delirium in hospitalized adults: a systematic review and meta-analysis. J Am Geriatr Soc. 2016;64(4):705–14. https://doi.org/10.1111/jgs.14076.

117. Hovaguimian F, Tschopp C, Beck-Schimmer B, Puhan M. Intraoperative ketamine administration to prevent delirium or postoperative cognitive dysfunc-

tion: a systematic review and meta-analysis. Acta Anaesthesiol Scand. 2018;62(9):1182–93. https://doi.org/10.1111/aas.13168.

118. Siddiqi N, Harrison JK, Clegg A, Teale EA, Young J, Taylor J, et al. Interventions for preventing delirium in hospitalised non-ICU patients. Cochrane Database Syst Rev. 2016;3:CD005563. https://doi.org/10.1002/14651858.CD005563.pub3.

119. Teale E, Young J. Multicomponent delirium prevention: not as effective as NICE suggest? Age Ageing. 2015;44(6):915–7. https://doi.org/10.1093/ageing/afv120.

120. Harbarth S, Sax H, Gastmeier P. The preventable proportion of nosocomial infections: an overview of published reports. J Hosp Infect. 2003;54(4):258–66; quiz 321.

121. Al-Tawfiq JA, Tambyah PA. Healthcare associated infections (HAI) perspectives. J Infect Public Health. 2014;7(4):339–44. https://doi.org/10.1016/j.jiph.2014.04.003.

122. Allegranzi B, Storr J, Dziekan G, Leotsakos A, Donaldson L, Pittet D. The first global patient safety challenge "clean care is safer care": from launch to current progress and achievements. J Hosp Infect. 2007;65(Suppl 2):115–23. https://doi.org/10.1016/S0195-6701(07)60027-9.

123. Mehta Y, Gupta A, Todi S, Myatra S, Samaddar DP, Patil V, et al. Guidelines for prevention of hospital acquired infections. Indian J Crit Care Med. 2014;18(3):149–63. https://doi.org/10.4103/0972-5229.128705.

124. Heit JA, Silverstein MD, Mohr DN, Petterson TM, O'Fallon WM, Melton LJ 3rd. Risk factors for deep vein thrombosis and pulmonary embolism: a population-based case-control study. Arch Intern Med. 2000;160(6):809–15. https://doi.org/10.1001/archinte.160.6.809.

125. Kahn SR, Lim W, Dunn AS, Cushman M, Dentali F, Akl EA, et al. Prevention of VTE in nonsurgical patients: antithrombotic therapy and prevention of thrombosis, 9th ed: American College of Chest Physicians Evidence-Based Clinical Practice Guidelines. Chest. 2012;141(2 Suppl):e195S–226S. https://doi.org/10.1378/chest.11-2296.

126. Prandoni P, Samama MM. Risk stratification and venous thromboprophylaxis in hospitalized medical and cancer patients. Br J Haematol. 2008;141(5):587–97. https://doi.org/10.1111/j.1365-2141.2008.07089.x.

127. Decousus H, Tapson VF, Bergmann JF, Chong BH, Froehlich JB, Kakkar AK, et al. Factors at admission associated with bleeding risk in medical patients: findings from the IMPROVE investigators. Chest. 2011;139(1):69–79. https://doi.org/10.1378/chest.09-3081.

128. La Regina M, Orlandini F, Marchini F, Marinaro A, Bonacci R, Bonanni P, et al. Combined assessment of thrombotic and haemorrhagic risk in acute medical patients. Thromb Haemost. 2016;115(2):392–8. https://doi.org/10.1160/TH14-12-1050.

129. Gussoni G, Campanini M, Silingardi M, Scannapieco G, Mazzone A, Magni G, et al. In-hospital symptomatic venous thromboembolism and antithrombotic prophylaxis in internal medicine. Findings from a multicenter, prospective study. Thromb Haemost. 2009;101(5):893–901.

130. Tincani E, Crowther MA, Turrini F, Prisco D. Prevention and treatment of venous thromboembolism in the elderly patient. Clin Interv Aging. 2007;2(2):237–46.

131. Samama MM, Cohen AT, Darmon JY, Desjardins L, Eldor A, Janbon C, et al. A comparison of enoxaparin with placebo for the prevention of venous thromboembolism in acutely ill medical patients. Prophylaxis in medical patients with enoxaparin study group. N Engl J Med. 1999;341(11):793–800. https://doi.org/10.1056/NEJM199909093411103.

132. Rondina MT, Wheeler M, Rodgers GM, Draper L, Pendleton RC. Weight-based dosing of enoxaparin for VTE prophylaxis in morbidly obese, medically-ill patients. Thromb Res. 2010;125(3):220–3. https://doi.org/10.1016/j.thromres.2009.02.003.

133. Imberti D, Legnani C, Baldini E, Cini M, Nicolini A, Guerra M, et al. Pharmacodynamics of low molecular weight heparin in patients undergoing bariatric surgery: a prospective, randomised study comparing two doses of parnaparin (BAFLUX study). Thromb Res. 2009;124(6):667–71. https://doi.org/10.1016/j.thromres.2009.04.021.

134. Schmid P, Brodmann D, Fischer AG, Wuillemin WA. Study of bioaccumulation of dalteparin at a prophylactic dose in patients with various degrees of impaired renal function. J Thromb Haemost. 2009;7(4):552–8. https://doi.org/10.1111/j.1538-7836.2009.03292.x.

135. Turpie AG, Lensing AW, Fuji T, Boyle DA. Pharmacokinetic and clinical data supporting the use of fondaparinux 1.5 mg once daily in the prevention of venous thromboembolism in renally impaired patients. Blood Coagul Fibrinolysis. 2009;20(2):114–21. https://doi.org/10.1097/MBC.0b013e328323da86.

136. Mosarla RC, Vaduganathan M, Qamar A, Moslehi J, Piazza G, Giugliano RP. Anticoagulation strategies in patients with cancer: JACC review topic of the week. J Am Coll Cardiol. 2019;73(11):1336–49. https://doi.org/10.1016/j.jacc.2019.01.017.

137. Sullivan N, Schoelles KM. Preventing in-facility pressure ulcers as a patient safety strategy: a systematic review. Ann Intern Med. 2013;158(5 Pt 2):410–6. https://doi.org/10.7326/0003-4819-158-5-201303051-00008.

138. Moore ZE, Patton D. Risk assessment tools for the prevention of pressure ulcers. Cochrane Database Syst Rev. 2019;1:CD006471. https://doi.org/10.1002/14651858.CD006471.pub4.

139. Insitute for Healthcare Improvement. What is a bundle? 2016. www.ihi.org/knowledge/Pages/ImprovementStories/WhatIsaBundle.apsx. Last accessed 28 Oct 2019.

140. Lyder CH, Ayello EA. Annual checkup: the CMS pressure ulcer present-on-admission indicator. Adv Skin Wound Care. 2009;22(10):476–84. https://doi.org/10.1097/01.ASW.0000361385.97489.51.

141. Jankowski IM, Nadzam DM. Identifying gaps, barriers, and solutions in implementing pressure ulcer prevention programs. Jt Comm J Qual Patient Saf. 2011;37(6):253–64.

142. Buist M, Bernard S, Nguyen TV, Moore G, Anderson J. Association between clinically abnormal observations and subsequent in-hospital mortality: a prospective study. Resuscitation. 2004;62(2):137–41. https://doi.org/10.1016/j.resuscitation.2004.03.005.

143. Goldhill DR, McNarry AF. Physiological abnormalities in early warning scores are related to mortality in adult inpatients. Br J Anaesth. 2004;92(6):882–4. https://doi.org/10.1093/bja/aeh113.

144. Kause J, Smith G, Prytherch D, Parr M, Flabouris A, Hillman K, et al. A comparison of antecedents to cardiac arrests, deaths and emergency intensive care admissions in Australia and New Zealand, and the United Kingdom—the ACADEMIA study. Resuscitation. 2004;62(3):275–82. https://doi.org/10.1016/j.resuscitation.2004.05.016.

145. Jansen JO, Cuthbertson BH. Detecting critical illness outside the ICU: the role of track and trigger systems. Curr Opin Crit Care. 2010;16(3):184–90. https://doi.org/10.1097/MCC.0b013e328338844e.

146. Groarke JD, Gallagher J, Stack J, Aftab A, Dwyer C, McGovern R, et al. Use of an admission early warning score to predict patient morbidity and mortality and treatment success. Emerg Med J. 2008;25(12):803–6. https://doi.org/10.1136/emj.2007.051425.

147. Ludikhuize J, Brunsveld-Reinders AH, Dijkgraaf MG, Smorenburg SM, de Rooij SE, Adams R, et al. Outcomes associated with the nationwide introduction of rapid response systems in the Netherlands. Crit Care Med. 2015;43(12):2544–51. https://doi.org/10.1097/CCM.0000000000001272.

148. Correia N, Rodrigues RP, Sa MC, Dias P, Lopes L, Paiva A. Improving recognition of patients at risk in a Portuguese general hospital: results from a preliminary study on the early warning score. Int J Emerg Med. 2014;7:22. https://doi.org/10.1186/s12245-014-0022-7.

149. Jarvis S, Kovacs C, Briggs J, Meredith P, Schmidt PE, Featherstone PI, et al. Aggregate National Early Warning Score (NEWS) values are more important than high scores for a single vital signs parameter for discriminating the risk of adverse outcomes. Resuscitation. 2015;87:75–80. https://doi.org/10.1016/j.resuscitation.2014.11.014.

150. Smith GB, Prytherch DR, Schmidt PE, Featherstone PI. Review and performance evaluation of aggregate weighted 'track and trigger' systems. Resuscitation. 2008;77(2):170–9. https://doi.org/10.1016/j.resuscitation.2007.12.004.

151. Royal College of Physicians London. National Early Warning Score (NEWS): standardising the assessment of acute-illness severity in the NHS. Report of working party. London: Royal College of Physicians; 2012.

152. Tirkkonen J, Yla-Mattila J, Olkkola KT, Huhtala H, Tenhunen J, Hoppu S. Factors associated with delayed activation of medical emergency team and excess mortality: an Utstein-style analysis. Resuscitation. 2013;84(2):173–8. https://doi.org/10.1016/j.resuscitation.2012.09.021.

153. Watkinson PJ, Barber VS, Price JD, Hann A, Tarassenko L, Young JD. A randomised controlled trial of the effect of continuous electronic physiological monitoring on the adverse event rate in high risk medical and surgical patients. Anaesthesia. 2006;61(11):1031–9. https://doi.org/10.1111/j.1365-2044.2006.04818.x.

154. London RCoP. National Early Warning Score (NEWS): standardising the assessment of acute-illness severity in the NHS. Report of working party. London: Royal College of Physicians; 2012.

155. Davies O, DeVita MA, Ayinla R, Perez X. Barriers to activation of the rapid response system. Resuscitation. 2014;85(11):1557–61. https://doi.org/10.1016/j.resuscitation.2014.07.013.

156. Shearer B, Marshall S, Buist MD, Finnigan M, Kitto S, Hore T, et al. What stops hospital clinical staff from following protocols? An analysis of the incidence and factors behind the failure of bedside clinical staff to activate the rapid response system in a multi-campus Australian metropolitan healthcare service. BMJ Qual Saf. 2012;21(7):569–75. https://doi.org/10.1136/bmjqs-2011-000692.

157. Bunkenborg G, Samuelson K, Akeson J, Poulsen I. Impact of professionalism in nursing on in-hospital bedside monitoring practice. J Adv Nurs. 2013;69(7):1466–77. https://doi.org/10.1111/jan.12003.

158. Jones L, King L, Wilson C. A literature review: factors that impact on nurses' effective use of the Medical Emergency Team (MET). J Clin Nurs. 2009;18(24):3379–90. https://doi.org/10.1111/j.1365-2702.2009.02944.x.

159. Rhodes A, Evans LE, Alhazzani W, Levy MM, Antonelli M, Ferrer R, et al. Surviving sepsis campaign: international guidelines for management of sepsis and septic shock: 2016. Intensive Care Med. 2017;43(3):304–77. https://doi.org/10.1007/s00134-017-4683-6.

160. Dellinger RP, Carlet JM, Masur H, Gerlach H, Calandra T, Cohen J, et al. Surviving sepsis campaign guidelines for management of severe sepsis and septic shock. Crit Care Med. 2004;32(3):858–73. https://doi.org/10.1097/01.ccm.0000117317.18092.e4.

161. Levy MM, Pronovost PJ, Dellinger RP, Townsend S, Resar RK, Clemmer TP, et al. Sepsis change bundles: converting guidelines into meaningful change in behavior and clinical outcome. Crit Care Med. 2004;32(11 Suppl):S595–7. https://doi.org/10.1097/01.ccm.0000147016.53607.c4.

162. Improvement IfH. What is a bundle? 2016. www.ihi.org/knowledge/Pages/ImprovementStories/WhatIsaBundle.apsx.

163. Seymour CW, Gesten F, Prescott HC, Friedrich ME, Iwashyna TJ, Phillips GS, et al. Time to treatment and mortality during mandated emergency care for sepsis. N Engl J Med. 2017;376(23):2235–44. https://doi.org/10.1056/NEJMoa1703058.

164. Dellinger RP, Levy MM, Carlet JM, Bion J, Parker MM, Jaeschke R, et al. Surviving sepsis campaign: international guidelines for management of severe sepsis and septic shock: 2008. Crit Care Med. 2008;36(1):296–327. https://doi.org/10.1097/01.CCM.0000298158.12101.41.

165. Dellinger RP, Levy MM, Rhodes A, Annane D, Gerlach H, Opal SM, et al. Surviving sepsis campaign: international guidelines for management of severe sepsis and septic shock, 2012. Intensive Care Med. 2013;39(2):165–228. https://doi.org/10.1007/s00134-012-2769-8.

166. Levy MM, Evans LE, Rhodes A. The surviving sepsis campaign bundle: 2018 update. Crit Care Med. 2018;46(6):997–1000. https://doi.org/10.1097/CCM.0000000000003119.

167. Kumar A. Systematic bias in meta-analyses of time to antimicrobial in sepsis studies. Crit Care Med. 2016;44(4):e234–5. https://doi.org/10.1097/CCM.0000000000001512.

168. Casserly B, Phillips GS, Schorr C, Dellinger RP, Townsend SR, Osborn TM, et al. Lactate measurements in sepsis-induced tissue hypoperfusion: results from the surviving sepsis campaign database. Crit Care Med. 2015;43(3):567–73. https://doi.org/10.1097/CCM.0000000000000742.

169. Lyu X, Xu Q, Cai G, Yan J, Yan M. [Efficacies of fluid resuscitation as guided by lactate clearance rate and central venous oxygen saturation in patients with septic shock]. Zhonghua Yi Xue Za Zhi. 2015;95(7):496–500.

170. Jones AE, Shapiro NI, Trzeciak S, Arnold RC, Claremont HA, Kline JA, et al. Lactate clearance vs central venous oxygen saturation as goals of early sepsis therapy: a randomized clinical trial. JAMA. 2010;303(8):739–46. https://doi.org/10.1001/jama.2010.158.

171. Zadroga R, Williams DN, Gottschall R, Hanson K, Nordberg V, Deike M, et al. Comparison of 2 blood culture media shows significant differences in bacterial recovery for patients on antimicrobial therapy. Clin Infect Dis. 2013;56(6):790–7. https://doi.org/10.1093/cid/cis1021.

172. Kleinpell R. Promoting early identification of sepsis in hospitalized patients with nurse-led protocols. Crit Care. 2017;21(1):10. https://doi.org/10.1186/s13054-016-1590-0.

173. Goulding L, Adamson J, Watt I, Wright J. Lost in hospital: a qualitative interview study that explores the perceptions of NHS inpatients who spent time on clinically inappropriate hospital wards. Health Expect. 2015;18(5):982–94. https://doi.org/10.1111/hex.12071.

174. Stylianou N, Fackrell R, Vasilakis C. Are medical outliers associated with worse patient outcomes? A retrospective study within a regional NHS hospital using routine data. BMJ Open. 2017;7(5):e015676. https://doi.org/10.1136/bmjopen-2016-015676.

175. Friends and Family test 2018–2019. https://www.southwestyorkshire.nhs.uk/about-us/performance/friends-and-family-test/2018-19-annual-results/. Last accessed 25 Oct 2019.

176. The Newcastle upon Tyne Hospitals NHS Foundation TrustBed Management and Escalation Policy. 2016. http://www.newcastle-hospitals.org.uk/downloads/policies/Operational/BedManagementPolicy201602.pdf. Last accessed 25 Oct 2019.

177. NHS Clinical Policies. Portsmouth Hospitals. https://www.porthosp.nhs.uk/about-us/policies-and-guidelines/clinical-policies.htm. Last accessed 28 Oct 2019.

178. Knight S, Mallory MNS, Huecker MR. Medical mimics of psychiatric conditions—part 1. MDedge. 2016. www.emed-journal.com.

179. McKee J, Brahm N. Medical mimics: differential diagnostic considerations for psychiatric symptoms. Ment Health Clin. 2016;6(6):289–96. https://doi.org/10.9740/mhc.2016.11.289.

180. NICE Guideline. Care of dying adults in the last days of life. https://www.nice.org.uk/guidance/ng31/resources/care-of-dying-adults-in-the-last-days-of-life-pdf-1837387324357. Last accessed 28 Oct 2019.

Risks in Oncology and Radiation Therapy

18

Adriano Marcolongo, Glauco Cristofaro,
Aldo Mariotto, Maurizio Mascarin,
and Fabio Puglisi

Learning Objectives

This chapter aims to promote awareness by providing essential scientific elements about the risks associated with clinical oncology, with a particular focus on chemotherapy and radiotherapy.

Here as follows is the range of covered subjects:

- First, the epidemiologic and cultural context is addressed in order to understand the peculiarity of oncology, a medical discipline in which the risk is directly related to the daily clinical practice, almost inseparable from the intervention that must be conducted, probably more than in any other branch of medicine.

- To increase specific knowledge, in a public health perspective, described herein is the epidemiology of the different adverse effects, listed according to their frequency of occurrence. The central topic of modern health organization in relation to the existing volume of activities, herein limited to surgery, and the quality of health services, which can arouse debates of professional and organizational nature. Finally, safety practices, which were proven to be effective, and the strategies to implement them are also addressed.

A. Marcolongo (✉) · A. Mariotto
IRCCS Centro di Riferimento Oncologico, National
Cancer Institute, Aviano, PN, Italy
e-mail: aldo.mariotto@cro.it

G. Cristofaro
Ophthalmology, Hospital University Careggi,
Florence, Italy

M. Mascarin
AYA Oncology and Pediatric Radiotherapy Unit,
IRCCS Centro di Riferimento Oncologico, National
Cancer Institute, Aviano, PN, Italy
e-mail: mascarin@cro.it

F. Puglisi
Department of Medicine, School of Medical
Oncology, University of Udine, Udine, Italy

Unit of Medical Oncology and Cancer Prevention,
Department of Medical Oncology, IRCCS Centro di
Riferimento Oncologico, National Cancer Institute,
Aviano, PN, Italy
e-mail: fabio.puglisi@uniud.it

18.1 Introduction

Developments in science and technology, together with the improved organization of health systems, have allowed remarkable progress in cancer diagnosis, care, and rehabilitation. In terms of assessment and management of the clinical risk, however, considerable issues are raised by the continuously increasing frequency of the disease, the super specialization in care, the elevated media attention, and the growing competence of patients and their associations.

Due to the complexity of their disease, cancer patients have access to different methodologies

© The Author(s) 2021
L. Donaldson et al. (eds.), *Textbook of Patient Safety and Clinical Risk Management*,
https://doi.org/10.1007/978-3-030-59403-9_18

and therapeutic strategies, all of which can be used with both curative intent and palliation:

- Cancer surgery
- Medical oncology
  - Chemotherapy
  - Hormonal therapy
  - Immunotherapy
  - Drug targeting
  - Gene therapy
  - Cell therapy
- Radiation therapy
  - External beam radiotherapy
  - Brachytherapy
  - IORT intraoperative radiotherapy
  - Radiometabolic therapy

Several therapeutic strategies can be adopted for treating oncology patients, including specific or combined/adjuvant approaches. Each strategy carries risks and adverse effects, which are not always acceptable, with the aim to achieve real benefits with the undertaken treatment.

The different, possible causes of these adverse events or errors, which can be frequent in certain situations, are discussed in this chapter.

Additionally, the chapter focuses on several strategies and organizational options aimed to minimize the risk and reduce therapeutic side effects, which can be negligible in some instances but very severe in others.

18.2   The Epidemiological Context

Tissue damage is unfortunately unavoidable during radiation therapy and chemotherapy, as both approaches work by means of a mechanism of destruction of nucleic structures essential to cancer cells, in order to reduce cell multiplication. The setback is that most healthy cells are just as susceptible as cancer cells to the damaging effects of the treatments. Radiotherapy is based on ionizing radiations that must go through healthy tissues in order to reach the tumor. Even though new technologies are being developed, each more sophisticated and better able to precisely target the cancerous areas, the tissues sur-

rounding the tumor still tend to get damaged, but this is also due to the fact that the tissues surrounding cancer cells are susceptible to microscopic invasion by the malignant cells. Chemotherapy, as a pharmacological, systemic treatment, exerts its effects on the whole organism. Therefore, although in theory therapy could eliminate cancer cells, in practice it is often impossible as it becomes difficult to expose all cancer cells to adequate doses without damaging healthy tissues. Hence, the central issue of clinical oncology consists in balancing cancer treatment effects and the effects that therapies could have on the healthy tissues, reaching an equilibrium that, for a particular patient with a specific cancer type, the best possible therapeutic ratio could be obtained, meaning the best possible balance between the risk of damaging healthy cells versus killing cancer cells.

It is therefore accepted by the scientific community that collateral damage to healthy cells in oncology is often unavoidable. In other words, it has been accepted that during treatment with curative intent, adverse effects, including severe ones, can be expected to occur more than in other medical fields. Adverse events can occur during and after treatments with radiotherapy and with chemotherapy. Short-term or acute adverse effects occur during or shortly after treatment, and they usually last for a few days or up to 2 weeks. Long-term or chronic adverse effects are more common in radiotherapy than in chemotherapy. They occur usually after treatment and sometimes even years later. These effects are usually irreversible and sometimes yield slowly progressive outcomes with severe consequences in terms of morbidity and, therefore, in terms of complaints and legal actions [1].

Approximately, one third of people may develop cancer during their lives. Today, about 40% of cancer cases are curable. However, a number of patients can keep the disease under control for long periods of time though not achieving a complete recovery. As can be expected, at least half of them will die from their disease. The reason the numbers of simple complaints and legal actions have dramatically increased in recent years lies in the high mortality of the disease and the high toxicity rates of therapies, on the one hand, and in the higher expectations of citizens regarding health services, on the other. This new perspective has been favored by higher cultural resources and by a higher awareness of their own rights due to democratic progress.

The main areas of risk in clinical oncology include misdiagnosis (e.g., anticancer treatment delivered to patients without cancer, or to patients who had cancer in the past without disease recurrence, or for the wrong type of cancer), medication errors in preparation or administration, therapeutic toxicity, and negligence [1].

Two more categories can be added: delayed treatments, due to a delayed diagnosis, or delayed initiation or continuation of therapy, causing harm to the patient; over diagnosis risks in oncology (e.g., PSA and TSH).

These are the most frequent categories of unfavorable outcomes afflicting patients. Some of the distinguishing characteristics of the specialty of oncology should be kept in mind. Oncology differs above all in the central role of the dedicated nurses and technicians who are specifically trained in the administration of sophisticated therapies. In radiotherapy in particular, a peculiar specificity exists, namely medical physicists who are called upon to run systematic quality checks of the linear accelerators' performance and to realize radiation treatment plans. Furthermore, oncology has come to act according to multidisciplinary and multiprofessional organizational models, following specific decisional protocols of clinical behavior.

18.3   Epidemiology of Adverse Effects

The most frequent adverse effects of cancer therapies belong to the category of toxicity. In general, radical treatments can result in very severe adverse effects in a small proportion of patients and in moderately severe adverse effects in a bigger proportion, even when conducted correctly and in accordance with to the appropriate clinical direction. The studies which have investigated the epidemiology of adverse effects mainly relate to chemotherapy.

In a cohort of 449 patients with cancer of the breast or lung or colon-rectum who underwent chemotherapy and followed up for a median time of 6 months, 86% reported at least one adverse effect during the study period and 27% an adverse effect of fourth degree, most often fatigue or dyspnea. Fatigue was the most frequent effect (85%), followed by diarrhea (74%), and constipation (74%). Prevalence and incidence rates of the adverse effects were similar among all types of cancer, and older age represented the only significantly associated demographic factor [2].

In another cohort study, patients in treatment with antineoplastic drugs were followed up for 2 years. Overall, 591 cases of adverse effects were reported, a 58.6% incidence rate. The prevalence of adverse effects was recorded among women (constituting 73% of the cohort). Of the patients with adverse effects, 50.2% requested a treatment, 12.9% were deemed severe cases, 87% moderate, and 51% unpredictable [3].

An important further study was conducted on 458 oncologic patients followed up for 8 months, investigating hospital stay. Among the unplanned hospital admissions, 13% were caused by a pharmacological event, 13% by an adverse drug reaction, and 2% by a major interaction between different drugs. In conclusion, one in 10 unplanned hospital admissions of cancer patients was caused by a pharmacological effect [4].

It is estimated that between half and two thirds of new cancer cases receive treatment plans that include radiotherapy. Seventy-five percent of them are aimed to cure the patients. Radiotherapy-related adverse effects are the most frequent and they are described below.

Prevalence of depression among cancer patients is extremely variable, ranging from 0% to 60% in different case studies, according to study criteria, methodology, and populations. Depression is associated in particular with cancers of the oro-pharynx, lung, breast, brain, and pancreas, but rarely with gynecologic tumors and colorectal cancers. Since comorbidity and treatment regimen are combined, in particular, with chemotherapy, it is often difficult to evaluate the direct effect of radiotherapy on depression as well as on several other symptoms.

Patients often indicate fatigue as the most disturbing adverse effect of radiotherapy, more than pain, nausea, and vomit. Fatigue correlated with radiotherapy occurs acutely in 80% of patients and chronically in 30% of patients. For this reason, patients should be evaluated for this symptom at regular intervals.

Dermatitis caused by radiation is a common adverse effect of radiotherapy, often complicating treatment of breast, prostate, perineum, and head and neck cancers. It is, however, difficult to evaluate the real burden of the phenomenon as clinical practice in this field is biased by unreliable and contradictory evidence. Early reactions include skin rash and dry and humid exfoliation, while delayed events include pigmentation changes, telangiectasias, hair loss, atrophy, and ulcerations.

Concerning vascular diseases due to radiotherapy, a well-known adverse effect occurs mostly in Hodgkin lymphoma patients, and in lower numbers, in breast and lung cancer patients. It is estimated that the relative risk of cardiovascular events after mediastinal radiation ranges from 2.2% to 7.2% for Hodgkin lymphoma cases and from 1% to 2.2% for cancer of the left breast.

Concerning lung effects, pneumonia due to radiation occurs in 5.15% of patients undergoing radiation for mediastinal cancers and breast and lung cancers. The risk is directly associated with the volume of the irradiated lung, intensity of radiation, and any concurrent chemotherapy. Toxicity of the digestive tract due to damage to the salivary glands is common in the radiation of the head and neck, especially in the case of concurrent chemotherapy. Esophagitis is also a common, early adverse effect whose frequency grows with the increasing of radioactive doses and in the presence of concurrent chemotherapy. Acute enteritis after radiotherapy is usually a self-limiting process by means of a correction to the diet and the administration of anti-diarrheal medications. Usually, the symptoms start 3 months after the end of radiotherapy and can last indefinitely. Another frequent symptom is the emesis induced by radiotherapy. The main risk factors

include the completion of chemotherapy before radiation of the upper abdomen and the width of the irradiated areas. Patients who receive total-body radiations are at higher risk. Acute bladder infection, including the most severe hemorrhagic cystitis, is a less common effect of radiotherapy, and the risk is augmented by concurrent chemotherapy.

Sexual dysfunctions, including impotence, are common after radiotherapy for cancers of the prostate and, to a lesser extent, of the colon-rectum. They are primarily a concern for older patients, who show a higher frequency of prostate cancer diagnosis. Erection dysfunction is more common with brachytherapy and with external radiotherapy. Among women, sexual dysfunctions are more common after radiotherapy for cervical and endometrial cancers. The adverse effects include a lower sex drive, vaginal dryness, and general sexual dissatisfaction.

18.4 Medication Errors in Oncology Practice

The publication of the report "To err is human" by the Institute of Medicine of Washington (IOM) in 1999 has led to a radical change in healthcare organizations with regard to the understanding of the phenomenon of medical error. In oncology, the current definition of medication error, i.e., any "preventable event that may cause or lead to inappropriate medication use or patient harm while the medication is in the control of the healthcare professional, patient, or consumer," is provided by the National Coordinating Council for Medical Error Reporting and Prevention.

A recent review of the literature from 1980 to 2017 has shown that medical errors in chemotherapy occur at a frequency ranging from 1 to 4 cases per 1000 prescriptions, concerning at least 1–3% of patients and appearing in all phases of the cure process [5]. The definition of medication error applies to all areas of medicine but can have different implications depending on the complexity of the discipline and the magnitude of the potential damage it can cause.

Cancer care is going through a revolutionary period both in the diagnostic and the therapeutic fields. At the same time, the substantial increase in scientific data is making the system increasingly complex and constitutes a challenge for health professionals [6]. For example, the current rate of new therapeutic indications in hematology-oncology is about one per week, preventing the general medical oncologist from keeping up.

In oncology, several factors may expose patients to increased risk that can result in serious adverse effects (AEs) [5]. The greater vulnerability of cancer patients may be due to the fragility induced by the disease itself, to the narrow therapeutic index of many anticancer agents, or to the use of innovative therapies of which potential side effects and their management are not fully known. In addition, cancer care is often provided by inter-professional teams that need to be perfectly in tune when it comes to communication [7].

Quite surprisingly, although oncologists pay high attention to treatment-related toxicities of anticancer agents, oncology as a discipline lags behind other areas of medicine in focusing on understanding the nature of medication errors and the extent of their effects. Of note, only a few studies have analyzed the incidence and consequences of medication errors in oncology [5, 8].

In December of 1994, a tragedy occurred that turned the spotlight on to the need to work systematically to ensure and strengthen safety measures in the administration of anticancer therapies. The incident occurred at the Dana-Farber Cancer Institute in Boston, a Harvard teaching hospital and a prestigious US institution, and caused the death of a young health journalist, Betsy A. Lehman, who died of a massive overdose of chemotherapy for breast cancer. A similar event occurred 2 days apart and caused permanent heart damage in a patient cared for by the same medical team. Both patients were treated with autologous stem-cell transplant, in the context of an experimental protocol that included high doses of cyclophosphamide. However, because of misinterpretation of the study protocol and subsequent miscalculated dosage, they received about four times the intended dose. The error was missed by other doctors, nurses, and pharmacists, including some senior members of the team.

Further attention was drawn to the importance of safe administration and management of chemotherapy after another lethal event occurred in December of 2015, two decades after the death of Betsy Leman. The death of a 49-year-old man caused again by an unintended chemotherapy overdose catalyzed a call to action for healthcare systems to recognize and to implement safety principles and practices to prevent patient harm. Increased awareness and sensitivity regarding the risk of errors related to anti-tumor treatments and, in particular, to chemotherapy, has led the American Society of Clinical Oncology (ASCO) and the Oncology Nursing Society (ONS) to set standards to minimize treatment-related risks. The most updated version of the standards was published in 2016 and focused on four main points [9]:

- The environment and routine procedures
- Treatment planning and patient education before the start of treatment
- Specific standards for ordering, preparing (including labeling), and administering treatment (chemotherapy)
- Monitoring adherence to, and toxicity from, chemotherapy to promote safety both while on treatment and subsequently

In particular, great attention is paid to the definition of the healthcare setting that includes the policy to ensure the relevant qualifications of the various professional figures involved in the order, preparation, and administration of the treatments.

Special emphasis is placed on training programs, on participation in basic life support courses by the clinical staff, and on information that must be reported in the medical record and verified before treatment (e.g., diagnosis, stage of illness, clinical history, physical examination, history of allergies, level of information shared with and understood by the patient and/or caregivers, description of the treatment plan). In addition, the healthcare setting includes a policy on documents that standardizes the process for obtaining treatment consent and valid proof of consent. Patients must be sufficiently informed about the treatment plan, the potential side effects, the management of adverse events, the handling of medicines at home, the follow-up visits, and the procedures they may be subjected to for monitoring during the therapy. Furthermore, patients must be provided with contact information in case of need.

Regarding therapeutic orders, it is recommended that they be signed by hand or electronically. Verbal orders are not allowed, with the exception of those for holding or stopping therapy. New orders or changes to orders (e.g., dose adjustments) must be documented in the medical record. It is important that a chemotherapy order be extremely detailed and include the following information: the patient's name, a second patient identifier, the date of the prescription order is written, the regimen or protocol identifier (name and number), the cycle number and day, all medications listed using full, generic names, the drug dose (to be written following the standards regarding abbreviations, trailing zeros, and leading zeros), the dose calculation, the date of administration, the route of administration, the presence of allergies, any supportive care treatments appropriate for the regimens (e.g., premedications, hydration, growth factors), parameters that would require holding or modifying the dose (e.g., laboratory tests, patient clinical status), the sequencing of drug administration, and the rate of drug administration. Special recommendations are given for prescriptions of oral chemotherapy.

The standards also include requirements for the preparation of chemotherapy which must be entrusted to licensed pharmacists, pharmacy technicians, physicians, or nurses with specific skills acquired as a result of specific education and training programs. Before preparation, a second person has the task of independently verifying the patient's identifiers, the name of the drug, the dose, the route of administration, the rate of administration, the calculation of the dose, the treatment cycle, and the cycle day.

Upon preparation, one of the two operators must verify the drug vial(s), the concentration, the drug volume or weight, the diluent type and volume, and the administration fluid type, volume, and tubing.

Before each chemotherapy administration, at least two practitioners have to verify eight essential elements: the drug name, the drug dose, the infusion volume, the rate of administration, the route of administration, the expiration dates and/or times, the physical integrity of the drugs, the rate set on the infusion pump.

Chemotherapy drugs—and ideally any drug used to treat cancer patients—must be labeled immediately upon preparation, including the following details [10]: patient's name, a second patient identifier, full generic drug name, drug dose, drug administration route, total volume required to administer the drug, date the medication is to be administered, expiration dates and/or times, sequencing of drug administration and total number of products to be given when medication is provided in fractionated doses (e.g., one of five, two of two), and a warning about storage and handling.

Before the administration, the practitioner administering the treatment has to confirm it with the patient, reporting at least the following information: drug name, infusion time, route of administration, and any infusion-related symptoms they should report. At least two individuals, in the presence of the patient, must verify the patient identification using at least two identifiers. Documentation of chemotherapy administration must report the verification of the aforementioned eight elements that had to be checked before the administration (see above). Procedures to manage extravasation must be defined and must follow the most up-to-date guidelines. The antidote sets must be accessible within the appropriate timeframe. After the administration of the treatment, appropriate procedures must be adopted to monitor adherence, toxicity, and possible complications.

Some studies have analyzed the different clinical and management settings in which the medication errors were reported. Interestingly, most them were intercepted and corrected before they reached the patient [11–14]. Pharmacists or nurses usually detected order-writing errors and informed clinicians, thus preventing harm to the patient. Therefore, no harm occurred as a result of error, in part thanks to the diligence of the staff and the special alertness of the team in questioning any unclear or ambiguous orders. This proactive approach allows the team to frequently intercept errors before they cause serious AEs. In addition, it produces cultural changes among health professionals, consequently improving medication prescription processes (e.g., development and adoption of specific computerized and noncomputerized order templates). In contrast, behaviors such as the hiding of errors or the sanctioning attitudes are an obstacle to the creation of a culture of patient safety among health professionals. Of note, hospital-based or center-based incident reporting systems have often performed better than nationwide systems, in which the problem of underreporting is more common [15, 16].

18.5   Safety Practices and Implementation Strategy in Clinical Oncology

Different strategies have been proposed in order to reduce the risk of medication errors during cancer care or to mitigate their effects or harm to the patient (Table 18.1). Therapeutic orders should be drawn up from standardized and continuously monitored dictionaries. By using computer technology, errors stemming from a misunderstanding of handwriting can be avoided. In the literature, there are some recommendations that mainly concern the way in which to report orders related to the prescription of chemotherapy. In particular, some information should always be present in each order report, including patient data such as name, height, weight, and body surface area, and treatment characteristics such as route of administration, timing, and dose. Furthermore, specific checklists that include

Table 18.1 Strategic measures to improve safe management of anticancer medication[a]

Strategic areas	Examples of intervention measures
Training	• All health professionals involved in treating cancer patients (i.e., physicians, pharmacists, nurses, technicians) must have the necessary knowledge and skillset to perform their functions. • Continuous education programs must be aimed at all staff members. • Periodic audits must be implemented for accreditation by authorized independent organizations.
Resources	• Staff and technological resources must be commensurate with the volume of work. • High pressure placed upon care staff must be avoided. • Information and communication technology-based integrated system focused on the management of cancer patients has to be part of the hospital infrastructures.
Operating procedures	• The healthcare setting must have in place standard operating procedures which include strategies for preventing errors. • The operating procedures must contain clear definitions of the processes for prescribing, pharmaceutical reviewing, preparing, dispensing, administering, and monitoring anticancer therapy. • Responsibilities of each member of the staff must be clearly indicated in each process. • The Center Cancer must have up-to-date dictionaries with evidence-based treatment protocols, clearly and unambiguously written, and accessible to all health professionals involved in cancer patient care.
Informing the patient and caregivers	The involvement of the patient and one or more caregivers is encouraged in order to facilitate the care process. To this end, it is crucial to pay attention to the completeness and clarity of the information provided.
Process of prescribing the treatment	• Standardization of treatment orders. • The use of a computerized physician order entry (CPOE) system integrated into the medical records, equipped with a clinical decision support system (CDSS) that allows to minimize prescribing errors (e.g., dose calculation alerts, adjustments according to clinical situations, allergies, maximum doses).

(continued)

Table 18.1 (continued)

Strategic areas	Examples of intervention measures
Process of preparing/ dispensing the treatment	• The staff of the pharmacy must follow standard guidelines or protocols related to the composition, reconstitution, dilution, stability, labeling of each drug used at the site. • Anticancer therapy must be prepared by the pharmacy staff in a safety cabinet, which can be automated or not, for one patient at a time, and each drug must be prepared individually. • Preparation of anticancer therapy should be completed by the pharmacy staff in such a way that no further preparation is required by the health professional responsible for administering the treatment (i.e., nurses). • A standardized labeling method must be used for ensuring easy identification of patient, medication, route, and dose. Labels must be printed (not handwritten). • The components of intravenous mixtures of cancer drugs must be verified using bar codes or a similar system. The preparation phase of cytotoxic drugs should be centrally managed within the hospital facility and guaranteed by dedicated pharmacists and technicians.
Process of administering the treatment	• Anticancer therapy must be administered by a qualified member of nursing staff. • Before each drug administration, patient ID must be verified by the nurse in the presence of the patient, using at least two identifiers. • In addition, an expert nurse must confirm the treatment with the patient. Drug name, infusion time, route of administration, and infusion-related symptoms must be reported, establishing any symptoms the patient must promptly report.
Monitoring process	After anticancer drug administration, patients must be monitored for adherence, toxicity, and complications.

[a]Many of these statements are also appropriate for radiation therapy.

safety parameters to be evaluated before the prescription should always be available. Examples of such checklists are forms with information on white blood cell counts, creatinine clearance, liver function indices, and drug interactions, among others.

It should be acknowledged that computer technology does not eliminate the risk of errors. Although Computerized Physician Order Entry (CPOE) systems and Clinical Decision Support Systems (CDSS) may limit some specific errors linked to incorrect order entry, many order entry alerts can be ignored or manually bypassed by physicians.

Prescription errors can be sensibly reduced by 55–80% by a CPOE system with the aid of a CDSS [17]. The introduction of computerized information systems in clinical practice and the use of medical records have been reported to have positive effects on the reduction of clinical risk, not only in relation to the cycle of medication (i.e., planning of treatment, prescription, preparation, administration, follow-up) but also for diagnostic and therapeutic evaluation in general.

The importance of documenting the occurrence of errors is independent of the extent of the damage caused to the patient or even whether any damage has been caused.

It is well known that underreporting of errors is widespread; errors that cause less serious damage often go untracked. However, the importance of providing information on near-miss or lesser injury events is increasingly clear. Policies that start from metrics and reporting are essential for improvement and the appropriate use of data is extremely useful when implementing management practices that target-specific risks.

Barriers to compliance with reporting include low staff awareness, cumbersome interfaces for documenting and sharing data among healthcare professionals, the perception of wasted time and uselessness, or fear of repercussions in the form of punitive measures.

On the other hand, strategies for improvement include simplification, standardization, and use of information technology.

Patient safety must not be limited hierarchies. Everyone must be involved in proactive error prevention. The physician, nurse, and pharmacist should all double-check therapeutic prescriptions [5, 18]. Patients, in turn, must be fully informed about the characteristics of the therapy and its administration. Everyone must feel encouraged to express any doubts. Each must share their work with the others; this is the key to success in preventing a large proportion of potential errors.

18.6 Radiotherapy

Radiotherapy (RT) is one of the major treatment options in cancer management and "it is widely known to be one of the safest areas of modern medicine, yet, for some, this essential treatment can bring harm, personal tragedy and even death" (Sir Liam Donaldson).

It is estimated that between one half and two thirds of new cancer cases receive RT [19], which is used with curative intent in 75% of the cases that receive it. RT is a highly effective treatment option for palliation and symptom control; however, its adverse effects are quite common.

RT has distinctive risk features owing to the invasiveness of the irradiating techniques used and to the seriousness of neoplastic disease [20]. The RT process is complex and makes use of highly specialized technical equipment. The technical advancement has played a decisive role for precision in treatment delivery, creating highly conformal dose distribution with steep dose gradients [21]. Whatever the changes might have been, the objective remains the same: to eradicate tumors and to eliminate all cells in the regions at risk with minimized normal tissue toxicity [22]. The radiation treatment process is represented can be broken down into a sequence of steps. A high level of accuracy is needed at every step for maximum tumor control with minimal risk to normal tissue, defined as Organ at Risk (OAR) [23] (Fig. 18.1).

Over the last two decades, numerous studies have reported an association between dosimetric parameters and normal tissue outcomes. In 2007, a joint task force of physicists and physicians was formed with the support of the American Society for Therapeutic Radiology and Oncology (ASTRO) and the American Association of Physicists in Medicine (AAPM) to summarize in the QUANTEC the available data in a format useful to clinicians and to update and refine the estimates provided [24, 25]. Recently, PENTEC (Pediatric Normal Tissue Effects in the Clinic) has tried to explore and define normal tissue tolerance in developing children as a function of dose and volume of radiation, type and scheduling of chemotherapy, and surgery. This information can ideally be used to inform radiation oncologists, patients, and parents of the risks and benefits of multimodality therapy involving radiation therapy, to define radiation dose constraints for treatment planning, and to propose new research directions [26].

In general, RT-related symptoms depend on the site, volume irradiated, technique, total dose, dose fractionation, age of patient, concurrent therapy, and biology of involved tissue. RT adverse effects are classically divided into acute adverse effects (i.e., arising during the treatment and lasting for about 3 months) and late ones (i.e., arising 6 months after treatment). RTOG/EORTC hoped to standardize the way of reporting late effects on both sides of the Atlantic [27]. This has been succeeded by the CTCAE scale (Common Toxicity Criteria for Adverse Events), whose most prominent features are the merging of early and late effects criteria into a single uniform document and the development of criteria applicable to all treatment methods (e.g., chemotherapy, RT, surgery, new biotechnological drugs) [28]. RT-related symptoms can be divided into general symptoms associated with the procedure or disease and specific symptoms related to the site of irradiation. Among the former, patients often indicate fatigue as the most disturbing adverse effect of radiotherapy, ahead of pain, nausea, and vomit. Fatigue correlated with radiotherapy occurs acutely in 80% of patients and chronically in 30% of patients. For this reason, patients should be evaluated for this symptom at regular intervals. The prevalence of depression among cancer patients is extremely variable, ranging from 0% to 60% in the different case studies, depending on study criteria, methodology, and populations. Depression is associated particularly with cancers of the oropharynx, lung, breast, brain, and pancreas, and rarely with gynecologic tumors and colorectal cancers. Since comorbidity and treatment regimens are usually combined with chemotherapy,

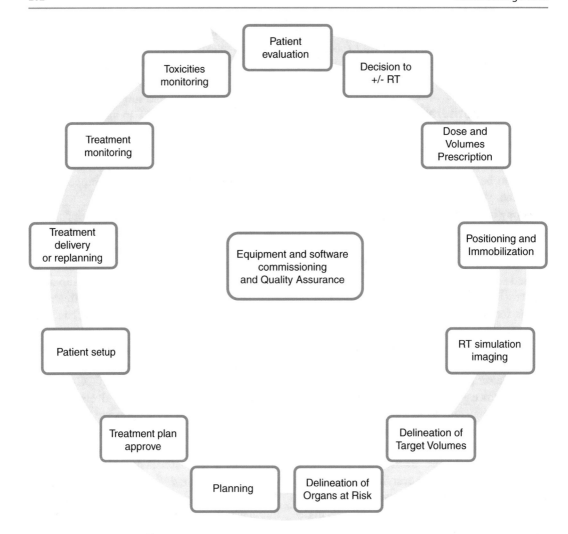

Fig. 18.1 Radiotherapy process of care from the first evaluation to follow-up. (Modified from WHO World Alliance for Patient Safety Radiotherapy Safety Expert Consensus Group)

it is often difficult to evaluate the direct effect of radiotherapy on depression as well as several other symptoms [29].

Specific symptoms relating to the irradiation of specific regions involve several organs. Here, we summarize only the main ones.

Acute and late effects of RT on the central nervous system are common and represent a significant source of morbidity. In particular, patients with tumor-related neurocognitive dysfunction may exhibit exacerbated deficits after RT [30].

Dermatitis caused by radiation is a common adverse effect of radiotherapy, often complicating treatment of breast, prostate, perineum, and head and neck cancers. It is, however, difficult to evaluate the real burden of the phenomenon as clinical practice in this field is biased by unreliable and contradictory evidence [31]. Early reactions include skin rash, and dry and humid exfoliation, while delayed events include pigmentation changes, telangiectasias, hair loss, atrophy, and ulcerations.

With regard to vascular diseases due to radiotherapy, patients who received left-sided radiotherapy as compared with those receiving right-sided radiotherapy experienced increased risks of developing coronary heart disease (RR 1,29) and cardiac death (RR 1,22). Radiotherapy for breast cancer was associated with cardiac absolute risk increase of 76.4 cases of coronary heart disease and 125.5 cases of cardiac death per 100,000 person per year [32].

With regard to effects on the lungs, pneumonia due to radiation occurs in 5.15% of patients undergoing radiation for mediastinal cancers as well as breast and lung cancers. The risk is directly associated with the volume of the irradiated lung, intensity of radiations, fractionation and concurrent chemotherapy [30].

Toxicity of the digestive tract deriving from damage to the salivary glands is common in the radiation of the head-neck area, especially in the case of concurrent chemotherapy [33]. Esophagitis is also a common, early adverse effect whose frequency grows with increasing radioactive doses and in the presence of concurrent chemotherapy [34]. Acute enteritis after radiotherapy is usually a self-limiting process, mitigated by correcting the diet and administering anti-diarrheal medications. The main risk factors include the completion of chemotherapy before the radiation of the upper abdomen and the width of the irradiated areas. Patients at higher risk are those who receive total-body radiations [35].

Acute bladder infection, including the most severe hemorrhagic cystitis, is a less common effect of radiotherapy, and the risk is elevated by concurrent chemotherapy [36].

Sexual dysfunctions, including impotence, are common after radiotherapy for cancers of the prostate and, to a lesser extent, the colon-rectum. It mainly concerns older patients, who exhibit a higher frequency of prostate cancer diagnosis. Erection dysfunction is more common with brachytherapy and with external radiotherapy [37]. In women, sexual dysfunctions are more common after radiotherapy for cervical and endometrial cancers. The adverse effects include a lower sex drive, vaginal dryness, and an overall sexual dissatisfaction [38].

Of no less importance is the role of RT in the multimodal treatment for many childhood tumors, offering an important opportunity when the limits of surgical possibilities have been reached. Due to growing tissue, children are particularly sensitive to radiation-induced adverse effects and the induction of secondary malignancies [39]. The significant developments in radiation therapy techniques together with risk-adapted treatment strategies have proven to offer advantages for the treatment of children in limiting dose exposure. The basic principle of pediatric radiotherapy is to tailor treatment intensity according to the individual risk profile (Fig. 18.2).

Quality Assurance (QA) programs improve the effectiveness of RT programs. Indeed, QA in RT involves all the procedures that ensure consistency of the dose/volume prescription, together with minimal dose to normal tissue and minimal exposure of the health operators [40].

Clinical, biological, and technical characteristics, dose delivery, organizational and training aspects can all have an impact on the efficacy, safety, and risk of the treatment [41].

The reference model in literature for clinical risk management is "clinical governance." It indicates all the activities of healthcare compa-

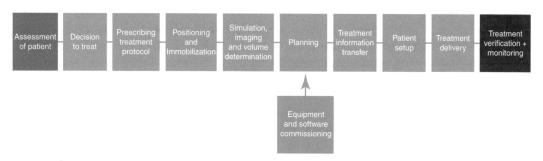

Fig. 18.2 Risk-adapted RT in pediatric cancer patients. The process should take in account the host characteristic (children/adolescent), the tumor site and volume, the treatment planned (photons, protons, multimodality treatment, etc.), the specific risk of organ dysfunction and finally the risk of secondary malignant neoplasm (SMN)

nies that are aimed at building relationships between different components with clinical and organizational responsibilities, based on quality, safety, and continuous improvement.

Typically, errors include unauthorized acts, operative errors, equipment failures, initiating events, accident precursors, near-misses, and other mishaps [42]. The event can occur anywhere in the entirety of the patient's clinical care process. Most of the errors are discovered in setup/treatment and during follow-up. There are still errors that are not covered by regular QA checks so individual clinics should perform a risk analysis of their own practice, classifying and learning from mistakes, to determine appropriate testing frequencies that maximize physicist time efficiency and patient treatment quality and to improve existing processes or implement new workflows [43]. The detection of errors is essential in the RT process as it minimizes the risk of repetition, activates mechanisms of correction, and instills in the staff a drive to improve the quality of daily activities.

The potential for errors in radiotherapy is high as it involves a complete patient pathway with many links in the chain. The interaction of many healthcare workers collaborating on highly technical measurements and calculations can in itself present a risk of error.

The United States Nuclear Regulatory Commission (NRC) maintains a large database of RT incidents and has estimated that about 60% or more of RT incidents are due to human error [44].

Beyond the rare cases in which there is inappropriate indication of treatment, there is still potential risk inherent to the treatment method. Three types of risk and consequent litigation exist: (1) correct RT treatment without the patient having given consent or being correctly informed of the risks and possible (potentially serious) side effects; (2) correct RT treatment not accompanied by a satisfactory therapeutic response in terms of tumor control and OAR sparing; (3) incorrect RT treatment [20].

An example of the first type is the lack of adequate explanation of fertility problems related to pelvic irradiation. Of the second type, possible,

subjective biological factors or unrecognized variables can be considered; for example, the exclusive use of RT treatment instead of multimodality treatment is less justified in younger patients to limit and/or avoid serious, late side effects. The third case—incorrect RT treatment— falls under malpractice due to inexperience, carelessness, or negligence. Such malpractice leads to civil and criminal liability where demonstrated and where there is definite cause of injury to the patient.

The WHO presents in "Radiotherapy Risk" a summary of all widely reported and major radiotherapy incidents that led to significant adverse events for patients (such as radiation injury and death) and which have occurred in the last three decades (1976–2007) [41]. In total, 3125 patients were affected, of whom 38 patients (1.2%) were reported to have died due to radiation overdose toxicity. Overall, 55% of incidents occurred in the planning stage, while 45% occurred during the introduction of new systems and/or equipment such as megavoltage machines.

The ROSIS database, a voluntary safety reporting system for Radiation Oncology for RT incidents in Europe [45] reports a total of 1074 incidents between 2003 and 2008: 97.7% were related to external beam radiation treatment delivered with Linear Accelerator or Cobalt, and 50% resulted in incorrect irradiation. Many incidents arise during the pretreatment phase but only about 25% of the reported process-related incidents were detected prior to treatment. Of the cases in which an incident was not detected prior to treatment, an average of 22% of the prescribed treatment fractions were delivered incorrectly. The most commonly reported detection methods were "found at time of patient treatment" and during "chart-check." The majority of the reported incidents (56%) were detected by radiation therapists in the treatment unit. While the majority of incidents that are reported are of minor dosimetric consequence, on average they affect more than 20% of the patient's treatment fractions.

Criteria for assessing treatment correctness are the following: (1) correspondence of the treatment schedule for administration of RT dose and technical performance by the radiographer or portal images or CT on board (IGRT); (2) identification of the most restricted field of radiation possible, taking into account the assistance provided by modern diagnostic imaging devices in preparing the treatment plan and centering; (3) safety through quality control of the device and exactness of the dose delivered, which mainly falls under the competence of the medical physicist.

The definition of organized protocols is fundamental; they should provide methods for the constant monitoring of radiotherapy devices and identification of the person responsible for each process. To prevent any risk of incorrect calibration, devices should be submitted to quality control at the beginning of each new working cycle. Specific competence of the radiotherapist for the organ or system being treated has become accepted among the current criteria for treatment quality.

Due to rapidly increasing complexity during the last few years, comprehensive QA has become even more important for treatment planning software, information handling, and treatment delivery.

The main health professionals involved in the delivery of RT are Radiotherapist Physicians, Radiation Therapists, and Medical Physicists, while the final guarantor of the process is the Radiotherapist Physician, who must acquire the patient's informed consent, which is a process, not a form. The need to obtain informed consent for treatment is based on the patient's right to self-determination and the fiduciary relationship between the patient and physician [46]. The Radiotherapist assumes responsibility for protecting the patient from errors and damage caused by the incorrect use of ionizing radiation (whether or not associated with drugs).

In the present era, RT is being enriched by big digital data and intensive technology. Modern radiotherapy departments transfer a great quantity of data from diagnosis to planning and treatment machines. The new technologies can help in reducing the risks but, when not used correctly or if the personnel is not adequately trained, can paradoxically act as a new source of error for manual procedures [47].

Multimodality image registration, intelligence-guided planning, real-time tracking, image-guided RT (IGRT), radiomics, and automatic follow-up surveys are the products of the digital era. Enormous amounts of digital data are created in the process of treatment, carrying both benefits and risks. Generally, decision-making in RT tries to balance these two aspects based on the archival and retrieving of data from various platforms.

Modern risk-based analyses show that many errors occurring in radiation oncology are due to failures in workflow [43, 48]. Medical imaging is crucial to RT; its application, referred to as IGRT, encompasses tumor diagnosis, staging, prognosis, treatment planning, radiation targeting, and follow-up care [49]. Setup errors, ranges of organ motion, and changes in tumor position and volume are most likely to be detected during an RT course with frequent imaging, which is becoming an essential requirement in order to attain the best local control of tumors and OAR sparing [50]. Various studies indicate that inconsistencies in anatomy contouring may be larger than errors in the other steps of the treatment planning and delivery process [51]. Some semiautomatic and automatic contouring methods have been proposed, such as probabilistic atlases and machine-learning technologies, to minimize manual input and increase consistency in delineating clinical target volume (CTV) and planning target volume (PTV). Image guidance is suggested, allowing margin reduction to several millimeters and dose escalation while maintaining the sparing of the OAR. However, respiratory motion and artifacts may distort target volume. This can be compensated for with the use of four-dimensional CT (4DCT) or instruments like "breath holding" that are able to facilitate the delivery of RT to a dynamic target rather than to a static volume. Tumor motion management has been a part of the IGRT effort and it markedly impacts radiation dose and volume of irradiated, normal tissue, as well as secondary cancer risk (SMN) [43].

The risks for RT-related SMN depend on the technique used (e.g., the risk for all tumors increases with the increase of number of fields, with higher energy, and with modulated/dynamic techniques) and vary in different organs and tissues. Both size and shape of the PTV influence the risk of secondary malignancy. If we consider only SMN causing risk for life (e.g., sarcoma, carcinoma), they usually occur in healthy tissues near volumes irradiated with high-intermediate doses [52–55]. Of 30,000 adult patients treated between 1969 and 1989 with RT, 203 were re-admitted for RT due to an SMN. About 70% of SMNs occur in intermediate-high dose regions. The stomach, lungs, and colon are the most common sites for SMN after radiation exposure [54].

With the use of modern RT photon techniques such as intensity-modulated radiation therapy IMRT, the above-target, high dose volumes in healthy tissue have been drastically reduced compared with conventional 2D- or 3D-RT. One might expect a decrease in the number of sarcomas induced and (maybe with less certainty) a small decrease in the number of carcinomas. By contrast, the move from 3D-RT to IMRT involves more fields, and the dose–volume histograms show that as a consequence a larger volume of normal tissue is exposed to lower doses [56].

The greatest challenge in determining risk is that secondary cancers after RT have onset latencies of 5–10 years for leukemia and about 10–60 years for solid tumors after the initial treatment. Only longer term follow-up will allow a true assessment of the SMN risk. A risk-adapted strategy can be taken to optimize the routine follow-up, the screening frequency, and the follow-up duration.

While IMRT marks the crowning achievement of photon-based external beam radiation therapy, the next step in improving physical-dose distribution naturally points to heavy-charged particle beams using the clinical application of Bragg peak. The recent introduction of particle therapy into clinical practice offers to minimize the radiation dose to healthy tissues near cancer targets, offering significantly lower second cancer incidence rates than photon-based therapy [53].

Problems related to the harmonious development of RT in a growing multidisciplinary context lie at the center of a growing interest to scientific groups. The scientific community of radiation oncologists is generally used to monitor the acute and late side effects related to treat-

ment, and consequently to adopt and to adapt methods from clinical Risk Management. The optimal use of preventative and integrated treatment interventions based on a logical and systematic methodology is carried out through multiple, linked phases to improve the quality of health services and guarantee patient safety. Risk management is effective through the identification, knowledge and analysis of risks and errors (via report systems, folder review, use of indicators, etc.), identification and correction of causes (via Root Causes Analysis, Process Analysis, Failure Mode and Effect Analysis, etc.), monitoring of preventive measures, and implementation and active support of proposed solutions.

Only integrated risk management can lead to changes in clinical practice and promote the growth of a healthcare culture that is more attentive to patients and operators. It contributes indirectly to the decrease in the cost of services and encourages the allocation of resources towards interventions aimed at developing safe and efficient health organizations and structures.

18.7 Safety Practices and Implementation Strategy for Radiotherapy

Modern radiotherapy depends considerably on the transfer of patient data between different operative units, information systems, and staff of different disciplines.

The steps of the process are presented as follows in "Safety is No Accident—ASTRO" (American Society for Radiation Oncology, 2019):

- Assessment of patient, or patient evaluation
- Radiation treatment preparation
- Clinical treatment planning
- Therapeutic simulation
- Dosimetric treatment planning
- Pretreatment quality assurance and plan verification
- Radiation treatment delivery
- Radiation treatment management
- Follow-up evaluation and care

Care has to be taken at each step and general strategies are also needed to reach the theoretical goal of no accidents occurring.

One basic strategy for the improvement of safety in the radiotherapy process is the development of a stable incident reporting and analysis structure. This could be designed in two steps. First, a systematic cross-check of the procedures should be established, at least at the end of the main subprocesses: clinical assessment and decision, target volume and organ at risk outlining, dosimetric treatment planning, and pretreatment checks. As a second step, it is important to instill in all operators the idea of error discovery and disclosure. This part of the process requires that all professionals (i.e., physicians, physicists, radiation therapists, etc.) are clearly informed about the potential advantages of a mandatory and tightened-up second check (i.e., a cross-check) of their actions, in order to create or maintain a no-blame culture within the department. To improve the global effectiveness of the check, every operator should be encouraged to record potential errors and report them within a well-structured reporting system or to dedicated professionals.

As stated by several authors, the quantitative and qualitative understanding of mistakes, gained by reporting, allows professionals to identify potential, necessary corrections to their organization or its processes, or to the technology available, in order to prevent future incidents.

If no incidents are known, that is, if operators do not report problems, no improvement will be possible.

18.8 Volumes–Outcomes Relationship in Surgery

Patient safety in oncology should also be considered from the perspective of the outcomes associated with complex surgical activities or the procedures that comprise a broader therapeutic approach, in order to find a significant application to solid tumors. The risk for cancer patients undergoing surgical procedures are linked, in the first place, to the generic risks that are typical of each surgical procedure, such as infection, selection of the wrong site, etc.; however, this section discusses only the risks associated with outcomes such as complications, hospitalization within 30 days from surgery, or death for surgery performed in specialized surgery centers, which differ by number of performed surgeries.

Since the earliest observations published about a century ago [57], a vast amount of studies have come to the conclusion that higher volume correlates to better outcomes in a number of medical and surgical procedures, especially in high-risk surgery. The relation between workload and the latter was regarded as a key factor in the regionalization of healthcare providers, particularly those offering surgery with a higher technology content [58]. For an overview of the medical and surgical specialties for which volumes–outcomes relationship has been found, three recent works [59–61] are available in literature. The latest report [59] highlighted for surgical procedures in oncology a positive association of considered outcomes with a high hospital volume for 14 out of 18 studied conditions (i.e., cancers of the colon, colon-rectum, esophagus, breast, ovaries, pancreas, lung, prostate, kidney, bladder, and head and neck), while for other surgical procedures no sufficient evidence was found to evaluate the association (i.e., for testis, brain, and pediatric cancers).

Workload volume thus acts as a proxy measure for various processes and provides characteristics that in turn may directly influence outcomes. The causes of this association have been investigated since the first statistical evidence of an association with mortality [62]. It has been hypothesized that for high-risk surgical procedures with relatively short lengths of stay the relationship could be largely explained by surgeon volume. A systematic review recently investigated whether high-volume surgeons of various surgical specialties perform better surgeries, (i.e., the surgeon's volume–outcome relationship) [61]. A positive volume–outcome relationship is apparent for most procedures/conditions (e.g., colorectal cancer, bariatric surgery, and breast cancer) and can be related to the "learning curve" of a surgeon. The simple concept of "learning by doing" and the idea that "practice makes perfect" are often used to exemplify this notion. A drawback of this work is that these results are partly based on systematic reviews with methodological weaknesses, in particular the possible risk of bias in the primary studies. On the other hand, the hospital volume–outcome relationship has been investigated, as in one recent, German work [63]. Policy makers need good evidence for policy making around the standardization of surgical procedures. For procedures requiring an extended length of stay, intensive care unit admission, and/or multidisciplinary inpatient or outpatient care (i.e., esophagectomy, pneumonectomy, hepatobiliary resection), the relationship can be largely explained by hospital volume, due to a large multidisciplinary team and many hospital processes of care required to achieve high-quality care.

Drawing parallels between the "experience curve" describing a decline in unit costs as function of cumulative production experience, a relation well documented in industrial economics, the Author underlines that a substantial number of deaths could be averted if all patients were treated in hospital having results similar to those of high-volume hospitals. Such consideration would represent a strong support in favor of regionalizing certain surgical procedures. To make a long story short: larger volumes lead to better outcomes. At a more fundamental level, one may ask whether a model focusing on volumes may be appropriate. Many questions arise concerning the relationship between outcomes and experience accumulated over several years, the significance of the procedure alone compared with the more general set of procedures to which a specific procedure belongs to. Moreover, it should be clarified whether to regionalize operations into larger medical centers even when smaller hospitals with high volumes of specific procedures exists. This perspective raises some issues with medical students and young physicians learning curve. In summary, volume alone

probably does not automatically result in better performance, but acts as a proxy measure for various processes and provides characteristics that in turn may directly influence outcomes.

In a large national dataset of Medicare patients, it was found that, after more than three decades, both absolute and relative differences in adjusted mortality persist between hospitals with the lowest and highest volume [64]. Two recent overviews of systematic reviews [61, 63] found evidence synthesis based on systematic reviews instead of primary studies. This result supports a positive volume–outcome association for the surgeon/practitioner performing most procedures/conditions. However, results are partly based on systematic reviews with methodological weaknesses, as to say the lack of consideration of the risk of bias in the primary studies [61]. The authors suggest that forthcoming reviews, to compare better findings across studies, should pay more attention to methodology specific to volume–outcome relationship.

A recent systematic review and meta-analysis on volume–outcome associations in head and neck oncology identified six studies that assessed long-term survival with conflicting results of limited external validity [65]. Of the studies analyzed, only one was able to assess both hospital and surgeon volume concurrently. This is a significant limitation because it has been previously demonstrated that, depending on the procedure, either surgeon or hospital volume can explain most of the effect on outcome. Thus, these studies cannot delineate between the relative importance of hospital- and surgeon-volume effects [65].

Considering head and neck cancer patients, the same authors took into account data coming from a single payer national healthcare system. The results of the meta-analysis were consistent with the hypothesis: for head and neck cancer resections that often require an extended hospital stay and inpatient and outpatient multidisciplinary care delivered by a large team, the relationship appears to be explained not only by surgeon volume but more strongly by hospital volume [66].

18.9 Case History

1. A 55-year-old woman with a recent diagnosis of early-stage triple negative breast cancer was admitted to the breast unit of a National Cancer Center to receive the second cycle of a regimen with epirubicin and cyclophosphamide. Although an apparently correct order was written by the physician, and the pharmacist entered the right dose of both drugs through the computerized provider order entry system, 7 days after the treatment administration the patient experienced a severe toxicity (i.e., febrile neutropenia and G3 stomatitis). Therefore, a deep verification process was started in order to exclude potential medication errors responsible for the observed side effects. In particular, a rigorous examination of the medical record together with the analysis of the various steps of the therapeutic course were performed. Notably, the second pharmacist, who was charged with independently verify the computerized order, signed the drug preparation as correct. In turn, before treatment administration, two nurses were charged to appropriately check for the pharmacists' signatures, and to independently compare the dose on the medication to the written physician order. Both nurses confirmed the correctness of the process, and the drug administration was initiated. Subsequently, before all of the medication had infused and according on standard procedures, the dose on the medication bag was compared to the written order, but no errors were found. Appropriately, every step about treatment prescription, preparation, and administration were adequately reported on the medical chart. This approach allowed us to recapitulate the whole event and to identify the error that had consisted into a wrong programming of the interval between the two cycles of therapy, administered at a distance of 2 weeks instead of 3. Therefore, the patient received an unintentional dose-dense regimen without support of pegfilgrastim. The physician was misled by the normal values of the blood count before starting the second cycle of chemotherapy. This is a clear example of an error due to a failure of a CPOE system to provide a proper alert about the wrong interval between two cycles of treatment, and it underlines the importance of a correct set of protocols with each distinct variable unequivocally detailed.

2. Patient undergoing two subsequent treatments with tomotherapy on two different areas of the same anatomical site. For the two treatments, two different immobilization and positioning masks were made with different positioning points. The IGRT (Image-Guided Radiation Therapy) procedure, mandatory before each treatment, requires the acquisition of images with the patient wearing the mask, positioned on the treatment bed, and a comparison of the acquired images with the simulation images, on which the dosimetry plan was conducted. For this patient, the IGRT procedure indicated an anomaly of a few centimeters along the cranial-caudal direction and a different rotation of the patient body on the transversal plan. The repositioning needed to return to the correct anatomical reference point was interpreted as a positioning error of the LASER during the planning phase. In addition, no investigation was conducted on the different rotation of the patient's body on the transversal plan. The repositioning according to the IGRT procedure movements was conducted and the patient received therapy in three sessions. After the third session, an evaluation of the images revealed that the positioning pre-IGRT did not coincide with that of the simulation and that the repositioning post-IGRT did not guarantee the precision required in these cases. The treatment was suspended, and an investigation indicated that the immobilization and positioning mask of the first treatment had not been destroyed as by requirement, and that at the first three sessions of the second treatment, the patient had been immobilized and positioned using the same mask of the first treatment. The second treatment was modified, in consideration of what had

happened during the first three sessions, and the patient continued therapy with the new treatment and the correct mask for the subsequent sessions without adverse effects.

18.10 Final Recommendations

Implementation of best practices in clinical oncology, to reduce the risk of error and preventing harm to the patient, must be seen as a priority among professionals and health organizations. The growing complexities of modern medicine require continuous updates and adjustments to meet new necessities. The safest possible administration of chemotherapy drugs requires a continuous surveillance of the methods through which the drugs are administered. The implementation of an orderly method of administration of the drugs is, today, a mandatory process of revision, if we want to obtain a significant reduction in the risk of error that can result in harm to the patient. The preparation of cytotoxic drugs can often lead to error. Therefore, it should be centrally managed in the hospitals and possibly guaranteed by dedicated technicians and pharmacists. The procedures not only must be kept in writing and shared with the team, but they also need to be monitored and revised in order to avoid the introduction of new types of errors. They can take advantage of integrated electronic systems, such as Computerized Provider Order Entry (CPOE) and Clinical Decision Support System (CDSS). Each hospital where oncology practices are provided must have a pharmacy staff trained to guarantee the appropriate preparation of drugs, which can also benefit from new technologies that include always improving monitoring systems and bar coding. The organization must enforce a safety culture among the hospital staff members, so that they can feel competent and involved in the processes of improving quality of services and preventing pharmacological errors. Patients should be encouraged to contribute to their own care through patient education programs with focus on self-evaluation and on monitoring the effect of their treat-

ments. Efforts must be made with the aim of improving systems to report and analyze errors. Coherently, strong strategies must be introduced to promote inter-professional and patient–provider communication.

Concerning radiotherapy, it is necessary: to document in detail the different phases of the process; to be able to rely on adequate information systems; to work in team; to support and implement a culture of safety training; to increment a system of error reporting and near-misses; to start methods of error analysis; to support continuous education and training, especially in case of introduction of new technologies.

In conclusion, there should be an open communication among the different professionals involved in management of treatment with the aim to take inspiration from the best practices, which must be defined on the basis of scientific evidence. Moreover, the Hospital Organization must ensure a peaceful environment and a serene atmosphere, warranting necessary organizational conditions.

References

1. Rees G. Risk management in clinical oncology. In: clinical risk management, enhancing patient safety, second edition, edited by charles vincent. BMJ. 2001;197–217.
2. Pearce A, Haas M, Viney R, Pearson SA, Haywood P, et al. Incidence and severity of self-reported chemotherapy side effects in routine care: a prospective cohort study. PLoS One. 2017;12(10):e0184360.
3. Chopra D, Rehan HS, Sharma V, Mishra R. Chemotherapy-induced adverse drug reactions in oncology patients: a prospective observational survey. Indian J Med Paediatr Oncol. 2016;37(1):42–6.
4. Miranda V, Fede A, Nobuo M, et al. Adverse drug reactions and drug interactions as causes of hospital admission in oncology. J Pain Symptom Manag. 2011;42(3):342–53. https://doi.org/10.1016/j.jpainsymman.2010.11.014.
5. Weingart SN, Zhang L, Sweeney M, Hassett M. Chemotherapy medication errors. Lancet Oncol. 2018;19(4):e191–9. https://doi.org/10.1016/S1470-2045(18)30094-9.
6. Sledge GW. Patients and physicians in the era of modern cancer care. JAMA. 2019;321(9):829–30.
7. Knoop T, Wujcik D, Wujcik K. Emerging models of interprofessional collaboration in cancer care. Semin Oncol Nurs. 2017;33(4):459–63.

8. Lipitz-Snyderman A, Pfister D, Classen D, Atoria CL, Killen A, Epstein AS, et al. Preventable and mitigable adverse events in cancer care: measuring risk and harm across the continuum. Cancer. 2017;123(23):4728–36.

9. Neuss MN, Gilmore TR, Belderson KM, et al. Updated American Society of Clinical Oncology/Oncology Nursing Society chemotherapy administration safety standards, including standards for pediatric oncology. J Oncol Pract. 2016;12(12):1262–71. Erratum in: J Oncol Pract. 2017;13(2):144.

10. Trudeau M, Green E, Cosby R, et al. Key components of intravenous chemotherapy labeling: a systematic review and practice guideline. J Oncol Pharm Pract. 2011;17:409–24.

11. Serrano-Fabiá A, Albert-Marí A, Almenar-Cubells D, Jiménez-Torres NV. Multidisciplinary system for detecting medication errors in antineoplastic chemotherapy. J Oncol Pharm Pract. 2010;16:105–12.

12. Díaz-Carrasco MS, Pareja A, Yachachi A, Cortés F, Espuny A. Prescription errors in chemotherapy. Farm Hosp. 2007;31:161–4.

13. Markert A, Thierry V, Kleber M, Behrens M, Engelhardt M. Chemotherapy safety and severe adverse events in cancer patients: strategies to efficiently avoid chemotherapy errors in in- and outpatient treatment. Int J Cancer. 2009;124:722–8.

14. Ford CD, Killebrew J, Fugitt P, Jacobsen J, Prystas EM. Study of medication errors on a community hospital oncology ward. J Oncol Pract. 2006;2:149–54.

15. Fyhr A, Akselsson R. Characteristics of medication errors with parenteral cytotoxic drugs. Eur J Cancer Care. 2012;21:606–13.

16. Rinke ML, Shore AD, Morlock L, Hicks RW, Miller MR. Characteristics of pediatric chemotherapy medication errors in a national error reporting database. Cancer. 2007;110:186–95.

17. Nerich V, Limat S, Demarchi M, et al. Computerized physician order entry of injectable antineoplastic drugs: an epidemiologic study of prescribing medication errors. Int J Med Inform. 2010;79:699–706.

18. Schulmeister L. Preventing chemotherapy errors. Oncologist. 2006;11(5):463–8.

19. Delaney G, et al. The role of radiotherapy in cancer treatment: estimating optimal utilization from a review of evidence-based clinical guidelines. Cancer. 2005;104:1129–37.

20. Luca A, Fileni A. Risk management in radiotherapy: analysis of insurance claims. Radiol Med. 2006;111:733–40.

21. Sullivan R, Peppercorn J, Sikora K, et al. Delivering affordable cancer care in high-income countries. Lancet Oncol. 2011;12(10):933–80.

22. Wu X. The technical infrastructure of a Modern Radiation Oncology Department. In: Radiation oncology an evidence-based approach. Berlin: Springer; 2008. p. 641.

23. Walker SJ. The management of treatment incidents: an analysis of incidents in radiotherapy. In: Faulkner K, Harrison RM, editors. Radiation incidents. London: British Institute of Radiology; 1996. p. 29–35.

24. Emami B, Lyman J, Brown A, Coia L, Goitein M, Munzenrider JE, et al. Tolerance of normal tissue to therapeutic irradiation. Int J Radiat Oncol Biol Phys. 1991;21(1):109–22.

25. Marks LB, Ten Haken RK, Martel MK. Guest editor's introduction to QUANTEC: a users guide. Int J Radiat Oncol Biol Phys. 2010;76(3):S1–2.

26. Constine LS, Ronckers CM, Hua CH, Olch A, Kremer LCM, Jackson A, Bentzen SM. Pediatric normal tissue effects in the clinic (PENTEC): an international collaboration to analyse normal tissue radiation dose–volume response relationships for paediatric cancer patients. Clin Oncol (R Coll Radiol). 2019;31(3):199–207.

27. Anonymous. Late effects consensus conference. Radiother Oncol. 1995;35(1):5–7.

28. https://ctep.cancer.gov/protocolDevelopment/electronic_applications/ctc.htm. Accessed 28 Feb 2020.

29. Berkey FJ. Managing the adverse effects of radiation therapy. Am Fam Physician. 2010;82(4):381–8, 394.

30. Lawrence YR, Li XA, el Naqa I, Hahn CA, Marks LB, Merchant TE, et al. Radiation dose-volume effects in the brain. Int J Radiat Oncol Biol Phys. 2010;76(3):S20–7.

31. Lam E, Yee C, Wong G, Popovic M, Drost L, Pon K, et al. A systematic review and meta-analysis of clinician-reported versus patient-reported outcomes of radiation dermatitis. Breast. 2020;50:125–34.

32. Cheng YJ, Nie XY, Ji CC, et al. Long-term cardiovascular risk after radiotherapy in women with breast cancer. J Am Heart Assoc. 2017;6(5):e005633. https://doi.org/10.1161/JAHA.117.005633.

33. Deasy JO, Moiseenko V, Marks L, Chao KS, Nam J, Eisbruch A. Radiotherapy dose-volume effects on salivary gland function. Int J Radiat Oncol Biol Phys. 2010;76(3):S58–63.

34. Werner-Wasik M, Yorke E, Deasy J, Nam J, Marks LB. Radiation dose-volume effects in the esophagus. Int J Radiat Oncol Biol Phys. 2010;76(3):S86–93.

35. Kavanagh BD, et al. Radiation dose-volume effects in the stomach and small bowel. Int J Radiat Oncol Biol Phys. 2010;76(3):S101–7.

36. Viswanathan AN, Yorke ED, Marks LB, Eifel PJ, Shipley WU. Radiation dose-volume effects of the urinary bladder. Int J Radiat Oncol Biol Phys. 2010;76(3):S116–22.

37. Roach M 3rd, Nam J, Gagliardi G, El Naqa I, Deasy JO, Marks LB. Radiation dose-volume effects and the penile bulb. Int J Radiat Oncol Biol Phys. 2010;76(3):S130–4.

38. White ID. Sexual difficulties after pelvic radiotherapy: improving clinical management. Clin Oncol (R Coll Radiol). 2015;27(11):647–55.

39. Steinmeier T, Schulze Schleithoff S, Timmermann B. Evolving radiotherapy techniques in paediatric oncology. Clin Oncol (R Coll Radiol). 2019;31(3):142–50. https://doi.org/10.1016/j.clon.2018.12.005.

40. World Health Organization (WHO). Quality assurance in radiotherapy. Geneva: WHO; 1988.

41. Radiotherapy risk profile. Technical manual. WHO; 2008.

42. Portaluri M, Fucilli FI, Gianicolo EA, et al. Collection and evaluation of incidents in a radiotherapy department: a reactive risk analysis. Strahlenther Onkol. 2010;186(12):693–9.

43. Jin F, Luo HL, Zhou J, He YN, Liu XF, Zhong MS, et al. Cancer risk assessment in modern radiotherapy workflow with medical big data. Cancer Manag Res. 2018;10:1665–75.

44. Duffey RB, Saull JW. Know the risk: learning from errors and accidents: safety and risk in today's technology. Butterworth-Heinemann Publications: Boston, MA; 2003.

45. Cunningham J, Coffey M, Knöös T, Holmberg O. Radiation oncology safety information system (ROSIS)—profiles of participants and the first 1074 incident reports. Radiother Oncol. 2010;97(3):601–7.

46. Reuter SR. An overview of informed consent for radiologists. Am J Roentgenol. 1987;148:219–22.

47. Patton G, Gaffney D, Moeller J. Facilitation of radiotherapeutic error by computerized record and verify systems. Int J Radiat Oncol Biol Phys. 2003;56(1):50–7.

48. Huq MS, Fraass BA, Dunscombe PB, et al. The report of Task Group 100 of the AAPM: application of risk analysis methods to radiation therapy quality management. Med Phys. 2016;43(7):4209.

49. Verellen D, De Ridder M, Linthout N, Tournel K, Soete G, Storme G. Innovations in image-guided radiotherapy. Nat Rev Cancer. 2007;7(12):949–60.

50. Dawson LA, Sharpe MB. Image-guided radiotherapy: rationale, benefits, and limitations. Lancet Oncol. 2006;7(10):848–58.

51. Segedin B, Petric P. Uncertainties in target volume delineation in radiotherapy—are they relevant and what can we do about them? Radiol Oncol. 2016;50(3):254–62.

52. Berrington de Gonzalez A, Gilbert E, Curtis R, et al. Second solid cancers after radiation therapy: a systematic review of the epidemiologic studies of the radiation dose-response relationship. Int J Radiat Oncol Biol Phys. 2013;86(2):224–33.

53. Hall EJ. Intensity-modulated radiation therapy, protons, and the risk of second cancers. Int J Radiat Oncol Biol Phys. 2006;65(1):1–7.

54. Dörr W, Herrmann T. Cancer induction by radiotherapy: dose dependence and spatial relationship to irradiated volume. J Radiol Prot. 2002;22(3A):A117–21.

55. Schneider U, Besserer J, Mack A. Hypofractionated radiotherapy has the potential for second cancer reduction. Theor Biol Med Model. 2010;7:4.

56. Hall EJ, Wuu CS. Radiation-induced second cancers: the impact of 3D-CRT and IMRT. Int J Radiat Oncol Biol Phys. 2003;56(1):83–8.

57. Codman EA. The product of a hospital. Surg Gynecol Obstet. 1914;18:491–6.

58. Luft HS, Bunker JP, Enthoven AC. Should operations be regionalized? The empirical relation between surgical volume and mortality. Surv Anesthesiol. 1980;24:395. https://doi.org/10.1097/00132586-198012000-00060.

59. Amato L, Fusco D, Acampora A, Bontempi K, Rosa AC, Colais P, et al. Volumi di attività ed esiti delle cure. Prove scientifiche in letteratura ed evidenze empiriche in Italia. Epidemiol Prev. 2017;41:130.

60. Halm EA, Lee C, Chassin MR. Is volume related to outcome in health care? A systematic review and methodologic critique of the literature. Ann Intern Med. 2002;137:511. https://doi.org/10.7326/0003-4819-137-6-200209170-00012.

61. Morche J, Mathes T, Pieper D. Relationship between surgeon volume and outcomes: a systematic review of systematic reviews. Syst Rev. 2016;5:204. https://doi.org/10.1186/s13643-016-0376-4.

62. Luft HS. The relation between surgical volume and mortality: an exploration of causal factors and alternative models. Med Care. 1980;18:940–59. https://doi.org/10.1097/00005650-198009000-00006.

63. Pieper D, Mathes T, Neugebauer E, Eikermann M. State of evidence on the relationship between high-volume hospitals and outcomes in surgery: a systematic review of systematic reviews. J Am Coll Surg. 2013;216:1015–25. https://doi.org/10.1016/j.jamcollsurg.2012.12.049.

64. Reames BN, Ghaferi AA, Birkmeyer JD, Dimick JB. Hospital volume and operative mortality in the modern era. Ann Surg. 2014;260:244–51. https://doi.org/10.1097/SLA.0000000000000375.

65. Eskander A, Irish J, Groome PA, Freeman J, Gullane P, Gilbert R, et al. Volume-outcome relationships for head and neck cancer surgery in a universal health care system: universal healthcare outcomes in HNSCC. Laryngoscope. 2014;124:2081–8. https://doi.org/10.1002/lary.24704.

66. Eskander A, Merdad M, Irish JC, Hall SF, Groome PA, Freeman JL, et al. Volume-outcome associations in head and neck cancer treatment: a systematic review and meta-analysis: volume-outcome in head and neck cancer treatment. Head Neck. 2014;36:1820–34. https://doi.org/10.1002/hed.23498.

Patient Safety in Orthopedics and Traumatology

Guido Barneschi, Francesco Raspanti, and Rodolfo Capanna

Learning Objective

Surgical specialties have a higher risk of errors and adverse events as represented in literature [1]. Orthopedics is one such specialty in which the clinical risk is more conspicuous and, consequently, it has a high exposure to medical-legal disputes [2, 3]. The aim of this work is to analyze the clinical risk and alleged malpractice in medical practice, in order to map professional risk and identify recurrent pitfalls.

19.1 Introduction

Orthopedics and traumatology are particularly risky specialties for various reasons:

- The very high volume of surgery.
- The reliance on extremely varied skills depending on the nature of treatments (casting and splinting immobilization, open and closed surgery, arthroscopy, etc.), the anatomical sites (hand surgery, shoulder surgery, spine surgery, etc.), and the age of patients (pediatric and geriatric orthopedics), a fact which renders impossible the acquisition of high levels of reliability in all disciplines.
- A progressive increase in surgical indications for traumatic pathologies and/or lesions that, in the past, were generally treated conservatively with casts. Today, patients no longer accept treatments that require long periods of immobilization. The evolution of surgical techniques offers tantalizing alternatives that allow a faster recovery, but involve greater risk related to surgery.
- The ever-increasing complexity of interventions. Within just a few years, orthopedics has grown from a limited number of relatively simple interventions to an enormous range of surgical possibilities, often highly technical (e.g., intraoperative computerized navigation). Where the complexity is high, there is a greater risk of making mistakes.
- Two distinct flavors of specialization: orthopedics and traumatology. The latter is characterized by a clinical path that begins suddenly, due to time-sensitive diagnostic and therapeutic choices conditioned by the time factor, often offering no opportunity for proper planning. The acceleration of any diagnostic-therapeutic procedure generates a greater risk of error, adverse events, or harm.
- The fact that any damage caused produces unavoidable functional repercussions that lead to obvious clinical consequences.

G. Barneschi (✉) · F. Raspanti
Department of Orthopaedics, University of Florence, Florence, Italy

R. Capanna
Department of Orthopaedics, University of Pisa, Pisa, Italy
e-mail: rodolfo.capanna@unipi.it

L. Donaldson et al. (eds.), *Textbook of Patient Safety and Clinical Risk Management*,
https://doi.org/10.1007/978-3-030-59403-9_19

- The growing attention to repercussions on physical appearance, in addition to those on functioning. Many surgical procedures attempt to correct deformities and any failures cause obvious aesthetic damage.

For these reasons, orthopedics is among the medical specialties most prone to clinical risk, together with oncology, obstetrics/gynecology, and general surgery; "clinical risk" refers to the probability that a patient is a victim of an adverse event and, consequently, suffers any damage that is attributable (even if unintentionally) to medical care.

The damage may consist of a worsening of health conditions, but also of an increase in the duration of treatment and/or higher care expenses. It may be due to an error which in turn can be defined as the failure to complete a planned action, or the adoption of procedures not suitable for the intended purpose; in this case, the damage can be preventable and the underlying error correctable. The damage may also be due to an accident (due to a cause that is independent of a real error) and, consequently, not always preventable; this is an adverse event in the strictest sense.

An error is often the result of various components: human, technological, organizational, procedural, and cultural. Adverse events are difficult to assess, due to their complexity, and require careful investigation in order to implement primary prevention measures, whenever possible. In Sweden, the analysis of adverse events in the orthopedic branch showed that errors in this specific discipline have a high degree of predictability [4]. This type of error deserves the highest dedication of attention and resources.

Of the errors which can be classified through a *Root Cause Analysis* [5], the main types are (1) diagnostic errors, (2) treatment errors, (3) communication errors, (4) evaluation errors, and (5) environmental or system-related problems. In the context of diagnostic errors, further categories can be distinguished, among which the most important are delayed diagnosis, missed diagnosis (unidentified pathology or lesion) or wrong diagnosis (different pathology diagnosis), failure to prescribe diagnostic tests, and incorrect inter-

pretation of diagnostic tests. Treatment errors include treatment delay, incorrect surgical technique, treatment failure, unnecessary treatment, and improper surgical wound care. Communication errors are divided into verbal and written communication mistakes. Evaluation errors include misevaluation of indications for surgery, non-fulfillment of protocols, and inadequate planning. Finally, various organizational aspects are considered with regard to problems inherent to the system, ranging from poor environmental safety to inadequate resources.

19.2 Epidemiology of Adverse Advent

The highest number of clinical negligence claims comes from surgical specialties, orthopedic surgery being the worst offender, responsible for 29.8% of all cases [1]. Casali et al. [6] carried out a retrospective study on orthopedic claims based on an archival data analysis from one of the largest medical malpractice insurance brokers in Italy. Their analysis indicates that orthopedics is the specialty with the highest risk of malpractice claims. Most of the claims studied originated in civil litigation and malpractice was mainly suspected in perioperative and operative cases arising in general hospitals. The anatomical sites most commonly invoked in claims were the hip and the knees (constituting 40% of all claims), and sciatic nerve lesions were the main contributor. Malpractice was ascertained in about half of the analyzed claims, typically cases of elective surgery that resulted in the permanent impairment of a patient. On the other hand, death resulting from orthopedic malpractice was rare.

19.3 Most Frequent Errors

In orthopedics, risk is mainly related to two types of procedures: diagnostic and therapeutic [6–8]. Therefore, subsequent discussion will be concentrated on these two types. However, it is necessary to remember that a strict classification of risk is not possible, since the categories of adverse events are numerous and since a causal chain can combine various causes from within each category. For example, the most classic typology in the category of treatment errors, that of surgery performed on the wrong limb, often sees a communication error as the main causal element.

Hospitals are the main sites of error in orthopedics and traumatology. In the patient's clinical route, there are three main phases: intake, hospitalization, and discharge. Intake usually happens through an outpatient appointment, an emergency room visit, or a transfer from another department. Patient intake is the phase in which diagnostic errors mainly occur. These errors have a high incidence in orthopedics and traumatology, comparable to that of therapeutic errors [9], even though diagnostic errors have been the subject of fewer studies. Although the causes of diagnostic error are numerous, the main mistakes are the insufficient collection of anamnestic data and clinical examination results, a failure to check previous health records (laboratory tests, reports of previous hospital admissions, etc.), insufficient knowledge of diseases compatible with the clinical presentation, a failure to generate diagnostic hypotheses or the formulation of incorrect diagnostic hypotheses (a differential diagnosis focused on the most striking or the most recently encountered diseases rather than the most statistically probable hypothesis), a lack of consideration of diseases or associated therapies that modify the diagnostic approach, a lack of time or an overload of work, the lack of knowledge or a failure to assess the accuracy limits of tests, among others.

Intake from the emergency department runs a higher risk of error than intake from an outpatient clinic. The importance of a diagnostic error during an intake from the emergency department is very variable. It can be relatively negligible, such as the failure to highlight a fracture of a distal phalanx of a finger, or it can have devastating consequences, such as neurological damage caused by a vertebral fracture that goes unrecognized and, consequently, not adequately immobilized. A lack of an initial diagnosis most often delays the start of therapy, possibly leading to a worse outcome or a more difficult treatment; fur-

thermore, in all cases of delayed injury identification, the prolongation of pain until a definitive diagnosis represents a significant source of discomfort. Finally, even if the physical consequences are minimal, there is always the concern of psychological stress trauma, deterioration of the doctor-patient relationship, or a loss of confidence in doctors or the hospital.

Traumatologic emergency care has been described as "the perfect storm" for a traumatologist (or radiologist) [10, 11], as the following conditions can occur simultaneously: an unstable patient, a difficulty to collect a complete anamnesis, a need to make important decisions quickly, a confluence of different specialist skills, a need for different treatments at once, overcrowding, and working with young or trainee health staff.

The polytrauma patient has the highest concentration of risk factors. In these circumstances, some orthopedic lesions often go initially unnoticed, both because of the need to focus clinical and instrumental diagnostics on conditions that endanger the patient's life and because of the multiplicity of lesions, some of which distract from fractures that are more difficult to identify through clinical examination (such as vertebral fractures). The initial evaluation is not always reliable; for example, it may happen that attention is initially drawn to more striking injuries that actually have lower priority: a severe facial trauma evokes a visceral response but, if the airways are clear, rarely constitutes a serious threat to the patient's life, while it can divert attention away from an unstable cervical spinal cord lesion of critical importance.

The most frequently misunderstood lesions are fractures, followed far behind by ligament injuries, dislocations, and tendon injuries. Vascular-nerve lesions are even less frequent but they are of high importance due to the risk of irreversible damage. The need for an accurate neurovascular evaluation of the limbs of the trauma-orthopedic patient is certainly well-recognized, but often overlooked: an interesting study published in 2012 in the American Journal of Medical Quality [12] highlights the existence of a statistically significant association between the increased experience of the examiner and the reduced or inadequate documentation of the neurovascular status of extremities.

A fracture may go unrecognized for many reasons; the following main groups can be distinguished: the absence of targeted instrumental examinations, the failure to observe the fracture even with a targeted instrumental examination, the incorrect interpretation of an examination, and the effective absence of radiographic evidence.

The failure to prescribe a radiographic exam is the second most frequent cause of diagnostic error, preceded only by the failure to observe a fracture in correctly performed radiographs [13]. Prescription error can be caused by various factors. First, it must be recognized that, however simple it may be to perform a targeted X-ray examination on a conscious patient who can pinpoint the origin of pain to the site of a fracture, the examination becomes extremely challenging when performed on a patient who is unconscious or in an altered sensory state. Furthermore, even in lucid patients, pain may not always be present; this may be especially true for elderly patients, in whom the frequent occurrence of bone fragility may cause the severity of trauma to be underestimated.

Failure to observe the fracture even through a targeted instrumental examination occurs relatively frequently in some anatomical regions that do not appear in standard projections. For example, fractures in the lower cervical/upper thoracic spine are often invisible due to the overlapping of the shoulders in a lateral projection; therefore, if the clinical presentation or the dynamics of the accident cannot exclude the presence of such lesions, an in-depth diagnostic analysis with CT is necessary.

The misinterpretation of the results of a correctly performed exam is primarily due to error in diagnostic imaging [13], while the actual absence of radiological signs, even in the presence of a lesion (a true false negative), is a rare but possible event (Fig. 19.1). These errors are mainly relevant to the radiological specialty, for which reference should be made to the respective literature [14, 15].

The most frequent locations of unrecognized fractures are hand, wrist, and foot and ankle; each anatomical site has a characteristically prevalent type of unrecognized lesion, posing very different degrees of danger: in the wrist, the most frequently unrecognized fracture occurs at the distal end of the radius (more so than all greenstick

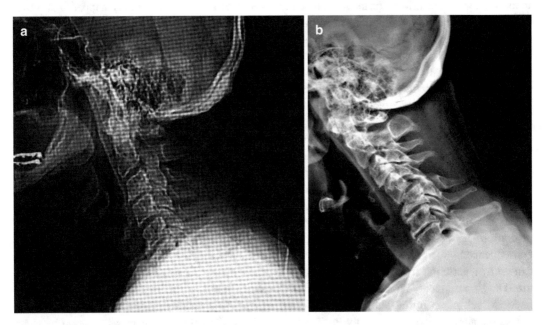

Fig. 19.1 (a) CT scan normal, performed on the day of the accident; (b) cervical radiograph performed 2 months later demonstrating C4–C5 subluxation

fractures in growing subjects); however, the scaphoid fracture, often completely invisible in initial radiograms, is the most important for its clinical consequences. In the elbow, fractures of the radial head are the most often ignored; in the hip, fractures of the branches are the least identified lesions, even though the consequences are definitely more serious in the less frequently undetected fractures of the femur neck. In the knee, the diagnosis of intercondylar eminence fracture is not frequently made, but the rarest joint fractures of the tibial plateau produce the most serious consequences. At the level of the ankle and foot, fractures of the external malleolus and calcaneal apophyses are those that most often escape the initial diagnosis, but more care must be taken when excluding thalamic calcaneal fractures, fractures of the talar neck, and the rarer fracture-dislocation of Lisfranc, which are determining factors in the severity of aftereffects when not promptly treated.

Regarding the spine, most of the missed diagnoses entail substantial risks: at the cervical level, fractures of the atlas and axis (and in particular of the odontoid process) can cause serious if not fatal neurological damage or pseudoarthrosis. At the level of the thoracic spine, compression fractures of the first vertebrae are frequently overlooked, since, as with lower cervical vertebrae, they are not visible on standard radiographs. The most frequently underestimated fractures are those of the thoracolumbar passage in elderly subjects or those with bone fragility. Even though these vertebrae are often the site of compression fractures (as well as low-energy trauma), the area is not sufficiently investigated either because the trauma is considered an insufficient cause for concern, or because the examination is incorrectly centered around the lumbosacral rachis (the site of radiating pain).

On the other hand, diagnostic errors may also be contrary to those previously described. They may consist of an unindicated radiographic examination or a radiographic diagnosis of fracture where it is absent (i.e., radiographic false positives, for overlapping artifacts or anatomical variants). In the former case, this leads to potentially damaging ionizing radiation exposure and,

in the latter case, to the unnecessary prescription of treatments (usually orthosis). The percentage of radiographic false positives in the radiology of the skeletal system in an emergency department can even reach 18% of cases if the radiologist has not yet gained sufficient competence [16].

Not all diagnostic errors result in therapeutic errors. Even if in orthopedic traumatology small fractures may go unnoticed relatively frequently and consequently be misdiagnosed as bruises or distortions, treatment (e.g., immobilization, rest, or weight-bearing restrictions) is often compatible with a favorable final result.

Hospitalization in the orthopedic-traumatological ward occurs by various means and, given the nature of the specialty, the purpose of hospitalization is typically surgery. Considering that surgical errors are the most frequent among the therapeutic errors, studies in literature have focused more on these than on others. In a work published in the Archives of Surgery of 2009 [17], all incorrect surgical and/or invasive procedures due to errors made in or outside the operating room were analyzed; data collected from the Veterans Health Administration (VHA) Medical Centers from 2001 to 2006 were analyzed and it was found that about 50% of the adverse events had occurred in operating rooms, and the rest outside. Orthopedic surgery was ranked among the first places for adverse events occurring in the operating room, while interventional radiology set the record for errors outside the surgical theater. Across the board, the most common cause of error was a lack of communication.

Incorrect surgical and/or invasive procedures represent a challenge both in and out of the operating room. Surgical errors can be classified in the following main groups: patient identification, surgical technique, and postoperative surgical complications.

Patient identification errors can be further subdivided into three subgroups: wrong patient, wrong anatomical site, and wrong procedure [18, 19]. Anatomical site errors have two peculiar characteristics that make them particularly of note in the context of clinical risk management: the first is that the consequences are particularly serious in terms of damage to the patient; the second is the high level of preventability, which renders viable their complete elimination and transformation into never events.

This type of error is not so rare: it has been calculated that the risk of making an anatomical site error within 35 years of an orthopedist's professional career is about 25%, particularly in arthroscopies for side errors and in vertebral surgery for level errors [20].

Anatomical site errors can be prevented by implementing various types of procedures: (1) preoperative checks, with clinical/instrumental exams and the use of specific items of the preoperative checklist. The identification of the patient, the side to be operated on, and the type of intervention should always take place in all phases, starting from the addition to the waiting list to the admittance into the operating room, always actively involving the patient, if their state of consciousness and the level of vigilance has not been compromised by concomitant pathologies; (2) marking the site with ink resistant to aseptic procedures. The mark must be visible even after the preparation of the sterile field. If it is possible to make an error even when the side is correct (for example, in the case of the various fingers of the hand), the mark must be specifically located on the anatomical part to be operated on, possibly precisely tracing the incision. In any case, the mark must not be ambiguous: it must be made by the first operator and known to the whole team; furthermore, there must be no other marks on the body. In spinal surgery, the use of specific radiological techniques may be necessary in order to identify the cutaneous region corresponding with the surgical level or the single vertebra; (3) "timeout," the last check performed by team members immediately before the surgical incision. Each activity must be suspended for a moment and the correctness of the site must be checked once again, verifying that the marked site agrees with the checklist.

Despite the implementation of protocols, reports of site errors are constantly increasing [2], probably in part thanks to improved transparency. Consequently, the risk of making mistakes in this sector is not negligible, above all because site errors tend to be underestimated by the ortho-

pedist who, often due to an excess of confidence, does not consider it as a possibility.

Surgical technique errors are extremely variable and a detailed discussion is outside the scope of this chapter. Spinal surgery is the most frequently involved [21] (e.g., neurological damage) together with prosthetic hip and knee surgery [22, 23] (e.g., mobilization of prosthetic components). Infectious complications, which were included in the next group, also weigh heavily in this context.

Most failures in orthopedic surgery are related to postoperative surgical complications, often arising from a failure to take adequate preventative measures. In traumatic and orthopedic pathology, surgical complications can be classified as local or general. The main local complications are related to infections, which occur in surgery at a constantly increasing rate despite improvements in aseptic procedures. This increase is probably due to the continuous evolution of implants and osteosynthesis systems, which require increasingly complex and prolonged interventions, on top of fears of new, resistant bacterial strains. The risk of infection cannot be completely eliminated; nevertheless, it is essential to reduce the risk as much as possible through the most accurate execution of each sanitary procedure according to the rules of asepsis, both in the ward before and after surgery, and in the operating room during the surgical phase. The key to preventing infections is sterility in the operating room and the management of surgical wounds in the ward.

General complications are extremely variable but thromboembolism is the most widely involved in orthopedic risk management. Antithromboembolic (ATE) prophylaxis and therapy, when needed, are a highly debated and controversial topic. There are various guidelines drawn up by the leading experts in the field, which are continuously reviewed and updated. The assessment of a patient's overall thromboembolic risk is tailored to the various departments in which this complication is more prevalent (with orthopedics at the top of the list). Adequate antithromboembolic prophylaxis must always be established while taking into account its counterpart: the risk of bleeding. In the context of general complications in orthopedic departments, the mortality rate is widely used as a safety indicator. Panesar et al. [24] analyzed deaths in the orthopedic environment using a qualitative approach to identify causative factors: the conclusions were that most deaths were due to avoidable or treatable complications.

Even patient discharge is a critical moment along the clinical route. It is essential to give the patient clear and detailed information highlighting all the possible risks (e.g., risks relating to an incorrectly performed thromboembolic prophylaxis or antibiotic therapy).

The medication reconciliation and handover [25] represent crucial moments for the care of a patient at home and for communication between the hospital doctor and the general practitioner. Communication in the discharge phase is very important; it must be certain that all information is understood by the patient and that they are invited to re-read the prescriptions of drugs or repeat the recommendations made.

Furthermore, it is appropriate to consider the socio-cultural background and the personality of the patient, in order to be sure that the indications are well understood and do not cause problems for their family.

During the discharge phase, checklists are useful to remind the doctor of all the necessary checks to be made before discharging the patient, including the removal of any devices and reporting to the general practitioner in particularly complex cases.

19.4 Safety Practices and Implementation Strategy

In absolute terms, the number of orthopedic patients suffering preventable adverse events is high. Critical phases of the clinical route are usually divided into tasks by organization, technology, and professional skill. Diagnosis errors are mainly linked to a lack of professional skill and organizational problems. In the case of professional skill, the specific training of health personnel must be improved. Various therapeutic protocols cover the most important steps in cases of polytrauma, especially those needed to rule out vertebral lesions. Providing information about the most easily misunderstood injuries, especially potentially serious ones, draws and maintains a high level of attention towards specific anatomical sites. For example, in the case of wrist trauma, tenderness of the snuffbox could indicate a possible compound fracture despite the absence of clear lesions of the scaphoid upon radiographic examination; it may therefore be appropriate to immobilize the wrist along with the first finger and re-evaluate the patient clinically and radiographically after a period of 7–10 days, when a possible compound fracture would be more evident after the initial bone resorption. In the case of cervical whiplash, there are specific protocols that determine if a radiographic examination is required. Finally, a fracture of the thoracolumbar passage in an osteoporotic subject with low back pain will not go unnoticed if guidelines are provided for acute low back pain and the epidemiology of fractures, such as the recommendations that patients over the age of 55 receive radiographic control of the spine and that X-ray control must be extended to the L1–T12 vertebrae which are the most frequent fracture sites.

With regard to organizational problems, individual phases of the diagnostic-therapeutic path must be distinguished. In urgent care and in emergency facilities, it is essential to regulate the access to prevent overcrowding.

In the orthopedics and traumatology departments, the main critical points are patient and surgical site identification, proper ward management including the compilation of the medical record and therapy, peripheral vascular-nervous status assessment, prevention of venous thromboembolism and infections, control of pre- and postoperative bleeding, and correct indications in the postoperative period as well as at discharge. Some of these problems are common to every other department while others are more specific. An inadequately completed medical record, besides representing a serious danger for the patient, is also an act of negligence. Without a precise clinical diary, it will be difficult, or even impossible, to clearly reconstruct the diagnostic-therapeutic course of that patient, which is essential to understand the context of an adverse event if one should occur.

The main critical tasks for the prevention of surgical error are also organizational and professional. From an organizational point of view, the surgical checklist is the most fundamental tool; it must be concise, complete, intuitive, and easily understandable to all the personnel involved, both in the operating theater and in the ward. A checklist is useless if its compilation, involving each actor, is not complete across every sector and within the pre-established timetable. Subsequent contributions by a single operator are useless and harmful. Consequently, efforts must be directed towards two main areas to ensure the quality of care and of future investigations: those in which the error has a higher incidence rate (e.g., communication, instrumentation), and those in which the error, even if less frequent, represents a serious risk for the patient (e.g., management of drugs/medications, surgical site errors) [2].

Taking into account the professional criticalities, it is possible to limit surgical technique errors by improving the training of personnel, even in simulated settings. It is desirable, especially in large hospitals, to promote super-specialized disciplines through the creation of subsets of surgeons dedicated to specific sectors, such as hand and spine surgery.

Most complications in orthopedics and traumatology can be treated or prevented thanks to the knowledge and the implementation of strategies for clinical risk management. It is more correct to say "risk management" than "risk elimination," because risk cannot be realistically eliminated. Risk is an ever-present condition and our aim must be the identification, understanding, management, and finally reduction of adverse events. The main purpose of clinical risk management is primary prevention, which includes continuous updating and professional training, aimed at improving health care; in addition, communication skills and the prevention of

surgical errors must be improved, with the help of protocols and checklists already widely distributed and available.

We must learn from our mistakes. Hence the importance of clinical audits and Mortality and Morbidity meetings. Adverse events and errors must be contextualized; the risks and criticalities present in context must be identified in order to introduce control and prevention measures. This is possible when there is adequate communication, consultation, control, and review of cases and, above all, when a health organization believes in safety management.

A modern approach to clinical risk management is represented by the *Failure Mode and Effects Criticality Analysis* (FMECA), a technique that allows to identify defects or errors of the system in a simulated way. Data relating to this interesting procedure, also tested in orthopedic departments [6], are still preliminary but definitely useful in the context of clinical risk management.

19.5 Clinical Cases

19.5.1 Case 1

A 68-year-old man was injured in a car accident. The first treatment was performed in a local hospital. The physical examination revealed a head injury and cervical pain. The cranial CT scan was normal. The lateral X-ray cervical view was normal until the level C6. The injury mechanism involved high energy and a cervical CT scan was performed. The cervical CT scan was also normal (Fig. 19.1). Two months later, the patient visited due to a persistence of the cervical pain. The clinical examination revealed pain and a deficiency in the range of cervical spine motion, without neurological impairment. No radiologic examination was ordered and the patient was prescribed analgesics and physiotherapy. After a month, the persistence of pain led to a second assessment: a cervical radiograph was ordered and demonstrated C4–C5 subluxation. There are only a few cases of neglected cervical spine dislocations reported in the literature and no clear guidelines regarding the management of such injuries. Therefore the treatment of delayed presentations of such cases is very difficult and the patient now needs a risky and complex surgical intervention. The diagnosis of cervical spine injuries remains a significant problem for many blunt trauma patients. Correct and early diagnosis of these injuries is imperative, as delayed or missed diagnoses result in increased morbidity and mortality.

The first error of diagnosis was radiologic: the sensitivity of the CT scan to cervical trauma is 98% but may fail to identify ligamentous injuries. Only an MRI can detect this type of lesion before the subluxation.

This case report underscores the importance of integrating all aspects of patient history, precise physical examination, diagnostic imaging, and clinical judgment. Re-evaluation is necessary when the CT scan does not correlate with physical examination. The diligent integration of both physical examination and the review of images obtained will undoubtedly lead to a decrease in claims of medical malpractice.

19.5.2 Case 2

The patient is a 16-year-old girl with no known family history of neurofibromatosis. She had noticed some deformity in her spine when she was 8 years old, and was diagnosed with neurofibromatosis type I (NF-1) and followed up by a neurologist. She had a scoliotic deformity of the spine, more pronounced during a forward Adam's test. During the neurologist's initial follow-up, serial plain radiographs that had been performed every 2 years revealed progression of the scoliosis. Then, 5 years ago, when she was 11 years old, the patient was treated with a brace. However, the curve rapidly progressed as she entered the adolescent growth spurt, with scoliosis measuring 50° Cobb, kyphosis 56°, and Risser 1 (Fig. 19.2). Even so, the brace treatment was continued. When the patient presented herself at our hospital, she was Risser 5 and the radiological imaging showed a classic dystrophic kyphoscoliosis with Cobb angles measuring 88° scoliosis (T5–T8) and 85° kyphosis (T2–T101) (Fig. 19.3).

Neurofibromatosis is an autosomal, dominant chromosomal disorder and scoliosis is the most common skeletal presentation, with incidence ranging from 10% to 60%. Our patient had a kyphoscoliotic curve of the proximal thoracic spine, with severe apical rotation from T5 to T8. The clinical presentation and radiological imaging in this patient were very suggestive of dystrophic features and included: (a) short segment and acute angular deformity; (b) early occurrence at the young age of 8 years old; (c) sagittal plane kyphoscoliosis; (c) pencilling of the ribs; and (d) defective pedicles. Early surgical stabilization was indicated in this patient at an early age of onset because of the risk of substantial progression of the curve. However, the doctor had opted for nonsurgical treatment in the initial stages, using a brace: this is an error of treatment and it was not surprising that bracing had failed nor that the curve had rapidly progressed. Now the patient needs multiple, complex, and risky surgical interventions.

19.6 Recommendations

To conclude, two important elements must be mentioned in orthopedic risk management. The first is that the biggest danger comes not from the risk itself but from ignorance, as many orthopedists do not fully appreciate the level of risk and so do not feel the need for more scrutiny.

The second is that a good doctor-patient relationship is as essential as both professional competence and compliance with protocols and guidelines. When approaching clinical practice, the principles of classical medicine, from the Hippocratic oath onwards, must always be kept in mind. According to Nebel [26], the best prevention against both adverse events and their legal implications can be summed up by the ancient precept "love thy patient."

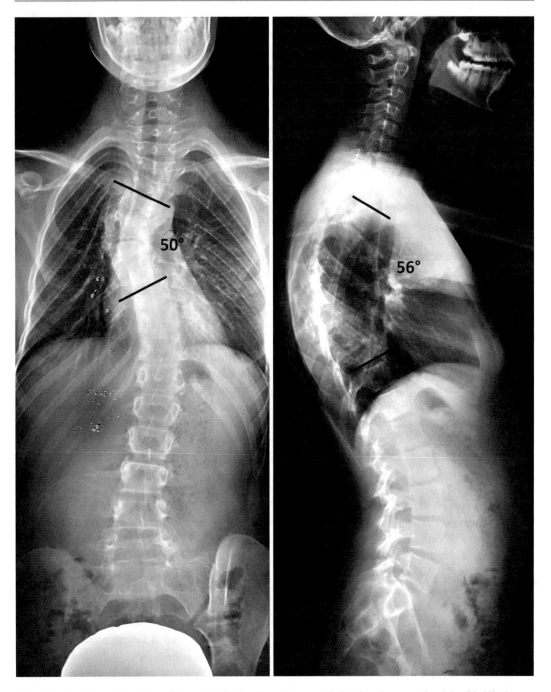

Fig. 19.2 Standing whole spine radiographs in NF1 patient 12 years old, showing sharp angular right-sided kyphosco-liosis: dystrophic curves have always surgical indication and the conservative treatment is contraindicated

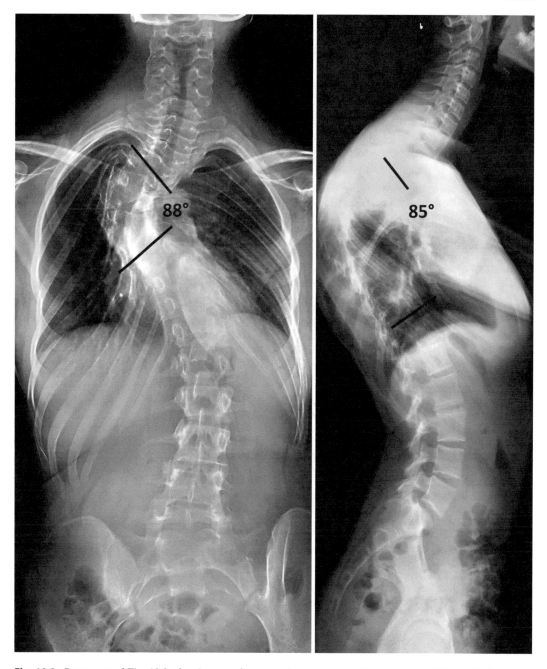

Fig. 19.3 Same case of Fig. 19.2 after 4 years of conservative treatment with progression of the scoliotic and the kyphotic curve

References

1. Von Laue NC, Schwappach DL, Koeck CM. The epidemiology of medical errors: a review of the literature. Wien Klin Wochenschr. 2003;115(10):318–25.

2. Wong DA, Herndon JH, Canale ST, et al. Medical errors in orthopaedics. Results of an AAOS member survey. J Bone Joint Surg Am. 2009;91(3):547–57.

3. Jena AB, Seabury S, Lakdawalla D, Chandra A. Malpractice risk according to physician specialty. N Engl J Med. 2011;365(7):629–36.

4. Unbeck M, Muren O, Lillkrona U. Identification of adverse events at an orthopedics department in Sweden. Acta Orthop. 2008;79(3):396–403.

5. Stahel PF, Sabel AL, Victoroff MS, et al. Wrong-site and wrong-patient procedures in the universal protocol era: analysis of a prospective database of physician self-reported occurrences. Arch Surg. 2010;145(10):978–84.

6. Casali MB, Blandini A, Del Sordo S, et al. Alleged malpractice in orthopaedics. Analysis of a series of medmal insurance claims. J Orthop Traumatol. 2018;20:7.

7. De Palma A, Flore E, Galluccio P, et al. La malpractice in ortopedia e traumatologia. Analisi dei dati della sinistrosità in tre regioni italiane. Giornale Italiano di Ortopedia e Traumatologia. 2016;42:61–7.

8. Morelli P, Vinci A, Galetto L, et al. FMECA methodology applied to two pathways in an orthopaedic hospital in Milan. J Prev Med Hyg. 2007;48:54–9.

9. Kohn LT, Corrigan JM, Donaldson MS, editors. To err is human: building a safer health system. Washington, DC: Committee on Quality of Health Care in America, Institute of Medicine, National Academy Press; 1999.

10. Gruen RL, Jurkovich GJ, McIntyre LK, et al. Patterns of errors contributing to trauma mortality: lessons learned from 2,594 deaths. Ann Surg. 2006;244:371–80.

11. West RW. Radiology malpractice in the emergency room setting. Emerg Radiol. 2000;7:14–8.

12. Tan EW, Ting BL, Jia X, et al. Diagnostic errors in orthopedic surgery: evaluation of resident documentation of neurovascular examinations for orthopedic trauma patients. Am J Med Qual. 2012;28(1):60–8.

13. Ng CH, Lau FL. A retrospective review of patients with radiological missed fractures in an emergency department in Hong Kong. Hong Kong J Emerg Med. 2003;10:215–22.

14. Pinto A, Brunese L. Spectrum of diagnostic errors in radiology. World J Radiol. 2010;2(10):377–83.

15. Wei CJ, Tsai WC, Tiu CM, et al. Systematic analysis of missed extremity fractures in emergency radiology. Acta Radiol. 2006;47(7):710–7.

16. Williams SM, Connelly DJ, Wadsworth S, Wilson DJ. Radiological review of accident and emergency radiographs: a 1-year audit. Clin Radiol. 2000;55(11):861–5.

17. Neily J, Mills PD, Eldridge N, et al. Incorrect surgical procedures within and outside of the operating room. Arch Surg. 2009;144(11):1028–34.

18. Panesar SS, Noble DJ, Mirza SB, et al. Can the surgical checklist reduce the risk of wrong site surgery in orthopaedics? Can the checklist help? Supporting evidence from analysis of a national patient incident reporting system. J Orthop Surg Res. 2011;18(6):18.

19. Robinson PM, Muir LT. Wrong-site surgery in orthopaedics. J Bone Joint Surg Br. 2009;91(10):1274–80.

20. American Academy of Orthopaedic Surgeons Council on Education. Report of the Task Force on Wrong-Site Surgery. Rosemont, IL: American Academy of Orthopaedic Surgeons; 1998.

21. Imagama S, Kawakami N, Tsuji T, et al. Perioperative complications and adverse events after lumbar spinal surgery: evaluation of 1012 operations at a single center. J Orthop Sci. 2011;16(5):510–5.

22. Kirschner S, Lützner J, Günther KP, et al. Adverse events in total knee arthroplasty: results of a physician independent survey in 260 patients. Patient Saf Surg. 2010;4(1):1–7.

23. Öhrn A, Elfstr MJ, Tropp H, Rutberg H. What can we learn from patient claims? A retrospective analysis of incidence and patterns of adverse events after orthopaedic procedures in Sweden. Patient Saf Surg. 2012;6:2.

24. Panesar SS, Carson-Stevens A, Mann BS, et al. Mortality as an indicator of patient safety in orthopaedics: lessons from qualitative analysis of a database of medical errors. BMC Musculoskelet Disord. 2012;13(1):93.

25. Toccafondi G, Albolino S, Tartaglia R, et al. The collaborative communication model for patient handover at the interface between high-acuity and low-acuity care. BMJ Qual Saf. 2012;21(Suppl 1):i58–66.

26. Nebel EJ. Malpractice: love thy patient. Clin Orthop Relat Res. 2003;407:19–24.

Patient Safety and Risk Management in Mental Health

20

Alessandro Cuomo, Despoina Koukouna,
Lorenzo Macchiarini, and Andrea Fagiolini

Learning Objectives

This chapter will review the most common *adverse events* that happen in a psychiatric unit and the safety measures that are needed to decrease the risk of errors and adverse events. The adverse events and errors that may happen in a psychiatric unit are unique and will be examined in detail. This section will also highlight the role of staff members and patients in preventing or causing the error.

A section of this chapter will describe the unique structural requirements that a psychiatric unit needs for optimal patient safety. The role of the doctors, nurses and staff to ensure safety will be discussed in detail.

A. Cuomo
Department of Molecular Medicine,
University of Siena, Siena, Italy

D. Koukouna
Department of Molecular Medicine,
University of Siena, Siena, Italy

L. Macchiarini
Private Practice, Bologna, Italy

A. Fagiolini (✉)
Department of Molecular Medicine,
University of Siena, Siena, Italy
e-mail: andrea.fagiolini@unisi.it

20.1 Introduction

'Patient safety' refers to the prevention of harm, errors and adverse events to patients receiving healthcare. Despite the growing interest in patient safety, its application to mental health context is still largely unexplored [1]. Indeed, mental health hospitals or units face unique patient safety issues, such as those related to self-harm, suicide and use of restraints/seclusion [1, 2].

The Institute of Medicine (US) categorizes patient safety events as either adverse events or medical errors [3]. An adverse event consists of an incident that causes harm to the patient and negatively affects the patient's health and quality of life, causing illness, injury, disability, suffering or death, and negatively affecting his or her social, physical or psychological structure [4]. A medical error is basically consisting of any mistake which is made during the diagnosis and treatment process [5].

The terms *medical errors* and *adverse events* are often used interchangeably. Medical errors can happen regardless of whether they lead to adverse events or cause no harm to the patient. Adverse events can be a consequence of a medical error but may well be also a result of appropriate care. For example, an event in which a patient, who has been appropriately assessed for not being at risk of a fall, accidentally trips and falls resulting in a fractured hip would be considered an adverse event. On the contrary, when a

© The Author(s) 2021
L. Donaldson et al. (eds.), *Textbook of Patient Safety and Clinical Risk Management*,
https://doi.org/10.1007/978-3-030-59403-9_20

person who has been assessed to be at risk of a fall does not receive the prerequisite fall prevention implements, and then the person falls, the event is to be considered as a medical error even if the individual does not experience any injury [3].

20.2 Epidemiology of Adverse Events in Patients Receiving Mental Healthcare

Adverse events resulting from psychiatric conditions are influenced by various clinical, social and patient factors [3]. As for other disciplines, adverse events during mental healthcare may be described as unintended injuries caused by mental health management, resulting in an increased hospital stay or diminished function/disability at the time of discharge. Severe adverse events include those that result in the death of patients or permanent disability [6]. A system for categorizing events is needed to understand the multitude of factors leading to it [4]. Marcus et al. classified adverse events into nondrug-related events and medication-related events [3].

Nondrug adverse events include falls, assault, sexual contact, self-harm and other injuries [3].

20.2.1 Nondrug-Related Adverse Events

20.2.1.1 Falls

Falls in hospitals are common and can result in conditions ranging from prolonged hospitalization to death [7]. Falls in psychiatric units are more common than observed in many other medico-surgical units [8], and falls in geropsychiatric patients result in more severe outcomes [9].

According to the National Database of Nursing Quality Indicators, the rate of patient falls in psychiatric units is in the range of 13–25 per 1000 patient days, compared with 4 per 1000 patient days in medico-surgical areas [8]. The higher rate of falls in psychiatric inpatients is likely influenced by side effects of psychotropic

medications, such as sedation, orthostatic hypertension [10] and medication-induced parkinsonism [9]. Lavsa et al. reported that the significant predictor of falls in the psychiatric population includes Alzheimer's disease, dementia, use of drugs like alpha-blockers, non-benzodiazepines sleep aids, benzodiazepines, H_2 blockers, lithium, atypical and conventional antipsychotics, anticonvulsants and mood stabilizers, laxatives, and stool softeners [7]. Chan et al. found that adjustment or change in psychotropic drugs is also one of the major factors for falls in psychiatric units [9]. Other risk factors include orthostasis, gait instability, fluctuations in blood pressure and physical limitations [10]. All patients undergoing electroconvulsive therapy are assumed to be at a higher fall risk thereafter [11].

20.2.1.2 Assault

Assault refers to forcible physical contact and may include slapping, kicking, biting, punching and pulling hair. The assault need not result in an injury to be considered an adverse event. The exception is when a patient assaults a staff member, which is considered as an adverse event only if the staff member sustains an injury. No assaultive violence like the destruction of hospital property is usually not regarded as a patient safety event [3].

Studies have found that assaults, aggression or violence from a patient to staff members is more common than the same events directed towards another patient. Staggs found that higher levels of staffing by non-registered nurses resulted in higher rates of injurious assaults, regardless of who the victim (hospital personnel/other patients) was. Higher levels of staffing by registered nurses were associated with lower rates of injurious assaults against patients and higher rates of injurious assaults against hospital personnel [12]. A research conducted in a Norwegian psychiatric hospital showed that 100% of nurses had experienced a violent assault during their career [13].

Violence may cause an emotional effect like fear, anger, depression and sleeplessness on other inpatients. It can also result in increased absenteeism of staff members and high staff turnover [14]. Several negative variables that increase the risk for violence in mental hospitals have been identified in the interaction between inpatients and hospital staff [15] and multiple studies have identified variables such as extended hospital stay, previous episodes of aggression, and substance abuse, among the most significant predictors of violence in mental health units [4, 15].

20.2.1.3   Sexual Contact

Sexual contact is always considered as a patient safety adverse event when it is not voluntary. However, even voluntary sexual intercourses may be adverse events, given that patients admitted to an inpatient unit are often cognitively impaired and unable to give full consent. Also, risks may arise from the possibility of getting/transmitting a sexually transmitted disease and/or of starting an unwanted pregnancy [3]. Sexual contact includes touching directly or indirectly, through the clothing, of the anus, breasts, genitalia, groin, buttocks and inner thigh. Sexual contact does not include non-physical contact such as sexual talk or non-sexual physical contact such as a pat on the back, hugging or kissing on the cheek greetings between a patient and a visitor, and where a staff member was an unwanted recipient of sexual contact from a patient [16]. Lawn and colleagues summarized a series of studies reporting that a high percentage of females experienced molestation or unwanted sexual comments during their stay in a psychiatric inpatient unit and that up to 56% of women reported having been troubled by men, with 8% stating that they had participated in sexual acts against their will. The authors note that consenting sexual activity on inpatient wards is a controversial issue but point to the fact that it is relatively common that inpatients have sexual intercourse. As an example, they report that in a study at Imperial College, 30% of the patients had engaged in some form of sexual intercourse, a percentage that was similar to the one (38%) that was found in a survey of chronic patients in a facility of British Columbia, Canada [17].

20.2.1.4   Self-Harm

Psychiatric illnesses such as anxiety, depression and alcohol use disorders are well-known fac-

tors for self-harm [18]. Self-harm has been described in many terms, including self-injury, deliberate self-harm, self-mutilation, attempted suicide or parasuicide [19]. People who self-injure may be at an increased risk of suicide [18]. Exceptions include suicidal ideations that are not followed by actions to self-harm and minor injuries without any bruises, swelling or need for treatment [16].

A study conducted among acute inpatients found that the most common method of self-harm is ripping of the skin. The study also reported that men would more likely use outwardly aggressive methods to self-harm. Another study found out that among the inpatients who engage in self-harm episodes, women with no suicidal risk comprised the largest group. The chances of the patient trying to re-engage in self-harm are highest in the first 2 years after the first episode of self-harm, but the risk may persist over the next few years [19].

Patients who self-harm often describe feelings of upset, anger, loneliness, periods of inner tension, or feeling unreal, numbness or emptiness inside. James et al. cited psychological distress as the most common reason for self-harm. Studies found that environmental restriction increased the risk of self-harm. Other reasons for self-harm include refusal of a request by staff, feeling of being controlled by the staff, conflict with other patients and disappointment with the doctor [20].

20.2.1.5   Other Nondrug Adverse Events

These adverse events are usually caused by medical examination or treatment other than medications, such as electroconvulsive therapy [3]. The events may include difficulty in breathing or walking, seeing, hearing, or standing [16] and often result in stopping the treatment and causing functional impairments.

20.2.2   Drug Adverse Events

Adverse drug reaction (ADR) refers to the response of a drug that results in unintended and harmful consequences when the medication is given at doses that are typically used in humans for diagnosis, prevention or modification of physiological functions. These reactions result in increased mortality, morbidity, cost of treatment and non-adherence to treatment [21]. ADRs pose a significant problem in the treatment of patients with mental illness because these patients often lack adequate insight into their condition and treatment, and the ADR further complicates the situation [23]. Weight gain, constipation and tremors are among the most common ADRs that have been reported [21].

ADRs in psychiatry units are common and somewhat preventable. Rothschild et al. reported that 13% of all ADRs were preventable and atypical antipsychotics accounted for 37% of reported ADRs [22]. A study on the referrals of psychiatric inpatients to general hospitals found out that 76% of transfers were because of neurological reactions and 32% of transfers were because of the use of more than one psychotropic drug [23].

Studies conducted in New England and Kolkata, India, found that atypical antipsychotics were responsible for the majority of the ADRs reported in psychiatry units [21]. Thomas et al. conducted a study that involved the analysis and evaluation of ADRs reported in a psychiatric hospital for 3 years. The study found that the most frequent drugs associated with ADRs were antiepileptics, cardiovascular agents and second-generation antipsychotics. The study also found a 20.4% ADR preventability rate in the mental care units, which is lower than the preventability rates found in general inpatients and long-term facilities [24].

20.3 Medical Errors in Psychiatric Care

As in the general medical setting, medical errors in psychiatric care lead to significant injuries, up to death, as well as to an increase in the healthcare system costs.

Medical errors are classified into diagnostic errors, preventive errors, treatment errors and 'other errors'. Diagnostic failure includes failure to diagnose, including failure to order a diagnos-

tic test. Preventive errors include failure in preventing disease or in monitoring the disease processes. Treatment errors include failure in providing medical interventions. Other errors include system error caused by a failure in the operating system or defective medical equipment.

The chain of events that leads to medical error is complex, but factors that lead to errors can be broadly classified as patient factors, provider factors and system factors.

(a) **Patient Factors**

Acute psychiatric symptoms such as impulsive, homicidal, suicidal and poor-judgement behaviour could result in either mistakes or slips. Mistakes include inaccurate treatment plans, whereas slips result from the deviation from the action plan. Psychiatric patients may not be able to accurately report their symptoms to the physician, which may delay treatment and complicate the differential diagnosis of diseases. Violent patients may induce distress and interfere with the decision-making process. For instance, even providers who are well knowledgeable of the dosing guidelines may end up administering excessive doses to these patients [25].

(b) **Provider Factors**

Mental healthcare providers have a considerable effect on patient safety [4]. Workplace stress and mental workload of the staff may impact on patients' safety and treatment. Communication deficiency is a commonly observed contributor to errors in psychiatry units [26]. Factors that may affect communication include fatigue, high staff turnover, lack of experience and interpersonal conflict [4]. Decreased length of stay by medical personnel in psychiatry units could raise the chances of missing out on crucial clinical information, such as medical comorbidities, medication allergies or medication dosing errors. The fear of aggression may result in an increased use of seclusion or restraint, as well as in insufficient therapeutic engagement [27].

(c) **System Factors**

Non-clinical systems such as training programmes, human resources, manualized admission and discharge processes are beyond the individual control of care providers but are relevant to patient safety [4]. Various factors pertaining to the general organization of mental healthcare delivery may have a significant effect on patient safety or lack thereof [4]. Institutional structures, operations and processes may be strained and vulnerable to errors [25].

Individuals with mental disorders are susceptible to the same type of errors that are seen in the general medical hospitals, such as diagnostic error, preventive error, treatment error and other errors.

(a) **Diagnostic Errors**

No biomarkers are available for the diagnosis of specific psychiatric conditions; therefore, the practitioner has to rely on subjective clinical assessment, to establish the diagnosis of the illness [28]. Establishing a diagnosis when adequate information about the patient's history is not available, especially of patients admitted on an emergency basis, is challenging and poses several risks. For instance, a missed diagnosis of bipolar disorder may lead to prescribing treatment with an antidepressant in mono therapy and result in agitation, impulse dyscontrol or manic switch.

(b) **Preventive Errors**

This type of error includes inadequate monitoring of patients and failure to provide prophylactic treatment. Inpatient psychiatric settings with inadequate protection systems such as locked wards and with a lack of 'no-sharps' policies result in patient self-harm. Failure to monitor patients with suicidal risk may place patients in danger.

(c) **Treatment Errors**

Treatment errors include errors in administering treatment and medications, improper care and avoidable delays in initiating treatment. Another error in treatment is over

sedation by handlers when the patient becomes aggressive or violent. Improper use of tranquillizers may over sedate patients which may result in severe patient falls.

(d) **Other Errors**

Other frequent errors include poor communication between patients, staff members and physicians. Effective communication between patients and service providers in psychiatric units is essential to understand patient history, conduct assessments and provide proper care [25].

20.3.1 Common Errors and Dangerous Outcomes

A summary of the most common errors associated with treatment in a mental health setting, as well as a review of their most dangerous outcomes, is provided below, with special reference to the errors that are associated with medication treatment, restraint, seclusion, and suicide.

20.3.1.1 Medication Errors

Medication errors are associated with an increase in morbidity and healthcare costs [29]. Medication administration error (MAE) may be the most commonly cited medication error in psychiatric hospitals. MAEs refers to a deviation from the instructions given by the psychiatrist, manufacturer and relevant institutional policies [26]. MAEs may occur due to failure in any of the five rights (right patient, dose, route, time and medication). These errors may arise both from mistakes committed by the provider and from system failures such as understaffing or inadequate prescribing or administration procedures [30].

20.3.1.2 Restraint and Seclusion

Restraint and seclusion, ordered to prevent aggressive patients from harming themselves, staff members and other patients, are controversial practices [4, 25]. They are perceived by some as an infringement of human rights and by others as unavoidable last resource to maintain patient safety.

Restraint is categorized into environmental constraint, physical/mechanical constraint and chemical constraint. Environmental restraint (seclusion) refers to limiting the mobility of patients to a specifically designed and securely locked room. Physical/mechanical restraint refers to the use of any technique to manually restrict the free body movement of a person or any part of the body. Mechanical restraint refers to the use of appliances and devices like body vests, multiple-point ligatures, blankets and bedside rails to immobilize the patient. Chemical restraint refers to the use of drugs to rapidly tranquillize or sedate the patient. The drugs that are commonly used for this practice include benzodiazepines and antipsychotics [4].

Errors relating to restraint and seclusion primarily result from the misuse of restraints or holding techniques. Errors also result from failure in monitoring the patients from using sharp objects or cigarette lighter to relieve themselves from the restraint. Also, patients with comorbid illnesses like asthma, cocaine intoxication, cardiomyopathy, pulmonary hypertension or coronary artery disease are at an increased risk of sudden death by restraint devices. Failure in documenting and assessing these risk factors may affect patient safety [25].

20.3.1.3 Suicide

Suicide is described as deliberate physical self-harm leading to death [4]. Suicide attempts tend to peak during early admission to psychiatric institutes and soon after discharge [31]. As compared to the genera; population, the risk of dying by suicide while being admitted to a psychiatric unit is much higher. An English study reported that among the patients who died by suicide, 39% were on agreed leave, 29% were absconding and 32% died in the ward [32]. Researchers have demonstrated that despite using sophisticated methods, it is impossible to predict suicide even in high-risk patients completely [11].

The most common predictors of inpatient suicide include a history of deliberate self-harm, depressive symptoms upon admission, and a diagnosis of schizophrenia [32]. The suicide incidences in patients who are suffering from schizophrenia are 10–13% [33]. The method of suicide largely depends on the means that are available in

the wards and includes hanging, strangulation, asphyxiation and cutting; among absconders the methods include drowning, jumping from a height, jumping in front of a vehicle and overdosing [31]. A large-scale study reported no difference in the risk of suicide in patients admitted to wards with and without doors [32]. However, the variables involved in suicide risk are multiple and there are situations in which an inpatient unit with closed doors is safer than a unit with open doors. Also, a closed unit avoids the need for nurses to spend time watching the door as opposed to talking and interacting with patients. However, there are situations in which a closed unit increases anxiety and agitation, over the feeling of being trapped, which might increase suicide risk. What is clear is that a poor assessment of suicide risk level and inadequate monitoring of patients at risk of suicide invariably leads to decreased safety [25].

20.3.2 Nondrug Medical Error

These include omitted, incorrect or delayed tests or procedures. They also include issues such as excessively low level of monitoring or observation, communication errors and failure to eliminate environmental dangers [16]. The three main categories of nondrug medical errors are errors proximal to the elopement, errors proximal to contraband and other errors [3].

20.3.2.1 Errors Contributing to Elopement

Elopement is the unauthorized absence of a patient from the psychiatric unit. Common reasons for elopement include the feeling of being trapped/confined, desire to use drugs or alcohol, feeling to be cut off from family and friends, boredom, being afraid of the other patients, objection over taking medications and stigma about being in a psychiatric unit. Involuntarily admitted patients have a higher chance of eloping from the psychiatric unit [34]. Elopement by itself is not an error, but the use of unguarded doors or windows may be considered as an error which allows the patient to flee from the unit [3].

20.3.2.2 Errors Contributing to Contraband

Contrabands are potentially hazardous items prohibited in the psychiatry unit. These include rope-like items such as shoelaces, headphone wires and belts; sharp objects such as scissors and razors; matches and lighters, illegal drugs and alcohol; plastic bags and balloons [16]. Detection of contraband is not an error, but a partial search of the body and belongings of the patients and visitors in the psychiatric unit is an error [3].

20.3.2.3 Other Errors

These include any other error that occurs during the hospitalization. Examples include performing a wrong or undue test or procedure, not performing test or procedures that were ordered, or issues such as administering food to a patient known to be allergic to that specific food [3].

20.4 Safety Practices and Implementation Strategies

Inpatient psychiatric care is often necessary to administer medications and procedures that cannot be administered on an outpatient basis. However, admission to an inpatient unit may also be due to the need for other reasons, such as the need to protect a patient from dangerous behaviours [16].

The most common strategies to reduce medical errors and adverse events and to provide a safe and therapeutic environment for inpatient psychiatric care are reported below.

20.4.1 Role of the Hospital Environment in Patient Safety

The unique structure of psychiatric ward plays a vital role in patient safety. Replacing the hazardous things in the psychiatric ward with non-hazardous materials may help in preventing the harm caused by the patient to self or others [35]. Avoiding anchors for ligatures and materials used

for ligatures during construction or renovation of a psychiatric unit may help to prevent many adverse events [11]. Ligature anchor points are protrusions capable of supporting body weight for patients who hang themselves [31].

The most common ligature points are hooks or handles, doors, curtain rods, closet clothing rods, towel rods and sprinkler heads [31, 36]. The facility should be regularly inspected, given that the bathroom, closet, bedroom, and a hidden area of a unit are places where patients can self-harm [11]. Doors should be removed from places where not required. It has been reported that the number of suicides following absconding from a locked door was the same as those that occurred in open wards [31]. Door hinges should be in the continuous piano style from the top to the bottom of the door, in an unbroken manner, to avoid that patients to tie the cord to the hinge [36]. Wardrobe cabinets should not have doors, and hangers and rods should be replaced with shelves.

Exposed utility pipes should be covered. Fire safety sprinklers and showerheads should have a flush-mounted design. Shower curtain rods should be removed or designed such that they break away even when a least-heavy patient tries to commit suicide. Shower controls, sink faucets and handles should be such that they will not support a cord. A rounded design can be incorporated. Plastic or unbreakable windows and mirrors should be used throughout the unit. Dining utensils should not be able to cause self-injury or to others. The dishes should also be unbreakable.

Patients can also use structures close to the floor for asphyxiation. Fixtures close to the floor should have a design such that they do not support a strangulation device. Items that can be used by patients for strangulation or hanging should be avoided inside the unit. These items include handkerchiefs, ties, belts, drawstring belts and shoelaces. Because patients can also use straps associated with bras for strangulation, it is necessary to assess women patients who are at a high risk of suicide and consideration should be made whether such women should be allowed to wear a bra [36].

The use of latest technology for safety, security and medicine administration helps in the safety of patients. The use of security system helps the patients feel well protected and protects them from unwanted visitors, robbery and access to alcohol and drugs [35].

20.4.2 Role of Organizational Management in Patient Safety

Organizational management plays a major role in patient safety [37]. The time spent by hospital managers and board of directors to visit and inspect the inpatients units positively influence safety performance [38]. Leadership comprises three areas: availability, experience and understanding patient safety plan. The role of leadership is to enhance learning, teamwork, feedback and improvement in individual worker's safety behaviour. They provide support for the staff and help in creating a good working environment. Also, if any adverse event occurs, they act as a support system for the staff [37].

20.4.3 Role of Staff in Patient Safety

Nurses play an important role in patient safety, especially in inpatient psychiatric wards [37]. According to a study conducted by Ajalli et al., the role of nurses is defined in two terms, 'close observing' and 'vigilant care' [39]. The head nurse plays an important role in encouraging patient safety culture among other nursing staff. The head nurse should do the following: communicate effectively, contribute to leadership, maintain a positive culture and provide patient-centred care. The presence of nurses with experience in dealing with psychiatric patients is strongly connected to the high quality of patient care and to better outcomes [35].

The staff members should possess skills to help with the disorders that are being treated in the unit, and skills to help patients with self-care. They should be able to provide reassurance, and basic information and knowledge about the ill-

ness, the treatment and its administration procedures. Also, they should be able to identify and address trauma-related needs [37].

Staff load is also a concern in patient safety. The number of patients is assigned to each nurse and staff member depending up on many factors which include the experience and qualification of the staff and patient's condition. Nurses who lack experience in dealing with patients with mental illnesses negatively impact the quality of care provided and this should be accounted for when the number of persons allocated to a shift is decided. Also, patients that are better stabilized should preferably be assigned to the nurses with less experience [35].

Staff safety, health and well-being are important in dealing with psychiatric patients [35, 37]. Hospital administration should take care that staff do not suffer from stress, fatigue or distraction from work. Staff members should have a healthy state of mind to be able to help patients experiencing an acute mental disease.

Staff members need to have good communication skills (written and verbal) to understand the patient's condition and minimize errors. Failure in communication is a known source for adverse events. Appropriate communication is also important during the transfer of a patient as an error in transferring the medical and psychiatric history may lead to serious adverse events. Communication also helps patients to seek help and safety when they feel a threat [37].

20.4.4 Role of the Patient in Patient Safety Practices

Involving patients in safety issues is key to reducing risks and preventing errors [37]. Establishing a safe nurse–patient environment is important for effective patient care, and helps to better understand the patient's needs [35, 37]. Whenever possible, patient's preference should be considered so that the decision made aligns with the patient's values. Patient's health condition and personality also play an important role because it influences communication and interest to become involved in the care [37].

Research has found that inpatients are active in making their environment safer for themselves by avoiding excessive interactions with risky individuals or situations, by contributing to de-escalating potential risky situations, and seeking surveillance or other safety interventions from staff. These findings underline the importance of fully involving patients in safety initiatives [4].

20.5   Conclusion

Several adverse events and medical errors are unique to inpatient psychiatric care. Several safety measures are able to decrease the risk of errors and adverse events. The most important strategies to improve safety in mental health facilities include an appropriate consideration of the structural requirements that a psychiatric unit needs to have in place to ensure the optimal patient safety. Also, administrators, doctors, nurses and staff play a proactive role to ensure safety. Whenever possible, patients themselves should be involved in procedures able to increase their safety.

20.6   Case Studies

The case examples below are fictitious and for didactic purposes only

20.6.1 Case Example 1

Mr. Mario, a 40-year-old man, was admitted to the emergency room, accompanied by his parents, for his 'strange and anomalous' behaviour in the last days. He lived with his parents and is their only child. He unemployed and had no sentimental ties.

Family members traced the onset of his symptoms when he was approximately 20 years old. At the time, Mario was a university student and began to manifest the bizarre symptoms and behaviours. He reduced the time spent in class and the relationships with his peers. He spent most of his time isolated in his room. He slept through the entire day and stayed awake at night. After a few months, the situation worsened, and he stopped communicating with everyone, including his parents, appeared confused, anguished and disturbed. He neglected basic needs such as personal hygiene and eating. One day he barricaded himself in his room, refusing to leave because he was convinced that the mafia had spies and cameras all over his life. His parents took him to a hospital, where an antipsychotic drug therapy was started, and a diagnosis of paranoid schizophrenia was made at discharge after a few days in the inpatient unit. Over the years, he was relatively stable, but his insight remained limited and his parents had to constantly convince him taking the prescribed treatment.

Six months ago, Mario's mother was diagnosed with breast cancer. She was initially hospitalized to undergo mastectomy and later received chemotherapy. This situation resulted in the reduced presence of parents at home and decreased her support in Mario's everyday life. Mario stopped his medication without informing neither the parents nor the reference psychiatrist. Persecutory delusions reappeared; he spent all his time locked in his room, had no relationship with anyone, remained naked in the dark and neglected his basic needs.

Mario was admitted to inpatient care and re-started being treated with an antipsychotic. In the following days, he improved and went gradually towards remission. His parents visited and spend time with him every day. After 5 days, however, the mother was hospitalized because of a severe infection and could no longer visit her son. Mario did not verbalize his concern for his mother's health but refused to talk and was apathetic. He was no longer a participant in the activities of the psychiatry unit and began to show indifference to everything and everyone, including his father who visited him regularly.

One night, when the health workers were busy to admit two new patients in the psychiatry department, Mario managed to steal the belt of a newly arrived patient and tried to hang himself in the shower of his room. Fortunately, the patient with whom he shared the room noticed what was happening and promptly warned the nurses who intervened and saved Mario's life.

20.6.1.1 Discussion

This case outlines that the level of stability and the required level of care may quickly change during the periods of inpatient admission. It is a reminder for the need to talk to the patients, check their suicidal ideation and constantly monitor their level of stability. Also, it reminds us about the need to not decrease the level of attention on the other patients when new patients are admitted to the inpatient unit. Finally, it reminds us of the key role of other patients in increasing their and other patients' level of safety.

20.6.2 Case Example 2

Ms. Alice was a patient admitted to the geriatric psychiatric unit because of a severe major depressive episode.

She is 78 years old. Her married daughter lived in another city. She suffered from arterial hypertension that was being treated pharmacologically with ACE inhibitor (ramipril 5 mg/day). She was also taking an oral opioid analgesic (tramadol 200 mg/day), for the past 2 months, to cope with severe pain and functional limitation of the right knee associated with medial femoral-tibial gonarthrosis. After her husband passed away 3 months ago, Ms. Alice did not sleep well at night and did not eat much. She preferred staying in bed most of the day and no longer seemed interested in any of her usual daily activities. Two weeks earlier, a general practitioner prescribed her antidepressant therapy with sertraline, which was started at 50 mg/day but did not lead to any improvement in her symptoms.

Upon admission, her sertraline was increased to 100 mg/day.

Five days after, she started to present with tremors, increased sweating, confusion, hyperpyrexia (39 °C), tachycardia, arterial pressure of 170/80 mmHg and respiratory rate of 30 acts/min. She also presented with chills, diarrhoea, vomiting, mydriasis and marked neuromuscular hyperactivity (more prominent in the lower extremities) with tremor plus hyperreflexia, hypertonia and muscle stiffness, myoclonus, spontaneous clonus and plantar extensor responses.

Based on history taking, laboratory and physical examination, Alice was diagnosed with serotonin syndrome. Treatment with tramadol and sertraline were stopped, and the patient was hydrated with intravenous fluids. The mental state of the patient improved within 24 h.

The hospital regime diagnostic-instrumental investigations excluded the presence of other organic pathologies of a neurological, infective or metabolic nature.

Upon discussion of the case, it turned out that the staff members had noticed—since her first day of admission—that she had sweating, hypertonia and tremors while drying her off after the daily shower. However, they did not report this finding to the attending nurses and physician.

20.6.2.1 Discussion

It is imperative to pay attention when a patient is taking a selective serotonin reuptake inhibitors (SSRIs), tramadol, in addition to a CYP2D6 inhibitor. These isoenzymes are involved in extensive metabolism of SSRIs in the liver. The CYP2D6 system, one of the key enzymes involved in adverse drug reactions, has a high degree of genetic polymorphism. Studies cite that 7% of white patients lack the capacity to metabolize drugs by CYP2D6 enzyme. Consequently, the serum levels of tramadol would be higher; and such patients would be at an increased risk for serotonin syndrome if a second serotonergic agent is added to the pharmacological protocol. The attending physician who admitted the patient likely made an error in continuing the medications that the patient was taking at home. The attending physician in the unit likely made an error in increasing the dose of sertraline, without considering the interaction with tramadol and without carefully examining the patient for symptoms of the serotonin syndrome. The staff members that noticed her tremor, sweating and hypertonia likely made an error in not communicating the above to the nurses and psychiatrists. A careful evaluation of the interactions of the medications that are prescribed in combination, a thorough physical exam conducted before and after raising the dose of sertraline, and a more appropriate communication to the nurses and physician of the observations from staff members could have prevented the onset of a potentially fatal event.

References

1. D'Lima D, Crawford MJ, Darzi A, Archer S. Patient safety and quality of care in mental health: a world of its own? BJPsych Bull. 2017;41(5):241–3.
2. Brickell TA, McLean C. Emerging issues and challenges for improving patient safety in mental health: a qualitative analysis of expert perspectives. J Patient Saf. 2011;7(1):39–44.
3. Marcus SC, Hermann RC, Cullen SW. Defining patient safety events in inpatient psychiatry. J Patient Saf. 2018; https://doi.org/10.1097/PTS.0000000000000520.
4. Brickell AT, et al. Patient safety in mental health. BC Mental Health and Addiction Services, p. 9, 16, 12.
5. Medication errors and patient safety in mental health. [Internet]. Available from: https://www.medscape.org/viewarticle/563039.
6. Jayaram G. Measuring adverse events in psychiatry. Psychiatry (Edgmont). 2008;5(11):17–9.
7. Lavsa SM, Fabian TJ, Saul MI, Corman SL, Coley KC. Influence of medications and diagnoses on fall risk in psychiatric inpatients. Am J Health Syst Pharm. 2010;67(15):1274–80.
8. Abraham S. Managing patient falls in psychiatric inpatient units: Part 2. Health Care Manag (Frederick). 2016;35(2):121–33.
9. Chan CH, Gau SS, Chan HY, Tsai YJ, Chiu CC, Wang SM, Huang ML. Risk factors for falling in psychiatric inpatients: a prospective, matched case-control study. J Psychiatr Res. 2013;47(8):1088–94.
10. Khurshid T, Lantz MS. Falls and inpatient geriatric psychiatry: a simple solution to a chronic and difficult problem. Am J Geriatr Psychiatry. 2016;24(3):S90–1.
11. Burke WJ, Rubin EH, Zorumski CF, Wetzel RD. The Safety of ECT in Geriatric Psychiatry. J Am Geriatr Soc. 1987;35(6):516–21.
12. Staggs VS. Injurious assault rates on inpatient psychiatric units: associations with staffing by registered nurses and other nursing personnel. Psychiatr Serv. 2015;66(11):1162–6.
13. Quirk A, Lelliott P, Seale C. Service users' strategies for managing risk in the volatile environment of an acute psychiatric ward. Soc Sci Med. 2004;59(12):2573–83.
14. Iozzino L, Ferrari C, Large M, Nielssen O, de Girolamo G. Prevalence and risk factors of violence by psychiatric acute inpatients: a systematic review and meta-analysis. PLoS One. 2015;10(6):e0128536.
15. Cornaggia CM, Beghi M, Pavone F, Barale F. Aggression in psychiatry wards: a systematic review. Psychiatry Res. 2011;189(1):10–20.
16. Marcus SC, Hermann RC, Frankel MR, Cullen SW. Safety of psychiatric inpatients at the veterans health administration. Psychiatr Serv. 2018;69(2):204–10.
17. Lawn T, McDonald E. Developing a policy to deal with sexual assault on psychiatric in-patient wards. Psychiatr Bull. 2009;33:108–11.
18. Singhal A, Ross J, Seminog O, Hawton K, Goldacre MJ. Risk of self-harm and suicide in people with specific psychiatric and physical disorders: comparisons between disorders using English national record linkage. J R Soc Med. 2014;107(5):194–204.
19. Tofthagen R, Talseth AG, Fagerstom L. Mental health nurses' experience of caring for patients suffering from self harm. Nurs Res Pract. 2014;2014:905741.
20. James K, Stewart D, Bowers L. Self-harm and attempted suicide within inpatient psychiatric services: a review of the literature. Int J Ment Health Nurs. 2012;21(4):301–9.
21. Chawla S, Kumar S. Adverse drug reactions and their impact on quality of life in patients on antipsychotic therapy at a tertiary care center in Delhi. Indian J Psychol Med. 2017;39(3):293–8.
22. Rothschild JM, Mann K, Keohane CA, Williams DH, Foskett C, Rosen SL, Flaherty L, Chu JA, Bates DW. Medication safety in a psychiatric hospital. Gen Hosp Psychiatry. 2007;29(2):156–62.
23. Popli AP, Hegarty JD, Siegel AJ, Kando JC, Tohen M. Transfer of psychiatric inpatients to a general hospital due to adverse drug reactions. Psychosomatics. 1997;38(1):35–7.
24. Thomas M, Boggs AA, DiPaula B, Siddiqi S. Adverse drug reactions in hospitalized psychiatric patients. Ann Pharmacother. 2010;44(5):819–25.
25. Nath SB, Marcus SC. Medical errors in psychiatry. Harv Rev Psychiatry. 2006;14(4):204–11.
26. Keers RN, Plácido M, Bennett K, Clayton K, Brown P, Ashcroft DM. What causes medication administration errors in a mental health hospital? A qualitative study with nursing staff. PLoS One. 2018;13(10):e0206233.
27. Slemon A, Jenkins E, Bungay V. Safety in psychiatric inpatient care: the impact of risk management culture on mental health nursing practice. Nurs Inq. 2017;24(4):e12199.
28. Phillips J. Detecting diagnostic error in psychiatry. Diagnosis (Berl). 2014;1(1):75–8.
29. Maidment ID, Parmentier H. Medication error in mental health: implications for primary care. Ment Health Fam Med. 2009;6(4):203–7.
30. Medication administration errors. [Internet] [Sept 2019]. Available from: https://psnet.ahrq.gov/primer/medication-administration-errors.
31. Sakinofsky I. Preventing suicide among inpatients. Can J Psychiatr. 2014;59(3):131–40.

32. Madsen T, Erlangsen A, Nordentoft M. Risk estimates and risk factors related to psychiatric inpatient suicide – an overview. Int J Environ Res Public Health. 2017;14(3):253.

33. Hussein ZN, Solomon H, Yohannis Z, Ahmed AM. Prevalence and associate factors of suicide ideation and attempt among people with schizophrenia at Amanuel Mental Specialized Hospital, Addis Ababa, Ethiopia. J Psychiatry. 2015;18:1.

34. Brumbles D, Meister A. Psychiatric elopement: using evidence to examine causative factors and preventative measures. Arch Psychiatr Nurs. 2013;27(1):3–9.

35. Alshowkan A, Gamal A. Nurses' perceptions of patient safety in psychiatry wards. IOSR J Nurs Health Sci. 2019;8(1):3.

36. Lieberman DZ, Resnik HLP, Holder-Perkins V. Environmental risk factors in hospital suicide. Suicide Life Threat Behav. 2004;34(4):448–53.

37. Kanerva A, Lammintakanen J, Kivinen T. Patient safety in psychiatric inpatient care: a literature review. J Psychiatr Mental Health Nurs. 2012;20(6):541–8.

38. Parand A, Dopson S, Renz A, Vincent C. The role of hospital managers in quality and patient safety: a systematic review. BMJ Open. 2014;4:e005055.

39. Ajalli A, Fallahi-Khoshknab M, Hosseini MA, Mohammadi E, Nir MS. Explanation of patient safety provided by nurses in inpatient psychiatric wards in Iran: a qualitative study. Iran J Psychiatry Behav Sci. 2018;12(4):e67951.

Patient Safety in Pediatrics

21

Sara Albolino, Marco De Luca,
and Antonino Morabito

Learning Objectives/Questions Covered in the Chapter

- What are the most common adverse events in pediatrics?
- Which are the approach and solutions to prevent harm?
- What are the most critical issues for quality and safety in the process of care of children?
- Which are the most effective practices and strategies for implementing them?

21.1 Epidemiology of Adverse Events in Pediatrics: Some Numbers and Some Reflections

Since the publication of the 1999 IOM report "To Err Is Human: Building a Safer Health System,"

S. Albolino (✉)
Centre for Clinical Risk Management and Patient Safety, WHO Collaborating Centre in Human Factors and Communication for the Delivery of Safe and Quality Care, Tuscany Region, Florence, Italy
e-mail: albolinos@aou-careggi.toscana.it

M. De Luca
Simulation and Risk Management, A. Meyer Children Hospital, Florence, Italy
e-mail: marco.deluca@meyer.it

A. Morabito
Pediatric Surgery, Meyer Children's Hospital, University of Florence, Florence, Italy
e-mail: antonino.morabito@unifi.it

much has been learned about pediatric patient safety. However, adverse events still affect one-third of all hospitalized children [1]. The main areas of adverse events are hospital-acquired infections, intravenous line complications, surgical complications, and medication errors [2].

The area of medication errors that has been considered the major priority by WHO through the campaign "medication without harm" [3] for children is even more critical because of childhood development, demographics, dependency on parents and other care providers, and the different epidemiology of medical conditions [4].

In a study conducted in 2 pediatric hospitals, on 1120 admission, including more than 10,000 orders, there were 616 medication errors (5.7%) [5]. In recent years the transition to digital healthcare has been identified as a significant element that concur to medication errors, in fact the electronic clinical records can affect the safety of prescription until they are modified with customized decision support, such as weight-based and body surface area-based dosing [2].

Concerning the most critical settings for quality and safety, a study published in 2012, conducted in Canada in 8 teaching hospitals and 14 local healthcare agencies underlined that the 79% of adverse events in children happened in intensive care unit, of which more than 40% are preventable and the incidence on admissions is of 6.5% [6]. These results are similar to the studies conducted in the adult population.

Other studies show other types of errors with total rates as high as 40 harms per 100 patients. Events reported include accidental extubation, pressure ulcers, patient misidentification, delays in diagnosis, intravenous infiltrates, and other adverse events attributed to systemic causes like communication, training, and systems failures [7].

Concerning the ambulatory setting, a recent study [8] revealed that the largest group of errors was attributed to medical treatment (37%). Other errors included patient identification (22%), preventive care (15%), diagnostic testing (13%), and patient communication (8%).

In a meta-analysis conducted in 2018, with the analysis of 388 primary studies related to interventions to improve patient safety, the most common critical issues to address were medication (189 studies, 48.7%) and general medical (81 studies, 20.9% errors) whereas the 53.1% (206 studies) addressed healthcare systems and technologies [9].

From these and other evidences, we can affirm that over the last 20 years many efforts and advancements have been done to improve patient safety, even in pediatrics, but the trend doesn't seem to have changed, as the complexity of the healthcare systems and their dynamicity is a big challenge for improving quality and safety of care. Also the centrality of the human being, the continuous interaction of clinicians and patients with the other components of the system, makes risks and errors in healthcare an unavoidable fact.

Error is part of normal human behavior as highlighted by James Reason "Human error is both universal and inevitable—human fallibility can be moderated but it can never be eliminated [10]. However, when errors have significant consequences or occur in high-risk industries, they become of paramount importance (ibidem)". Reason wrote that "Errors are consequences not causes, they have a history" and that only by understanding the history of the circumstances can there be progress to limit the chances of a recurrence (ibidem).

As a result of high-profile errors which have caused many deaths, industries like aviation, space travel, military, nuclear, and oil rigs have spent the last decades investing in the understanding, identification, and error prevention training in their respective industries [11].

In order to understand and prevent that errors result in adverse events, it is important to adopt a patient safety approach with some key elements: awareness of the epidemiology of adverse events and establishment of methods for risk identification; integration of improvement science principles and techniques into daily work; and creation, customization, and application of evidence- and context-based patient-safety solutions. Each of these key elements can be incorporated into pediatric patient safety risk assessment and solution development [12].

Some of the most common and severe types of adverse events, also in pediatrics, are the ones that happen in surgery. All surgery involves risk and potential complications—both known and unexpected. Medical errors may be decreased if there are clear standards of care described and adhered to; however it is clear that no two surgeries are identical; therefore every surgical error (and the underlying cause of the error) has the potential to be unique [13].

In high-reliability organizations variability is a constant and the focus is on minimizing that variability and its effects, this strategy in high-hazard industries have contributed in a significant decrease of severe adverse events. But in the specific setting of healthcare, with the high complexity of medical care there are usually more difficulties in creating a culture of safety. In this case, as underlined by Pascale Carayon in her SEIPS model [14], the science of human factors (the focus on how people interact with each other and their environment) provides healthcare professionals with an important view that can give them the resilience to avoid adverse events. An optimal culture of safety focuses on human fallibility by concentrating on the conditions under which people work and on building defenses to prevent adverse events or mitigate their effects.

Going back to the surgical adverse events in pediatrics, not all surgical errors constitute medical malpractice and not all errors lead to adverse events. Studies indicate that nearly 75% of surgical errors occur during surgery, with the remaining occurring either during pre- or postoperative care. There are well-recognized factors for surgical errors [15–18]:

- Environment—Factors in the organizational and management structure/culture may impact on the individual surgeon performance from lack of a safety culture, lack of effective leadership and workplace communication procedures.
- Lack of Surgical Competency—be that lack of the appropriate individual technical skills or technique, poor decision-making, poor teamwork.
- Insufficient Preoperative Planning—It is critical that a surgeon be well prepared for surgery with a full knowledge of the individual patient to be operated on the intended techniques. The preparation of the patient is also important including a robust preoperative workup and multidisciplinary discussions if necessary of any known or anticipated issues/complications. Preoperatively the surgeon should try and forward plan and anticipate complications that have a potential to occur. The wider theater team needs to also have had the opportunity for forward planning, ensuring the correct skill mix is present, the correct equipment available with personnel familiar with the operative procedures to be undertaken and equipment to be used.
- Inappropriate workplace conduct—Either professionally by utilizing improper surgical techniques and employing improper surgical haste or "shortcuts" or personal by, e.g., disruptive behavior and poor leadership.
- Poor Communication—This can be as an individual or within the team. Poor communication can occur prior to the operation, e.g., marking the wrong site for surgery, miscommunication of the procedure to occur, and lack of forward communication about surgical equipment required. To improve communication prior to the start of the theater list Team Briefing is now employed.

- Fatigue, personal stresses, drugs, and alcohol can all impair decision-making and technical performance.
- Patient factors may make the surgery more complex such as the ASA grade, age, BMI, and surgical pathology (e.g., previous surgery) and these can all influence performance and postoperative recovery.

Surgical competency involves a combination of good decision-making (preoperatively, operatively and postoperatively), team performance and communication with all colleagues and the appropriate technical skills. These skills coupled with a high patient volume operating rate tend to achieve a reduced patient mortality and morbidity [19, 20]. There are three important "red flag" times to check the correct patients/procedures/skill and equipment mix—before induction of anesthesia, before skin incision, and before the patient leaves the theater suite. During the procedure the lead surgeon should be constantly re-evaluating the ongoing surgical progress with salient communications; they should be re-appraising the clinical and theater setting, and constantly re-evaluating the patient's care and the conduct of the operation. Protocols have been introduced to reduce surgical error (e.g., safer surgery checklists) [21]. However, the occurrence of surgical error is part of a multifaceted phenomenon and protocol use is only part of the overall solution. A cascade of errors from varying aetiologies, with different controlling factors, can/may culminate into a catastrophe or adverse event [22].

Practicing surgery and medicine in the twenty-first century will embrace new medications, technologies, equipment, operations, etc. which aim to improve the treatment and care of patients. However the focus must also remain on evaluating and minimizing the impact of adverse events in the healthcare environment to provide a sustained, high level of surgical care.

Pediatric healthcare providers in all practice environments can benefit from having awareness of the need for understanding patient safety starting from a systemic and human factor approach.

Knowing the patient safety concepts and language can help pediatricians to adopt the best practices and attend risks that are unique to children, and leading efforts to reduce avoidable harm for their patients [2].

21.2 The Importance of Understanding the Context for Patient Safety Practices for Pediatrics

Epidemiological data and evidences from the literature are few for patient safety in pediatrics and there is a need for comparing experiences and applied solutions in different contexts. At the European level some recommendations have been defined and the need for applying specific solutions and patient safety practices has been underlined. We have now a list of evidence-based patient safety practices at the international level. These practices need to be adapted by trials in order to be useful also for the pediatric settings. The patient safety manifesto by the American Academy of Pediatrics whose last version was published in 2019 underlines the importance to evaluate the patient's specific characteristics every time that a safety intervention for children is planned [2].

In fact the analysis of patient safety practices in pediatrics literature underlines that there is no list of interventions strongly recommended [23], in contrast with the adult context where some priority interventions have been identified [24], while there are several groups of practices that can be adopted according to the specificity of the pediatric setting and issue you have to address. The concern with a compiled unique list, say the authors, is to give priority to practices which are less expensive or more adapted to the hospital setting. Especially in pediatrics it is instead important to consider the complexity of the care, the inestimable value of saving a life and the fragility of the patients. Besides that, it is important to consider that in general there is a need for moving from simple to complex interventions which include not just the application of single

actions but the identification of more advanced model for evaluating complexity and promote a system change.

21.2.1 Simulation as a Key Factor for Implementation of Solutions for Safety in Pediatrics

One of the most effective methodologies for evaluating the complexity, developing technical and nontechnical skills, and testing a system change is simulation. Pediatrics is among the disciplines that benefits most from the introduction of simulation, the health personnel who take care of the health of children have the possibility of exercising and improving their skills, without risk and without the emotional stress of damaging their little patients [25]. This is an extraordinary context to experiment new solutions for safer care.

The pediatric patient has unique characteristics, both from a physiopathological and psychobehavioral point of view. "The child is not a small adult" and this assumption also applies to simulation. The pathology of the critically ill pediatric patient is often a rare but high-risk pathology. This involves the use of medical devices and supplies specific for the child, with calibers and dosages that vary with the weight and age of the patient. All this adds complexity and risks to an already complex situation.

However, the simulation is an added value not only for training on technical skills. It is now clear that many errors in the medical field are consequent to problems related to the organization and not to the inexperience of the professionals or to negligence or incorrect individual conduct. Research has also shown that through the development of a process-centered model in the health system, it is possible to reduce adverse events and improve the quality and safety of care. Since 2000, the Institute of Medicine [26] mentions simulation as a key strategy for improving patient safety.

It is also important to mention that in order to apply solutions for improving quality and safety of health in an effective way, the simulation is a key element. Especially simulation on site had a significant diffusion in relation to this purpose. In fact simulation on site is less expensive and can be performed in the everday working environment, so that a major number of healthcare operators can participate and experience the advantage of testing a solution. With the application of a structured debriefing, it is possible to evaluate the positive and negative aspects of the designed solution and tailor it for a better compliance to the specific setting.

The use of simulation offers undoubtable advantages, among the most relevant are:

- Eliminates all the problems related to fear, embarrassment, possible legal implications that can arise during a real event.
- Allows, once the causes of an adverse event or near-miss has been identified, to define corrective measures which, if applied in a subsequent planned simulation, offer the possibility of verifying their feasibility and effectiveness in the field.
- Allows to evaluate the clinical risk of processes that in reality are only exceptionally implemented, but which can be tested several times as part of a simulation project.
- In addition to the ethical and moral implications of providing the highest quality in care, there are important financial reasons for introducing simulation more frequently within health systems. Whereas it is now clear that adverse events significantly increase the cost of treatments. It is likely that decision makers will be more receptive in incorporating the simulation within healthcare organizations, if the value of this training, also in terms of return on investments, can be demonstrated tangibly.

In the next paragraph we present a clinical case, based on a true reported event, that is also used, in a large network of healthcare trusts for training by simulation pediatricians in the emergency area (Simpnet—Tuscany regional network for pediatric simulation).

21.2.2 Clinical Case: Safe Care in Pediatric Emergency

21.2.2.1 9.15 pm

Anna arrives in PS, transported by an ambulance with a doctor on board, Anna is a 3-year-old patient with perinatal suffering quadriparesis. Anna has been suffering from high fever gastroenteritis for the last 2 days. In the past 12 h, she has had numerous episodes of vomiting and diarrhea. For the last 4 h, she has been more sleepy and less interactive with her mother, who worried and called the emergency service, when after the last episode of vomiting, the daughter did not respond to verbal stimuli.

These are the vital signs recorded during ambulance transportation:

- RF 36/min
- satO$_2$ not detectable due to the presence of peripheral vasoconstriction
- CF 150/min
- T 37.6 °C
- AP 72–41

When the ambulance arrives at the ER, Anna is transferred directly to the red code room (resuscitation room). Giulia, the triage nurse, asks the mother to stay at the triage with her for collecting the personal and clinical data of the patient. The door of the red code room closes and Anna's mom will never enter that room during the resuscitation phases. She will wait sitting on a chair just outside the door of the red code room.

Critical Issues
International literature and guidelines agree in making the family members of pediatric patients to assist to the resuscitation phases, if they wish, and in any case to encourage their presence. This presence should not be perceived as invasive for the resuscitation team. Evidences show that the parents' presence benefits the child and allows the family members to have a realistic view of the resuscitation attempts and of the expertise of the operators. In addition, it helps the parents in

developing greater adaptability if the patient dies and in experiencing a better mourning process.

21.2.2.2   9.18 pm
In the room there are:

- Mario—Pediatrician with 6-year experience in the ER
- Sara—Pediatrician with a temporary contract for 3 months in the ER
- Lucia—Expert nurse in the ER
- Claudio—nurse transferred to the ER for 6 months from a geriatric ward
- Paolo—doctor working at the emergency territorial service
- Cesare—volunteer of the emergency territorial service

Mario asks Sara to get Anna's vital signs and talks to Paolo, (a doctor from the emergency territorial service), about the patient and her assessments. Paolo reports that he was unable to take any vascular access. He admits that he has no experience with pediatric patients and that in any case the patient was very vasoconstricted with cold ends and that was the reason why they were unable to achieve O_2 saturation and that the HR was elevated 150 min despite a feverish temperature of 37.6 °C. Paolo repeatedly apologizes for not having taken venous access, Mario listens absently to Paolo's indications on the patient and to his apologies, he is distracted by the appearance of the parameters on the monitor and by the difficulty in finding a saturation value.

Paolo knows he often faces difficulties with pediatric patients and this leads to further stress in their management.

Critical Issues
In this unstructured handover, Paolo forgets to report that he had performed a glycemic stick (42 mg/dl) which is also reported on the form filled up in the ambulance and left at the access to ER. At the triage, Giulia has inserted the patient into the waiting list through the ER software and she doesn't notice the filled format on the coun-

ter. A structured handover, even in an emergency situation, can make a difference, especially in those situations where the team is aware of conditions that can generate stress, as in the case of Paolo that is unfamiliar with pediatric patients. The fact that Mario is distracted by the work of nurses in taking the parameters does not facilitate communication in such an important situation.

21.2.2.3   9.20 pm
The nurse Claudio began to place the electrodes on Anna's chest, and the oximeter probe on the index finger of the right hand.

- HR is 78 min down
- RR 16 min with gasping
- $satO_2$ not detectable due to the presence of peripheral vasoconstriction
- T 37.4 °C
- BP 52–31 after some measurement attempts

Mario asked Sara to begin clinical evaluations and Lucia to take venous access.

21.2.2.4   9.24 pm
Paolo and Cesare have left the room and are preparing to go to the ambulance for another territorial service.

Anna does not even respond by now to the painful stimulus of venous access attempts.

In fact, in the meantime, Lucia has not been able to take the venous access, she has already been trying for 4 min, on the patient's skin there are already signs of Paolo's ambulance attempts. Lucia knows she is very good at finding venous access in critically ill pediatric patients and does not accept failing in this case. She has lost track of time.

Sara has difficulty finding a peripheral pulse and assessing the patient's breathing. Mario sees Lucia's difficulties and begins to seek access to the veins of the hand.

The Claudio went to get a new oximeter probe.

HR has fallen below 60 min, a frequency that is now insufficient to maintain an effective cardiac output.

Critical Issues

Anna's conditions because quickly compromised, but at the moment there is no real leadership, there is not an Event Manager who manages the situation. There is no explicit distribution of roles. Everyone is engaged in specific activities and even Mario, who initially seemed to assign the tasks, is busy with venous access. All the team is victim of an error of fixation: Mario and Lucia on the venous access, Claudio on the oximeter probe that seems not to work for evaluating the peripheral vasoconstriction, Sara in the search for the pulse and evaluation of the breathing in a clinical situation of imminent cardiac arrest. The perception of time and the possibility of a plan B regarding venous access are also lacking. International guidelines show that in the critical child, if it is not possible to find venous access within 1 min, it is a priority to insert an intraosseous device.

21.2.2.5   9.27 pm

- HR is 38 min down
- RR 6 min with gasping
- satO$_2$ undetectable
- BP undetectable

Claudio in attempts to have a parameter of saturation is repeatedly looking at the monitor and he noticed that the HR has dropped to 44 min and communicates it to the team in a generic way:

– "The heart rate is 44 min." Mario and Lucia are concentrated on the vascular access attempts and do not notice the communication, which is received by Sara. Sara, however, cannot understand if Mario's lack of response to this critical information is because he is distracted, but she does not stress the message because at that moment he has managed to cannulate a peripheral vein and they can start with taking the exams and starting a bolus of physiological solution at 20 ml/kg. They don't know the weight, Claudio looks out of the door to ask the mother.

"11 kg, but how's Anna doing? What's up?"—but the door has already closed the door.

Sara finally manages to attract Mario's attention with this sentence:

– "I don't feel the pulse, the heart rate is 34 on the monitor, she has gasping, we start cardiopulmonary resuscitation and we are calling the anesthesiologists to help us and intubate the patient."

21.2.2.6   9.32 pm

Beginning of CPR and contact the anesthesiologists.

As there is no real leadership, or an Event Manager who manages the patient with a 360° view, communication skills has not been effective. The message is not addressed to a specific person. There was no feedback, no closing of the circle. Claudio's message on bradycardia did not reach Mario, the expert doctor and Sara, who got the message, does not want to interrupt Mario who is managing to cannulate a peripheral vein. Only later she kept Mario's attention by summarizing the clinical situation and proposing fundamental actions.

21.2.2.7   9:34 pm

CPR was on for 2 min when Martina, the anesthesiologist, and Giorgio, the nurse, arrive from the Intensive care.

She is informed that the patient is under cardiac arrest and that they have been massaging and ventilating her for about 2 min.

Martina wants them to stop for 10 s to do a reassessment.

HR is 12 min electric activity without a pulse. RR, satO$_2$, PA not detectable.

Martina decides to intubate the patient and gets help from Giorgio and asks Claudio.

"Meanwhile, get ready the adrenaline, 1 mg."

Claudio has some doubts about this drug, but prepares a 2.5 cc syringe with 1 ml of undiluted Adrenaline 1:1000, as he used to do in the geriatric ward, where he previously worked. Martina is on the third unsuccessful intubation attempt, and when she sees the syringe with undiluted adrenaline she is upset lashing out her frustration for the failed intubation on Claudio.

"it is not possible! In pediatric arrest you always have to dilute 1 to 10,000, always!!!" She takes the syringe and throws it in a corner of the room.

Critical Issues

Martina's request for adrenaline dosage is incorrect. Under the pressure of the moment she got confused between mg and ml, asking a dose ten times higher than that required by guidelines. Besides the exchange related to the dosage, the rest of the communication on adrenaline was also incorrect, the dilution, the preparation method and Claudio's failure to explain the preparation explicitly led to a further waste of time. This technical error is frequent in pediatrics and numerous studies show that patients in this age group are exposed three times more than adults to potentially harmful therapeutic errors. In infants or low-weight patients, for example, there is a high risk of error: a minimal difference in the dosage of an additional drug can produce lethal effects since the low body mass and the immaturity of the organs cannot buffer the overdose. Martina's irritation related to the difficulties of intubation and the altered tone towards Claudio, definitively compromised a good team collaboration.

Luisa re-prepares the diluted adrenaline, but realizes that at the site of the cannulation of the vein there was an extravasation of Synovial Fluid and the vein is irrecoverable. She tells Mario that is massaging the patient, he tries to see if the Synovial rilli sis really leaking, but this worsens the quality of the massage.

Martina listens to the conversation and decides for an intraosseous access and sends Giorgio to take the drill in the intensive care unit. The same intraosseous is present in the ER, but at this point Sara and Claudio, who know about that, don't want to contradict Martina. Mario thinks that in the intensive care unit there could be a more advanced technological device to do this procedure, but does not have the courage to ask for it.

Critical Issues

The tense atmosphere within the team again leads to unshared choices, and the lack of information (the presence of the ER intraosseous drill)

with the consequent further loss of time and resources (Giorgio leaves the room to go to intensive care unit). ER and intensive care unit teams were taking care of the same patient without speaking enough and without sharing priorities.

Anna is in asystole.

After about 40 minutes CPR without ever resuming a pulse compatible rhythm, Martina declares Anna's death. And now someone has to open that door to communicate it to the mother.

21.2.2.8 Final Considerations

Pediatrics is one of the most challenging areas in patient safety. There is a need for basic and advanced research and for a rigorous application of the evidence-based solutions already tested and validated in pediatric settings. The application of these solutions remains a challenging issue. The clinical case we presented and the previous evidences discussed in the chapter underlines the importance of understanding the context as a key factor for safety, and especially for safety in pediatrics. The importance of understanding context has been highlighted by research underlining that proven safety solutions can be less effective in settings different from the ones they were developed and firstly applied in [27]. This opens a large debate about the effectiveness of the proposed interventions but also on the capability of the new contexts, in terms of organizational, cultural, and economic resources, to apply that solution [ibidem]. In this scenario we believe that quality improvement methodology together with the human factor approach can provide fundamental insight for the transferability and success of the application of the patient safety solutions in different contexts and especially in pediatrics. Among the key elements responsible for the comprehension and the enabling of the context are:

- Patient and family engagement, which has been identified as a priority in the WHO patient safety Declaration during WHA 2019 [28] and is one of the most important elements for setting up agendas at all levels for promoting patient safety.
- Leadership and culture which are the engines for fostering patient safety as a strategic asset

of healthcare organizations, usually more developed and advanced in pediatrics.

- Governance, which is the basic framework in which developing patient safety actions.
- Teamwork and education, which are the infrastructure for creating new generations of clinicians able to provide care having in mind safety as a priority for our kids.

References

1. Walsh KE, Bundy DG, Landrigan CP. Preventing health care–associated harm in children. JAMA. 2014;311(17):1731–2. https://doi.org/10.1001/jama.2014.2038.
2. Mueller BU, Daniel RN, Stucky Fisher ER, Council on Quality Improvement and Patient Safety, Committee on Hospital Care. Principles of pediatric patient safety: reducing harm due to medical care. Pediatrics. 2019;143(2):e20183649. https://doi.org/10.1542/peds.2018-3649.
3. The WHO's Global Patient Safety Challenge: Medication without harm. May 2017. WHO/HIS/SDS/2017.
4. Santell JP, Hicks R. Medication errors involving pediatric patients. Jt Comm J Qual Patient Saf. 2005;31(6):348–53.
5. Kaushal R, Bates DW, Landrigan C, et al. Medication errors and adverse drug events in pediatric inpatients. JAMA. 2001;285(16):2114–20.
6. Matlow AG, Baker GR, Flintoft V, et al. Adverse events among children in Canadian hospitals: the Canadian Paediatric Adverse Events Study. CMAJ. 2012;184(13):E709–E7181.
7. Khan A, Furtak SL, Melvin P, Rogers JE, Schuster MA, Landrigan CP. Parent reported errors and adverse events in hospitalized children. JAMA Pediatr. 2016;170(4):e154608.
8. Mohr Julie J, Carole ML, Thoma Kathleen A, Woods D, et al. Learning from errors in ambulatory pediatrics. In: Henriksen K, Battles JB, Marks ES, et al., editors. Advances in patient safety: from research to implementation, Research findings, vol. 1. Agency for Healthcare Research and Quality: Rockville, MD; 2005.
9. Stang A. Safe care for pediatric patients: a coping review across multiple health care settings. Clin Pediatr. 2018;57(1):62–7.
10. Reason J. Human error. 1st ed. Cambridge: Cambridge University Press; 1990.
11. Barach P, Small SD. Reporting and preventing medical mishaps: lessons from non-medical near miss reporting systems. BMJ. 2000;320:759–63.
12. Woods D, Thomas E, Holl J, Altman S, Brennan T. Adverse events and preventable adverse events in children. Pediatrics. 2005;115(1):155–60.
13. Thomas EJ, Brennan TA. Errors and adverse events in medicine: an overview. In: Vincent CA, editor. Clinical risk management. Enhancing patient safety. London: BMJ Publications; 2001.
14. Carayon P, Schoofs Hundt A, Karsh B, et al. Work system design for patient safety: the SEIPS model. BMJ Qual Saf. 2006;15:i50–8.
15. Seymour NE, Gallagher AG, Roman SA, O'Brien MK, Bansal VK, Andersen DK, et al. Virtual reality training improves operating room performance: results of a randomized, double-blinded study. Ann Surg. 2002;236(4):458–63.
16. Sarker SK, Chang A, Vincent C, Darzi AW. Surgical technical errors in performing open & laparoscopic surgery. Br J Surg. 2004;91:s78.
17. Sarker SK. Courses, counsellors & cadavers: reducing errors in the operating theatre. BMJ. 2003;327:s10.
18. Hadjianastassiou VG, Tekkis PP, Poloniecki JD, Gavalas MC, Goldhill DR. Surgical mortality score: risk management tool for auditing surgical performance. World J Surg. 2004;28(2):193–200.
19. Birkmeyer JD, Siewers AE, Finlayson EVA, Stukel TA, Lucas FL, Batista I, et al. Hospital volume and surgical mortality in the United States. N Engl J Med. 2002;346:1128–37.
20. Begg CB, Riedel ER, Bach PB, Kattan MW, Schrag D, Warren JL, et al. Variations in morbidity after radical prostatectomy. N Engl J Med. 2002;346:1138–44.
21. World Health Organization. Patient safety curriculum guide. Available from: http://www.who.int/patientsafety/education/curriculum/tools-download/en/.
22. Rasmussen J. Skills, rules, knowledge: signals, signs and symbols and other distinctions in human performance models. IEEE Trans Syst, Man, Cybern, SMC-13. 1983. p. 257–67.
23. Fitzsimons J, Vaughan D. Top 10 interventions in paediatric patient safety. Curr Treat Options Peds. 2015;1:275–85. https://doi.org/10.1007/s40746-015-0035-3.
24. Shekelle PG, Wachter RM, Pronovost PJ, et al. Making health care safer II: an updated critical analysis of the evidence for patient safety practices. Evid Rep Technol Assess. 2013;211:1–945.
25. Mirza A, Winer J, Garber M, Makker K, Maraqa N. Primer in patient safety concepts: simulation case-based training for pediatric residents and fellows. MedEdPORTAL. 2018;14:10711. https://doi.org/10.15766/mep_2374-8265.10711.
26. Institute of Medicine (US) Committee on Quality of Health Care in America. In: Kohn LT, Corrigan JM, Donaldson MS, editors. To err is human: building a safer health system. Washington, DC: National Academies Press; 2000.
27. Dixon-Woods M, Leslie M, Tarrant C, Bion J. Explaining Matching Michigan: an ethnographic study of a patient safety program. Implement Sci. 2013;8:70.
28. Patient safety resolution, Global action on patient safety. Reported by General Director, Seventy-Second World Health Assembly A72/26, 25 Mar 2019. http://apps.who.int/gb/ebwha/pdf_files/WHA72/A72_26-en.pdf. Accessed 04 Jan 2020.

Patient Safety in Radiology

22

Mahdieh Montazeran, Davide Caramella, and Mansoor Fatehi

Learning Objectives
- Recognize the importance of multidimensional patient safety issues in radiology.
- Discuss the level of awareness of radiation protection in the different categories of health care workers and among patients.
- Explain MRI hazards and identify their preventive approaches.
- Analyse the clinical use and adverse effects of contrast media and the management of contrast agent-related risks.

22.1 Introduction

Medical imaging (in short radiology) includes diagnostic and interventional procedures and has an essential role in the diagnosis and treatment of diseases. The objective in this field of medicine is focused on providing diagnostic and therapeutic benefit to the patients along with protecting them from the possible hazards associated with the procedures. By continuously upgrading imaging technologies and improving imaging modalities, such as ultrasonography, X-ray-based imaging (radiography, fluoroscopy, and computed tomography), magnetic resonance imaging (MRI), and interventional radiology, safety has become more and more crucial. The potential hazards in radiology for the patients and the staff are multidimensional:

- some possible errors could take place during handling the patients, acquisition of imaging, or image reporting that could be harmful to the patients. The examples of these errors include the wrong patient, site, or side during image acquisition, diagnostic errors of perception or interpretation of imaging, and transcription errors in radiology reports [1, 2]
- the potential hazards and side effects of unique aspects of medical imaging such as ionizing radiation, the strong magnetic field of MRI, and the contrast agents are critical issues in radiology safety.
- considering the ubiquitary diffusion of information technology in medical imaging, cybersecurity strategies are becoming necessary to avoid incidents that could threaten patient safety [3].

In radiology, like the other medical fields, new approaches to patient safety are needed: a patient-

M. Montazeran
Shahid Sadoughi University of Medical Sciences, Yazd, Iran

Hôpital Nord Franche-Comté, Belfort, France

D. Caramella (✉)
University of Pisa, Pisa, Italy
e-mail: davide.caramella@unipi.it

M. Fatehi
Chief of Imaging Informatics, Virtual University of Medical Sciences, Tehran, Iran

© The Author(s) 2021
L. Donaldson et al. (eds.), *Textbook of Patient Safety and Clinical Risk Management*,
https://doi.org/10.1007/978-3-030-59403-9_22

centered approach and a high-tolerance system vis-a-vis the errors rather than eliminating them by individual blaming [1]. Team working and continuous training about radiology hazards and their prevention are essential for all radiology professionals, to improve the system quality and to provide radiology safety for the patients and the staff [4].

In this chapter, we will discuss the main radiology safety aspects: radiation protection, MRI hazards, and contrast agent-related risks.

22.2   Radiation Protection

"Radiation protection" includes all measures useful to ensure the protection of man and the environment against the hazards of ionizing radiation. In medical imaging, X-ray-based modalities, especially computed tomography (CT), are the main area of concern for radiation exposure and its biological effects [5]. Indeed, radiation from imaging procedures comprises a significant amount of exposure to the general population.

Radiation effects can be classified as follows: (1) somatic effect (appears in the person exposed) and genetic effect (emerges in the offspring); (2) deterministic effect (with a radiation threshold level, such as burning) and stochastic effect (without a radiation threshold level). Stochastic effects are the most significant matter of concern of radiation exposure in radiology [5]. These effects can arise from exposure to low-level ionizing radiation which is responsible for long-term disease induction (both cancer and non-oncological diseases). The linear no-threshold model states that any exposure to ionizing radiation, however small, has the potential to cause harm [6].

Several papers have shown a small but significant increase of cancer risk in children and young patients with previous exposure to CT scans [7] paralleled by a measurable increase in radiation-induced DNA damage following several radiologic examinations [8].

The European Commission issued guidelines on radiation protection education and training of medical professionals in the European Union that recommend [9]:

- a course on radiation protection should be included in the basic curriculum of medical and dental schools
- continuing education and training after qualification should be provided, and, in the special case of the clinical use of new techniques, training should be provided on these techniques and the relevant radiation protection requirements
- knowledge of the advantages and disadvantages of the use of ionising radiation in medicine, including basic information about radioactive waste and its safe management, should be part of radiation protection education and training for medical students.

However, several studies have reported an alarming lack of knowledge among health professionals about radiation protection issues and radiation doses of commonly performed imaging procedures [10–12]. For example, the overall radiation doses associated with various imaging modalities are underestimated by a substantial number of professionals, and in some cases, professionals are unable to correctly differentiate between ionizing and nonionizing radiation-based imaging techniques [13]. Furthermore, patients' knowledge of the risk associated with radiation exposure is generally low. They should be better informed concerning the dose and the potential risk of medical radiation [14]. The referring physicians, as well as radiologists, have the responsibility to communicate dose information to patients in an easily understandable and useful way.

The European Directive BSS 59/13 is an essential document in this field, which has forcefully restated the importance that all stakeholders are informed and committed to the reduction of unnecessary exposure of patients during imaging procedures [15]. Article 57, which deals with the responsibilities, explains the requirements to optimize the radiation dose and to provide information to patients. It is emphasized that the professionals have to provide adequate information to the patient or his/her representative, and have to ensure that he/she is aware of the benefit and the risk of radiation based procedures [15].

The radiographers play a vital role as the last gatekeeper in the radiation protection chain. To do so radiographers should [13, 15]:

- be provided with intensive education programs on typical doses for each type of examination, risk/benefit analysis and biological effects of radiation
- attend obligatory radiation safety courses during their undergraduate studies, as well as postgraduate radiation protection and radiation safety training
- attend updating courses about new technologies and devices which can limit radiation dose without compromising image quality
- be familiar with software which allows radiation dose monitoring of the procedures carried out in the daily activity (DMS: Dose Management System)
- participate in projects of radiological procedures benchmarking
- be included in multidisciplinary teams to set up and periodically review diagnostic reference levels both for adult and paediatric patients.

A poorly informed radiographer can put the patient at a higher risk by not optimizing the pertinent imaging parameters. For instance, during CT imaging, it is crucial to select the correct tube voltage and current rotation time, depending on patient age and diagnostic query. Further to this, the use of automated tube current modulation and correct patient centering on the CT table have proved useful in lowering radiation dose while preserving diagnostic image quality. The localizer radiograph shows a significant influence on radiation exposure but with different outcomes depending on the manufacturer of the CT scanner [16].

Radiologists and radiographers should have a thorough understanding of these differences to assure patients the best examination in terms of a correct trade-off between radiation dose and image quality. Moreover, particular attention should be given to ensure that radiation dose variability is minimized in patients undergoing repeat CT examination [17]. Because of the strict correlation between image noise and radiation exposure, the iterative reconstruction approach has the potential to be employed with data acquired at lower radiation doses while preserving clinical information [18].

All this highlights the importance of education and awareness of the operators. The lack of awareness represents a small risk for individual patients; however, the danger becomes significant when considered at a population level. Un-awareness may depend on [13, 19]:

- lack of proper preparation during university courses
- inadequate training for staff already in employment, and lack of interest, especially of the senior staff
- growth of technological complexity, which requires a continuous update of the knowledge of the radiological staff
- lack of accountability, i.e. dose performances are seldom evaluated.

Comprehensive and well-coordinated actions must be set up to increase awareness of radiation risks and to promote education and knowledge in radiation protection. This is why information campaigns such as Image Gently®, Image Wisely®, and the more recent Eurosafe Imaging campaign have paid specific attention to the fundamental role of staff training in radiation protection, emphasizing the role of effective multi-professional cooperation [20].

22.3 Magnetic Resonance Imaging (MRI) Hazards

Magnetic resonance imaging (MRI), as a nonionizing radiation modality, poses unique hazards to the patients and the staff. These hazards are mainly related to the static magnetic field (SMF), the gradient magnetic field (GMF), and the radiofrequency (RF) field. The interaction between these three components and human body tissues, as well as ferromagnetic objects/devices, presents the more relevant safety concerns. Other MRI safety issues include: gadolinium-based contrast media, cryogen-related issues, metallic implants, pregnancy, and paediatric examinations.

The following paragraphs will briefly explain the hazards and safety issues of MRI in further detail.

22.3.1 Static Magnetic Fields (SMF)

Biological effects on the human body: The SMF strength used in clinical applications is typically between 0.2 and 3.0 T; however, the clinical utilization of 7 T MRI is increasing. Magnet strengths as high as 17.5 T are currently being used in research [21]. There is no evidence indicative of significant or permanent biological effects of the SMF on the human body [22]. However, patients within a strong magnetic field (7 T or above) can undergo transient symptoms including nausea, vertigo, tinnitus, hearing loss, nystagmus, motion disturbances, dizziness, and a metallic taste [23]. For certain occupations, such as a surgeon, during an operation within an open MRI device, the occurrence of these acute symptoms may present a safety threat for patients [24]. Simultaneous exposure to SMF and low-frequency movement-induced time-varying magnetic fields from a 7 T MRI can result in neurocognitive effects such as reduced verbal memory and visual acuity [25]. There is no consensus in the scientific literature regarding the ability of SMF to damage DNA, to be carcinogenic, or to have other biological effects [21, 26].

Translational force and torque on ferromagnetic objects: Torque (twisting force) and translational magnetic force (the force that causes a magnetic object to move toward a magnet) are the results of the interaction between the SMF and ferromagnetic objects, which are proportional to the strength and spatial gradient of the magnetic field (MF), respectively [22]. Objects which may be affected by these forces include implanted medical devices—such as surgical sutures, stents, clips, prostheses, and cardiac pacemakers—and unintended metallic foreign bodies. These forces can dislodge the objects resulting in injury to the patient or may even be fatal if located in dangerous anatomic zones such as aneurysm clips [21, 27]. The compatibility of MRI with any implant and medical devices has to be evaluated before entering into the MRI environment. Therefore, it is necessary to perform accurate and thorough screening procedures for patients and other individuals to avoid all the MR non-safe objects entering the MR environment (see Sect. 22.3.4 below).

All patients who are suspected of having ferromagnetic foreign objects within their bodies must undergo further investigation. For example, in patients with a history of orbital trauma, orbital radiography is recommended to exclude possible intraocular metallic foreign body before MR examination [23, 28].

Projectile injury: The projectile or missile effect is a dangerous event caused by the attraction of ferromagnetic objects (external to the patient) by the SMF. Accelerated movements of medical support equipment such as oxygen tanks, cylinders filled with anesthetic gas, intravenous stands, beds, and chairs towards the magnetic bore can cause patient injury and damage to the hardware [22, 27]. To prevent projectile injuries, all patients and non-MR personnel must pass device and object screening before entering the MR environment [28]. There should be restrictions into the MR zone in order to preserve a safe environment. Hence, the accessibility of the MR site is classified into four zones according to the potential risk of danger: zone I (freely accessible to the public), zone II (the interface between zone I and the strictly controlled zones), zone III (in which free access by unscreened non-MR personnel or ferromagnetic objects can result in serious injury), and zone IV (MR unit magnet room: the presence of the individuals in this zone is subject to direct visual observation of MR imaging personnel) [28].

22.3.2 Gradient Magnetic Fields (GMF)

Nerve and muscle stimulation: The fast-switching gradient magnetic coils used within the MR unit produce spatial information [21]. The time-varying (gradient) magnetic field induces tiny currents in the peripheral nerve cells and muscle fibers resulting in a sensation of tingling or pain. The U.S. Food and Drug Administration (FDA) does not provide a specific number for dB/dt to avoid peripheral neurostimulation and only requires to operate below levels that may result in adverse effects [27]. Another potential side effect of GMF is magneto-phosphenes, the perceived flashing sensation in the eye, due to stimulation of the retina/optic nerve. Current MR systems operate below the threshold for cardiac stimulation or ventricular fibrillation [22]. GMF may also induce electronic currents in conductive materials which may be hazardous for patients with electronically active devices like cardiac pacemakers or neurostimulators that can undergo temporary or permanent malfunctioning [29].

Acoustic noise: Due to the rapidly switching currents in the coils, another effect of GMF is the production of acoustic noise. Hearing protection devices should be provided for all patients during MR examinations with noise pressure exceeding 99 dB to avoid acoustic injuries [28].

22.3.3 Radiofrequency (RF) Magnetic Field

Thermal injury and burns: The RF coil produces the RF magnetic field (in the order of µT), which excites nuclear magnetization inside the body and receives nuclear MR signal which is used to form the images [21]. The absorbed RF energy by the human body may result in whole-body or localized tissue heating. Heat stress and heat exhaustion might be produced due to excessive body heating, and in certain conditions, localized RF burns may occur because of intense heat transmission. The level of RF energy deposited into body tissues can be quantified by the Specific Absorption Rate (SAR, W/kg) and Specific Energy Dose (SAD, J/kg). SAD can be calculated by multiplying the SAR with the duration of exposure to the RF power [23]. Patients who have the highest risk of experiencing dangerous levels of whole-body heating include those with thermoregulatory dysfunctions such as obesity, diabetes, old age, and those unable to sense or communicate an increase in temperature [21, 23]. Therefore, it is essential to maintain the core body temperature below 40°C, and it must not increase more than 1°C to ensure patient safety [30]. The FDA recommends that the maximum level of SAR for individuals with normal thermoregulatory function should be: 4 W/kg for the whole body over 15 min, 3 W/kg to the head, and 8 W/kg for any 1 cm^3 of tissue (e.g., in the extremities) over 5 min [22]. Recent data proposed that the SAD should be below 4 kJ/kg to prevent an excessive core temperature rise of 1.3°C, which is the updated threshold limit [30]. The other safety points are to keep the temperature in the MRI system below 22°C, to avoid the use of blankets, to consider active cooling, and to provide rest (cooling-off) periods for patients in the case of higher SAD or prolonged MR examinations [23, 30].

The RF magnetic field induces the current in conducting objects, primarily those with an elongated shape or those with a loop of a specific diameter. This interaction between the RF field and conducting objects can produce excessive heat, which may lead to thermal injuries or burns of adjacent tissue [30]. Hence, conductive objects such as implants, medical devices, wires, leads, sensors, and jewelry, can be problematic. Another important recommendation is to remove all clothing of the patients and to use MR-safe clothing during the MR examination [23]. Moreover, it is recommended to use cold compresses or ice packs in areas at high risk of burning, for example, where leads are placed on the skin or extensively tattooed areas [28]. Localized burns can also potentially be caused by conductive loops resulting in excessive energy deposition due to skin-to-skin contact, for example, thigh-to-thigh contact. In order to prevent these kinds of injuries, thermal insulation should be placed in areas with risk of skin-to-skin contact. Finally, it is mandatory to use insulation pads between the patient and the RF coils to reduce the risk of burns [27].

22.3.4 Implants and Devices

Potentially relevant MR safety hazards can occur as the result of magnetic field-induced movement and dislodgment of ferromagnetic objects, induction of electrical currents, excessive heat production, and misinterpretation due to imaging artifact [30]. Moreover, the MR electromagnetic field may interfere with the regular operation of electronically active devices such as cardiac pacemakers, implantable cardioverter-defibrillators, neurostimulators, implanted medication pumps, and cochlear implants. Non-clinical testing is required for all medical implants and devices to determine their safety in the MR environment [30]. Three types of labeling—typically provided by the device manufacturer—apply for the implants/devices according to either the scientifically based rationale or device testing data: MR safe (no known hazards), MR non-safe, and MR conditional [31]. MR conditional devices are objects that are tested and considered safe only under specific MR conditions. Information on these conditions, including maximum SMF, maximum spatial magnetic field gradient (dB/dx), and the maximum whole-body averaged SAR, are provided by the device manufacturer [30, 32].

Effective screening to identify possible implants/devices within the patients is necessary before the MR examination to preserve a safe MR environment. In the patient with implants/devices, it is essential to obtain the MR safety information of the implant/devices to document its compatibility with the MR environment [29].

With the development of new technologies and devices, adherence to continuously updated guidelines is crucial. Fortunately, large databases exist that provide updated safety ratings and recommendations for medical devices, and manufacturers publish MR safety information on their websites [33, 34].

22.4 Contrast Agent-Related Risks

Contrast agents (CA) are frequently employed to improve radiology diagnostic capacity in certain indications. Although these agents generally considered safe, they can cause some adverse effects ranging from minor reactions to severe life-threatening events [35]. These agents include:

- Iodinated contrast agents for X-ray-based studies (radiography, fluoroscopy, CT).
- Gadolinium-based contrast agents (GBCA) for MRI.
- Microbubbles for ultrasonography.

The side effects of CA consist of acute adverse events, injection site problems such as CA extravasation, or the adverse effects related to a specific group of CA such as nephrotoxicity, thyrotoxicity, and systemic nephrogenic fibrosis. The general considerations and precautions related to the contrast-enhanced examinations to provide patient safety are summarized as follows.

22.4.1 Patient Selection

The best prevention of CA adverse effects is to avoid applying them. The referring physicians and the radiologists should always consider the risk-to-benefit of applying CA for the patients, assure about the real indication, and consider the possible better alternative diagnostic imaging without CA [35].

22.4.2 Identify the Risk Factors and Contraindications

It is necessary to obtain the medical and drug history of the patients before performing a contrast-enhanced examination. One example is the history of prior allergic-like reactions to CA, asthma, or allergies that could increase the risk of allergic-like contrast reactions and if necessary premedication should be prescribed with corticosteroids or changing the CA within the same CA group. Another example is the history of renal diseases: in these patients creatinine level should be obtained before administration of iodinated CA or GBCA. Drug history of using metformin (hypoglycemic agent) should be considered before the administration of iodinated

CA and in case of reduction of renal function temporary discontinuation of metformin is recommended.

22.4.3 Safe Injection of Contrast Agents

The injection of CA either by hand or by power injector can cause complications following contrast extravasation or air embolism. The health care professional performing the injection has to evaluate intravenous access, verify the catheter size, monitor the flow rate of injection, and adjust the power injector carefully for preventing the potential adverse events [35, 36].

22.4.4 Allergy-Like and Chemotoxic Reactions

These adverse reactions can occur following intravascular administration of any group of CA, specially iodinated CA and GBCA [35]. Most of these reactions are acute and occur in the first hour after contrast administration (many in the first 5 min), but in rare cases, there are delayed reactions after injection of iodinated CA [36].

The acute adverse events can be chemotoxic or allergy-like (idiosyncratic) reactions. They are classified into three severity categories: mild, moderate, and severe. Most of the acute adverse reactions are mild, but severe life-threatening reactions can rarely occur. Chemotoxic reactions are related to molecular and chemical characteristics and are frequently dose and concentration related. Vasovagal reactions and cardiovascular effects (especially in patients with underlying cardiac disease) and symptoms of warmth, metallic taste, and nausea/vomiting are examples of chemotoxic reactions [36]. Allergy-like reactions are independent of dose. The symptoms can include urticaria, pruritus, cutaneous edema, or rare anaphylactic reaction. The most important risk factor for an acute adverse reaction to CA is a previous reaction, and a prophylactic corticosteroid injection is indicated. A history of asthma and atopy can result in a mildly increased risk of acute adverse reactions [35]. The other risk fac-

tors include more massive doses, increased rate of administration, the use of higher osmolar nonionic CA, and intra-arterial (vs. intravenous) administration [37]. The properties of GBCA that increase the risk of acute allergic reactions are ionicity, protein binding, and having a macrocyclic structure [38].

The considerations required for ensuring the minimal contrast-related acute adverse events and their proper management are:

- providing enough education and training of the health professionals involved in CA side effects, their risk factors, and treatment
- screening the patients for detecting possible risk factors
- using nonionic CA whenever possible
- considering premedication in high-risk patients
- ensuring the availability of emergency and resuscitation equipment
- monitoring the patients and providing accessible communication between them and the radiology staff before, during, and after the injection [37, 39].

22.4.5 Adverse Events Related to Iodinated Contrast Agents

Nephrotoxicity: Iodinated contrast agents (ICA) can cause acute kidney injury or worsen pre-existing chronic kidney disease [40]. This effect is known as contrast-induced nephropathy (CIN). However, post-contrast acute kidney injury (PC-AKI) is a general term and describes any sudden deterioration in renal function within 48 h following the intravascular administration of iodinated contrast, regardless of the cause [35]. The pathophysiology of CIN is not precisely understood [40].

The critical risk factor is pre-existing severe renal insufficiency (eGFR <30 ml/min for intravenous, eGFR <30–45 ml/min for intra-arterial injection). Other risk factors include age >70 years, dehydration, diabetes mellitus, hypertension requiring medical therapy, nephrotoxic medication, and metformin or metformin-containing drug combinations [39, 40]. ICA with high osmolality, high viscosity, large doses, and multiple contrast injections within 48–72 h entail further risk [40].

- Follow the recommendations to prevent ICA-related nephrotoxicity [35, 39, 40].
- A baseline serum creatinine should be available or obtained before the injection of contrast medium in all patients considered at risk for CIN.
- Alternative imaging without using ICA (if possible) should be applied in high-risk patients.
- Volume, osmolality, and viscosity of the ICM should be as low as possible if the injection of ICA is necessary.
- Nephrotoxic treatments should be discontinued.
- Hydration before the injection of ICA in high-risk patients is extremely important.
- The use of antioxidants, such as statins or *N*-acetylcysteine, may be useful.

Thyrotoxicity: ICA can develop thyrotoxicosis in patients with a history of hyperthyroidism [35].

22.4.6 Adverse Events Related to Gadolinium-Based Contrast Agents (GBCA)

GBCA are MR contrast media. Different kinds of GBCA are available, with different chelate chemistry, viscosity, and osmolality. According to these properties, GBCA can be macrocyclic, linear, ionic, or nonionic [38]. In the following paragraphs, two main side effects of GBCA will be presented.

Nephrogenic systemic fibrosis (NSF): NSF is a rare and serious disease, related to the exposure of GBCA in patients with impaired renal function. It primarily involves the dermal/sub-dermal tissues but can also involve other organs such as lungs, heart, skeletal muscles, and esophagus. Most cases of NFS are reported in patients with severe chronic kidney disease (CKD4, eGFR

15–29 ml/min/1.73 m^2) and end-stage CKD (CKD5, eGFR <15 ml/min/1.73 m^2). Risk factors for developing NSF, include renal failure (acute or chronic), the pre-existing pro-inflammatory state of these patients, and type, dosage, and frequency of GCBA administration [41, 42]. The higher the dose of GBCA, either administered in a single dose or cumulative dose of multiple administrations, the higher is the risk of NFS [41].

The formulation of GBCA is an essential factor in developing NFS. Most reported cases of NFS are due to exposure to gadodiamide, gadopentetate dimeglumine, and gadoversetamide. The American College of Radiology Committee on drugs and contrast media, the European Medicines Agency, and the U.S. FDA have classified GBCA groups based on their risk for developing NFS [35, 42].

Therefore, low-risk GBCA and the lowest possible dose should be used in patients with renal insufficiency to prevent the development of NFS. For dialysis-dependent patients, a full 4-h dialysis session should be considered [35, 41, 42].

Tissue deposition of GBCA: GBCA can be deposited in some tissues, i.e., the brain, in patients with multiple exposures to GBCA. Linear GBCA are responsible for most reported cases of brain GBCA deposition, which can be seen as high T1 signal intensity in the dentate nucleus and globus pallidus. Although no neurological adverse effects of GBCA deposition have been reported, further evidence is needed before excluding any harmful consequence of such deposition [43].

22.5 Conclusion

Other aspects of patient safety in medical imaging, such as cybersecurity, radiology safety in children or pregnant women, and safety in interventional procedures are not addressed in this chapter. The aim of the chapter is to provide a basic coverage of the main safety concerns related to medical imaging that may be useful for further improving radiology as an enabling medical specialty [44].

References

1. Larson DB, Kruskal JB, Krecke KN, Donnelly LF. Key concepts of patient safety in radiology. Radiographics. 2015;35(6):1677–93.
2. Jabin SR, Schultz T, Hibbert P, Mandel C, Runciman W. Effectiveness of quality improvement interventions for patient safety in radiology: a systematic review protocol. JBI Database System Rev Implement Rep. 2016;14(9):65–78.
3. Ferrara A. Cybersecurity in medical imaging. Radiol Technol. 2019;90(6):563–75.
4. Abujudeh H, Kaewlai R, Shaqdan K, Bruno MA. Key principles in quality and safety in radiology. Am J Roentgenol. 2017;208(3):W101–9.
5. Kalra MK, Sodickson AD, Mayo-Smith WW. CT Radiation: Key Concepts for Gentle and Wise Use. Radiographics 2015;35(6):1706–21.
6. Hricak H, Brenner DJ, Adelstein SJ, Frush DP, Hall EJ, Howell RW, et al. Managing radiation use in medical imaging: a multifaceted challenge. Radiology. 2011;258(3):889–905.
7. Baysson H, Journy N, Roué T, Ducou-Lepointe H, Etard C, Bernier M-O. [Exposure to CT scans in childhood and long-term cancer risk: a review of epidemiological studies]. Bull Cancer. 2016;103(2):190–8.
8. Kuefner MA, Brand M, Engert C, Schwab SA, Uder M. Radiation induced DNA double-strand breaks in radiology. Rofo. 2015;187(10):872–8.
9. European Commission, Directorate-General for Energy. Guidelines on radiation protection education and training of medical professionals in the European Union. Luxembourg: Publications Office; 2014.
10. Faggioni L, Paolicchi F, Bastiani L, Guido D, Caramella D. Awareness of radiation protection and dose levels of imaging procedures among medical students, radiography students, and radiology residents at an academic hospital: results of a comprehensive survey. Eur J Radiol. 2017;86:135–42.
11. Brown N, Jones L. Knowledge of medical imaging radiation dose and risk among doctors. J Med Imaging Radiat Oncol. 2013;57(1):8–14.
12. Paolicchi F, Faggioni L, Bastiani L, Molinaro S, Caramella D, Bartolozzi C. Real practice radiation dose and dosimetric impact of radiological staff training in body CT examinations. Insights Imaging. 2013;4(2):239–44.
13. Paolicchi F, Miniati F, Bastiani L, Faggioni L, Ciaramella A, Creonti I, et al. Assessment of radiation protection awareness and knowledge about radiological examination doses among Italian radiographers. Insights Imaging. 2016;7(2):233–42.
14. Ria F, Bergantin A, Vai A, Bonfanti P, Martinotti AS, Redaelli I, et al. Awareness of medical radiation exposure among patients: a patient survey as a first step for effective communication of ionizing radiation risks. Phys Med. 2017;43:57–62.
15. European Society of Radiology (ESR). Summary of the European Directive 2013/59/Euratom: essentials for health professionals in radiology. Insights Imaging. 2015;6(4):411–7.
16. Paolicchi F, Bastiani L, Negri J, Caramella D. Effect of CT localizer radiographs on radiation dose associated with automatic tube current modulation: a multivendor study. Curr Probl Diagn Radiol. 2020;49(1):34–41.
17. Paolicchi F, Bastiani L, Guido D, Dore A, Aringhieri G, Caramella D. Radiation dose exposure in patients affected by lymphoma undergoing repeat CT examinations: how to manage the radiation dose variability. Radiol Med. 2018;123(3):191–201.
18. Barca P, Giannelli M, Fantacci ME, Caramella D. Computed tomography imaging with the Adaptive Statistical Iterative Reconstruction (ASIR) algorithm: dependence of image quality on the blending level of reconstruction. Australas Phys Eng Sci Med. 2018;41(2):463–73.
19. Ramanathan S, Ryan J. Radiation awareness among radiology residents, technologists, fellows and staff: where do we stand? Insights Imaging. 2014;6(1):133–9.
20. ESR. EuroSafe Imaging Together - for patient safety [Internet]. [cited 2020 Jan 28]. Available from: http://www.eurosafeimaging.org/.
21. Kim SJ, Kim KA. Safety issues and updates under MR environments. Eur J Radiol. 2017;89:7–13.
22. Biological effects of magnetic resonance imaging. In: Radiation biology of medical imaging [Internet]. John Wiley & Sons, Ltd; 2014 [cited 2019 Oct 24]. p. 281–95. Available from: https://onlinelibrary.wiley.com/doi/abs/10.1002/9781118517154.ch17.
23. Greenberg TD, Hoff MN, Gilk TB, Jackson EF, Kanal E, McKinney AM, et al. ACR guidance document on MR safe practices: Updates and critical information 2019. J Magn Reson Imaging [Internet]. [cited 2019 Oct 24]. Available from: https://onlinelibrary.wiley.com/doi/abs/10.1002/jmri.26880.
24. International Commission on Non-Ionizing Radiation Protection. Guidelines on limits of exposure to static magnetic fields. Health Phys. 2009;96(4):504–14.
25. van Nierop LE, Slottje P, van Zandvoort M, Kromhout H. Simultaneous exposure to MRI-related static and low-frequency movement-induced time-varying magnetic fields affects neurocognitive performance: a double-blind randomized crossover study. Magn Reson Med. 2015;74(3):840–9.
26. Critchley WR, Reid A, Morris J, Naish JH, Stone JP, Ball AL, et al. The effect of 1.5 T cardiac magnetic resonance on human circulating leucocytes. Eur Heart J. 2018;39(4):305–12.
27. Tsai LL, Grant AK, Mortele KJ, Kung JW, Smith MP. A practical guide to MR imaging safety: what radiologists need to know. Radiographics. 2015;35(6):1722–37.
28. Expert Panel on MR Safety, Kanal E, Barkovich AJ, Bell C, Borgstede JP, Bradley WG, et al. ACR guidance document on MR safe practices: 2013. J Magn Reson Imaging. 2013;37(3):501–30.

29. Manker SG, Shellock FG. Chapter 24 - MRI safety and neuromodulation systems. In: Krames ES, Peckham PH, Rezai AR, editors. Neuromodulation (2nd Edition) [Internet]. Academic Press; 2018 [cited 2019 Oct 30]. p. 315–37. Available from: http://www.sciencedirect.com/science/article/pii/B9780128053539000243.

30. van den Brink JS. Thermal effects associated with RF exposures in diagnostic MRI: overview of existing and emerging concepts of protection. Concepts Magn Reson B. 2019;2019:1–17.

31. Shellock FG, Woods TO, Crues JV. MR labeling information for implants and devices: explanation of terminology. Radiology. 2009;253(1):26–30.

32. Magnetic resonance procedures: health effects and safety [Internet]. CRC Press. [cited 2019 Oct 28]. Available from: https://www.crcpress.com/Magnetic-Resonance-Procedures-Health-Effects-and-Safety/Shellock/p/book/9780849308741.

33. ASTM F2503-13. Standard practice for marking medical devices and other items for safety in the magnetic resonance environment [Internet]. [cited 2019 Oct 30]. Available from: http://www.astm.org/cgi-bin/resolver.cgi?F2503-13.

34. Shellock FG. MRI safety home [Internet]. [cited 2019 Oct 30]. Available from: http://mrisafety.com/.

35. American College of Radiology, Committee on Drugs and Contrast Media. ACR manual on contrast media [Internet]. 2015 [cited 2019 Oct 30]. Available from: http://www.acr.org/~/link.aspx?_id=29C40D1FE0EC4E5EAB6861BD213793E5&_z=z.

36. Beckett KR, Moriarity AK, Langer JM. Safe use of contrast media: what the radiologist needs to know. Radiographics. 2015;35(6):1738–50.

37. Morzycki A, Bhatia A, Murphy KJ. Adverse reactions to contrast material: a Canadian update. Can Assoc Radiol J. 2017;68(2):187–93.

38. Behzadi AH, Zhao Y, Farooq Z, Prince MR. Immediate allergic reactions to Gadolinium-based contrast agents: a systematic review and meta-analysis. Radiology. 2017;286(2):471–82.

39. European Society of Radiology (ESR), European Federation of Radiographer Societies (EFRS). Patient safety in medical imaging: a joint paper of the European Society of Radiology (ESR) and the European Federation of Radiographer Societies (EFRS). Insights Imaging. 2019;10(1):45.

40. Faucon A-L, Bobrie G, Clément O. Nephrotoxicity of iodinated contrast media: from pathophysiology to prevention strategies. Eur J Radiol. 2019;116:231–41.

41. Hazelton JM, Chiu MK, Abujudeh HH. Nephrogenic systemic fibrosis: a review of history, pathophysiology, and current guidelines. Curr Radiol Rep. 2019;7(2):5.

42. Khawaja AZ, Cassidy DB, Al Shakarchi J, McGrogan DG, Inston NG, Jones RG. Revisiting the risks of MRI with Gadolinium based contrast agents—review of literature and guidelines. Insights Imaging. 2015;6(5):553–8.

43. Choi JW, Moon W-J. Gadolinium deposition in the brain: current updates. Korean J Radiol. 2019;20(1):134–47.

44. Caramella D, Cappelli C, Cervelli R, Strowig G. Contribution of radiology as an enabling medical specialty. In: Boggi U. (eds) Minimally invasive surgery of the pancreas. Updates in Surgery. Springer, Milano. 2018; https://doi.org/10.1007/978-88-470-3958-2_7.

Organ Donor Risk Stratification in Italy

23

Adriano Peris, Jessica Bronzoni, Sonia Meli,
Juri Ducci, Erjon Rreka, Davide Ghinolfi,
Emanuele Balzano, Fabio Melandro,
and Paolo De Simone

23.1 Background

23.1.1 The Donor Risk

Assessment of suitability of organ and tissue donors is aimed at the best donor-to-recipient matching and minimization of the risk of disease transmission. Basically, there are two types of communicable disease: infectious and neoplastic. In addition, some toxic agents (i.e., acute poisoning of the organ donor) can inadvertently be

A. Peris
Organizzazione Toscana Tapianti, The Regional Health Ministry, Florence, Italy

J. Bronzoni · S. Meli
Hepatobiliary Surgery and Liver Transplantation, University of Pisa Medical School Hospital, Pisa, Italy

University of Pisa, Pisa, Italy

J. Ducci · E. Rreka · D. Ghinolfi · E. Balzano
F. Melandro
Hepatobiliary Surgery and Liver Transplantation, University of Pisa Medical School Hospital, Pisa, Italy

P. De Simone (✉)
Hepatobiliary Surgery and Liver Transplantation, University of Pisa Medical School Hospital, Pisa, Italy

Department of Surgical, Medical and Molecular Pathology and Intensive Care, University of Pisa, Pisa, Italy
e-mail: paolo.desimone@unipi.it;

transmitted to graft recipients. In the setting of organ transplantation, disease transmission may be **intentional** (i.e., deliberate, anticipated) or **inadvertent** (Table 23.1).

For instance, use of hepatitis C positive (HCV) liver grafts may be contemplated for HCV-positive liver recipients due to recent availability of pangenotypic, direct acting antivirals (DAA). In such cases, the risk of viral transmission is considered minimal with respect to the anticipated benefit for the transplant recipient. The higher the need of transplantation for a given patient, the greater is the risk that can potentially be taken: i.e., risk assessment requires evaluation of both donors and recipients. The organ donor evaluation process entails collection of available information, laboratory investigations, clinical examinations, and surgical exploration findings. It is intrinsically multidisciplinary and multiphase, and its span ranges from donor referral to long-term survival of organ recipients. Transmissible disease is any condition for which available scientific evidence or clinical reports confirm the risk of transmission. In clinical practice, however, communicable disease is the one that is considered such by clinical experts or whose risk of transmission cannot entirely be excluded.

In Italy, the donor risk assessment process is based on guidelines provided to all transplant network professionals by the national agency for transplantation (Centro Nazionale Trapianti, CNT). Due to complexity of clinical practice,

L. Donaldson et al. (eds.), *Textbook of Patient Safety and Clinical Risk Management*,
https://doi.org/10.1007/978-3-030-59403-9_23

Table 23.1 Categories of donor-derived disease transmission in organ transplantation

Category	Definition	Instances
Inadvertent	Unintentional transmission of infections, malignancies or toxic agents from organ donors to recipients	• Transmission of unknown donor hepatocellular carcinoma or HIV infection
Intentional	Anticipated transmission based on possibility of treatment and/or benefit for the recipient	• ver transplantation from HBsAg, anti-HBc or anti-HCV-positive donors • Transplantation from donors with low-grade malignancies (i.e., skin, kidney, prostate)

Table 23.2 The basic principles of the donor risk evaluation process

#	Definition
1	No donor can be excluded from evaluation unless there is any clinical condition contraindicating donation (i.e., metastatic malignancy)
2	The risk is never zero
3	Risk evaluation is an ongoing process based on available clinical information

Table 23.3 The donor risk evaluation algorithm

Phase	#	Definition
Pretransplant	1	Clinical history
	2	Physical exam
	3	Laboratory and imaging
	4	Surgery
Posttransplant	5	Ongoing clinical evaluation and prompt reporting of adverse events

however, consultation with national experts in infectious disease, pathology, hematology, and legal issues has been provided on a routine basis since 2004 to assist transplant professionals.

23.1.2 The Principles of Donor Risk Evaluation

There are three basic tenets in the donor evaluation process (Table 23.2). Firstly, in the absence of formal contraindications to donation (i.e., active systemic infections from multidrug-resistant bacteria or invasive malignancies with metastatic dissemination), the risk of disease transmission must be assessed against the potential benefit for the transplant recipient. Apart from a limited number of clinical conditions unfit to donation (unacceptable risk), no donor can be excluded from evaluation and their organs might benefit potential candidates. Secondly, patients awaiting organ transplantation must be informed that the risk of disease transmission is small but finite (standard risk). Finally, risk evaluation is an ongoing process based on information collected longitudinally after transplantation. To this regard, CNT is committed to updating of current guidelines based on clinical data derived from clinicians and on evaluation of posttransplant graft and patient survival rates.

23.1.3 The Risk Evaluation Process

The donor risk evaluation process is multi-phase and multidisciplinary and involves all healthcare professionals along the entire continuum of the donation-transplantation journey. Risk assessment is based on the following (Table 23.3).

23.1.3.1 Organ Procurement

(a) **Donor's clinical history**, with special focus on infectious diseases and malignancies. This entails use of all available sources of information (attending physicians; family members; healthcare staff, etc.), and attention should be paid to (1) sexual habits; (2) use of drugs; (3) travels to areas with endemic infectious disease (i.e., malaria; West Nile virus; trypanosomiasis); (4) bite-marks (dogs; bats; hamsters, etc.), and (5) previous or current disease of infectious, neoplastic or autoimmune etiology.

(b) **Donor's physical examination**: This should focus on the presence of scars (i.e., previous surgeries), skin or mucous lesions with special attention to: (1) tattoos; (2) jaundice; (3) rashes (especially in infants and children); (4) lymph node enlargement; and (5) signs of active drug use (venipuncture). Exploration of thyroid, breast, testes, superficial lymph nodes and rectal examination is strongly recommended if the donor is >50 years.

(c) **Laboratory and imaging**: There is great variability in number and type of investigations as per local clinical practice, but the basic set should include blood count; kidney and liver function tests; and HBV, HCV, HIV serology. Additional tests may be contemplated, based on local practice or individual donor's clinical conditions. In the presence of massive blood and fluid administration (i.e., traumas), all viral serology should be interpreted with care. Current European Union directives recommend long-term storage of a whole blood or buffy coat sample of both donor and recipient for longitudinal risk assessment.

(d) **Donor surgery**: Irrespective of number and type of procured organs, surgeons are requested to explore thoracic and abdominal organs, including kidneys in case of anticipated lack of allocation. Exploration should be combined with sampling and biopsies when needed.

23.1.3.2 Posttransplant Course

Continued monitoring of transplant recipients and prompt reporting of donation-related and unrelated adverse events is crucial to collection of evidence and updating of current recommendations.

23.1.4 The Donor Risk Categories

Based on procurement data and information, any referred donor can be further categorized in one of the following (Table 23.4):

1. **Standard-risk donor**: this group includes any organ donor with no particular disease transmission risk. The probability of disease transmission is extremely low, but not zero.
2. **Nonstandard-risk donor**: This group is further divided into:
   (a) *Donor with a negligible risk profile*: This category includes donors with disease that either will not affect the posttransplant graft and patient outcome or do not require special treatment versus standard-risk donors.
   (b) *Donor with an acceptable risk profile*: In these cases, use of organs is based on availability of treatment (i.e., anti-hepatitis B virus (HBV) prophylaxis for recipients of HBsAg and/or anti-HBc donor organs) or benefit to recipients (i.e., risk of dropout from the waiting list due to native disease progression). In both cases, recipients shall be informed at the time of wait listing and transplantation and informed consent is to be docu-

Table 23.4 The donor risk categories according to the Italian Center for Transplantation (CNT)

Risk category	Definition	Organ allocation
Standard	No risk factors have been detected during donor referral evaluation and procurement	No restriction
Nonstandard	Negligible Presence of disease that will not affect transplant outcome or require treatment (i.e., skin basalioma, low-Gleason score prostate cancer)	No restriction Informed consent required
	Acceptable Presence of disease that might affect transplant outcome if untreated (i.e., transplantation from HBsAg and/or anti-HBc and/or anti-HCV-positive donors)	Selection of appropriate transplant recipients is required (i.e., anti-HCV-positive recipients for anti-HCV-positive donors) Posttransplant treatment should be implemented Informed consent required
	Acceptable for patients in relative clinical urgency Presence of disease that might affect transplant outcome	Allocation directed to recipients at risk of disease progression and waitlist dropout Informed consent required
Unacceptable	Presence of risk factors of communicable, ominous disease (i.e., metastatic malignancy)	Avoid transplantation

mented in their clinical records. The category of acceptable risk profile also includes transplantation for patients in relative clinical urgency, i.e., those with severe clinical status, impending disease progression, and consequent risk of dropout from the waiting list (e.g., advanced hepatocellular carcinoma, high model for end-stage disease (MELD) liver transplant candidates or long-standing kidney transplant patients with pretransplant sensitization).

3. **Unacceptable-risk donor**: This group includes donors with overt risk factors for disease transmission, with special regard to active infectious disease from multidrug-resistant bacteria and metastatic malignancies. In such cases we assume that the risk of transplantation greatly exceeds the benefits of dying on the transplant waiting list.

23.2 Discussion

Organ transplantation carries a small but finite risk of disease transmission [1, 2]. The risk of transmission of malignancies in organ transplantation is currently estimated between 0.01% and 0.05% [1, 2] when strict criteria for donor selection and evaluation are implemented. In such series [3, 4], only one case of melanoma is reported, thus underscoring the benefit of transplantation as compared to a 2% mortality risk for kidney and up to 17% for liver waitlist candidates in the same study period. On the opposite, lack of guidelines and inaccurate medical histories are at the basis of case reports of donor-to-recipient transmission of malignancies [5–19].

Due to stagnant donation rates, donor selection criteria have been expanded and use of nonstandard risk donors has been introduced in many countries [20]. This clearly poses considerable ethical issues that should be analyzed and taken into consideration by the competent authorities and institutions. In Italy, introduction of donor risk categories in 2004 has allowed safe use of organs from donors with malignancies, HBsAg and/or anti-HBc donors and, recently, from anti-HCV-positive and HCV RNA-positive donors in negative recipients in light of the availability of DAAs for hepatitis C treatment with no negative impact on the overall graft and patients survival rates [20].

Implementation of national guidelines and risk stratification has been crucial to achievement of favorable results. This underlies the important role of regional and national authorities/agencies and of multidisciplinary integration of all healthcare professionals along the entire continuum of the donation-transplantation process. Retrieval of clinical information can be challenging in the setting of donation after brain death (DBD) and even more in the setting of uncontrolled donation after cardiocirculatory death (uDCD), when time pressure urges professionals to achieve results (i.e., organ procurement) as quickly as possible. To this regard, active participation of donor families, general practitioners, and healthcare institutions to the donation process is pivotal to an efficient algorithm and reduction of the uncertainty margin to the lowest level (standard risk). Organ donation is truly an instance of social enterprise, and relies on efficient integration of all levels of care (primary, secondary, and tertiary). Risk control strategies can be effective only if based on comprehensive policies encompassing the entire spectrum of the donation-transplantation process.

References

1. Kauffman HM, McBride MA, Cherikh WS, Spain PC, Delmonico FL. Transplant tumor registry: donor related malignancies. Transplantation. 2002;74:358–62.
2. Desai R, Collett D, Watson CJ, Johnson P, Evans T, Neuberger J. Cancer transmission from organ donors – unavoidable but low risk. Transplantation. 2012;94:1200–7.
3. Desai R, Collett D, Watson CJE, Johnson P, Evans T, Neuberger J. Estimated risk of cancer transmission from organ donor to graft recipient in a national transplantation registry. BJS. 2014;101:768–74.
4. Kauffman HM, Cherikh WS, McBride MA, Cheng Y, Hanto DW. Deceased donor with a past history of malignancy: an Organ Procurement and Transplantation Network/United Network of Organ Sharing update. Transplantation. 2007;84:272–4.

5. Sack FU, Lange R, Mehmanesh H, Amman K, Schnabel P, Zimmermann R, Dengler T, Otto HF, Hagl S. Transferral of extrathoracic donor neoplasm by the cardiac allograft. J Heart Lung Transplant. 1997;16(3):298–301.

6. Barrou B, Bitker MO, Delcourt A, Ourahma S, Richard F. Fate of renal tubulopapillary adenoma transmitted by an organ donor. Transplantation. 2001;72(3):540–1.

7. Llamas F, Gallego E, Salinas A, Virseda J, Pérez J, Ortega A, Nam SH, Gómez C. Sarcomatoid renal cell carcinoma in a renal transplant recipient. Transplant Proc. 2009;10:4422–4.

8. Ferreira GF, Azevedo de Oliveira R, Jorge LB, Nahas WC, Saldanha LB, Ianhez LE, Srougi M. Urothelial carcinoma transmission via kidney transplantation. Nephrol Dial Transplant. 2010;25:641–3.

9. Forbes GB, Goggin MJ, Dische FE, Saeed IT, Parsons V, Harding MJ, Bewick M, Rudge CT. Accidental transplantation of bronchial carcinoma from a cadaver donor to two recipients of renal allografts. J Clin Pathol. 1981;34(2):109–15.

10. Winter TC, Keller PR, Lee FT Jr, Pozniak MA. Donor-derived malignancy: transmission of small-cell lung cancer via renal transplantation. J Ultrasound Med. 2001;20(5):559–62.

11. Lipshutz GS, Baxter-Lowe LA, Nguyen T, Jones KD, Ascher NL, Feng S. Death from donor-transmitted malignancy despite emergency liver retransplantation. Liver Transpl. 2003;9(10):1102–7.

12. Nair BT, Bhat SH, Narayan UV, Sukumar S, Saheed M, Kurien G, Sudhindran S. Donate organs not malignancies: postoperative small cell lung carcinoma in a marginal living kidney donor. Transplant Proc. 2007;39(10):3477–80.

13. Zelinkova Z, Geurts-Giele I, Verheij J, Metselaar H, Dinjens W, Dubbink HJ, Taimr P. Donor-transmitted metastasis of colorectal carcinoma in a transplanted liver. Transpl Int. 2012;25(1):e10–5.

14. Ison MG, Nalesnik MA. An update on donor-derived disease transmission in organ transplantation. Am J Transpl. 2011;11:1123–30.

15. Zwald FO, Christenson LJ, Billingsley EM, Zeitouni NC, Ratner D, Bordeaux J, Patel MJ, Brown MD, Proby CM, Euvrard S, Otley CC, Stasko T, Melanoma Working Group of the International Transplant Skin Cancer Collaborative and Skin Care in Organ Transplant Patients, Europe. Melanoma in solid organ transplant recipients. Am J Transplant. 2010;10(5):1297–304.

16. Strauss DC, Thomas M. Transmission of donor melanoma by organ transplantation. Lancet Oncol. 2010;11:790–6.

17. MacKie RM, Reid R, Junor B. Fatal melanoma transferred in a donated kidney 16 years after melanoma surgery. N Engl J Med. 2003;348:567–8.

18. Bajai NS, Watt C, Hadjiliadis D, Gillespie C, Haas AR, Pochettino A, Mendez J, Sterman DH, Schuchter LM, Christie JD, Lee JC, Ahya VN. Donor transmission of malignant melanoma in a lung transplant recipient 32 years after curative resection. Transpl Int. 2010;23(7):e26–31.

19. Braun-Parvez L, Charlin E, Caillard S, Ducloux D, Wolf P, Rolle F, Golfier F, Flicoteaux H, Bergerat JP, Moulin B. Gestational choriocarcinoma transmission following multiorgan donation. Am J Transplant. 2010;10(11):2541–6.

20. Petrini C, Trapani S, Riva L, Floridia G, Gainotti S, Lombardini L, Masiero L, Rizzato L, Costa AN. Organ transplantation from nonstandard risk donors: midway between rigid and flexible rules. Transplant Proc. 2019;51(9):2856–9.

Patient Safety in Laboratory Medicine

24

Mario Plebani, Ada Aita, and Laura Sciacovelli

Learning Objectives

The notion of patient safety in laboratory medicine can be loosely interpreted as the assurance that harm to patients is prevented, safe care outcomes are enhanced through error prevention, and the system is continuously improved. However, this somewhat simplistic interpretation hides the concept's true complexity. A clear definition of the laboratory professional's role and competencies in the diagnostic process is therefore required, as is the use of suitable quality assurance tools.

The concept of a "brain-to-brain loop" of laboratory testing encompasses the different steps involved, starting with appropriate test requesting and concluding with the appropriate use of laboratory information (Fig. 24.1). Moreover, it highlights the importance of integrating laboratory information in the care pathways, calling for system quality and patient safety, and also elucidates the value of laboratory medicine.

In the last few decades, changes in the nature of laboratory services have underscored a paradigmatic transformation of the laboratory scenario [1] thanks to technological innovation, the introduction of ever more complex tests in emerging diagnostic fields, more advanced diagnostics, and other internal and external drivers. The transformation will become even more marked in the future. In the ten points identified in the "Manifesto for the future of Laboratory Medicine professionals" (Table 24.1), great emphasis is placed on the importance of cooperation in reducing the risk of diagnostic errors, the implementation of reliable laboratory medicine stewardship, the involvement of laboratory medicine professionals in interdisciplinary teams, and the promotion of professional expertise. A large body of evidence demonstrates that this integration is crucial to the rational utilization of laboratory information [2].

The issue of patient safety, which impacts every diagnosis, involves numerous stakeholders. No single intervention to prevent errors is available, and there is a pressing need for the rigorous evaluation of possible solutions that will be beneficial, will obviate unintended consequences, and, above all, will safeguard patients.

In the healthcare setting, medical laboratories should always be a driver in ensuring patient safety through:

- The integration of laboratory professionals with new competencies and skills in

M. Plebani (✉) · A. Aita
Department of Laboratory Medicine, University-Hospital of Padova, Padova, Italy

Department of Medicine-DIMED, University of Padova, Padova, Italy
e-mail: mario.plebani@unipd.it

L. Sciacovelli
Department of Laboratory Medicine, University-Hospital of Padova, Padova, Italy
e-mail: laura.sciacovelli@aopd.veneto.it

© The Author(s) 2021
L. Donaldson et al. (eds.), *Textbook of Patient Safety and Clinical Risk Management*,
https://doi.org/10.1007/978-3-030-59403-9_24

Fig. 24.1 The brain-to-brain-loop: description of the total testing process (from reference 8 modified)

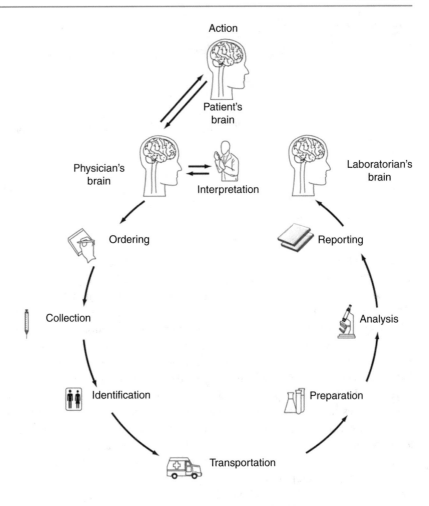

Action

Patient's brain

Physician's brain

Interpretation

Laboratorian's brain

Ordering

Reporting

Collection

Analysis

Identification

Preparation

Transportation

Table 24.1 Manifesto for the future of laboratory medicine professionals [1]

1. Convert results in clinical information
2. Cooperate in reducing the risk of diagnostic errors
3. Implement a reliable laboratory medicine stewardship
4. Combine data of all laboratories subspecialties and diagnostic imaging in the same report
5. Establish reliable reference ranges and decision limits
6. Facilitate more effective teamwork and be actively involved in interdisciplinary teams
7. Promote the shift from volume based reimbursement models to clinical values
8. Improve and update the way laboratory medicine is taught
9. Do not neglect administrative competence and duties
10. Promote the value of the profession

multidisciplinary teams, in which all stakeholders are involved.

- Awareness of the impact of laboratory errors in patient management.
- The implementation of effective quality assurance tools to identify and prevent potential laboratory errors.

24.1 Epidemiology of Adverse Events

24.1.1 Laboratory Medicine as a Driver in Ensuring Patient Safety

The phrase "clinical laboratory stewardship" effectively clarifies the indispensable role of laboratory medicine in healthcare and points to the need to promote a new vision for the discipline in which some novel ideas must be stressed and focused on. Diagnostic and therapeutic networks must be promoted in order to improve patient-centered and end-to-end support in clinical pathways and to transform laboratory data into effective information. Studies in literature highlight the urgent need for clinicians to make better use of diagnostic testing and to be confident that laboratory information issued to them is accurate. Important issues must be shared in order to achieve compliance with the above needs. In order to reduce errors and improve quality of care, laboratory professionals must be made aware of the impact laboratory results have on the patient and, on the other hand, clinicians must have a thorough understanding of the tools implemented and used in the laboratory [3–5].

In the healthcare system, Laboratory Medicine is still considered a low-risk speciality with respect to other specialities such as emergency and intensive care medicine [6]. This is because the main activities in laboratory medicine are accurately defined [7, 8] and are more easily controlled than procedures in an emergency department, where they are strictly dependent on the healthcare professionals. However, laboratory errors tend to be more insidious and difficult to immediately identify because they involve several steps, numerous providers, and a greater time lapse between testing, physician action, and patient outcome [9].

During the healthcare process, failures occurring in a phase nearest to patient intervention are more likely to result in patient harm due to the presence of active and defensive barriers designed to identify the event before it impacts patient outcome. However, despite the common belief that errors in laboratory testing have less of an impact on patient safety than those occurring in the operating or resuscitation rooms, several examples in literature demonstrate that errors in the testing process can result in a negative patient outcome. In a survey, anatomic pathologists and medical laboratory directors were asked questions on error rates, on barriers to error disclosure, and on

their experience with pathology and laboratory error disclosure. Of the 95.2% of respondents who reported having experienced an error, 43.6% reported involvement with a serious error, 69.1% a minor error, and 77.6% a near miss [10]. Himmel et al. described a case of unnecessary hemodialysis being performed in a healthy patient due to an erroneously transcribed methanol result (6 mmol/L instead of 0.06 mmol/L) [11]. In 2007 in Italy, a transcription error in an HIV result led to the death of three transplant recipients [12]. Adverse events have been also associated with false glucose readings when using glucose dehydrogenase pyrroloquinoline quinone (GPD-PQQ) test strips: out of 82 erroneous reports, 16 (20%) led to death, 46 (56%) severe hypo-glycemia, and 12 (15%) minor hypo-glycemia [13]. Other authors have reported that about 30% of cases of error in total laboratory testing translate into a patient care problem (e.g., inappropriate admission to critical care units, inappropriate transfusions, modifications in heparin and digoxin therapies) [14–16].

These data demonstrate the importance of laboratory information in clinical decision-making since it can significantly affect the diagnosis and subsequent patient management [17]. The reliability of laboratory information is therefore the prerequisite for assuring a quality healthcare process and reducing the risk of harm to patients.

Although it is acknowledged worldwide that the fundamental role of laboratory medicine is to ensure patient safety, more could be done to highlight this role in order to make the laboratory's work visible to the patient.

24.1.2 From Laboratory-Related Errors to Diagnostic Errors

The understanding of errors in terms of type, frequency, causes, and impact on patients is crucial to identifying and implementing control measures to prevent failures and reduce risk. In the laboratory field, the meaning of "error" has changed over time, in parallel with the transformation of the organizational methods of the medical laboratory and the definition of the laboratory testing process itself.

In the late 1990s, the promotion of patient-centered care prompted laboratory professionals to investigate any defects in the TTP that could negatively impact the patient. A series of papers published between 1989 and 2007 documented a high error rate in the pre- and post-analytical steps, thus demonstrating the high vulnerability of these phases [15, 16, 18, 19]. Accordingly, the accepted definition of laboratory error became "a defect occurring at any part of the laboratory cycle, from ordering tests to reporting results and appropriately interpreting and reacting on these," which was also incorporated into the ISO Technical Report 22367:2008 "Medical laboratories— Reduction of error through risk management and continual improvement—Complementary elements" [20].

In 2011, the Institute of Medicine (IOM) included the service of laboratory medicine among the ten categories of essential services in the United States health system, marking a new era for the medical laboratory. As the medical laboratory becomes an integral part of the health-care system, laboratory-related error becomes part of a much wider issue, known as "diagnostic error" [21, 22]. Diagnostic errors have been defined as failures to provide an accurate and timely explanation of the patient's health problems and/or communicate that explanation to the patient. Diagnostic errors are typically subdivided into errors in which diagnosis has been (a) *delayed*, despite sufficient available information, (b) *wrong*, because a diagnosis was made before the correct one was determined, or (c) *missed*, when no diagnosis was made [23]. The concept of "diagnostic errors" definitively links laboratory-associated errors to patient safety problems. The fundamental role of the medical laboratory in the diagnostic process was high-lighted by a survey administered to clinicians to assess type and causes of missed and delayed diagnoses. The results showed that errors occurred most frequently in the testing phase (i.e., failure to order, report, and follow-up laboratory results) (44%), followed by errors in clinician assessment (overruling or failing to consider a competing diagnosis) (32%), history taking

(10%), physical examination (10%), and referral or consultation errors and delays (3%) [24].

Failure to order appropriate diagnostic tests, including laboratory tests, has also been linked to missed and delayed diagnoses in the ambulatory setting (55%) [25], and in emergency departments (58%). Likewise, failure to note abnormal test results (7%) has been related to delay in diagnosing cancer. The incorrect interpretation of laboratory tests, resulting in diagnostic errors, has also been documented in the primary care setting (37%), internal medicine (38%), and emergency departments (37%) [25, 26].

Current research into laboratory-related diagnostic errors highlights the following.

- *Pre- and post-analytical phases are more vulnerable to errors*, accounting for 46–68% and 19–47% of errors, respectively. The management of the interface between the clinical setting and laboratory remains a challenge for healthcare professionals [27].
- *Analytical quality is a persistent issue*. Initial studies on laboratory-related errors focused on the analytical phase, the only phase completely performed within the laboratory walls and under direct laboratory control. Furthermore, only errors in the measurement of clinical chemistry analytes were considered. Despite their limited design, these studies offered a wide range of strategies to improve analytical performance and provide clinicians with timely and reliable results. The strategies adopted (e.g., the development of external quality assurance (EQA) programs, the improvement of internal quality control (IQC), regulation and standardization of analytical techniques and reagents, automation and computerization of laboratory processes) led to a dramatic decrease in analytical error rates and to a significant increase in test demand and utilization.
- *Analytical interferences must be focused on.* Despite the optimism of clinical pathologists, analytical interferences still affect many tests, such as glucose, bilirubin, C-reactive protein, creatinine, and albumin [28]. These errors, also known as irregular errors, represent one of the greatest challenges for laboratory pro-

fessionals because they are not detectable by quality control procedures, are reproducible within the test system, and may be clinically plausible. Furthermore, their frequency is variable and probably underreported [29]. Immunoassays are the most affected tests, with an analytical error rate of 0.4–4%, considerably higher than those for other routine tests and in some cases associated with an adverse clinical outcome (e.g., unnecessary hysterectomy and chemotherapy in a 22-year-old woman due to false-positive hCG results caused by heterophilic antibodies) [30]. The issue of irregular analytical errors presents an opportunity to reframe the mission of laboratory medicine as the provision of key information for effective clinical decision-making and optimal patient outcome [31].

- *Errors do not only concern clinical chemistry tests.* New pathophysiological knowledge and technologies have led to the introduction of novel, ever more sophisticated tests into clinical practice, calling for further efforts to ensure competency of laboratory staff as well as other healthcare professionals [1]. Although the test cycle is the same across laboratory medicine tests and disciplines, this cannot be said for the distribution of the errors within the test cycle. In molecular-genetic testing or mass spectrometry, many steps of the analytical process are not yet automated and are closely linked to the inherent judgment of the laboratory professional, thus making the results more subjective than those of other clinical laboratory tests. In molecular-genetic testing for example, it has been demonstrated that 60% of errors occur in the pre-analytical phase, 32% in the analytical phase, and 8% in the post-analytical phase [32].

24.2   Safety Practices and Implementation Strategy

In recent years, the evolution of the role of laboratory medicine in patient management and the growing attention to cost containment have underscored an evaluation of the service provided by the medical laboratory based on efficacy criteria. In this context, improvement has been observed in quality control techniques, from improvements in the analytical phase to the promotion and development of quality assurance systems for the entire analysis process; several quality improvement initiatives have been undertaken to support sustainable outcomes based on systematic and organizational criteria.

A body of scientific evidence shows that it is now essential to identify opportunities for improvement while considering all TTP activities, especially those in the pre- and post-analytical phases. Systems for the identification and monitoring of errors are important quality assurance tools, as are proactive and reactive analysis methods that focus not only on the processes themselves but also, and above all, on any risk to the patient.

Of the procedures to be implemented in medical laboratories, the identification and monitoring of errors is paramount to ensure proper performance because it calls for continuous data analysis and the implementation of preventive, corrective, and ameliorative actions whenever necessary. The monitoring of result accuracy, a traditional laboratory process, is conducted using IQC procedures and through participation in EQA programs. In the last few decades, the responsibility of laboratory professionals has widened thanks to awareness of the brain-to-brain loop (Fig. 24.1) [33]. The systematic use of approved quality indicators (QIs) to control critical TTP activities over time has expanded to the monitoring of the extra-analytical phases and the description of the efficiency and effectiveness of performance.

Moreover, a robust, well-structured, and well-managed quality management system can provide a wide variety of information generated by both symptomatic events (e.g., incident reporting) and asymptomatic events (e.g., analysis of strengths, weaknesses, opportunities, and threats) for measuring and monitoring different aspects of the process and its outcomes.

Examples of information sources are:

- Reports on participation in EQA programs.
- Quality indicator data.

- Findings of external accreditation and/or certification audits.
- Records of non-conformities (e.g., errors, complaints, adverse events, non-compliance).
- Findings of surveys investigating user satisfaction, where the user is understood to be one who utilizes the service (e.g., citizen, patient, clinician, doctor) or one who works within the process as a user of one sub-process and a supplier of another.
- Assessments of staff competency.

The analysis of all data collected contributes to the definition of organizational and quality objectives and of intervention priorities. However, the effectiveness of the information for improvement purposes is influenced by the criteria and methods with which the information is collected and subsequently managed.

Only a small proportion of laboratory errors give rise to actual patient harm and adverse events, thanks to several checks and defensive layers implemented to guarantee the reliable release of laboratory information; however, each and every error that does occur must serve as an important learning opportunity [34].

24.2.1 ISO 15189 Accreditation

The reliability of laboratory tests has increased dramatically in line with technological progress and the refinement of techniques, methods, and professional skills. For a medical laboratory to reliably deliver routine services at high volumes continuously and broadly, it must emphasize the importance of drawing maximum attention to the quality of its processes, starting with the biological sample quality (i.e., collection, handling, and transport), followed by analytical accuracy, and then the quality of report communication (e.g., timeliness, appropriateness of reference intervals/decision levels, controls in place to ensure the correct communication is received by clinicians).

Although a robust quality management system is crucial for the correct management and traceability of all processes, it is now more important than ever to understand how to optimize efficiency and effectiveness while overcoming the mentality of blind compliance with requirements. The definition and application of criteria, procedures, and quality assurance tools must be driven by laboratory professionals on the basis of practice and data analysis, rather than by requirements defined outside the laboratory.

Improvement action plans for laboratory activities are multiple and varied due to the complexity of the relationships and interactions between the different processes and activities. Success depends on:

- The commitment of leadership to improving quality as a modus operandi.
- An organization-wide culture that recognizes the need for and calls for the involvement of all personnel in improvement activities.
- Integrated and defined processes and procedures describing the ways in which improvement can be implemented and responsibilities articulated.
- The application by management and all staff members of knowledge and skills relevant to the continuous improvement of concepts, models, and tools [35].

Laboratory medicine is increasingly recognized as a fundamental component of patient care and therefore laboratory professionals are requested to improve not only analytical but also clinical competence. Great efforts have been made by laboratory professionals to supplant the belief that the recognition of performance quality might be assured with the granting of ISO 9001 certification, highlighting instead the suitability of the ISO 15189 accreditation process.

Accreditation in compliance with ISO 15189 (*Medical laboratories—Requirements for quality and competence*) is designed to demonstrate the reliability of laboratory performances to patients and users, and general stakeholders [36]. This assurance is based on the implementation of an adequate quality management system and, above all, on the availability of qualified staff with the technical competence needed to carry out specific examinations.

The ISO 15189 is a worldwide International Standard, specifically designed for the accreditation of medical laboratories. The ISO 15189 accreditation is issued by the national accreditation body, a unique body recognized by the national government for the issuing of accreditation. Obligatory in some countries and voluntary in others, accreditation is based on comparative logics between homogeneous organizations, typical of benchmark systems. Its purpose is not to satisfy a fixed target but goals that vary continuously over time and space and hinge upon quality of professional performance (best practice). Since best practice is affected by contextual change, technological evolution, scientific advancements, and so forth, the aim of accreditation is to help the laboratory achieve continued improvement and compare its performance with the best possible performance, as determined by the state-of-the-art and/or the reference model. The maintenance of accreditation, a dynamic process, calls for continuous evaluation of excellence in the respective discipline.

24.2.2 Quality Indicators

Despite the availability of laboratory accreditation and compliance with mandatory and/or voluntary standards calling for the application of the best available criteria and procedures, and the harmonization of staff behavior, its effectiveness is closely related to continuous monitoring of all TTP steps and outcomes.

In recent years, laboratory professionals have developed and implemented a number of QIs focusing on the main critical TTP steps that are to be included in a coherent and well-integrated quality improvement system [36–41]. This has come about because of the need to reduce error rates, the difficulty in recognizing and isolating undesired events, and a willingness to meet ISO 15189 accreditation requirements.

An internal evaluation process and participation in an inter-laboratory comparison must be implemented in order to guarantee the effectiveness of QIs.

The internal evaluation process includes the definition of:

- A list of QIs focused on the critical activities.
- A document for each indicator describing its specifications (e.g., what must be measured, how to collect data, measurement limitations, acceptability limits of results, areas of application, responsibilities).
- A standard operating procedure describing all steps to be followed in order to guarantee effective use of QIs.

Moreover, participation in inter-laboratory comparison aims to evaluate the quality level achieved in comparison with other national or international laboratories. This calls for the use of common QIs and of criteria and procedures for data collection. A coordinator center is needed to perform data processing that complies with approved quality specifications and to provide each laboratory with a report describing the resulting performance evaluation pertaining to each QI.

The Working Group on "Laboratory Errors and Patient Safety" (WG-LEPS) of the International Federation of Clinical Chemistry and Laboratory Medicine (IFCC) has put in motion a project for the definition of a Model of Quality Indicators (MQI) along with data collection specifications, to be used in all laboratories regardless of logistics, technological level, and complexity. In two Consensus Conferences held in 2013 and 2016, experts on this topic discussed and ultimately approved the list of QIs, the procedure for data collection, the criteria for performance evaluation, and the information to be included in a periodic report concerning the analysis of data for participating laboratories. The progress of the project and its findings are reported in literature as well as through a dedicated website that is www.ifcc-mqi.com.

Currently the MQI includes 53 measurements to evaluate 26 indicators concerning key processes, support processes, and outcome measures. To facilitate implementation, a priority

Fig. 24.2 Model of
Quality Indicators
proposed by WG-LEPS
of IFCC

IFCC Working Group "Laboratory Errors and Patient Safety"

Model of Quality Indicators

26 Indicators ➡ 53 Measurements

	Indicators	Measurements
Key Processes	20	43
Pre-analytical phase	11	25
Intra-analytical phase	5	6
Post-analytical phase	4	12
Support Processes	3	5
Outcome Measures	3	5

Fig. 24.3 Model of
Quality Indicators
proposed by WG-LEPS
of IFCC per priority
index

Model of Quality Indicators = 53 Measurements

Key Processes = 43	Priority	1	2	3	4
Pre-analytical phase		19	2	2	2
Intra-analytical phase		6	0	0	0
Post-analytical phase		9	0	0	3

Support Processes = 5	Priority	1	2	3	4
		0	4	1	0

Outcome Measures = 5	Priority	1	2	3	4
		5	0	0	0

index has been assigned to each QI (from 1 to 4, with 1 being the highest and 4 the lowest) based on the importance of the QI and the difficulty of data collection (Figs. 24.2 and 24.3).

However, sufficient effectiveness of the system cannot be achieved without the correct identification and analysis of the causes for error as well as the implementation of adequate corrective actions. In order to reduce error rates and improve laboratory performance, it is extremely important for laboratory professionals to periodically analyze the QI data and:

- Highlight declines in performance in comparison with previous data and with the state-of-the-art (i.e., other laboratories).
- Identify any error-related causes of undesirable performance as well as any room for improvement.
- Implement preventative and/or corrective and/or improvement actions.
- Evaluate any risk to patient safety.

QI data are an effective starting point for evaluating error probability in risk management procedures. Some authors have reported on their experience applying Failure Mode and Effect Analysis (FMEA) to critical activities using QI data. The reported findings demonstrate that the use of QIs to monitor errors and implement risk management procedures reduces the error rate, maximizes performance quality, and improves patient safety and health system outcomes [42]. The promotion of continued improvement centers about the commitment of laboratory professionals to the management of QIs. The last few years have confirmed that the utility of QIs is closely linked to the recognition by all personnel involved of their importance and of the need to guarantee appropriate data collection as well as effective data analysis. To raise awareness in professionals, there has been a diffusion of consensually approved MQI and results that highlight achieved improvement, and professionals have been encouraged to assume responsibility. The continuous exchange of experiences among laboratory professional aim therefore to improve both the quality of the project and of laboratory services [41].

24.2.3 Professional Competence: Education and Skill

In order to make the role of laboratory medicine in the context of patient care more visible, laboratory professionals must accept that they are members of a multidisciplinary team. Greater visibility in the form of rounds, committees, consultation, demonstration of knowledge, and self-promotion will be judged chiefly in relation to the clinical value they bring. Laboratory professionals must develop new competencies to highlight the contribution of laboratory information to patient management. Even knowledge of less traditional areas is required; this will bring new insights and approaches from other disciplines. Moreover, laboratory professionals must realize that the level of recognition achieved will be profoundly affected by continuous advancements in areas such as computerization, technology, clinical decision tools, informative media, and artificial neural networks. Laboratory medicine is a con-

tinuously evolving clinical discipline and emerging challenges require a revision and improvement of operational flows to enhance quality and safety in patients care. Laboratory professionals must maintain a high level of skills for achieving efficiency and effectiveness when delivering laboratory services [43]. To reduce diagnostic errors, the first-line intervention consists of education and training designed to improve knowledge and skills to guarantee relevant competency [23]. Given the data reported above, it might be necessary to act on graduate education and training by rescheduling national programs, enhancing the duration and contents of courses given in laboratory medicine. Currently, however, only postgraduate initiatives are underway. The EFLM published the fifth edition of a syllabus for laboratory medicine outlining requirements for the postgraduate skills, knowledge, and competency needed to direct laboratory medicine services. The syllabus would not replace existing postgraduate programs, the aim being to harmonize the common principles of education and training of professionals working Europe in order to guarantee high standards of quality and safety. This initiative paves the way for the free migration of professionals and patients across EU national borders. While the fourth version of the syllabus was built with the specialist's generic skills, knowledge, and competencies in mind, the fifth version details individual discipline requirements (such as those in clinical chemistry, immunology, hematology, blood transfusion, microbiology/virology, genetics, and in vitro fertilization) and includes new analytical techniques and statistics. Laboratory organization, quality, safety, and clinical governance have also been included as fundamental aspects of training, thus enabling the specialist in Laboratory Medicine to operate as a clinical leader who can support and transform healthcare services [44]. Given the recent changes in the nature of laboratory service and its role in the healthcare process, the new generation of laboratory professionals and leaders are then called upon to incorporate specific technical skills into a broader vision of healthcare and of patients' needs. As shown in Table 24.1, the recently published "Manifesto for the future of laboratory medicine professionals" specifies the tasks of laboratory professionals in ten specific points. Clinical laboratory stewardship appears to be the new, shared strategy for guaranteeing patient safety while simultaneously maximizing efficacy and efficiency [1]. With this approach, quality and safety are held to be just as essential in daily laboratory practice as they are in clinical practice; yet, neither topic appears in national education and training programs.

The World Health Organization (WHO) has developed initiatives for professionals training in the field of patient safety, beginning with the publication of a "Multi-professional's patient safety curriculum guide" to provide assistance in the teaching of patient safety in universities and schools. This manual, originally published in 2011, has been translated into many different languages (i.e., Chinese, Czech, English, French, German, Indonesian, Italian, Japanese, Polish, and Spanish) [45]. In 2018, WHO organized the first international meeting on safety in healthcare addressed to students and residents in the medical field. More than 200 residents of different specialities and coming from 30 nations were divided into 18 working groups and enhanced the new clinical generation's perspective on healthcare safety through their participation. The survey administered at the end of the sessions highlighted that for 90% of respondents this was the first time attending an international meeting on patient safety, that 80% of residents had not been aware of the existence of the "WHO Multi-professional Patient Safety Curriculum Guide" prior to attending, and that only 40% of the participants had already received training in the field of patient safety and clinical risk.

The above percentages show that in the areas of quality, safety, and risk management the training of young laboratory and clinical professionals is still linked to the sensitivity of leadership towards these issues. However, professionals cannot overlook this issue: they must all be aware that many laboratory errors stem from personnel-related factors, and that other factors can positively or negatively affect laboratory activities, factors such as the social

environment, developments in technology, economic parameters, rules and regulations, and safety precautions [46–48].

24.2.4 Risk Management Procedures

Risk management, the systemic process designed to identify and manage the actual and potential risks associated with laboratory testing, is becoming an integral part of quality management systems and plays an important role in providing quality services [49].

Although ISO 15189 [36] and ISO 9001 [50] include risk management requirements, they do not specify the means to this end. Laboratory professionals generally choose risk assessment techniques recommended by ISO/TS 22367 [20] or suggested by CLSI EP18-A2 [51] while using differing approaches to define goals and identify risks.

Available reviews of risk management procedures in literature focus on different steps and activities. Some authors use FMEA and the Failure Reporting, Analysis and Corrective Action System (FRACAS) to estimate, respectively, potential and actual risks associated with operational (i.e., pre-analytical, analytical, and post-analytical) and strategic and support processes [52]. Other authors use the FMEA technique for specific examination procedures to reduce the occurrence of multiple failures recorded throughout the entire testing process, in particular risks concerning Factor V Leiden mutation or parathyroid and adrenocorticotropic hormones [53, 54], or risks pertaining to the pre-analytical phase using QI data [42].

The use of QI data in risk management procedures is a valid mean for evaluating the probability of error occurrence. The Australasian QI program, Key Incident Monitoring and Management System (KIMMS), provides participants with the KIMMS risk matrix among other statistical tools in order to encourage laboratories to examine high-risk steps and analyze causes of error. For each QI, the system automatically multiplies together the frequency imputed by lab participants, the harm as defined in advance by a consensus of lab professionals, and the ability to detect errors [55]. Flegar-Meštrić et al. [42] also retrospectively studied data collected from 22 harmonized QIs of MQI launched by the IFCC WG-LEPS for risk analysis and error reduction in pre-analytical steps in an emergency department with a higher error rate [33].

24.3   Clinical Cases

In our laboratory, the IFCC-MQI reports provided by WG-LEPS—including the mean and sigma value of laboratory performances for each quality indicator—are analyzed annually to identify high-risk processes. In 2018, the most frequent errors were related to sample unsuitability (e.g., hemolyzed, clotted, or insufficient samples, and samples with inappropriate sample-anticoagulant volume ratio of 0.262%); as a result, the blood collection phase was analyzed to identify the high-risk steps and procedures. Errors in blood collection can generate incorrect results, delays in the release of results, delays in diagnosis and treatment, the release of incomplete testing panels, and repeated blood collection resulting in a negative final outcome for the patient. Checks already in place to prevent procedural errors included standard operating procedures and a training course for blood collection, as well as a checklist serving as an auxiliary tool to guide phlebotomists. All procedural errors can be detected in the laboratory by means of serum indices. To analyze the blood collection phase and identify causes of errors, a selection was made of five wards (i.e., neonatal pathology, clinical medicine, hematology, clinical immunology and day-hospital, and general medicine) with different organizational structure and patient characteristics. The blood collection phase was mapped out in each ward and the risk index (RI) estimated. The highest risk index was found for neonatal pathology (RI = 226), followed by hematology (RI = 165), clinical medicine (RI = 138), clinical immunology day-hospital (RI = 107), and general medicine (RI = 63). The

risk analysis demonstrated that the major causes of error were partial knowledge of the standard operating procedures relating to blood sampling and the storage and sending of the sample (for example, due to insufficient user credentials to access an internal website containing standard operating procedures), insufficient and/or inadequate staff training, partial use of the blood collection checklist, incorrect storage of the sample, human factors (e.g., stress, fatigue, lack of sleep), and the patient's condition (e.g., fragile veins). In order to reduce the error rate during blood collection and minimize risk to patients, several corrective actions were implemented: divulgation of the existing standard operating procedures on blood collection and on sample storage and transportation to the laboratory; request-based authorization to access the documentation found in the internal website; a training course on blood collection addressed to all phlebotomists; and encouraging use of the checklist. Six months after the implementation of the corrective actions, the risk index was re-evaluated to verify effectiveness. We found risk had been reduced in all the studied wards, in particular hematology (58% risk minimization; RI = 69), followed by neonatal pathology (32%; RI = 153), clinical medicine (30%; RI = 98), clinical immunology day-hospital (28%; RI = 77), and general medicine (19%; RI = 51).

The detection, identification, and monitoring of errors through a set of harmonized, evidence-based, and patient-centered QIs have allowed a better understanding and management of the more critical stages of the processes. QIs incorporated in the laboratory quality management system proved to be effective tools for risk assessment and minimized the possibility of errors occurring, consequently guaranteeing patient safety.

24.4   Recommendations

The prevention of errors in healthcare is still a worldwide priority for ensuring patient safety. Data reported by the World Health Organization

(WHO) website on the incidence and magnitude of errors in healthcare are discouraging: it has been estimated that approximately 43 million patient safety incidences occur every year, and as many as one in ten patients are harmed while receiving healthcare. Medical record reviews have demonstrated that 6–17% of all adverse events in hospital are due to diagnostic errors, which have therefore been listed among the ten factors affecting patient safety [56].

The IOM defined patient safety as "the prevention of harm to patients," considering it "indistinguishable from the delivery of quality healthcare," and defined quality of care as "the degree to which healthcare services for individuals and populations increase the likelihood of desired health outcomes and are consistent with current professional practices" [46, 57]. It is clear from these definitions that safety is an essential building block for high-quality performance and that it is strictly connected to the other dimensions of quality of care, such as patient-centeredness, effectiveness, timeliness, efficiency, and equity [58].

Quality assurance tools in laboratory medicine must be integrated within the everyday work of all laboratory professionals, who must shift from focusing on individual human errors to adopting a systematic approach.

References

1. Plebani M, Laposata M, Lippi G. A manifesto for the future of laboratory medicine professionals. Clin Chim Acta. 2019;489:49–52.
2. Plebani M. The future of laboratory medicine: navigating between technology and professionalism. Clin Chim Acta. 2019;49:816.
3. Plebani M. Towards a new paradigm in laboratory medicine: the five rights. Clin Chem Lab Med. 2016;54:1881–91.
4. Brush JE, Brophy JM. Sharing the process of diagnostic decision making. JAMA Intern Med. 2017;177:1245–6.
5. Schiff GD, Martin SA, Eidelman D, Volk I, Ruan E, Cassel C, et al. Ten principles for more conservative, care-full diagnosis. Ann Intern Med. 2018;169(9):643–64.
6. Kalra J. Medical errors: impact on clinical laboratories and other critical areas. Clin Biochem. 2004;37:1052–62.
7. Lundberg GD. Acting on significant laboratory results. JAMA. 1981;245:1762–3.
8. Plebani M, Laposata M, Lundberg GD. The brain-to-brain loop concept for laboratory testing 40 years after its introduction. Am J Clin Pathol. 2011;136:829–33.
9. Plebani M. The CCLM contribution to improvements in quality and patient safety. Clin Chem Lab Med. 2013;51:39–46.
10. Dintzis SM, Stetsenko GY, Sitlani CM, Gronowski AM, Astion ML, Gallagher TH. Communicating pathology and laboratory errors: anatomic pathologists' and laboratory medical directors' attitudes and experiences. Am J Clin Pathol. 2011;135:760–5.
11. Himmel ME, Lam K, Fralick M. Hemodialysis in a healthy patient - a case of an erroneous laboratory result: a teachable moment [published erratum appears in JAMA Intern Med 2016;176:1037]. JAMA Intern Med. 2016;176:431–2.
12. Bellandi T, Albolino S, Tartaglia R, Filipponi F. Unintended transplantation of three organs from an HIV-positive donor: report of the analysis of an adverse event in a regional health care service in Italy. Transplant Proc. 2010;42:2187–9.
13. Frias JP, Lim CG, Ellison JM, Montandon CM. Review of adverse events associated with false glucose readings measured by GDH-PQQ-based glucose test strips in the presence of interfering sugars. Diabetes Care. 2010;33:728–9.
14. Ross JW, Boone DJ. Institute on Critical Issues in Health Laboratory Practice, vol. 173. Wilmington, DE: DuPont Press; 1989.
15. Plebani M, Carraro P. Mistakes in a stat laboratory: types and frequency. Clin Chem. 1997;43:1348–51.
16. Carraro P, Plebani M. Errors in a stat laboratory: types and frequencies 10 years later. Clin Chem. 2007;53:1338–42.
17. Plebani M, Lippi G. Improving diagnosis and reducing diagnostic errors: the next frontier of laboratory medicine. Clin Chem Lab Med. 2016;54:1117–8.
18. Laposata M, Dighe A. "Pre-pre" and "post-post" analytical error: high-incidence patient safety hazards involving the clinical laboratory. Clin Chem Lab Med. 2007;45:712–9.
19. Astion ML, Shojania KG, Hamill TR, Kim S, Ng VL. Classifying laboratory incident reports to identify problems that jeopardize patient safety. Am J Clin Pathol. 2003;120:18–26.
20. International Organization for Standardization (ISO). ISO Technical Report 22367:2008. Medical laboratories—reduction of error through risk management and continual improvement—complementary elements. Geneva: International Organization for Standardization; 2008.
21. Committee on Patient Safety and Health Information Technology, Institute of Medicine. Health IT and patient safety: building safer systems for better care. Washington, DC: National Academies Press; 2011.
22. Plebani M. Laboratory-associated and diagnostic errors: a neglected link. Diagnosis (Berl). 2014;1:89–94.

23. World Health Organization. Diagnostic errors: technical series on safer primary care. Licence: CC BY-NC-SA 3.0 IGO. Geneva: World Health Organization; 2016.
24. Schiff GD, Hasan O, Kim S, Abrams R, Cosby K, Lambert BL, et al. Diagnostic error in medicine: analysis of 583 physician-reported errors. Arch Intern Med. 2009;169:1881–7.
25. Gandhi TK, Kachalia A, Thomas EJ, Puopolo AL, Yoon C, Brennan TA, Studdert DM. Missed and delayed diagnoses in the ambulatory setting: a study of closed malpractice claims. Ann Intern Med. 2006;145:488–96.
26. Kachalia A, Gandhi TK, Puopolo AL, Yoon C, Thomas EJ, Griffey R, et al. Missed and delayed diagnoses in the emergency department: a study of closed malpractice claims from 4 liability insurers. Ann Emerg Med. 2007;49:196–205.
27. Plebani M. Errors in clinical laboratories or errors in laboratory medicine? Clin Chem Lab Med. 2006;44:750–9.
28. Vogeser M, Seger C. Quality management in clinical application of mass spectrometry measurement systems. Clin Biochem. 2016;49:947–54.
29. Vogeser M, Seger C. Irregular analytical errors in diagnostic testing – a novel concept. Clin Chem Lab Med. 2018;56:386–96.
30. Ismail AA. When laboratory tests can mislead even when they appear plausible. Clin Med (Lond). 2017;17:329–32.
31. Plebani M. Errors in laboratory medicine and patient safety: the road ahead. Clin Chem Lab Med. 2007;45:700–7.
32. Hofgärtner WT, Tait JF. Frequency of problems during clinical molecular-genetic testing. Am J Clin Pathol. 1999;112:14–21.
33. Sciacovelli L, Lippi G, Sumarac Z, West J, Garcia Del Pino Castro I, Furtado Vieira K, et al. Working Group "Laboratory Errors and Patient Safety" of International Federation of Clinical Chemistry and Laboratory Medicine (IFCC). Quality indicators in laboratory medicine: the status of the progress of IFCC Working Group "Laboratory Errors and Patient Safety" project. Clin Chem Lab Med. 2017;55:348–57.
34. Plebani M. The journey toward quality and patient safety in laboratory medicine continues. North Am J Med Sci. 2014;6:229–30.
35. Boone DJ. Assessing laboratory employee competence. Arch Pathol Lab Med. 2000;124:190–1.
36. International Organization for Standardization. ISO 15189:2012. Medical laboratories—Requirements for quality and competence. Geneva: International Organization for Standardization; 2012.
37. Wagar EA, Tamashiro L, Yasin B, et al. Patient safety in the clinical laboratory: a longitudinal analysis of specimen identification errors. Arch Pathol Lab Med. 2006;130:1662–8.
38. Lippi G, Blanckaert N, Bonini P, et al. Causes, consequences, detection, and prevention of identification errors in laboratory diagnostics. Clin Chem Lab Med. 2009;47:143–53.
39. Plebani M. Quality indicators to detect pre-analytical errors in laboratory testing. Clin Biochem Rev. 2012;33:85–8.
40. Plebani M, Sciacovelli L, Aita A, et al. Quality indicators to detect pre-analytical errors in laboratory testing. Clin Chim Acta. 2014;432:44–8.
41. Plebani M, Sciacovelli L, Marinova M, et al. Quality indicators in laboratory medicine: a fundamental tool for quality and patient safety. Clin Biochem. 2013;46:1170–4.
42. Flegar-Mestric Z, Perkov S, Radeljak A, Marijana M, Paro K, Prkacin I, Devcic-Jeras A. Risk analysis of the pre-analytical process based on quality indicators data. Clin Chem Lab Med. 2017;55:368–77.
43. McQueen MJ. Will physicians and scientists have any role in managing laboratory resources in the year 2002. Eur J Clin Chem Clin Biochem. 1996;34:867–71.
44. Jassam N, Lake J, Dabrowska M, Queralto J, Rizos D, Lichtinghagen R, et al. The European Federation of Clinical Chemistry and Laboratory Medicine syllabus for postgraduate education and training for Specialists in Laboratory Medicine: version 5–2018. Clin Chem Lab Med. 2018;56:1846–63.
45. World Health Organization. Multi-professional patient safety curriculum guide. Geneva: World Health Organization; 2011.
46. Institute of Medicine (US) Committee on Quality of Health Care in America. In: Kohn LT, Corrigan JM, Donaldson MS, editors. To err is human: building a safer health system. Washington, DC: National Academies Press; 2000.
47. Plebani M. System-related and cognitive errors in laboratory medicine. Diagnosis (Berl). 2018;5:191–6.
48. Laposata M. Obtaining a correct diagnosis rapidly in the United States is associated with many barriers not present in other countries. Am J Clin Pathol. 2018;149:458–60.
49. Scally G, Donaldson LJ. The NHS's 50 anniversary. Clinical governance and the drive for quality improvement in the new NHS in England. BMJ. 1998;317:61–5.
50. International Organization for Standardization (ISO). ISO 9001:2015. Quality management system. Geneva: International Organization for Standardization (ISO); 2015.
51. Clinical and Laboratory Standards Institute (CLSI). CLSI EP18-A2. Risk management techniques to identify and control error sources. Approved Guideline. 2nd ed. USA; 2009.
52. Lao EG, García AS, Figuerola MB, Moreno E, Paraire AH. Errors of clinical laboratories and its impact on patient safety. Open J Soc Sci. 2017;5:243–53.
53. Serafini A, Troiano G, Franceschini E, Calzoni P, Nante N, Scapellato C. Use of a systematic risk analysis method (FMECA) to improve quality in a clinical laboratory procedure. Ann Ig. 2016;28:288–95.

54. Magnezi R, Hemi A, Hemi R. Using the failure mode and effects analysis model to improve parathyroid hormone and adrenocorticotropic hormone testing. Risk Manag Healthc Policy. 2016;9:271–4.

55. Badrick T, Gay S, Mackay M, Sikaris K. The key incident monitoring and management system - history and role in quality improvement. Clin Chem Lab Med. 2018;56:264–72.

56. World Health Organization: WHO. http://www.who.int/features/factfiles/patient_safety/en/.

57. Institute of Medicine. Medicare: a strategy for quality assurance: executive summary IOM Committee to design a strategy for quality review and assurance in Medicare. Washington, DC: National Academy Press; 1990.

58. National Patient Safety Foundation. Free from harm: accelerating patient safety improvement fifteen years after. To err is human. National Patient Safety Foundation: Boston, MA; 2015.

Patient Safety in Ophthalmology

25

Myrta Lippera, Jacques Bijon, Chiara Eandi, and Gianni Virgili

Learning Objects and Questions Covered in the Chapter

- Patient safety in the field of surgical ophthalmic care.
- Intraoperative and postoperative adverse events of cataract surgery and intravitreal injection therapy, possible prevention strategies, and management of the complications.
- Patient care and assessment prior, during, and after ophthalmic surgery.
- How to improve the surgical training process.
- Introduction to ophthalmic surgical errors and implications for the patient and the surgeon, with special focus on cataract and intravitreal injection therapy.
- How medical errors occur: the Swiss Cheese model of system accident.
- Causes and risk factors of wrong site surgery and preventing strategies.
- How to avert medication-related errors.

25.1 Introduction

In the *"Guidance on Patient Safety in Ophthalmology,"* the Royal College of Ophthalmologists (RCO) defines patient safety as *"the process by which an organization makes patient care safer. This should involve the following: risk assessment; the identification and management of patient-related risks; the reporting and analysis of incidents; and the capacity to learn from and follow-up on incidents and implement solutions to minimize the risk of them recurring"* [1].

Patient safety is particularly relevant in ophthalmology and regards the surgical part more than the clinical one. In particular, the Veteran Health Administration (VHA) reported in 2009 and 2011 that ophthalmology was the specialty with the highest number of incorrect surgical procedures [2]. However, Mayo Clinic defines ophthalmic surgery, and in particular cataract surgery, as safe for patients. This apparent contradiction is due to the fact that cataract surgery is a very common operation, and thus even rare adverse outcomes are frequent in absolute terms.

According to the World Health Organization (WHO), cataract causes 51% of world blindness.

Myrta Lippera and Jacques Bijon contributed equally so both are co-first author.

M. Lippera · G. Virgili
Eye Clinic, Department NEUROFARBA, Careggi University Hospital, University of Florence, Florence, Italy
e-mail: gianni.virgili@unifi.it

J. Bijon (✉) · C. Eandi
Department of Ophthalmology, University of Lausanne, Lausanne, Switzerland

Jules-Gonin Eye Hospital, Fondation Asile des Aveugles, Lausanne, Switzerland
e-mail: Jacques.bijon@fa2.ch; chiara.eandi@fa2.ch

© The Author(s) 2021
L. Donaldson et al. (eds.), *Textbook of Patient Safety and Clinical Risk Management*, https://doi.org/10.1007/978-3-030-59403-9_25

In 2010 this condition represented about 20 million people. In fact, in many countries barriers exist that prevent patients to access surgery. Nonetheless, worldwide approximately ten million surgeries are performed each year. In economically well-developed countries, cataract surgeries were performed at a rate of 4000–6000 per million population annually in 2000 [3]. In 2011, in the United States of America (USA), the rate reached 1100 per 100,000 residents and the number of people who undergo cataract surgery seems to grow steadily [4].

In the same way, the amount of intravitreal injections continues to increase year by year [5]. Between 2010 and 2015 it was registered in England a 215% rise of anti-VEGF injections and 388,031 procedures were registered between 2014 and 2015 [6]. In 2016 it was reported that 5.9 million injections were administered only in the USA [5].

Since the two mentioned procedures are the most common and consequently the ones that contribute the most to adverse events and errors in the ophthalmic practice, they will be the focus of the chapter.

25.2 Epidemiology of Adverse Events: Safety Practices and Implementation Strategy

25.2.1 Cataract Surgery

Greenberg et al. reported the prevalence of ocular complications associated with cataract surgery in 45,082 United States veterans. The study showed that 3.8% patients had intraoperative ocular complications and 9.8% patients had postoperative ocular complications within 90 days from surgery. The most common intraoperative ocular complications were posterior capsular tear and vitreous loss, sometimes both (3.5%). The most common 90-day postoperative ocular complication was posterior capsular opacification (4.2%). Cystic macular edema (3.3%) and retained lens fragments (1.7%) followed [7].

Ophthalmology trainees execute 21–39% of all the cataract surgeries performed in developed countries [8, 9]. It is interesting to notice that, with proper supervision and patients' selection, cataract surgery performed by residents have a similar risk of complications to cataract surgery performed by attending staff. In detail, Rutar et al. reported a major intraoperative complication rate of 4.7% in cataract surgery performed by residents in the USA, the rate included 3.1% cases of vitreous loss [10]. The USA Accreditation Council for Graduate Medical Education (ACGME) assessed at 86 the required minimum number of procedures as primary surgeon for graduating residents in ophthalmology [11].

Similarly, a study conducted in Australia found no difference in the rate of posterior capsule tear, vitreous loss, or dropped lens rates between trainees and consultants. However, an increased rate of wound burns when trainees were operating was registered (2.2% versus 0.4%) [12].

The same trend was confirmed by a Canadian study [13]. Unfortunately, further recent studies regarding the complication rate of cataract surgery performed by residents are missing in other countries, for instance Europe.

Therefore, the reported data might not reflect the standards worldwide. Nevertheless, it can be said that residents can always add a positive value to the quality of patient's care. As a matter of fact, trainees often spend additional time with patients and create a supportive relationship with them. This attitude improves patient experience before surgery, with a more attentive preoperative assessment for risk factors. In addition, there are also benefits after surgery, with increased vigilance for postoperative complications [14].

25.2.1.1 Intraoperative Adverse Events

- **Local anesthesia** is nowadays the technique most frequently used. In specific it is performed in 95.5% of cataract surgeries. In particular, topical and sub-Tenon anesthesia are considered effective and safe procedures [15]. In fact, sub-Tenon anesthesia consists in the insertion of a blunt cannula in the episcleral space in order to release the anesthetic. Topical anesthesia consists in administration of anesthetic eye drops.

On the contrary, retro-bulbar and peri-bulbar anesthesia imply the use of a sharp needle to inject the anesthetic [16]. This action can lead to sporadic but serious adverse events like retrobulbar hemorrhage (0.03%), globe injury (0.01%), and, more rarely, optic nerve atrophy, muscular palsy, and brain-steam anesthesia [17].

The main adverse event of topical and sub-Tenon anesthesia is patient discomfort or ocular pain during and after the procedure. A Cochrane review established that topical anesthesia showed intensification of intraoperative pain and decrease of postoperative pain at 24 h, when compared to sub-Tenon's anesthesia. Since there was not enough evidence to declare which of the two techniques was associated with less intraoperative complications, both types of anesthesia can be considered adequate for cataract surgery [16].

- **Posterior capsule rupture (PCR)** incidence rate has recently decreased due to the introduction of advanced techniques, newer instrumentation and technology. It is the most common intraoperative complication and in uncomplicated cases of cataract surgery can range from 1.9% [18] to 3.5% of [7]. It can lead to consequences such as vitreous loss (1–5%), drop of lens fragments or nucleus in the vitreous, placement of the intraocular lens in the ciliary sulcus or anterior chamber, and occasionally the need for additional surgical interventions [19].

  Intraocular risk factors for PCR include: pseudoexfoliation syndrome; small pupils and reduced working place; excessive anterior chamber depth, which can occur in high myopic eyes or after pars plana vitrectomy; certain types of cataract, as posterior polar ones; dense asteroid hyalosis; etc. [20].

  The American Academy of Ophthalmology (AAO) described cardinal signs that can help a non-expert surgeon in recognizing PCR: sud-

den deepening of the anterior chamber, momentary pupillary dilatation, excessive movement of the nucleus that do not come toward the phaco tip, or vision of a focal sharp red reflex.

Recommendations in order to prevent PCR include considering intracameral phenylephrine in floppy iris syndrome; small capsulorhexis enlargement before hydrodissection; application of one of the existing different techniques in case of rhexis tears [20]; and use of capsular tension rings whenever the capsular bag is unstable or in case of zonular dehiscence [21]. Moreover, a thorough knowledge of phacoemulsification machine and its parameters is essential both to prevent and manage unexpected events while operating [20].

In the eventual case of PCR, the National Institute for Health and Care Excellence (NICE) suggests following a protocol. The protocol should include: removing vitreous from the wound and anterior chamber; minimizing traction on the retina; removing lens fragments in the posterior chamber or vitreous cavity when possible; removing soft lens matter; and proceeding to intraocular lens (IOL) insertion when possible [21].

In conclusion, identifying the presence of predisposing factors, early recognition, and appropriate modification of the surgical plan can decrease the overall incidence of PCR.

25.2.1.2   Postoperative Adverse Events

- **Posterior capsular opacification (PCO)** rate varies in literature from 3% [22] to 47% [23, 24]. PCO is caused by migration toward the posterior capsule, proliferation, and differentiation of the residual lens epithelial cells on the anterior capsule [25]. Young age is a significant risk factor for PCO [26]. Surgery-related factors that can be modified in order to prevent PCO are: achieving good hydrodissection and cortical cleanup, implanting both haptics in the capsular bag, performing a continuous curvilinear capsulorhexis diameter which should be slightly smaller than the IOL optic diameter [22].

The treatment is provided by YAG capsulotomy, a noninvasive, quick, and effective technique. However, it should be remembered that YAG capsulotomy can cause rare but possible risks, including retinal detachment, damage to the IOL, cystoid macular edema, increase in intraocular pressure, iris hemorrhage, corneal edema, IOL subluxation, and exacerbation of localized endophthalmitis [27]. A follow-up after YAG capsulotomy is therefore recommended.

- **Retinal detachment (RD)** rate is described being between 0.26% at 1 year [28] and 1.79% at 20 years from cataract surgery [29].

It was hypothesized to be caused by postsurgical anatomical and biochemical alterations in the vitreous [30]. Specifically, the smaller volume of IOL, compared to the volume of the cataractous lens, increases the total vitreous volume and consequently mobility of the vitreous [31]. Moreover, biochemical changes and alterations in the protein composition of the vitreous fluid after phacoemulsification contribute to the development of retinal disease [32].

Predisposing factors are young age, male gender, long axial length, and intraoperative complications, like capsular tear with vitreous loss [33]. Pars plana vitrectomy for removal of posteriorly dislocated lens fragments was additionally associated with a significantly shorter time interval between cataract surgery and retinal detachment (3.9 versus 15.7 months) [34].

Whenever this complication occurs, the patient should be immediately referred to a vitreoretinal surgeon. Haddad et al. showed achievement, after retinal reattachment, of 20/60 best-corrected visual acuity (BCVA) or better in only 50% of cases [34].

- **Cystoid macular edema (CME)** is a frequent cause of decreased BCVA after uncomplicated cataract surgery [35]. The incidence of CME in patients without risk factors was 1–2% [36]. However, its incidence has been reported to be between 1% and 30%, due to

the heterogeneity of diagnostic criteria. In addition, its rate can be increased whenever other ocular comorbidities are present, like diabetes, previous CME, previous retinal vein occlusion, epiretinal membrane or by prostaglandin use [37].

CME is normally a self-limiting condition: 95% of CME due to Irvine-Gass, or post-cataract CME, has been shown to resolve within 6 months without additional therapy. Some cases, however, can determine long-term visual impairment [37]. The NICE recommends the use of topical steroids in combination with non-steroidal anti-inflammatory drugs (NSAIDs) in order to manage CME. Moreover, NICE recommends their use after cataract surgery for people at increased risk of cystoid macular edema, for example, people with diabetes or uveitis [21].

In 2015, Kim et al. reported that topic NSAIDs hasten the speed of short-term visual recovery after cataract surgery when compared with placebo or corticosteroid eye drop with limited intraocular penetration. However, at 3 months or more, prophylactic use of NSAIDs showed lack of evidence in reducing CME-related vision loss [38]. A 2016 Cochrane review concluded that topical NSAIDs can be useful in preventing CME, but possible effects on postoperative BVCA are uncertain [39]. In 2018 the European Society of Cataract & Refractive Surgeons (ESCRS) PREMED Study I reported that use of topical bromfenac 0.09%, compared with topical dexamethasone 0.1%, can lower macular thickness and total volume after uneventful cataract surgery in patients with no risk factors for CME. However, a reduced risk of developing clinical significant macular edema was shown in eyes treated with combination of the two drugs, compared with patients treated with a single drug [40, 41].

- **Suprachoroidal Hemorrhage (SCH)** is a sight-threatening complication where blood accumulates between the choroid and the sclera. The etiopathogenesis is long or short posterior ciliary arteries rupture [19, 42]. It is defined as a hemorrhage that can cause extrusion from the eye of the intraocular contents, or that can force the inner retinal surfaces into or near apposition [42]. The incidence varies from 0.03% to 0.28%, in the case of extracapsular cataract extraction [42, 43]. Risk factors include myopia, glaucoma, diabetes, atherosclerotic vascular diseases, and hypertension [42].

Clinical signs of an intraoperative choroidal hemorrhage include shallowing of the anterior chamber, iris prolapse, expulsion of the lens and vitreous outside the eye, and dark retinal and choroidal detachment with loss of the red reflex [44]. Whenever it occurs, the surgical wound should be immediately closed with sustainable sutures [42]. As systemic hypertension is also a risk factor, intravenous administration of hypotensive agents might help in patients with high blood pressure.

In case of massive SCH, with BVCA of light perception, surgical interventions such as transcleral drainage, vitrectomy, and silicone oil tamponade are valuable options to improve the poor prognosis [45].

Consideration of all risk factors and avoidance of predisposing events are a priority in order to prevent SCH.

- **Endophthalmitis** is a severe infective inflammation of intraocular fluids. It is frequently a postoperative complication but can also occur after traumas. Rarely it can be sterile or with an endogenous etiology, arising from systemic infections or inflammatory disorders [46].

The epidemiology of post-cataract endophthalmitis varies in the literature. A systematic review conducted by Taban et al. reports an overall endophthalmitis rate of 0.128% between the years 1963 and 2003. Specifically, a 0.327% rate occurred in the 1970s, 0.158% in the 1980s, 0.087% in the 1990s. It is interesting to notice that a 0.265% rate was registered between 2000 and 2003 [47]. On the contrary, the ESCRS endophthalmitis study group reported a decrease of postoperative endophthalmitis from rates near 0.3–1.2% to 0.014–0.08% after the institution of intracameral cefuroxime [48].

The main finding is a red eye with blurred vision. Although an aching eye is often present, 25% of the patients do not complain of pain. Signs include hypopyon (85% of cases) and hazy media (80% of cases) [49].

The mainstay treatment is with antibiotic intravitreal injections; vancomycin and ceftazidime are the first choice. The Endophthalmitis Vitrectomy Study (EVS) showed no benefits in systemic intravenous antibiotics administration [49]. On the contrary, in case of severe purulent infections the ESCRS Guidelines for Prevention and Treatment of Endophthalmitis encourage the prescription of a systemic antibiotic therapy, not necessarily intravenous. For those cases, the same drug class from the one contained in the intravitreal therapy should be administered [50].

BCVA was a discriminant factor for endophthalmitis management. In 1995 the EVS reported that only patients presenting with a visual acuity of light-perception showed benefit from immediate core vitrectomy. However, more recently Kuhr suggested offering a complete vitrectomy whenever those clinical signs were present: poor red reflex or no detection of retinal details, no improvement after 24 h from intravitreal injection [51, 52]. The study is, however, conducted on a limited number of patients and it is not randomized.

25.2.1.3 Safety Practices and Implementation Strategy in Cataract Surgery

A. Preoperative Care

Patient Assessment
NICE guidelines recommend using optical biometry for axial length measurements [21]. In facts, this technique is easy and quick to perform. It is automated, user-independent, and precise, since the patient is fixating on a target while the measurement is taken [53, 54]. However, its limitation is due to the fact that the machine uses an average velocity to determine the eye axial length, which is extrapolated from the time

needed by the pulse waveform to cover the cornea-retina distance. Due to this, in an eye longer than 26 mm the real axial length could be overestimated, and the opposite could occur in an eye shorter than 22 mm. In those cases, special formulas are required to balance the final calculation.

Ultrasound biometry is nowadays necessary when optical biometry pulse waveform does not manage to measure the axial length, for example, in case of very dense cataracts or vitreous hemorrhage; or whenever the optical biometry results cannot be considerate precise, as it can occur in case of macular retinal detachment.

Corneal topography should be used whenever any abnormality of the cornea surface is present or suspected: high or low K-values, high astigmatism, keratoconus, etc. In particular, topography should be performed in case of a precedent refractive surgery correction. Since the relationship between the anterior and posterior curvature is iatrogenic modified in those eyes, additional calculations and sometimes more than one intervention can be necessary to achieve the desired refractive target [21].

Supplemental Evaluation

Patient comorbidities can worsen and cause systemic adverse events during or after cataract surgery. Cavallini et al. registered those complications to occur in 0.63% of cataract cases, in particular arterial hypertension showed to complicate the 0.31% of the surgeries [55]. Systemic adverse events are a matter of concern, in terms of absolute numbers, due to the large number of elderly who undergo cataract surgery with cardiac or pulmonary diseases [56]. In the past decade, the request of blood test results and of an electrocardiogram prior to surgery was common. Nowadays, different geographical areas have various approaches.

The AAO Preferred Practice Pattern, as well as the RCO Guidelines and the National Health Service (NHS), discourages asking for routine exams before cataract surgery [21, 53, 57]. But, in case of serious comorbidities, the AAO advises requiring supplemental testing and a systemic visit [53].

On the other hand, in 2019 a Cochrane review certified that routine preoperative testing does not increase the safety of cataract surgery in terms of total medical adverse events, total hospitalization, total deaths, cancellation of cataract surgery, and total ocular adverse events. As an alternative, questionnaires about general health can be administered and completed by the patient or the primary care physician. Doing so, a better identification of patients at risk of systemic adverse events is possible [56].

Risk Stratification

NICE Guidelines suggest relying on a validated risk stratification system in the preoperative assessment. If a high surgical risk is identified, its implications and the new risk-benefit ratio for surgery should be discussed with the patient. Whenever an unsuccessful surgery could have a severe impact on life, as it might be for instance in monocular vision, surgical risks should be attenuated and a close supervision is necessary if a trainee is performing the surgery [21].

Muhtaseb et al. developed a risk stratification system by reviewing different risk factors for cataract surgery from the literature and associating a value to each of them. According to the total sum of the points related to single risk factors, each patient was categorized into a risk group predictive of intraoperative complications: group 1 with no added risk; group 2 with low risk; group 3 with moderate risk; and group 4 with high risk. In addition to individualized counseling, risk stratification can be useful to select cases that could be operated by nonexpert surgeons and to standardize patients in groups for scientific studies [9].

Butler et al. described a similar system with weighted scores based on the severity of risk factors reported by Narendran et al [58, 59]. Scores less than 3 are appropriate for junior trainees; cases scoring from 3 to 5 are appropriate for more senior trainees; and cases scoring higher than 5 for consultants [58]. Although this system was meant to predict intraoperative complications, a correlation was also observed between the score and postoperative complications, as well as postoperative corrected-distance visual acuity outcomes [60]. Other risk stratification systems exist, like the New Zealand Cataract Risk Stratification or the Najjar-Awwad cataract surgery risk score for resident phacoemulsification surgery [60–62].

B. Perioperative Care

Patient Alimentation and Therapy

The Joint Guidelines from the RCO and the Royal College of Anesthetists declared that it is not mandatory for patients to be fasted the day of the surgery in case of topical anesthesia without sedation. As a matter of fact, no aspiration event was ever described. In detail, a special attention is required for diabetic patients in therapy with insulin. For them, local protocols should be developed in order to avoid hypoglycemia, considering also catering whenever the surgery is going to be performed late in the day [63].

The RCO also suggests to tell patients to take their normal medication on the day of the surgery [57, 63]. In particular, a review conducted in 2015 showed how continuation of anticoagulant and antiplatelet therapy before and during an uncomplicated cataract surgery is safe. However, in case of small pupils, floppy iris syndrome, iris neovascularization, significant pseudoexfoliation, or phacodonesis, discontinuation of the therapy can be discussed with an internist or cardiologist [64]. Indeed, Warfarin increases the risk of orbital hemorrhage from 0.2% to 1.0% [57]. It might also increase other hemorrhagic complication risk, like hyphema, dot retinal or retrobulbar and choroidal hemorrhages [64]. In addition, anticoagulant exposure worsen the severity of an already onset bleeding [65]. Nevertheless, it was demonstrated that warfarin reduces life-threatening thrombotic events and decreases the risk for stroke to 1 in 100 [57]. Therefore, when older oral anticoagulants are used, the International Normalized Ratio (INR), when possible, should remain in the desired therapeutic range [57].

Prophylaxis of Infections and Sterility

Endophthalmitis prevention is crucial. The ESCRS Endophthalmitis Study Group demonstrated that the risk for contracting postoperative endophthalmitis was reduced by an intracameral injection of 1 mg cefuroxime at the end of the surgery. The lowest incidence rate of endophthalmitis was observed in the group who received, in addition to intracameral cefuroxime, an intensive pulsed dose regimen of three drops levofloxacin, each drop separated by 5 min, also given at the close of surgery, along with two drops given preoperatively, 30 min apart [50, 66]. A Cochrane review confirmed, with high-certainty evidence, the role of intracameral cefuroxime for prevention of intraocular infections. On the other hand, the perioperative use of antibiotic eye drops, levofloxacin or chloramphenicol, showed to lower the possibility of endophthalmitis only with moderate certainty evidence [46].

Since the patient's own ocular surface flora contains also pathogenic microorganisms that can infect the eye during surgery, preoperative antisepsis is an important point in prophylaxis [67]. Prior to the start of operation, the surgeon must irrigate the cornea, conjunctival sac and periocular skin with povidone-iodine 5% ophthalmic solution, or chlorhexidine 0.05% in case of allergy [50]. In this way, the microorganisms of patient ocular flora are reduced up to 90%. The application of the antiseptic for at least 3 min before surgery showed to decrease the postoperative endophthalmitis rate [50, 68].

A systematic review demonstrated that, excluded patient ocular flora, another cause of postoperative endophthalmitis is contamination from the surgical environment. In particular, it occurs from solutions, phacoemulsification machines, ventilation systems, and defective sterilization of ocular surgical instruments [69]. Consequentially, endophthalmitis prevention includes standardized quality control systems, surveillance, and infection control measures in the operating theater. Regular maintenance of proper filters in the airflow systems is mandatory. In the same way, maintenance of closed doors during surgery is recommended and a constant positive pressure in the room should always be present. Bacterial filters on bottles of solutions are necessary since wet areas are easily contaminated with *Pseudomonas aeruginosa*, which leads to a particularly severe form of endophthalmitis [50]. All instruments must be limited to single use and washed properly prior to sterilization. More recommendations regarding intraocular surgical instruments cleaning and sterilization can be found in the article written by Hellinger et al. [70].

C. Postoperative Care

After surgery, teaching the patient which symptoms might be an early sign of a possible complication is crucial for fast access to emergency care. In particular, it should be remarked that significant reduction in vision, increasing pain, progressive redness, or periocular swelling could indicate a possible intraocular infection [53].

Since it was demonstrated that, in case of an uncomplicated operation, a visit within 24 h from surgery did not reduce the rate of severe adverse events, a first postoperative visit postponed at 2 weeks did not seem to increase the postoperative risk [71, 72]. However, a 24-h check is still recommended in patients who underwent intraoperative complications, have high postoperative risk, or have monocular vision [53].

Moreover, during the postoperative visits, a dilated fundus examination is not mandatory since the incidence of peripheral retinal findings at 1 month after cataract surgery was demonstrated to be low [53, 73]. However, it should be performed whenever a posterior segment complication is suspected or in patients with high risk of peripheral retinal pathologies like diabetic retinopathy, retinal vein occlusions, or high myopia [74].

According to the AAO, "*the surgeon's obligation to the patient is not discharged with the conclusion of a successful operation. Unless terminated by the parties, his relationship to the patient continues until ended by the cessation of the necessity which gave rise to the relation.*" Therefore, the same ophthalmologist who performed the surgery should provide postoperative eye care. Whenever this is not possible, the patient can be referred to another ophthalmologist only with agreement between the three figures involved: the patient and the two ophthalmologists [75].

D. Training

The ACGME states that trainees approaching the end of their ophthalmic residency should be able to perform the diagnostic, medical, and surgical procedures expected for an ophthalmologist entering a comprehensive ophthalmic practice [76]. This goal has to be achieved always providing high-quality patient care.

The ACGME also exhorts University Hospitals to build their own Ophthalmic Educational Programs. Each program should include goals for the trainee. The aims cannot be standardized since they depend on the needs of the community where the hospital works, on the hospital working team propensity toward specific ophthalmic fields, as well as on the resident talent or inclination. Because of this, the Program may be more focused on research, leadership, public health, etc. Nevertheless, faculty members should approve it and review it regularly [76].

The "*Guide for delivery of Ophthalmic Specialist Training (OST)*" of the RCO recommends protected time for education. Lessons should be organized, and residents should be able to attend at least one session per week of a regional teaching program. In addition, at least one fully protected research session a week is expected [77].

The International Council of Ophthalmology (ICO) Residency Curriculum, available online, offers an international perspective on what should be taught during residency [78].

Methods to teach and learn surgical procedures are not standardized worldwide. Moreover, the surgical skills and possibility to learn for residents vary widely among the residency training programs and even within the same program. For instance, in the USA the average number of phacoemulsification performed during residency is about 113, but it might vary from 80 to 140 cases, and 25% of residents perform fewer than 80 cases; United Kingdom (UK) registered a number of 500–600 cases per resident [79], and Canada a number of 200–400 [79, 80]. However, in other countries less than 50 phacoemulsification are performed at the end of residency.

Implementation strategies to improve the process of training, while reducing risk for the patient, have been proposed [79].

Enhancement made by hospital and program administration might regard expansion of clinic and operating theater where residents work. In addition, teaching should be encouraged, also with incentives.

Regarding trainers, the RCO strongly exhorts them to regularly attend a course that learns how to teach. Whenever possible, part of the operating lists should be specifically reserved for training, and specific time in the surgery room should be dedicated for junior doctors [81].

Lastly, residents should study and be familiar with the surgical procedures and possible complications [79]. Indeed, they should also actively participate to the pre- and postoperative care [79]. In facts, good data collection with continuous monitoring of complication rates for each individual resident is important, as well as successive audit about the cataract outcomes [81].

Wet labs and surgical simulators should be included in residents' experience in order to improve the trainee learning curve and increase patient safety [82]. In fact, a significant decrease of cataract intraoperative complications was shown in junior surgeons who trained with additional surgical simulator [83].

25.2.2 Intravitreal Injection Therapy

Intravitreal injection therapy (IVT) is the treatment of choice for many retinal diseases. This is used mainly in case of choroidal neovascularization in macular degeneration or in case of macular edema, which can be present in diabetic retinopathy or retinal vein occlusion.

Types of drug released mainly belong to the anti-VEGF family, which blocks the vascular endothelial growth factor in order to obtain regression of abnormal vessels, or corticosteroids, which act as a nonspecific anti-inflammatory agent, but also showed a role in VEGF downregulation [84].

25.2.2.1 Adverse Events, Safety Practices, and Implementation Strategy

- **Ocular hemorrhage** is the most frequent adverse event. In fact, subconjunctival hemorrhages can occur in 10% of intravitreal injections, especially if the patient is under antiaggregant medications [85]. Massive subretinal and choroidal hemorrhages are rare but

present in the literature as possible complications [86, 87]. It is important though not to interrupt antiaggregant, neither anticoagulation drugs prior to IVT. In fact, the risk of serious ocular hemorrhage is low. On the contrary, in case of discontinuation the risk of severe thromboembolic events is high [88].

- **Endophthalmitis** is the most severe of IVT adverse events. The frequency of this complication ranges from 0.02% to 1.6% [89, 90].

  Streptococcus species showed to be the causative pathogen approximately three times more frequently when compared with intraocular surgery. The bacteria can be isolated in the salivary flora, indeed aerosolization or droplet spread can be the source of operative field contamination. For this reason, talking, sneezing, and coughing should be avoided while performing IVT and a surgical mask should be worn during the whole procedure [89].

  Streptococcus mitis or *oralis* were also found in unused syringes of Bevacizumab. Bevacizumab is an anti-VEGF approved by the Food and Drug Administration for colon-rectal cancer metastasis. Nevertheless, this drug showed good results also in case of neovascular macular degeneration, for which it might be used off-label [91]. On one hand, Bevacizumab use reduces public health care costs due to its price 4–40 times lower than the on-label drugs. On the other hand, in order to reduce the costs, the drug needs to be repackaged for intravitreal injections by the local pharmacy. This action increases the risks of contamination, and therefore protocols and guidelines which stress the need of asepsis during syringe preparation have been made available [92].

  Other strategies to reduce the rate of postinjection endophthalmitis are treatment of patient's external infections like conjunctivitis or blepharitis, use of 5% povidone–iodine, and avoidance of needle contact with eyelids or lashes by the use of a blepharostat [93].

  A systematic review conducted in 2018 showed that topical antibiotic prophylaxis prior to IVI injections does not reduce the rate of risk for endophthalmitis [94].

- **Sterile intraocular inflammation** frequency ranges from 1.4% to 2.9% [95]. It is an acute ocular reaction without infection; consequently it can be treated with topical steroids and showed good visual outcomes at resolution [96]. This condition goes in differential diagnosis with endophthalmitis, although it is more frequent. Signs that might help a correct diagnosis include:

- Time of presentation: 2.55 days (between 1 and 6 days) for endophthalmitis versus 1 day or less in ocular inflammation.
- Symptoms: decreased vision and severe pain are more frequently associated with endophthalmitis.
- Severity of anterior chamber reaction and vitreitis.

However, it is recommended to administer early intravitreal antibiotic injections whenever a high infection suspicion is present [97].

- **Rhegmatogenous retinal detachment (RRD)** incidence was around 0.013% as reported by Meyer et al. [98]. The hypothesized cause is the vitreous detachment due to an incorrect injection technique. For this reason, particular attention to the site of injection and use of small needles are required [93].
- **Intraocular pressure (IOP)** acute and transitory elevation, lasting maximum some hours and with individual variations, is caused by the injection of fluid in the eye [99]. However, cases of sustained IOP elevation following anti-VEGF have been described, although they are rare [100]. On the contrary, intravitreal injections of corticosteroids, and in particular of Dexamethasone, showed to cause chronic ocular hypertension in almost one out of three patients [101]. Risk factors are a family history for glaucoma or previous glaucoma diagnosis. Regular check of IOP after intravitreal injection is recommended. Fifty percent of all cases with chronic IOP elevation did not require any treatment, while topical hypotensive drugs were needed in most of the other cases and a glaucoma surgery was rarely performed [101].
- **Posterior subscapular cataract** is known to be correlated with corticosteroid use [102]. Dexamethasone intravitreal implant

showed a role in cataract development and was confirmed by a meta-analysis conducted in 2018 [103].

The setting of care for IVT is not necessarily an operating theater. The procedure can also be safely performed in a suitable sterile room with adequate ventilation system. More information about sterility requirements, patient information and consent, pre-injection checks and preparation, as well as post-injection care can be found in the Ophthalmic Service Guidance for Intravitreal Injection Therapy [104].

25.3 Most Frequent Errors: Safety Practices and Implementation Strategy

Since humans are fallible, patient safety cannot only rely on the ophthalmologist experience or proficiency. Reliable systems must be put in place to reduce human errors, considered as events that should *never* occur (i.e., "never event"). For instance, invasive procedure on the wrong eye, as published in the *"Never Events List 2018"* by the NHS, is not acceptable [105]. Moreover, the occurrence of even a single "never event" constitutes a red flag.

Thereby, despite being in training, a young ophthalmologist must become aware of this fundamental issue: preventable medical errors are not tolerated, especially in the eye of the patient's opinion [106]. This topic is further significant for a specialty that trains not only physicians but also future eye surgeons.

For instance, as previously said, cataract surgery constitutes one of the most common procedures performed, making it a top priority for error avoidance [4, 107, 108]. Indeed, Neily et al. found 342 reported incorrect surgical procedures from VHA Medical Centers from 2001 to 2006. Ophthalmology was the specialty with the most reported errors, representing 1.8 surgical confusions for every 10,000 cases: wrong IOL implantation occupied the highest percentage [109]. This observation was also reported by Simon et al. where 67% of surgical confusion cases (67/106) were accountable to wrong IOL implantation [106]. Their findings emphasize the importance of awareness among young trainees attending ophthalmological surgery.

In a retrospective analysis of medical professional liability (MPL) claims in the US from 2006 to 2015, 2.6% out of the 90,743 closed malpractice claims were filed against ophthalmologists, with 50% being accountable to cataract and corneal surgery [110]. Even though this study concluded that compared with other specialties, ophthalmology had a relative low number of malpractice claims (ranked 12th out of 29 specialties in a 10-year period), it should be reminded that study results on this topic probably represent the tip of the iceberg as many medical errors might be unreported [106, 111, 112]. Furthermore, Ali et al. analyzed a decade of claims due to clinical negligence on the NHS Litigation Authority database for ophthalmology (from 1995 to 2006) [113]: their results estimated that an ophthalmologist of any grade had a 30% chance to be confronted to a claim in a 10-year period, representing one medical claim due to malpractice in a 30-year career. An even higher risk was predicted for consultants, with 90% chance of being faced to a claim in a 10-year period.

25.3.1 The Most Common Medical Errors and Preventive Strategies in Ophthalmology

To be successful at preventing a medical error, knowledge of how it occurs is fundamental. The Swiss Cheese model of system accident, proposed by Reason et al., allows to understand how an incident could happen despite defense mechanisms in place [114]. This model represents a "cumulative act effect" phenomenon. For example, in an elaborate medical system, a series of barriers (metaphorically considered as a slice of cheese) are built to prevent a mishap to occur. However, each barrier has its own dynamic weakness (i.e., holes in a Swiss cheese). Taken individually, they do not create an adverse event for the patient but when the holes of the slices are

aligned, there is the opportunity for a given hazard to reach the patient [115]. Those weaknesses come from the combination of two main reasons [114]: active failures and latent conditions. James Reason defines active failures as "*the unsafe acts committed by people who are in direct contact with the patient or system,*" while latent condition "*arise from decisions made by designers, builders, procedure writers, and top-level management.*"

In summary, young trainees could hardly be entirely responsible for an error but can participate in the occurrence of such, especially within a system where many latent conditions lie dormant. It takes minor mistakes from multiple aspects of the management of a patient to provoke a preventable error: thus, every medical action has its importance.

It is important for trainees to be aware of the causes and consequences of possible medical errors (including surgical confusions) in ophthalmology. It would allow implementing strategies from the beginning to prevent such mistakes and thus improve patient safety. The list of medical errors and strategies is non-exhaustive; therefore acknowledging their existence is the very first step toward avoiding malpractice. When properly considered, medical errors are an opportunity to learn. Indeed, this allows for actions to be taken in response to such unfortunate and evitable events. Consequently, this will lead to risk reduction for recurrence.

25.3.1.1 Wrong-Site Eye Surgery

Introduction
Wrong-site surgery is defined as "*surgery on the wrong site or the wrong side, the wrong procedure, the wrong implant, or the wrong patient*" [116]. In a large systematic review of surgical never events published in 2015, the median incidence of wrong-site surgery in ophthalmology ranged from 0.5 to 4 events per 10,000 procedures [116]. In comparison, the median incidence for general surgical procedures across seven American studies was 0.09 events per 10,000 procedures with, however, a wide variation in the results. Parikh et al. recently conducted a

large retrospective cohort study of errors in ophthalmological surgical procedure between 2006 and 2017 [117]: they intended to characterize the incidence, causes and consequences of ophthalmological surgical confusions on patients and specialists. Out of the 143 cases of surgical confusions reported, cataract-related errors occupied the first position. Incorrect eye blocks were the second most common surgical confusions, representing 14.0% of cases. Incorrect eye procedure was in third position, with incorrect patients or operation (3.5%) being the fifth. Similarly, these results are consistent with a previous retrospective series of 106 cases investigated by Simon et al. more than 10 years earlier [106]. Indeed, 15 cases had surgery on the wrong eye. Wrong eye block was performed in 14 cases. In another 8 cases, either the operation occurred on the wrong patient or the wrong procedure was performed.

Causes and Risk Factors

Some examples of common root causes and risk factors for the occurrence of surgical confusion identified among the different studies mentioned include [106, 116, 117]:

- Inadequate time-out: it represented the main cause of surgical confusion according to Parikh et al.
- Inadequate site markings: absent, washed off during preparation, poorly visualized, hidden under surgical capes or drapes.
- Inadequate communication: breakdown of communication between the patient and the surgeon, inadequate communication among staff (e.g., OR schedule changes not adequately communicated to all staff members).

Preventive Strategies

The following are the main prevention strategies of wrong-site surgery proposed across the studies:

A. The Universal Protocol

This protocol was introduced by the Joint Commission on Accreditation of Healthcare Organizations in 2004 and is aimed to prevent confusions in all surgical procedures. For instance, Parikh et al. concluded that 64.3% of ophthalmological cases would have been preventable by using the universal protocol [117]. The same conclusion was initially made by Simon et al. where, conscientiously applied, 85% of the ophthalmological surgical confusions in their retrospective series of 106 cases could have been prevented [106].

The protocol focuses on three complementary steps [118]: (1) Preoperative verification, (2) site marking, and (3) time-out before starting the surgery [106].

However, the universal protocol does not cover steps prior the surgery day where a lot of negligence can be the cause of medical errors occurring in the OR.

The AAO Wrong-site Task Force has managed to fill this gap by bringing specific recommendations tailored to ophthalmological surgery [119]. Their guidelines are divided into three stages:

1. Steps taken prior to surgery day.
2. Steps taken on the day of surgery.
3. Procedures dependent upon preoperative calculations.

Interestingly, communication is central. Indeed, the first step emphasizes on medical records of the patient with proper surgical data available. It outlines the importance of passing the information adequately between ward or clinic and operative room. Other examples include the active participation of the patient and all staff members especially on the day of surgery. Moreover, adherence to the steps and communication would be facilitated by the use of checklists, further reducing the incidence of wrong-site surgery [118].

Nonetheless, certain issues are yet not covered by these strategies. For instance, Simon et al. suggested that patient confusion could ultimately lead to failure of the protocol's efficacy [106]. Furthermore, if staff members do not take seriously into consideration the time-out, which represents the final step of the universal protocol, it would be ineffective. Thus, prevention strategies are only tools to help reduce risks, but eventually it is the duty of the surgeon to make sure these tools are thoroughly followed.

These basic rules must be learned from the beginning of training in order to ensure their efficient application. For example, the inconsistent engagement of staff members in the WHO surgical safety checklist is thought to contribute to persistence of surgical errors in the NHS. Experience of the surgical safety checklist training was therefore investigated through a survey among UK medical and nursing undergraduates by Kilduff et al. [120]. Students that received teaching about the checklist or that were included in the time-out before the beginning of the procedure had a significant better understanding of the checklist's purpose. Their results, however, highlighted the suboptimal teaching of surgical checklists among undergraduates: they did not meet the WHO minimum standards. They postulated that teaching about perioperative patient safety systems and continuous participation in safety protocols were important skills to be taught early in training. Interestingly, they recommended principles and educational interventions in order to guide such endeavor (introductory lectures, surgical rotations, clinical skills, surgical safety checklist assessment through examination questions and clinical evaluation, etc.). The need for formal assessment in the prevention of surgical errors was already suggested through results from a survey mailed to U.S. ophthalmology residents [121]. Most residents responded that their program provided training in preventing surgical errors, mostly through observation and participation to OR protocols. Hands-on experience was found to be the most effective method. However, a gap still remained in formally assessing residents' knowledge about this subject.

B. Consent Form

This is entirely a part of the universal protocol as mentioned in the WHO guidelines [118]. Full consent from the patient is mandatory for any procedure. The patient must be awake, alert, and have a full capacity of discernment in order to understand the details and potential complications of the surgery that will be performed. This includes therefore a proper explanation from the physician and an active participation of the patient or representative. Consequently, the site of the surgery and the laterality must be clearly stated and written on the form. Finally, once agreement between the surgeon and the patient has been achieved, the latter must sign the consent form to confirm its approval.

25.3.1.2   Cataract Surgery-Related Errors

Introduction
Cataract surgery occupies a central part in understanding and preventing medical and surgical errors in ophthalmology. Studies treating about the incidence of surgical confusions in ophthalmology unequivocally agreed that the top surgical error is related to IOL implants. Indeed, the use of incorrect IOL represented 66.4% of surgical confusion cases in Parikh et al. series [117]; 48.9% of adverse events in Neily et al. descriptive study [109], and 63% in the retrospective series of Simon et al. [106]. Interestingly, these results match the number of claims reported in the literature among ophthalmological procedures. For example, two different studies made across the UK showed that one third of malpractice claims filed against ophthalmologists were accountable to cataract surgeons [113, 122]. Moreover, socioeconomic consequences of cataract malpractice are considerable [110]. Therefore, young ophthalmologists must be well prepared regarding legal aspect when starting their surgical training especially in cataract surgery.

Causes and Risk Factors
In the "*Cataract Surgery Guidelines*" released by the RCO in 2010 [57], they presented a list of risk factors for unsafe cataract surgery for surgeons to be attentive to. Here are some examples that could lead to medical errors especially for residents:

- Clinical staff not following guidelines or not relying on evidence-based medicine.
- Lack of team working or team training.

- Lack of appropriate skills.
- Distractions or interruptions during intervention.
- Rushing during surgery with inappropriate focusing on personal performance rather than patient safety and quality of care.
- Lack of patient involvement.
- Poor communication (e.g., of information within the medical file or between the surgeon and the patient…).

Interestingly, such factors have been linked to the occurrence of surgical claims. Ali et al. separated predisposing factors (communication errors, inattention…) from precipitating factors (lack of adequate care, mistakes, system errors…) for litigation [111]. They suggested that in the absence of predisposing factors, precipitating factors are unlikely to lead to litigation in clinical practice. Furthermore, studies have shown that a breakdown in communication is the root cause of up to 70% of claims [123]. Thus, knowing these causational risk factors for young trainees would reasonably improve patient care by reducing the risk of medical errors occurrence.

There are different stages of the patient care in cataract surgery: (1) identification of refractive goals, (2) biometry measurement, (3) IOL selection, and (4) implantation. These sequential steps involve various staff members in different times. Often, communication is crucial to allow a proper transmission of data. Thus, this complicated process carries out an increased risk for error occurrence. In the following are examples of specific preventable human errors (i.e., never events) that were identified for leading to IOL-related incident [57, 124]:

1. **IOL measurement (biometry, formula)**
   (a) Inaccurate biometry
   (b) Wrong formula
   (c) Failure of routine bilateral biometry measurement
   (d) Failure of re-measurement of axial length asymmetry
2. **IOL selection**
   (a) Confusion in postoperative refractive goals (e.g., the patient agreed for postop-

erative myopia and the surgeon aimed for emmetropia during surgery)
   (b) Wrong-patient biometric data used for surgery
   (c) Wrong-eye biometric data used for surgery
   (d) Wrong type of IOL data selected (e.g., confusion between anterior chamber and posterior chamber IOL data)
   (e) Failure to adequately communicate the selected IOL type and power due to transcription errors
3. **IOL preoperative preparation**
   (a) Failure to check availability of the IOL before starting the surgery
   (b) Failure to adequately label the IOL box with the correct patient
4. **IOL surgical implantation**
   (a) Failure to bring the correct IOL in the OR
   (b) IOL confusion due to a second IOL (not belonging to the patient) already present in the OR
   (c) Failure to check the IOL characteristics before implantation [106]
   (d) Failure to correctly place a toric IOL in the right meridian

Finally, improper use of the universal protocol is also among the errors identified for incorrect IOL placement.

Preventive Strategies

Examples of preventive strategies could be divided into two definite periods according to the NICE guideline for cataract management in adults (for details, refer to paragraph 1.5, "*Preventing wrong lens implant errors*") [21]:

1. **The day before the surgery**
   (a) Confirm the patient's correct medical notes.
   (b) Biometry assessment: confirm that the results belong to the proper patient; use electronic data and transfer the biometry results to the patient's medical record; print the results and fix them appropriately into patient's medical notes.

(c) Communication with the patient: explain the different types of IOL and their refractive implications; discuss the refractive target; record the IOL chosen by the patient and any specificities mentioned during the discussion.

2. **The day of the surgery**
   (a) Have the patient's note, especially biometry results available in the OR.
   (b) Use the modified WHO Surgical Checklist: confirm the patient's identity and match the information with the consent form, the biometry results and the medical notes; check and mark the eye to be operated; have only the selected IOL in the OR with one another identical IOL in stock and an alternative type of IOL ready if complications occur. Some of these steps are repeated before anesthesia and one last time before starting the procedure by the surgeon.
   (c) Confirmation by two distinct staff members that the IOL formulas, calculations, and constants are appropriate.

Moreover, in attempt to learn from any wrong IOL implantation and establish further preventive strategies, the NICE guidelines advocate for multidisciplinary analysis of actual incidents.

Interestingly, these guidelines are, for instance, based on the IOL safety protocol for routine cataract surgery that is merged with the WHO Surgical Checklist as introduced by the Royal Victorian Eye and Ear Hospital in Australia [124]. Similar strategies were described in the third section of the recommendations proposed by the AAO wrong-site task force, regarding the procedures that are dependent upon preoperative calculations [119].

25.3.1.3 Intravitreal Therapy-Related Errors

Introduction

Despite IVT being more frequently performed than cataract surgery, studies have shown that there is less surgical confusion occurring during intravitreal injection [117]. Parikh et al. only found one case of an incorrect eye intravitreal injection. An under-report of errors could justify this paradigm. As suggested, the latter could be explained by the procedure being mainly performed by single ophthalmologists in nonhospital-based clinics, a substantial number of patients having bilateral conditions which would therefore minimize the consequence of wrong-side intervention, the procedure itself being of low-risk for complications, and substances used to be similar in action with few adverse effects [117].

Preventive Strategies

In a retrospective review of anti-VEGF-related incidents from 2003 to 2010 in NHS care, a substantial number of patient safety incidents were accountable to medical and surgical confusions [1]. Some suggestions by the authors to reduce these incidents included electronic patient records or prescriptions, audit tools, or the use of checklists with an appropriate time-out before injection. Therefore, most of medical and surgical confusions related to intravitreal injections belong to the category of "wrong-site surgery" and its preventive strategies.

25.3.1.4 Medication-Related Errors in Ophthalmology

Introduction

The National Coordinating Council for Medication Error Reporting and Prevention defines medication errors as *"any preventable event that may cause or lead to inappropriate medication use or patient harm while the medication is in the control of the health care professional, patient, or consumers (…)."* They propose this standard definition to be used by researchers and institutions to better identify errors [125]. Medication errors constitute a common cause for malpractice in medicine. Ophthalmology is thus not spared, especially due to the high volume of prescriptions in this specialty. Indeed, in a large data report collected in the United States in 1995 and 1996 from the National Ambulatory Medical Care Survey, half of ophthalmological consultations in the office resulted in a medication prescription [126]. Furthermore, a prospective study over a 4-week period that recorded the number of prescription errors at an ophthalmic hospital in the UK found that 8% of prescription sheets had errors (144/1952) [127]. Therefore, drug prescription is a sensible step in a patient care, especially after a surgical intervention, and identifying the causes and strategies to prevent errors are critical to ensure patient safety.

Causes and Risk Factors

In the following are highlighted common contributing factors that lead to medication errors as listed in the Communication about Drug Orders released by the AAO in 2015 [128]:

- Lack of information about the patient (e.g., allergies, contraindication) and the drug (e.g., interactions).
- Failure in adequate communication of drug orders (e.g., illegible prescription, improper use of decimal points and zeros, confusion with abbreviations).
- Environmental stress (e.g., fatigue, distractions affecting performance during prescription writing).

Additionally, young ophthalmologists are more likely to commit medication errors than the senior physicians, as suggested by the results of the prospective study conducted by Utman et al. [129]. This finding emphasizes the importance of training and prevention among residents in this topic.

The causes of medication errors could be divided into two categories, prescription errors and drug-related errors [127, 129]:

1. Prescription errors
   (a) Erroneous patient information
   (b) Erroneous format
   (c) Unreadable prescription
   (d) Unclear instructions
   (e) Failure to note allergy status
2. Drug-related errors.
   (a) Erroneous dosage
   (b) Erroneous frequency
   (c) Erroneous route of administration

Preventive Strategies

In the following are some strategies regarding writing of prescription to improve patient safety [128]:

- Include: date, patient name, drug name, dosage, route of administration, frequency, prescriber name and signature.
- Use capital letters.
- Avoid abbreviations (e.g., q.h.s., t.i.d., …): instead transcribe in full (every night at bedtime, three times a day).
- Use the metric system.
- Use leading zero (0.1 instead of .1) and avoid trailing zero (2 instead of 2.0).
- If available, prefer computer-based prescribing systems (participates in decreasing the incidence of prescription errors [129–132]).

Finally, other types of error and their corresponding strategy are proposed by the AAO Quality of Care Secretariat. For example, regarding drugs with similar names, they propose to communicate the generic and brand name to minimize confusions. Other suggestions include limiting verbal orders to urgent situations when other ways of prescription orders are not available [128].

25.4 Clinical Case

We report the clinical case of a 45-year-old man who attended left eye (LE) cataract surgery in September 2019. The patient was allergic to Novocaine. The patient worked for a sewer and drain cleaning service. He was known for cardiovascular risk factors under treatment, with history of myocardial infarction and transitory ischemic attack a year prior to the event. He was pseudophakic in his right eye (RE).

The surgeon prescribed a preoperative therapy with eyelid cleansing pads and Bromfenac eye drops 0.9 mg/ml, twice per day, 2 days before surgery. The day of the surgery, topical anesthesia without sedation and preoperative antisepsis were administered in the left eye. The surgeon performed small incisions, capsulorhexis, hydrodissection, and hydrodelineation. During phacoemulsification, wound burn of the tunnel occurred. During the whole procedure the patient was irritated and complained intraoperative pain. The tunnel where the wound burn occurred was sutured and the IOL was implanted. Due to the constant eye squeezing and scarce patient compliance, the surgeon decided not to inject intracameral cefuroxime, which was however used to irrigate the cornea. A contact lens was applied on the left eye.

Postoperative therapy included antibiotic and corticosteroid drops, four times per day each, and topical NSAIDs twice per day. The day after the operation corneal edema was present, and corticosteroids were increased to six times per day. No signs of anterior chamber inflammation were detected. A new visit was programmed in 7 days.

Three days after surgery, the patient came to the emergency room with left eye pain. The patient reported that he went back to work the day before. Visual acuity was light perception and the ocular examination detected a 4 mm hypopyon. The IOP was within normal limits. The eye fundus was not explorable. Endophthalmitis was diagnosed and the patient underwent a pars plana vitrectomy. During the surgery, corneal melting with perforation on the sutured wound burn was detected. The corneal suture was removed; vitreous and aqueous humor taps were collected and sent to the microbiology. The surgeon performed then a complete vitrectomy and Oxane was left as tamponade. Intravitreal injections of vancomycin and ceftazidime were performed. An amniotic membrane was sutured on the cornea. Postoperative therapy consisted in ciprofloxacin 500 mg twice a day for 6 days, luxazone eye drops one drop four times a day for 15 days, fortified vancomycin 25 mg/ml eye drop one drop every 2 h and fortified tobramycin 14 mg/ml one drop every 2 h.

At the 15-day visit visual acuity was still light perception, the amniotic membrane was correctly positioned and did not allow vision of the underlying structures. The therapy was changed based on the antibiogram sent by the microbiology that detected a *Staphylococcus aureus* infection. The surgeon prescribed tobramycin 0.3%/dexamethasone 0.1% one drop four times a day and ciprofloxacin drops 0.3% one drop four times a day.

An audit on the clinical case was successively discussed.

25.4.1 Clinical Case Recommendations

1. A good pre-anesthesia assessment of the patient is important. In fact, topical anesthesia without sedation is not always the appropriate technique for cataract surgery. A good anamnesis and examination are necessary to rule out the type of anesthesia that better suits the patient and ophthalmologist needs.
2. Whenever there are no contraindications, always inject 1 mg cefuroxime in the anterior chamber since it contributes to prevent ocular infections.
3. Avoid premature return to the patient's work, especially if this condition exposes the operated eye to a high bacterial load.
4. Close follow-up is necessary for a high-risk patient.
5. Wound burns might complicate cataract surgery. They are a risk factor for endophthalmitis because of the continuing leakage, anterior chamber shallowing, corneo-scleral melting, and the possible presence of a corneal fistula. Performance of larger corneal incisions and adjustment of phacoemulsification settings can prevent this complication.

25.5 Recommendations

High-quality care and safety are important issues in ophthalmology. Prevention is crucial.

Knowledge of ophthalmic surgical complications and their management is fundamental, especially whenever a non-expert surgeon is operating.

Young ophthalmologists should consider the possibility of making medical errors in order to be cautious during daily practice.

Attention to guidelines and the use of a surgical checklist can help in reducing both adverse events and medical errors. Periodical check of the Ophthalmic Safety Alert website page from the Quality and Safe group is recommended to keep updated.

The educational process should involve different figures: the resident, who actively take part in the patient care; the trainers, who dedicate their time and knowledge to young doctors; and the hospital administration. In particular, wet labs and surgical simulators should be introduced in resident training. A proactive behavior is important to be adopted while on training.

Each program should have a structure that promotes safe, interprofessional, and team-based care [133]. Therefore, this is the duty of each resident and young trainee to know the different rules that apply for each individual program.

It is expected from residents to pay particular attention to patient safety. In facts, residents' perceptions of perioperative safety were defined as suboptimal in different scientific papers [120, 134, 135]. Establishing a culture of safety in ophthalmology and training young doctors in this field is important in order to improve patient care standards.

25.6 Conclusion

The purpose of this chapter was to sensitize young trainees to some of the most common adverse events and medical errors in ophthalmology with a special focus on surgery, and the tools to overcome such burden by presenting existing safety practices and strategies. We did not intend to be exhaustive, but we aimed to raise curiosity and self-awareness about this topic. Indeed, the occurrence of such events could have unacceptable consequences for the patient and severely impact young ophthalmologists that are building their career. We thus believe that the sooner we modify our behavior, the higher the impact on patient safety and on each individual future profession.

References

1. Kelly SP. Guidance on patient safety in ophthalmology from the Royal College of Ophthalmologists. Eye. 2009;23:2143.
2. Custer PL, Fitzgerald ME, Herman DC, Lee PP, Cowan CL, Cantor LB, et al. Building a culture of safety in ophthalmology. Ophthalmology. 2016;123:S40.
3. Foster A. Vision 2020: the cataract challenge. J Commun Eye Health. 2000;13(34):17–9.
4. Gollogly HE, Hodge DO, St. Sauver JL, Erie JC. Increasing incidence of cataract surgery: population-based study. J Cataract Refract Surg. 2013;39:1383.
5. Grzybowski A, Told R, Sacu S, Bandello F, Moisseiev E, Loewenstein A, et al. Update on intravitreal injections: Euretina Expert Consensus Recommendations. Ophthalmologica. 2018;239(4):181–93.
6. Hollingworth W, Jones T, Reeves BC, Peto T. A longitudinal study to assess the frequency and cost of antivascular endothelial therapy, and inequalities in access, in England between 2005 and 2015. BMJ Open. 2017;7(10):e018289.
7. Greenberg PB, Tseng VL, Wu WC, Liu J, Jiang L, Chen CK, et al. Prevalence and predictors of ocular complications associated with cataract surgery in United States veterans. Ophthalmology. 2011;118(3):507–14.
8. Pingree MF, Crandall AS, Olson RJ. Cataract surgery complications in 1 year at an academic institution. J Cataract Refract Surg. 1999;25(5):705–8.
9. Muhtaseb M, Kalhoro A, Ionides A. A system for preoperative stratification of cataract patients according to risk of intraoperative complications: a prospective analysis of 1441 cases. Br J Ophthalmol. 2004;88(10):1242–6.
10. Rutar T, Travis C, Porco AN. Risk factors for vitreous complications in resident-performed phacoemulsification surgery. Ophthalmology. 2009;116(3):431–6.
11. ACGME. Required minimum number of procedures for graduating residents in ophthalmology [Internet]. Accreditation Council for Graduate Medical Education (ACGME). 2013. Available from: https://www.acgme.org/acgmeweb/Portals/0/PFAssets/ProgramResources/240_Oph_Minimum_Numbers.pdf.
12. Fong CSU, Mitchell P, de Loryn T, Rochtchina E, Hong T, Cugati S, et al. Long-term outcomes of phacoemulsification cataract surgery performed by trainees and consultants in an Australian cohort. Clin Exp Ophthalmol. 2012;40(6):597–603.
13. Low SAW, Braga-Mele R, Yan DB, El-Defrawy S. Intraoperative complication rates in cataract surgery performed by ophthalmology resident trainees compared to staff surgeons in a Canadian academic center. J Cataract Refract Surg. 2018;44(11):1344–9.
14. Oetting TA. Managing risk in cataract surgeries performed by resident ophthalmologists. Am Med Assoc J Ethics. 2010;12(12):913–6.
15. Thevi T, Godinho MA. Trends and complications of local anaesthesia in cataract surgery: an 8-year analysis of 12992 patients. Br J Ophthalmol. 2016;100:1708.
16. Guay J, Sales K. Sub-Tenon's anaesthesia versus topical anaesthesia for cataract surgery. Cochrane Database Syst Rev. 2015;(3):CD006291.
17. El-Hindy N, Johnston RL, Jaycock P, Eke T, Braga AJ, Tole DM, et al. The Cataract National Dataset

electronic multi-centre audit of 55 567 operations: anaesthetic techniques and complications. Eye. 2009;23(1):50–5.

18. Jaycock P, Johnston RL, Taylor H, Adams M, Tole DM, Galloway P, et al. The Cataract National Dataset electronic multi-centre audit of 55 567 operations: updating benchmark standards of care in the United Kingdom and internationally. Eye. 2009;23:38.

19. Stein JD. Serious adverse events after cataract surgery. Curr Opin Ophthalmol. 2012;23(3):219–25.

20. Chakrabarti A, Nazm N. Posterior capsular rent: prevention and management. Indian J Ophthalmol. 2017;65:1359.

21. NICE. Cataracts in adults: management [Internet]. Cataracts in adults: management. 2017. Available from: https://www.nice.org.uk/guidance/ng77.

22. Schmidbauer JM, Vargas LG, Apple DJ, Escobar-Gomez M, Izak A, Arthur SN, et al. Evaluation of neodymium:yttrium-aluminum-garnet capsulotomies in eyes implanted with AcrySof intraocular lenses. Ophthalmology. 2002;109:1421.

23. Thompson AM, Sachdev N, Wong T, Riley AF, Grupcheva CN, McGhee CN. The Auckland Cataract Study: 2 year postoperative assessment of aspects of clinical, visual, corneal topographic and satisfaction outcomes. Br J Ophthalmol. 2004;88:1042.

24. Raj SM, Vasavada AR, Johar SRK, Vasavada VA, Vasavada VA. Post-operative capsular opacification: a review. Int J Biomed Sci. 2007;3(4):237–50.

25. Wormstone IM. Posterior capsule opacification: a cell biological perspective. Exp Eye Res. 2002;74(3):337–47.

26. Pandey SK, Apple DJ, Werner L, Maloof AJ, Milverton EJ. Posterior capsule opacification: a review of the aetiopathogenesis, experimental and clinical studies and factors for prevention. Indian J Ophthalmol. 2004;52:99–112.

27. Awasthi N, Guo S, Wagner BJ. Posterior capsular opacification: a problem reduced but not yet eradicated. Arch Ophthalmol. 2009;127:555.

28. Stein JD, Grossman DS, Mundy KM, Sugar A, Sloan FA. Severe adverse events after cataract surgery among medicare beneficiaries. Ophthalmology. 2011;118(9):1716–23.

29. Erie JC, Raecker ME, Baratz KH, Schleck CD, Robertson DM. Risk of retinal detachment after cataract extraction, 1980–2004: a population-based study. Trans Am Ophthalmol Soc. 2006;113(11):2026–32.

30. Kassem R, Greenwald Y, Achiron A, Hecht I, Man V, Ben Haim L, et al. Peak occurrence of retinal detachment following cataract surgery: a systematic review and pooled analysis with internal validation. J Ophthalmol. 2018;2018:1.

31. Hermann MM, Kirchhof B, Fauser S. Temporal occurrence of retinal detachments after cataract surgery. Acta Ophthalmol. 2012;90(8):e594–6.

32. Neal RE, Bettelheim FA, Lin C, Winn KC, Garland DL, Zigler JS. Alterations in human vitreous humour following cataract extraction. Exp Eye Res. 2005;80(3):337–47.

33. Olsen T. The incidence of retinal detachment after cataract surgery. Open Ophthalmol J. 2012;6:79.

34. Haddad WM, Monin C, Morel C, Larricart P, Quesnot S, Ameline B, et al. Retinal detachment after phacoemulsification: a study of 114 cases. Am J Ophthalmol. 2002;133(5):630–8.

35. Bellan L, Ahmed IIK, MacInnis B, Mann C, Noël F, Sanmugasunderam S. Canadian Ophthalmological Society evidence-based clinical practice guidelines for cataract surgery in the adult eye. Can J Ophthalmol. 2008;43(Suppl. 1):S7–33.

36. Ray S, D'Amico DJ. Pseudophakic cystoid macular edema. Semin Ophthalmol. 2002;17:167.

37. Grzybowski A, Sikorski BL, Ascaso FJ, Huerva V. Pseudophakic cystoid macular edema: update 2016. Clin Interv Aging. 2016;11:1221–9.

38. Kim SJ, Schoenberger SD, Thorne JE, Ehlers JP, Yeh S, Bakri SJ, et al. Topical nonsteroidal anti-inflammatory drugs and cataract surgery: a report by the American Academy of Ophthalmology. Ophthalmology. 2015;122:2159.

39. Lim BX, Lim CHL, Lim DK, Evans JR, Bunce C, Wormald R. Prophylactic non-steroidal anti-inflammatory drugs for the prevention of macular oedema after cataract surgery. Cochrane Database of Systematic Reviews. 2016;11(11):CD006683.

40. Wielders LHP, Lambermont VA, Schouten JSAG, Van Den Biggelaar FJHM, Worthy G, Simons RWP, et al. Prevention of cystoid macular edema after cataract surgery in nondiabetic and diabetic patients: a systematic review and meta-analysis. Am J Ophthalmol. 2015;160:968.

41. Wielders LHP, Schouten JSAG, Winkens B, van den Biggelaar FJHM, Veldhuizen CA, Murta JCN, et al. European multicenter trial of the prevention of cystoid macular edema after cataract surgery in nondiabetics: ESCRS PREMED study report 1. J Cataract Refract Surg. 2018;44(4):429–39.

42. Obuchowska I, Mariak Z. Risk factors of massive suprachoroidal hemorrhage during extracapsular cataract extraction surgery. Eur J Ophthalmol. 2005;15:712.

43. Eriksson A, Koranyi G, Seregard S, Philipson B. Risk of acute suprachoroidal hemorrhage with phacoemulsification. J Cataract Refract Surg. 1998;24:793.

44. Ling R, Cole M, James C, Kamalarajah S, Foot B, Shaw S. Suprachoroidal haemorrhage complicating cataract surgery in the UK: epidemiology, clinical features, management, and outcomes. Br J Ophthalmol. 2004;88(4):478–80.

45. Laube T, Brockmann C, Bornfeld N. Massive suprachoroidal hemorrhage: surgical management and outcome. GMS Ophthalmol Cases. 2015;5:Doc10.

46. Gower EW, Lindsley K, Tulenko SE, Nanji AA, Leyngold I, McDonnell PJ. Perioperative antibiotics for prevention of acute endophthalmitis after cataract surgery (Review). Cochrane Database Syst Rev. 2017;(2):CD006364.

47. Taban M, Behrens A, Newcomb RL, Nobe MY, Saedi G, Sweet PM, et al. Acute endophthalmitis following cataract surgery: a systematic review of the literature. Arch Ophthalmol. 2005;123(5):613–20.

48. Barry P, Gettinby G, Lees F, Peterson M, Revie C, Seal D, et al. Prophylaxis of postoperative endophthalmitis following cataract surgery: results of the ESCRS multicenter study and identification of risk factors. J Cataract Refract Surg. 2007;33(6):978–88.

49. Group EVS. Results of the Endophthalmitis Vitrectomy study: a randomized trial of immediate vitrectomy and of intravenous antibiotics for the treatment of postoperative bacterial endophthalmitis. Arch Ophthalmol. 1995;113(12):1479–96.

50. Barry P, Cordovés L, Gardner S. ESCRS guidelines for prevention and treatment of endophthalmitis following cataract surgery. 2013. https://www.escrs.org/downloads/Endophthalmitis-Guidelines.pdf.

51. Kuhn F, Gini G. Complete and early vitrectomy for endophthalmitis (CEVE) as today's alternative to the endophthalmitis vitrectomy study. Vitr Surg. 2007:53–68.

52. Kuhn F, Gini G. Vitrectomy for endophthalmitis. Ophthalmology. 2006;113:714.

53. Olson RJ, Braga-Mele R, Chen SH, Miller KM, Pineda R, Tweeten JP, et al. Cataract in the adult eye preferred practice pattern. Am Acad Ophthalmol. 2017;124(2):P1–119.

54. Vogel A, Dick B, Krummenauer F. Reproducibility of optical biometry using partial coherence interferometry: intraobserver and interobserver reliability. J Cataract Refract Surg. 2001;27:1961.

55. Cavallini GM, Saccarola P, D'Amico R, Gasparin A, Campi L. Impact of preoperative testing on ophthalmologic and systemic outcomes in cataract surgery. Eur J Ophthalmol. 2004;14:369.

56. Keay L, Lindsley K, Tielsch J, Katz J, Schein O. Routine preoperative medical testing for cataract surgery (review). Cochrane Syst Rev. 2019;(1):CD007293.

57. The Royal College of Ophthalmologists. Cataract Surgery Guidelines 2010. The Royal College of Ophthalmologists: London, 2010. Available at: https://www.rcophth.ac.uk/wp-content/uploads/2014/12/2010-SCI-069-Cataract-Surgery-Guidelines-2010-SEPTEMBER-2010-1.pdf.

58. Butler TKH. Risk stratification and assessment in cataract surgery. J Cataract Refract Surg. 2012;38:184.

59. Narendran N, Jaycock P, Johnston RL, Taylor H, Adams M, Tole DM, et al. The Cataract National Dataset electronic multicentre audit of 55 567 operations: risk stratification for posterior capsule rupture and vitreous loss. Eye. 2009;23(1):31–7.

60. Kim BZ, Patel DV, Sherwin T, McGhee CNJ. The Auckland Cataract Study: assessing preoperative risk stratification systems for phacoemulsification surgery in a teaching hospital. Am J Ophthalmol. 2016;171:145–50.

61. Han JV, Patel DV, Wallace HB, Kim BZ, Sherwin T, McGhee CNJ. Auckland Cataract Study III: refining preoperative assessment with cataract risk stratification to reduce intraoperative complications. Am J Ophthalmol. 2019; https://doi.org/10.1016/j.ajo.2018.09.026.

62. Blomquist PH, Sargent JW, Winslow HH. Validation of Najjar-Awwad cataract surgery risk score for resident phacoemulsification surgery. J Cataract Refract Surg. 2010;36:1753.

63. Royal College. Local anaesthesia for ophthalmic surgery. Joint guidelines from the Royal College of Anaesthetists and the Royal College of Ophthalmologists. Curr Anaesth Crit Care. 2012.

64. Grzybowski A, Ascaso FJ, Kupidura-Majewski K, Packer M. Continuation of anticoagulant and antiplatelet therapy during phacoemulsification cataract surgery. Curr Opin Ophthalmol. 2015;26:28.

65. Benzimra JD, Johnston RL, Jaycock P, Galloway PH, Lambert G, Chung AKK, et al. The Cataract National Dataset electronic multicentre audit of 55 567 operations: antiplatelet and anticoagulant medications. Eye. 2009;23:10.

66. Barry P, Seal DV, Gettinby G, Lees F, Peterson M, Revie CW. ESCRS study of prophylaxis of postoperative endophthalmitis after cataract surgery. Preliminary report of principal results from a European multicenter study. J Cataract Refract Surg. 2006;32(3):407–10.

67. Speaker MG, Milch FA, Shah MK, Eisner W, Kreiswirth BN. Role of external bacterial flora in the pathogenesis of acute postoperative endophthalmitis. Ophthalmology. 1991;98(5):639–49.

68. Wood A, Conner R. Guideline for preoperative patient skin antisepsis. In: Guidelines for perioperative practice. Denver, CO: Association of Perioperative Registered Nurses; 2015.

69. Pathengay A, Flynn HW, Isom RF, Miller D. Endophthalmitis outbreaks following cataract surgery: causative organisms, etiologies, and visual acuity outcomes. J Cataract Refract Surg. 2012;38:1278.

70. Hellinger WC, Bacalis LP, Edelhauser HF, Mamalis N, Milstein B, Masket S, et al. Recommended practices for cleaning and sterilizing intraocular surgical instruments. J Cataract Refract Surg. 2007;33(6):1095–100.

71. Tinley CG, Frost A, Hakin KN, McDermott W, Ewings P. Is visual outcome compromised when next day review is omitted after phacoemulsification surgery? A randomised control trial. Br J Ophthalmol. 2003;87:1350.

72. Tan JHY, Newman DK, Klunker C, Watts SE, Burton RL. Phacoemulsification cataract surgery: is routine review necessary on the first post-operative day? Eye. 2000;14(Pt 1):53–5.

73. Borkar DS, Moustafa GA, Eton EA, Koulisis N, Kloek CE, Borboli-Gerogiannis S, et al. Incidence of unexpected peripheral retinal findings on dilated examination 1 month after cataract surgery: results in the Perioperative Care for Intraocular Lens Study. J Cataract Refract Surg. 2018;44:780.

74. Tan CS, Lim LW, Ting DS. The role of dilated fundus examination following cataract surgery. J Cataract Refract Surg. 2019;45(1):113.

75. AAO. Ophthalmologist's duties concerning postoperative care policy statement. Am Acad Ophthalmol Policy statement. 2012.

76. Accreditation Council for Graduate Medical Education. ACGME program requirements for graduate medical education in ophthalmology [Internet]. 2020. Available from: https://www.acgme.org/Portals/0/PFAssets/ProgramRequirements/240_Ophthalmology_2020.pdf?ver=2019-02-19-121341-650.

77. Spencer F. The Royal College of Ophthalmologists. Guide for delivery of Ophthalmic Specialist Training (OST). R Coll Ophthalmol. 2018.

78. International Council of Ophthalmologists. International Council of Ophthalmology residency curriculum. 2016. icoph.org/curricula.html.

79. Alfawaz AM. Ophthalmology resident surgical training: can we do better? Saudi J Ophthalmol. 2019;33(2):159–62.

80. Le K, Bursztyn L, Rootman D, Harissi-Dagher M. National survey of Canadian ophthalmology residency education. Can J Ophthalmol. 2016;51(3):219–25.

81. The Royal College of Ophthalmologists. Practice guidance: cataract surgery guidelines. 2010. www.rcophth.ac.uk.

82. Belyea DA, Brown SE, Rajjoub LZ. Influence of surgery simulator training on ophthalmology resident phacoemulsification performance. J Cataract Refract Surg. 2011;37:1756.

83. Staropoli PC, Gregori NZ, Junk AK, Galor A, Goldhardt R, Goldhagen BE, et al. Surgical simulation training reduces intraoperative cataract surgery complications among residents. Simul Healthc. 2018;13(1):11–5.

84. Nauck M, Roth M, Tamm M, Eickelberg O, Wieland H, Stulz P, et al. Induction of vascular endothelial growth factor by platelet-activating factor and platelet-derived growth factor is downregulated by corticosteroids. Am J Respir Cell Mol Biol. 1997;16:398.

85. Ladas ID, Karagiannis DA, Rouvas AA, Kotsolis AI, Liotsou A, Vergados I. Safety of repeat intravitreal injections of bevacizumab versus ranibizumab: our experience after 2,000 injections. Retina. 2009;29:313.

86. Brouzas D, Koutsandrea C, Moschos M, Papadimitriou S, Ladas I, Apostolopoulos M. Massive choroidal hemorrhage after intravitreal administration of bevacizumab for AMD followed by controlateral sympathetic ophthalmia. Clin Ophthalmol. 2009;3:457–9.

87. Karagiannis DA, Mitropoulos P, Ladas ID. Large subretinal haemorrhage following change from intravitreal bevacizumab to ranibizumab. Ophthalmologica. 2009;223(4):279–82.

88. Mason JO, Frederick PA, Neimkin MG, White MF, Feist RM, Thomley ML, et al. Incidence of hemorrhagic complications after intravitreal bevacizumab (Avastin) or ranibizumab (Lucentis) injections on systemically anticoagulated patients. Retina. 2010;30:1386.

89. McCannel CA. Meta-analysis of endophthalmitis after intravitreal injection of anti-vascular endothelial growth factor agents: causative organisms and possible prevention strategies. Retina. 2011;31:654.

90. Scott IU, Flynn HW. Reducing the risk of endophthalmitis following intravitreal injections. Retina. 2007;27(1):10–2.

91. Ferraz D, Bressanim G, Takahashi B, Pelayes D, Takahashi W. Three-monthly intravitreal bevacizumab injections for neovascular age-related macular degeneration: short-term visual acuity results. Eur J Ophthalmol. 2010;20:740.

92. Sodré SL, Barbosa IAF, Pacheco IE, Ferreira F d QT, David MA, Nascimento MA, et al. Costs and benefits of bevacizumab vial sharing for the treatment of retinal diseases. BMC Public Health. 2019; https://doi.org/10.1186/s12889-019-7562-y.

93. Falavarjani KG, Nguyen QD. Adverse events and complications associated with intravitreal injection of anti-VEGF agents: a review of literature. Eye (Basingstoke). 2013;27(7):787–94.

94. Menchini F, Toneatto G, Miele A, Donati S, Lanzetta P, Virgili G. Antibiotic prophylaxis for preventing endophthalmitis after intravitreal injection: a systematic review. Eye (Basingstoke). 2018;32(9):1423–31.

95. Tolentino M. Systemic and ocular safety of intravitreal anti-VEGF therapies for ocular neovascular disease. Surv Ophthalmol. 2011;56:95.

96. Hahn P, Kim JE, Stinnett S, Chung MM, Dugel PU, Flynn HW, et al. Aflibercept-related sterile inflammation. Ophthalmology. 2013;3(9):753–9.

97. Mezad-Koursh D, Goldstein M, Heilwail G, Zayit-Soudry S, Loewenstein A, Barak A. Clinical characteristics of endophthalmitis after an injection of intravitreal antivascular endothelial growth factor. Retina. 2010;30(7):1051–7.

98. Meyer CH, Michels S, Rodrigues EB, Hager A, Mennel S, Schmidt JC, et al. Incidence of rhegmatogenous retinal detachments after intravitreal antivascular endothelial factor injections. Acta Ophthalmol. 2011;89(1):70–5.

99. Bakri SJ, Pulido JS, McCannel CA, Hodge DO, Diehl N, Hillemeier J. Immediate intraocular pressure changes following intravitreal injections of triamcinolone, pegaptanib, and bevacizumab. Eye. 2009;23(1):181–5.

100. Demirel S, Yanik O, Batioglu F, Ozmert E. Intraocular pressure changes related to intravitreal injections of ranibizumab: analysis of pseudophakia and glaucoma subgroup. Int Ophthalmol. 2014;35(4):541–7.

101. Mazzarella S, Mateo C, Freixes S, Burés-Jelstrup A, Rios J, Navarro R, et al. Effect of intravitreal injection of dexamethasone 0.7 mg (Ozurdex®) on intraocular pressure in patients with macular edema. Ophthalmic Res. 2015;54(3):143–9.

102. Urban RC, Cotlier E. Corticosteroid-induced cataracts. Surv Ophthalmol. 1986;1(2):102–10.

103. He Y, Ren XJ, Hu BJ, Lam WC, Li XR. A meta-analysis of the effect of a dexamethasone intravitreal

implant versus intravitreal anti-vascular endothelial growth factor treatment for diabetic macular edema. BMC Ophthalmol. 2018;18(1):121.

104. RCO. Ophthalmic Service Guidance. Intravitreal injection therapy. R Coll Ophthalmol. 2018;1–16.

105. NHS Improvement. Never events list 2018. 2018;22. Available from: https://improvement.nhs.uk/documents/2266/Never_Events_list_2018_FINAL_v5.pdf.

106. Simon JW, Ngo Y, Khan S, Strogatz D. Surgical confusions in ophthalmology. Arch Ophthalmol. 2007;125(11):1515–22.

107. Schein OD, Cassard SD, Tielsch JM, Gower EW. Cataract surgery among medicare beneficiaries. Ophthal Epidemiol. 2012;19(5):257–64.

108. Bhan A, Dave D, Vernon SA, Bhan K, Bhargava J, Goodwin H. Risk management strategies following analysis of cataract negligence claims. Eye. 2005;19(3):264–8.

109. Neily J, Mills PD, Eldridge N, Dunn EJ, Samples C, Turner JR, et al. Incorrect surgical procedures within and outside of the operating room. Arch Surg. 2009;144(11):1028–34.

110. Thompson AC, Parikh PD, Lad EM. Review of ophthalmology medical professional liability claims in the United States from 2006 through 2015. Ophthalmology. 2018;125(5):631–41.

111. Ali N, Little BC. Causes of cataract surgery malpractice claims in England 1995–2008. Br J Ophthalmol. 2011;95(4):490.

112. International Council of Ophthalmology. ICO's global call for action to eliminate eye surgical errors [Internet]. International Council of Ophthalmology. 2016. Available from: http://www.icoph.org/downloads/ICO_Global_Call_for_Action_to_Eliminate_Eye_Surgical_Errors.pdf.

113. Ali N. A decade of clinical negligence in ophthalmology. BMC Ophthalmol. 2007;7:20.

114. Reason J. Human error: models and management. Br Med J. 2000;320:768.

115. Perneger TV. The Swiss cheese model of safety incidents: are there holes in the metaphor? BMC Health Serv Res. 2005;5:1–7.

116. Hempel S, Maggard-Gibbons M, Nguyen DK, Dawes AJ, Miake-Lye I, Beroes JM, et al. Wrong-site surgery, retained surgical items, and surgical fires a systematic review of surgical never events. JAMA Surg. 2015;50(8):796–805.

117. Parikh R, Palmer V, Kumar A, Simon JW. Surgical confusions in ophthalmology: description, analysis, and prevention of errors from 2006 through 2017. Ophthalmology. 2019;127(3):296–302.

118. World Health Organization. WHO guidelines for safe surgery. Geneva: WHO; 2009. p. 2009.

119. AAO Wrong-Site Task Force. Recommendations of American Academy of Ophthalmology Wrong-Site Task Force - 2014 [Internet]. American Academy of Ophthalmology. 2014. Available from: https://www.aao.org/patient-safety-statement/recommendations-of-american-academy-ophthalmology-.

120. Kilduff CLS, Leith TO, Drake TM, Fitzgerald JEF. Surgical safety checklist training: a national study of undergraduate medical and nursing student teaching, understanding and influencing factors. Postgrad Med J. 2018;94:143.

121. Chen AJ, Havnaer AG, Greenberg PB. Training in the prevention of surgical errors in ophthalmology: the resident perspective. J Cataract Refract Surg. 2014;40:2157.

122. Mathew RG, Ferguson V, Hingorani M. Clinical negligence in ophthalmology: fifteen years of National Health service litigation authority data. Ophthalmology. 2013;120:859.

123. Beckman HB, Markakis KM, Suchman AL, Frankel RM. The doctor-patient relationship and malpractice. Lessons from plaintiff depositions. Arch Intern Med. 1994;154(12):1365–70.

124. Zamir E, Beresova-Creese K, Miln L. Intraocular lens confusions: a preventable " never event" - the Royal Victorian Eye and Ear Hospital Protocol. Surv Ophthalmol. 2012;57:430.

125. National Coordinating Council for Medication Error Reporting and Prevention. About medication errors. What is a medication error? NCCMERP. 2016.

126. Schappert SM, Nelson C. National ambulatory medical care survey: 1995–96 summary. Vital Heal Stat Ser 13 Data Heal Resour Util; 1999.

127. Mandal K, Fraser SG. The incidence of prescribing errors in an eye hospital. BMC Ophthalmol. 2005;5:4.

128. AAO Quality of Care Secretariat. Minimizing medication errors: communication about drug orders - 2015 [Internet]. American Academy of Ophthalmology. 2015. Available from: https://www.aao.org/patient-safety-statement/minimizing-medication-errors-communication-about-d.

129. Utman SAK, Atkinson PL, Baig HM. Methods to reduce prescription errors in ophthalmic medication. Saudi J Ophthalmol. 2013;27:267.

130. Papshev D, Peterson AM. Electronic prescribing in ambulatory practice: promises, pitfalls, and potential solutions. Am J Manag Care. 2001;7(7):725–36.

131. S.T C. Electronic prescribing: a review of costs and benefits. Top Health Inf Manage; 2003.

132. Nightingale PG, Adu D, Richards NT, Peters M. Implementation of rules based computerised bedside prescribing and administration: intervention study. BMJ. 2000;320(7237):750–3.

133. Accreditation Council for Graduate Medical Education. Program requirements for graduate medical education in ophthalmology [Internet]. 2019. Available from: https://www.acgme.org/Portals/0/PFAssets/ProgramRequirements/240-Ophthalmology_2019.pdf?ver=2018-08-21-132333-400.

134. Putnam LR, Levy SM, Kellagher CM, Etchegaray JM, Thomas EJ, Kao LS, et al. Surgical resident education in patient safety: where can we improve? J Surg Res. 2015;199(2):308–13.

135. Alper E, Rosenberg EI, O'Brien KE, Fischer M, Durning SJ. Patient safety education at U.S. and Canadian medical schools: results from the 2006 clerkship directors in internal medicine survey. Acad Med. 2009;84(12):1672–6.

Part IV

Healthcare Organization

Community and Primary Care

Elisabetta Alti and Alessandro Mereu

WHO defined primary care "as socially appropriate, universally accessible, scientifically sound first level care provided by a suitably trained workforce supported by integrated referral systems and in a way that gives priority to those most needed, maximizes community and individual self-reliance and participation and involves collaboration with other sectors, including health promotion, illness prevention, care of the sick, advocacy and community development" [1].

Therefore, primary care services are at the integrated people-centered healthcare in many countries where they provide an entry point into the health system and have directly impact on people's well-being and their use of other health and care resources. Unsafe or ineffective primary care may increase morbidity and preventable mortality, and may lead to the unnecessary hospitalization and specialist resource and, in some cases, disability and even death [2].

Patient safety is the absence of preventable harm to a patient during the process of healthcare and reduction of risk of unnecessary harm associated with healthcare to an acceptable minimum. An acceptable minimum refers to the collective notions of given current knowledge, resources available and the context in which care was delivered weighed against the risk of non-treatment or other treatment [2]. Therefore, it is the minimum prerequisite for high-quality care.

Studies on patient safety have traditionally focused on hospital care. The reason for this is that it reflects the dominance of hospital-based care in many health systems and is the result of a perception that this is where most serious incidents occur.

Primary care has been perceived for many years as a low technology environment where safety would not be a problem. However, in England, 90% of contacts with the National Health Service take place in primary care, and more than 750,000 patients consult their GP each day. In many countries, it is estimated that 85% of all healthcare contacts occur in primary care [1].

European data show that the issue of patient safety is ongoing and that, for example, in the United Kingdom between 5 and 80 safety incidents occur per 100,000 primary care consultations, which translates to between 370 and 600 incidents per day [3].

For this reason, patient safety and preventable harm to patients in primary care is becoming a rising issue because it represents the largest volume of healthcare encounters.

Attention towards patient safety was renewed in 2016 by the World Health Organisation (WHO) with its "Technical Series on Safer Primary Care" aiming at raising awareness about the underlying

E. Alti (✉)
Tuscan Health Service, Florence, Italy

A. Mereu
Movimento Giotto - WONCA Italy, Florence, Italy

L. Donaldson et al. (eds.), *Textbook of Patient Safety and Clinical Risk Management*,
https://doi.org/10.1007/978-3-030-59403-9_26

causes of safety incidents and consequences of unsafe primary care [2].

There is lack of a formal reporting mechanism for medical errors in primary care. Incident reporting is practiced as a self-reporting process and the magnitude of errors could have been underestimated. Among existing strategies to help improve clinical effectiveness and enhance patient safety there are the Quality and Outcomes Framework (QOF), appraisal, revalidation, significant event analysis (SEA), and critical incident reporting systems (CIRS) One of the first comprehensive and coordinated attempts to improve patient safety in primary care is the Scottish Patient Safety Program in Primary Care (SPSP-PC), established in March 2013.

Recent years have seen more researches located in primary care settings which have different features compared to secondary care. Attempts to classify medical errors and preventable adverse events in primary care have proved challenging due to the lack of an evidence base and are yet to be reliably quantified. Data on the most frequent misdiagnosed conditions are scarce, and little is known about which diagnostic processes are most vulnerable to breakdown. Most of them are derived from studies of malpractice claims or self-report surveys. These methods introduce significant biases that limit the generalizability of findings to routine clinical practice [4].

Many countries have implemented strategies to reduce avoidable harm or "never event" defined as "a serious, largely preventable patient safety incident that should not occur if the available preventable measures were implemented by healthcare workers." In 2014, De Wet published a never event list based on general practice identified eight items (Mistaken patient identity, Acts of omission, Investigations, Medication, Medico-legal and ethical incidents, Clinical management Practice systems, Teamwork and communication) and, if there is some evidence of reduction of patient safety incidents in some item of never event list, it is unclear whether all of the never events in the list are truly preventable, or which of the available interventions will be acceptable or effective [5, 6].

The difficulties in identifying and monitoring the never event list is due to the specific context of General Practice.

> "Marshall Marinker has characterised the role of the GP as being to 'marginalise danger', contrasting this with the specialist, whose diagnostic role is to 'marginalise uncertainty'. In other words GPs have the often difficult task of identifying the minority of patients whose presenting symptoms represent serious illness from the majority who do not have something seriously wrong" [7].

Patients in primary care setting can have many health problems (multimorbidity), complex needs (both social and medical), and frequent interactions with healthcare staff in a number of different clinical contexts. There is a range of challenges for GPs, due to the specific primary care setting based on deliver optimal disease management and patient-centered care in a time-limited consultation. The many and varied diseases encountered in primary care make comprehensive measurement of guideline adherence difficult (especially for guidelines that change frequently). Decision-making in primary care often relies on complicated care algorithms specific to numerous diseases. The complexity and inadequacy of single disease guidelines, evidence-based medicine and barriers to shared decision-making were managed through the use of relational continuity of care.

This peculiar care relationship involves a many patient factors, including sex, age, the nature of the illness, earlier experiences and perceived control on the illness, education, financial considerations, personal values, and cultures and traditions [8].

Studies suggests inappropriate care with patients presenting the same conditions, as a result of gender, ethnicity, or socioeconomic disparities and some vulnerable social groups are more likely to experience adverse patient safety events. A recent research confirms that, in primary care, women and black patients are more likely to receive inappropriate diagnosis, treatment, or referrals compared to men and Whites, respectively. However, our findings interestingly suggest that social disparities in patient safety vary among social groups depending on the type of disease, treatment, or health service [9].

High-quality and safe care should be equally achievable for all patients and we need further studies to matching data on patient's gender, educational, ethnic, and socioeconomical status with the data of critical incident registers.

26.1 Epidemiology of Adverse Event

Most published literature originated from the USA and the UK within the last 10 years.

The most common approaches for measuring harm in primary care include self-reporting by staff, analysis of existing databases, reviewing patient records manually or using automation, and asking professionals or patients to recall errors.

Most of these methods suffer from potential bias. Staff incident reports and patient and staff surveys are all affected by recall bias and potential social desirability bias.

Trigger tools are commonly used to identify events in hospital care but only a few studies have tested this approach in primary care [10, 11].

Furthermore, the majority of the studies published on medical errors in primary care show different error reporting methods and several definitions and classifications of types of medical errors (rate severity or preventability, etc.) and sources (estimated, legal reported or hospital referrals, etc.).

International reviews suggests that 1–2% of general practice consultations may result in adverse events, potentially preventable in 45–76% of cases, with estimated serious harm in 4–7% of all adverse event (resulted in permanent harm such as disability, death or long-lasting physical or mental consequences). Other authors report the occurrence of incidents to be between 5 and 80 times per 100,000 [3, 12–14].

In many studies, safety incidents are identified in three categories: administrative and communication incidents; diagnostic incidents; and prescribing and medication management incidents.

Some studies estimated that administration incidents occurred in at least 6% of patient contacts. Most of these incidents related to issues such as incomplete, unavailable, unclear, or incorrect documentation (coding/record keeping); inappropriate monitoring of laboratory tests (e.g., repeat blood tests for patients with repeat prescription or not checking results); or insufficient communication between professionals and patients (e.g. referral pathway for chronic diseases). Documentation errors are in high rate in undeveloped countries because of the lack of electronic records, while in developed countries they are less reported.

Diagnostic incidents are responsible for 4–45% of all patient safety related incidents. Common diagnostic incidents related to misdiagnosis or missed diagnoses and their effect can take months to years to manifest. Examining faulty clinical decision-making, shortcuts in reasoning (heuristics) emerges as an important entity. Misattributing presenting symptoms and signs to an obvious or readily available diagnosis may be a key issue, known as availability heuristics, or even anchoring heuristics, which occurs when doctors tend to maintain initial impressions once they are solidly formed. Any previous diagnostic label can reduce the clinician's ability to reconsider an appropriate differential diagnosis list.

Researchers estimate an overall prescribing error rate from 3% to 65%, potentially occurred in any step of the medication process such as prescribing, transcribing, dispensing, administration, and monitoring (e.g., drug error, information error, or administrative error). Older persons are at higher risk than the general population for these adverse events and this probability increases to 75% in older people with four or more medications (polypharmacy) especially those residing in nursing homes. The reason of such high rate is probably related to elderly physiologic changes, frequent low health literacy, and drugs misuse for cognitive dysfunction.

26.2 Most Frequent Errors

The international medical community identifies three classes of factors as source of harm in primary care:

- Human factors such as teamwork, communication, stress, and burnout.
- Structural factors such as reporting systems, processes, and the environment.
- Clinical factors such as medication.

The classification proposed here of the error areas is a function of the moment of citizen-professional meeting for simplicity here called "clinical moment" [15].

26.2.1 Preclinical Errors

Preclinical errors are due to the organizational activities of primary care professionals. In the preclinical setting, we can make further dimensional distinctions based on the specific competencies involved. We can thus distinguish access management errors of spontaneous citizens' presentations (accesses postponed to days away for time-dependent pathologies with diagnostic and therapeutic delay; immediate accesses for self-resolving conditions with the risk of overmedicalization and overdiagnosis), administrative errors (errors of compilation and use of personal data sheets, error in the management and storage of sensitive data), reception problems (lack of or confusing reception and orientation to services both at the front office level and at the level of web information; lack or defect of architectural elements aimed at to accommodate the inconvenience of mobilization such as elevators, chairs, comfortable environments, absence of reception for people with audio-visual-linguistic barriers on a cultural or disability basis), problems linked to the physical achievement of primary care facilities (reachability by public transport or private, usability during day or night hours), problems related to the communication methods with the structure and the professionals (availability of telephone or web contacts, receipt of communications in the appropriate channels and quality of their management).

These dimensions at the risk of generating errors can variably cause damage in the short to medium or long term.

A citizen who fails to reach or communicate with the primary care facility may suffer a diagnostic or therapeutic delay, or turn to an improper setting with avoidable risks and improper use of resources to the detriment of other citizens.

A citizen who is not welcomed and oriented may delay the spontaneous presentation of the problem he perceives, may manifest anxiety or violent attitudes, or he can decide to postpone it and present it later with the risk of developing more demanding conditions.

This also has ethical, equity, and right to healthcare implications.

An incorrect management of personal data files, sensitive data, and poor care of electronic medical records can expose the patient to problems and damages even without a concurrent consultation with a professional. The risk of using erroneous or missing data can occur for exchanges in personal or administrative data or different clinical history used in subsequent meetings with professionals.

26.2.2 Clinical Errors

Clinical errors are those that are classically identified as a central element of safety problems, both among professionals and in the public. The authors agree that this type of error is an important part of the possible errors but not the most relevant.

Usually clinical errors in primary care have less impact than clinical errors in high-intensity settings; at the same time, the outcomes of these errors can reverberate at a distance.

A first group of errors concerns the prescriptive error of pharmacotherapy. LASA drugs (looks alike sounds alike) prescriptions are always possible and often avoided thanks to the electronic health record (EHR) software with its numerous checks necessary for the issue of the prescription and a last check at the time of delivery of the drugs in pharmacy. These errors often occur due to fatigue or distraction, rarely due to incompetence. To this end, EHR software, through its own alerts and security systems, can greatly limit errors with drugs and their dosages.

A second group of errors is the doctor's diagnostic process. The errors of this group are in the scarce technical-medical competences during the medical examination and the anamnesis, the errors on the relationship and communication plan, the difficult management and communication of the diagnostic uncertainty, the erroneous prescription of lab tests and imaging tests. The latter represents a particular subgroup worthy of interest that calls for quaternary prevention. In the event that the primary care physician ask for a consultation to another doctor or prescribes further tests, this determines a certain risk of subjecting the patient to useless and sometimes harmful medical practices: unnecessary examinations, increased costs and time, over-use of resources of the health system and patient, sensitive iatrogenic risk investigations such as those with ionizing radiation, and accesses in specialized healthcare settings.

A third group of errors is the malfunctioning of the team or its ineffective use and its lack. It is internationally shared options that primary care established in multidisciplinary teams where more skills can be present at the patient's closest level may be able to respond to health needs. Malfunctioning teams with staff shortages or lack of leadership can generate clinical errors: lack of sharing and planning of care plans, failure to share information, non-assignment and recognition of professional responsibilities.

A fourth group of errors consists of delayed diagnoses. As said for the second group the diagnosis is a social fact, an error placed in its social determinants will produce a clinical error. An example is precisely delayed diagnosis or delayed prevention. Both underlie the presence of a lack of clinical and organizational competence. By way of example, the diagnosis of advanced diabetic foot lesions can be characterized by a diagnostic delay in initial lesions or even by a failure to prevent the diabetic foot (an activity that must be organized) if not precisely by the failure to prevent diabetes. It appears obvious here that the question of error goes beyond the ideal boundaries of primary care as the near or distant respon-

sibilities lie in individual behavior and in the social determinants of disease, but it is equally evident that the problem emerges in the clinical setting of primary care among physicians and patient.

A fifth group of errors is in the promotion-preventive sector. The banal absence of preventive and health-promoting activities is notorious that involves development of disease and represents a mistake. This type of error is intertwined in preventive skills and competences and in organizational skills. This is a very important point because in the medicine of the twenty-first century the attention and resources to prevention must grow in order to pass effectively from an acute organization to an organization for complex problems and chronic cases.

26.3 Clinical Cases

26.3.1 Clinical Case: Being Alert

The wife of a 68-year-old patient calls the switchboard of the group medicine because her husband has been suffering from dyspnea for a few days and is worried, he calls at 4.00 pm and the doctor invites him to present himself the same evening, having time to dedicate to him. The patient arrives after about an hour, on foot (his house is about 1500 m away) accompanied by his wife and daughter. It appears dyspnoic. The patient is known to the doctor, has a low socioeconomic condition. As a chronic diseases, he has type 2 diabetes mellitus in oral antidiabetic therapy, COPD 2b in inhalation with LABA and LAMA, he has an essential tremor on propranolol therapy. The doctor investigates any concurrent events, the patient denies fever denies trauma and denies coughing. He denies chest pain. The vital parameters are good (PA 130/70 FC 75r Sat 97% T 36.3). Being a patient with an elevated cardiovascular risk (previous tobacco smoker, diabetic) the doctor proceeds with the execution of an ECG in the office. The ECG demonstrates an elevation of V1, V2, V3, and V4 and suspecting an acute coronary syndrome alerting the territorial emergency-urgency service for rapid access to the Emergency Room. Furtherly the doctor will be informed by the children about the diagnostic confirmation, which will be followed by an urgent coronary angiography with medicated DES and then the setting up of an antiplatelet therapy and cardiological rehabilitation.

Compared to the safety practices adopted we can identify some hidden but absolutely important elements.

The availability for urgent visits is the essential element that allows citizens to be able to have a confrontation with the doctor for situations that alarm them but that do not lead them to independently access emergency services. This availability cannot be causal but is the result of an organization, and therefore of an organizational, multidisciplinary competence that involves physician and ancillary staff (front office). The possibility of receiving phone calls during daytime means setting up a service capable not only of receiving phone calls during daylight hours but also of making the doctor interact with these requests for attention. This service is substantiated with the presence of dedicated staff and doctors available during the daytime hours. A triage, run by medical or nursing professionals, can be added to this organization, which could significantly increase the quality of the management of urgent requests, but today there is little literature on the subject and in any case does not fit into the clinical case scenario.

The presence of time and space is an element of safety. The organization of primary care must foresee the unforeseen and equip itself with effective response capacities: it is necessary that unpredictable visits can take place in times and places consistent with the need for each single clinical case.

On the instrumental level we can see how a doctor experienced in the diagnostic use of medical equipment represents a critical element. For the patient's condition, probably the doctor would still have had to send it to the emergency service as it would have been considered necessary the troponin curve not feasible in another setting. But the early diagnostic suspicion made it possible to activate the further medical service in order to optimize the management with times

and strategies typical for a life-threatening condition. This technical element, of medical competence, conceals the element of safety that concerns the continuity of care in setting transitions which also represents a competence, though not merely clinical.

26.3.2 Clinical Case: A Foreseeable Error

In the hottest days of summer, Aldo, a diabetic 83-year-old man, is recovering from a weekend gastroenteritis with 2 days of vomiting and diarrhea. He is not worried because his nephew had a similar condition few days before and told him what to do. In a certain way, he hopes to lose weight faster and reduce his high glycemic level. He didn't take all medications in the last days, except those for blood pressure and diabetes (ACE-I and metformin). He tried to call his doctor, but the line was always busy and the secretary told him that first office appointment available would have been the next week, so he decided to postpone the consultation, also because he is tired and his back pain has increased in the past few days. Before going to bed, he takes three pills of an over-the-counter painkiller (NSAID) to reduce back pain. Two days after, his fatigue has increased and he urinates very little, almost nothing from midnight, even if he has doubled the dose of diuretic. His worried nephew tells him call the doctor but Aldo decides to wait until the afternoon, when the doctor is in office, but he is a little confused and go to bed and he sleeps all evening waking up only for dinner. Aldo is very tired and little inclined to speak and also he doesn't trust the young doctors on call. When he calls, he only talks about his tiredness The doctor who answers doesn't investigate about his comorbidities or medication and reassures him saying that this is the normal course of acute viral gastroenteritis.

During the night, Aldo is not doing well, he is confused, extremely tired, sick, and when dyspnea occurs, he decide to call the Emergency Department. Admitted in the Emergency Room, his diagnosis is acute kidney injury.

Acute kidney injury (AKI) is a sudden episode of kidney failure or kidney damage that happens within a few hours or a few days. AKI occurs in approximately 10–15% of patients admitted to hospital. It is a serious condition with fourfold increased hospital mortality. It is defined by a rapid increase in serum creatinine, decrease in urine output, or both. Comorbid conditions including CKD, diabetes, hypertension, coronary artery disease, heart failure, liver disease, and chronic obstructive pulmonary disease are risk factors for AKI as well as age (over 65 years), nephrotoxic exposures (iodine products and drugs as NSAIDs, ACE-I, diuretics, etc.) major surgery, sepsis, fluid resuscitation, and volume status (dehydration by Inadequate fluid intake, excessive vomiting, diarrhea, and fever).

In this clinical case, Aldo had not been sufficiently informed of the side effects of the medicines he was taking or of the measures to be taken in the event of a fever or vomiting or diarrhea. Prescribing a medicine, with reviewing side effects, contraindications, and drugs interactions, is an essential part of the primary care visit. Using a tool to monitor that step during the visit would be useful to avoid medication incident. Another communicative incident is also the difficulty of accessing a medical consultation with his primary doctor, both by phone and by visit. The lack of confidence in the unknown doctor leads him to silence parts of his condition and the doctor on call does not sufficiently investigate patient's condition (age, comorbidities, etc.). This diagnostic error is due to both clinical and organizational competence. The incomplete anamnestic review leads to superficial diagnosis and underestimated severity with potential serious harm (from intensive care to dialysis or death). A more organized primary care team would have shared medical records, avoiding misunderstanding.

A further element of safety that those scenario predicts, but does not described, is the possibility of a review of the case through the SEA model (significant event analysis). The diagnosis, during the acute phase, of a life-threatening disease is a significant event in primary care. This phenomenon represents an excellent opportunity for the multidisciplinary team to review its skills and competences and understand if mistakes have been made, regardless of the positive outcome of the specific case.

26.4 Safety Procedures

Safety is a major concern in four main areas: diagnosis, prescribing, communication, and organizational change [16].

26.4.1 Diagnosis

Diagnosis in primary care is by its very nature uncertain and uses a hypothetic-deductive approach. A general practitioners deals with a very broad range of symptoms and signs with no clear diagnosis in most cases and his longitudinal care leads to practice related to individualized needs, preferences, and values. Therefore, the use of guidelines and protocols is likely to have some, but limited, success in improving safety. Some procedures are known to be safer than others, and those could be the best practices to improve in primary care. Decision support tools and (electronic) information systems can be hypothetically useful, but this has not yet been proved empirically. But, many safety problems can be overcome by design, for example, the use in specific circumstances of reminders such as message alerts on screen or insertion of checks or forcing steps instead of relying on memory and observance.

26.4.2 Prescribing

Prescribing is the most analyzed area. Hospital-based studies have shown that use of a computer system for prescribing is likely to improve accuracy. In many computer medical records, there is the opportunity to highlight possible drug-drug interactions, individual known drug hypersensitivities, and relative and absolute contraindications related to clinical conditions. But, many computer systems currently use alerts so often that many doctors simply choose to ignore them (the "cry wolf" phenomenon) and the increasing use of complementary treatments including herbal remedies is often not reported by patient because they are not considered medicine.

26.4.3 Communication

Communication is a common cause of harm to patients, but it is probably a symptom of organizational problem rather than a cause. Medical errors can occur due to a lack of communication both between colleagues and between doctor and patient.

Electronic communication can reduce problems in sharing clinical information or therapies or allergies among clinicians. The "patient held record" (better if held on the internet) would ensure that clinicians have immediate access to all relevant clinical information and assure consistency across primary and secondary care.

A poor doctor–patient relationship can have negative outcomes for patient satisfaction, treatment compliance, and even the health status of the patient (missed or inadequate diagnosis, for example). Agreed methods of communicating would be developed and established at the first visit, well known by team members and secretarial staff. Each therapy should be reviewed and re-explained at each visit in writing form. While respecting patient privacy, all clinical information should be known to the primary care team.

26.4.4 Organizational Change

The reporting of incidents can help healthcare professionals learn from mistakes. Leaders within the system should reward and encourage doctors to report problems in order to take specific action to prevent the problem occurring again. The understanding how system fails, reporting and analysis of the medical errors, the use of technology, and the continuous attention to the safety culture can lead to a quick improvement of the primary care. **Where primary care is organized in teamwork, it has the ability of** sharing and analyzing medical errors, actual or perceived, and implements those organizational changes necessary for a better development of the safety culture [17].

26.5 Recommendations

Patient safety incidents (PSIs) in primary care are perceived as a relatively lower-risk endeavor, but about 4–7% of the errors have the potential to cause serious harm, either in the short or long term. Most of them are preventable. In secondary care settings, targeted strategies have been implemented and reported but in primary care we have limited data and the World Health Organization has noted the pressing need to study and address patient safety in this setting.

As Dr. De Wet pointed out, improving patient safety in general practice requires "action on at least three fronts: greater evidence-based knowledge of patient safety, time and space to conduct the required, appropriate reflection and a strong safety culture within practices, characterised by excellent leadership, effective communication, and team members who support each other and learn together" [14].

The importance of "human factors" and the complexity of doctor–patient interactions in primary care can influence any health system and need to be investigated to better understanding their role in causing patient safety incidents.

To reduce harm and improve patient safety is essential to overcome the diversity in the reported frequency and nature of errors and to develop an understanding of both the causation and prevention of error in primary care. Actually, we have an opportunistic incident reporting rather than a systematic and proactive approach and we need a more specific intervention in the definition of "error" in primary care, a common rate for severity and preventability and in collecting data.

In 2019, González-Formoso shows that education is a key pillar of quality improvement and is considered the most important factor in improving patient safety, especially in primary care where the effectiveness of the educational intervention given to residents and their tutors in family medicine teaching units was measured by the number of events reported [18]. Training in patient safety improves knowledge and the process of care. The effectiveness of specific interventions to reliably reduce harm in general practice remains unknown. Further studies are needed to examine whether and how the professionals participating in the educational intervention have modified their behavior with respect to patient safety and whether patients' outcomes did improve.

References

1. World Health Organization. Conceptual framework for the international classification for patient safety. Contract No.: WHO/IER/PSP/2010.2. Geneva: WHO; 2009.
2. World Health Organization. Medication errors: WHO technical series on safer primary care. Geneva: World Health Organization; 2016.
3. Sandars J, Esmail A. The frequency and nature of medical error in primary care: understanding the diversity across studies. Fam Pract. 2003;20(3):231–6.
4. Wallace E, Lowry J, Smith SM, et al. The epidemiology of malpractice claims in primary care: a systematic review. BMJ Open. 2013;3:e002929. https://doi.org/10.1136/bmjopen-2013-002929.
5. de Wet C, O'Donnell C, Bowie P. Developing a preliminary 'never event' list for general practice using consensus-building methods. Br J Gen Pract. 2014;64(620):e159–67.
6. de Wet C, Bradley N, Bowie P. Significant event analysis: a comparative study of knowledge, process and attitudes in primary care. J Eval Clin Pract. 2011;17:1207–15.
7. Jones R. Editor's briefing. Br J Gen Pract. 2014;64:161–208.
8. Harmsen CG, et al. Communicating risk using absolute risk reduction or prolongation of life formats: cluster-randomised trial in general practice. Br J Gen Pract. 2014;64(621):e199–207. https://doi.org/10.3399/bjgp14X677824.
9. Piccardi C, et al. Social disparities in patient safety in primary care: a systematic review. Int J Equity Health. 2018;17(1):114. https://doi.org/10.1186/s12939-018-0828-7.
10. Houston N, Bowie P. The Scottish patient safety programme in primary care: context, interventions, and early outcomes. Scott Med J. 2015;60:192–5. https://doi.org/10.1177/0036933015606577.
11. Esmail A. Measuring and monitoring safety: a primary care perspective. London: The Health Foundation; 2013.
12. The Health Foundation. Evidence scan: levels of harm in primary care. 2011. https://www.health.org.uk/publications/levels-of-harm-in-primary-care.
13. Panesar SS, deSilva D, Carson-Stevens A, et al. How safe is primary care? A systematic review. BMJ Qual Saf. 2016;25:544–53.
14. De Wet C. Editorial: Patient safety and general practice: traversing the tightrope. Br J Gen Pract. 2014;64(621):164–5.
15. Elder NC, Dovey SM. Classification of medical errors and preventable adverse events in primary care: a synthesis of the literature. J Fam Pract. 2002;51(11):927–31.
16. WHO patient safety curriculum guide: multi-professional edition. Il Manuale del Percorso Formativo sulla Sicurezza del Paziente. Edizione multidisciplinare. © Azienda ULSS 20 di Verona; 2014.
17. McKay J, Bradley N, Lough M, Bowie P. A review of significant events analysed in general practice: implications for the quality and safety of patient care. BMC Fam Pract. 2009;10:61. https://doi.org/10.1186/1471-2296-10-61.
18. González-Formoso C, et al. Effectiveness of an educational intervention to improve the safety culture in primary care: a randomized trial. BMC Fam Pract. 2019;20(1):15. https://doi.org/10.1186/s12875-018-0901-8.

Complexity Science as a Frame for Understanding the Management and Delivery of High Quality and Safer Care

Jeffrey Braithwaite ⓘ, Louise A. Ellis ⓘ,
Kate Churruca ⓘ, Janet C. Long ⓘ, Peter Hibbert ⓘ,
and Robyn Clay-Williams ⓘ

Learning Objectives and Questions Covered in the Chapter

- How does a linear view of improvement contrast with a complexity science approach?
- The complexity frame makes it harder to manage and deliver high quality and safer care—does it therefore need to be rejected in favour of simpler improvement models?
- What examples can be brought to bear to show how studies in the complexity frame can lead to good outcomes and positive change?

27.1 The Complexities of Healthcare

Over the past two decades, prominent researchers such as Greenhalgh [1], Plsek [2], Leykum [3], Lanham [4], Petticrew [5] and Hawe [6, 7] and their colleagues and teams have promoted using complexity theory to describe and analyse the various dimensions of healthcare organisation [8–12]. Internationally, in parallel, governments have recognised the need to 'think differently'

about healthcare policy and service delivery, but without much traction on how that might be done and what it might mean. Nevertheless, it has now become more common—but by no means universal—to apply a complexity lens to understanding healthcare services and to improving them. This involves greater appreciation of elaborate, intricate, multi-faceted care networks, healthcare ecosystems, layered parts in composite settings, contextual differences across care settings, clinical cultures, multi-agent environments, and the convoluted, challenging, wicked problems [13] these systems throw up. However, with some relatively limited exceptions, the quality and safety fields' interest in complexity has, to date, been largely superficial, both theoretically and empirically [1].

Although it is seen as an emerging field, complexity science is not new; it sprang from knowledge and studies accumulating in disciplines such as sociology, ecology, and evolutionary biology in the 1940s, and with antecedents even earlier in what is broadly called 'systems thinking'. Taking a systems view, healthcare is not just complicated, or layered, or socially dense, or varied, although it is certainly all of these things. Rather, the systems view is based on several fundamental ideas: essentially, that all systems are composed of a set of seemingly discrete but actually interdependent components, defined not just by their inter-relations but by the permeable and shifting boundaries between them. The

J. Braithwaite (✉) · L. A. Ellis · K. Churruca
J. C. Long · P. Hibbert · R. Clay-Williams
Australian Institute of Health Innovation, Macquarie University, Sydney, NSW, Australia
e-mail: jeffrey.braithwaite@mq.edu.au;
louise.ellis@mq.edu.au; kate.churruca@mq.edu.au;
janet.long@mq.edu.au; peter.hibbert@mq.edu.au;
robyn.clay-williams@mq.edu.au

© The Author(s) 2021
L. Donaldson et al. (eds.), *Textbook of Patient Safety and Clinical Risk Management*,
https://doi.org/10.1007/978-3-030-59403-9_27

components (people, technology, artefacts, equipment, departments, professions) are combined sometimes in organised and expected ways, and sometimes opportunistically and in unexpected ways. The components are constantly changing, and aggregate such that their collective behaviour is more than the sum of their parts. Complex systems are multidimensional, and characterised by eddying, recurring patterns of behaviour [14]. Complexity has been described as 'a dynamic and constantly emerging set of processes and objects that not only interact with each other, but come to be defined by those interactions' [15].

Healthcare and care delivery systems are powerful examples of a *complex adaptive system* (CAS) [8, 14]. A healthcare CAS consists of dynamic interactions between different individuals and groups (agents of different types such as bureaucrats, clinicians and patients), as well as their affordances (buildings and artefacts, ranging from stethoscopes to computers to pathology tests to pharmaceuticals). The groups and affordances cohere in a system of relationships which produce roles and behaviours that emerge from those interactions, and which in turn produce outcomes: care, treatment, errors, referrals, discharges and deaths, for example. In essence, CASs are rich in collective behaviour: in healthcare, this means assemblies of loosely or tightly networked doctors, nurses, allied health staff, and scientists; managers of different hues; and policymakers of various kinds and at varying levels, as well as patients and patient groups. They all interact, inter-relating and mediating their behaviours via tools, rules, procedures and equipment, each exercising their skills for common purpose [2, 8]—to provide quality care to large numbers of patients.

The interconnections between the agents are dynamic, and the stakeholders interrelate in often surprising ways [16]. This provides challenges to understanding the way systems unfurl over time, to apprehending the system's performance and what drives it, to designing interventions to alter that performance, to improving processes and workflows, and to measuring the outcomes of any interventions in the system [5, 17, 18]. CASs are

inherently unpredictable, or it is probably more apt to say that behaviours within them and organisational and clinical outcomes cannot be forecast very far ahead.

27.2 Managing Complexity

These complexities of healthcare systems give rise to a range of challenges that clinicians, managers, administrative and support staff, policymakers and researchers face as they carry out their various roles and responsibilities and seek over time to care for, and improve the care for, patients. Yet, the simplest way to manage healthcare is to ignore or deny its complexities. It is easier to imagine a 1:1 correspondence between the intentions for healthcare and the consequential result of those intentions, as seen in Fig. 27.1.

Many people do this: they imagine that the next policy or guideline or mandated change, or quality improvement programme, or procedure, or test result, or new IT system, will be taken up unproblematically on the front lines of care. Contrary to that kind of thinking, there are multiple layers to healthcare complexity [19]; in addition to the dynamics of the care setting (systems complexity), patients come with a range of complex conditions and needs, and diagnosis, treatment and follow-up are rarely unproblematic (medical complexity). As well, patients have intricate life histories, home lives, socioeconomic circumstances, and families, partners, children and parents (situational complexity). All of these complexities co-evolve to evince intractable problems (Fig. 27.2). Indeed, it is at the interstices of these three kinds of complexity depicted in Fig. 27.2 that much wickedness manifests [20]. By wickedness, we mean problems

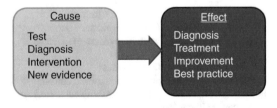

Fig. 27.1 Examples of linear thinking in healthcare. (Authors' conceptualisation)

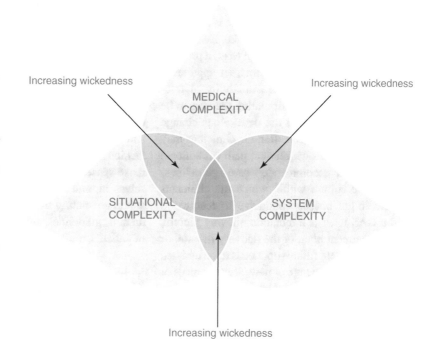

Fig. 27.2 Three kinds of complexities that co-evolve to wicked problems. (Reproduced from Kuipers, P., Kendall, E., Ehrlich, C., McIntyre, M., Barber, L., Amsters, D. & Brownie, S. (2011). Complexity and health care: Health practitioner workforce, services, roles, skills and training to respond to patients with complex needs. Clinical Education and Training Queensland, Queensland Health. ISBN: 9781921707551)

that have considerable degrees of difficulty, are difficult even to define, making them often impossible in principle to solve. How, and the extent to which, any one individual or group (e.g., an executive member or group, or a clinician or clinical team) can effectively manage complexity, or the wicked problems that ensue from that complexity, is not at all clear.

In a complex system, it is not just the different types of complexity that overlap to create challenges, but there are profound uncertainties generated by the inherent complexities [21]. These uncertainties interact (Fig. 27.3). For example, and depicted in Fig. 27.3, uncertainties about the processes of care may be compounded by an unclear diagnosis (labelled in the model scientific uncertainty) and further by a patient's unstable mental state (characterised as personal uncertainty). In many such situations the systems and structures are not understood (denoted as practical uncertainty).

Even more challenging, it is not always possible in healthcare environments for every piece of the jigsaw puzzle to be in place before acting. In fast-paced clinical practice, things happen rapidly, and a prompt response is required. While

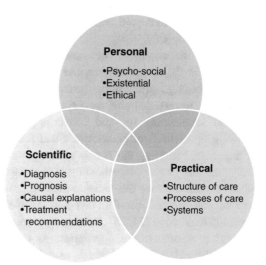

Fig. 27.3 Example of uncertainties interacting in healthcare. (Reproduced from Pomare C, Churruca K, Ellis LA, Long JC & Braithwaite J. (2019). A revised model of uncertainty in complex healthcare settings: A scoping review. Journal of evaluation in clinical practice, 25(2), 176–182)

clinicians are always under pressure to be exhaustive, they must also be pragmatic, and make room for the next patient. Hollnagel calls this the efficiency-thoroughness trade-off (ETTO) [22].

Hence, clinicians must be able to tolerate uncertainty and act even where there is imperfect data and no clearly right path to take. Even when there is thought to be a right path (e.g., a presenting patient with clear symptoms, an apparently accurate diagnosis, and the availability of relevant clinical guidelines stipulating the care to be delivered), the course of the disease can change or the treatment plan can alter, the clinicians may be following their own clinical path (mindlines) rather than the recommended care (guidelines) [23], or the culture within which the clinicians operate might not be conducive to teamwork. And a CAS itself is a dynamic, moving picture, so any treatment plan, or the delivery of care, or the post-treatment follow-up, needs to be updated in the light of the change or new circumstances or information. Even in a stable, well-run organisational ecosystem with a receptive, non-toxic, trustful culture, things can go wrong, variables can alter, the team's composition can change, the carers can come under pressure, or the path to progress can be disrupted and therefore things will not run smoothly.

Another characteristic of complexity in healthcare is the sheer number and variety of stakeholders (e.g., professional groups, clinical specialities, managers, policymakers, regulators) involved in planning for and delivering care. Drawing upon different perspectives and forms of expertise, including the patient's, can potentially facilitate greater understanding of uncertain situations and improve the decision-making process but can also add manifold layers of involvement and interaction [24, 25]. Indeed, in complex systems it is often more appropriate to think about stakeholders and individuals as collective sense-makers [26] rather than rational decision-makers in the 'if X, then Y' mode. This notion focuses on the social aspects of meaning-making: people in CASs spend a considerable amount of energy figuring out what's going on, and what to do next in the light of imperfect information. Indeed, individuals often, even typically, have conflicting understandings of uncertain situations. Sense-making theory says that we must recognise the relative value of the plausibility of a decision or explanation to people over its accuracy [12, 26]. For example, healthcare 'huddles', which have been shown to have positive effects on patient safety, leverage complexity principles such as fluidity, adaptiveness, sense-making, trade-offs and meaningful interaction [3, 27]. They provide feasible, credible decisions that the group can accommodate to, live with and action, rather than absolute answers. Clinicians and clinical teams do not make decisions in textbook fashion, or via a structured decision tree, but make sense of the circumstances they find themselves in, and create meaning and take ensuing action emanating from the convergence of information, guidelines, others' perspectives, wishes of patients, and what is viable and possible.

27.3 Responding to Complexity

Responding to these inherent complexities of healthcare systems requires letting go of many simplistic explanations and 'one-size-fits-all', or cause-and-effect, solutions. Indeed, in CASs, changes in variables over time are normal, and often appear suddenly, even at times unfathomably or chaotically. Surprise and unpredictability occur frequently: indeed, it has been said that things that have never happened, happen all the time.

Responses to induced or orchestrated or mandated changes can yield unexpected or counter-intuitive outcomes. Complex systems, because of their multi-layered nature, exhibit emergence: the properties of the system that arise from interactions at one level down, for example, group behaviour emerges from the relationships and interdependencies of the individuals which make up the group. Healthcare CASs constantly create and re-create such emergent behaviours which by their very nature are unforecastable. This is why the work day people experience as it unfolds is never the same as the one they planned for at the start of the shift.

In addition, in homing in on any part of a CAS, we can discern elements of both self-similarity and local nuances. Self-similarity can manifest fractally, at different scales (e.g., features of the culture of the organisation at the team level approximate to that of the culture of the department, and then division, and then the whole organisation) or laterally (e.g., one department looks comparable structurally to another). It might seem paradoxical, but healthcare levels or departments, despite being self-similar in some respects, also each operate as unique entities. There are always localised contextual, cultural and structural distinctions. Such local nuances occur as the result of the particular configurations of agents (e.g., nurses, doctors, quality managers, patients) following their internalised rules and shared mental models (e.g., put the patients first, project a good reputation to the outside world, prioritise safety) in that unique setting.

Against such a backdrop, any efforts to introduce a change or quality improvement initiative can be hampered if the complexities of the local context are not taken into account; things don't always work the same in different places and indeed are never adopted as intended, but are always modified by local agents and cultures to suit circumstances [28]. Hence, for change proponents, engagement with agents on a local-level is required and while some aspects of an improvement initiative may be standardised or readily imported from elsewhere, most things will need to be adapted to suit these variable contexts [7]. Even a rigid, highly structured, imposed IT system intended for application universally across a health organisation will be used in vastly different ways by local teams and individuals [29–32].

Responding to complexity also requires letting go of traditional notions of organisational management. CASs manifest in such a way as to thwart attempts at tightly centralised control [33]. No one person can fully comprehend the entire system or claim consistent influence over all agents, for example, something that the issue of localised, nuanced context also underscores. In short, strictly hierarchical management, because it relies on the putative ability of a single person or executive grouping 'at the top' to be in charge, can in reality never cope with all the complexities present in a system such as a hospital or busy community setting, let alone an entire chain, health region or jurisdiction [34]. Alternative models of managing with complexity in mind focus instead on mechanisms or strategies such as distributed leadership, decentralised responsibility, communities of practices, relationship-building, opinion leaders, shared mental models, and networked influence (Fig. 27.4). These hold greater promise in being better able to manage complex environments because information, power and control are spread throughout a CAS, and information that matters is often situated locally [35, 36]. Control is also distributed, and does not simply reside at the organisational apex. Top-level leaders and managers in complex organisations, then, essentially must focus on broad goals rather than prescriptive instructions—that is, negotiating with colleagues, employees or contractors over *what* needs to be achieved and then leaving it up to such

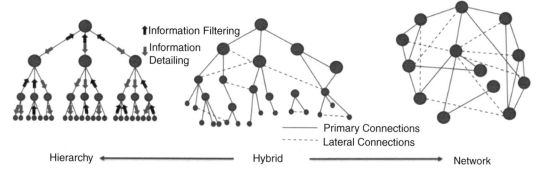

Fig. 27.4 Three types of organisational structures. (Reproduced from Yaneer Bar-Yam (2002) Complexity rising: From human beings to human civilisation, a com-plexity profile. Encyclopedia of Life Support Systems. Oxford, UK: UNESCO Publishers)

stakeholders to figure out *how* they get there [37]. Rather than command and control, ongoing dialogue and feedback between the parties is needed. In CASs, people navigate, manoeuvre and negotiate rather than carry out mandates, prescriptions and detailed requirements. Agency is everywhere; and blind adherence to instructions is in short supply. That is a very considerable dilemma and challenge for managers and leaders in healthcare.

27.4 Researching Quality and Safety Using Complexity Thinking

Despite the increasing prominence of complexity, traditional methods for investigating safety, improving quality and implementing risk management in healthcare have typically been based more on linear than complex systems thinking. In linear thinking, unwanted system variability can be controlled and outcomes from an intervention can be generalised, scaled and spread. That logic suggests that the top-down mandates of the apex decision-makers directly, or through causal stages, lead to front-line change. Local problems can be addressed by executives independently of what might be going on in the larger system, and once a problem is solved it is permanently addressed and will no longer need to be monitored. If the intervention is effective, we will see immediate, or almost immediate, results, or at least, responses causally related to or attributed to the top-down decisions, as a chain of events. In linear thinking, we can also apply multiple interventions simultaneously, while assessing them individually.

As we have seen, healthcare is not such a system: it is dynamic, and causality is never fully knowable. Local problems will affect, and be affected by, the larger system. Validity of results will vary with context, and there is a time lag—sometimes many years for things that change slowly, such as culture or a new clinical practice—between intervention and results. 'Fix and forget' does not work: we must consider variability, unpredictability and work towards common goals. Planning broadly, but not in detail, for the

longer term, and exercising influence, are key methods. Nudge-and-encourage, giving people room to manoeuvre, are more likely to be effective rather than instruction-and-adherence, asking people to comply with organisational requirements.

In such a world, making improvements to care systems, and implementing risk management in healthcare, is more effective when applying multiple methods and respecting the system characteristics rather than searching for one optimal solution. Because systems interact at micro-, meso- and macro-levels, and are configured laterally, across heterarchical structures, we need to capture local and systems-wide information. We also need to understand the *interactions* between micro-, meso- and macroelements of the CAS, and laterally across the heterarchies. To answer the what?, when? and how much? questions, we can use multilevel statistical modelling. Even more pertinent, we can also model the systems and subsystems, using computational methods such as system dynamics modelling (for aggregated, longitudinal data), social network analysis (for connections and influence), agent-based modelling (for individual or more granular data), and Functional Resonance Analysis Method (FRAM; to understand system variability). To answer the why? and how? questions, we will also need to use more qualitative methods, such as ethnographies, simulations and interviews or focus groups. Integrating multi-method data enables researchers to triangulate. This can help build a rich picture to represent the system we seek to influence, enabling identification of critical issues, key leverage points and potential solutions to improving patient safety or care quality.

27.5 Real World Examples

We turn to an analysis of five studies, each of which exemplify our own research, evaluation and interventional efforts in attempting to create safer, better care, and to manage associated risks. Each is a study using complexity science and systems thinking, but in various ways and with differing foci, aims and purposes. We present them at differing levels of granularity, from close to the patient, to meso-level studies, to those attempting to influence macro, systems-wide change. The studies are of a group of carers alongside action researchers seeking to improve the way they deliver services to patients with a single clinical condition (our Lynch syndrome study) [38]; an investigation of a coal-face solution to deteriorating patients in acute settings (research on Medical Emergency Teams) [39–41]; studies of departmental decision-making, communication and teamwork (social networks in a ward and an emergency department) [42, 43]; an examination of social processes in aggregate, with aligned clinicians, scientists and researchers creating a learning community (Australian Genomics) [44, 45]; and a systems-level enquiry into patient safety (the Deepening our Understanding of Quality in Australia research programme) [46].

27.5.1 The Lynch Syndrome Study

The complexities of work or organisational processes are not always evident at the start of a quality improvement project. An initial or superficial view will end up missing the underlying interdependencies, social processes and emergent behaviours which need to be explored and understood. One way of proceeding is to identify and visualise the focal process as they manifest (work-as-done), rather than as it is believed they manifest (work-as-imagined) [47]. Only then can we design useful interventions. By talking through the steps of how things usually go, and questioning why they are done that way, underlying complexities can be revealed. One of our projects aimed to increase the referral rates of

patients with cancer that receive a high-risk result from a screening test [38, 48, 49]. When we initially scoped the project and reviewed the guidelines, it was easy to imagine the system that the clinicians were working in as a relatively simple, linear process of:

1. Screening tests carried out to assess the risk of the cancer being hereditary.
2. Results reported as high or low risk.
3. People with a high-risk result were referred to the genetic service (Fig. 27.5).

It took nine iterations across multiple consultations between the stakeholders involved (surgeons, medical and radiation oncologists, pathologists and genetic specialists) and the research team to develop a process map that was agreed upon as depicting 'referral as done' [38] as seen in Fig. 27.6.

The number of factors influencing whether a high-risk result triggered a referral or not was surprising to all participants in the study. Factors included reluctance to initially overwhelm patients with a 'new' issue ('The results arrive in the first days post-op when the patient is dealing with pain, incontinence and fear of the cancer returning'), failure to remember to refer later, practical issues ('Referral forms are never available', 'There's nowhere in the electronic medical record to record if a referral has been made'), lack of consensus on roles ('It's not my role to refer, just report'), and confusion ('I'm not exactly sure what the report means. Do I refer or not?'). A suite of interventions was developed to effect changes in practices. By mapping the multiplicity of issues arising from the complexity of the context, and presenting them, we allowed

Fig. 27.5 Linear conceptualisation of clinical work amongst Lynch Syndrome clinicians: referral as imagined. (Authors' simplification extracted from Taylor N, Long JC, Debono D, Williams R, Salisbury E, O'Neill S, Eykman E, Braithwaite J & Chin M. (2016) Achieving behaviour change for detection of Lynch syndrome using the Theoretical Domains Framework Implementation (TDFI) approach: a study protocol. BMC Health Services Research 16:89)

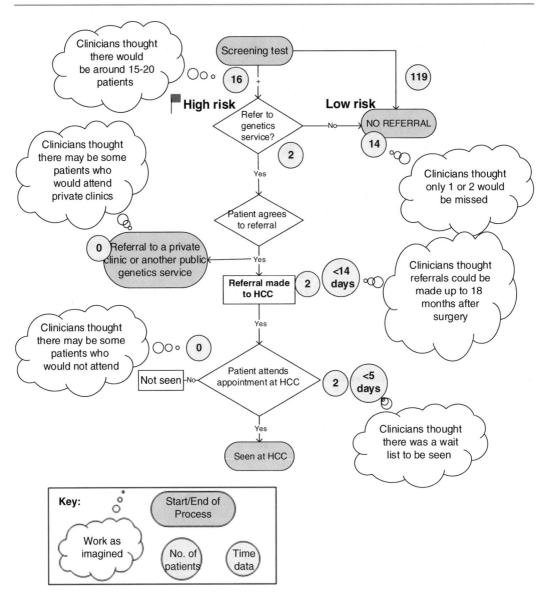

Fig. 27.6 Mapping the referral process for Lynch syndrome. (Authors conceptualisation based on Taylor N, Long JC, Debono D, Williams R, Salisbury E, O'Neill S, Eykman E, Braithwaite J & Chin M. (2016) Achieving behaviour change for detection of Lynch syndrome using the Theoretical Domains Framework Implementation (TDFI) approach: a study protocol. BMC Health Services Research 16:89)

individual clinicians and the team to see processes undertaken in their own and other nearby departments and enabled them to appreciate how their actions could affect up- and down-stream processes. Bringing clinicians from different departments together with the patient as the focus, provided a deeper understanding of other's roles and barriers, helped create a shared mental model, and fostered a whole-of-system approach to the care for patients with this condition.

27.5.2 Research on Medical Emergency Teams

Other features of complexity that confound quality and safety or improvement endeavours are social and cultural influences. The introduction of Medical Emergency Teams in acute settings across the world illustrates this point. When a hospital patient's condition deteriorates, urgent action is required to prevent irreversible harm ('the slippery slope' as seen in Fig. 27.7). Designed by colleagues originally in the USA and Australia, and then involving people internationally, Medical Emergency Teams were developed to provide a rapid response in this situation. If deterioration is detected the Medical Emergency Team can be called in from the intensive care unit to directly manage the patient's decline, the earlier the better.

Two sites where early trials of these teams were conducted had very different outcomes [28], illuminating the effect of social and cultural norms [50]. The trial was not successful in a well-established hospital in London where the Medical Emergency Teams faced opposition from an entrenched cultural belief that patients were 'owned' by their admitting doctor. This belief clouded both whether the teams were authorised to treat the patient, and where accountability lay for the care of the patient. These issues often caused delays in response which rendered the team's efforts ineffective. The other site was Liverpool Hospital in Sydney, Australia, a newer hospital with an openness to innovation and less opposition to shared accountability for patient outcomes. Here the trial, led by our colleague Ken Hillman, was a success. Today, Medical Emergency Teams are credited with reducing inpatient mortality and cardiac arrests in deteriorating patient cohorts by up to one-third wherever they have been introduced [39, 40, 51].

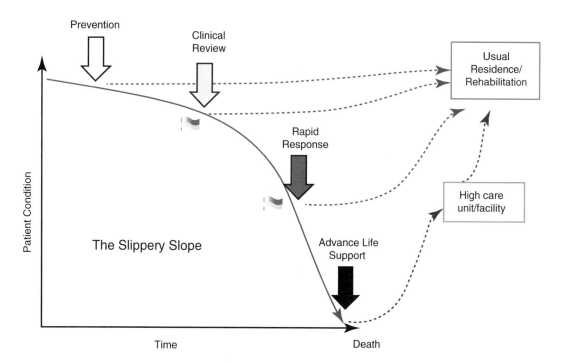

| 'Between the Flags' intervention on the 'Slippery Slope' of patient deterioration.

Fig. 27.7 Deterioration as a slippery slope in the 'Between the Flags' intervention. (Reproduced from © Copyright Clinical Excellence Commission (CEC) 2010)

27.5.3 Social Networks in a Ward and an Emergency Department

Communication and advice-seeking pathways are other key social processes that can affect patient safety and clinical risk but which are often not clearly understood before interventions are commenced [52]. Creswick and colleagues used social network analyses to map these pathways in an Australian Emergency Department, a respiratory and a renal ward [42, 43, 53], to test assumptions around the nature of communication in the units, who were the key knowledge brokers, and how united their teams were. In one study, the researchers asked staff (Emergency Department $n = 109$; respiratory ward $n = 47$): from whom

had they sought advice for medication-related problems recently? They then constructed a sociogram from their replies as seen in Fig. 27.8. They noted that while Emergency Departments are often construed as a single interdisciplinary team, the results show clearly that communication is siloed, with nurses preferring to interact with nurses, doctors with doctors and allied health with allied health. Self-similarity was evident, with the same pattern seen on the ward.

The data facilitated an analysis of key knowledge brokers in the system, including the pharmacist on the ward, and highlighted the need for protecting the roles of those key sources of information. It also revealed the complexities of the 'hidden work' being done by those staff members who were sought out for advice.

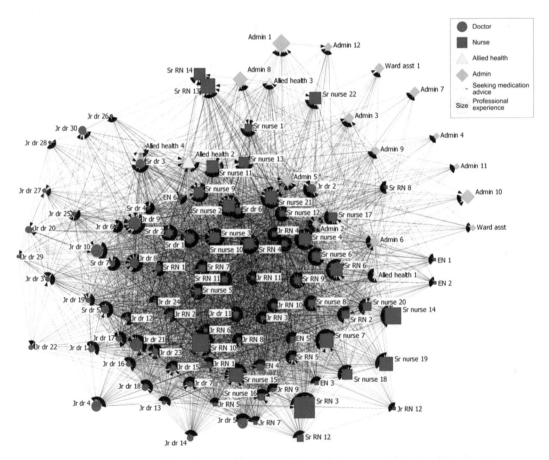

Fig. 27.8 Medication advice-seeking network in an Emergency Department. (Reproduced from: Creswick N, Westbrook JI & Braithwaite, J. (2009). Understanding communication networks in the emergency department. BMC Health Services Research, 9(1), 247)

27.5.4 Australian Genomics as a Learning Community

Much work has shown how social influences can be potent barriers to interventions and can drive undesirable behaviour [54–56]. They can also be drivers of positive change, of course [38]. But visualising and quantifying social processes is rarely done [44]. Social network analysis is a unique methodology that, as we have seen, maps the interactions between agents in a system and can identify the key players, areas of poor or high connection, and relationship strengths and risks. We used this methodology to examine social influences in the implementation of clinical genomics across Australia [57].

The *Australian Genomics Health Alliance* (hereafter, Australian Genomics) is a research-funded, nation-wide collaboration of genomic researchers, practitioners, consumers and operational staff tasked with leading the adoption of clinical genomics into routine healthcare in Australia [58]. Clinical genomics holds great promise for more accurate and rapid diagnosis of rare genetic diseases as well as guiding optimal treatment regimes for people with cancer, producing high quality care. Successful use of clinical genomics relies on interdisciplinary teams of clinical specialists, laboratory scientists, genetic specialists and counsellors to review and interpret the gigabytes of data produced by each genome tested. Early implementation projects with members of Australian Genomics suggested that a potent driver of the successful use of clinical genomics was social influence: learning from one another in the context of actually 'doing genomics'. To map the extent and strength of this influence, we surveyed all members of Australian Genomics ($n = 384$). We asked them: 'What are the strongest influences on the work you are doing towards adoption of clinical genomic practice', and the socially based question: 'Which other members are part of your genomic learning community?'

Results from the 222 respondents confirmed the influence of socially based activities with the most nominated factors being: 'hands on learning' and 'shared decision-making'. 'Formal courses' in contrast did not rate strongly—they were only weakly influential. A sociogram was constructed from respondents' nomination of people in their learning community across Australian Genomics settings (Fig. 27.9).

The largest nodes indicate the people with the most interaction in the network, i.e., the key players. It can be seen that the operational staff are particularly active and that the various groups, while tending towards being clustered, are not insular. Computations of the network show that there is a great deal of mixing across groups. We are using this information to foster more and better learning across groups, to protect key linking and coordinating roles and ultimately to improve care quality.

27.5.5 The Deepening Our Understanding of Quality in Australia Studies

The 'Deepening our Understanding of Quality in Australia' (DUQuA) studies represent the culmination of a 5-year multilevel, cross-sectional research programme aiming to identify how quality management systems, clinician leadership and safety culture in Australian hospitals are related to care delivery and patient outcomes [46]. Based on the 'Deepening our Understanding of Quality in Europe' (DUQuE) research in 188 hospitals across seven European countries [59, 60], DUQuA was also able to compare aspects of the Australian and European findings to better understand how quality management is enacted in acute settings. Evidence- or consensus-based measurement tools were designed or modified and then utilised to collect quantitative data on quality management systems at hospital and care pathway levels, department-level clinician safety culture and leadership, clinical treatment processes, patient outcomes, and patient perceptions of safety (Fig. 27.10).

Collection methods included paper-based and electronic surveys, medical record reviews, external audits, and accessing large national datasets. Linear and multilevel modelling were used to identify   relationships   between   quality

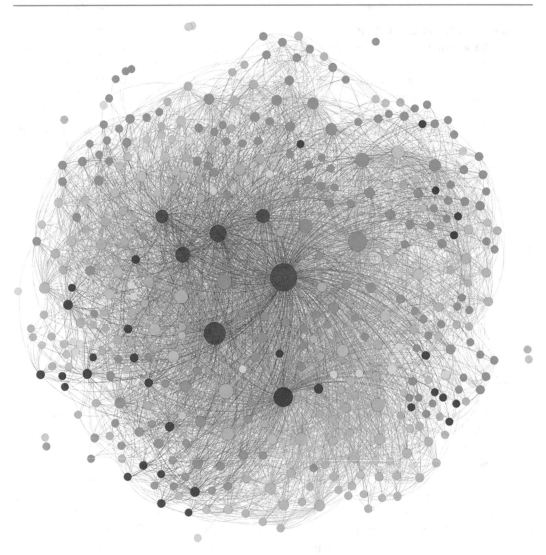

Fig. 27.9 Genomic learning community of members of the Australian Genomics Health Alliance in 2018, where nodes are members and lines are ties. Size of node indi- cates importance in the network. Colours represent the various working groups ($n = 22$); red indicates national operational staff. (Created with Gephi 0.9)

management, safety culture and leadership, care delivery and patient outcomes.

DUQuA participants included nearly half ($n = 32$) of the large, acute care public hospitals in Australia. Despite the apparent homogeneity of the group, the variability and complexity of the settings limited our ability to identify strong associations between quality management sys- tems and processes, and patient outcomes. Variation, for example, was often greater *within* hospitals than *between* them. In some instances, such as implementation of evidence-based patient safety measures, Australia's mandatory accredi-

tation programme involving assessment of per- formance against ten National Standards [61], meant that there was little variability between comparative hospital safety performance at the organisation level. At the care pathway level, however, for the acute myocardial infarction, stroke and hip fracture conditions that were assessed, there was significant variation in lead- ership and safety culture between conditions within the same hospital.

At individual hospitals, DUQuA has enabled us, through statistical modelling, to answer the what?, when? and how much? questions about

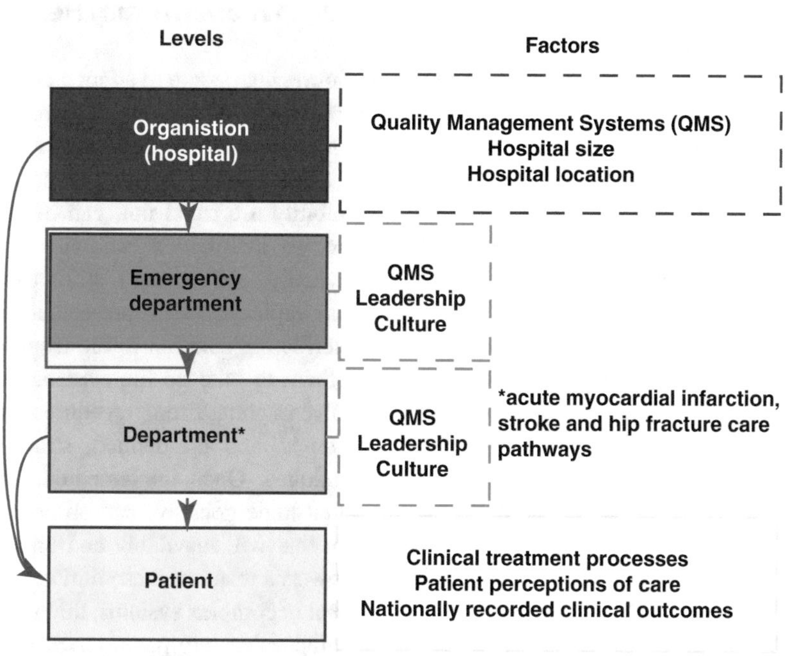

Fig. 27.10 Levels and factors investigated in the Deepening our Understanding of Quality in Healthcare in Australia study. (Reproduced from Braithwaite J, Clay-Williams R, Taylor N, Ting HP, Winata T, Hogden E, Li Z, Selwood A, Warwick M, Hibbert P, Arnolda G. Deepening our Understanding of Quality in Australia (DUQuA): an overview of a nation-wide, multilevel analysis of relationships between quality management systems and patient factors in 32 hospitals. International Journal for Quality in Health Care. 2020;32(S1):8–2.)

our acute care hospitals, and pointed to where we might best concentrate our efforts for future work. It has also enabled us to provide customised benchmarking data and links to evidence-based ideas for improvement for each hospital in the form of a report, alongside validated measurement tools to aid hospital executives and clinical leaders in implementing future quality improvement activities, and measuring their efficacy.

27.6 Extending These Ideas and Studies to the Future Organisation of Quality and Safety

We have made the case that complexity science is a gateway to understanding healthcare organisations and the quality and safety of the care they provide. Complexity science aids understanding of the intricate, multi-agent, interactive system under consideration. As we have seen, thinking of healthcare settings as CASs rather than linear systems facilitates a deeper appreciation of care-as-delivered rather than as-imagined-to-be-delivered, and adds texture and richness to the understanding of what needs to be tackled in the pursuit of safer, higher quality, better care.

The alternative, a more linear depiction of the system within which care takes place, misses much and assumes or portrays that the task of improvement is more manageable than it is. Complexity thinking does not make the problems we are trying to solve in intervening to create safer and higher quality care any easier. To the contrary, it is in reality a frontal attack on simplistic thinking, and those who assume the readiness of systems to accommodate new ideas, techniques, programmes and technology and who believe that take-up, scale and spread inevitably flow from decisions made at the top of the organisation chart or in response to research findings. Traditional thinking also assumes there is sufficient absorptive capacity: the system can do what is being asked of it when safer or higher quality care is demanded of it. In linear representations the essential logic is chain rea-soning, i.e., one thing leads to another in a cas-cading sequence. That change model at its most basic is 'do this' in a prescribed way, and when things don't work out 'do more' or 'try harder'. In complexity representations, the essential logic is different. Complexity thinking is predicated on understanding multi-stakeholder, interacting relationships, giving consideration to the fact that the whole is greater than, or at the very least dif-ferent from, the sum of the parts. That change model is based on non-linearity: the system is governed by feedback and is constantly adapting, with emergent behaviours and, due to the sheer amount of interactions and interdependencies, is inherently unpredictable. What seems on the sur-face as a caused result (attributed to the actions of a decision-maker, or the executive team), can be coupled, and related to that decision and the accompanying actions, but can also be unlinked—a mirage correlation, or an independent event, or an outcome of multiple interactions, or net-worked influence [62]. What masquerades in a CAS as causality, in summary, is sometimes, even mostly, not.

As we have seen, complexity science led us to ask, of Lynch syndrome-type studies, how does clinical work actually unfold, in contradistinction to how people think it does? We considered, of Medical Emergency Team-type interventions: how long does spread take, even of a relatively easy-to-apprehend idea, but whose time has come, and what cultural factors enabled or impeded the emergence of Medical Emergency Teams, and their subsequent take-up? A complexity science lens was also mobilised to point to how networked behaviours were mapped to understand the con-nections on the front line of care (in Emergency Departments and wards) and social processes in learning communities across a country (in Australian Genomics). And, in our final example, it helped us to home in on the care actually pro-vided in multiple large hospitals, uncovering which variables are important (but not determinis-tic) in quality improvement, systems-wide (the DUQuA research programme).

27.7 Where to From Here?

Encouraging people to adopt a complexity frame of reference, and doing research or designing interventions using such an approach, where strict generalisability, direct causation, and pre-dictability are ruled out, can be daunting. It is easier to maintain a rationalisation that says, essentially: let's design straight-line interven-tions, implement such projects as intended, and prescribe the solution to the front lines in order for them to take up the evidence directly. This involves standardised procedures, mandated pro-grammes, and pre-defined, structured tools or techniques. Once implemented, so this instru-mental logic goes, we can observe the improve-ment that will inevitably and unproblematically follow as a result of these initiatives.

But in complex systems, things are not readily decomposable into parts. CASs are organic, not mechanistic; frogs, not bicycles [63].

We believe linear models have limited appli-cations in CASs generally, and healthcare specifi-cally. The job of scholars, improvement agents, quality and safety specialists and policymakers is not to ice-skate elegantly over the top of prob-lems or to construe them simply, but to grapple with them in all their gritty reality. In non-linear, complex systems, end-point changes can be dis-proportional to the inputs. Newton's clockwork universe of logical, machine-like health systems that change in direct response to the requirements placed on them can only take us—and indeed has only taken us—so far. Quantum mechanics, with its inherent complexity, unpredictability and uncertainty principle is a much more apt meta-phor for change. As more people realise this, they will be more likely to appreciate the multidimen-sional task of improving care quality and making things safer for patients. This way leads to tools such as FRAM [64], social network analyses [57] and system dynamics modelling. It paves the way to an understanding of the resilient properties of health systems [47]. It tells us to search for a deeper appreciation for the characteristics of the system, e.g., its absorptive capacity, contextual richness and nuanced cultures. It invited us to consider the characteristics of the agents and stakeholder groups who manoeuvre, negotiate, trade-off and navigate their settings. These are the features of healthcare that anyone interested in researching, leading or delivering high quality care, or managing clinical risk, must factor into their thinking and practices.

27.8 Recommendations

1. Sensitise those with responsibility for leading, managing, improving or researching care settings to a systems view.
2. Train sufficient staff in the tools of complexity: FRAM, network analyses, system dynamics modelling, process mapping, and the like.
3. Approach quality and safety and risk management activities with a knowledge of complexity science, sense-making, and non-linearity rather than as a set of linear problems amenable to simplistic causal change logic.
4. Consider how our studies, borrowing from complexity theory, have resisted simplifying the challenges, but have nevertheless made progress in understanding care systems and their improvement.

References

1. Greenhalgh T, Papoutsi C. Studying complexity in health services research: desperately seeking an overdue paradigm shift. BMC Med. 2018;16:95.
2. Plsek PE, Greenhalgh T. The challenge of complexity in health care. BMJ. 2001;323:625.
3. Provost SM, Lanham HJ, Leykum LK, McDaniel RR Jr, Pugh J. Health care huddles: managing complexity to achieve high reliability. Health Care Manage Rev. 2015;40:2–12.
4. Lanham HJ, Leykum LK, Taylor BS, McCannon CJ, Lindberg C, Lester RT. How complexity science can inform scale-up and spread in health care: understanding the role of self-organization in variation across local contexts. Soc Sci Med. 2013;93:194–202.
5. Petticrew M. When are complex interventions 'complex'? When are simple interventions 'simple'? Eur J Pub Health. 2011;21:397–8.
6. Hawe P. Lessons from complex interventions to improve health. Annu Rev Public Health. 2015;36:307–23.
7. Hawe P, Shiell A, Riley T. Complex interventions: how "out of control" can a randomised controlled trial be? BMJ. 2004;328:1561.
8. Braithwaite J, Clay-Williams R, Nugus P, Plumb J. Health care as a complex adaptive system. In: Hollnagel E, Braithwaite J, Wears RL, editors. Resilient health care. Surrey, UK: Ashgate Publishing; 2013. p. 57–73.
9. Anderson RA, Issel LM, McDaniel RR Jr. Nursing homes as complex adaptive systems: relationship between management practice and resident outcomes. Nurs Res. 2003;52:12–21.
10. Anderson RA, Corazzini KN, McDaniel RR Jr. Complexity science and the dynamics of climate and communication: reducing nursing home turnover. Gerontologist. 2004;44:378–88.
11. Miller WL, McDaniel RR, Crabtree BF, Stange KC. Practice jazz: understanding variation in family practices using complexity science. J Fam Pract. 2001;50:872–8.
12. McDaniel RR, Dean JD. Complexity science and health care management. In: Friedman LH, Goes J, Savage GT, editors. Advances in health care management, vol. 2. Bingley, UK: Emerald Group Publishing Limited; 2001. p. 11–36.
13. Cunningham FC, Ranmuthugala G, Westbrook JI, Braithwaite J. Tackling the wicked problem of health networks: the design of an evaluation framework. BMJ Open. 2019;9:e024231.
14. Braithwaite J, Churruca K, Ellis LA, Long JC, Clay-Williams R, Damen N, Herkes J, Pomare C, Ludlow K. Complexity science in healthcare – aspirations, approaches, applications and accomplishments: a white paper. Sydney: Australian Institute of Health Innovation, Macquarie University; 2017.
15. Cohn S, Clinch M, Bunn C, Stronge P. Entangled complexity: why complex interventions are just not complicated enough. J Health Serv Res Policy. 2013;18:40–3.
16. Rychetnik L, Frommer M, Hawe P, Shiell A. Criteria for evaluating evidence on public health interventions. J Epidemiol Commun Health. 2002;56:119.
17. Craig P, Dieppe P, Macintyre S, Michie S, Nazareth I, Petticrew M. Developing and evaluating complex interventions: the new Medical Research Council guidance. BMJ. 2008;337:a1655.
18. Datta J, Petticrew M. Challenges to evaluating complex interventions: a content analysis of published papers. BMC Public Health. 2013;13:568.
19. Braithwaite J, Churruca K, Ellis LA. Can we fix the uber-complexities of healthcare? J R Soc Med. 2017;110:392–4.
20. Rittel HWJ, Webber MM. Dilemmas in a general theory of planning. Policy Sci. 1973;4:155–69.

21. Pomare C, Churruca K, Ellis LA, Long JC, Braithwaite J. A revised model of uncertainty in complex healthcare settings: a scoping review. J Eval Clin Pract. 2019;25:176–82.

22. Hollnagel E. The ETTO principle: efficiency-thoroughness trade-off. Boca Raton, FL: Routledge; 2018.

23. Gabbay J, Al M. Evidence based guidelines or collectively constructed "mindlines?" Ethnographic study of knowledge management in primary care. BMJ. 2004;329:1013.

24. Politi MC, Street RL. The importance of communication in collaborative decision making: facilitating shared mind and the management of uncertainty. J Eval Clin Pract. 2011;17:579–84.

25. Pomare C, Long JC, Ellis LA, Churruca K, Braithwaite J. Interprofessional collaboration in mental health settings: a social network analysis. J Interprof Care. 2019;33:497–503.

26. Weick KE. Sensemaking in organizations. Thousand Oaks, CA: SAGE Publication; 1995.

27. Jordan ME, Lanham HJ, Crabtree BF, Nutting PA, Miller WL, Stange KC, McDaniel RR Jr. The role of conversation in health care interventions: enabling sensemaking and learning. Implement Sci. 2009;4:15.

28. Braithwaite J, Churruca K, Long JC, Ellis LA, Herkes J. When complexity science meets implementation science: a theoretical and empirical analysis of systems change. BMC Med. 2018;16:63.

29. Debono D, Braithwaite J. Workarounds in nursing practice in acute care: a case of a health care arms race? In: Wears RL, Hollnagel E, Braithwaite J, editors. Resilient health care, The resilience of everyday clinical work, vol. 2. Surrey, UK: Ashgate Publishing; 2015.

30. Westbrook JI, Duffield C, Li L, Creswick NJ. How much time do nurses have for patients? A longitudinal study quantifying hospital nurses' patterns of task time distribution and interactions with health professionals. BMC Health Serv Res. 2011;11:319.

31. Greenhalgh T, Wherton J, Papoutsi C, Lynch J, Hughes G, A'Court C, Hinder S, Fahy N, Proctor R, Shaw S. Beyond adoption: a new framework for theorizing and evaluating nonadoption, abandonment, and challenges to the scale-up, spread, and sustainability of health and care technologies. J Med Internet Res. 2017;19:e367.

32. Greenhalgh T, Wherton J, Papoutsi C, Lynch J, Hughes G, A'Court C, Hinder S, Proctor R, Shaw S. Analysing the role of complexity in explaining the fortunes of technology programmes: empirical application of the NASSS framework. BMC Med. 2018;16:66.

33. Greenhalgh T, Plsek P, Wilson T, Fraser S, Holt T. Response to 'The appropriation of complexity theory in health care'. J Health Serv Res Policy. 2010;15:115–7.

34. Bar-Yam Y. Complexity rising: from human beings to human civilization, a complexity profile. In: UNESCO, editor. Encyclopedia of life support systems. Oxford, UK: UNESCO Publishers; 2002.

35. Braithwaite J, Runciman WB, Merry AF. Towards safer, better healthcare: harnessing the natural properties of complex sociotechnical systems. Qual Saf Health Care. 2009;18:37.

36. Greenfield D, Braithwaite J, Pawsey M, Johnson B, Robinson M. Distributed leadership to mobilise capacity for accreditation research. J Health Organ Manag. 2009;23:255–67.

37. Wilson T, Holt T, Greenhalgh T. Complexity and clinical care. BMJ. 2001;323:685.

38. Long JC, Debono D, Williams R, Salisbury E, O'Neill S, Eykman E, Butler J, Rawson R, Phan-Thien K-C, Thompson SR, Braithwaite J, Chin M, Taylor N. Using behaviour change and implementation science to address low referral rates in oncology. BMC Health Serv Res. 2018;18:904.

39. Chan PS, Jain R, Nallmothu BK, Berg RA, Sasson C. Rapid response teams: a systematic review and meta-analysis. JAMA Intern Med. 2010;170:18–26.

40. Chen J, Bellomo R, Flabouris A, Hillman K, Finfer S, The MERIT Study Investigators for the Simpson Centre, the ANZICS Clinical Trials Group. The relationship between early emergency team calls and serious adverse events. Crit Care Med. 2009;37:148–53.

41. Hughes C, Pain C, Braithwaite J, Hillman K. 'Between the flags': implementing a rapid response system at scale. BMJ Qual Saf. 2014;23:714.

42. Creswick N, Westbrook JI. Social network analysis of medication advice-seeking interactions among staff in an Australian hospital. Int J Med Inform. 2010;79:e116–e25.

43. Creswick N, Westbrook JI, Braithwaite J. Understanding communication networks in the Emergency Department. BMC Health Serv Res. 2009;9:247.

44. Long JC, Cunningham FC, Carswell P, Braithwaite J. Who are the key players in a new translational research network? BMC Health Serv Res. 2013;13:338.

45. Long JC, Pomare C, Best S, Boughtwood T, North K, Ellis LA, Churruca K, Braithwaite J. Building a learning community of Australian clinical genomics: a social network study of the Australian Genomic Health Alliance. BMC Med. 2019;17:44.

46. Braithwaite J, Clay-Williams R, Taylor N, Ting HP, Winata T, Arnolda G, Sunol R, Grone O, Wagner C, Klazinga NS, Donaldson L, Dowton SB. Bending the quality curve. Int J Qual Health Care. 2020;32(Suppl_1):1–7.

47. Braithwaite J, Wears RL, Hollnagel E, editors. Resilient health care, Reconciling work-as-imagined and work-as-done, vol. 3. Abingdon, UK: Taylor & Francis; 2017.

48. Long JC, Winata T, Debono D, Phan-Tien K-C, Zhu C, Taylor N. Process evaluation of a behaviour change approach to improving clinical practice for detecting hereditary cancer. BMC Health Serv Res. 2019;19:180.

49. Taylor N, Long JC, Debono D, Williams R, Salisbury E, O'Neill S, Eykman E, Braithwaite J, Chin M. Achieving behaviour change for detection of Lynch syndrome using the Theoretical Domains Framework Implementation (TDFI) approach: a study protocol. BMC Health Serv Res. 2016;16:89.

50. Braithwaite J, Clay-Williams R, Vecellio E, Marks D, Hooper T, Westbrook M, Westbrook J, Blakely B, Ludlow K. The basis of clinical tribalism, hierarchy and stereotyping: a laboratory-controlled teamwork experiment. BMJ Open. 2016;6:e012467.

51. Chen J, Ou L, Flabouris A, Hillman K, Bellomo R, Parr M. Impact of a standardized rapid response system on outcomes in a large healthcare jurisdiction. Resuscitation. 2016;107:47–56.

52. The Joint Commission—Office of Quality and Patient Safety. Sentinel event data - root causes by event type 2004–2015. Oak Brook, IL: The Joint Commission—Office of Quality and Patient Safety; 2016.

53. Creswick N, Westbrook JI. Who do hospital physicians and nurses go to for advice about medications? A social network analysis and examination of prescribing error rates. J Patient Saf. 2015;11:152–9.

54. Lipworth W, Taylor N, Braithwaite J. Can the theoretical domains framework account for the implementation of clinical quality interventions? BMC Health Serv Res. 2013;13:530.

55. Kelly MP, Barker M. Why is changing health-related behaviour so difficult? Public Health. 2016;136:109–16.

56. Damschroder LJ, Aron DC, Keith RE, Kirsh SR, Alexander JA, Lowery JC. Fostering implementation of health services research findings into practice: a consolidated framework for advancing implementation science. Implement Sci. 2009;4:50.

57. Long JC, Hibbert P, Braithwaite J. Structuring successful collaboration: a longitudinal social network analysis of a translational research network. Implement Sci. 2016;11:19.

58. Australian Genomic Health Alliance. 2019. https://wwwaustraliangenomicsorgau/. Accessed 18 Oct 2019.

59. Wagner C, Groene O, Thompson CA, Dersarkissian M, Klazinga NS, Arah OA, Sunol R, et al. DUQuE quality management measures: associations between quality management at hospital and pathway levels. Int J Qual Health Care. 2014;26:66–73.

60. Groene O, Klazinga N, Wagner C, Arah OA, Thompson A, Bruneau C, Sunol R, on behalf of the DUQuE Research Project. Investigating organizational quality improvement systems, patient empowerment, organizational culture, professional involvement and the quality of care in European hospitals: the 'Deepening our Understanding of Quality Improvement in Europe (DUQuE)' project. BMC Health Serv Res. 2010;10:281.

61. Australian Commission on Safety and Quality in Health Care. National safety and quality health service standards. Sydney: Australian Commission on Safety and Quality in Health Care; 2012.

62. Sugihara G, May R, Ye H, Hsieh C-H, Deyle E, Fogarty M, Munch S. Detecting causality in complex ecosystems. Science. 2012;338:496.

63. Mant A. Intelligent leadership. 2nd ed. Sydney: Allen & Unwin; 2000.

64. Hollnagel E. FRAM: The Functional Resonance Analysis Method: modelling complex socio-technical systems. Boca Raton, FL: CRC Press; 2012.

Michela Tanzini, Johanna I. Westbrook,
Stefano Guidi, Neroli Sunderland,
and Mirela Prgomet

28.1 What Is Clinical Workflow?

Clinical workflow at its most simple is the sequence of steps associated with delivering healthcare—the 'who, what, when, where, for how long, and in what order' of each task. However, healthcare is complex and dynamic with many interdependencies. In such an environment, tasks are rarely completed in a linear, step-wise fashion. Work tasks may be paused, interrupted, performed simultaneously, or be inter-dependent on other tasks or other clinicians. In many settings clinicians manage the care of multiple patients concurrently [1]. While information technology may assist in streamlining some processes and providing guidance during task completion, it often changes workflows in both expected and unexpected ways [2].

Quantitatively measuring clinical work patterns requires some form of classification for categorising elements of work. For example, clinical work can be conceptualised in terms of broad categories of: direct care with patients; communication with patients/families/colleagues; test ordering and reviewing results; documentation; managing medications; indirect care tasks associated with organising equipment, information, co-ordination of care tasks; teaching and mentoring; social interactions and breaks; and administration. The complexity of clinical work increases with each additional person, process or technology added to the system.

Each step in a process is a point at which clinical work (healthcare) can go right or wrong. Thus, each step in clinical workflows is a potential target for improving the safety and quality of care delivered. Many factors will impact the safety of clinical work, from an individual's level of fatigue, to the organisational culture, e.g. whether staff feel able to seek advice. An understanding of clinical work, including the characteristics of individuals and the environments in which work is performed, is essential for the targeting of safety interventions. Safe clinical work is responsive to contextual factors, many of which may not be predictable. Thus, understanding how clinicians use strategies to manage and adapt their work in response to contextual factors [3] is central to understanding how to support resilient and safe health systems.

Since the publication of the Institute of Medicine's report To Err Is Human in 1999 [4],

M. Tanzini (✉) · S. Guidi
Centre for Clinical Risk Management and Patient Safety, Tuscany Region - WHO Collaborating Centre in Human Factors and Communication for the Delivery of Safe and Quality Care, Florence, Italy
e-mail: tanzinim@aou-careggi.toscana.it

J. I. Westbrook · N. Sunderland · M. Prgomet
Centre for Health Systems and Safety Research, Australian Institute of Health Innovation, Macquarie University, Macquarie Park, NSW, Australia
e-mail: johanna.westbrook@mq.edu.au;
neroli.sunderland@mq.edu.au;
mirela.prgomet@mq.edu.au

© The Author(s) 2021
L. Donaldson et al. (eds.), *Textbook of Patient Safety and Clinical Risk Management*,
https://doi.org/10.1007/978-3-030-59403-9_28

there has been growing concern about the potential for medical errors due to the disruptive nature of clinical work environments. Hospital environments have been characterised by dynamism, complexity, interrelations, time and resource constraints, and have been identified to be at greater risk of errors than many other settings [5–8]. Due to the interconnected nature of clinical work, the introduction of a new technology or other system interventions may have unintended knock-on effects. A thorough understanding of clinical workflow contributes to the anticipation and containment of such unintended consequences.

28.2 Studying Clinical Workflow

28.2.1 Approaches for Studying Clinical Workflows

Some traditional methods used to study clinical work and its resultant outcomes (safety), include compiling and assessing medicolegal claims, medical record review, performance assessment, international quality and safety indicator benchmarking, and initiatives such as the Italian National Outcome Plan (Italian PNE). Each of these approaches contributes data to provide information on particular safety issues on which there may be potential to intervene. Often evaluations of safety rely upon such administrative data but many of these sources fail to reveal the context in which clinical care was performed: the social dynamics, the interactions with devices and tools, behaviours that adapt to circumstances, and the patient's changing condition.

Direct observation of clinical work in situ provides an opportunity to gain new insights into the relationships between the way work is performed in everyday situations and the safety of care delivered. Data focusing on clinical workflow and clinical outcomes are essential for identifying critical issues and organisational solutions to improve quality of care, ensuring reasonable workloads and the well-being and safety of both healthcare providers and patients.

Quantitative studies of clinical work can deliver data on the time spent managing different types of activities, their frequency and duration, along with the frequency, duration and sources of interruptions and disruptions to work. The extent to which clinicians work on multiple tasks (multitasking) can also be assessed. These data can be compared with staff perceptions of their work patterns. For example, measuring observed sources of interruptions compared to reports of interruption sources by staff may identify types of interruptions which cause the most disruption/annoyance to clinical staff [9]. Thus, sharing quantitative direct work observational data with staff provides a valuable source of evidence to raise awareness of actual work practices and can inform the design of interventions to support safe work.

Gathering comprehensive information about clinical workflows within a wider organisational context is not a simple matter; at best, data will represent a snapshot related to a specific time frame and be closely related to specific social and organisational dynamics. Further linking work patterns to specific outcomes can be methodologically challenging.

28.2.2 Time and Motion Studies

'Time and motion' research is an overarching term for a range of direct observation methods that aim to continuously observe and record an individual's activities over a certain period of time. Early examples of time and motion studies in healthcare often focused on efficiency. Time and motion clinical workflow studies have more recently been moving towards linking workflows and clinical outcomes, but this is more challenging.

The development of technological tools for collecting time and motion observations has allowed the design of more comprehensive, multidimensional studies. A variety of computer-based tools are available for recording time and motion data to study clinical workflow [10]. Such tools free observers from recording, for example, detailed time-task information, as electronic timestamps are automated. Such tools have moved beyond just collection of information about task frequency and time to consider dimensions such as the location of work, people involved, and tools/equipment used. Given research evidence of the potential safety implications of excessive interruptions to clinical work [11], most tools will also seek to collect information about interruptions/disruptions and multitasking behaviours.

One such tool is the Work Observation Method By Activity Timing (WOMBAT) technique [12], originally developed in 2007, which provides a reliable method for investigating clinical work and communication patterns, and how these are impacted by the implementation of interventions such as health information technologies. WOMBAT advanced existing time and motion methods by enabling the collection of multiple dimensions of work (e.g. who, what, when, why and how) that are all accurately timestamped, thus better reflecting the complexity of clinical work. Rather than only being able to record one task at a time, WOMBAT can record multiple tasks occurring simultaneously (multitasking), capture all the characteristics of the tasks that are occurring, as well as automatically timestamping the duration of each task and the duration of overlapping (multitasking) time. WOMBAT can also be used to record tasks that have been interrupted by another task, capture the characteristics of the interrupting task, capture the duration that the task remains interrupted, as well as if, and when, the interrupted task is returned to. Comprehensive contextual information about the other people involved in tasks (e.g. patients, colleagues), time of day/week, location and any other characteristics can be included in a WOMBAT data collection template to capture and build a picture of how clinical work is performed in the real world. These rich, multidimensional data assist in elucidating the links between workflow and safety. The workflow time study approach combined with surveys or interviews increases the potential to capture work complexity, social dynamics and personal motivations. Obtaining baseline data about current patterns of work is also important

for assessing the effects of interventions designed to improve care delivery models.

28.2.3 What Types of Questions Can Clinical Workflow Studies Answer?

Clinical workflow studies can be used to investigate a range of questions related to the relationship between work and safety. For example, to:

- Describe and compare the work patterns of different professional groups to consider implications for cognitive load and safety. Also, to allow comparisons between groups, settings, time and countries [13–15].
- Assess compliance with safety procedures. For example, Gon et al. investigated specific hand hygiene practices among birth attendants in Zanzibar [16].
- Identify workflow effects on cognitive load (e.g. interruptions, multitasking) and errors. For example, by examining the extent of interruptions to work, response to interruptions and also whether these interruptions were associated with task errors [1, 5, 11, 17, 18].
- Measure the impact of interventions or new practices on clinical workflows, and the potential impacts of any changes to safety [15, 19–21]. For example, Westbrook et al. conducted a study of pharmacists' work in the UK and Australia before and after the implementation of an electronic medication management system to assess changes in their task-time distribution and interruption rates [15] (Table 28.1).

28.2.4 Interruptions

One area of clinical workflow that has received more intensive study has been the association between errors and work interruptions [44]. Interruption science represents one of the models for how we can approach the broader study of socio-technical systems in patient safety [45]. The combination of multitasking (carrying out multiple tasks simultaneously) and interruptions

Table 28.1 Studies using the Work Observation Method By Activity Timing (WOMBAT) technique to measure clinical workflow and relationships with patient safety

Clinical workflow studies measuring work patterns of different groups			
Ampt et al. [22]	2007	Registered nurses	Australia
Ampt and Westbrook [23]	2007	Nurses (geriatric, respiratory, renal/vascular)	Australia
Ballerman et al. [24]	2011	ICU staff (physicians, nurses, respiratory therapists, unit clerks)	Canada
Bellandi et al. [25]	2018	Doctors and nurses in surgical units	Italy
Cavaye et al. [26]	2018	Community pharmacists	Australia
Graham et al. [27]	2018	ED physicians	Canada
Hand et al. [28]	2019	Renal dialysis dieticians	USA
Holmqvist et al. [29]	2018	Nurses in home healthcare	Sweden
Lehnbom et al. [30]	2016	Paediatric hospital pharmacists	Australia
Shaw et al. [31]	2011	ICU nurses	Canada
Westbrook et al. [32]	2011	Nurses	Australia
Westbrook and Ampt [12]	2009	Nurses	Australia
Westbrook et al. [33]	2008	Hospital doctors	Australia
Sinsky et al. [34]	2016	Physicians (primary, cardiology, orthopaedics)	USA
Clinical workflow studies examining contextual factors that impact workflow			
Arabadzhiyska et al. [35]	2013	Junior doctors	Australia
Hefter et al. [36]	2015	ICU physicians and physician assistants	USA
Hefter et al. [37]	2015	ICU physicians	USA
Hefter et al. [38]	2016	ICU physicians	USA
Li et al. [39]	2016	ICU physicians	Australia
Richardson et al. [13]	2016	Junior doctors	Australia
Walter et al. [17]	2014	ED clinicians, ward doctors, ward nurses	Australia
Walter et al. [3]	2017	ED physicians	Australia
Walter et al. [1]	2019	ED physicians	Australia
Clinical workflow studies examining cognitive load, interruptions, multitasking, errors			
Ballerman et al. [40]	2010	ICU staff (physicians, nurses, respiratory therapists, unit clerks)	Canada
Ballerman et al. [21]	2012	ICU staff (physicians, nurses, respiratory therapists, unit clerks)	Canada
Ballerman et al. [41]	2010	ICU staff (physicians and nurses)	Canada
Bellandi et al. [25]	2018	Doctors and nurses in surgical units	Italy
Hefter et al. [37]	2015	ICU physicians	USA
Hefter et al. [38]	2016	ICU physicians	USA
Walter et al. [17]	2014	ED clinicians, ward doctors, ward nurses	Australia
Walter et al. [3]	2017	ED physicians	Australia
Walter et al. [1]	2019	ED physicians	Australia
Westbrook et al. [11]	2018	ED physicians	Australia
Westbrook et al. [33]	2008	Hospital doctors	Australia
Clinical workflow studies examining effect of interventions or changes in practice			
Ballerman et al. [42]	2011	ICU staff (physicians, nurses, respiratory therapists)	Canada
Callen et al. [19]	2013	Nurses (Rheumatology dept)	Australia
Georgiou et al. [20]	2017	ED physicians	Australia
Westbrook et al. [2]	2013	Hospital physicians and nurses	Australia
Westbrook et al. [9]	2017	Nurses	Australia
Westbrook et al. [15]	2019	Hospital pharmacists	UK and Australia
Westbrook et al. [14]	2016	Hospital pharmacists	UK and Australia
Lo et al. [43]	2010	Hospital pharmacists	Australia
Clinical workflow studies examining compliance with specific safety procedures			
Gon et al. [16]	2018	Birth attendants in labour wards	Zanzibar
Westbrook et al. [9]	2017	Nurses	Australia

is a potent latent source of clinical error [33, 46, 47]. Direct observation in situ can assist in understanding the nature of interruptions and their impacts. For example, a study of emergency department physicians measured the relationships between interruptions and prescribing errors and demonstrated that physicians were nearly three times as likely to make a clinical prescribing error when interrupted [11].

The strategies that clinicians use to respond to interruptions can also be observed [3, 17]. Such data may provide insights into why many interruptions do not result in harm [44] and point to interventions which may effectively reduce unnecessary interruptions, as well as mitigate their negative effects. Considerable attention during the study design phase must be placed on clearly defining what constitutes an interruption and the types of response behaviours which may be observed [46].

28.2.5 Multitasking

Multitasking is an important dimension of clinical work. Workflow measurements have often not accounted for multitasking in a sophisticated way, that is, they have often had observers identify the primary task and ignore the collection of data on secondary tasks. More recent studies have started to develop methods for capturing concurrent work tasks and investigating their effects on cognitive load. For example, Westbrook et al. showed that among emergency physicians, multitasking while prescribing medication was associated with making more administrative/procedural errors (for example not using standard terminology), but not associated with an increase in clinical prescribing errors (e.g. wrong dose) [11].

28.3 Cultural and Organisational Considerations in Conducting Clinical Workflow Studies

Although tools such as WOMBAT provide a standardised methodology for conducting clinical workflow research, there are many important local factors to be considered when conducting these types of studies.

Examples of practical issues that must be considered include:

- *Study design.* Consider if a validated study data collection template (e.g. modelled on a published workflow study) would be suitable or if customisation is required to suit the local context (e.g. physical locations, types of clinical work tasks to be observed) or the particular research focus.
- *Ethical considerations.* Considerations around local ethics approval requirements, voluntary recruitment of study participants, obtaining consent from participants to be observed, procedures for study withdrawal, how to inform patients, and procedures for what observers should do if they observe a potential safety issue.
- *Patient privacy.* Clinicians may need to conduct procedures, physically assess the patient or discuss sensitive aspects of patient care, and thus observers need to always be cognisant of and respect patient privacy and dignity.
- *Engagement.* To facilitate buy-in from hospital management and staff, it is helpful to hold information sessions to discuss the research and introduce the observers, develop a positive rapport with staff, alleviate potential concerns about scrutiny of individual work practices (i.e. data from multiple participants is aggregated), and arrange feedback sessions to report key research findings.

28.4 Data Quality, Analysis and Interpretation in Clinical Workflow Studies

There are several challenges in analysing and interpreting data collected in time and motion studies [48]. Some difficulties concern the data processing steps needed in order to perform further statistical modelling, and stem from the data format and nature. Others are related to data quality and inter-observer variability, and further ones concern sampling units and the type of statistical tests that can be applied.

28.4.1 Important Practical Considerations with Ensuring Data Quality in Workflow Studies

- *Study data collection*
  Whenever practicable, it is preferable to use a validated data collection tool/technique. This ensures that the data variables to be collected have been previously tested and their definitions/scope well developed. Use of validated data collection categories also allows for direct comparison across study findings.
- *Sample selection*
  Consider the research questions and, thus, the type of staff that need to be included in the study sample (e.g. all staff or a specific professional group). Develop a sampling strategy to ensure that the collected data are representative across the sample of staff (i.e. proportion of time each participant or participant group is observed should be distributed appropriately, so that no one participant's/group's work practices are overrepresented proportionally to their contribution to the staff mix).
- *Observational period*
  With the study research objectives in mind, consideration needs to be given to determining the observation period (e.g. day/evening/night shifts, weekdays, weekends, public holidays). Observation periods should be equally distributed, and observation of participants should be randomised across the selected times/days/observers. The length of each observation session also needs to be considered. Depending on the work activities being captured, observer fatigue may set in after 2 h of intensive observation and impact data quality.
- *Observers*
  Observers are integral to the success of any observational workflow study. Consideration needs to be given to observer selection (e.g. is it vital for the observer to be a clinician or have clinical knowledge/understanding?). For example, in a study about nursing activities, ward nurses have the advantage of being familiar with the organisational process but

must acquire skills and experience in using and interacting with the observation tool. External observers, on the other hand, can be more facilitated in interacting with WOMBAT, but require more training and discussion with healthcare workers to correctly identify and record observed activities. Observer training is also critical to ensure they understand the methods of data collection and are intimately familiar with the definitions/scope of the work activity variables to be collected. Where more than one observer is collecting data, inter-rater reliability among the observers needs to be measured to ensure data consistency and integrity. For studies with a long period of data collection, random inter-observer reliability measures should be undertaken throughout the data collection period to ensure the consistency of observers over time.

28.4.2 Analysis

A dataset from a time and motion study typically comprises data collected in different observation sessions, conducted at different times during the day/week, and possibly by different observers. In its minimal form, the dataset will have as many records as the number of "tasks" observed in the various sessions, one record (i.e. row) for each task. Observer, session and task-related information will be stored in several columns, along with other timing information (e.g. start and end times). In the presence of multitasking, to be able to accurately compute task-specific statistics, such as interruption rates or proportions of task times, for each task categories one must first identify all the instances of multitasking involving tasks of the same category. In these cases, in fact, simply summing up the durations of all the observed tasks in a category to get the denominators for computing rates or proportions (but also for regression modelling) would lead to underestimation of these statistics, since all multitasking instances (i.e. time intervals) involving two or more tasks of the same category would be counted twice or more. Identifying these instances and correcting the computation of the statistics from raw data is not a trivial task and algorithms can have issues of computational time complexity.

To estimate confidence intervals and test hypotheses about differences between groups, valid methods can be, respectively, bootstrap resampling and Monte Carlo permutation tests. For both goals, in fact, parametric methods have limitations when the test measure is the proportion of a continuous variable (such as time on specific types of tasks), since the sample size is not clearly defined (there are conceptual ambiguities related to task definition), and the few proposed methods can have drawbacks such as allowing nonsensical intervals extremes (i.e. upper limit above 100%). Multilevel regression modelling is also an appropriate method for association studies, since it allows inclusion of covariates to control for factors that can be hard to control for in observational studies in a real context, and also to account for individual variability between participants, observers and setting/location. This is particularly suitable for multicentric studies in which multiple observers are used, and random variability related to these factors could reduce statistical power and undermine the possibility to draw conclusions on the effectiveness of interventions and/or limit the generalisability of the results.

28.4.3 Inter-observer Reliability

Finally, inter-observer reliability assessment, required when several observers are involved and to verify learning progress during training of observers, also presents many challenges, due to the multivariate, timestamped and ordered nature of the data from observation studies, which limits the applicability of traditional inter-rater reliability assessment methods [49]. First of all, measures such as Cohen's kappa, are only applicable to one variable at the time, so that high k scores for one aspect can be achieved even if two observers disagree substantially on other variables object of their observation (e.g. the presence/absence of multitasking, the category of the second tasks). Secondly, computing these measures

first requires matching pairs of tasks from different observers' data referring to the same task, a problem that cannot be done with perfect certainty. A way to overcome this issue could be that of either using non parametric tests to compare aggregate proportions between different observers, which avoids completely the need of pairing tasks, or to restructure the data in smaller time windows (e.g. 1 s) which can be perfectly aligned and matched, although restructuring can be tricky and sometimes computationally costly. Janson and Olsson, moreover, proposed a measure of agreement between two or more observers on multivariate categorical data which could be used on the time window data to overcome the limitations concerning single measures [50, 51]. More generally speaking, it is necessary to be aware that a single method for assessing IOR will be always necessarily insufficient to address all the different aspects on which observers in time and motion studies can disagree, that there can be trade-offs between different possible alternatives that should be considered in the light of the specific study's aims, and strive to adopt a composite method whenever possible to limit the impact of observers' bias, and to be as transparent and detailed as possible in reporting the exact methods used.

28.4.4 Disseminating Findings to Influence Practice and Policy

An aspect that is often overlooked is the importance of disseminating the results of time and motion studies. It is clear that disseminating the outcome of a study in scientific peer-reviewed journals and at conferences is essential for increasing our understanding of workflow in healthcare contexts and of complex—and possibly disruptive—phenomena such as interruptions and multitasking. As was previously highlighted, given the great variability in workflow studies and in the light of the unique challenges they posit, it is very important to be explicit in reporting the details of the methodology, including the definitions of task categories, interruptions and multitasking, as well as the IOR assessment strategy and methods used, beside the actual measures, to ease results interpretation and comparisons with different studies/contexts.

Less considered is the relevance of results dissemination within the organisational context in which a study was conducted. After a study was conducted workshops or dedicated ad hoc events should always be organised to present the results to the healthcare workers that were observed and the organisation's management team. Besides increasing staff awareness of the relevance of these phenomena and of their possible consequences in terms of errors, presenting and discussing results is a way to better understand and interpret the results. Involving all actors in the identification and refinement of possible organisational solutions to reduce or minimise the negative impact of these phenomena and ultimately increase safety and quality of care is also likely to increase the uptake of future interventions.

28.5 Conclusion

There is much to be learnt from the specific analysis of clinical workflow and how it relates to patient safety [5]. Time and motion studies provide a robust method by which to measure clinical workflows, particularly taking advantage of new electronic tools for data collection. Close collaborations between clinical staff and researchers conducting such studies is central for success, from the design stage to the final interpretation of results. Most importantly is ensuring that new information is used to inform changes in practice and policy which support clinical staff in their work to deliver safe care to patients.

References

1. Walter SR, Raban MZ, Westbrook JI. Visualising clinical work in the emergency department: understanding interleaved patient management. Appl Ergon. 2019;79:45–53.
2. Westbrook JI, Li L, Georgiou A, et al. Impact of an electronic medication management system on hospital doctors' and nurses' work: a controlled pre-post, time and motion study. J Am Med Inform Assoc. 2013;20(6):1150–8. https://doi.org/10.1136/amiajnl-2012-001414.
3. Walter SR, Raban MZ, Dunsmuir WTM, et al. Emergency doctors' strategies to manage competing workload demands in an interruptive environment: an observational workflow time study. Appl Ergon. 2017;58:454–60. https://doi.org/10.1016/j.apergo.2016.07.020.
4. Institute of Medicine Committee on Quality of Health Care in America. In: Kohn LT, Corrigan JM, Donaldson MS, editors. To err is human: building a safer health system. Washington, DC: National Academies Press; 2000.
5. Westbrook JI, Coiera E, Dunsmuir WT, et al. The impact of interruptions on clinical task completion. Qual Saf Health Care. 2010;19(4):284–9. https://doi.org/10.1136/qshc.2009.039255.
6. Westbrook JI, Woods A, Rob MI, et al. Association of interruptions with an increased risk and severity of medication administration errors. Arch Intern Med. 2010;170(8):683. https://doi.org/10.1001/archinternmed.2010.65.
7. Flynn EA, Barker KN, Gibson JT, et al. Impact of interruptions and distractions on dispensing errors in an ambulatory care pharmacy. Am J Health Syst Pharm. 1999;56(13):1319–25. https://doi.org/10.1093/ajhp/56.13.1319.
8. Coiera E. When conversation is better than computation. J Am Med Inform Assoc. 2000;7(3):277–86. https://doi.org/10.1136/jamia.2000.0070277.
9. Westbrook JI, Li L, Hooper TD, et al. Effectiveness of a 'Do not interrupt' bundled intervention to reduce interruptions during medication administration: a cluster randomised controlled feasibility study. BMJ Qual Saf. 2017;26(9):734–42. https://doi.org/10.1136/bmjqs-2016-006123.
10. Tzu-Yu Wu D. Computer-based tools for recording time and motion data for assessing clinical workflow. In: Zheng K, Westbrook J, Kannampallil TG, et al., editors. Cognitive informatics: reengineering clinical workflow for safer and more efficient care. Switzerland: Springer Nature; 2019. p. 181–90.
11. Westbrook JI, Raban MZ, Walter SR, et al. Task errors by emergency physicians are associated with interruptions, multitasking, fatigue and working memory capacity: a prospective, direct observation study. BMJ Qual Saf. 2018;27(8):655. https://doi.org/10.1136/bmjqs-2017-007333.
12. Westbrook JI, Ampt A. Design, application and testing of the Work Observation Method by Activity Timing (WOMBAT) to measure clinicians' patterns of work and communication. Int J Med Inform. 2009;78(Suppl 1):S25–33. https://doi.org/10.1016/j.ijmedinf.2008.09.003.
13. Richardson LC, Lehnbom EC, Baysari MT, et al. A time and motion study of junior doctor work patterns on the weekend: a potential contributor to the weekend effect? Intern Med J. 2016;46(7):819–25. https://doi.org/10.1111/imj.13120.

14. Westbrook JI, Shah S, Lehnbom EC, et al. Collaborative cross-country study to measure the impact of electronic medication management systems. Int J Qual Health Care. 2016;28(Suppl_1):10–1. https://doi.org/10.1093/intqhc/mzw104.11.

15. Westbrook JI, Li L, Shah S, et al. A cross-country time and motion study to measure the impact of electronic medication management systems on the work of hospital pharmacists in Australia and England. Int J Med Inform. 2019;129:253.

16. Gon G, de Bruin M, de Barra M, et al. Hands washing glove use, and avoiding recontamination before aseptic procedures at birth: a multicenter time-and-motion study conducted in Zanzibar. Am J Infect Control. 2019;47(2):149–56.

17. Walter SR, Li L, Dunsmuir WTM, et al. Managing competing demands through task-switching and multitasking: a multi-setting observational study of 200 clinicians over 1000 hours. BMJ Qual Saf. 2014;23(3):231–41. https://doi.org/10.1136/bmjqs-2013-002097.

18. Reed CC, Minnick AF, Dietrich MS. Nurses' responses to interruptions during medication tasks: a time and motion study. Int J Nurs Stud. 2018;82:113–20. https://doi.org/10.1016/j.ijnurstu.2018.03.017.

19. Callen J, Hordern A, Gibson K, et al. Can technology change the work of nurses? Evaluation of a drug monitoring system for ambulatory chronic disease patients. Int J Med Inform. 2013;82(3):159–67. https://doi.org/10.1016/j.ijmedinf.2012.11.009.

20. Georgiou A, McCaughey EJ, Tariq A, et al. What is the impact of an electronic test result acknowledgement system on emergency department physicians' work processes? A mixed-method pre-post observational study. Int J Med Inform. 2017;99:29–36. https://doi.org/10.1016/j.ijmedinf.2016.12.006.

21. Ballermann M, Shaw NT, Mayes DC, et al. Impact of a clinical information system on multitasking in two intensive care units. Electron J Health Informatics. 2012;7(1):2.

22. Ampt A, Westbrook J, Creswick N, et al. A comparison of self-reported and observational work sampling techniques for measuring time in nursing tasks. J Health Serv Res Policy. 2007;12(1):18–24. https://doi.org/10.1258/135581907779497576.

23. Ampt A, Westbrook JI. Measuring nurses' time in medication related tasks prior to the implementation of an electronic medication management system. Stud Health Technol Inform. 2007;130:157–67.

24. Ballermann M, Shaw N, Mayes D, et al. Validation of the Work Observation Method By Activity Timing (WOMBAT) method of conducting time-motion observations in critical care settings: an observational study. BMC Med Inform Decis Mak. 2011;11(1):32.

25. Bellandi T, Cerri A, Carreras G, et al. Interruptions and multitasking in surgery: a multicentre observational study of the daily work patterns of doctors and nurses. Ergonomics. 2018;61(1):40–7. https://doi.org/10.1080/00140139.2017.1349934.

26. Cavaye D, Lehnbom EC, Laba T-L, et al. Considering pharmacy workflow in the context of Australian community pharmacy: a pilot time and motion study. Res Soc Adm Pharm. 2018;14:1157. https://doi.org/10.1016/j.sapharm.2018.01.003.

27. Graham TA, Ballermann M, Lang E, et al. Emergency physician use of the Alberta Netcare Portal, a province-wide interoperable electronic health record: multi-method observational study. JMIR Med Inform. 2018;6(3):e10184.

28. Hand RK, Albert JM, Sehgal AR. Quantifying the time used for renal dietitian's responsibilities: a pilot study. J Ren Nutr. 2019;29:416.

29. Holmqvist M, Ekstedt M, Walter SR, et al. Medication management in municipality-based healthcare: a time and motion study of nurses. Home Healthc Now. 2018;36(4):238–46.

30. Lehnbom EC, Li L, Prgomet M, Lam WY, Westbrook JI. Little things matter: a time and motion study of pharmacists' activities in a paediatric hospital. In: Digital Health Innovation for Consumers, Clinicians, Connectivity and Community: Selected Papers from the 24th Australian National Health Informatics Conference (HIC 2016). Amsterdam: IOS Press; 2016.

31. Shaw NT, Ballermann MA, Hagtvedt R, et al. Intensive care unit nurse workflow during shift change prior to the introduction of a critical care clinical information system. Electron J Health Inform. 2011;6(1):5.

32. Westbrook J, Duffield C, Li L, et al. How much time do nurses have for patients? A longitudinal study quantifying hospital nurses' patterns of task time distribution and interactions with health professionals. BMC Health Serv Res. 2011;11(1):319.

33. Westbrook JI, Ampt A, Kearney L, et al. All in a day's work: an observational study to quantify how and with whom doctors on hospital wards spend their time. Med J Aust. 2008;188(9):506–9.

34. Sinsky C, Colligan L, Li L, et al. Allocation of physician time in ambulatory practice: a time and motion study in 4 specialties. Ann Intern Med. 2016;165(11):753–60. https://doi.org/10.7326/M16-0961.

35. Arabadzhiyska PN, Baysari MT, Walter S, et al. Shedding light on junior doctors' work practices after hours. Intern Med J. 2013;43(12):1321–6. https://doi.org/10.1111/imj.12223.

36. Hefter Y, Madahar P, Eisen L, et al. A time motion study to describe workflow of attendings and residents in medical and surgical ICUs. C94 high impact clinical trials in critical care. Am J Respir Crit Care Med. 2015;201:A5126.

37. Hefter Y, Madahar P, Eisen LA, et al. Relationship of ICU strain factors and allocation of physician time in the ICU. C103 optimizing limited ICU resources. Am J Respir Crit Care Med. 2015;191:A5233.

38. Hefter Y, Madahar P, Eisen LA, et al. A time-motion study of ICU workflow and the impact of strain. Crit Care Med. 2016;44(8):1482–9. https://doi.org/10.1097/ccm.0000000000001719.

39. Li L, Hains I, Hordern T, et al. What do ICU doctors do? A multisite time and motion study of the clinical work patterns of registrars. Crit Care Resusc. 2015;17(3):159.

40. Ballermann MA, Shaw NT, Arbeau KJ, Mayes DC, Gibney RTN. Intensive care unit health care providers spend less time multitasking after the introduction of a critical care clinical information system. HIC 2010: 18th Annual Health Informatics Conference: Informing the Business of Healthcare, 24–26 Aug 2010, Melbourne Convention and Exhibition Centre. Health Informatics Society of Australia.

41. Ballermann MA, Shaw NT, Arbeau KJ, et al. Impact of a critical care clinical information system on interruption rates during intensive care nurse and physician documentation tasks. Stud Health Technol Inform. 2010;160(Pt 1):274–8.

42. Ballermann M, Shaw NT, Mayes DC, et al. Critical care providers refer to information tools less during communication tasks after a critical care clinical information system introduction. Stud Health Technol Inform. 2011;164:37–41.

43. Lo C, Burke R, Westbrook JI. Electronic medication management systems' influence on hospital pharmacists' work patterns. J Pharm Pract Res. 2010;40(2):106–10.

44. Sanderson P, McCurdie T, Grundgeiger T. Interruptions in health care: assessing their connection with error and patient harm. Hum Factors. 2019;61(7):1025–36. https://doi.org/10.1177/0018720819869115.

45. Coiera E. The science of interruption. BMJ Qual Saf. 2012;21(5):357. https://doi.org/10.1136/bmjqs-2012-000783.

46. Walter SR, Dunsmuir WTM, Westbrook JI. Studying interruptions and multitasking in situ: the untapped potential of quantitative observational studies. Int J Hum Comput Stud. 2015;79:118–25. https://doi.org/10.1016/j.ijhcs.2015.01.008.

47. Tucker AL, Spear SJ. Operational failures and interruptions in hospital nursing. Health Serv Res. 2006;41(3 Pt 1):643–62. https://doi.org/10.1111/j.1475-6773.2006.00502.x.

48. Walter SR, Dunsmuir WT, Raban MZ, et al. Understanding clinical workflow through direct continuous observation: addressing the unique statistical challenges. In: Zheng K, Westbrook J, Kannampallil T, Patel V, editors. Cognitive informatics. Switzerland: Springer; 2019.

49. Walter SR, Dunsmuir WTM, Westbrook JI. Inter-observer agreement and reliability assessment for observational studies of clinical work. J Biomed Inf. 2019;100:103317. https://doi.org/10.1016/j.jbi.2019.103317.

50. Janson H, Olsson U. A measure of agreement for interval or nominal multivariate observations. Thousand Oaks, CA: Sage Publications; 2001. p. 277–89.

51. Lopetegui MA, Bai S, Yen PY, et al. Inter-observer reliability assessments in time motion studies: the foundation for meaningful clinical workflow analysis. AMIA Annu Symp Proc. 2013;2013:889–96.

Shiftwork Organization

29

Giovanni Costa, Eleonora Tommasi,
Leonardo Giovannini, and Nicola Mucci

29.1 Introduction to Shift Work

29.1.1 Definition and Main Features

The correct organization of health worker shift-work is essential to ensure continuous 24-h patient care. Healthcare is the perfect example of the "24-h society," whose milestones are the various types of shift work (night work, split shifts, on-call work, part-time work, irregular and flexible working hours) and new technologies. In general, "shiftwork" means any structure of work in which the operating time of a company is extended beyond the usual 8 or 9 h (typically between 7–8 a.m. and 5–6 p.m.), to cover the entire 24 h, through the alternation of different groups of workers [1, 2].

To ensure 24-h coverage, shift work must also include night work which, according to International Labour Organization Convention No. 171 [3], is defined as "all work which is performed during a period of not less than seven consecutive hours, including the interval from midnight to 5 a.m. (night time)." The European Directive 2003/88/EC [4] defines a "night worker" as "(a) any worker who, during the night, works at least three hours of his daily working time as a normal course; (b) any worker who works a certain proportion of his annual working time, as defined at the choice of the Member State concerned."

Shift scheduling may differ with respect to various parameters including:

- *Duration of duty period*: predominantly ranging from 6 to 8 or 9 h, but it can last up to 12 h or more, or be reduced to 4 h (in the case of part-time work).
- *Semicontinuous* or *continuous rota systems*: depending on the inclusion of weekends or Sundays.
- *Presence and frequency of work during the "nighttime."*
- *Number and type of shifts*: mainly two shifts (morning and afternoon) or three shifts (including the night) of 7–9 h, or four shifts of 6 h (morning, afternoon, evening, night, in the so-called "6 × 6" shift system).
- *Start and end times of each shift:* for example, morning shift (starting after 03:00 and ending before 18:00), day shift (starting after 08:00 and ending before 18:00), evening shift (starting at any time between 18:00 and 23:00 and not categorized as a night shift), night (≥ 3 h between 23:00 and 06:00).

G. Costa
Department of Clinical Sciences and Community Health, University of Milano, Milan, Italy
e-mail: giovanni.costa@unimi.it

E. Tommasi · L. Giovannini · N. Mucci (✉)
Department of Experimental and Clinical Medicine, University of Florence, Florence, Italy
e-mail: eleonora.tommasi@unifi.it;
leonardo.giovannini@unifi.it; nicola.mucci@unifi.it

© The Author(s) 2021
L. Donaldson et al. (eds.), *Textbook of Patient Safety and Clinical Risk Management*,
https://doi.org/10.1007/978-3-030-59403-9_29

- *Direction of shift rotation*: clockwise or phase-delayed (morning-afternoon-night), counterclockwise or phase-advanced (afternoon-morning-night).
- *Speed of rotation among shifts*: fast (every 1–3 days), intermediate (every 4–6 days), slow (7 or more days), null (in the case of fixed shifts).
- *Regularity/irregularity and length of the entire shift cycle* (i.e., from 5 days up to 6 months or more).

Shift work can have adverse effects on the health and well-being of the worker who must be operative at all times and on days off. In particular, shift work causes significant interference in the different domains of human life (biological, behavioral, social) and alters the psychophysical balance of a person, in particular: (1) the perturbation of circadian rhythms; (2) a reduction in vigilance and performance, leading to a consequently greater risk of errors and accidents; (3) adverse health effects both in the short-term (sleep, digestive, mental and menstrual disorders) and in the medium- to long-term (increased gastrointestinal, neuropsychic, metabolic, cardiovascular diseases); (4) difficulties in maintaining social roles, which have negative consequences on interpersonal relationships and family care. Several studies suggest that shiftwork also increases the risk of breast, prostate, and colorectal cancers.

Shift workers must be adequately informed about this occupational risk factor and must be guaranteed adequate organization of working times based on proven ergonomic criteria as well as appropriate compensatory measures to mitigate adverse effects.

29.1.2 Chronobiological Aspects

"Circadian rhythm" describes the physiological oscillations occurring in biological functions over the course of 24 h. The word "circadian" comes from Latin, where "circa" means "around" and "diem" means "day." In humans, the circadian master clock resides in the suprachiasmatic nucleus of the anterior hypothalamus and is synchronized by environmental factors, in particular light/dark alternation. By way of the retino-hypothalamic tract, external light influences the expression of the CLOCK and BMAL1 genes, which are the main regulators of the periodic oscillations that occur during the light/dark cycle. The binding of CLOCK and BMAL1 activates other genes such as the *Period* genes that are also responsible for the physiological oscillation of the circadian rhythm by means of an inhibitory feedback loop. *Period* genes encode for the PER protein, whose level rises during the night and decreases during the day. Based on the light stimuli received and the genes activated as a result, the suprachiasmatic nucleus regulates the secretion of melatonin from the pineal gland: melatonin levels increase during the dark of night and decrease under the exposure to light during the day [5].

Shift work, in particular night work, modifies human exposure to the light/dark cycle and consequently the normal circadian oscillation of biological functions. This alteration involves a flattening of the amplitude and a shift of the acrophase of circadian rhythms, the extent of which depends on the number of consecutive night shifts and the direction of rotation, clockwise or counterclockwise, of the on-duty periods. The type of shift work, whether rotating or fixed, can also affect the oscillation of circadian rhythms. Workers involved in continuously rotating shifts, the most widely used in the health sector, are forced to adapt as quickly as possible to changing work times, resulting in significant work-stress. Fixed-shift workers, on the other hand, are more likely to keep their sleep/wake cycle stable, provided they keep a consistent schedule even on days off.

29.2 Effects of Shift Work on Worker Health and Impact on Patient Safety

29.2.1 Sleep Deprivation and Vigilance

The disturbance of the psychobiological functions, linked to the modification of the sleep/wake cycle, plays an important role in influencing work ability. Shift workers can suffer from a series of symptoms commonly known as "jet-lag syndrome," characterized by fatigue, drowsiness, insomnia, digestive troubles, and the slowing down of mental functions and performance.

The timing of shifts (especially night and early-morning), the environmental conditions, and workers' lifestyles can negatively affect both quantity and quality of sleep. After the night shift, a worker should be placed in favorable conditions for psychophysical recovery. However, falling asleep and sleeping longer are very difficult due to environmental interference such as light and noise. Sleep is generally reduced by about 2–4 h: in particular, phase 2 of non-rapid eye movement sleep (NREM) and rapid eye movement sleep (REM) are disturbed. The REM phase is also particularly reduced by the early-morning shift (starting at 6 a.m. or earlier) because of a truncation of the last part of the sleep cycle; moreover, this advanced waking time usually causes excessive daytime sleepiness during the waking period. The direction of rotation of shifts can also influence sleep patterns and circadian rhythms: clockwise-rotating shift schedules are less disruptive than counterclockwise ones. In very quickly rotating shifts for example, the intervals between shifts rotating clockwise (1M-1A-1N) are longer (always 24 h) than those between shifts rotating according to a counterclockwise system (1A-1M-1N) which places the morning shift immediately after the afternoon shift and before the night shift of the very same day ("quick return"): in the latter case, rest intervals between shifts are very short (only 8 h), thus implying the truncation of sleep preceding the morning shift and the possibility of only a very short sleep or nap before the night shift [6].

It is well known that sleepiness, sleep deprivation, chronic fatigue, and fluctuations in vigilance are key factors in creating the conditions that lead to human errors and accidents through interactions with other organizational factors, such as environmental conditions, workload, job content, and time pressure. Insomnia, one of the core symptoms of shift work disorder, has a prevalence of about 6% in the general population and between 29% and 38% in shift workers [7].

Symptoms include difficulties falling asleep, reduced sleep duration, frequent waking, and an intense preoccupation with the act of sleeping itself.

Fatigue, drowsiness, and insomnia resulting from a disturbed sleep-wake cycle can manifest themselves as the so-called "shift work sleep disorder," which negatively affects physical and mental health, quality of life, performance, and productivity. A study by Drake et al. [8] investigating 2570 US workers aged 18–65 years reported that 14% of night workers and 8% of rotating shift workers met the criteria for shift work sleep disorder. Such individuals had significantly higher rates of ulcers (odds ratio of 4.18), sleepiness-related accidents, absenteeism, and depression, and missed family and social activities more frequently compared to shift workers who did not meet the criteria.

Concerning personal characteristics, Kalmbach et al. [9] reported that in a group of normal sleeping, non-shift workers, the chances of developing shift work disorder after transitioning to rotating shifts were over five times greater for highly sleep-sensitive individuals. In a longitudinal study including 1533 Norwegian nurses, Waage et al. [10] showed that the risk of developing a shift work disorder was significantly associated with the number of night shifts worked in the previous year, the Epworth sleepiness score, the use of melatonin, the use of bright light therapy, and symptoms of depression.

29.2.2 Interference in Performance Efficiency and Patient Safety

Shift and night work, as well as prolonged and/or irregular working hours, are also risk factors for patient safety, a fact well documented by many epidemiological studies. The working conditions of the night shift differ from those of the day shift. In particular, the night shift involves fewer employees who have to take care of many patients. The increased workload and the alteration of the sleep-wake rhythm increases the risk of making clinical errors.

Studies in the industrial sector have shown that risk grows with the number of consecutive night shifts (6% increase for the second night, 17% for the third, and 36% for the fourth) and with the lengthening of work shifts, noting an exponential increase in the occurrence of accidents after the eighth hour of work and estimating a doubling of the risk for 12-h shifts compared to 8-h shifts, for which there is no corresponding reduction in workload or introduction of adequate breaks.

Similar results are also reported for the hospital workers, including a higher relative risk of accidents in afternoon and night shifts, resulting in longer periods of absence, as well as reduced levels of attention and vigilance and increased error associated with long shifts (24 h or more) [11–13]. On the other hand, it is also known that a significant improvement of these outcomes can come from limiting the length of work shifts [14, 15].

According to a study of 2737 US medical residents [16], the incidence of at least one major mistake was 3.8%, 9.8%, and 16%, in the case of 0 shifts, 1–4 shifts, and more than 4 shifts of prolonged duration (32 h on average), respectively, with a 300% increase in preventable adverse events due to fatigue and/or sleep deprivation resulting in the death of the patient. Other core symptoms of fatigue are exhaustion, tiredness, and lethargy, resulting in loss of efficiency, difficulty in concentrating, as well as a decrease in productivity and safety at work.

In the case of nurses, too, an increase has been documented in the occurrence of errors, that jeopardize patient safety, dependent on the duration of a shift beyond 8 h, overtime, and night work shifts [17–19]. In addition, other studies have shown that, when coupled with high patient turnover, extended shifts or a reduced number of staff are associated with an increase in hospital mortality. In addition, other studies reveal significant association between increased hospital mortality rates and extended shifts or reduced staff along with high patient turnover (YES IT IS) [20, 21].

A very recent national survey on work patterns and fatigue-related outcomes carried out on 3133 nurses of 6 practice hospital areas (child health including neonatology, cardiac care/intensive care, emergency and trauma, inpatient mental health, medical, and surgical nursing) in New Zealand showed that 30.8% of errors in the previous 6 months were fatigue-related while 64% of responders reported having felt sleepy at the wheel in the previous 12 months. Fatigue-related outcomes were associated with shift timing and sleep. Risk increased with more night shifts and decreased with more nights of sleep between 11 p.m. and 7 a.m. during which nurses had enough sleep to feel fully rested. Risk also increased with roster changes and more shift extensions greater than 30 min, and decreased with more flexibility regarding shifts [22].

29.2.3 Health Disorders

The literature in recent years shows that shift work can cause serious medium- and long-term effects on the worker health due to the disruption of physiological circadian rhythms [1, 23]). Hence, the socioeconomic and health-related consequences of sleep and circadian rhythm disorders in shift workers, such as absenteeism and mood disorders, should likewise not be underestimated [24].

Irritability, nervousness, and anxiety are frequent complaints from shift workers, relating to more stressful working conditions. In association with persistent disruption of circadian rhythms and sleep deficit, they may lead to mood disorders, chronic anxiety, and/or depression, fostering absenteeism and often requiring the administration of sedatives and hypnotics [25].

After the aforementioned sleep troubles, gastrointestinal disorders are the most frequent morbidities found among shift workers. In particular, the risk of gastroduodenitis, peptic ulcer, and irritable bowel syndrome is two to five times higher for shift and night workers [26]. The mismatch between circadian phases of the gastrointestinal tract (i.e., gastric, bile, and pancreatic secretions, intestinal mobility, hunger and satiety hormones) and meal times is one of the causes for this increased prevalence among shift workers, who are most frequently forced to consume "junk food," which are pre-packaged and more caloric, and "pep" and soft drinks [27].

Many epidemiological studies have demonstrated a significant association between shift work and metabolic syndrome [28], insulin resistance, and type 2 diabetes [29, 30].

Moreover, according to several authors, shift workers have a 40% higher risk than day workers of suffering from ischemic heart disease [31, 32], relating to circadian disruption along with disturbed cardiac autonomic control and detrimental lifestyle changes, such as obesity and smoking [33]. A recent meta-analysis by Manohar et al. [34] also reported a significant association between hypertension and rotating shift work.

Night shift work negatively affects female fertility and reproductive health and is associated with an increased risk of adverse pregnancy outcomes such as miscarriage and impaired fetal development, including pre-term birth and low birth weight [35]. In 2007, "shift work involving circadian disruption" was classified as "probably carcinogenic to humans" (Group 2A) by the International Agency for Research on Cancer (IARC) on the basis of sufficient evidence in animal models and limited evidence in humans, in particular for breast cancer. A positive association between high-intensity, long-duration night shift work and breast cancer has also been reported in large populations of nurses [36]. Experimental animal and cellular studies found immunosuppression, chronic inflammation, and cell proliferation caused by the disruption of the light-dark cycle. According to recent epidemiological studies, weaker evidence is also emerging for colorectal and prostate cancer: this has lead the IARC to confirm very recently its assessment of night shift work as a probable carcinogen [37].

29.3 Preventive Actions and Recommendations

29.3.1 Ergonomic Criteria for the Organization of Shift Schedules

Healthcare companies must also consider the well-being of their employees when organizing shift work. Shifts must be planned based on ergo-

nomic criteria that protect the psychophysical integrity and social well-being of workers. These criteria must take into account biological adaptation, work performance, health status, and personal and social problems, and can be summarized as follows [38, 39]:

- The amount of night work and the number of consecutive night shifts should be reduced as much as possible (2–3 at most) to limit interference with circadian rhythms and sleep.
- Quickly rotating shift systems should be chosen over slowly rotating ones, since they interfere less with circadian rhythms and minimize the extent of any cumulative sleep deficit.
- Clockwise rotation (morning-afternoon-night) should be preferred to counterclockwise rotation (afternoon-morning-night) since it is better adapted to endogenous circadian rhythms (which show a periodicity slightly longer than 24 h in "free-running" experiments), avoids quick changeovers (e.g., having morning and night shifts within the same day), and allows for longer rest periods for immediate recovery from fatigue and sleep deficit.
- Setting the start of morning shifts too early should be avoided in order to reduce the truncation of sleep (of the REM phase in particular) and the consequent sleepiness and risk of error.
- Prolonged work shifts (9–12 h) should only be considered when the workload is suitable, adequate pauses may be taken, and the shift system is designed to minimize the accumulation of fatigue as well as the exposure to toxic substances.
- Shift cycles should be as regular as possible and should ensure as many weekends free as possible, in order to allow workers to better plan and enjoy their leisure and social time.
- Fixed night work should be implemented only for particular work situations, which require a complete adjustment to night work to ensure the highest levels of safety.
- Flexible working time arrangements should be promoted in order to meet workers' needs and preferences.

However, there doesn't exist a "best" shift system that can be recommended across the board. Each shift-based work schedule should be planned around and tailored to the different job activities and demands involved, as well as the specific traits, social habits, and personal backgrounds of the workers involved. Workers must participate in the analysis, design, and implementation of the shift system chosen. This is important for motivating workers and improving their psychophysical tolerance: indeed, shift schedules often fail because they do not reflect the conditions and needs of workers. On the other hand, workers sometimes prefer less favorable shift patterns (i.e., 12-h shifts or counterclockwise rotation) in order to have longer rest periods between cycles. As previously mentioned, in several cases the rapid transition from morning to night shift in the same day, in particular waking early in the morning, prefigures an extremely stressful and risky condition.

The duration of work shifts should be adjusted according to workload and the type of task, as well as the number of workers available. Jobs requiring high levels of vigilance and physical activity (i.e., emergency and intensive care units) should have shorter shifts while, on the other hand, shifts may be longer for jobs with a lighter workload (i.e., basic assistance or support activities) or jobs during which workers can take breaks.

29.3.2 Other Organizational Aspects

When introducing or modifying a shift scheme, an effective methodology should follow precise steps, including in particular:

1. A preliminary, general plan taking into account the various conditions at play, such as legislative and contractual provisions, service and/or production requirements, working conditions.
2. A careful analysis of the traits of the persons involved, with a focus on demographic aspects (e.g., age, gender), workloads in the different shifts, risk factors, personal conditions (e.g., family and social status, commuting).

3. The structure of the shift schedule based on the previously mentioned ergonomic criteria.
4. The shift system's introduction and a verification of the degree of acceptability by a sample group of workers for a given period, including the recording of appropriate indicators (e.g., subjective assessment, working behavior, absenteeism, errors).
5. The final implementation of the new shift system after adequate adjustments addressing any indications emerging from the previous phase.

The planning of shift work in hospitals is complex because it involves multiple organizational aspects based on the type of assistance provided (e.g., intensive care, medical, surgical, laboratory, and specialist services) and the operational standards in terms of the staff/patient ratio, the type of intervention, and the quantity and type of professionals available and/or necessary in each shift. Various interventions aimed at compensating for the inconveniences caused by shift work have been proposed and adopted in recent years, often in very different and empirical ways depending on the different working conditions and specific, company-wide problems. According to Thierry [40], these interventions can be divided into two categories:

(a) The "counterweights," intended solely to compensate for inconveniences or disturbances caused by the shift system. One that is usually (and often uniquely) adopted is the increase in remuneration for work performed at night and during holidays. This constitutes a simple translation of the various aspects of the problem into monetary terms, which often has no direct connection to their specificity or seriousness, as the increase in remuneration may differ considerably as a function of contractual rules, trade union power, economic conditions, and company production needs. Other, more useful "counterweights" represent actions aimed at improving working conditions such as environmental hygiene, workload, and pace.
(b) The "counter-values," aiming at reducing or eliminating the causes of adverse conse-

quences or inconveniences. Among these, the following must be reported at an organizational level: the reduction of night work by limiting the number of night shifts during the year and/or reducing the duration of the shift itself; the introduction of scheduled breaks providing an opportunity to enjoy hot meals and take short naps; a higher number of compensatory rest days or holidays proportional to the number of night shifts worked; the provision of adequate social services (e.g., transportation, nursery schools, kindergartens) through appropriate agreements with local authorities and commercial organizations; the possibility to switch to day work temporarily, at regular intervals, and/or permanently after a certain number of years assigned to the night shift or at a certain age.

29.4 Some Considerations for Resident Doctors

The path to becoming a doctor is notoriously difficult. Medical residencies are institutional internships and are therefore structured to serve the dual, often competing, purposes of training new generations of professionals while responding to the working needs of a hospital. Despite improvements brought about by good-faith efforts, the physical and emotional demands on residents have few comparisons in modern society. Some of these pressures are inherent to the nature of the profession. Most people cannot imagine a workday when a mental lapse or an error in judgment can deprive another person of their hearing, brain functioning, or even life. But those in the medical profession are expected to grin and bear it, and come back the next morning for their 6 a.m. shift.

Other demands are less easily explicable. Residents in the USA are expected to spend up to 80 h a week in the hospital and endure single shifts that routinely last up to 28 h, with such workdays required on average about four times a month [41]. Overall, residents usually work more than twice as many hours annually as their peers in other white-collar professions, such as attorneys in corporate law firms, and face a grueling

schedule that potentially puts both caregivers and patients at risk. In Europe, on the other hand, residents are subject to a maximum workweek of 48 h, with no "apparent" harm to patient care or to the educational component of residencies. This workweek policy in Europe is just considered to be a legal formality, as the extension of work hours is common practice in any hospital and clinical ward. This disregard for the law, due to economical and organizational deficiencies, is not just an injustice to the worker, but also a serious clinical risk to patient safety. Residents are a cheap source of skilled labor that can fill gaps in staff coverage while being paid a fixed, modest salary. Hence the non-compliance with the European directive is something even more important in the context of residency. Residents are usually the last step in the health ladder and the more expendable.

This misconduct is so deeply rooted within the health system not only by systemic problems (such as a shortage of trained medical doctors, a lack of nurses, and difficulties in logistics) but also because of an overreliance on residents. In fact, usually owing to their willingness to learn more and learn faster, residents choose to work more than dictated by the law, without concern for their condition and, unfortunately, for patient safety. Surely there is a bigger problem among US residents in particular, seeing as, before 2011, it was routine for them to spend 100 or even 120 h a week in the hospital, with single shifts extending up to 48 h and beyond. In 2011, the Accreditation Council for Graduate Medical Education established additional restrictions [42] among other things, by reducing the maximum shift duration to 16 h for first-year residents (also known as "interns") and to 28 h for more experienced residents [43]. But looking closely at the effects of the new rules, it is unclear how much residents' working lives have actually changed. Averaging 80-h workweeks and regularly putting in 28-h shifts is still brutal by any measure. On the other hand, in 2017, the limit placed by the 2011 law was reverted back to 24 h per shift for first-year surgery residents. This change was justified by the publication of the Bilimoria study [44], which claimed that longer shifts may be better for patients and for the training of young doctors. The findings of this article have been confirmed by another article written about residents of internal medicine and published in 2019, in which it was shown that the exposure of internists to working time reforms during their residency was not associated with post-training differences in patient mortality, readmissions, or costs of care [45].

References

1. Costa G. Shift work and health: current problems and preventive actions. Safety Health Work. 2010;1:112–23. https://doi.org/10.5491/SHAW.2010.1.2.112.
2. Costa G. Introduction to problems of shift work. In: Iskra-Golec I, Barnes-Farrell J, Bohle P, editors. Social and family issues in shift work and non standard working hours. Switzerland: Springer International Publishing; 2016;19–35.
3. ILO International Labour Organization. C171-night work convention, 1990 (No. 171). 1990. https://www.ilo.org/dyn/normlex/en/f?p=NORMLEXPUB:12100:0::NO::P12100_INSTRUMENT_ID:312316. Accessed 30 Sept 2019.
4. European Parliament and Council. Directive 2003/88/EC of 4 November 2003 concerning certain aspects of the organisation of working time. 2003. https://eur-lex.europa.eu/legal-content/EN/ALL/?uri=CELEX:32003L0088. Accessed 30 Sept 2019.
5. Seifalian A, Hart A. Circadian rhythms: will it revolutionise the management of diseases? J Lifestyle Med. 2019;9(1):1–11. https://doi.org/10.15280/jlm.2019.9.1.1.
6. Costa G. Sleep deprivation due to shift work. Handb Clin Neurol. 2015;131:437–46. https://doi.org/10.1016/B978-0-444-62627-1.00023-8.
7. Doi Y. An epidemiologic review on occupational sleep research among Japanese workers. Ind Health. 2005;43:3–10. https://doi.org/10.2486/indhealth.43.3.
8. Drake CL, Roehrs T, Richardson G, Walsh JK, Roth T. Shift work sleep disorder: prevalence and consequences beyond that of symptomatic day workers. Sleep. 2004;27:1453–62.
9. Kalmbach DA, Pillai V, Cheng P, Arnedt JT, Drake CL. Shift work disorder, depression, and anxiety in the transition to rotating shifts: the role of sleep reactivity. Sleep Med. 2015;16:1532–8. https://doi.org/10.1016/j.sleep.2015.09.007.
10. Waage S, Pallesen S, Moen BE, Mageroy N, Flo E, Di Milia L, et al. Predictors of shift work disorder among nurses: a longitudinal study. Sleep Med. 2014;15:1449–55. https://doi.org/10.1016/j.sleep.2014.07.014.
11. Gaba DM, Howard SK. Fatigue among clinicians and the safety of patients. N Engl J Med. 2002;347:1249–55. https://doi.org/10.1056/NEJMsa020846.
12. Howard SK, Gaba DM, Smith BE, Weinger MB, Herndon C, Keshavacharya S, Rosekind MR. Simulation study of rested versus sleep-deprived anesthesiologists. Anesthesiology. 2003;98:1345–55. https://doi.org/10.1097/00000542-200306000-00008.
13. Weinger MB, Ancoli-Israel S. Sleep deprivation and clinical performance. JAMA. 2002;287:955–7.
14. Landrigan CP, Rothschild JM, Cronin JW, Kaushal R, Burdick E, Katz JT, et al. Effect of reducing interns' work hours on serious medical errors in intensive-care units. N Engl J Med. 2004;351:1838–48. https://doi.org/10.1056/NEJMoa041406.
15. Lockley SW, Cronin JW, Evans EE, Cade BE, Lee CJ, Landrigan CP, et al. Effect of reducing interns' weekly work hours on sleep and attentional failures. N Engl J Med. 2004;351:1829–37. https://doi.org/10.1056/NEJMoa041404.
16. Barger LK, Ayas NT, Cade BE, et al. Impact of extended-duration shifts on medical errors, adverse events, and attentional failures. PLoS Med. 2006;3(12):e487.
17. Rogers AE, Hwang W-T, Scott LD, Aiken LH, Dinges DF. The working hours of hospital staff nurses and patient safety. Health Aff (Millwood). 2004;23:202–12. https://doi.org/10.1377/hlthaff.23.4.202.
18. Scott LD, Rogers AD, Hwang WT, Zhang Y. Effects of critical care nurses' work hours on vigilance and patients' safety. Am J Crit Care. 2006;15:30–7.
19. Tanaka K, Takahashi M, Hiro H, Kakinuma M, Tanaka M, Miyaoka H. Differences in medical error risk among nurses working two- and three-shift systems at teaching hospitals: a six-month prospective study. Ind Health. 2010;48:357–64. https://doi.org/10.2486/indhealth.48.357.
20. Needleman J, Buerhaus P, Pankratz VS, Leibson CL, Stevens SR, Harris M. Nurse staffing and impatient hospital mortality. N Engl J Med. 2011;364:1037–45. https://doi.org/10.1056/NEJMsa1001025.
21. Trinkoff AM, Johantgen M, Storr CL, Gurses AP, Liang Y, Han K. Nurses' work schedule characteristics, nurse staffing, and patient mortality. Nurs Res. 2011;60:1–8. https://doi.org/10.1097/NNR.0b013e3181fff15d.
22. Gander P, O'Keeffe K, Santos-Fernandez E, Huntington A, Walker L, Willis J. Fatigue and nurses' work patterns: an online questionnaire survey. Int J Nurs Stud. 2019;98:67–74. https://doi.org/10.1016/j.ijnurstu.2019.06.011.
23. ANSES Rapport d'expertise Collective. Évaluation des risques sanitaires pour les professionnels exposés à des horaires de travail atypiques, notamment de nuit. Paris: Agence Nationale de Sécurité Sanitaire, Alimentation, Environnement, Travail; 2016. p. 1–408.
24. Rajaratnam SMW, Barger LK, Lockley SW, Shea SA, Wang W, Landrigan CP, et al. Sleep disorders, health, and safety in police officers. JAMA. 2011;306:2567–78. https://doi.org/10.1001/jama.2011.1851.
25. Nakata A, Haratani T, Takahashi M, Kawakami N, Arito H, Kobayashi F, et al. Association of sickness absence with poor sleep and depressive symptoms

in shift workers. Chronobiol Int. 2004;21:899–912. https://doi.org/10.1081/cbi-200038104.

26. Knutsson A, Boggild H. Gastrointestinal disorders among shift workers. Scand J Work Environ Health. 2010;36:85–95. https://doi.org/10.5271/sjweh.2897.

27. Lennernas M, Hambraeus L, Åkerstedt T. Nutrient intake in day and shift workers. Appetite. 1994;8:332–42. https://doi.org/10.1006/appe.1995.0060.

28. De Bacquer D, Van Risseghem M, Clays E, Kittel F, De Backer G, Braeckman L. Rotating shift work and the metabolic syndrome: a prospective study. Int J Epidemiol. 2009;38:848–54. https://doi.org/10.1093/ije/dyn360.

29. Strohmaier S, Devore EE, Zhang Y, Schernhammer ES. A review of data of findings on night shift work and the development of DM and CVD events: a synthesis of the proposed molecular mechanisms. Curr Diab Rep. 2018;18(12):132. https://doi.org/10.1007/s11892-018-1102-5.

30. Suwazono Y, Dochi M, Oishi M, Tanaka K, Kobayashi E, Sakata K. Shiftwork and impaired glucose metabolism: a 14-year cohort study on 7104 male workers. Chronobiol Int. 2009;26:926–41. https://doi.org/10.1080/07420520903044422.

31. Frost P, Kolstad HA, Bonde JP. Shift work and the risk of ischemic heart disease – a systematic review of the epidemiologic evidence - Scand J Work Environ Health. 2009;35:163–79. https://doi.org/10.5271/sjweh.1319.

32. Puttonen S, Härmä M, Hublin C. Shift work and cardiovascular disease – pathways from circadian stress to morbidity. Scand J Work Environ Health. 2010;36:96–108. https://doi.org/10.5271/sjweh.2894.

33. van Amelsvoort LG, Jansen NW, Kant I. Smoking among shift workers: more than a confounding factor. Chronobiol Int. 2006;23:1105–13. https://doi.org/10.1080/07420520601089539.

34. Manohar S, Thongprayoon C, Cheungpasitporn W, Mao MA, Herrmann SM. Associations of rotational shift work and night shift status with hypertension: a systematic review and meta-analysis. J Hypertens. 2017;35(10):1929–37. https://doi.org/10.1097/HJH.0000000000001442.

35. Nurminen T. Shift work and reproductive health. Scand J Work Environ Health. 1998;24(Suppl 3):28–34.

36. Wegrzyn LR, Tamimi RM, Rosner BA, Brown SB, Stevens RG, Eliassen AH, et al. Rotating night-shift work and the risk of breast cancer in the nurses' health studies. Am J Epidemiol. 2017;186(5):532–40. https://doi.org/10.1093/aje/kwx140.

37. IARC Monographs Vol 124 Group. Carcinogenicity of night shift work. Lancet Oncol. 2019;20(8):1058–9. https://doi.org/10.1016/S1470-2045(19)30455-3.

38. Knauth P. Designing better shift systems. Appl Ergon. 1996;27(1):39–44. https://doi.org/10.1016/0003-6870(95)00044-5.

39. Knauth P. Innovative worktime arrangements. Scand J Work Environ Health. 1998;24(Suppl 3):13–7.

40. Thierry H. Compensation for shiftwork: a model and some results. In: Colquhoun WP, Rutenfranz J, editors. Experimental studies of shiftwork. London: Taylor & Francis; 1980. p. 449–62.

41. Ladouceur R. Twenty-four-hour shifts for residents. Can Fam Physician. 2013;59(2):123.

42. ACGME Accreditation Council for Graduate Medical Education. Duty hour standard enhancing quality of care, supervision and resident professional development. 2011. https://www.acgme.org/Portals/0/PDFs/jgme-monograph[1].pdf. Accessed 30 Sept 2019.

43. Park R. Why so many young doctors work such awful hours. The Altantic 21. 2017. https://www.theatlantic.com/business/archive/2017/02/doctors-long-hours-schedules/516639/. Accessed 30 Sept 2019.

44. Bilimoria KY, Chung JW, Hedges LV, Dahlke AR, Love R, Cohen ME, Hoyt DB, Yang AD, Tarpley JL, Mellinger JD, Mahvi DM, Kelz RR, Ko CY, Odell DD, Stulberg JJ, Lewis FR. National cluster-randomized trial of duty hour flexibility in surgical training. N Engl J Med. 2016;374:713–27. https://doi.org/10.1056/NEJMoa1515724.

45. Jena AB, Newhouse RL, Farid M, Blumenthal D, Bhattacharya J. Association of residency work hour reform with long term quality and costs of care of US physicians: observational study. BMJ. 2019;366:l4134. https://doi.org/10.1136/bmj.l4134.

Stavros Prineas, Kathleen Mosier, Claus Mirko, and Stefano Guicciardi

30.1 Introduction

Non-Technical Skills (NTS) can be defined as *a constellation of cognitive and social skills, exhibited by individuals and teams, needed to reduce error and improve human performance in complex systems*. NTS have been described as generic 'life-skills' that can be applied across all technical domains [1]; they are deemed to be 'non-technical', in that they have traditionally resided outside most formal technical education curricula. While the importance of human factors in the performance of technical tasks has been appreciated for over 80 years [2, 3], NTS as a formal training system is derived from aviation Crew Resource Management (originally called Cockpit Resource Management). CRM was first adopted by United Airlines in 1981 [4] after a series of high-profile air crashes in the late 1970s, in which human elements such as poor communication, teamwork and situation awareness were identified as key contributing factors [5–7]. CRM is now fully integrated into all commercial pilot training worldwide; in a constant state of evolution, it is currently in its sixth generation [8].

In healthcare, it was not until the 1990s that the significance of human factors in patient safety became more widely publicised [9], coinciding with the rise in medical simulation [10]. In 1999, an emergency medicine team training project, MedTeams, was launched [11]. The following year two landmark reports were published within weeks of each other: *To Err is Human* in the USA [12] and *An Organisation with a Memory* in the UK [13]. These inspired a burgeoning of research into applied human factors in healthcare. Flin pioneered a behavioural marker system known as Anaesthetists' Non-Technical Skills (ANTS: [14]), followed by Non-Technical Skills for Surgeons (NOTTS: [15]). The disciplines of anaesthesia, critical care and surgery remain at the forefront of NTS training in medicine. Several other multidisciplinary clinical NTS frameworks, including the Oxford NOTECHs system [16] and TeamSTEPPS™ [17], have also been implemented and studied in real and simulated clinical environments.

As NTS evaluation and/or training systems become increasingly incorporated within undergraduate and postgraduate technical curricula, and specific techniques are developed (especially

S. Prineas (✉)
ErroMed Pty Ltd, Sydney, NSW, Australia

K. Mosier
International Ergonomics Association, San Francisco, CA, USA
e-mail: kmosier@sfsu.edu

C. Mirko
School of Hygiene and Preventive Medicine, University of Padova, Padova, Italy

S. Guicciardi
Local Health Authority Unit of Bologna, Bologna, Italy

Department of Biomedical and Neuromotor Sciences, University of Bologna, Bologna, Italy

© The Author(s) 2021
L. Donaldson et al. (eds.), *Textbook of Patient Safety and Clinical Risk Management*,
https://doi.org/10.1007/978-3-030-59403-9_30

in communication skills) supported by a growing body of research, a paradox arises: many non-technical skills no longer qualify as being 'non-technical'. Moreover the term 'non-technical' appears to subordinate these skills to their technical counterparts, when in reality the two skill sets are both essential and inseparable, especially during the management of medical crises. In time new terms may be required (e.g. 'paratechnical' skills, Clinical Resource Management) to define and describe this group of skills, and to consolidate their true place in the clinician's armamentarium.

30.1.1 Practical Overview of NTS Training Topics in Healthcare

The standard NTS training topics are summarised in Table 30.1 and detailed in the rest of this chapter. It is important to recognise that these skills are intertwined not only with the more traditional skills they support, but also with each other. Proficiency in one non-technical skill is, to no small extent, dependent on proficiency in the others. Newer generations of aviation CRM have introduced new topics, e.g. the acquisition of expertise and managing automation. It is foreseeable therefore that these topics will be incorporated into future clinical NTS training programmes.

30.2 Performance Shaping Factors

Most work environments operate on the assumption that adequate training, experience and motivation are enough to ensure successful performance. These prerequisites are necessary

Table 30.1 Typical NTS training topics

• Performance shaping factors
• Planning, preparation and prioritisation
• Situation awareness and perception of risk
• Decision-making
• Communication
• Teamwork and leadership

but not sufficient, especially in a complex adaptive system such as healthcare. There are many factors that can influence human performance—over long periods of time, from day to day, or in a given moment. *Performance Shaping Factors* (PSFs) can be classified according to a clinical adaptation of Reason's 'Three Buckets' model [18] where the traditional categories of 'task' (factors inherent to the nature of the task), 'self' (internal and personal factors) and 'context' (environmental factors) are each sub-divided into 'task/patient', 'individual/team' and 'workplace/organisation' factors, respectively (Fig. 30.1).

The ability to identify and evaluate PSFs in everyday practice may be a useful skill for front-line clinicians. The Three Buckets model can be applied both prospectively and retrospectively. In 2008, the UK National Patient Safety Agency launched a Foresight Training Resource Pack [19], based on a simplified version of the Three Buckets model, to help nurses and midwives better foresee clinical risks. This package is currently used in a number of NHS Trusts. As a retrospective incident analysis tool, Contributory Factors Analysis, also known as the 'London Protocol' [20], is based on a similar principle, as is the HEAPS incident analysis tool used in Queensland Health [21] and other health networks in Australia. A quick Three-Bucket summary can be used to highlight PSFs relevant to cases presented at, e.g. Grand Rounds or M&M meetings.

30.3 Planning and Preparation Skills

Popular culture is full of references stressing the importance of planning and preparation before performing complex tasks: 'Be Prepared', 'Plan the Dive and Dive the Plan', 'Luck favours prepared', 'P to the seventh power' ('Prior Preparation and Planning Prevents P—Poor Performance'), etc. In teaching hospital settings, medical and nursing trainees are often asked to perform tasks for which they are ill-prepared. In these efforts they are not only hampered by the opportunistic nature of teaching in

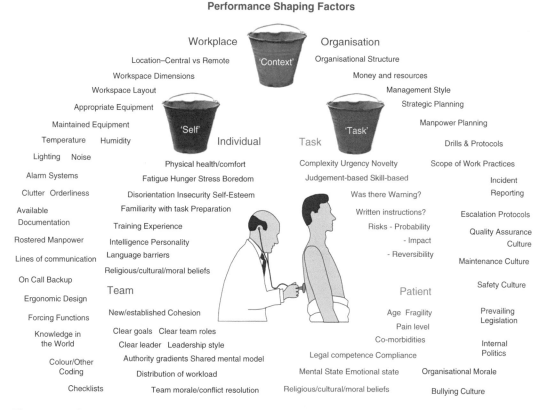

Fig. 30.1 Performance Shaping Factors. A clinical expansion of Reason's Three Buckets model

clinical settings, but also by the culture of 'see one, do one, teach one', a tradition that is counter-intuitive to human-factors thinking and seemingly peculiar (among high-risk endeavours) to medical and nursing education. 'SODOTO' training has both critics [22] and defenders [23]. Simulation Based Education (SBE) can be used to demonstrate the consequences of poor preparation and planning in a safe setting [24].

While there are a number of system tools that can help and guide staff (orientation days, checklists, pre-prepared procedural kits, etc.), the question arises as to whether there is a set of definable human competencies/aptitudes that optimise planning and preparing for tasks, and whether this can be taught. The answer to the first part of this question appears to be 'yes', in that evaluation of planning, preparation and prioritisation skills are key elements of the ANTS behavioural marker system. These help researchers identify

'good' and 'poor' task management behaviours in simulated settings, with the highest inter-rater reliability of the four main ANTS categories [25]. However, the ANTS system is not designed to address *how to train* practitioners to plan and prepare better.

30.4 Situation Awareness and Perception of Risk

Situation awareness (SA) is defined as 'the perception of elements in the environment, the comprehension of their meaning in terms of task goals, and the projection of their status in the near future' [26]. *Perception* is essentially being aware of and/or gathering available information relevant to a situation. In a clinical context this correlates with taking a clinical history, examining a patient, reviewing the results of investigations and tests, receiving a handover, conducting a

Fig. 30.2 Situation Awareness (SA) in a clinical context. (Courtesy of ErroMed, reproduced with permission)

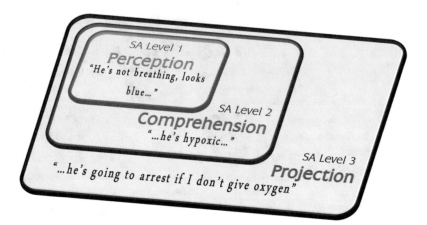

briefing, etc. *Comprehension* is the ability to form a mental model that makes sense of the available information. In clinical practice, this would be similar to forming a diagnosis, or a differential of diagnoses. *Projection* is the ability to use an operating mental model of a situation to foresee potential future states, or as clinicians would say, to make a prognosis. A simple example is given in Fig. 30.2.

In traditional medical training, these levels of awareness are built upon each other. For example, trainees are (rightly) encouraged to take a history and examine a patient (Level I SA) before venturing a diagnosis (Level II SA). The SBAR/ISBAR communication tool (see below) is a way of serially organising information to facilitate situation awareness between individuals. In real life however, perception, comprehension and projection may not occur in that order. In many emergency situations it is possible, indeed potentially crucial, to prognose the need to resuscitate (Level III) before one has made a complete examination (Level I) or a definitive diagnosis (Level II). This concept of *parallel* rather than *serial* cognitive processing of SA is the hallmark of Naturalistic or Recognition-Primed Decision-Making, and a feature of expert cognition [27], described figuratively as 'seeing the past, present and future at the same time' [28].

In anaesthetic practice, [29] described a model of 'distributed situation awareness', emphasising that during an operation the patient's condition is constantly being modified by the interventions of the anaesthetist and the surgeon in real time. Thus, in this model, ideal SA is the result of a *dynamic* and *iterative* process of regularly scanning the environment, matching one's mental model with incoming information, modifying the anaesthetist's plan and actions accordingly, and cycling through this process repeatedly until the patient is safely in the recovery unit.

30.4.1 'Perception of Risk'

When thinking about potential adverse future states, a number of terms—*hazard*, *threat* and *risk*—are often used interchangeably, when they would perhaps be better used to connote overlapping but distinct concepts. A *hazard* is anything that could potentially go wrong or cause harm, without any qualification of its likelihood or severity. For example, when asked to list the possible complications of central venous catheter insertion, a medical student will often recite a list of early and late complications, subcategorised according to anatomical location, structure type, etc. The student has no direct experience of central line insertion and therefore limited ability to rank this list of *hazards* according to their likelihood of occurring in routine practice, or what the real impact of each complication would be.

A *threat* is the *subjective* perception of a hazard. It is important to recognise, independently of whatever data exists for a given situation, that a number of factors influence the perception of danger, including gender [30], healthcare role and length of experience [31], primacy (the disproportionately 'formative' impact of early experiences or first impressions: [32]), recency (the disproportionate impact of most recent experiences: [33]), whether a person has volunteered to accept the hazard or had the hazard imposed upon them [34], whether the hazard is familiar or hitherto unknown [35], whether the effects are immediate or delayed [36], etc. If, for example, the medical student above, now a resident, were unlucky enough to cause a chylothorax with an early central line insertion, the complication would tend to figure prominently in that resident's future assessments for a considerable time afterwards, even though in objective terms such a complication is very rare.

Subjective factors influence threat assessments, which in turn can influence clinical decision-making. For example, a Canadian study of the prescribing practices of family physicians treating patients with atrial fibrillation showed that a substantial proportion stopped prescribing warfarin altogether after one of their patients suffered a haemorrhagic stroke, whereas physicians who did not routinely prescribe anticoagulants tended not to change their practice even when one or more of their patients suffered an thromboembolic stroke [37]. In this case, the negative consequences of electing to intervene (i.e. prescribing) had a greater impact on perception of risk than the negative consequences of electing not to intervene (i.e. not prescribing).

A *risk* is a calculated evaluation of the likelihood and impact of a hazard, based on objective assessments and measurements rather than subjective interpretation. For example, the same medical student, now a consultant intensivist, might be able to cite a personal log of their last 1000 central line insertions, quote literature reviews on the topic, and assert that the top three risks in their practice are, e.g. infection, pneumothorax and accidental arterial cannulation. This is what Klein [28] would call seeing the 'choke points'—another feature of expertise—the ability to identify quickly where the material dangers

are in a situation, what actions are more likely to lead to failure, and what actions better ensure success ('leverage points').

In light of this, the term 'perception of risk' should be approached with a little caution. In the absence of hard data, most of what clinicians call 'risk assessments' in day-to-day practice would in large part actually be 'threat assessments'. Despite the subjective and potentially distorting nature of threat assessments, this is not necessarily a bad thing. Reliable data for a given risk situation often may not exist, let alone be to hand. Moreover, expert clinicians are often called upon to make decisions in urgent and complex situations, and their 'threat assessments' are usually better than a novice's 'risk assessments'. To understand why and when this might be true (and when it might not be) requires a deeper analysis.

30.5 Expert Decision-Making

Efficient and accurate decision-making is critical to patient safety—and it is important that the people responsible for making decisions that impact patient safety are as experienced and as expert as possible. Research on expert decision-making in complex, dynamic domains, often referred to as Naturalistic Decision Making (NDM: [27, 38]), has demonstrated that the most important step in making a decision in these domains is to accurately assess the situation—identify the problem, formulate a diagnosis, evaluate the risks. Mosier and Fischer [39] refer to this as the *front end* of the decision-making process. Once the situation is known, the retrieval of a workable course of action, the *back end* of the process, is facilitated.

Expertise impacts the decision process in several specific ways. First, expert decision makers exhibit high levels of competence and knowledge within the domain, and have experienced a wide variety of situations, instances, and cases they can draw upon (e.g. [40]). This means that a current case will often have features that match an event from the expert's repertoire, facilitating quick and accurate situation assessment. Second, experts see and process information differently than novices do. They can quickly identify critical cues—that is, the subset of information most critical to accurate situation assessment—and attend to or categorise them. This impacts their ability to develop situation awareness and to create an accurate mental model of the situation [41]. Experts are sensitive to changing values of information and can adapt their mental models to accommodate them [42]. They may use an iterative process, using feedback from the environment to adjust their actions and incorporate changes resulting from incremental decisions. In healthcare, for example, physicians often monitor results of a treatment to refine their diagnoses [43]. They also employ strategies to cope with dynamic situations—anticipating developments, prioritising tasks, and making contingency plans—and employ knowledge-based control to address conflicts or contradictions [39, 44]. The NDM framework relies heavily on expertise and on intuitive rather than analytical processing, and capitalises on decision makers' abilities to pattern match, to mentally simulate a course of action, and to use sense-making strategies to improve their understanding of a given situation.

30.5.1 Metacognition

Experts not only monitor the situation but also how they are thinking and whether it is appropriate for the situation at hand. They critique and correct their diagnosis until they arrive at a satisfactory mental model of the situation, or further processing is too costly [45, 46]. They are able to shift strategies when faced with high uncertainty or unmet expectancies, taking an incremental approach or engaging in more analytical processes [47, 48]. For example, expert surgeons perform many routine tasks automatically, but 'slow down' and engage in effortful processing in preparation for nonroutine events or in response to unexpected events [49].

30.5.2 Affect

Expertise also attunes the decision maker to affect that is in response to critical elements of the task context and that may have significance for their decisions. The affective reaction to a situation—particularly comfort or discomfort—may represent a knowledge-based informational cue for decision-making. For example, when a situation is not recognised as familiar, affective responses such as unease or discomfort ('something's not right') can motivate the expert to engage in more information gathering, or more substantive sense-making processes. Dominguez [50], for instance, reported that physicians frequently refer to their comfort level while deciding on whether or not to continue with laparoscopic surgery. This function of affect is similar to the role of 'hunches' in split-second decision-making.

30.5.3 Communication and Decision-Making

All individuals involved in ensuring a patient's safety must function collaboratively as a team. Because healthcare is a dynamic task environment, team members need to respond adaptively to changing conditions. Communication plays a pivotal role in this process [51], especially in healthcare as team members often perform sequentially and rely on information from the previous shift to guide their decisions and actions. Team members let others in on their reasoning and inform them about their intentions and expectations [52]. Critically, expert teams ensure common ground and shared mental models by providing feedback [53], and work to mitigate decision-making and other errors through team-centred communication [54, 55].

30.5.4 Stress and Decision-Making

Stress related to the working conditions is defined by the World Health Organization as the response people may have when presented with work demands and pressures that are not matched to their knowledge and abilities, and which challenge their ability to cope. It occurs in a wide range of circumstances and may have a profound impact on decision-making which, in the medical context, could negatively affect clinical outcomes. Stress-related reductions in cognitive performance (e.g. accuracy, reaction time, attention, memory) resulted in poorer patient safety outcomes such as hospital acquired infections or medication errors [56].

It is therefore essential to address the causes of stress, which can be found both at the individual and at the organisational level. In the first case, it must be highlighted that medical practice has a solid rational basis made explicit through the clinical reasoning but, given the relationships doctors necessarily build with patients and other professionals, it also entails a strong emotional dimension that must be acknowledged [57]. Healthcare professionals experience emotions differently, quantitatively and qualitatively, and should be aware of their 'emotional intelligence' and trained on their ability to cope and react in case of stressful situations without stigmatisations [58, 59].

In the second case, from a system perspective, stressful conditions in the work environment must be identified and possibly mitigated—if not removed—in terms of both contents (working hours, monotony, participation and control) and contexts (job insecurity, teamwork, organisational culture, work-life balance). Doctors are requested to take charge of greater responsibilities and demands, but resources are often limited resulting in risks of overload and burnout. Adequate staffing levels, human-capital investments, respect of working times and cultural changes in the medical organisations with a radical shift from competitiveness to collaboration and teamwork are therefore needed to reduce stress and its consequences [60].

30.6　Communication

'Effective communication' is recognised as a core non-technical skill [17], a means to provide knowledge, institute relationships, establish predictable behaviour patterns, and as a vital component for leadership and team coordination [61, 62]. It is crucial for delivering high-quality healthcare and has been acknowledged together with effective teamwork as an essential component for patient safety [61, 63]. 'Communication failures' have long been recognised as a leading cause of unintentional patient harm [64]. More recently a report of 2587 sentinel medical adverse events, reviewed by the US Joint Commission over a 3-year period, cited 'communication' as a contributing factor in over 68% of cases [65].

However, 'communication' is a very broad term; pinning down a practical definition is difficult. In the wider academic literature, communication has been classified according to at least seven distinct philosophical approaches [66], of which at least two are relevant to non-technical skills training in healthcare: the information engineering ('cybernetic') approach and the social construction ('sociocultural') approach [67, 68]. The first defines communication as the linear transmission of 'signal packages' from a 'transmitter' to a 'receiver' through a medium. The latter emphasises how team communication can create the dynamic context in which people work, implying that communication, rather than a neutral mean, is the primary social process through which a meaningful shared world is built [67]. There is also the field of 'semiotics'—the study of signals and the nature of 'meaning' itself across different populations, demographics and cultures. These varied perspectives underscore the *sociotechnical* nature of all healthcare communication.

For the purposes of developing workable patient safety tools (and mindful of this very narrow context), communication can be defined as *the transfer of meaning from one person to another* [69]. In teams comprising health professionals with different backgrounds, roles, training and perspectives on care, the main purpose of communication is to facilitate among team members a *shared mental model* of a situation: the context, the goals, the tasks, the methods to be used, who will do what, etc. (i.e. 'team situation awareness'). Thus, it is important to recognise that 'meaning' is different to 'information' or 'knowledge', and effective communication therefore depends to some extent on the existing level of situation awareness of individual team members. For example, stating clearly that 'the patient's blood pressure is 80/50' is not per se effective communication of its *meaning* if the person hearing it does not know that this finding usually represents critical hypotension in an adult.

While effective teamwork requires much more than communication (see below), specific failures in communication can hinder the process of building a shared understanding of the situation between team members, leading to poor performance and errors [70]. It follows that effective communication in healthcare teams can only be the result of dynamic iterative 'two-way' processes that lead to an 'equilibrium of understanding' among team members [69], and which can and must change with the input of new people and new information. Refining these processes can be seen as the basis for developing better 'communication skills'.

30.6.1 Specific/Directed/ Acknowledged Communication

For ensuring effective team communication two aspects have been highlighted as fundamental [71]: the sharing of unique information held by team members in face-to-face environments and openness of information in virtual environments [72, 73]. To this one can add the implementation of closed-loop communication procedures that acknowledge the receipt of information and clarify any inconsistencies in information interpretation [74].

The concept of 'specific/directed/acknowledged' communication comes from simulation training [10]. 'Specific' refers to speaking clearly and the use of salient unambiguous descriptions, ideally using a 'controlled vocabulary' of terms with unique meanings as agreed by a discrete population of practitioners. An obvious example is the 'military speak' used in formal mission communications between soldiers, both in Hollywood movies and real life; however it should also be apparent that much of the diagnostic and therapeutic jargon used by clinicians, based mostly on Latin and Greek terminology, is already a form of controlled vocabulary. Specificity is also reflected in a number of other practical ways [69]:

- Using the word 'right' only to mean chirality (as in 'left' or 'right') and avoiding its use to mean 'Ok' or 'correct' (as in 'the left leg is the right leg for this operation, right?')
- Using numbers rather than vague terms where applicable ('the systolic is 200' rather than 'the blood pressure's high', 'I should be there in 10–20 min' versus 'I'll be down soon').
- Using the 'five rights' convention for prescribing and administering medications: checking the correct *drug* in the correct *dose* via the correct *route* at the correct time for the correct *patient* [75]; a convention routinely taught to nurses but not so consistently to doctors.
- Recognising and avoiding non-standard and ambiguous clinical abbreviations and acronyms [76].

'Directed' means that information or instructions are explicitly directed to a nominated person. For example, 'Fran, please pass me the Yankauer sucker' instead of 'Somebody give me something for the bleeding'. Of course, the ability to direct information requires team members to know others' names in the first place. One of the consistent elements of the WHO Surgical Safety Checklist is that team members introduce themselves by name and role [77]. A survey of OR teams showed that participants believed that knowing team member's name and rank was important not only to team bonding but also to patient safety [78]. While intuitively attractive, more studies are required to determine whether directed vs. undirected communication has a reproducible impact on clinical safety.

'Acknowledged' communication seeks to confirm that what was said was not only heard, but also that what was heard *matches* what was said. In *closed-loop communication*, also known as 'read-back' [79], the sender initiates communication, the receiver confirms that the communication has been heard and repeats the content, finally the sender verifies the accuracy of that content including an explicit accuracy check with the recipient [62]. Closed communication loops improve the reliability of communication by having the receiver of communication restate what was said by the sender to confirm understanding. [67]. Organisations requiring this type of closed-loop communication can help smooth the communication process and ensure critical information is correctly conveyed and understood. This seems to be most useful, e.g. during surgery to confirm sponge count, during high-risk patient handovers to ensure comprehensive information exchange and during medication ordering [67].

30.6.2 Briefings and Handovers

Briefings are discrete meetings to provide members of a team with specific information and/or instructions. *Handovers* (also called *handoffs* in the USA) are briefings that occur at a changeover between personnel who share similar roles. Briefings set the scene for team interaction, ensuring that care providers have a shared mental model of what is going to happen during a process, and raising team situation awareness to identify any risk points and plan for contingencies. When done effectively, briefings can establish predictability, reduce interruptions prevent delays and build social relationships and capital for future interactions [80]. Briefings are designed to prepare teams to counter threats and minimise error potential. Formal and informal protocols, checklists, scenario planning, and open team discussion are commonly used [81].

Handover problems have been implicated in a number of adverse event studies [82, 83]. Perioperative briefings have been proven effective in improving surgical teams climate and their efficiency of their work [84]. Interprofessional checklist briefings have been shown to reduce the number of communication failures and to promote proactive and collaborative team communication [85]. Nevertheless, there remain definitional and methodological problems with using the existing literature to support any conclusions of what best practice should be [86]. This appears to be reflected in a recent retrospec-

tive study of over 300,000 adult patients undergoing major surgery, where the risk of complications, hospital readmissions and/or death was 44% in cases where there was a complete handover of anaesthetic care from one practitioner to another during the case, compared with 29% when no handover occurred [87]. There is clearly still a lot to learn about how to preserve continuity of care safely from one caregiver to another; meanwhile, specific techniques have earned substantial worldwide popularity.

30.6.3 SBAR

A structured communication technique called Situation, Background, Assessment, and Recommendation (SBAR) has been developed by the U.S. Navy nuclear submarine industry for high-risk situations and for its versatility has been adapted in healthcare setting [88]. The communication process involving SBAR is as follows: the Situation is conveyed by the initiating individual and establishes the topic of discussion; the Background involves any information needed to make an informed decision for the patient such as the list of current medication, or recent vital signs; in Assessment, the individual initiating the SBAR report the patient's situation and status; finally, the Recommendation is what the individual initiating the SBAR offers in terms of what they think should take place or be done [67].

A lower number of incident reports related to communication errors has been linked to SBAR tool in specific context such as effective in improving perception of communication between professionals and of the safety climate [89]. A recent review found moderate evidence for improved patient safety through SBAR implementation, especially when used to structure communication over the phone.

One study reported problems with the traditional SBAR tool during its implementation at a number of West Australian hospitals [90], most notably that (a) it was not intuitively obvious that personnel introduce themselves as part of the Situation phase, (b) sometimes certain members disputed the recommendations, and (c) sometimes not all parties clearly understood the recommendations. The researchers proposed 'iSoBAR' (where 'I' stands for Introductions, 'O' stands for Observations and replaces 'A' for Assessment, which in turn becomes Agreed Plan, and 'R' becomes Readback to confirm the agreed plan of action). At the time of publication, this variant was still in use in West Australia [91]. A simpler variant, ISBAR (where 'I' stands for 'Identify') has been adopted by healthcare authorities in other Australian States [92]; indeed in Australia implementation of some version of SBAR has been adopted as part of a national standard of clinical handover [93]. However, high-quality research on this widely used communication tool, in whichever variant, is still wanting [94].

30.6.4 Escalation of Concern: Graded Assertiveness

In most clinical situations, where there is a clear and agreed pathway for action and appropriate leadership, safety is best maintained by cooperating with the plan and deferring to one's superiors. However plans do not always proceed as expected; if errors or mishaps occur, or an imminent threat to safety arises, it is sometimes necessary for healthcare providers to assert themselves in a clear and timely fashion to support patient safety [67]. As there are many hierarchical structures in healthcare with many authority gradients between individuals, speaking up to senior colleagues does not come naturally to many people, especially junior personnel, even in the face of an overt safety issue. Organisations that employ clinicians with a duty of care to patients must therefore seek to empower staff by providing them with training in assertion techniques.

An example of assertive language is the two-challenge rule, where a concern is stated at least two times to better ensure it has been heard. The CUS tool (Concerned, Uncomfortable, Safety issue) also part of the TeamSTEPPS framework escalates communication from an expression of

concern through a command to stop. The escalation of concern consists of, 'I'm concerned', 'I'm uncomfortable', 'this is unsafe', meaning 'This is a potential serious problem. Stop and listen to me'. [148]. Frankel and Leonard [95] suggest that the true 'test' of teams and leaders occurs when the 'line is stopped' after someone raises a concern, which then turns out to have been a false alarm.

Another tool, derived from the aviation-based PACE algorithm [96], is Graded Assertiveness. The tool comprises four levels of assertion—Observation, Suggestion, Challenge and Emergency—and has been adapted for use in clinical environments [69]. An example of the tool is given in Fig. 30.3.

30.7 Teamwork and Leadership Skills

A *team* can be defined as '*a distinguishable set of two or more individuals who interact dynamically, adaptively, and interdependently; who share common goals or purposes; and who have specific roles or functions to perform*' [97]. Successful teams are the product of time, effort and trust. As teams are also defined as *social* entities [98] that at times perform highly technical functions, there may be value in regarding healthcare teams as microcosms of a wider *sociotechnical* system, particularly in regard to improving patient safety [99].

Be it in a community health service or a large hospital, teams come in many forms: teams overlapping with other teams, teams nested within teams, teams dispersed in time and geographical space. It is therefore not surprising that there is a large variation among doctors in their conceptualisations of what and where teams are [100]. It may not be obvious to an individual practitioner where the team is, or even if one exists, for the task they are trying to perform. Moreover, there is a growing (albeit belated) recognition that patients and their families should be considered as part of the healthcare team [101].

Situation
A trainee anaesthetist is working with a consultant, who has been up all night on call.
The consultant has just intubated a patient. The trainee suspects an oesophageal intubation.

Level 1: Observation
Make a neutral factual observation about the situation
"The patient's chest doesn't appear to be moving."

Level 2 : Suggestion
Offer a face-saving alternative
"Perhaps I could ventilate manually while you listen to the chest."

Level 3 : Challenge
Question the plan and/or the assumptions
"Excuse me Sir, I don't see any sign of gas exchange, the O_2 sats are starting to fall.
Are you sure the endotracheal tube is in the right place?"

Level 4 : Emergency
Give order using standardised language and formal title, with consequence of failure to comply
"Dr Smith, *you must listen*. The patient is hypoxic.
Check the tube now or I will take over/call for help/hit the emergency button"

Fig. 30.3 Graded Assertiveness. (Courtesy of ErroMed Pty. Ltd. (Reproduced with permission))

30.7.1 The 'Anatomy' of Teams

While apparently 'leaderless' teams do exist, especially in nature, in the human world most successful teams have *leaders* and *followers*. The concept of leadership is complex, and is explored later in this chapter. In broad terms a leader is someone chosen (by the team itself or by others) to exercise authority and influence over the team. While good 'followership' requires a cooperative attitude, it too is not as straightforward a concept as it may seem. For example, followers need to know when and how to be assertive, even to their leader, when there is an overt threat to patient safety ([69]; see Sect. 30.6.4 above). Leaders and followers exhibit different characteristics in different types of teams.

30.7.2 Unidisciplinary Teams

A unidisciplinary team is one where most of the members, if not all, essentially share the same skill set—an army of soldiers, for example. Unidisciplinary teams tend to be hierarchical, with ranks according to seniority or experience,

and leaders of unidisciplinary teams have usually risen through these ranks, and thus share a common training background with their team members. Ranks may be explicit ('sergeant', 'lieutenant', 'general') or implicit (the 'grand dame' of a department, the 'elder statesmen' of a college or the 'green' registrar).

Unidisciplinary teams are very common in healthcare, e.g. clinical departments within a hospital ('Neurology', 'Physiotherapy', 'Anaesthesia', etc.). Unidisciplinary team structures are task/service focused and therefore are great for training and producing results (e.g. provision of a service) of a reproducible standard. It is also more likely that one member of the team can be substituted for another. When members of a unidisciplinary team communicate, there is usually a pre-existing level of shared understanding; as a result, a lot of meaning in conversations, briefings and handovers can be conveyed *implicitly* (through assumptions, 'shorthand' jargon/acronyms and non-verbal communication) rather than *explicitly*.

Unfortunately, unidisciplinary teams tend to form 'silos'—isolated hierarchies of expertise that communicate poorly with each other—a problem well known to healthcare [102].

30.7.3 Multidisciplinary Teams

In multidisciplinary teams people with diverse backgrounds and skills are brought together for a particular purpose. Leaders of such teams will usually not share the same background or experience with many of their team members. Members tend to have discrete technical roles rather than hold rank.

An operating theatre team is an example of a multidisciplinary team (containing unidisciplinary sub-teams—anaesthesia, surgery, nursing, wardsmen, etc.—*as well as* the patient). In healthcare the output of these teams is tailored to individual patients, and heavily influenced by the input of all individuals in the team who each play a discrete role. Frequently it is difficult (if not impossible) to substitute one team member for another, or to do without a member who has a specific technical role. Unless such teams have worked closely together for a while, there is often little shared understanding between team members; consequently, implicit communication is unreliable, especially early in the life of the team.

Multidisciplinary teams counteract the negative effects of silos and have been shown to improve patient outcomes in a range of in-hospital settings [103]. However, cohesive multidisciplinary teams are much harder to establish and maintain [104]. Successful multidisciplinary team leaders tend to employ *situational leadership* and *transferable command and control* (see below).

30.7.4 Committees

A committee is a group of interested but diverse individuals ('stakeholders') assembled in a structured forum governed by agreed rules and motions through which collective decisions can be made. The group is presided over by a chairperson with limited nominal authority. A committee has the anatomical appearance of a team but its individual members are under no obligation per se to function like one, unless the com-

mittee has been convened to perform a specific function (e.g. a 'steering committee' or a 'task force'), and even that is no guarantee that it will function well. There is surprisingly little research on how healthcare committees function. 'The psychology of committees is a special case of the psychology of mobs' [105].

30.7.5 Improving Team Performance

Developing a behavioural marker system for team performance in high-risk clinical environments such as the operating theatre has been an ongoing global endeavour for at least three decades ([10, 14, 106, 107], [108]). The following is a summary of the more commonly used markers.

30.7.6 Calling for Help Early: Team Assembly

Declaring the need to form a team is a fundamental team competency. Calling for help early is the first step in the 'chain of survival' for improving outcomes from cardiac arrest ([109, 110]). Other examples of team assembly include a trainee knowing when to call their on-call superior, or a practitioner calling a colleague for advice, or to assist them if they are feeling unwell or overwhelmed.

30.7.7 Team Structure: Clear Leader, Roles and Goals

In traditional command-and-control systems, a clear team structure and process is important. Trauma and resuscitation teams are more effective where there is a clearly defined team leader (see below) with other team members assuming functional roles [111, 112]. Neonatal cardiothoracic teams that rehearsed a 'pit-crew' style handover process with designated roles resulted in a faster handover with fewer technical errors [113].

30.7.8 Team-Oriented Communication

Effective teams employ a number of team-oriented communication techniques such as briefings and handovers, specific/directed/acknowledged communication, tools for enquiry/advocacy/escalation of concern, etc. (see Sect. 30.6 above). It is important for the leader to create an atmosphere that fosters open exchange between team members [10] and encourages cooperative and assertive communication styles that are focused on the task at hand and 'what is right', rather than submissive and aggressive styles that are focused on power and 'who is right' [10, 69].

30.7.9 Decision-Making

Decisions in teams are usually made by the leader, either autocratically or in consultation with other team members, depending on the urgency and clarity of the situation, and skills and experience of the team involved (see Sect. 30.7.15 below).

The emergence of shared decision-making between clinicians and patients in a range of healthcare domains [114–116] is further validation of incorporating patients and their families as part of the wider clinical team. This is a variant of consultative leadership where the physician informs and guides the patient along a process of making decisions about their own care, which are then executed by the rest of the team.

30.7.10 Managing Workload and Time

A team approach allows distribution of physical and cognitive workload across the human resources at hand [10]. For example, trauma teams work faster when members perform pre-allocated roles [117], and the time to complete the primary survey has a direct bearing on patient outcomes [118, 119].

30.7.11 Team Situation Awareness

Getting all members of a team to share a mental model of what needs to be done by whom and how is fundamental to effective team function. In using the term 'shared mental model' one can reinterpret Endsley's SA model of shared perceptions, shared comprehension and shared projection to infer the need for a 'team situation awareness' that evolves with time and new information just as individual SA does [120]. Creating a shared mental model has been shown to improve overall team performance in simulated settings, both in aviation [121] and in medical trauma [122]. Establishing and maintaining a dynamic and appropriate team SA may be considered an important communication role of the team leader (see below).

30.7.12 Team Familiarity, Group Climate and Interpersonal Conflict

People who work together regularly perform better together. Teams where members are already familiar with each other tend to use their (shared) cognitive resources more effectively, which in turn improves their performance [123]. Cumulative team experience and team familiarity significantly reduce surgical operative time [124]. Moreover, teams that are made up of friends usually perform better than teams of ad hoc acquaintances, especially in larger groups and with high-output/high-turnover tasks [125].

In a complex dynamic workplace, differences of opinion and indeed conflict are inevitable. With appropriate resolution practices in place, conflict can be marshalled as a positive way to sharpen clinical decision-making [126]. More usually however, conflict that involves intimidation, bullying or verbal abuse over time has been cited as a cause of occupational stress, which in turn increases absenteeism and staff turnover [127, 131]. This effect appears to be more likely among female workers who have children [127], a dominant demographic of healthcare workers, especially in nursing and allied health. It seems intuitive that interpersonal conflict within healthcare teams would be a threat to patient safety; indeed surveys and structured interviews confirm that healthcare workers strongly hold this perception [128, 129]. Interpersonal conflict is a key feature of whistle-blower cases of serious and serial patient harm [130]; however the conspicuous conflict in these cases is mostly a *consequence* of poor individual or team performance (and conflict over reporting this) rather than a *cause*. While there are some relevant case reports [132], there is to date surprisingly little systematic research linking team conflict to adverse patient outcomes; this would suggest an avenue for future study.

30.7.13 Debriefing

Debriefings are concise exchanges that occur after tasks or events, allowing team members to review what happened [67]. Debriefings may be *psychological* (especially after traumatic events), where team members are allowed a safe space to express their feelings about what occurred and to receive consolation and support; they may be *technical* (e.g. after a mission or procedure), where events and team/individual actions are systematically reviewed to improve future performance; or they may contain elements of both. Persons debriefing teams after a difficult clinical procedure, particularly where there was a negative patient outcome, should be prepared to conduct both a psychological and a technical debrief, or to defer one in favour of the other, as circumstances may demand. Debriefing may also be used to brainstorm new solutions to problems encountered during a procedure, or to consult experts from other clinical domains by the experts to enrich the collective wisdom of a care team. In this respect a well-run morbidity and mortality meeting can be viewed as a form of educational debriefing.

The benefit of providing single-session Critical Incident Stress Debriefing [133] or other variations of formalised psychological debriefing, which is standard procedure in many healthcare institutions to personnel after traumatic adverse events, has been brought into question in a number of studies [134–136]. For a healthcare manager faced with personnel exposed to a traumatic event, the most practical advice can be summarised as follows [135]:

- The exposed person(s) should, in a timely and empathic manner, be offered information about the possible reactions they may experience, what they can do to help themselves if these occur, and where to get help if they want or need it.
- Early support should be made ready and available, but instigating interventions, if at all, should be based on an accurate assessment of need. Different people cope with stress in different ways.
- Interventions should be customised to the culture, personality and developmental level of the person.
- A rapid recovery, or even freedom from distress, may not be desired outcomes. This will depend on the goals and motivations of the individual person.
- Evaluate any interventions early and be prepared to abandon something that isn't helping, and design a new intervention as needed.

Thus, with certain staff, and in the hands of an experienced, vigilant and compassionate facilitator, there may be greater therapeutic value in an informal but personalised debriefing process over time.

In any case it has been argued that putting the information gained from debriefing into an improvement process is more important than the debriefing itself [95]. A timely debriefing at the end of a session facilitates appropriate feedback [137] Teams should document items that did not go well and make suggestions for improvement. By documenting problems, teams can move towards fixing them and prevent issues later on [67].

30.7.14 Leadership, Command and Control

These are three distinct but overlapping concepts.

- *Leadership* can be defined simply as *the art of influencing others* to achieve common objectives in specific situations. Dixon [138] observed that people who are chosen to be leaders tend to be 'task specialists' or 'social specialists' or, rarely, both. These two leader types correlate with more modern descriptors of 'transactional' (task-oriented) vs. 'transformational' (team/relationship-oriented) healthcare leaders [139]. Ideal leadership combines proficiency in technical *command* (see below) with at least two additional social roles—that of a 'role model' (someone who 'shows the way' by taking initiative and inspiring junior members of the team to follow a shared vision) and that of a 'shepherd' (someone who cares for and protects the team, and encourages an environment in which the team can be most productive).

- It follows that just being a good technician/tactician without social skills, or an affable 'people person' without technical skills, does not per se make for a good clinical leader. [140] proposed a research-based framework for global evaluation of ED leadership behaviours that covers evaluation and planning behaviours (mission analysis, specifying goals, formulating strategy and reflection), action behaviours (patient and systems monitoring, providing guidance, error identification and coordination) and interpersonal skills (conflict resolution, affect management, motivation and communication).

- *Command* is the *exercise of authority* in the course of a task or a mission. Exercising authority usually involves assessing a situation, making decisions, giving orders and evaluating performance. Thus, command entails more than the mere wielding of resources (the definition of *control*—see below). For example, a consultant anaesthetist who is supervising a resident intubating a patient is *in command*, while the resident holding the laryngoscope is *in control*. A lone anaesthetist intubating a patient has both *command* and *control*.

- Command in complex emergencies can be divided into strategic ('why are we doing this'), tactical ('how are we doing this') and operational ('we're doing this'). This command structure is known as 'Gold-Silver-Bronze' in the UK and its application has extended from police responses to civil unrest [141] to the NHS management of large-scale medical incidents [142]. These principles apply equally to smaller scale command challenges, such as the running of a clinical department or a busy outpatients clinic.

- *Control* is the actual *wielding of resources* in the course of performing a task or series of tasks. For example, the person holding the laryngoscope *has control* of an intubation (whether or not they were directed by others to do it) but may *command* others to perform supporting manoeuvres (e.g. cricoid pressure), to get equipment or administer drugs.

- Understanding how these concepts interact influences leadership practice. For example, it is often difficult to maintain strategic and tactical oversight of a complex task if one is burdened with being technically 'hands-on'. Cardiac arrest teams whose leaders took an active part in resuscitating were often less well structured, less dynamic and performed resuscitation less effectively, leading to the concept of team leaders standing back and guiding the team remotely, or 'lighthouse leadership' [143]; this is now a standard part of advanced resuscitation team training.

30.7.15 Leadership Styles and Situational Leadership

Leadership styles can also be classified by the steepness of the *authority gradient* between the team leader and team members. In an *autocratic* style, the authority gradient is steep, i.e. the leader expects orders to be followed without question, and team members have little or no opportunity to query, challenge, or offer input to the leader. In a *consultative* style, the authority gradient is more shallow: the leader more actively solicits views and input from the team, and it is easier for team members to question or advocate suggestions, although the leader makes the final decision ('everyone gets their say but not everyone gets their way').

Which style is better? In one theoretical model, the answer depends on the situation. For example, in a complex ill-defined scenario involving an experienced multidisciplinary team, a consultative approach would seem more constructive; on the other hand, in a well-defined time-critical emergency with a novice team, invoking an autocratic drill would be more efficient. This is the concept of *situational leadership*—that good leaders adapt their style according to the available human resources and the needs of the situation [144].

Correlations have been found between Myers-Briggs personality types and leadership styles [145]. This suggests that clinicians in charge may gravitate naturally to one or other leadership style—autocratic or consultative, 'task-specialist' or 'social-specialist'—according to their personality. It is important therefore for clinicians to recognise their own natural tendencies, and (e.g. through simulation) to seek out training in being *the opposite*; naturally deferential types could practice being more assertive; naturally autocratic types could practice active listening. In this way the leader is better prepared to apply whatever appropriate style a situation may demand.

30.7.16 Transferable Command and Control

In helicopter medical retrievals, the pilot is in overall *tactical* command and can modify or abort the mission at any time. However, as the rescue moves through different phases, different team members hold *operational* command, directing other team members (even the pilot) during the performance of key tasks. The pilot is in charge of getting the team to the site; the winchman oversees getting the medical crew to ground; the medical officer assesses the patient and is in charge of initial resuscitation; the paramedic ensures the patient is safely secured on the stretcher; then it's the winchman again, in charge of getting the patient and crew back into the helicopter; then back to the pilot, getting the chopper to the receiving hospital; and finally the medical officer is in charge of handing the patient over to the receiving emergency team. This concept of 'taking the con' is a form of *transferable leader-*

ship [146] or *transferable command and control*, and can be applied to many multidisciplinary situations in healthcare, e.g. running an operating theatre, a busy diabetes outpatient clinic, or a community mental health service. It requires multidisciplinary team leaders to know and trust the different skill sets of their team members, and to balance autocratic and consultative leadership styles (see Sect. 30.7.15—see above).

30.8 Teaching Non-technical Skills

Training to ensure effective decision-making for patient safety should contain components of deliberate practice and feedback [147]. It is essential to expand the number and range of scenarios that decision makers have in their repertoires, and to develop the sense of what is important. High- and low-fidelity simulations are increasingly being used for research and training in dynamic domains such as healthcare (e.g. operating rooms; [148]). Low-fidelity approaches such as the ShadowBox™ method are effective ways to expose decision makers to a range of possible decision scenarios with coaching from experts on cues to monitor, issues to worry about, and interpretations of ambiguous situations [149, 150]. Higher-fidelity training may include contextual features, such as the hospital or operating environment, and incorporate communication and teamwork in realistic simulations.

Over the last decade there has been increasing interest in the interprofessional team training—doctors, nurses and allied staff training together as opposed to training within their craft groups—to overcome the challenges of cultivating effective multidisciplinary teams and patient-centred care, particularly in crisis management scenarios [151, 152].

30.9 Summary

Supported by a large base of theoretical literature on human factors in both medical and non-medical domains, non-technical skills are fast becoming an established and indispensable building block of patient safety, and increasingly incorporated into many undergraduate and postgraduate healthcare curricula. A growing body of research suggests that good NTS training improves healthcare processes and outcomes, mostly in simulated environments, but also in real-world environments, especially in critical care fields such as anaesthesia, surgery and emergency medicine. While there remain substantial challenges in developing methodologies to better define and refine the role of NTS in improving healthcare outcomes, this domain is a rich seam for future study.

References

1. Nasir ANB, Ali DF, et al. Technical skills and non-technical skills: predefinition concept. Presentation at the IETEC'11 Conference, Kuala Lumpur, Malaysia. 2011. http://ietec.apaqa.org/wp-content/uploads/IETEC-2011-Proceedings/papers/Conference%20Papers%20Refereed/Monday/MP2/MP2.320.pdf. Accessed 20 Oct 2019.
2. Beaty D. The human factor in aviation accidents. New York: Stein & Day; 1969.
3. Vernon HM. Accidents and their prevention. Cambridge: Cambridge University Press; 1936.
4. Helmreich RL, Merritt AC, Wilhelm JA. The evolution of crew resource management training in commercial aviation. Int J Aviat Psychol. 1999;9(1):19–32.
5. Job M. "Did he not clear the runway – the Pan American?" (The 1977 Tenerife air disaster). In: Air disaster, vol. 1. Australia: Aerospace Publications; 1994. p. 164–80.
6. Job M. "I don't like this…" (The 1979 Mt Erebus air disaster). In: Air disaster, vol. 2. Australia: Aerospace Publications; 1996a. p. 61–82.
7. Job M. "Mayday! We're not going to make it to the airport!" (The 1978 Portland air disaster). In: Air disaster, vol. 2. Australia: Aerospace Publications; 1996b. p. 36–46.
8. Muñoz-Marrón D. Human factors in aviation: CRM (Crew Resource Management). Psychologist Pap. 2018;39(3):191–9.
9. Leape LL. Error in medicine. JAMA. 1994;272(23):1851–7.
10. Gaba DM, Fish KJ, Howard SK. Crisis management in anesthesia. Philadelphia, PA: Churchill Livingstone; 1993.
11. Risser DT, Rice MM, Salisburt ML, Simon R, Jay GD, Berns SD, The MedTeams Research Consortium. The potential for improved teamwork to reduce medical errors in the emergency department. Ann Emerg Med. 1999;34(3):373–83.
12. Institute of Medicine. To err is human: building a better Health system. Washington, DC: National Academies Press; 1999.
13. Department of Health [UK]. An organization with a memory: report of an expert group on learning from adverse events in the NHS. London: Stationery Office; 2000.
14. Fletcher G, Flin R, et al. Anaesthetists' Non-Technical Skills (ANTS): evaluation of a behavioural marker system. Br J Anaesth. 2004;90(5):580–8.
15. Yule S, Flin R, et al. Development of a rating system for surgeons' non-technical skills. Med Educ. 2006;40(11):1098–104.
16. Mishra A, Catchpole K, McCulloch P. The Oxford NOTECHS system: reliability and validity of a tool for measuring teamwork behaviour in the operating theatre. Qual Saf Health Care. 2009;18(2):104–8.
17. King HB, Battles J, Baker DP, Alonso A, Salas E, Webster J, Toomey L, Salisbury M. TeamSTEPPS™: team strategies and tools to enhance performance and patient safety. In: Henriksen K, Battles JB, Keyes MA, et al., editors. Advances in patient Safety: new directions and alternative approaches, Performance and tools, vol. 3; 2008. http://www.ncbi.nlm.nih.gov/pubmed/21249942.
18. Reason J. Beyond the organisational accident: the need for "error wisdom" on the frontline. BMJ Qual Saf. 2004;13:ii28–33.
19. National Patient Safety Agency. Foresight training resource pack. 2008. https://webarchivenationalarchivesgovuk/20171030133314/http://wwwnrlsnpsanhsuk/resources/patient-safety-topics/human-factors-patient-safety-culture/?entryid45=59840&p=2. Accessed 21 Oct 2019.
20. Taylor-Adams S, Vincent C. Systems analysis of clinical incidents: the London protocol. Clin Risk. 2004;10:211–20.
21. Queensland Health. Best practice guide to clinical incident management. 2014. p. 67. https://clinicalexcellence.qld.gov.au/sites/default/files/2018-01/clinicalincidentguide.pdf. Accessed 21 Oct 2019.
22. Rodriguez-Paz JM, Kennedy M, Salas E, Wu AW, Sexton JB, Hunt EA, Provonost PJ. Beyond "see one, do one, teach one": toward a different training paradigm. BMJ Qual Saf. 2009;18:63–8.
23. Kotsis SV, Chung KC. Application of See One, Do One, Teach One Concept in Surgical Training. Plast Reconstr Surg. 2013;131(5):1194–1201.
24. Weller JM, Nestel D, et al. Simulation in clinical teaching and learning. Med J Aust. 2012;196(9):594.
25. Zwaan L, Len LTS, et al. The reliability and usability of the anesthesiologists' non-technical skills (ANTS) system in simulation research. Adv Simul. 2016;1(18) https://doi.org/10.1186/s41077-016-0013-2.
26. Endsley MR. Towards a theory of situation awareness in dynamic systems. Hum Factors. 1995;37(1):32–64.
27. Klein G. Naturalistic decision making. Hum Factors. 2008;50(3):456–60.

28. Klein GA. Sources of power: how people make decisions. Cambridge, MA: MIT Press; 1998.

29. Fioratou E, Flin R, Glavin R, Patey R. Beyond monitoring: distributed situation awareness in anaesthesia. BJA. 2010;105(1):83–90.

30. Flynn J, Slovic P, Mertz CK. Gender, race, and perception of environmental health risks. Risk Anaysisl. 1994;14(6):1101–8.

31. Braun BI, Harris AD, Richards CL, Belton BM, Dembry L-M, Morton DJ, Xiao Y. Does health care role and experience influence perception of safety culture related to preventing infections? Am J Inf Control. 2010;41(7):638–41.

32. Greenwald AG. The totalitarian ego: fabrication and revision of personal history. Am Psychol. 1980;35(7):603–18.

33. Ubel PA, Smith DM, Zikmund-Fisher BJ, Derry HA, McClure J, Stark A, Wiese C, Greene S, Jancovic A, Fagerlin A. Testing whether decision aids introduce cognitive biases: results of a randomized trial. Patient Educ Couns. 2009;80(2):158–63.

34. Renn O. Concepts of risk: a classification. In: Krimsky S, Golding D, editors. Social theories of risk. Westport, CT: Praeger; 1992. p. 53–79.

35. Slovic P. Perception of risk. Science. 1987;236(4799):280–5.

36. Oh S-H, Paek H-J, Hove T. Cognitive and emotional dimensions of perceived risk characteristics, genre-specific media effects, and risk perceptions: the case of H1N1 influenza in South Korea. Asian J Comm. 2015;25(1):14–32.

37. Choudry NK, Anderson GK, Laupacis A, Ross-Degnan D, Norman ST, Soumerai SB. Impact of adverse events on prescribing warfarin in patients with atrial fibrillation: matched pair analysis. BMJ. 2006;332(7534):141–5.

38. Klein GA. A recognition-primed decision (RPD) model of rapid decision making. In: Klein GA, Orasanu J, Calderwood R, Zsambok CE, editors. Decision making in action: models and methods. Norwood, NJ: Ablex Publishing; 1993. p. 138–47.

39. Mosier KL, Fischer UM. Judgment and decision making by individuals and teams: issues, models and applications. In: Harris D, editor. Reviews of human factors, vol. 6. Santa Monica, CA: Human Factors and Ergonomics Society; 2010. p. 198–256. Reprinted in Harris D, Li W, editors. Decision making in aviation. Burlington, VT: Ashgate; 2015. p. 139–97.

40. Charness N, Tuffiash M. The role of expertise research and human factors in capturing, explaining, and producing superior performance. Hum Factors. 2008;50(3):427–32.

41. Endsley MR. Expertise and situation awareness. In: Ericsson KA, Hoffman RR, Kozbelt A, Williams AM, editors. The Cambridge handbook on expertise and expert performance. Cambridge: Cambridge University Press; 2018. p. 714–41.

42. Waag WL, Bell HH. Situation assessment and decision making in skilled fighter pilots. In Zsambok, CE, Klein, G. Naturalistic decision making. Mahwah, NJ: Lawrence Erlbaum Associates, Publishers. 1997:247–54.

43. Orasanu J, Connolly T. The reinvention of decision making. In: Klein GA, Orasanu J, Calderwood R, Zsambok CE, editors. Decision making in action: models and methods. Norwood, NJ: Ablex; 1993. p. 3–20.

44. Morineau T, Morandi X, LeMoëllic N, Diabira S, Riffaud L, Haegelen C, Hénaux P-L, Jannin P. Decision making during preoperative surgical planning. Hum Factors. 2009;51(1):67–77.

45. Cohen M. Knowns, known unknowns, and unknown unknowns: synergies between intuitive and deliberative approaches to time, uncertainty, and information. In: Mosier KL, Fischer UM, editors. Informed by knowledge: expert performance in complex situations. New York: Taylor & Francis; 2011. p. 371–91.

46. Khoo L, Mosier K. The impact of time pressure and experience on information search and decision-making processes. J Cogn Eng Decis Making. 2008;2:275–94.

47. Klein G. The power of intuition. New York: Doubleday; 2003.

48. Moulton CE, Regehr G, Mylopoulos M, MacRae HM. Slowing down when you should: a new model of expert judgment. Acad Med. 2007;82(10):S109–16.

49. Moulton CE, Regehr G, Lingard L, Merritt C, MacRae H. 'Slowing down when you should': initiators and influences of the transition from the routine to the effortful. J Gastrointest Surg. 2010;14(6):1019–26.

50. Dominguez CO. Expertise and metacognition in laparoscopic surgery: a field study. In: Proceedings of the Human Factors and Ergonomic Society 45th Annual Meeting, Minneapolis/St. Paul; 2001. p. 1298–303.

51. Orasanu J, Fischer U. Team cognition in the cockpit: Linguistic control of shared problem solving. In:Proceedings of the 14th Annual Conference of the Cognitive Science Society. Hillsdale, NJ: Erlbaum. 1992:189–94.

52. Manser T, Foster S, Flin R, Patey R. Team communication during patient handover from the operating room: more than facts and figures. Hum Factors. 2013;55(1):138–56.

53. Johannesen L. Maintaining common ground: an analysis of cooperative communication in the operating room. In: Nemeth CP, editor. Improving healthcare team communication: building on lessons from aviation and aerospace. Aldershot, UK: Ashgate; 2008. p. 179–203.

54. Fischer U, Orasanu J. Error-challenging strategies: their role in preventing and correcting errors. In: Proceedings of the Human Factors and Ergonomics Society 44th Annual Meeting, San Diego, CA, vol. 1; 2000. p. 30–3.

55. Mosier K, Fischer U, Hoffman R, Klein G. Expert professional judgments and "Naturalistic Decision Making". In: Ericsson KA, Hoffman RR, Kozbelt A, Williams AM, editors. The Cambridge handbook

on expertise and expert performance. New York: Cambridge University Press; 2018. p. 453–75.

56. Tawfik DS, Profit J, Morgenthaler TI, Tutty MA, West CP, Shanfelt TD. Physician Burnout, Well-being, and Work Unit Safety Grades in Relationship to Reported Medical Errors. Mayo Clin Proc. 2018;93(11):1571–80.

57. Croskerry P, Abbass A, Wu AW. Emotional influences in patient safety. J Patient Saf. 2010;6(4):199–205. http://www.ncbi.nlm.nih.gov/pubmed/21500605.

58. Heyhoe J, Birks Y, Harrison R, O'Hara JK, Cracknell A, Lawton R. The role of emotion in patient safety: are we brave enough to scratch beneath the surface? J R Soc Med. 2016;109(2):52–8. https://doi.org/10.1177/0141076815620614.

59. Kozlowski D, Hutchinson M, Hurley J, Rowley J, Sutherland J. The role of emotion in clinical decision making: an integrative literature review. BMC Med Educ. 2017;17(1):255. https://doi.org/10.1186/s12909-017-1089-7.

60. Walsh G, Hayes B, Freeney Y, McArdle S. Doctor, how can we help you? Qualitative interview study to identify key interventions to target burnout in hospital doctors. BMJ Open. 2019;9(9):e030209. https://doi.org/10.1136/bmjopen-2019-030209.

61. Flin R, Winter J, Sarac C, Raduma M. Human factors in patient safety: review of topics and tools. World Health Organisiation; 2009. https://wwwwhoint/patientsafety/research/methods_measures/human_factors/human_factors_reviewpdf. Accessed 3 Nov 2019.

62. Salas E, Wilson KA, Murphy CE, King H, Salisbury M. Communicating, coordinating, and cooperating when lives depend on it: tips for teamwork. Jt Comm J Qual Patient Saf. 2008c;34(6):333–41. https://doi.org/10.1016/s1553-7250(08)34042-2.

63. Kodate N, Ross AJ, Anderson JE, Flin R. Non-technical skills (NTS) for enhancing patient Safety: achievements and future directions. In: Working papers 201227. Dublin: Geary Institute, University College Dublin; 2012.

64. Leonard M, Graham S, Bonacum D. The human factor: the critical importance of effective teamwork and communication in providing safe care. Qual Saf Health Care. 2004;13:i85. https://doi.org/10.1136/qshc.2004.010033.

65. The Joint Commission. Sentinel event data: root causes by event type 2004–2015. 2016. https://hcupdatefileswordpresscom/2016/02/2016-02-se-root-causes-by-event-type-2004-2015pdf. Accessed 21 Oct 2019.

66. Craig RT, Muller HL. Theorizing communication: readings across traditions. Passim. Los Angeles: Sage Publishers; 2007.

67. Lo LCPSI. Teamwork and communication in healthcare a literature review. Canadian Patient Safety Institute; 2011. https://www.patientsafetyinstitute.ca/en/toolsResources/teamworkCommunication/Documents/. Accessed 3 Nov 2019.

68. Prineas S, Smith AF, Tan SGM. To begin…. In: Cyna AM, Andrew MI, Tan SGM, Smith AF, edi-tors. Handbook of communication in anaesthesia and intensive care. Oxford: Oxford University Press; 2011. p. 3–16.

69. Prineas S. Safety-critical communication. In: Cyna AM, Andrew MI, Tan SGM, Smith AF, editors. Handbook of communication in anaesthesia and intensive care. Oxford: Oxford University Press; 2011. p. 189–200.

70. Stout RJ, Cannon-Bowers JA, Salas E, Milanovich DM. Planning, shared mental models, and coordinated performance: an empirical link is established. Hum Factors. 1999;41(1):61–71. https://doi.org/10.1518/001872099779577273.

71. Salas E, Shuffler ML, Thayer AL, Bedwell WL, Lazzara EH. Understanding and improving teamwork in organizations: a scientifically based practical guide. Hum Resour Manag. 2015;54(4):599–622. https://doi.org/10.1002/hrm.21628.

72. Mesmer-Magnus J. Information sharing and team performance: a meta-analysis. CREWS. 2009;94:535. https://doi.org/10.1037/a0013773.

73. Mesmer-Magnus JR, DeChurch LA, Jimenez-Rodriguez M, Wildman J, Shuffler M. A meta-analytic investigation of virtuality and information sharing in teams. Organ Behav Hum Decis Process. 2011;115(2):214–25. https://doi.org/10.1016/j.obhdp.2011.03.002.

74. McIntyre RM, Salas E. Measuring and managing for team performance: Emerging principles from complex environments. In R. Guzzo and E. Salas, (Eds.): Team effectiveness and decision making in organizations. San Francisco: Jossey-Bass. 1995:9–45.

75. ASHP. ASHP guidelines on preventing medication errors in hospitals. Am J Hosp Pharm. 1993;50(5):305–14.

76. Davis NM. Medical abbreviations: 55,000 conveniences at the expense of communication and safety. 16th ed. Warminster, PA: Neil M Davis Publishing; 2020.

77. World Alliance for Patient Safety. Implementation manual, surgical safety checklist. Geneva: World Health Organistaion; 2008. https://wwwwhoint/patientsafety/safesurgery/ss_checklist/en/. Accessed 19 Nov 2019.

78. Bodor R, Nguyen BJ, Broder K. Were are going to name names and call you out! Improving the team in the academic operating theatre environment. Ann Plast Surg. 2017;78(5 Suppl 4):S222–4.

79. Brown JP. Closing the communication loop: using readback/hearback to support patient safety. Jt Comm J Saf Qual. 2004;30(8):460–4.

80. Makary MA, Thompson D, Rowen L, Heitmiller ES, Maley WR, Black JH, et al. Operating room briefings: working on the same page. Jt Comm J Qual Patient Saf. 2006;32(6):351–5. https://doi.org/10.1016/S1553-7250(06)32045-4.

81. Allard J, Bleakley A, Hobbs A, Coombes L. Pre-surgery briefings and safety climate in the operating theatre. BMJ Qual Saf. 2011;20(8):711–7. https://doi.org/10.1136/bmjqs.2009.032672.

82. Arora V, Johnson J, et al. Communication failures in patient sign-out and suggestions for improvement: a critical incident analysis. Qual Saf Health Care. 2005;14:401–7.

83. Pezzolesi C, Schifano F, Pickles J, Randell W, Hussain Z, Muir H, Dhillon S. Clinical handover incident reporting in one UK general hospital. Int J Qual Health Care. 2010;22(5):396–401.

84. Makary MA, Mukherjee A, Sexton JB, Syin D, Goodrich E, Hartmann E, et al. Operating room briefings and wrong-site surgery. J Am Coll Surg. 2007;204(2):236–43. https://doi.org/10.1016/j.jamcollsurg.2006.10.018.

85. Lingard L, Espin S, Rubin B, Whyte S, Colmenares M, Baker GR, et al. Getting teams to talk: development and pilot implementation of a checklist to promote interprofessional communication in the OR. Qual Saf Health Care. 2005;14(5):340–6. https://doi.org/10.1136/qshc.2004.012377.

86. Cohen MD, Hilligoss PB. The published literature on handoffs in hospitals: deficiencies identified in an extensive review. Qual Saf Health Care. 2010;19(6):493–7.

87. Jones PM, Cherry RA, et al. Association between handover of anesthesia care and adverse postoperative outcomes among patients undergoing major surgery. JAMA. 2018;319(2):143–53.

88. Guttman OT, Lazzara EH, Keebler JR, Webster KLW, Gisick LM, Baker AL. Dissecting communication barriers in healthcare: a path to enhancing communication resiliency, reliability, and patient safety. J Patient Saf. 2018; https://doi.org/10.1097/PTS.0000000000000541.

89. Randmaa M, Mårtensson G, Swenne CL, Engström M. SBAR improves communication and safety climate and decreases incident reports due to communication errors in an anaesthetic clinic: a prospective intervention study. BMJ Open. 2014;4(1):e004268. https://doi.org/10.1136/bmjopen-2013-004268.

90. Porteous J, Stewart-Wynne EG, Connolly M, Crommelin PF. iSoBAR – a concept and handover checklist: the National Clinical Handover Initiative. Med J Aust. 2009;190(11):S152–6.

91. Department of Health [West Australia]. Clinical handover guideline. 2017. https://ww2health-wagovau/~/media/Files/Corporate/general%20documents/Quality/PDF/Clinical-Handover-Guidelinepdf. Accessed 2 Nov 2019.

92. SA Health, Safety and Quality Unit. ISBAR - a standard mnemonic to improve clinical communication. 2016. https://www.sahealth.sa.gov.au/wps/wcm/connect/public+content/sa+health+internet/clinical+resources/clinical+topics/communicating+for+safety/isbar+-+identify+situation+background+assessment+and+recommendation. Accessed 3 Nov 2019.

93. Australian Commission for Quality and Safety in Health Care. Safety and quality improvement guide - standard 6: clinical handover. 2012. https://wwwsafetyandqualitygovau/sites/default/files/migrated/Standard6_Oct_2012_WEBpdf. Accessed 2 Nov 2019.

94. Müller M, Jürgens J, Redaèlli M, Klingberg K, Hautz WE, Stock S. Impact of the communication and patient hand-off tool SBAR on patient safety: a systematic review. BMJ Open. 2018, August 1;8:e022202. https://doi.org/10.1136/bmjopen-2018-022202.

95. Frankel A, Leonard M. Essential components for a patient Safety strategy. Periop Nurs Clin. 2008;3:263. https://doi.org/10.1016/j.cpen.2008.08.004.

96. Besco RO. To intervene or not to intervene? The co-pilot's "catch 22." Developing flight crew survival skills through the use of "P. A. C. E." Paper presented at the Twenty-Fifth International Seminar of the International Society of Air Safety Investigators, Paris, France, 3–7 Oct 3–7 1994.

97. Salas E, Diaz Granados D, Klein C, Burke CS, Stagl KC, Goodwin GF, Halpin SM. Does team training improve team performance? A meta-analysis. Hum Factors. 2008b;50(6):903.

98. Salas E, Cooke NJ, Rosen MA. On teams, teamwork, and team performance: discoveries and developments. Hum Factors. 2008a;50(3):540–7.

99. Carayon P. Sociotechnical systems approach to healthcare quality and patient safety. Work. 2012;41(1):3850–4.

100. Rydenfält C, Borell J, Erlingsdottir G. What do doctors mean when they talk about teamwork? Possible implications for interprofessional care. J Interprof Care. 2019;33(6):714–23.

101. Okun S, Schoenbaum SC, Andrews D, Chidambaran P, Cholette V, Gruman J, Leal S, Lown BA, Mitchell PH, Parry C, Prins W, Ricciardi R, Simon MA, Stock R, Strasser DC, Webb E, Wynia MK, Henderson D. Patients and health care teams forging effective partnerships. New York: Institute of Medicine of the National Academies; 2014. https://nam.edu/wp-content/uploads/2015/06/PatientsForgingEffectivePartnerships1.pdf. Accessed 9 Nov 2019.

102. Hajek AM. Breaking down clinical silos in healthcare. Front Health Serv Manag. 2013;29(4):45–50.

103. Epstein NE. Multidisciplinary in-hospital teams improve patient outcomes: a review. Surg Neurol Int. 2014;5(Suppl 7):S295–303.

104. Firth-Cozens J. Multidisciplinary teamwork: the good, the bad and everything in between (Editorial). BMJ Qual Saf. 2001;10(2):65–6.

105. Green C. The decline and fall of science. London: Hamish Hamilton; 1976.

106. Helmreich RL, Shaefer H-G. Team performance in the operating room. In: Bogner MS, editor. Human error in medicine. Mahwah, NJ: Lawrence Erlbaum Associates Inc.; 1994. p. 225–54.

107. Klampfer B, Flin R, Helmreich RL, Häusler R, Sexton B, Fletcher G, Field P, Staender S, Lauche K, Dieckmann P, Amacher A. Enhancing performance in high-risk environments: recommendations for the use of behavioural markers. Workshop presented at

the Swissair Training Centre, Zurich, 5–6 July 2001. https://www.raes-hfg.com/reports/notechs-swiss. pdf. Accessed 18 Nov 2019.

108. Rosenman ED, Branzetti JB, Fernandez R. Assessing Team Leadership in Emergency Medicine: The Milestones and Beyond. J Grad Med Educ. 2016;8(3): 332–40.

109. Nolan J, Soar J, Eikeland H. The chain of survival. Resuscitation 2006;71(3):270–1.

110. Perkins GD, Lockley AS, de Belder MA, Moore F, Weissberg P, Gray H. National initiatives to improve outcomes from out-of-hospital cardiac arrest in England. Emerg Med J. 2016;33(7):448–51.

111. Ford K, Menchine M, Burner E, Arora S, Inaba K, Demetriades D, Yersin B. Leadership and teamwork in trauma and resuscitation. West J Emerg Med. 2016;17(5):549–56.

112. Holcomb JB, Dumire RD, Crommett JW, Stamateris CE, Fagert MA, Cleveland JA, Dorlac GR, Dorlac WC, Bonar JP, Hira K, Aoki N, Mattox KL. Evaluation of trauma team performance using an advanced human patient simulator for resuscitation training. J Trauma. 2002;52(6):1078–85; discussion 85–6.

113. Catchpole KR, de Leval MR, McEwan A, Pigott N, Elliott MJ, McQuillan A. Patient handover from surgery to intensive care: using Formula 1 pit-stop and aviation models to improve safety and quality. Pediatr Anaesth. 2005;17(5):470–8.

114. Elwyn G, Frosch D, Thomson R, Joseph-Williams N, Lloyd A, Kinnersley P, Cording E, Tomson D, Dodd C, Rollnick S, Edwards A, Barry M. Shared decision making: a model for clinical practice. J Gen Intern Med. 2012;27(10):1361–7.

115. Grad R, Légaré F, Bell NR, Dickinson JA, Singh H, Moore AE, Kasperavicius D, Kretschmer KL. Shared decision making in preventive health care: what it is; what it is not. Can Fam Physician. 2017;63(9):682–4.

116. Hoffman TC, Légaré F, Simmons MB, McNamara K, McCaffery K, Trevena LJ, Hudson B, Glasziou PP. Shared decision making: what do clinicians need to know and why should they bother? Med J Aust. 2014;201(1):35–9.

117. Driscoll PA, Vincent CA. Organising an efficient trauma team. Injury. 1992a;23(2):107–10.

118. Driscoll PA, Vincent CA. Variation in trauma resuscitation and its effect on patient outcome. Injury. 1992b;23(2):111–5.

119. Tiel Groenestege-Kreb D, van Maarseveen LL. Trauma team. BJA. 2014;113(2):258–65.

120. Endsley MR, Jones WM. A model of inter- and intrateam situation awareness: implications for design, training and measurement. In: McNeese M, Salas E, Endsley M, editors. New trends in cooperative activities: understanding system dynamics in complex environments. Human Factors and Ergonomics Society: Santa Monica, CA; 2001. p. 46–67.

121. Mathieu JE, Heffner TS, Goodwin GF, Salas E, Cannon-Bowers JA. The influence of shared mental models on team process and performance. J Appl Psychol. 2000;85(2):273–83.

122. Westli KH, Johnsen BH, Eid J, Rasten I, Brattebø G. Teamwork skills, shared mental models, and performance in simulated trauma teams: an independent group design. Scand J Trauma Resus Emerg Med. 2010;18(47):47. https://doi.org/10.1186/1757-7241-18-47.

123. Hayes P. The impact of team familiarity on performance: ad hoc and pre-formed emergency service teams. In: Owen C, editor. Human factors challenges in emergency service management. Boca Raton, FL: CRC Press; 2017. p. 97–124.

124. Maruthappu M, Duclos A, Zhou CD, Lipsitz SR, Wright J, Orgill D, Carty MJ. The impact of team familiarity and surgical experience on operative efficiency: a retrospective analysis. J R Soc Med. 2016;109(4):147–53.

125. Chung S, Lount RB, Park HM, Park ES. Friends with performance benefits: a meta-analysis on the relationship between friendship and group performance. Pers Soc Psych Bull. 2018;44(1):63–79.

126. Haraway DL, Haraway WM III. Analysis of the effect of conflict-management and resolution training on employee stress at a healthcare organization. Hosp Top. 2005;83(4):11–7.

127. Bridger RS, Day AJ, Morton K. Occupational stress and employee turnover. Ergonomics. 2013;56(11):1629. https://doi.org/10.1080/0014013 9.2013.836251.

128. El-Hosany WA. Interpersonal conflict, job satisfaction, and team effectiveness among nurses at Ismalia General Hoispital. J Nurs Ed Prac. 2017;7(3):115–27.

129. Cullati S, Bochatay N, Maitre F, Laroche T. When team conflicts threaten quality of care: A study of healthcare professionals' experiences and perceptions. Mayo Clin Proc. 2019;3(1):43–51.

130. Cleary S. Nurse Whistleblowers in Australian Hospitals: a Critical Case Study. PhD Thesis submitted to Deakin Unversity. 2014; available at http://dro.deakin.edu.au/eserv/DU:30067381/cleary-nurse-2014A.pdf accessed 071020.

131. Gilioli R, Campanini P, Fichera GP, Punzi S, Cassito MG. Emerging aspects of psyochosocial risks: violence and harassment at work. Med Lav. 2006;97(2):160–4.

132. Patton CM. Conflict in health care: a literature review. Internet J Healthcare Admin. 2014;9(1):1–11.

133. Mitchell JT. When disaster strikes: the critical incident stress debriefing process. J Emerg Med Serv. 1983;8:36–9.

134. Bisson JI, McFarlane AC, Rose S. Psychological debriefing [Special issue: Guidelines for treatment of PTSD]. J Traum Stress. 2000;4:555–8.

135. Bisson JI, McFarlane AC, Rose S, Ruzek JI, Watson PJ. Psychological debriefing for adults. In: Foa EB, Keane TM, Friedman MJ, Cohen JA, editors. Effective treatments for PTSD. 2nd ed. New York: Guilford Press; 2009. p. 83–105.

136. van Emmerich AA, Kamphuis JH, Hulsbosch AM, Emmelkamp PM. Single session debriefing after

psychological trauma: a meta-analysis. Lancet. 2002;360(9335):766–71.

137. Salas E, Wilson KA, Burke CS, Priest HA. Using simulation-based training to improve patient safety: what does it take? Jt Comm J Qual Patient Saf. 2005;31(7):363–71. https://doi.org/10.1016/S1553-7250(05)31049-X.

138. Dixon NS. Leaders of men. In: On the psychology of military incompetence. London: Pimlico Books; 1976. p. 216–8.

139. Sfantou DF, Laliotis A, Patelarou AE, Sifaki-Pistolla D, Matalliotakis M, Patelarou E. Importance of leadership style towards quality of care measures in healthcare settings: a systematic review. Healthcare (Basel). 2017;5(4):73. https://doi.org/10.3390/healthcare5040073.

140. Cooper S, Wakeham A. Leadership of resuscitation teams: "lighthouse leadership". Resuscitation. 1999;42:27–45.

141. Home Office, United Kingdom. Critical incident management. 2018. https://assets.publishing.service.gov.uk/government/uploads/system/uploads/attachment_data/file/736743/critical-incident-management-v12.0ext.pdf. Accessed 11 Nov 2019.

142. Nursing Times. Strategic command arrangements for the NHS during a major incident. 2009. https://wwwnursingtimesnet/archive/strategic-command-arrangements-for-the-nhs-during-a-major-incident-14-08-2009/. Accessed 11 Nov 2019.

143. Stefanidis D, Sevdalis N, Paige J, Zevin B, Aggarwal R, Grantcharov T, Jones DB et al. Simulation in Surgery: What's needed next? Ann Surg. 2015;261(5):846–53.

144. Stoller JK. The clinician as leader: why, how and when. Ann Am Thorac Soc. 2017;14(11):1622–6.

145. Ojala A-K. Leadership styles and traits in the public sector. 2013. https://pdfs.semanticscholar.org/fec6/d955dc878484802da99172f39c44c2668ad8.pdf. Accessed 11 Nov 2019.

146. Prineas S, Wynne D, Cartmill J, Morris R, Dunn S, Mackender D, The ErroMed Group. Teamwork. In: Human factors and patient safety training programme [Programme de formation sur les facteurs humains en relation avec la sécurité des patients]. Quebec: Health and Social Services; 2008. ISBN 978-2-550-53753-3.

147. Ericsson KA. The differential influence of experience, practice, and deliberate practice on the development of superior individual performance of experts. In: Ericsson KA, Hoffman RR, Kozbelt A, Williams AM, editors. The Cambridge handbook on expertise and expert performance. New York: Cambridge University Press; 2018. p. 745–69.

148. Agency for Healthcare Research and Quality. CUS Tool - Improving Communication and Teamwork in the Surgical Environment Module. (Content last reviewed May 2017). Agency for Healthcare Research and Quality, Rockville, MD. Available at https://www.ahrq.gov/hai/tools/ambulatory-surgery/sections/implementation/training-tools/cus-tool.html accessed 7 Oct 2020.

149. Klein G, Borders J. The ShadowBox approach to cognitive skills training: an empirical evaluation. J Cogn Eng Decis Making. 2016;10:268–80.

150. Klein G, Hintze N, Saab D. Thinking inside the box: the ShadowBox method for cognitive skill development. In: Chaudet H, Pellegrin L, Bonnardel N, editors. Proceedings of the 11th International Conference on Naturalistic Decision Making, Marseille, France, 21–24 May 2013. Paris, France: Arpege Science Publishing; 2013.

151. Manser T. Teamwork and patient safety in dynamic domains of healthcare: a review of the literature. Acta Anaesth Scand. 2009;53(2):143–51.

152. Stephens T, Hunningher A, Mills H, Freeth D. An interprofessional training course in crises and human factors for perioperative teams. J Interprof Care. 2016;30(5):685–8.

Medication Safety

Hooi Cheng Soon, Pierangelo Geppetti, Chiara Lupi, and Boon Phiaw Kho

31.1 Introduction

Ensuring patient safety during health services delivery is fundamental for an efficient healthcare system [1]. A strong organisational culture of patient safety and quality enables service providers to be better prepared for health emergencies, promote healthier populations and contribute to the achievement of universal health coverage [2].

Pharmacotherapy is the most common therapeutic intervention in healthcare to improve health outcomes of patients. Despite the intent to benefit patients, there are many instances where effectiveness of medications is undermined by poor medication use process and practices that could promote avoidable medication errors, thus putting patients' health in jeopardy [2]. Safe care requires that all individuals, patients and care providers are protected from medication-related harm when using the essential health services they need. A medication error is defined by the United States National Coordinating Council for Medication Error Reporting and Prevention as *"Any preventable event that may cause or lead to inappropriate medication use or patient harm while the medication is in the control of the health care professional, patient, or consumer. Such events may be related to professional practice, health care products, procedures, and systems, including prescribing, order communication, product labelling, packaging, and nomenclature, compounding, dispensing, distribution, administration, education, monitoring and use"* [3].

Unsafe medication practices leading to medication errors are among the leading causes of morbidity and mortality in health services delivery. A medication safety fact file released by the World Health Organization (WHO) in 2019 shows that medication errors harm millions of patients yearly [4]. The resultant financial burden of harm was estimated at USD42 billion each year, representing approximately 1% of global expenditure on health [5]. More importantly, these errors are *preventable*. Identifying the causes of errors and building safeguards in the healthcare system are key steps towards providing safe, quality, people-centred, timely, equitable, efficient and integrated health services.

H. C. Soon
Department of Pharmacy, Kulim Hospital, Kedah, Malaysia

P. Geppetti (✉) · C. Lupi
Pharmacology and Oncology Unit, Department of Health Sciences, University of Florence, Florence, Italy

Headache Centre, Careggi University Hospital, Florence, Italy
e-mail: pierangelo.geppetti@unifi.it; chiara.lupi@unifi.it

B. P. Kho
Department of Pharmacy, Sarawak General Hospital, Sarawak, Malaysia

© The Author(s) 2021
L. Donaldson et al. (eds.), *Textbook of Patient Safety and Clinical Risk Management*,
https://doi.org/10.1007/978-3-030-59403-9_31

31.1.1 A Focus on Transitions of Care, Polypharmacy and High-Risk Situations

Medication errors often occur as a result of gap in medication use process and practice, from prescribing and ordering to transcribing and/or documenting, and from preparing and dispensing to administering and monitoring. Transition points of care, such as admissions to hospital from a community or primary care setting, transfer from one area within the hospital to another or discharge from hospital to another care setting, are particularly vulnerable to medication errors [2]. Moreover, medications prescribed can be contraindicated for a particular patient, or in combination with his or her concomitant medications. The risk of harm is further heightened in high-risk situations associated with the use of high-risk medications.

The available evidence indicates that a substantial amount of medication-related harm is focused on transitions of care, polypharmacy and high-risk situations. In March 2017, the WHO launched the third *Global Patient Safety Challenge: Medication Without Harm* with the goal of reducing the risk of severe avoidable medication-related harm by 50%, over 5 years, globally [2]. It was envisioned that when these areas are appropriately managed, the risk of avoidable harm to many patients could be reduced, leading to improved patients' trust towards the healthcare system, as well as healthcare workers' job satisfaction, ultimately achieving safer hospital and primary care.

31.1.2 Learning Objectives

This chapter aims to highlight inherent risks and weaknesses in the medication use process in healthcare facilities, focusing on the three main areas identified as having the greatest burden of harm, as well as on the strategies that can be applied to mitigate them. After completing this chapter, readers will be able to appreciate the prevalence and incidence of common medication safety issues, as well as approaches that can be employed to reduce avoidable medication-related harm associated with transitions of care, polypharmacy and high-risk situations. As health service delivery requires inter-disciplinary involvement, this chapter also aims to engage and empower young or experienced students or residents from different specialties to work together in ensuring medication safety while delivering health services.

31.1.3 Learning Outcomes: Knowledge and Performance

31.1.3.1 Knowledge Requirements

At the end of this chapter, a health professional should know:

- The relationship between medication errors and adverse drug events (ADEs).
- The scale of medication errors at three priority areas of medication safety.
- Common points in the medication use process where errors can take place.
- Ways to ensure medication safety at three priority medication safety areas.
- The benefits of inter-professional approach.

31.1.3.2 Performance Requirements

Healthcare professionals who understand that medication errors are preventable harm and appreciate risks of unnecessary harm associated with the three priority areas of medication safety will strive to:

- Improve quality and availability of information during transitions of care.
- Engage with and educate patients, families and caregivers.
- Carry out medication reconciliations.
- Perform medication reviews.
- Practice deprescribing.
- Use generic names.
- Be extra vigilant during high-risk situations or treating high-risk patients with high-risk medications.
- Understand and practice drug calculations, e.g. adjustments of dosage based on clinical parameters.

- Be familiar with the medications prescribed, prepared, dispensed, and/or administered.
- Develop double-check habits.
- Appreciate human limitations and human factors as contributing factor of errors.
- Communicate clearly and be an effective team player.
- Report and learn from errors.

31.2 Medication Safety in Transitions of Care

Transitions of care involve movement of patients between different levels of care within the same setting or across settings, and consultations with different healthcare providers (see Fig. 31.1). Transitions of care may also involve other care providers, such as palliative care or social care. During transitions of care, changes to the current medication list of patients are very likely to occur. Therefore, ensuring medication safety involves implementation of safe medication practices to bridge critical communication gaps in medication use process. These could include appropriate prescription and risk assessment, medication review, patient engagement and communication, as well as medication reconciliation [6]. Figure 31.1 shows the medication use process for a patient within the same setting or across different levels of care, specifically at the interface between hospital and primary care.

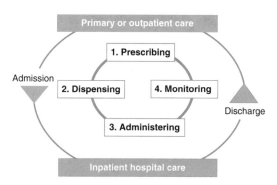

Fig. 31.1 Medication use process and communication during transitions of care

31.2.1 Prevalence of Medication Discrepancies

For patients who receive multiple medications from varied prescribers across different settings, obtaining a single medication list or a "gold standard" on what they should be taking can pose a significant challenge [7]. This invariably predisposes patients to a "mismatch" of the medications they take on a regular basis and what is prescribed to them at points of care, such as upon admission or at discharge. Technically, the use of the term "medication discrepancy" will be more appropriate than the term "error" when referring to the "mismatch", in efforts to capture potential medication errors that occur during transitions of care [7]. Medication discrepancy is, therefore, defined as "*Any difference between the medication use history and the medication orders. Discrepancies may be intentional, undocumented intentional or unintentional discrepancies*" [6].

The prescribing process, from starting a new medication, adding, withholding or stopping a medication, to alteration of dosages by prescribers when patient receives outpatient care or inpatient care, could lead to confusion among subsequent care providers (e.g. primary care counterparts and pharmacists). For instance, when reasons for changes in the preadmission medication list are not reported in the patient's discharge medication list, the next care providers have to conjecture to determine the rationale of these alternations, and whether the change is temporary or permanent [8]. Medication discrepancies owing to changes in medications during hospital admission can be intentional, attributed to the condition which caused the admission or unrelated to the reason for hospitalisation, such as to improve the management of existing chronic illnesses. Importantly, any undocumented intentional or unintentional medication discrepancy is a safety risk to patients. Studies indicate that more than half of patients experienced at least one unintended medication discrepancy during admission [9, 10]. One national multi-site audit found that nearly half of the patients with at least one new medication started had undocumented reason, while more than half of the cases with medication discontinued or withheld had undocumented reason. In addition, three out of ten patients had unintentional omissions of preadmission medication [11].

31.2.2 Medication-Related Harm During Transitions of Care

Prevention of medication-related harm for patients who seek hospital or primary care, including during transitions of care, is a top patient safety priority. While not all medication discrepancies occurring at transitions of care cause immediate patient harm, unidentified and unresolved discrepancies can increase the risk of ADEs, emergency department visits and hospital readmissions in the longer time frame, such as at 30-day time interval. A systematic review showed that 11–59% of medication discrepancies that occurred at transition points can lead to these outcomes [10]. In fact, about 33.3% of ADEs that led to hospital admission were attributable to preventable medication errors [12, 13]. Omission errors at discharge can also prove to be detrimental. For instance, myocardial infarction can be attributed to the failure to continue aspirin for secondary prevention during care transition. Such risks are further heightened for patients with low health literacy, as well as for those prescribed with high-risk medications or complex medications regimens. ADE is defined as:

> Any injury resulting from medical interventions related to a drug. This includes both adverse drug reactions that are not preventable and complications resulting from medication errors, which are preventable [6, 14].

31.2.3 Making Medication Use Safer During Transitions of Care

Ensuring medication safety during transitions of care often require a multifaceted systematic approach involving inter-disciplinary care teams such as doctors, pharmacists and nurses. Interventions with the goal of reducing medication-related harm during transitions of care focus on three essential areas:

- Medication reconciliation
- Information clarity and availability at all transition of care points
- Patients and family engagement and education

31.2.3.1 Medication Reconciliation

Medication reconciliation is a risk mitigation strategy for preventing ADEs. It is defined as *"The formal structured process in which healthcare professionals partner with patients to ensure accurate and complete medication information transfer at interfaces of care"* [6]. Medication reconciliation is an important component in health services delivery especially for patients during hospitalisation. The best possible medication history (BPMH) is obtained when information about all medications taken by a patient is recorded accurately. This is often carried out via interview of patients, their families or caregivers using a structured format. Obtaining BPMH followed by reconciliating the medication lists during transitions of care is essential to ensure medication safety and continuity of care, with the goal of communicating accurate and complete medication information to patients and subsequent care providers (Table 31.1).

Obtaining BPMH and carrying out medication reconciliation can take up to 30 min per patient [13]. Implementation of formal and structured medication reconciliation processes requires education and training of all healthcare professionals involved, including prescribers, nurses, pharmacists, and pharmacy technicians. Roles and responsibilities of each team member should be clearly elucidated and agreed upon. Targeting high-risk patients has the highest impact in contributing to the success of intervention, whereas having technologies and appropriate tools that aid standardisation could force completion of these processes [15]. The High 5s Project is a WHO initiative to standardise medication reconciliation processes to improve patient safety. Apart from reducing

Table 31.1 Steps in the medication reconciliation process to ensure medication safety during transitions of care [6, 13]

	On admission	On discharge/transfer
Verification	Verifying the information obtained from patient/caregivers against at least one reliable source of information.	Retrieving the BPMH (or completing this if it was not completed upon admission) and verifying the final medication list at the time of discharge or transfer.
Clarification	Returning to the patient and confirming the medication list with patient to build the BPMH.	Clarifying any inappropriate dosages or frequency and whether the change is temporary or permanent.
Reconciliation	Reconciling the BPMH with the medications prescribed on admission to identify and resolve any discrepancies.	Reconciling and deciding which medication is required after discharge or transfer and prescribing or listing it.
Documentation	Documenting reasons for intentional discrepancies and updating records.	Documenting reasons for changes or discontinuations to preadmission medication list and updating records, to indicate the discharge medication list and changes.

potential medication-related harm, one of the lessons shared in the High 5s Project on implementing medication reconciliation is that discrepancies that are resolved soon after admission will reduce delays in discharge and risk of human factor-related medication error [13].

31.2.3.2 Information Clarity and Availability at All Transition of Care Points

As mentioned earlier, BPMH is an important patient document for transitions of care. Hospitals and primary care teams should work together in a complementary manner to build the BPMH, and both patients and healthcare professionals should have access to an up-to-date medication list to ensure continuity of care [16]. Various facilitating tools and technologies described below are now available to ensure information availability and clarity during transitions of care.

Appropriate Tools and Technology

Having a checklist and form to standardise each stage of medication reconciliation processes can be helpful in improving medication safety, and an added benefit of this intervention is that it is feasible also in low resource settings. The form (either in paper format or a simple electronic format) should be designed to enable listing of all current medications and have a space to communicate changes in therapy, whether addition or discontinuation, temporary or permanent, with rationale clearly stated [16, 17].

Electronic Health Records (EHRs)

EHRs are electronic versions of paper charts, which record patient information. A well-functioning EHR system improves the clarity and timeliness of medication information during transitions of care. While there has been steady growth in the adoption of EHRs globally, many are not integrated across or within settings, complicating the seamless transfer of information. Apart from sufficient funding, other major barriers include poorly developed infrastructures and communication technologies to support EHR systems, as well as the lack of human resources and capacity to develop and maintain such complex systems [18]. The discharge summary records should reflect the medication usage of the patient across transitions, as well as be accessible and editable by appropriate healthcare personnel [6]. When EHR and well-designed tools are available, up to a 45% reduction in unintentional discrepancies, improved patient-provider communication, optimisation of medication regimen and better patient medication adherence to treatment are achievable [19, 20].

Information to Support Safe Use of Medications

Promoting the use of the generic name (international non-proprietary name) of medicines in the prescribing and labelling process will help to improve clarity for both patients and healthcare professionals alike and minimise reconciliation errors. In addition, national pharmacovigilance centres, pharmacies or medication information services can improve understanding as well as support safe and effective use of medication by providing readily accessible information on medications and potential ADE for both patients and healthcare professionals.

31.2.3.3 Patient Engagement and Education

Navigating the complicated processes in transitions of care, especially across settings, requires high level of health literacy and active involvement from patients and their families or caregivers [21–23]. This is essential as they are the only constant in their respective healthcare journeys, and those with low health literacy will face challenges to identify and voice discrepancies in their medication list during care transitions.

As being inadequately educated regarding their medications increases the risk of ADEs or suboptimal therapy, various actions can be taken by healthcare professionals to engage and educate patients. For starters, healthcare professionals should ensure that all patients as well as their immediate families or caregivers are made aware of changes in their medication, the monitoring needs and whom to contact should problems arise during transitions of care [13]. This can be done by properly engaging and counselling them, especially during discharge from hospitals, including asking whether they understand what is being communicated.

Other strategies include developing standardised discharge instructions for patients, creating or updating patient-held medication list with rationale for changes in therapy stated and follow-up needs specified. This comprehensive medication list can also increase their understanding about their medical conditions as well as the indication of each medications, how to take them, what side effects to expect and when they should seek help.

31.2.3.4 Monitoring and Measurement

Successful implementation of transitions of care interventions requires extensive coordination and communication between healthcare providers from different institutions. Various interventions can be put to trial to improve transitions of care,

but they have to be adequately monitored and measured to determine their efficacy in reducing medication discrepancies and avoidable patient harm. Various standardised outcome measures are available, for instance process measures for the quality and effectiveness of medication reconciliation such as outstanding unintentional medication discrepancies and percentage of patients receiving medication reconciliation [13]. In addition, validated survey instruments for patient-centred measures, such as patient experience and understanding of medications, are also recommended to achieve a well-rounded evaluation [16, 24, 25].

31.3 Medication Safety in Polypharmacy

In order to have a rough estimate of the prevalence of polypharmacy, it is necessary to understand the definition of polypharmacy first. In its most simplistic definition, polypharmacy means "an individual on multiple medications" [26, 27]. This usually afflicts those with numerous chronic health conditions, and is highly prevalent in the elderly as the number of co-morbidities increases in tandem with age [28, 29]. Individuals with polypharmacy often consult more than one medical specialist and have prescription medications filled at multiple pharmacies, making their medication regimen complex. This is further complicated by usage of non-prescription as well as traditional and/or complementary medications [28].

There is however no exact definition for polypharmacy. It is often defined as taking five or more medications, but other numbers were also used as the cut-off point [30]. This numerical definition is criticised as being arbitrary, as the number of medications taken lacks correlation with patients' clinical outcome. In fact, the use of multiple medications is warranted and rational in some health conditions, for example, heart or renal failure. This rational polypharmacy is contrary to the negative connotation associated with the term, where it is used to describe duplication of therapy, presence of drug interaction, non-indicated or excessive use of medicines [31, 32]. Hence, proponents now advocate for a distinction to be made between appropriate and inappropriate polypharmacy [31, 32].

For polypharmacy to be appropriate, the combination of medicines prescribed has to be optimised based on available best evidence and incorporates the patient's wishes to achieve the intended clinical outcomes [26, 33]. Failure to do so will result in inappropriate or problematic polypharmacy, where the risk of therapy outweigh the intended benefit, resulting in suboptimal treatment or patient harm. This includes potential prescribing omissions, where polypharmacy paradoxically results in under-prescribing of indicated medications due to an aversion towards potential ADR and non-adherence [33].

31.3.1 Prevalence of Polypharmacy

Most prevalence studies focused on the number of medicines, as well as frequency of potentially inappropriate medications (PIM) [34, 35]. Polypharmacy is usually defined as ≥ 5 medications, while the term excessive polypharmacy is used for ≥ 10 medications. Most of the research on polypharmacy focuses on the elderly (aged ≥ 65 years old), those living in managed care facilities and cancer patients, as these populations are more prone and vulnerable to the consequences of inappropriate polypharmacy. In the elderly population, a systematic review noted that those in primary care recorded a lower prevalence of patients having ≥ 5 medications at 27–59% compared to those who are hospitalised at 46–84% [35]. A study conducted across Europe established that one-third of community dwelling patients were on polypharmacy [36]. Rates of excessive polypharmacy were also reported, with around 10% of patients falling within this group [35, 37]. In long-term care facilities, 38–91% were on ≥ 5 medications, whereas 11–65% were on ≥ 10 medications [38].

31.3.2 Medication-Related Harm in Polypharmacy

The concern with polypharmacy that makes it a medication safety priority is that it increases the risk of adverse drug reactions (ADRs) due to drug-drug interactions and duplicity of therapy. These unwanted effects are a major source of iatrogenic medication-related harm for patients, and the elderly are more susceptible due to age-related physiologic decline [31, 39]. An adverse reaction can also result in a prescription cascade, where it is mistaken for an emerging medical condition and treated with new medicines [29]. These situations contribute to the incidence of intentional or non-intentional non-adherence among patients, as well as physical harm such as falls, fractures, cognitive impairments and dementia [29, 40]. In terms of economic implications, polypharmacy increases avoidable healthcare costs such as emergency department visits and hospitalisations [40, 41].

The main cause of polypharmacy is the emergence of multiple morbidities in an ageing population. The prevalence of having two or more chronic conditions increases with age, afflicting two-thirds of those aged more than 65 years old [42]. Multiple morbidity is a major confounder of the relationship between number of medications and health outcomes [43]. Other patient factors affecting polypharmacy include gender, with females having a greater preponderance to take more medications, ethnicity, and socioeconomic status, with those of poorer background and less education more prone to polypharmacy [34, 37, 44].

Health system changes causing an increase in polypharmacy include improved patient awareness and availability of treatment, wider insurance coverage, as well as pharmaceutical promotions [45, 46]. The rise of preventative medicine also contributes to polypharmacy, as patients are prescribed medicines to reduce their probability of being inflicted with stroke or acute myocardial infarctions [26]. Emphasis on evidence-based practice also results in the routine application of clinical guidelines in prescriptions. Unfortunately, these guidelines are often single condition specific and do not cater to potential medication-related problems due to treatment of multiple morbidities, further increasing the number of medications and potentially inappropriate medications being prescribed [26, 29, 40].

The number of medicines itself, regardless of appropriateness, also constitutes a risk for ADR as it increases the odds of drug interaction and inappropriate prescription [37, 40]. For example, the combined use of diuretics and blood pressure medications in a patient with heart failure can lead to postural hypotension and hyponatremia. Interactions can also occur with non-prescription medicines, complementary and alternative medicines as well as food [34]. In fact, the addition of a new medication in a patient with polypharmacy was found to elevate the risk of prescribing or monitoring error by 16% [27]. Prevalence of potential inappropriate medications meanwhile was found to range from 27% to 56% among the elderly in clinical care [35].

31.3.3 Approaches for Addressing Polypharmacy

Ensuring medication safety in polypharmacy entails the optimisation of medicines use, in which medicines prescribed for a patient are indicated and well considered in terms of their risk and benefit profiles, potential interactions and patient acceptability. Various interventions aimed at improving the appropriate use of polypharmacy had been carried out, but systematic reviews concluded that these interventions had yet to demonstrate significant clinical outcomes [33, 47]. However, this is more likely caused by deficiencies in the research designs rather than actual ineffectiveness of the interventions in the trials. Most of the studies also follow-up their subjects for less than 1 year, which may not be enough to detect significant changes in clinical outcomes.

Interventions were led by doctors, pharmacists or multidisciplinary endeavours, and involved structured pharmaceutical care programme, educational intervention and training, medication review, medication screening, prescription review, electronic medical record-based intervention, comprehensive geriatric assessment and multidisciplinary case conference [33, 47]. Some of the more established strategies are further discussed below.

For patients living in nursing homes or aged care facilities, similar multifaceted interventions were employed to optimise medications use. Medication review was the main recurring component along with multidisciplinary case discussion, education for staff, and utilisation of clinical decision support system [48]. Other interventions suggested include (1) implementing a medication reconciliation service by pharmacists, (2) conducting audits on high-risk medication use, (3) developing deprescribing scripts, (4) developing prescribing guidelines for geriatric patients with multiple co-morbidities, (5) making electronic medication charts and records accessible to all healthcare professionals, and (6) empowering facility level Medication Advisory Committee to determine medication appropriateness [49].

31.3.3.1 Measuring Appropriateness of Medications

In order to ensure medication safety in polypharmacy, medications taken by a patient, especially those with multiple morbidities, should always be assessed by physicians before the start of a new medication, or routinely by pharmacists during medication review and reconciliation [50]. The aim of this assessment is to increase medication appropriateness and decrease inappropriately prescribed medication and prescribing omissions.

Among the elderly, the Beers criteria is often used to determine appropriateness of medicines use [51]. Medicines that should generally be avoided in this population or in certain specific medical conditions are considered. A total of 48 medicines are deemed inappropriate to be used among the elderly, including benzodiazepines, anticholinergics and antihistamines, long-term non-steroidal anti-inflammatory drugs and stimulation laxatives. Other validated screening tools include Medication Appropriateness Index (MSI) and Screening Tool of Older Persons' Prescriptions and Screening Tool to Alert Doctors to Right Treatment (STOPP/START) [26]. Burt et al. developed a 12-item measure of polypharmacy appropriateness based on a systematic review and expert panel consensus, adding in measures on determinants of patient adherence, medication regimen complexity and non-pharmacological treatments [52].

31.3.3.2 Medication Reviews

Medication review is the foremost strategy to reduce polypharmacy. In medication reviews, patients' medications are evaluated by a trained healthcare professional and discussed together to identify drug-related problems. Interventional recommendations are then made to optimise treatment [41, 53, 54]. In 2018, the Scottish National Health Services published a comprehensive seven-step review process to serve as guidance in managing polypharmacy in a patient-centred manner. It involves (1) establishing treatment objectives with the patient, before working through the whole list of medications to determine drug therapies that are (2) essential as well as (3) potentially unnecessary. The current treatment is then assessed to determine its (4) effectiveness, (5) safety, (6) cost-effectiveness and (7) patient acceptance [50].

Medication reviews are often led by pharmacists, where other issues such as medication adherence, device use technique and monitoring of treatment are also considered [53, 54]. This service is available in most Western countries, including the United States, United Kingdom, Australia, Canada and New Zealand, and is often conducted in community pharmacies and reimbursable by the respective governments [54]. Outcome wise, medication reviews that are more comprehensive and conducted in the context of patients' clinical condition were found to significantly reduce hospitalisation [53]. Medication reviews with follow-up were also found to improve patients' quality of life, reduce medication-related hospitalisations and to be cost-effective [55, 56]. In the United States, medication reviews known as Medication Therapy Management (MTM) were found to improve medication appropriateness, adherence and hospitalisation for diseases such as heart failure and diabetes [57].

For a patient with polypharmacy, there is an increased risk of discrepancies during transition of care between different institutions. Hence conducting medication reviews and reconciliations during hospital admission and upon discharge are likely to have a high impact on medication safety. A mechanism has to be in place to ensure changes in medication are properly documented and conveyed to the receiving care team, as this vital information is often inaccurate or lacking [26, 27].

31.3.3.3 Rational Prescribing

Several guidelines on prescribing for the elderly exist, especially for conditions often affecting them such as management of constipation, chronic pain and rational usage of benzodiazepines, anticholinergics and anti-psychotics [50]. Guidelines for the management of patients with multiple chronic conditions are also being developed and this is the way forward for the management of polypharmacy [27]. Such guidelines are currently lacking, with only eight being identified by a systematic review [58]. Tools to assist in decision-making on polypharmacy are also available, for example, the Medicines Effectiveness Summary, where the annualised numbers needed to treat (NNT) to achieve a beneficial outcome for high-risk medications were calculated based on available trial evidence [50].

Computerised decision support systems are also increasingly being adopted to tackle polypharmacy. This includes assisted detection of inappropriate medicines and doses, which are then conveyed to prescribers via an alert system. This intervention has been found to modestly reduce ADEs [37]. PRIMA-eDS, a recently developed European-based electronic decision support system, is able to recommend medication discontinuation or modification based on patients' data and latest guidelines [59].

31.3.3.4 Deprescribing

Deprescribing entails going through a patient's medication list systematically to identify items that can be safely discontinued. It includes identifying the rationale of each previously prescribed medication, weighing the benefit of the regimen against risk of ADEs, assessing their potential to be discontinued, prioritising the discontinuation sequence, as well as monitoring the effect on patient care [60]. Due diligence is important in deprescribing, as inappropriately stopping a medication can lead to adverse drug withdrawal events. For these medications, a gradual tapering of doses is recommended [44]. Research findings suggested that deprescribing saves cost, reduces waste of medications and does not result in patient harm; however definitive impact on clinical outcomes as well as patients' medication adherence cannot be determined due to paucity of high quality, long-term trials [61, 62].

31.3.3.5 Health System Changes

In order to develop polypharmacy management programmes that are sustainable, change management principles such as Kotter's Eight step process for leading change, as well as implementation strategies that are grounded in established theories are recommended [41]. Multidisciplinary and multinational projects, engaging varied stakeholders including politicians, healthcare commissioners, educators, regulators, providers, and patients, such as the European Union's SIMPATHY consortium are also essential to spur innovation and drive change management [63].

31.3.3.6 Practical Tips

In addition to institutional changes, healthcare professionals can also address polypharmacy according to their individual capacities. The King's Fund (2013) suggested practical tips on polypharmacy management that can be carried out by all healthcare providers [26]. Tips include ensuring that medication regimens are as simple as possible for patients in terms of frequency and pill burden, for example, substituting rather than adding medications to the regimen. Making things easier is also recommended, such as providing clear and specific written instructions, dosing schedules, compliance aids as well as assessing their level of understanding.

31.3.3.7 Practicing Patient-Centred Care

The involvement of patients and their family members in shared decision-making on their treatment regimen is important to ensure medication safety in polypharmacy. Prescribers should always communicate with patients to ensure that their needs are met and concerns addressed. Involvement of patients is essential to ensure that they understand the medication regimen and will adhere to the medicines prescribed [26, 50, 52]. Tools to facilitate patient involvement can be used, including patient-held medication records, explanation materials for illnesses and medications as well as empowerment support materials such as WHO's 5 Moments for Medication Safety [41].

31.4 High-Risk Situations in Medication Safety

Regarding medication safety, high-risk situations are circumstances which are associated with significant harm due to unsafe medication practices or medication errors [64]. The inherent risk of use of certain drugs, defined as high-risk or high-alert medications, as well as certain work environments (e.g. hospital healthcare) and clinical scenarios (e.g. emergency and anaesthesia settings), which involve particular difficulties for healthcare professionals in complying with safe medication practices, represent some examples of high-risk situations. Similarly, there are also some conditions inherent to the individual, such as childhood and old age, and medical conditions, such as hepatic or renal impairment and cardiac failure, which predispose patients to an increased risk of medication errors and ADRs [64]. Pregnant women can even be included among high-risk patients due to the limited information about the safety of most medications in this population, because of a lack of randomised clinical trials [65]. High-risk situations, as a whole, require mechanisms to prevent medication errors and, in case they occur, should cover means of identification before they result in harm to the patient. In a recent consensus prioritisation exercise, a group of leading researchers in patient and medication safety, including experts from the WHO Global Patient Safety Network, identified development of guidelines and standard operating procedures for high-risk medications, patients and contexts, as well as the production of score-based approaches to predict high-risk situations as top priority research areas [66].

31.4.1 Medication Errors and Related Harm in High-Risk Situations

31.4.1.1 High-Risk Medications

High-risk medications are drugs that are more likely to cause harm to a patient when they are used in error or taken inappropriately. Although mistakes may or may not be more common with these drugs, the consequences of an error at any level of their management (i.e. prescription, storage, dispensing, preparation, administration and monitoring) are more devastating to patients compared to non-high-risk medications [67]. These medicines require particular attention in the medication use process, mainly because of their potential toxicity, low therapeutic index or high possibility of pharmacological interactions.

A recent systematic review, which focused on the epidemiology of prescribing errors with high-risk medications in the inpatient setting, highlighted that the prevalence of these errors was highly variable, ranging from 0.24 to 89.6 errors per 100 orders. This wide range reflected the lack of uniqueness on definitions of both prescribing errors and high-risk medications. Dosage errors, incorrect date of prescription, and omissions of required medications were the most common prescribing errors. Opioids and sedatives were the most frequent pharmacological categories associated with these errors [68]. In another systematic literature review aimed at defining high-risk drug classes, methotrexate and warfarin were the top two drugs resulting in fatal medication errors [69].

While the drugs identified as high-risk may vary between countries and healthcare settings in light of the types of molecules used and patients treated, analysis of incident data and review of the literature identified a group of medicines that should universally be considered as high-risk. In 2015, the New South Wales Clinical Excellence Commission summarised these drugs by the mnemonic acronym "A PINCH" (anti-infective agents, potassium and other electrolytes, insulin, narcotics and other sedatives, chemotherapeutic and immunosuppressive agents, and heparin and anticoagulants) [70]. The most frequent medication errors and ADRs associated with the use of the high-risk medication categories considered in "A PINCH" are reported in Table 31.2 [64, 70].

This list is not intended to be exhaustive, and tables should be developed locally in order to reflect the specificities of drugs used in different work environments. A wider list has been drawn up and is periodically updated by the Institute for Safe Medication Practices (ISMP), based on error reports submitted to the ISMP National Medication Errors Reporting Program, evidences from the literature and inputs from practitioners and safety experts. High-risk medications have been classified according to their different use in acute care, ambulatory healthcare and long-term care settings [71].

31.4.1.2 High-Risk Patients

Data from observational studies indicate that 5–27% of all paediatric medication orders resulted in error [72]. Children, especially neonates and infants, are particularly vulnerable to patient safety concerns, including the use of weight-based dosing, the need for stock medicine dilution to administer small amounts of medication, immature hepatic and renal systems and the inability to self-administer medications or communicate side effects [73].

In the elderly, as discussed in the previous section, long-term polypharmacy due to the emergence of multiple chronic morbidities and high probability of drug-drug interactions are the most critical factors in the medication safety field. It is also noteworthy that the elderly are generally poorly compliant to therapy and less likely to tolerate drugs. Indeed, age-related physiological changes, including the reduction of glomerular filtration rate, the decreasing liver volume and blood flow, as well as an increase of gastric acidity, affect pharmacokinetic processes,

Table 31.2 High-risk medication list [64, 70]

High-risk medication groups	Examples of medications	Examples of medication errors and adverse drug reactions
A: Anti-infective	Amphotericin	Dosage and administration errors (e.g. substitution of the lipid-base form with a high dose of the cardiotoxic conventional form)
	Aminoglycosides	Dosage and monitoring errors (e.g. dose-related damage to hearing and kidneys)
P: Potassium and other electrolytes	Injection of potassium, magnesium, calcium, hypertonic sodium chloride	Preparation and administration errors (e.g. intravenous infusions incorrectly prepared, concentrated solutions administered in place of diluted solutions)
I: Insulin	All insulins	Dosage and administration errors (e.g. incorrect use of non-insulin syringes, misunderstanding of doses expressed in U or UI for units)
N: Narcotics and other sedatives	Opioids (e.g. hydromorphone, oxycodone, morphine, fentanyl), benzodiazepines (e.g. diazepam, midazolam), short-term anaesthetics (e.g. thiopentone, propofol)	Prescribing, dosage and administration errors (e.g. cardiorespiratory toxicity due to overdosing, incorrect management of molecules with different durations of action, incorrect use of opioid analgesic patches)
C: Chemotherapeutic agents	Oral and parenteral chemotherapeutics	Dosage and monitoring errors (e.g. toxicity due to overdosing)
	Methotrexate	Administration errors (e.g. overdosing induced by daily administration instead of weekly administration)
H: Heparin and anticoagulants	Low molecular weight heparins (e.g. enoxaparin), orally active vitamin K antagonists (e.g. warfarin), newer oral anticoagulants (e.g. rivaroxaban)	Dosage and monitoring errors (e.g. risk of inefficacy due to underdosing, risk of bleeding due to overdosing)
Other high-risk medications identified at Local Health District/Facility/Unit Level	Paracetamol	Dosage errors (dose-related liver failure mainly in children)
	Non-steroidal anti-inflammatory drugs	Prescribing errors (long-term gastrointestinal, renal and cardiovascular toxicity mainly in high-risk populations)

thus exposing older people to an increased risk of ADRs [74].

Recent studies have reported that medication use is common among pregnant women. In a multinational web-based European study conducted in pregnant women and new mothers with a child less than 1-year-old, 28% of the women used medications classified as risky to the foetus or child. Having a chronic disorder was the factor with the strongest association with the use of risky medications during pregnancy [75]. Even fragile patient groups, such as those with chronic pain conditions, diabetes, cancer or major psychiatric disorders, need to be included among patients at increased risk of ADRs.

31.4.1.3 High-Risk Contexts

Two systematic reviews reported that prescribing errors are common in general practice and hospital inpatients [76, 77]. The hospital environment is particularly prone to error-provoking conditions. Hospital wards may be busy or understaffed, and clinicians may inadequately supervise the medication use process or fail to check important information. Tiredness and the need to multitask often interrupt critical processes, such as administration of medicines, cause adverse ramifications for patient safety [78]. For example, a study conducted in a Spanish tertiary-care hospital emergency department noted that medication errors occurred most frequently when medication were administered, especially during the afternoon or evening shift when staff were more tired [79].

Certain hospital specialties are associated with increased risk of medication administration error. In a prospective incident monitoring study conducted at a large Chinese tertiary hospital, the frequency of administration error during anaesthesia was 1.1%. The largest categories of errors were omissions, incorrect doses and substitutions. Even then, substantially more respondents who claimed that they were not fully rested reported inattention as a contributing factor to errors compared to those who were fully rested [80].

31.4.2 Some Ways to Ensure Medication Safety in High-Risk Situations

31.4.2.1 High-Risk Medications

Both at local and global level, the purpose of identifying a list of high-alert medications is to determine which drugs require special safeguards to reduce the risk of errors and minimise harm that can occur in the different phases of the medication use process [71]. Simplifying and standardising the ordering, storage, preparation, and dispensing of high-risk medications is the main strategy to reduce the risk of errors from high-risk medicines. In the fifth edition of the Accreditation Standards for Hospitals, the Joint Commission International identified improving the safety of high-risk medications in hospitals as a key objective, paying particular attention on the development and implementation of processes to manage the safe use of concentrated electrolytes [81]. Concentrated electrolyte solutions should always be stored in a controlled environment to prevent selection error and inadvertent administration of undiluted solutions, which have contributed to fatal outcomes.

Healthcare professionals are also involved in ensuring safe prescription, administration and monitoring of high-risk medications. In this regard, drugs with a narrow therapeutic index, such as chemotherapeutics and orally active

vitamin K antagonists, should be carefully dosed and monitored by clinicians, in order to perform dose adjustments when necessary. Indeed, even small increases in the concentration of these medications at their site of action, for example, due to pharmacological interaction or concomitant disease, may cause a significant increase in their effect, resulting in patient harm [64]. Therapeutic guidelines should be followed for drugs where dosing is complex and duration of therapy substantially increases the risk of toxicity, for example, aminoglycosides and opioids [70]. "Navigating opioids for chronic pain" is a tool that provides guidance on different opioids based on morphine equivalence to compare the relative potency of the different molecules [82]. The use of shelf reminders, auxiliary labels, checklists and automated alerts, better if built into information technology systems, is intended to improve information and stimulate the attention of the clinicians regarding high-risk medicines. A regular review of local and broader system incidents and near-misses and the use of prospective analysis and re-design of systems is fundamental to prevent reoccurrence of the same errors with these drugs [70].

31.4.2.2 High-Risk Patients

All patients should be supported by a prescribing team working in close partnership with other healthcare providers, to ensure that they are aware of the therapeutic objectives of the medications taken, their likely benefits and potential side effects [83]. Self-empowerment among patients is essential to promote medication safety, as they serve as the final barrier in preventing medication errors. For this purpose, the use of aide-memoire tools, such as WHO 5 Moments for Medication Safety, should be promoted especially among high-risk patients, their families and caregivers, at all levels of care and across all settings [84].

Among the paediatric population, improving medication safety across the spectrum of their medication use process remains an area of critical focus. In a prospective cohort study on prioritising strategies for preventing medication errors and ADEs in paediatric inpatients, computerised physician order entry with clinical decision support systems, ward-based clinical pharmacists and improved communication among physicians, nurses, and pharmacists were identified as having the greatest potential to reduce medication errors [85]. While some advanced technologies, such as computerised physician order entry with clinical decision support systems, are increasingly adopted worldwide, others, including barcode administration systems and "SMART pumps" (i.e. infusion delivery systems that provide decision support for users), are only mainstream in the United States [86]. Technologies to improve medication safety that are still in the pipeline include mobile apps to assist each step of the medication management process from ordering to delivery in real time and workflow management systems.

In outpatient paediatrics, focus of interventions should be on the administration stage considering that parents, rather than patients or trained nurses, administer most medications. This process is error-prone, including parental confusion regarding the correct use of teaspoons, tablespoons, and dose cups. Supplementing the often-rushed information from physicians and pharmacists regarding drug administration with accurate Internet-based information on drugs or a personal consultation with an office-based pharmacist could be helpful [73].

In the elderly population, rational prescribing is a crucial step to avoid ADRs resulting from unnecessary drug use, incorrect drug choices, inappropriate dosing regimens and therapeutic duplications [74]. Lists have been derived from consensus opinion to guide clinicians, and primarily general practitioners, about appropriate prescriptions for older people, including the Beers Criteria and STOPP/START tool [87, 88]. While the use of such criteria would reduce the risk of wrong prescription in older people, it is most effective if supplemented with periodic medication reviews, as reduction in the absolute number of prescribed medications, particularly non-indicated items, can minimise the risk of ADRs [74]. Multidisciplinary cooperation between nurses, physicists and pharmacists is essential in this aspect. By mak-

ing medical care plans together, errors associated with incorrect doses and noncompliance with regulations and laws can be prevented more effectively [89].

There is a paucity of information on medication safety during pregnancy. This underscores the important role healthcare providers play as trusted sources of information for women during this vital stage of their life. Interactions between women of childbearing age and their physicians and pharmacists will influence the decisions they make about medication use. Strategic messaging and improved informational resources could help maximise the effectiveness of these interactions by ensuring that women receive the clear, credible, and comprehensive information about medication risks during pregnancy at the right time [90].

31.4.2.3 High-Risk Contexts

The working environment in healthcare facilities, primarily hospital settings, are often suboptimal with fluctuations in workload, staffing absences, missing medical records, distractions, and time pressures. Thus, prescribers should be equipped with the knowledge, skills and resilience to cope with these eventualities [91]. Various strategies can be taken to mitigate inherent risks in high-risk situations. As an example, in the hospital setting, preparing and administering intravenous medications is particularly complex, error prone and dangerous. Mitigation of this risk entails conduct of error checking at each stage of the preparation. The use of pre-prepared injections may also help by eliminating errors in the reconstitution of drug and diluent [92]. Another risk reduction strategy is the implementation of electronic prescription. A recent systematic review and meta-analysis of 38 prospective interventional studies found that hospital-based electronic prescription strategies reduced medication errors, dosing errors and ADEs. Although the available evidence was heterogeneous and mainly represented by non-randomised studies, it provides early data to justify implementation and further evaluation of computerised strategies [93].

31.5 Final Recommendations and Conclusions

The complexity and vastness of the healthcare system as well as the rapid advancement in pharmacotherapy render medication safety challenging to achieve. A patient can now be seen by multiple prescribers in multiple facilities and started on multiple medications, some of which are high-risk. Healthcare workers are also working in an increasingly siloed environment, focusing on the specialisation of their unit, resulting in fragmented information exchange and lack of inter-departmental cooperation. All these factors increase the probability and propensity for unintentional medication errors to occur. Therefore, it is now vital for the next generation of healthcare professionals to appreciate the magnitude of the challenges faced in ensuring medication safety, using the current strategies as a reference to devise their own innovative solutions.

As a recap of the chapter, transitions of care is a major contributor to medication discrepancies. A lack of information sharing among healthcare professionals detailing medication changes when patients transfer from one hospital to another or between different setting of care, and inadequate patient health literacy are the main causes for this lapse in medication safety. Focusing on medication reconciliation, information clarity during care transition, as well as patient engagement and empowerment are keys to alleviate this issue.

The use of multiple medications or polypharmacy is a rising trend. This will inevitably increase medication-related adverse events leading to patient harm. Various measures have been taken to promote rationale prescribing, especially among elderly patients as well as to reduce inappropriate polypharmacy. Conducting robust research in this area is a priority, as there is insufficient evidences that current polypharmacy-related interventions significantly improve patients' clinical outcomes. Multifaceted interventions involving multiple stakeholders and health system changes should be the focus of future research to ensure medication safety in this aspect of care.

Some situations, including patients, specific medications and contexts of care, are associated with higher inherent safety risks. High-risk medications are often those with narrow therapeutic index and high potency, whereas some patient segments, especially children, geriatrics and pregnant women, are physiologically more vulnerable to errors. Chaotic and understaffed institutions, including poorly trained staff, also increase medication error risk. Use of alert systems, checklists and computerised technologies are strategies that can reduce the risk level. Safer hospital and primary care will be achievable when safety strategies and risk management skills are built into healthcare systems and practices of medication, safety and risk management is built into healthcare systems and processes.

References

1. World Health Organization. Patient safety: making health care safer. Geneva: World Health Organization; 2017.
2. World Health Organization. WHO global patient safety challenge: medication without harm. Geneva: World Health Organization; 2017.
3. About medication errors [website]. Rockville, MD: National Coordinating Council for Medication Error Reporting and Prevention; 2019. http://www.ncc-merp.org/about-medication-errors. Accessed 31 Oct 2019.
4. 10 facts on Patient Safety [website]. Geneva: World Health Organization; 2019. https://www.who.int/features/factfiles/patient_safety/en/. Accessed 31 Oct 2019.
5. Aitken M, Gorokhovich L. Advancing the responsible use of medicines: applying levers for change. Parsippany, NJ: IMS Institute for Healthcare Informatics; 2012.
6. World Health Organization. Medication safety in transitions of care. Geneva: World Health Organization; 2019.
7. Coleman EA, Smith JD, Raha D, Min S-J. Posthospital medication discrepancies: prevalence and contributing factors. Arch Intern Med. 2005;165(16):1842–7.
8. Eng JA, Steinman MA. Changing chronic medications in hospitalized patients—bridging the inpatient–outpatient divide. J Hosp Med. 2014;9(5):332–3.
9. Cornish PL, Knowles SR, Marchesano R, Tam V, Shadowitz S, Juurlink DN, et al. Unintended medication discrepancies at the time of hospital admission. Arch Intern Med. 2005;165:424–9.

10. Tam VC, Knowles SR, Cornish PL, Fine N, Marchesano R, Etchells EE. Frequency, type and clinical importance of medication history errors at admission to hospital: a systematic review. CMAJ. 2005;173(5):510–5.

11. Shah C, Hough J, Jani Y. Collaborative audit across England on the quality of medication related information provided when transferring patients from secondary care to primary care and the subsequent medicines reconciliation in primary care. London: NHS Specialist Pharmacy Service; 2016.

12. Lehnbom EC, Stewart MJ, Manias E, Westbrook JI. Impact of medication reconciliation and review on clinical outcomes. Ann Pharmacother. 2014;48(10):1298–312.

13. World Health Organization. The high 5s project: interim report. Geneva: World Health Organization; 2014.

14. Otero MJ, Schmitt E. Clarifying terminology for adverse drug events. Ann Intern Med. 2005;142(1):77.

15. Mueller SK, Sponsler KC, Kripalani S, Schnipper JL. Hospital-based medication reconciliation practices: a systematic review. Arch Intern Med. 2012;172(14):1057–69.

16. World Health Organization. Transitions of care: technical series on safer primary care. Geneva: World Health Organization; 2016.

17. Gleason KM, Brake H, Agramonte V, Perfetti C. Medications at transitions and clinical hand-offs (MATCH) toolkit for medication reconciliation. Agency for Healthcare Research and Quality: Rockville, MD; 2012.

18. World Health Organization. Global diffusion of eHealth: making universal health coverage achievable. Report of the third global survey on eHealth. Geneva: World Health Organization; 2016.

19. Ammenwerth E, Schnell-Inderst P, Hoerbst A. The impact of electronic patient portals on patient care: a systematic review of controlled trials. J Med Internet Res. 2012;14(6):e162.

20. Mekonnen AB, Abebe TB, McLachlan AJ, Brien JA. Impact of electronic medication reconciliation interventions on medication discrepancies at hospital transitions: a systematic review and metaanalysis. BMC Med Inform Decis Mak. 2016;16:112.

21. Coleman EA, Smith JD, Frank JC, Min SJ, Parry C, Kramer AM. Preparing patients and caregivers to participate in care delivered across settings: the Care Transitions Intervention. J Am Geriatr Soc. 2004;52(11):1817–25.

22. Kristeller J. Transition of care: pharmacist help needed. Los Angeles, CA: SAGE Publications.

23. McCray AT. Promoting health literacy. J Am Med Inform Assoc. 2005;12(2):152–63.

24. Ontario Hospital Association. Recommended patient experience surveys. Toronto, ON: Ontario Hospital Association; 2019.

25. Canadian Patient Safety Institute. Engaging patients in patient safety: a Canadian guide. Edmonton, AB: Canadian Patient Safety Institute; 2018.

26. Duerden M, Avery T, Rupert P. Polypharmacy and medicines optimisation: making it safe and sound. London: The King's Fund; 2013.

27. Molokhia M, Majeed A. Current and future perspectives on the management of polypharmacy. BMC Fam Pract. 2017;18(1):70.

28. Hajjar ER, Cafiero AC, Hanlon JT. Polypharmacy in elderly patients. Am J Geriatr Pharmacother. 2007;5(4):345–51.

29. Sergi G, Rui MD, Sarti S, Manzato E. Polypharmacy in the elderly. Drugs Aging. 2011;28(7):509–18.

30. Masnoon N, Shakib S, Kalisch-Ellett L, Caughey GE. What is polypharmacy? A systematic review of definitions. BMC Geriatr. 2017;17(1):230.

31. Bushardt RL, Massey EB, Simpson TW, Ariail JC, Simpson KN. Polypharmacy: misleading, but manageable. Clin Interv Aging. 2008;3(2):383–9.

32. Gillette C, Prunty L, Wolcott J, Broedel-Zaugg K. A new lexicon for polypharmacy: implications for research, practice, and education. Res Soc Adm Pharm. 2015;11(3):468–71.

33. Rankin A, Cadogan CA, Patterson SM, Kerse N, Cardwell CR, Bradley MC, et al. Interventions to improve the appropriate use of polypharmacy for older people. Cochrane Database Syst Rev. 2018;(9):CD008165.

34. Hovstadius B, Petersson G. Factors leading to excessive polypharmacy. In: Holmes HM, editor. Clinics in geriatric medicine, vol. 28. Elsevier Inc: Philadelphia, PA; 2012. p. 159.

35. Elmståhl SL, Linder H. Polypharmacy and inappropriate drug use among older people—a systematic review. Healthy Aging Clin Care Elderly. 2013;5:1.

36. Midão L, Giardini A, Menditto E, Kardas P, Costa E. Polypharmacy prevalence among older adults based on the survey of health, ageing and retirement in Europe. Arch Gerontol Geriatr. 2018;78:213–20.

37. Lim LM, McStea M, Chung WW, Nor Azmi N, Abdul Aziz SA, Alwi S, et al. Prevalence, risk factors and health outcomes associated with polypharmacy among urban community-dwelling older adults in multi-ethnic Malaysia. PLoS One. 2017;12(3):e0173466.

38. Jokanovic N, Tan ECK, Dooley MJ, Kirkpatrick CM, Bell JS. Prevalence and factors associated with polypharmacy in long-term care facilities: a systematic review. J Am Med Directors Assoc. 2015;16(6):535e1–e12.

39. Sheikh A, Dhingra-Kumar N, Kelley E, Kieny MP, Donaldson LJ. The third global patient safety challenge: tackling medication-related harm. Bull World Health Organ. 2017;95(8):546-A.

40. Garfinkel D, Ilhan B, Bahat G. Routine deprescribing of chronic medications to combat polypharmacy. Ther Adv Drug Saf. 2015;6(6):212–33.

41. World Health Organisation. Medication safety in polypharmacy. Geneva: World Health Organisation; 2019.

42. Barnett K, Mercer SW, Norbury M, Watt G, Wyke S, Guthrie B. Epidemiology of multimorbid-

ity and implications for health care, research, and medical education: a cross-sectional study. Lancet. 2012;380(9836):37–43.

43. Fried TR, O'Leary J, Towle V, Goldstein MK, Trentalange M, Martin DK. Health outcomes associated with polypharmacy in community-dwelling older adults: a systematic review. J Am Geriatr Soc. 2014;62(12):2261–72.

44. Gnjidic D, Le Couteur DG, Kouladjian L, Hilmer SN. Deprescribing trials: methods to reduce polypharmacy and the impact on prescribing and clinical outcomes. Clin Geriatr Med. 2012;28(2):237–53.

45. Charlesworth CJ, Smit E, Lee DSH, Alramadhan F, Odden MC. Polypharmacy among adults aged 65 years and older in the United States: 1988–2010. J Gerontol A. 2015;70(8):989–95.

46. Morin L, Johnell K, Laroche M-L, Fastbom J, Wastesson JW. The epidemiology of polypharmacy in older adults: register-based prospective cohort study. Clin Epidemiol. 2018;10:289–98.

47. Johansson T, Abuzahra ME, Keller S, Mann E, Faller B, Sommerauer C, et al. Impact of strategies to reduce polypharmacy on clinically relevant endpoints: a systematic review and meta-analysis. Br J Clin Pharmacol. 2016;82(2):532–48.

48. Alldred DP, Kennedy MC, Hughes C, Chen TF, Miller P. Interventions to optimise prescribing for older people in care homes. Cochrane Database Syst Rev. 2016;(2):CD009095.

49. Jokanovic N, Wang KN, Dooley MJ, Lalic S, Tan ECK, Kirkpatrick CM, et al. Prioritizing interventions to manage polypharmacy in Australian aged care facilities. Res Soc Adm Pharm. 2017;13(3):564–74.

50. Scottish Government Polypharmacy Model of Care Group. Polypharmacy guidance, realistic prescribing. 3rd ed. Edinburgh: Scottish Government; 2018.

51. Fick DM, Cooper JW, Wade WE, Waller JL, Maclean JR, Beers MH. Updating the Beers criteria for potentially inappropriate medication use in older adults: results of a US Consensus Panel of Experts. JAMA Intern Med. 2003;163(22):2716–24.

52. Burt J, Elmore N, Campbell SM, Rodgers S, Avery AJ, Payne RA. Developing a measure of polypharmacy appropriateness in primary care: systematic review and expert consensus study. BMC Med. 2018;16(1):91.

53. Hatah E, Braund R, Tordoff J, Duffull SB. A systematic review and meta-analysis of pharmacist-led fee-for-services medication review. Br J Clin Pharmacol. 2014;77(1):102–15.

54. Messerli M, Blozik E, Vriends N, Hersberger KE. Impact of a community pharmacist-led medication review on medicines use in patients on polypharmacy - a prospective randomised controlled trial. BMC Health Serv Res. 2016;16(1):145.

55. Jódar-Sánchez F, Malet-Larrea A, Martín JJ, García-Mochón L, López del Amo MP, Martínez-Martínez F, et al. Cost-utility analysis of a medication review with follow-up service for older adults with poly-

pharmacy in community pharmacies in Spain: the conSIGUE Program. PharmacoEconomics. 2015;33(6):599–610.

56. Malet-Larrea A, Goyenechea E, García-Cárdenas V, Calvo B, Arteche JM, Aranegui P, et al. The impact of a medication review with follow-up service on hospital admissions in aged polypharmacy patients. Br J Clin Pharmacol. 2016;82(3):831–8.

57. Viswanathan M, Kahwati LC, Golin CE, Blalock SJ, Coker-Schwimmer E, Posey R, et al. Medication therapy management interventions in outpatient settings: a systematic review and meta-analysis. JAMA Intern Med. 2015;175(1):76–87.

58. Muth C, Blom JW, Smith SM, Johnell K, Gonzalez-Gonzalez AI, Nguyen TS, et al. Evidence supporting the best clinical management of patients with multimorbidity and polypharmacy: a systematic guideline review and expert consensus. J Intern Med. 2019;285(3):272–88.

59. Rieckert A, Teichmann A-L, Drewelow E, Kriechmayr C, Piccoliori G, Woodham A, et al. Reduction of inappropriate medication in older populations by electronic decision support (the PRIMA-eDS project): a survey of general practitioners' experiences. J Am Med Inform Assoc. 2019;26:1323.

60. Scott IA, Hilmer SN, Reeve E, Potter K, Le Couteur D, Rigby D, et al. Reducing inappropriate polypharmacy: the process of deprescribing. JAMA Intern Med. 2015;175(5):827–34.

61. Thompson W, Farrell B. Deprescribing: what is it and what does the evidence tell us? Can J Hosp Pharm. 2013;66(3):201–2.

62. Ulley J, Harrop D, Ali A, Alton S, Fowler Davis S. Deprescribing interventions and their impact on medication adherence in community-dwelling older adults with polypharmacy: a systematic review. BMC Geriatr. 2019;19(1):15.

63. Stewart D, Mair A, Wilson M, Kardas P, Lewek P, Alonso A, et al. Guidance to manage inappropriate polypharmacy in older people: systematic review and future developments. Expert Opin Drug Saf. 2017;16(2):203–13.

64. Medication safety in high-risk situations. Geneva: World Health Organisation; 2019. https://www.who.int/patientsafety/medication-safety/HighRisk.pdf?ua=1. Accessed 15 Oct 2019.

65. Wood ME, Lapane KL, van Gelder MMHJ, Rai D, Nordeng HME. Making fair comparisons in pregnancy medication safety studies: an overview of advanced methods for confounding control. Pharmacoepidemiol Drug Saf. 2018;27(2):140–7.

66. Sheikh A, Rudan I, Cresswell K, Dhingra-Kumar N, Tan ML, Hakkinen ML, et al. Agreeing on global research priorities for medication safety: an international prioritisation exercise. J Glob Health. 2019;9(1):010422.

67. American Pharmacists Association. Medication errors. 2nd ed. Washington, DC: American Pharmacists Association; 2007.

68. Alanazi MA, Tully MP, Lewis PJ. A systematic review of the prevalence and incidence of prescribing errors with high-risk medicines in hospitals. J Clin Pharm Ther. 2016;41(3):239–45.

69. Saedder EA, Brock B, Nielsen LP, Bonnerup DK, Lisby M. Identifying high-risk medication: a systematic literature review. Eur J Clin Pharmacol. 2014;70(6):637–45.

70. Clinical Excellence Commission. High-risk medicines management policy. Sydney: NSW Ministry of Health; 2015. https://www1.health.nsw.gov.au/pds/ActivePDSDocuments/PD2015_029.pdf. Accessed 15 Oct 2019.

71. ISMP. High-alert medications. Institute for Safe Medication Practices: Horsham, PA; 2019. http://www.ismp.org/Tools/highAlertMedicationLists.asp. Accessed 15 Oct 2019.

72. Rinke ML, Bundy DG, Velasquez CA, Rao S, Zerhouni Y, Lobner K, et al. Interventions to reduce pediatric medication errors: a systematic review. Pediatrics. 2014;134(2):338–60.

73. Kaushal R, Jaggi T, Walsh K, Fortescue EB, Bates DW. Pediatric medication errors: what do we know? What gaps remain? Ambul Pediatr. 2004;4(1):73–81.

74. Hubbard RE, O'Mahony MS, Woodhouse KW. Medication prescribing in frail older people. Eur J Clin Pharmacol. 2013;69(3):319–26.

75. Trønnes JN, Lupattelli A, Nordeng H. Safety profile of medication used during pregnancy: results of a multinational European study. Pharmacoepidemiol Drug Saf. 2017;26(7):802–11.

76. Avery A, Barber N, Ghaleb M, Franklin BD, Armstrong S, Crowe S, et al. Investigating the prevalence and causes of prescribing errors in general practice: the PRACtICe study. London: General Medical Council; 2012. https://www.gmcuk.org/media/about/investigatingtheprevalenceandcausesofprescribingerrorsingeneralpracticethepracticestudyreoprtmay2012.pdf?la=en&hash=62C1821CA5CCC5A4868B86A83FEDE14283686C29. Accessed 15 Oct 2019.

77. Dornan T, Ashcroft D, Heathfield H, Lewis P, Miles J, Taylor D, et al. An in-depth investigation into causes of prescribing errors by foundation trainees in relation to their medical education: EQUIP study. London: General Medical Council; 2009. https://www.gmcuk.org/FINAL_Report_prevalence_and_causes_of_prescribing_errors.pdf_28935150.pdf. Accessed 15 Oct 2019.

78. Westbrook JI, Woods A, Rob MI, Dunsmuir WT, Day RO. Association of interruptions with an increased risk and severity of medication administration errors. Arch Intern Med. 2010;170(8):683–90.

79. Consuelo-Estrada JR, Gaona-Valle LS, Portillo-Rodríguez O. Lesiones por causa externa en el servicio de urgencias de un hospital en un periodo de cinco años. Gac Med Mex. 2018;154(3):302–9.

80. Zhang Y, Dong YJ, Webster CS, Ding XD, Liu XY, Chen WM, et al. The frequency and nature of drug administration error during anaesthesia in a Chinese hospital. Acta Anaesthesiol Scand. 2013;57(2):158–64.

81. Joint Commission International Standards for Hospital. 5th Edition. 2014. https://www.jointcommissioninternational.org/assets/3/7/Hospital-5E-Standards-Only-Mar2014.pdf. Accessed 15 Oct 2019.

82. University of Toronto, Institute for Safe Medication Practices Canada, Physicians for Responsible Opioid Prescribing. Navigating opioids for chronic pain. Toronto, ON: Institute for Safe Medication Practices Canada; 2019. https://www.ismpcanada.org/download/OpioidStewardship/navigating-opioids-11x17-canada.pdf. Accessed 15 Oct 2019.

83. Routledge PA. Safe prescribing: a titanic challenge. Br J Clin Pharmacol. 2012;74(4):676–84.

84. 5 Moments for medication safety. In: Patient Safety. Geneva: World Health Organization; 2019. https://www.who.int/patientsafety/medicationsafety/5moments/en/. Accessed 15 Oct 2019.

85. Fortescue EB, Kaushal R, Landrigan CP, McKenna KJ, Clapp MD, Federico F, et al. Prioritizing strategies for preventing medication errors and adverse drug events in pediatric inpatients. Pediatrics. 2003;111(4 Pt 1):722–9.

86. Kahn S, Abramson EL. What is new in paediatric medication safety? Arch Dis Child. 2019;104(6):596–9.

87. Beers MH, Ouslander JG, Rollingher I, Reuben DB, Brooks J, Beck JC. Explicit criteria for determining inappropriate medication use in nursing home residents. UCLA Division of Geriatric Medicine. Arch Intern Med. 1991;151(9):1825–32.

88. Gallagher P, O'Mahony D. STOPP (Screening Tool of Older Persons' potentially inappropriate Prescriptions): application to acutely ill elderly patients and comparison with Beers' criteria. Age Ageing. 2008;37(6):673–9.

89. Metsälä E, Vaherkoski U. Medication errors in elderly acute care—a systematic review. Scand J Caring Sci. 2014;28(1):12–28.

90. Lynch MM, Amoozegar JB, McClure EM, Squiers LB, Broussard CS, Lind JN, et al. Improving safe use of medications during pregnancy: the roles of patients, physicians, and pharmacists. Qual Health Res. 2017;27(13):2071–80.

91. Maxwell SRJ, Webb DJ. Improving medication safety: focus on prescribers and systems. Lancet. 2019;394(10195):283–5.

92. McDowell SE, Mt-Isa S, Ashby D, Ferner RE. Where errors occur in the preparation and administration of intravenous medicines: a systematic review and Bayesian analysis. Qual Saf Health Care. 2010;19(4):341–5.

93. Roumeliotis N, Sniderman J, Adams-Webber T, Addo N, Anand V, Rochon P, et al. Effect of electronic prescribing strategies on medication error and harm in hospital: a systematic review and meta-analysis. J Gen Intern Med. 2019;34(10):2210–23.

Digital Technology and Usability and Ergonomics of Medical Devices

32

Francesco Ranzani and Oronzo Parlangeli

32.1 Introduction

Trying to identify what digital medical technologies are today is a practically unresolvable task. Over the last few years, we have seen a radical change in these technologies; they have become not only extremely sophisticated and complex but also capable of maintaining evolving relationships with their users.

It is obvious that the benefits of this evolution are absolutely valuable, but several issues are linked to the evolutionary lines of medical devices and are often related to usability. In fact, the usability of digital medical devices (i.e., the level of effectiveness and efficiency provided by the device in interactive environments) and the level of user satisfaction in certain contexts of use [1] are definitely not satisfactory at present. Users of medical technology are among the most diverse, including doctors, nurses, technicians, administrators, and patients themselves or their families. Each type of user has different and sometimes conflicting needs, skills, and traits. The tools themselves can be so different that combining them under a single label seems excessively summary as well as inappropriate. We could define the term "medical device" to refer once and for all, say, to devices without any relational quality beyond those impressed on them by their designers (e.g., a scalpel). But the notion of a medical device also encompasses e-health records, robots that assist or take the place of human operators, and applications that inform and help patients, thus creating a dialogue between patients and healthcare professionals; often these systems create ecosystems in which, in addition to one or more human counterparts, they interact with each other.

On closer inspection, the problem of usability of medical devices cannot be tackled in isolation and must concern managerial and administrative aspects of the entire healthcare system. However, within this complexity, the design of each medical device must be tailored to the specific activities, objectives, competencies, and skills of those they assist. Just as the considerations relating to their evaluation both in the development phase and during their actual use are indispensable. Given the complexity of the socio-technical systems that are responsible for providing health services, the insufficient usability of medical devices is one of the major problems affecting the efficiency of the entire system and, more importantly, the health of the patient [2, 3]. Many

F. Ranzani (✉)
Centre for Clinical Risk Management and Patient Safety, Tuscany Region - WHO Collaborating Centre in Human Factors and Communication for the Delivery of Safe and Quality Care, Florence, Italy
e-mail: ranzanif@aou-careggi.toscana.it

O. Parlangeli
Department of Social, Political and Cognitive Sciences, University of Siena, Siena, Italy
e-mail: parlangeli@unisi.it

L. Donaldson et al. (eds.), *Textbook of Patient Safety and Clinical Risk Management*,
https://doi.org/10.1007/978-3-030-59403-9_32

studies in recent years have highlighted problems related to the usability of medical devices that have resulted in negative effects for the health of patients [4]. This paper will focus on a few studies in particular to shed some light on the nature of the problems and their consequences.

32.2   Some Studies on Medical Devices

Errors related to the use of medical devices can lead to serious damage to the patient and represent a frequent and sometimes silent cause of death. Numerous studies on errors in medicine clearly show a direct link between usability problems and errors, patient readmission, and injuries [5, 6]. As an example, it is worth noting that adverse events related to patient-controlled analgesia were reported almost 2500 times between 2003 and 2004. This figure seems even worse when we consider the fact that over 9000 adverse events occurred in the 5-year period from 2000 to 2005 [7, 8]. These errors are often attributable to bad interface design: cognitive ergonomics guidelines are very often violated though they could be beneficially applied to the design of healthcare systems and medical devices in order to minimize the chance of adverse events.

Nowadays, electronic medical devices have spread to all hospital and extra-hospital environments, including operating rooms, emergency rooms, radiology departments, laboratories, emergency vehicles, intensive care units, and even homes. The development process and the performance of these devices are affected by an infinite number of variables that are not always considered and whose consequences are not always foreseen. Among these variables it seems obvious to consider that the pervasive use of these instruments is compromised by sound interference, low lighting, reflections, and electrical interference. However, it is less commonly appreciated that operators, even experienced ones, are forced to continuously update their operational skills and develop new automatisms [9]. Performance can be further limited by stress, fatigue, and the application of incorrect procedures. This is compounded by the wide range of

devices that the operator uses over the course of a day. The physical, sensory, and mental capacities of health workers are variables that must be taken into account, especially since the use of equipment increases considerably from year to year.

Devices can only be used safely and effectively when the user, the activity, the context of use, the stress and fatigue levels, and the interactions between all these factors have been adequately evaluated during the design process. Keeping in mind the complexity of the factors involved, Schaeffer et al. [10] have studied the consequences of using two different models of insulin infusion pumps for patients. In their study, they linked the design principles of human factors with those of user interface design. More specifically, the authors correlated the programming errors of the instrument during data entry with different error categories, considering parameters such as blood glucose level or amount of carbohydrates. As a result of their evaluation, they were able to point out that, if certain developmental inefficiencies in the usability of the instrument had remained unresolved, adverse events could have occurred due to the release of inappropriate amounts of insulin, potentially having very serious consequences.

Other aspects relevant to the design of medical devices include population aging and consequent changes in users, such as reduced sensory capacities (e.g., decreased vision or hearing) and motor and cognitive abilities. Maša Isaković et al. [11] investigated elderly patients' ease in using a glucose self-monitoring application not specifically designed with them in mind. Their analysis showed that the most important points when designing an application for the elderly are the very basic aspects of the user interface: the size, visibility, and comprehensibility of buttons and symbols. For this purpose, the various distorting and illusory effects of perceptual processes should also be taken into account [12, 13]. Furthermore, the age-related deterioration of memory and a lack of familiarity with technology can cause user confusion and therefore lead to error. Although making applications suitable for all users would be a very difficult if not impossible task, creating different profiles for different accessibility groups seems to be the best performing solution. In this case, the involvement of users from the earliest stages of design has been shown to be essential.

In development teams, collaboration between people with different skills is fundamental. The study conducted by Fairbanks et al. [14] on defibrillators highlighted the importance of collaboration between clinicians and human factor experts. This study has pointed out that, although the collaborative design and the ergonomic evaluation of the user interface are well-established practices in the aeronautical and nuclear industry, most medical devices are not tested in all the contexts in which they will be used and with all future users. Defibrillators are perhaps the medical devices most exposed to critical situations. Problems such as the presence of too many buttons in a small area, the need for excessive scrolling to get to the desired setting, and lack of feedback in an emergency can be lethal. Whereas the market today offers many choices, an ergonomic approach should also guarantee the simplification of the organization of the health system, increasing the quality, efficiency, and safety of care. Managers and experts should consider medical devices that are truly functional for clinical-assistance activities and that aid workers in carrying out their daily tasks with greater satisfaction and effectiveness, with the added benefit of consequent savings in terms of a reduced need for training.

One of the aspects of evaluation studies that can prove to be difficult is the recruitment of subjects. Healthcare personnel, doctors, and nurses are often overworked professionals, which makes it difficult to involve them in evaluation circumstances beyond their working environments. To overcome this obstacle, Bond et al. [15] had evaluation sessions take place during a conference attended by end users, allowing direct interaction with the medical devices they wanted to evaluate. More specifically, their evaluations concerned one software application, a medical diagnostic tool (ECG viewer), and a medical research tool (electrode misplacement simulator). From their study, interesting possibilities emerge for conducting evaluations in a way that does not involve taking the end users inside laboratories, but instead finding large gatherings of end users and taking the opportunity to have end users interact with the device at their convenience.

Another study is particularly interesting for at least two reasons: it is a longitudinal analysis that was carried out in two different phases over 7 years, and concerns users who are sometimes neglected in usability studies, that is, radiology technicians. In this study [16], six radiology technicians were observed while performing radiological examinations (i.e., Computed Tomography) as part of their usual activities in a hospital emergency department. The authors considered variables such as the occurrence of errors and the time needed to conduct various aspects of the examination. The same technicians were interviewed about their thoughts on the diagnostic system they were using regarding aspects such as ease of use, cognitive effort required, and the possibility of it leading to errors. The results of this analysis highlighted several problems related to the usability of the system, both in itself and as part of a broader operational context. Most notably, it became apparent over the years that all noticeable improvements, such as a reduction in the time needed to carry out the examination, were in fact attributable to an increase in the skill of the operators. The system updates made between the first and second evaluations had not led to any improvement in usability.

32.3 Beneficiaries of Usable Medical Devices

Direct and indirect users of medical devices have different needs and characteristics. To varying degrees, any individual can take part in the improvement of device usability and effectiveness for their particular context and needs. In any case, however different the needs may be, the following objectives are universal when improving usability:

- To reduce the number of accidents and deaths due to incorrect, ineffective, or inappropriate use of medical devices.
- To improve the ease of use for users as well as users' well-being.
- To comply with current regulations and cultural needs of the various countries.

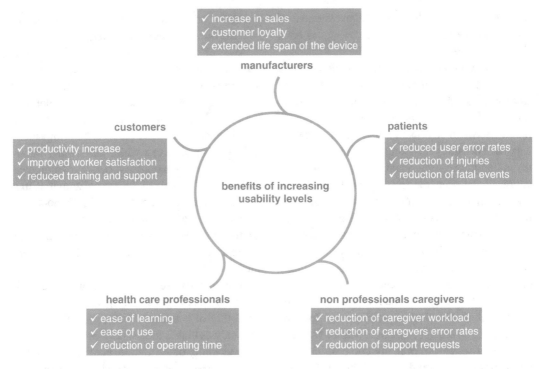

Fig. 32.1 The main beneficiaries of the increased levels of usability of medical instruments and their benefits

Based on these considerations, Wiklund et al. [17] stated that ensuring adequate usability of medical instruments is as much a moral imperative as a path to economic benefits (see Fig. 32.1).

Efforts to ensure adequate usability must involve all beneficiaries. Each user group is a vector of specific needs and requirements and is called to participate in the evolutionary development of medical devices.

32.4 Usability Evaluation

Various government authorities (see, for example, the FDA's webpage[1]) have recommended that the activities and processes necessary to ensure the usability of medical devices should be divided into (a) processes relating to devices not yet on the market and (b) processes relating to products already in use.

For devices not yet on the market, the indications, essentially addressed to the manufacturing

companies, guide the preparation of a final report that clearly expresses the results achieved regarding the usability of the product.

Therefore, the report must contain clearly and in detail:

- Any conclusions reached during evaluation.
- A description of the device's target users, applications, and contexts, and any training necessary for its operation.
- A description of the user interface.
- Any problems highlighted during evaluation.
- An analysis of the risks and dangers associated with the use of the device.
- A summary of preliminary results.
- A description and categorization of tasks along with their critical aspects.
- The details of the evaluation, based on the principles of human factors.

Following the release of the product on the market, issues may arise such as potentially or actually dangerous circumstances, errors during use, and improper use, even if the product was developed following correct usability guide-

[1] https://www.fda.gov/medical-devices/human-factors-and-medical-devices

Fig. 32.2 The process of user-centered design (UCD) in which, starting from user and market analysis, iterative evaluation cycles, with the user as the focal point, are carried out before the product launch

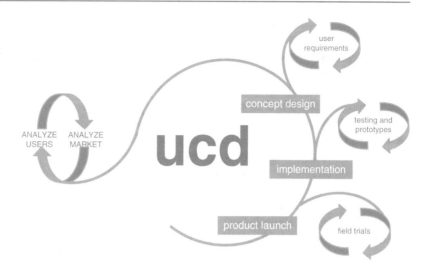

lines.[2] In this case, the priority becomes the clear communication of the event to the manufacturer of the device so that the device's usability may be improved further. Here also, the FDA recommends the preparation of a report describing with as much precision as possible the context in which the adverse event occurred. In particular, the following information is required:

- The device type, manufacturer, brand, and lot number if applicable.
- The exact location of the event.
- If a patient or device operator was harmed.
- If there was a problem with the device itself, such as a defect, malfunction, and break.
- Whether someone was directly operating the device at the time of the event, and if so, who.
- If there were other therapies being used on the patient at the time of the event that may have caused or contributed to the event.

Evidently, the FDA's statements have as their conceptual basis user-centered design (UCD) [18] (see Fig. 32.2). UCD considers the user its focal point, rather than technology. In the realization of a product, the specific needs, traits, and limitations of the end user are the most important

functional needs. To this end, development must be carried out at different levels by multidisciplinary teams of marketing representatives, developers, technicians, and usability experts. The goal of UCD is to understand what users really want and need in order to produce interactive tools that foster a productive and satisfactory dialogue between user and device.

What this team is specifically called to do can vary depending on many factors, from the company's positioning to how many products the company has already put on the market, from how innovative the product is to the type of target users and whether that type is more or less precisely defined. In "The invisible computer" [19], Donald Norman states that it is extremely important to perform a preliminary assessment of user needs and then move on to a market analysis. This sequence of analysis is already itself an iterative cycle, since the market analysis should serve to re-evaluate and reframe users' needs in terms of their definitive requirements and characteristics. Based on the results obtained, a series of iterative cycles is initiated, towards the specification of the product (concept design), its realization in the form of prototypes which gradually grow closer and closer to the final product (implementation), and experimentation on the usability of the product in the field before the product is definitively released (product launch).

Each of these cycles aims to make user-device interaction more fluid, responsive, and error-free.

[2] (https://www.fda.gov/medical-devices/human-factors-and-medical-devices/postmarket-information-device-surveillance-and-reporting-processes)

Any difficulty encountered by the user poses a challenge to form new design hypotheses leading to alternative design solutions. Ultimately, UCD aims to maximize the usability of a product. ISO 9241 [1] defines usability as the "the extent to which a product can be used by specified users to achieve specified goals with effectiveness, efficiency and satisfaction in a specified context of use." To achieve adequate usability, designers must be able to respond adequately to these questions:

- Effectiveness: does the product support the user in achieving their objective?
- Efficiency: does the product allow the user to achieve their goals without unnecessary effort, without wasting time, and without generating mistakes?
- Satisfaction: does the use of the product represent a positive experience for the user, meeting not only instrumental requirements but also cognitive and emotional needs?

As defined, these questions must be answered in the affirmative, taking into account the specified users and the specified contexts of use.

32.4.1 Methods for Usability Assessment

The methods that have been developed over the years for the assessment of usability can be divided into two main categories: those carried out exclusively by experts and those involving a variable number of the end users. The methods carried out exclusively by experts are observational or inspectional in nature, while those involving end users, whether conducted in the laboratory or in the field, almost always consist of having the users perform tasks with the device in order to measure the distance between what the users perceive and how they interpret it, as well as between intention and action. The time and resources available are very often the main factors in the choice of methods used for the collection of end user requirements. For this reason, the most pragmatic and rapid methods are described below, since they allow the collection of large amounts of data in a reasonably short time while minimizing

costs, possibly by leveraging several methodologies at once. The methods that involve expert analysis include cognitive task analysis, heuristic evaluation, cognitive walkthrough, and the Delphi Method. One method that involves both experts and end users is contextual inquiry. Users, on the other hand, are usually involved in usability tests and focus groups.

Cognitive task analysis

Cognitive Task Analysis is a technique—more accurately a set of techniques—which examines the cognitive nature of tasks by analyzing and breaking down the activities into specific actions, identifying their relative frequency and difficulty [20]. A fundamental part of the technique is the elicitation of the experts' own knowledge, even tacit knowledge. This type of analysis allows the designers to create a practical hierarchy of interventions and therefore plan the redesign of the system around the most critical elements.

Heuristic evaluation

Heuristic evaluation is a low-cost technique that works well for medical devices and can generally detect the main problems in a rather short time. It can also be very useful in cases where contextual observation cannot be applied or where confidentiality may be restrictive.

The technique is usually based on guidelines or heuristics which are used by experts to inspect the technology under evaluation [21–23]. The guidelines have been refined over the years in the field of cognitive ergonomics. The application of this technique usually requires at least two experts to independently explore all components of the system and detect any violations of the appropriate guidelines, noting the severity of each violation. The detection of violations may also provide indications for the redesign of the system.

Cognitive walkthrough

Like heuristic evaluation, cognitive walkthrough is entrusted to experienced staff and not to end users [24]. Often following task analysis, a heuristic evaluation requires an expert to complete a series of tasks to test the system's comprehensibility and learning curve for a novice user. Essentially, in situations where the availability of end users and financial resources proves restrictive, experts may leverage their theoretical and practical knowledge of usability issues to evaluate a product. Another advantage of this method is that the evaluator's sensitivity eliminates the bias often found in less experienced users who attribute shortcomings in performance to some weakness in the device rather than their lack of experience.

Delphi Method

After identifying all user-related requirements for a product, it may be difficult to set priorities. The Delphi method is by definition an iterated sequence of steps with the aim of ensuring that opinions converge as iterations progress [25]. Starting with fairly generic questions, experts discuss relevant issues and exchange opinions which can then be cross-referenced to provide the basis for a second session of deeper elaborations. From time to time, a summary of the previous session's discussion can be provided to the experts. In the third and usually last meeting, a series of questions are asked in order to arrive at a conclusive consensus on the importance of the different factors considered.

Contextual inquiry

Contextual inquiry is a particularly pragmatic technique suitable for the design of a new product or the redesign of an existing one. The activity of the expert tends to focus on the user: the expert asks the users questions about their experience as they interact with the device, such as questions about what is happening and why, and any possible improvements to the system [26]. Designer and user collaborate in this way in an almost symbiotic relationship to uncover information essential for product development. To implement this methodology in highly complex healthcare contexts it is often necessary to use simulations of real scenarios to avoid situations that could be dangerous for operators and patients.

Usability test

Usability tests conducted with users can identify and quantify different variables such as the frequency and type of errors made by users when interacting with a device, the time needed to complete different tasks, and the frequency and nature of requests for support [27, 28]. Whenever possible, these tests are conducted in the laboratory and involve a limited number of users that are representative of end users in general. In preparation for the execution of the test, it is important to establish the preliminary activity of selecting the tasks the user must try to perform and the techniques for recording the user's activity. In addition to highlighting critical issues of which the user is normally unaware, usability tests are also commonly chosen to collect information on the user's experience, satisfaction, and opinions on variables such as the attractiveness and the perceived usefulness of the system.

Focus groups

Focus groups are widely used, not only in healthcare but in all contexts that adopt a user-centered approach. A focus group consists of one (or more) experimenter(s)/facilitator(s) and a group of participants representing the end users [29]. The fundamental component of its success is the ability of the facilitator to animate the discussion among the group of people in search of useful ideas for the evaluation and/or development of a device. For focus groups to work it is essential that the facilitator follows simple rules such as providing everyone with clear, basic information about the purpose of the meeting, using terminology that is easily understandable by all, listening respectfully, and employing a strong dose of empathy.

Adequate tools (e.g., notes, audio recordings, video recordings) must be integrated into the realization of a focus group to keep track of all the information, whether implicit or explicit, provided by the participants.

32.4.2 The Usability Assessments in Reality

To date, there are no clear indications on which methodologies to adopt in order to maximize the amount of information gained from the evaluation of medical equipment. Very often the path followed by evaluators is the one that appears to be the most informative given the limitations of the context within which evaluations are to be carried out [30]. In order to identify the path usually taken by the various researchers involved in the evaluation of medical devices, Campoe [31] conducted a meta-analysis on relevant studies published between 1993 and 2012. Following preliminary research, she identified 886 papers that, after several rounds of refinement, were reduced to only 18. The analysis of these 18 papers showed that half of the studies on the usability of medical devices adopted only one analytical method which was either based on heuristics or involved end users. The other half adopted an approach integrating two or more methods.

The results of this review are not always methodologically sound. For example, the users had not been described in any detail: in most studies, only the demographics of the users were described, and in six of the studies not even those were considered. However, even when studies did report more information on user characteristics such as their level of professional experience, they did not use these variables to account for the results [31].

The task descriptions did not fare much better. In fact, only six studies reported in some detail the tasks used during the evaluation, relating them to the complexity, duration, and frequency of the operational process. However, the major weakness found in these studies lies in their lack of explanation of the reference environments used to evaluate tools that are often used in direct conjunction with other devices or that may have varying uses as determined by the operational context. The analysis by Campoe [31] showed that 11 studies reported the kind of environment in which the evaluation test took place (i.e., the hospital, operating room, etc.), but only 2

described the physical characteristics of the environment in which the device would be actually used. Complete negligence was found regarding the treatment of technical, social, and cultural characteristics of the reference environments: none of the 18 studies treated these characteristics as relevant factors for the usability of the device under evaluation.

32.5 Conclusion

The solution to this sort of methodological anarchy among usability studies cannot come from the enforcement of rules, codes, laws, or compliance with standards. The medical device ecosystem is in fact undergoing continuous and rapid evolution, which often produces solutions that exceed the development goals contemplated by rules and standards. In fact, regulatory systems can often steer the development of medical devices towards solutions that have little to do with everyday practice or even hamper day-to-day operations [32].

Therefore, many aspects of the processes that ensure the usability of medical devices need to be reformulated or reframed in an absolutely innovative way. In this regard, Vincent and colleagues [32] have argued that, with respect to several innovations in the medical field, it is not useful to reference pre-existing norms, standards, or well-established evaluation procedures. For example, 3D printers enable the rapid production of precisely shaped components. But there are obvious difficulties regarding the quality control of the components produced. If we then consider the usability of personal, mobile medical devices, it is clear that the standards developed so far do not effectively guide the realization of products to really meet the needs of each user. Finally, the issue of ensuring usability can be further exemplified by the fact that the increasingly ubiquitous smartphone applications, including various health-related applications that are now within each individual's reach, can receive formal certifications and approvals not on the basis of their real content, but mostly of how they are presented.

Technological advancement, as far as medical instruments are concerned, opens up obvious and serious problems, difficulties that clearly pose a challenge that has yet to be solved. However, the most innovative medical devices are also those that promise hitherto unexpected possibilities and benefits for the health of patients and broaden the horizon for the development of novel methods that will ensure proper usability [32].

References

1. International Organization of Standards. ISO 9241-11. Guidance on usability. Geneva, Switzerland: International Organization of Standards; 1998.
2. Middleton B, Bloomrosen M, Dente MA, et al. Enhancing patient safety and quality of care by improving the usability of electronic health record systems: recommendations from AMIA. J Am Med Inform Assoc. 2013;20(e1):e2–8. https://doi.org/10.1136/amiajnl-2012-001458.
3. Gardner RL, Cooper E, Haskell J, Harris DA, Poplau S, Kroth PJ, Linzer M. Physician stress and burnout: the impact of health information technology. J Am Med Inform Assoc. 2019;26(2):106–14. https://doi.org/10.1093/jamia/ocy145.
4. U.S. Food and Drug Administration. Draft guidance for industry and food and drug administration staff – applying human factors and usability engineering to optimize medical device design. Rockville, MD: Center for Devices and Radiological Health - Office of Device Evaluation; 2011. http://www.fda.gov/MedicalDevices/DeviceRegulationandGuidance/GuidanceDocuments/ucm259748.htm.
5. Powell-Cope G, Nelson AL, Patterson ES. Patient care technology and safety. In: Hughs RG, editor. Patient safety and quality: an evidence-based handbook for nurses. Rockville, MD: Agency for Healthcare Research and Quality; 2008.
6. Reed TL, Kaufman-Rivi D. Management & technology. FDA adverse event problem codes: standardizing the classification of device and patient problems associated with medical device use. Biomed Instrum Technol. 2010;44(3):248–56.
7. Meissner B, Nelson W, Hicks R, Sikirica V, Gagne J, Schein J. The rate and costs attributable to intravenous 2013 International Symposium on Human Factors and Ergonomics in Health Care: advancing the cause 129 patient-controlled analgesia errors. Hosp Pharm. 2009;44(4):312–24. https://doi.org/10.1310/hpj4404-312.
8. Hicks RW, Sikirica V, Nelson W, Schein JR, Cousins DD. Medication errors involving patient-controlled analgesia. Am J Health Syst Pharm. 2008;65(5):429–40. https://doi.org/10.2146/ajhp070194.
9. Cassano C, Colantuono A, De Simone G, Giani A, Liston PM, Marchigiani E, Talla G, Parlangeli O. Developments and problems in the man-machine relationship in computed tomography (CT). In: Bagnara S, Tartaglia R, Albolino S, Alexander T, Fujita Y, editors. Proceedings of the 20th Congress of the International Ergonomics Association (IEA 2018), Advances in intelligent systems and computing. Cham: Springer; 2019. p. 822. https://doi.org/10.1007/978-3-319-96077-7_52.
10. Schaeffer NE, Parks LJ, Verhoef ET, Bailey TS, Schorr AB, Davis T, Halford J, Sulik B. Usability and training differences between two personal insulin pumps. J Diabetes Sci Technol. 2015;9(2):221–30. https://doi.org/10.1177/1932296814555158.
11. Isaković M, Sedlar U, Bešter JJ. Usability pitfalls of diabetes mHealth apps for the elderly. J Diabetes Res. 2016;2016:1604609. https://doi.org/10.1155/2016/1604609.
12. Bridgeman B, Peery S, Anand S. Interaction of cognitive and sensorimotor maps of visual space. Percept Psychophys. 1997;59:456–69.
13. Guidi S, Parlangeli O, Bettella S, Roncato S. Features of the selectivity for contrast polarity in contour integration revealed by a novel tilt illusion. Perception. 2011;40:1357–75.
14. Fairbanks R, Shah M, Caplan S, Marks A, Bishop P. Defibrillator usability study among paramedics. Proc Hum Factors Ergonom Soc Annu Meeting. 2004;48:1768. https://doi.org/10.1177/154193120404801530.
15. Bond RR, Finlay DD, Nugent CD, Moore G, Guldenring D. A usability evaluation of medical software at an expert conference setting. Comput Methods Prog Biomed. 2014;113(1):383–95. https://doi.org/10.1016/j.cmpb.2013.10.006.
16. Parlangeli O, Liston PM, Marchigiani E, Bracci M, Giani A. Perceptions and use of computed tomography in a hospital emergency department: technicians' perspectives. Hum Factors. 2019;62:5. https://doi.org/10.1177/0018720819841758.
17. Wiklund M, Kendler J, Strochlic A. Usability testing of medical devices. Boca Raton, FL: CRC Press, Taylor & Francis Group; 2016.
18. Norman DA, Draper S. User centered system design: new perspectives on human-computer interaction. Mahwah, NJ: Lawrence Erlbaum Associates; 1986.
19. Norman DA. The invisible computer. Cambridge, MA: The MIT Press; 1999.
20. Luczak H. Task analysis. In: Salvendy G, editor. The handbook of human factors and ergnomonics. New York, NY: Wiley; 1997. p. 340–416.
21. Nielsen J, Molich R. Heuristic evaluation of user interfaces. In: Proceedings of the SIGCHI Conference on Human Factors in Computing Systems: empowering people, Seattle, WA; 1990. p. 249–56.
22. Cockton G, Lavery D, Woolrych A. Inspection-based methods. In: Jacko JA, Sears A, editors. The human-computer interaction handbook. Mahwah, NJ: Lawrence Erlbaum Associates; 2003. p. 1118–38.

23. Parlangeli O, Mengoni G, Guidi S. The effect of system usability and multitasking activities in distance learning. In: Proceedings of the CHItaly conference, 13–16 September. Alghero: ACM Library; 2011. p. 59–64.

24. Wharton C, Rieman J, Lewis C, Polson P. The cognitive walkthrough: a practitioner's guide. In: Nielsen J, Mack L, editors. Usability inspections methods. New York: Wiley; 1994. p. 105–40.

25. Goldman K, Gross P, Heeren C, Herman G, Kaczmarczyk L, Loui MC, Zilles C. Identifying important and difficult concepts in introductory computing courses using a Delphi process. ACM SIGCSE Bull. 2008;40(1):256–60.

26. Holtzblatt K, Wendell JB, Wood S. Rapid contextual design: a how-to guide to key techniques for user-centered design. San Francisco, CA: Morgan Kaufmann; 2005.

27. Dumas J, Redish J. A practical guide to usability testing (Revised edition). Exeter, UK: Intellect; 1999.

28. Rubin J, Chisnell D. Handbook of usability testing (2nd Edition): how to plan, design, and conduct effective tests. New York: Wiley; 2008.

29. Krueger RA, Casey MA. Focus groups: a practical guide for applied research. 3rd ed. Thousand Oaks, CA: Sage Publications; 2000.

30. Caratozzolo MC, Bagnara S, Parlangeli O. Use of ICT to supply health-care services to nomadic patients: an explorative survey. Behav Inform Technol. 2008;27(4):354–0.

31. Campoe KR. Medical device usability analyses: an integrative review. Proc Int Symp Hum Factors Ergonom Health Care. 2013;2(1):123–30. https://doi.org/10.1177/2327857913021024.

32. Vincent CJ, Niezen G, O'Kane AA, Stawarz K. Can standards and regulations keep up with health technology? JMIR Mhealth Uhealth. 2015;3(2):e64. https://doi.org/10.2196/mhealth.3918.

Lessons Learned from the Japan Obstetric Compensation System for Cerebral Palsy: A Novel System of Data Aggregation, Investigation, Amelioration, and No-Fault Compensation

33

Shin Ushiro, Antonio Ragusa, and Riccardo Tartaglia

Cerebral palsy is a pathological condition whose prevention and treatment have been immensely studied by experts in perinatal medicine and pediatric neurology. Despite this, it is still one of the main concerns nowadays in many countries, not only for scientific reasons but for legal ones also. For instance, in Japan, an increase in lawsuits relating to cerebral palsy was observed more than a decade ago, after healthcare resources in perinatal medicine had increasingly shrunk and had become fragile under the growing burden for physicians and midwives to provide advanced treatment, emergent care, high-risk treatment, and so on. Young physicians did not specialize in obstetrics because of the increased burden, which gave rise to a vicious cycle of shrinking resources in perinatal medi-

cine. To address this issue, the Japan Obstetric Compensation System for Cerebral Palsy (JOCS-CP) was urgently introduced in 2009 to investigate, develop preventive measures, and award monetary compensation on a no-fault basis, with the Japan Council for Quality Health Care (JQ) as its operating organization (Fig. 33.1). It has so far produced annual reports on the prevention of cerebral palsy for nine consecutive years including numerical data and specific themes relating to the occurrence and prevention of cerebral palsy. The success of the system is a good reference for responding to adverse events which may happen in and have a vast impact on perinatal care. Therefore, this chapter focuses on cerebral palsy with primary reference to materials published by the JOCS-CP in the field of perinatal medicine. The aim of this chapter is to learn about the issues mentioned above and to discuss the significance and impact of introducing a nationwide system like the JOCS-CP. It describes knowledge and idea to questions of "Why cerebral palsy is highlighted among adverse event in obstetrics?", "How the no-fault compensation/investigation/prevention system could be introduced?", "What has been achieved by the system?", and "How cerebral palsy is prevented?".

S. Ushiro
Division of Patient Safety, Kyushu University Hospital, Fukuoka, Japan

Japan Council for Quality Health Care, Tokyo, Japan
e-mail: ushiro@surg2.med.kyushu-u.ac.jp

A. Ragusa (✉)
Obstetrics and Gynecology Department, Fatebebefratelli Hospital; Isola Tiberina, Rome, Italy

R. Tartaglia
Institute of Management, School of Advance Studies Sant'Anna, Pisa, Italy

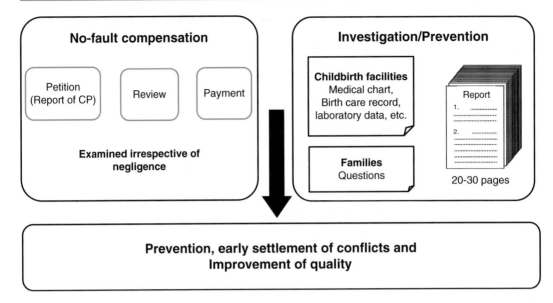

Fig. 33.1 No-fault compensation/investigation/prevention system for cerebral palsy. (The Japan Obstetric Compensation System (2009))

33.1 Context for the Introduction of the JOCS-CP: Increasing Conflict Over Cerebral Palsy and Hopes for a No-Fault Compensation System

According to the numbers of lawsuits filed in 2004 against each medical specialty, per registered physician, the obstetrics and gynecology rate was the highest (12.4%), a heavy burden for all obstetricians involved. One assumption made about the obstetrics lawsuits was that a significant portion of them related to cerebral palsy. It should be noted that recent studies have speculated that most cases of cerebral palsy were not related to procedures performed by obstetricians and midwives, although there actually are a small number of cases caused by violations of current quality-of-care guidelines and/or standards. In general, it is difficult to distinguish between negligence and other causes of cerebral palsy. For example, a child may develop profound cerebral palsy after a normal or seemingly normal pregnancy and delivery. The onset of cerebral palsy is

likely to provoke turmoil leading to legal action taken by the family, which raises questions about the delivery procedure itself and the family's worries and anxieties about the long-term care needed for rearing their disabled child. To address this issue, obstetricians and relevant experts in Japan have long studied and explored the possibility of introducing a no-fault compensation system for cerebral palsy at the national scale to reverse the persistent high frequency of conflict around cerebral palsy. Concurrently, the Japan Medical Association (JMA) has been considering no-fault compensation since the early 1970s. Its 1972 report entitled "The Legal Proceedings for Medical Accidents and the Relevant Theory" touched upon the following three items regarding institutionalization of such a system:

1. Prompt compensation should be provided in cases of medical accidents for which a physician is deemed responsible after a thorough review of the case.
2. A unique national compensation scheme should be devised to cover cases of accidents

not attributed to a medical procedure conducted by a physician, that is, cases that were inevitable during clinical care.

3. A unique national system should be established for settling disputes, functioning independently of the judicial court system.

Regarding the first point, the JMA Physician's Liability Compensation System was launched in 1973 in line with the indemnity insurance system. However, neither the second nor the third point were realized in the following decades. In the early 2000s, concerns about patient safety, the shortage of obstetricians and pediatricians, and low national birth rates rapidly emerged in Japan. This eventually prompted the JMA to publish a report entitled "Toward Compensation in Cases Related to Medical Management and Procedures" in January of 2006. It states that "although it is ideal to launch a compensation system to cover entire medical specialties, a compensation system with a narrower scope for cases with neurological sequela, i.e., cerebral palsy, should be given the highest priority for institutionalization." The JMA board member who supervised the compilation of the report was an obstetrician and vice president who, years later, became the president of the Japan Association of Obstetricians and Gynaecologists (JAOG). In August of 2006, the JMA published another report compiled by a project committee on the progress of the implementation of a compensation system for disabilities caused by cerebral palsy. It set forth concrete and detailed reasons to launch a no-fault compensation system specific to cerebral palsy. The project was further promoted by a report from the Policy Research Committee of the Liberal Democratic Party (LDP) which was at the time and still is a member of a leading political alliance. The report was titled "The Framework of No-fault Compensation System for Obstetric Care," commonly referred to as the "LDP Framework." The report described the perceived significance of launching no-fault compensation system for cerebral palsy by declaring, "It usu-

ally is difficult to identify malpractice regarding an adverse event during delivery, and those cases are apt to be contested in court. The frequency of disputes is one reason for the shortage of obstetricians." The LDP Framework proposes that, to secure safe and trustworthy perinatal care that benefits obstetricians, patients, and families, a new system should: (1) compensate patients who develop impairments possibly caused by adverse obstetric events, (2) swiftly resolve and settle all disputes, and (3) improve the quality of obstetrical care by investigating cerebral palsy cases. Immediately upon the release of the LDP Framework, significant official and unofficial attention focused on JQ, proposing that it should be an operating organization for the novel system. JQ was the natural choice because it had previously conducted projects on quality and safety improvement, such as hospital accreditation and Adverse Event Reporting and Learning Systems. In response to high expectations, JQ established in 2007 the Division of Introductory Work on the Japan Obstetric Compensation System for Cerebral Palsy (JOCS-CP) as a temporary agent to introduce the JOCS-CP in Japanese healthcare system. At this point, it should be noted that political decision added momentum to the growing demand by academic society to launch the JOCS-CP; JQ was considered to be the right choice to operate the JOCS-CP because it was a neutral body related to quality and safety improvement in healthcare. The secretary installed in JQ for working on the JOCS-CP during preparatory period intensively studied potential obstacles for the launch of a system and, in January of 2008, finally issued a report which described the detailed design of the system. After careful review of the report, the JQ board accepted the role of managing organization of the system in March of 2008. Subsequently, the JOCS-CP was launched on the 1st of January 2009, and has been in operation since, undergoing a revision in 2015 that saw the expansion of eligibility criteria with the full support of stakeholders.

33.2 The Meaning of "No-Fault Compensation" in the JOCS-CP

The term "no-fault compensation" could be defined in multiple ways. Besides the JOCS-CP, another compensation system in Japan—a system regarding medication side effects, managed by the governmental Pharmaceuticals and Medical Devices Agency (PMDA)—has been described as a no-fault compensation system because it compensates individuals who suffer medication side effects provided that the medication was prescribed and administered appropriately and that the medication is the probable cause of the adverse side effects. The system is designed based on the idea that adverse side effects can occur even when appropriate medication is prescribed and administered. On the other hand, no-fault compensation might refer to a system which provides compensation no matter the degree of any suspected negligence. This is an idea of the JOCS-CP which is different from the one adopted by the civil judicial system.

Specifically, the LDP Framework states that the JOCS-CP will compensate patients with cerebral palsy that was possibly caused by delivery procedures regardless of the extent of obstetrical negligence. Therefore, cerebral palsy cases obviously caused by congenital defects, such as cerebral anomalies, and thus not related to the obstetrical procedures are not eligible for compensation under the system.

33.3 Compensation Driven by the Indemnity Insurance Mechanism

The two main pillars of the JOCS-CP are compensation and investigation/prevention (Fig. 33.1). Compensation works through a mechanism of indemnity insurance services provided by the alliance of indemnity insurance companies under contract with JQ, as indicated in "The Framework of the No-fault Compensation System in Obstetric Care" (Fig. 33.2). As described within this framework, a childbirth

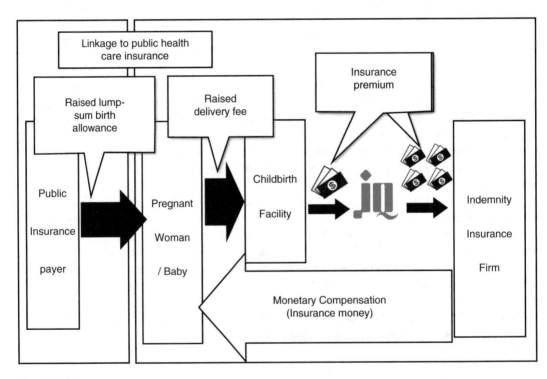

Fig. 33.2 Finance

facility (1) registers with the JOCS-CP under a unified agreement, and (2) agrees to pay a compensation premium to an indemnity insurance company through JQ when a baby is born and cooperate with JQ for investigation when a baby develops profound cerebral palsy. The facility must notify pregnant women of the compensation for a baby with profound cerebral palsy by submitting the "Registration Certificate for Pregnant Women" to them. Childbirth facilities pay insurance premiums as high as JPY 16,000 (USD 140/EUR 120) which are paid to the indemnity insurance companies through JQ. At the inception of the system, the premium was JPY 30,000 (USD 265/EUR 225) for every baby born between 2009 and 2014. The reason for the subsequent reduction of the premium will be described later. JQ mediates the transaction, collecting payments from the registered childbirth facilities and regularly depositing lump sums with the indemnity insurance companies. Children who develop profound cerebral palsy are assessed by the Review Committee to see whether they meet the eligibility criteria for compensation. When a case is approved, monetary compensation is awarded as required under the compensation agreement between the childbirth facility and the family. For practical reasons, the compensation is directly paid to the patient's guardian by the indemnity insurance company. According to LDP Framework, the Ministry of Health, Labour and Welfare (MHLW) increased the lump sum childbirth compensation by an amount equivalent to that of the insurance premium in response to the likely increase in childbirth costs set by childbirth facilities. Between 2009 and 2014, the amount was JPY 30,000 (USD 265/EUR 225), and, since 2015, the amount has been JPY 16,000 (USD 140/EUR 120). Thus, the lump sum payment of public health insurance for childbirth has served as a financial source of compensation in the JOCS-CP. This link between compensation and public health insurance appears to qualify the JOCS-CP as a quasi-public system. The amount of lump sum compensation was stable after the system launched, at JPY 420,000 (USD 3700/EUR 3150) for babies born in registered childbirth

facilities; then, in 2015, the insurance premiums reduced to JPY 16,000 from JPY 30,000. The standard compensation agreement stipulates that lump sum payments should generally be paid within 60 days of a petitioner's complete submission, while it has actually been paid as swift as 25 days or less after the petition. Similarly, annual installment should be paid within 60 days of the day of the month in which the child was born or of the receipt of all required forms, whichever comes first.

33.4 Monetary Compensation

The total monetary compensation per patient amounts to JPY 30,000,000 (USD 266,000/EUR 225,000) in two forms of payment: a lump sum of JPY 6,000,000 (USD 53,300/EUR 45,200) and annual installments of JPY 24,000,000 (USD 212,700/EUR 179,800). Installments of JPY 1,200,000 (USD 18,600/EUR 15,800) are paid once a year for 20 years starting in the birth year of the claimant and ending on their 19th birthday. For example, regarding the petition and review process of events that occurred in the first year of a baby's life, the review of all cases for children born in 2009 must be completed by 2015 because a petition may be filed until the claimant's fifth birthday (as stated in the standard compensation agreement). Petitions for patients born in 2010 (open until 2016) or later are processed under the same guideline.

33.5 Epidemiology of Adverse Events

1. **Prevalence of cerebral palsy**

   The prevalence of cerebral palsy has been reported on by various research groups. In designing the JOCS-CP, JQ explored existing data on Japanese childbirth from Okinawa Prefecture, Himeji City, and a part of the Tokyo metropolitan area. Among these studies, data from Okinawa Prefecture was statistically accurate enough to be used in the designing process of the JOCS-CP. It gave a figure of 2.3 cases of cerebral palsy per 1000 live births which is comparable to rates determined in other countries.

2. Estimates of annual numbers of eligible individuals in the JOCS-CP

Eligibility criteria and estimates of the numbers of eligible individuals are crucial elements of the system for appreciating the financial scale. These items were carefully assessed based on cerebral palsy registration data from Okinawa Prefecture, the city of Himeji, and a part of the Tokyo metropolitan area. The approximate number of eligible individuals per year was estimated to be "500–800 persons annually at maximum," which the system took into account to ensure its financial sustainability.

3. Revision of the JOCS-CP including re-estimation of the number of eligible individuals

In 2014, it became urgent to improve JOCS-CP financing because the excessive collection of insurance premiums since the system began was raising serious questions in the Japanese parliament, among public payers, in the MHLW, and among relevant entities and clinicians. Although the enumeration of eligible babies born in the first year had not yet been completed, the estimation was made again in 2015 in a more accurate way than that adopted on small scale at the inception of the system. In particular, cerebral palsy registration research had been expanded in Okinawa Prefecture and other institutional data were obtained from consulting facilities for physically impaired persons and relevant medical institutions in Tochigi Prefecture and Mie Prefecture with the help of researchers in those regions. Ultimately, it turned out to be difficult to make use of data from Tochigi Prefecture and Mie Prefecture as they were not reliable enough for making accurate estimations, and so only the data from Okinawa Prefecture was employed to compute a point estimate of 481 and an interval estimate of 340–623, with a 95% confidence interval. Concurrently, the JOCS-CP's eligibility crite-

ria were revised as "born at 32 or more weeks of gestational age and 1400-g or more birth weight" giving rise to new point and interval estimates of 571 and 423–719, respectively. The revised criteria were put into effect in January of 2015.

4. Statistics of eligible individuals— Epidemiology of profound cerebral palsy in the JOCS-CP

The review procedure is carried out along with the standard compensation agreement. Briefly, a childbirth facility insured by the JOCS-CP files a petition with JQ, which must be accompanied by certification verifying the diagnosis of profound cerebral palsy by a qualified physician. The certification form must provide relevant information, such as detailed diagnostic and clinical data on the patient. Since scientific knowledge and expertise are necessary for diagnosis, the certification must be issued by physicians certified by the Japanese Society of Child Neurology and/ or registered physicians as defined by Article 15 of the Physically Disabled Persons Welfare Act. Qualified physicians that agree to participate in the review process are voluntarily registered with the JOCS-CP, and their identities affiliations are disclosed on its website; as of June 2019, 511 qualified physicians were registered. The petition undergoes preliminary review and then enters a queue awaiting approval by the Review Committee based on the eligibility criteria. The review process is fundamentally based on documents that demonstrate compatibility with general criteria and exclusion criteria. Upon approval, the JQ board must authorize the petition, which is the final step of the review process. The petitioner (i.e., the childbirth facility) is notified of the approval, which is promptly followed by payment of monetary compensation in the form of a lump sum and annual installments. Petitioners whose cases do not satisfy the general criteria may still be approved in a case-by-case review under the relevant criteria. About 75% (2755) of the petitions had been approved as of June 2019. Regarding the

Table 33.1 Statistics of eligible case by birth year (as of June 30, 2019)

Birth year	No. case reviewed	Eligible	Not-eligible				Petition
		Eligible	Not eligible	Preliminary to review	Total	In process	
2009	561	**419**	142	0	142	0	Expired
2010	523	**382**	141	0	141	0	Expired
2011	502	**355**	147	0	147	0	Expired
2012	516	**361**	155	0	155	0	Expired
2013	476	**351**	125	0	125	0	Expired
2014–2018	1098	887	158	44	202	9	Valid
Total	3676	2755	868	44	912	9	

petitions of babies born in the system's first year (2009), the reviews were completed in early 2015, while petitions of patients born in 2010 or later were processed within the appropriate 5-year windows as described previously. There were 419 eligible cases among those born in 2009, followed by 382 in 2010, 355 in 2011, 361 in 2012, and 351 in 2013, which seems to demonstrate a downward trend (Table 33.1). As of June 2019, 868 (24%) of the petitions had been deemed ineligible. The reasons for rejection were studied in depth by the Steering Committee of the JOCS-CP. The most common reasons were that the petition did not meet the case-by-case review criteria in that the pH of umbilical arterial blood exceeded 7.1 and/or the fetal heart rate pattern did not meet the criteria for hypoxia during labor and delivery as specified by the standard compensation agreement. The next most common reasons for rejection were that the cerebral palsy was clearly congenital (i.e., caused by major brain anomalies, chromosomal abnormalities, genetic abnormalities, etc.) and/or caused by conditions that emerged during or after the neonatal period, such as meningitis. Petitions rejected by the Review Committee may petition the Appeal Review Committee by providing a rationale for the initial claim. Of the 181 cases rejected by the Review Committee that appealed, only four petitions had been approved. Thus, the Appeal Review Committee has mostly supported the Review Committee's decisions.

33.6 Investigation: Identifying Error During Delivery

Investigation is a primary pillar of the JOCS-CP process aimed not only at preventing cerebral palsy, but also at mitigating conflict and reaching speedy resolutions and settlements (Fig. 33.3). To achieve these goals, an Investigative Report is provided to the relevant childbirth facility and to the patients' guardians/family. Investigative Reports result from intensive scientific investigations using sufficient data from childbirth facilities and input from the patients' guardians/families. During the introductory and early years of the JOCS-CP, some obstetricians on the frontline who were not engaged in the operation of the JOCS-CP rigorously opposed sharing Investigative Reports with childbirth facilities and families because they feared that the report could provoke conflict and potentially lawsuits, which had not been the case before the JOCS-CP was commenced. On the contrary, another group of obstetricians and patient representatives claimed that the Investigative Reports would meet the families' expectations to learn the cause of cerebral palsy because scientific experts had generated them. Years later, the number of lawsuits did indeed decrease rapidly, as had predicted the latter group of obstetricians and patient representatives.

The JQ has equipped itself with seven sub-committees as working groups to produce the Investigative Reports. Each sub-committee comprises five obstetricians (the chair and four drafting members), two neonatologists, one midwife,

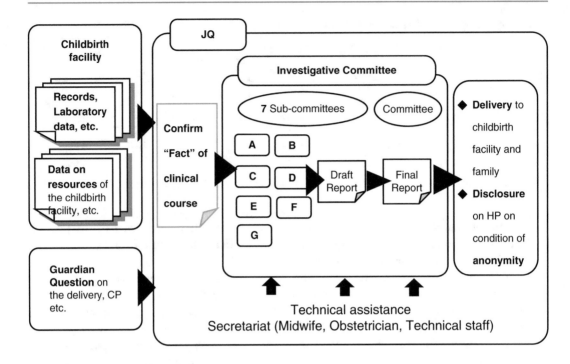

Fig. 33.3 Production of standardized investigative report

and two lawyers (one representing the physician and the other representing the family). The lawyers are appointed from a list of recommendations provided by the Japan Federation of Bar Associations in response to JQ's request. The investigative procedure proceeds as follows. Petitions approved by the Review Committee are sent to the sub-committees, which then draft Investigative Reports. The Investigation Committee handles about 400 such reports per year. The five physicians and the midwife mostly provide medical perspective and the two lawyers draft standardized Investigative Reports that include clear points of contention which are easy for lay people to understand. The reports are structured with tables of contents and uniform language within and across reports to clearly convey meaning. A manual was written to guide the standardization of the investigative work and reporting. The sub-committees produce drafts that are reviewed by the Investigative Committee to finalize them. Summaries of the final Investigative Reports with all personal identifiers deleted are posted on the JOCS-CP website for

scientific use and to ensure transparency. As of June 2019, 2369 Investigative Reports had been published. The website includes a keyword search engine so that users can locate cases of interest. Copies of the originals are also available on request with personal identifiers deleted after confirmation by JQ's ethics committee of the reason for the request and so on. Because Japan's Ethical Guidelines for Medical and Health Research Involving Human Subjects, revised on April 1, 2015, might influence the disclosure of Investigative Reports, JQ revised the disclosure process to conform to the revised ethical rules. Since November of 2015, JQ's ethics committee has put into effect revised procedures for disclosure. The concept and policy of producing Investigative Reports focuses on production of an Investigative Report that fully satisfies guardians/families. Therefore, the goals, concepts, and policies are stated in the manual of investigative work as described below:

1. The Investigative Report does not aim to accuse any party, but to elucidate the probable

causes of profound cerebral palsy and to specify ameliorative measures in order to prevent similar future events.

2. The Investigative Report should be simple enough for guardians/families, Japanese citizens, and lawyers to understand, and they should be trustworthy.

3. The investigations should be conducted using data gathered during the course of delivery as well as data providing context, such as medical histories of diseases and terms of pregnancy.

4. Delivery procedures, pregnancy management, and so on should be reviewed from a prospective viewpoint in terms of appropriate procedures or management when the event in question, such as hypoxia, occurred.

5. Ameliorative measures for the improvement of perinatal care should be explored from a retrospective viewpoint using all of the data collected from the childbirth facility.

6. The Investigative Committee highly prioritizes its consensus that the prospective viewpoint and the retrospective viewpoint should not be confused to avoid hindsight bias.

33.7 Controversy on Disclosing Preventability in Individual Cases

Since the inception of the system, there has been controversy regarding whether to include the "possibility of avoiding cerebral palsy" as determined by the Investigation Committee in an Investigative Report. Obstetricians have worried that stating that cerebral palsy might have been prevented could create conflict, potentially involving lawsuits. Obstetricians were afraid such statements might appear to be an accusation of negligence, despite the systems' goals and its policy of not placing blame. The chair of the Investigative Committee stressed that these statements should not be included in the Investigative Reports because the "possibility of avoidance" is often interpreted as the type of negligence feared by many physicians.

On the other hand, some of the Investigative Committee members, including patient representatives, argued that Investigative Reports should explore the possibilities for avoiding cerebral palsy to help in devising effective preventive measures. Ultimately, these members capitulated and agreed with the chair's position because investigations cannot be carried out without the cooperation and commitment of the medical professionals. The Investigative Committee reached an agreement on December 15, 2009, in which the members in support of the doctors' position presented ways to work on the "possibility of avoidance" issue in the Investigative Report. After controversial arguments, the chair put forth a conciliatory document as a compromise on the issue. The text of that document, which might be a useful reference for investigative work in general, reads as follows.

33.7.1 Guidance for "The Items to Consider for Better Obstetrical/Perinatal Care" Section of the Investigative Report

- Preventive measures that might be helpful should be described under "The items to consider for better obstetrical/perinatal care" in the Investigative Report after considering every possible preventive act through intense investigation of procedures and/or management during pregnancy and delivery in comparison with methods of prevention that have been successful in similar cases.

- Items under "The items to consider for better obstetrical/perinatal care" in the Investigative Report should be described using the tone and phrasing exemplified by "It is desirable to be educated and trained in neonatal resuscitation" and "It is strongly recommended that cesarean section or forceps delivery is immediately performed when vacuum delivery is not effective."

- If multiple preventive measures are proposed, they should be presented in order of importance.

- When cerebral palsy is caused by low-quality or dangerous managerial or procedural practices, the childbirth facility should be urged to improve those practices as soon as possible. To this end, the Investigative Report should clearly state the causes and the relevant preventive measures.

33.7.2 Guidance for Handling Questions from Guardians/Families During the Investigative Process

- In the Investigative Report, the Investigative Committee should answer all questions from the guardian/family from a medical perspective to the greatest extent possible.
- When a guardian/family member asks, "How could the cerebral palsy in our case have been prevented?" the Investigative Committee should provide as complete an answer as possible.
- Answers to questions from the guardian/family are written in a document entitled "Annex."
- The "Annex" must be provided to the childbirth facility and to the guardian/family.
- The contents of an "Annex" should not be disclosed by the JOCS-CP, and it is understood that disclosure by the guardian/family cannot be controlled.

33.8 Survey on the Investigative Report

The JOCS-CP initiated the investigative procedures in line with the LDP Framework on the premise that the Investigative Reports would be accepted by the childbirth facilities and the guardians/families and that they would be effective for improving perinatal quality of care and safety. In 2015, a survey on the effectiveness of the Investigative Report was conducted to ascertain whether the Investigative Reports had been embraced by both childbirth facilities and guardians/families. The results found that childbirth facilities and guardians/families mostly supported the Investigative Report's policy, with about 73% of the facilities and 65% of the guardians/families responding "very good" or "mostly good." The

most frequently cited reason for approving of the Investigative Report was that "analysis was conducted by a third party," suggesting that they attached significant importance to the neutrality and fairness of a third party. Also of note is that, in response to the question about how well the report worked, about 14% of the guardians/families but just 3% of the childbirth facilities answered "not very good." The difference in the figures is most likely closely related to the fact that 84% of guardians/families who answered "not very good" marked "the cause of cerebral palsy was not eventually determined" as the reason, compared to 58% of the childbirth facilities. Approximately 36.3% of the Investigative Reports concluded that the cause of cerebral palsy was uncertain or unknown. It seems that the guardian/family respondents tended to expect that the Investigative Committee can always identify probable causes of cerebral palsy given that it is made up of medical experts specializing in perinatal care.

33.9 Most Frequent Errors

1. **Prevention—Identification of probable cause of cerebral palsy**

   All Investigative Reports are aggregated and put through systematic analysis by the Prevention Committee to create knowledge for the prevention of cerebral palsy through improvements to obstetrical and perinatal care (Fig. 33.4). The JOCS-CP publishes an annual Prevention Report, the latest including 2113 Investigative Reports in its analysis. The JOCS-CP disseminates the preventive measures described in the Prevention Reports as effectively as possible by employing distribution methods which successfully worked in other JQ projects such as Adverse Event Reporting and Learning Systems. The annual Prevention Report specifically includes quantitative and epidemiological analyses of relevant data—such as maternal data, clinical course of pregnancy, delivery and neonatal periods, institutional human resources, and the healthcare provision system—and thematic analysis using data on the causes of cerebral palsy described in the Investigative

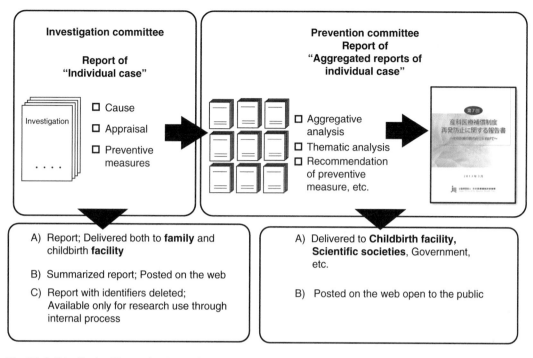

Fig. 33.4 Distributing "Prevention Report" to encourage quality improvement

Reports, fetal heart rate monitoring records, records on the administration of uterine-contracting agents and clinical procedures (such as forced delivery and neonatal resuscitation), availability of medical devices, organizational structure, and other childbirth-related resources and equipment. Aggregate analyses have been used to create tables of probable causes of cerebral palsy approved by the JOCS-CP. The JOCS-CP is the only institution in Japan that has data on probable causes of cerebral palsy on a large scale, although similar results on far smaller scales have been reported. Placental abruption and bleeding, and umbilical factors are the most common causes of cerebral palsy, followed by intrauterine infections and uterine ruptures. However, it should be noted that Investigative Reports failed to determine the causes of the cerebral palsy in 36.3% of the approved individual cases, suggesting that a significant proportion of cerebral palsy cases have unknown origins despite the current, advanced state of relevant research. The guardians/families and other non-experts generally do not know that knowledge of

medical science is limited at this point which potentially increases the likelihood of conflicts between guardians/families and medical professionals. Therefore, it is important for the JOCS-CP to disseminate among our society what is known and what is not known about the causes of cerebral palsy, including the fact that the causes of cerebral palsy have not yet been fully elucidated.

2. **Prevention—Frequent errors and thematic analysis**

The thematic analyses included in the Prevention Report are conducted in accordance with JQ's other projects, such as the Nationwide Adverse Event Reporting and Learning Systems, and are recognized as effective tools for medical professionals to apply to in-depth data on adverse events, in this case cerebral palsy and preventive measures. Twenty themes have been addressed to date. The themes treat error-prone procedures and management which deserve improvement. The themes are as follows:

(a)   Vacuum delivery
(b)   Uterine contracting agent

(c) Kristeller maneuver and Pressing maneuver on uterine fundus
(d) Fetal heart rate monitoring during delivery
(e) Umbilical factor except for umbilical prolapse
(f) Umbilical prolapse
(g) Intrauterine infection
(h) Uterine rupture
(i) Placental abruption
(j) Maternal education for early detection of placental abruption
(k) Premature birth
(l) Multiple pregnancy
(m) Pregnancy induced hypertension
(n) Detonated all transfusion syndrome
(o) Neonatal care
(p) Neonatal resuscitation
(q) Case in which neonatal resuscitation is not needed within 5 min after birth
(r) Follow-up statistics of the past themes
(s) Medical chart recording
(t) Emergent transfer system of the pregnant woman and/or baby

Prevention reports are based on thorough study of aggregated Investigative Reports and include assessments of procedures implemented during maternal screening, labor and delivery, and recommended preventive measures. Those elements are presented according to the standardized "Table of contents" in each Investigative Report. The standardization of individual reports enables quantitative and qualitative analysis and a better understanding of the prevention of profound cerebral palsy. The structure of the thematic analyses in the Prevention Report is also carefully standardized.

33.10 Safety Practices and Implementation Strategy

The information gleaned from the Prevention Report strongly influences obstetricians and midwives because it is generated from data on cases of cerebral palsy which actually took place in Japanese childbirth facilities. The Prevention

Reports published to date are available on the JOCS-CP website in PDF and CSV file formats. The thematic analysis is displayed in a particularly user-friendly fashion through a list of individual PDFs grouped by theme. In 2017, the Japan Society of Obstetricians and Gynecologists (JSOG) and JAOG revised the guidelines for obstetrical care, entitled "Guidelines for obstetrical practice in Japan." The guidelines address five clinical questions using knowledge gained from thematic analyses of the Prevention Reports and the book on Cardiotocogram interpretation for profound cerebral palsy. Therefore, it is increasingly apparent that the JOCS-CP is a provider of up-to-date knowledge on perinatal care for the medical professionals of Japan's scientific community. The information generated by the Prevention Reports is shared with pregnant women as well as medical professionals for better understanding their pregnancies. One of the leaflets for experts stresses the importance of consent in cases of induced labor using uterine-contracting agents. It recommends that the consent document includes indications of the agents, drug-related side effects, possible treatments related to side effects, alternative drug options, and procedures to ensure patient safety during labor and delivery. Similarly, a leaflet for pregnant women depicts the standard practice of early skin-to-skin contact and highlights key items such as informed, written consent, the safe positioning of the baby, the baby's expected body temperature, and so on. Patient representatives of the Prevention Committee have made enormous contributions to the leaflets for pregnant women, mothers with neonates, and family members.

33.11 Two Clinical Cases

The Prevention Report includes not only quantitative analysis but also qualitative and thematic analysis. The latter describes specific facts, procedures, management, and probable cause of cerebral palsy, along with recommendations. Here, we present two cases from the report which are closely related to patient safety.

33.11.1 Case 1

33.11.1.1 Clinical Course

The patient presented with genital bleeding and abdominal stiffness with lower abdominal pain and was admitted to the clinic. She was diagnosed with imminent birth, and ritodrine hydrochloride was therefore administered intravenously. A labor-monitoring device was applied to the patient and dosage of ritodrine hydrochloride was increased in relation to the continuation of symptoms. The baseline fetal heart rate was 130 bpm with late deceleration. On observing the fetal heart rate pattern, the physician paused labor monitoring. However, the monitoring resumed approximately 1 h and 30 min later and the device showed that the baseline variability of fetal heart rate (FHR) had decreased and mild variable deceleration manifested. Therefore, the patient was transferred to another hospital, where premature abruption of placenta was suspected. Cardiotocography (CTG) demonstrated a highly decreased FHR and mild variable deceleration. Ultrasonography revealed further thickened placenta. The physician suspected that a cesarean section was emergently needed and therefore suggested and explained the procedure to obtain consent of the patient and a member of their family. Testing for the surgery was conducted in a hurried manner. Subsequently, an emergent cesarean section was initiated approximately 1 h after consent was obtained. The baby was born 21 min after the cesarean section was initiated, with birth weight of 2540 g, umbilical cord arterial blood pH of 6.7, and BE of −27 mmol/L. Apgar score was determined to be 1 after 1 min and 1 after 5 min. Neonatal resuscitation was conducted by Bag-Valve-Mask (BVM) ventilation, tracheal intubation, and chest compression. The baby was diagnosed with premature birth and severe neonatal asphyxia. Pathological testing of the placenta displayed chorioamnionitis. Twelve days after the birth, MRI imaging revealed severe hypoxic encephalopathy (HIE).

33.11.1.2 Probable Cause of Cerebral Palsy

(a) Cerebral palsy was likely caused through hypoxia and academia of the fetus brought on by premature abruption of the placenta.

(b) Intrauterine infection might have affected the placental abruption.

(c) The abruption supposedly took place before admission although it is difficult to identify the time of occurrence precisely.

33.11.1.3 Evaluation of Procedures

(a) Ritodrine hydrochloride was increased and the patient was kept under observation with the clinical findings that fetal heart monitoring revealed decreased variability of the baseline and frequent mild and severe late deceleration. These findings are not commonly seen in clinical practice. The pattern should be interpreted as fetal insufficiency which requires subsequent decision-making by the physician, including cesarean section according to the clinical guidelines.

(b) It is common practice that the clinic would transfer the patient to the hospital based on findings of decreased variability of the baseline and mild variable deceleration.

(c) It is common that, based on the ultrasonography findings, the physician would conduct blood tests and recommend cesarean section, obtaining the written consent of the patient and the family member.

(d) It is a common finding that the fetal heart rate pattern shows decreased variability of the baseline and fluctuates repeatedly by a decrease of 15 bpm for 1 min followed by recovery to normal.

(e) However, it does not reflect common practice that the physician did not plan the cesarean section faster, making the decision to move the patient to the operating theater about 1 h after obtaining consent.

(f) It is common practice that the physician would plan grade A cesarean section after having identified fetal bradycardia from

115 bpm to 80 bpm and complete delivery by cesarean section in 21 min.

33.11.1.4 Recommendations

For the clinic:

(a) Participation in internal and/or external education and training with cardiotocograms is encouraged for better interpretation. In addition, staff may participate in conferences organized by the hospital about the transferred case.
(b) Staff are encouraged to study clinical guidelines on delivery to make correct differential diagnosis of placental abruption from imminent birth.

For the hospital:

(a) Participation in internal and/or external education and training with cardiotocograms is encouraged for better interpretation.
(b) Staff is encouraged to follow clinical guidelines when placental abruption is suspected in a patient.

33.11.2 Case 2

33.11.2.1 Clinical Course

The patient was in the clinical course of her first pregnancy and undergoing regular check-ups by the hospital. She was pregnant with dichorionic-diamniotic (DD) twins. The second twin eventually developed cerebral palsy. The patient was obese with a BMI of 33.9 before she became pregnant. She had been diagnosed with diabetes mellitus which was treated with insulin during the previous 5–6 years. She was diagnosed with imminent birth in the 33rd gestational week and treated with ritodrine hydrochloride. The intravenous injections were administered until the 35th gestational week. In the 36th week, the patient manifested spontaneous membrane rupture and labor pain was noted. The labor was induced by oxytocin as it was too weak to keep in observation. The first twin was delivered after 10 h and 53 min through a joint maneuver of uterus com-

pression and four-round vacuum delivery. Around the time of the first twin's birth, the fetal heart rate pattern of the second twin exhibited decreased variability of the baseline. The findings further deteriorated after the birth of the first twin, showing repetition of late deceleration and bradycardia. The second twin was eventually delivered through four rounds of uterus compressions and six rounds of vacuum delivery. The second twin was born in the 36th gestational week with birth weight of 2610 g. Analysis of umbilical arterial blood sample exhibited a pH of 6.6 and BE −34 mmol/L. The baby's Apgar score was determined to be 0 after 1 min and 0 after 5 min. The baby went into cardiac arrest at birth, and therefore cardiac resuscitation was immediately attempted through manual ventilation, chest compression, tracheal intubation, and injection of adrenaline. Spontaneous heartbeats were observed 14 min after the initiation of the resuscitation. The baby was subsequently moved to a NICU where mechanical ventilation was applied. Hypothermia was initiated for the baby 4 h after birth; however, it was terminated on Day 1 after birth when ultrasonography of the brain revealed extensive bleeding in the bilateral hypothalamus. As hemoglobin levels dropped to 7.4 g/dL, blood transfusion was conducted. Brain CT imaging reported (1) high density of the right ventricular wall suggesting subependymal hemorrhage, (2) enlarged ventricules and subaponeurotic hemorrhage, and (3) low density of cerebral white matter bilaterally suggesting previous hypoxia and immaturity of the brain structure.

33.11.2.2 Probable Cause of Cerebral Palsy

(a) The baby developed cerebral palsy probably due to hypoxic conditions and associated fetal circulatory failure which took place during the delivery of the first twin and continued for approximately 40 min eventually causing severe hypoxia in the second baby.
(b) Fetal hypoxia was supposedly caused by rapid uterine contraction after the birth of the first twin followed by increased intrauterine pressure and umbilical factors such as umbilical cord compression.

(c) Vacuum delivery of the first twin jointly performed with uterine compression maneuver may have caused hypoxia in the second twin.

(d) Furthermore, it cannot be denied that the application of the uterine compression maneuver in the delivery of the second twin contributed as a deteriorating factor.

(e) In addition, it is probable that the loss of circulatory volume due to subaponeurotic hemorrhage and to the cardiac arrest at birth that lasted for 14 min gave rise to cerebral palsy.

33.11.2.3 Evaluation of Procedures

(a) Management of imminent birth, procedural selection of delivery, description of risk in consent procedure of second baby during delivery of twins, the procedures that were applied when the patient underwent spontaneous rupture of the membrane in the 36th gestational week are all common practice.

(b) In contrast, it does not reflect common practice that the medical staff did not ensure intravenous line until full dilation in the patient with gestational diabetes mellitus who suffered hypoglycemia.

(c) Dosage of oxytocin to begin injection and dosage acceleration strayed from the guidelines.

(d) In terms of judgment and procedure, it is standard that the physician diagnosed the patient with prolonged active phase of delivery and decided to implement vacuum delivery; however, it is not standard that delivery ultimately ended with a contraction period of 43 min and that the uterine compression maneuver was applied to the delivery of the first twin.

(e) It does not reflect common practice that the physician increased the dosage of oxytocin and did not provide the patient with oxygen amid suspicion of fetal insufficiency.

(f) It is acceptable to select vacuum delivery as the method of emergent delivery for the second twin.

(g) It is controversial from a medical point of view to apply the uterine compression maneuver for the second twin because while some claim that it effectively helps vacuum

delivery, others claim that it may prompt uterine rupture or failure of placental circulation.

(h) It is common for the delivery to be conducted in the presence of a pediatrician upon request.

(i) The procedure of neonatal resuscitation was in compliance with standards.

33.11.2.4 Recommendations

For the hospital:

(a) Management of delivery of twins
- It is known that the proceedings of the clinical course of delivery vary even when carefully planned. Therefore, it is desirable that the decision of whether to continue to attempt vaginal delivery or to resort to emergent cesarean section should be made deliberately and swiftly.
- In addition, when attempting vaginal delivery of the second twin, cesarean section should always be a ready option for securing the well-being of the second twin.
- Uterine compression maneuver should be carefully applied during the birth of the first twin, taking into consideration that it may affect placental circulation for the second twin.

(b) Administration of uterine contracting agent
- Prescription and administration of uterine contracting agents should firmly abide by the latest clinical guidelines generated by academic and professional societies.

(c) Pathological testing of placenta
- It is recommended that pathological testing of placenta should be performed as it is vital to explore the cause of neurological symptoms of a baby that may be observed at and after birth.

(d) Management and monitoring system for vaginal delivery of twins
- The physician explained to the patient soon after birth that they had tried vacuum delivery as it would have taken 30 min to conduct a cesarean section no matter how fast they worked on delivery during the procedure.

- It is desirable that systems for an emergent cesarean section are always ready as a cesarean section for the second twin is seen with some frequency.
- A notice from the Ministry of Health, Labour and Welfare regarding the improvement of regional capabilities to provide perinatal care states that it is desirable for a regional center for perinatal care to be staffed with obstetricians, anesthesiologists, and other relevant staff to be able to conduct emergent cesarean section within 30 min.
- If this is not possible within the context of the hospital, the hospital should consider whether to conduct delivery in an operating room or conduct the cesarean section in the delivery ward.

For academic and professional society:

(a) It is desirable to produce in-depth guidance for the vaginal delivery of twins.

33.12 Recommendations

JOCS-CP has conducted preventive activities, particularly thematic analysis, which produce recommendations related to the aforementioned themes. It is vital for medical professionals to take into account the recommendations for providing high standards of healthcare in the perinatal system. Excerpts from the recommendations are listed below.

33.12.1 Vacuum Delivery

For obstetricians:

(a) Vacuum delivery should be done in a timely manner with the appropriate procedures.
- It should be conducted by a trained physician or a physician under guidance of trained physician.
- The physician to conduct vacuum delivery should consider the clinical course,

including the mother's well-being, the baby's station, and fetal head rotation, and strictly follow the rules of indication and relevant conditions for implementation.

(b) Procedures of delivery should be reviewed where necessary during delivery.
- Clinical guideline on delivery states that alternative measure such as cesarean section for delivery should be explored in expedited manner when delivery do not proceed with baby's head at zero station. If that is the case, it should be noted that trained staffs are ready for neonatal resuscitation.

(c) It should be recognized that delivery with uterine compression maneuver could bring harm to the well-being of the fetus.
- Uterine compression maneuver should be applied only a couple of times when needed to complete delivery.

(d) A baby delivered through vacuum delivery should be carefully observed for a certain period after birth.

For academic and professional societies:

(a) Education on vacuum delivery should be provided at the institutional level.
(b) Clinical guidelines developed by academic and professional societies should be shared among member physicians.
(c) The guideline should include with more detailed description items to be carefully noted about vacuum delivery and the observation of a baby delivered through vacuum delivery.

33.12.2 Administration of Uterine Contracting Agents

For obstetricians:

(a) Indications, condition, and contraindications should be carefully considered. Patient consent should be documented. In case of emergent administration after verbal consent, it should be recorded in writing.

- Fetal well-being should be reviewed before administration.
- The fetus should be carefully monitored with a fetal heart-monitoring device after the administration of uterine contracting agents because they may cause hypercontraction of the uterus. The administration should be reviewed upon observing bradycardia of the fetus.
- Uterine contracting agents should be prescribed and administered in accordance with the dosage and administration guidelines specified in the package insert.

(b) Concomitant administration of multiple uterine contracting agents.

- PGF2α and oxytocin should not be concomitantly administered with PGE2. A 1-h interval should be kept between their administrations.

(c) Labor induction procedure amid administration of uterine contracting agents.

- Cervical dilation should precede the administration of uterine contracting agents. Cervical dilating agents and uterine contracting agents should not be concomitantly given to patient.
- A balloon dilator may be applied preceding uterine contracting agents with a 1-h interval.

For academic and professional societies:

(a) Clinical guidelines should detail the dosages of uterine contracting agents and uterine dilating agents and the appropriate intervals of administration.

(b) If possible, a standard should be created for the monitoring of labor with administration of uterine contracting agents.

33.12.3 Fetal Heart Rate Monitoring

For medical facilities:

(a) Fetal heart rate should be carefully monitored, paying attention to the following items:

- During the latent phase of labor, no abnormal pattern should be initially observed by continuous monitoring with monitoring device for 20 min. The next period of continuous monitoring should be done within 6 h, with intermittent monitoring every 15–90 min during the same phase.
- In case of lack of monitoring devices in the facility (e.g., a midwife facility), the fetal heart rate should be monitored every 15 min during the latent phase of delivery and every 5 min during the active phase. Monitoring should be done for at least 60 s after uterine contraction to interpret any change in heart rate due to the contraction.
- Physicians and midwives may conduct continuous monitoring throughout the latent period.

(b) The clinical guidelines should include the requirement for 20 min of continuous monitoring.

(c) The clinical guidelines should include any other requirements for continuous monitoring of fetal heart rate.

(d) The transducers of the monitoring device should be correctly applied to the patient. The site of application and the belt to fix the transducers may be changed and fastened or loosened as needed for proper functioning.

(e) Recording of fetal heart rate should be done with attention to the following items:

- The time of the recording should be standardized.
- The fetal heart rate should be recorded on paper at a speed of 3 cm/min for accurate visualization of the heart rate pattern.
- The fetal heart recording should be stored with the medical chart which must be stored for 5 years by regulation.
- Clinical findings related to the monitoring (e.g., fetal heart rate and status of labor) should be appropriately described on the medical chart.

For academic and professional societies:

(a) The clinical guidelines should be revised to improve understanding of the general procedures of monitoring in delivery and the specific monitoring procedures (1) after appreciation of labor, (2) with administration of uterine contracting agents, (3) during TOLAC, (4) after full rupture of membrane, and (5) in high-risk pregnancy such as a prolonged active phase of delivery potentially causing fetal insufficiency. In addition, the revised guidelines should be distributed among medical professionals in perinatal care.

(b) Midwives should have access to facility guidelines on procedures of intermittent fetal heart rate monitoring and should understand the necessity of the periodic application of a monitoring device as well as continuous monitoring.

(c) That the fetal heart rate should be recorded on paper at a rate of 3 cm/min should be made widely known in academic and professional societies.

33.12.4 Care for Placental Abruption

For pregnant mothers:

(a) Patients should consult childbirth facilities as soon as possible if they perceive symptoms relating to placental abruption, rather than endure them. These symptoms include vaginal bleeding, abdominal pain, stiffness of the abdomen, and decrease or lack of fetal movement.

(b) Pregnant women must pay special attention to relevant symptoms if they may carry risk factors related to placental abruption, including pregnancy-induced hypertension syndrome, past history of placental abruption and trauma caused by traffic accident, and age of 35 years or older.

For obstetricians:

(a) Management of pregnancy
   • All patients should be informed of early onset symptoms of placental abruption (i.e., vaginal bleeding, abdominal pain,

stiffness of the abdomen, decrease of fetal movement) by the time they reach the 30th gestational week.
   • Health education and attentive health check-ups should be provided to patients who bear risk factors (e.g., pregnancy-induced hypertension) with a physician's full awareness of those factors.

(b) Diagnosis of placental abruption
   • Fetal heart rate monitoring device should be applied to the patient for a certain duration (20 min or longer) to check the well-being of the fetus on admission of all patients and during any consultation in which the patient manifests abnormal signs.
   • The possibility of placental abruption should be considered when symptoms suggestive of imminent birth and any abnormality in the fetal heart rate pattern are observed. Subsequently, differential diagnosis should follow in accordance with the clinical guidelines using ultrasonography, blood tests (i.e., CBC), serum chemistry, blood coagulation, and fetal heart rate monitoring.
   • Placental abruption should be clinically examined, noting not only typical manifestations (i.e., abdominal pain, stiffness of the abdomen, vaginal bleeding, decrease or lack of fetal movement) but also atypical ones such as lumber pain. Furthermore, symptoms suggestive of initiation of delivery, such as labor onset and the sensation of water breaking, could be observed.
   • All medical professionals relevant to childbirth should receive education and training on CTG interpretation, whether in-house or externally.

(c) Care to provide after the diagnosis with placental abruption is made
   • The fetus should be delivered as soon as possible, both under careful maternal management of DIC and fetal management of premature birth. When planning the delivery, the type of forced delivery,

presence of pediatrician, and necessary transfer of mother and/or baby should be taken into consideration among other factors.

- Neonatal resuscitation should be in line with the latest clinical guidelines. In addition, indication of hypothermia should be deliberated when baby is resuscitated.
- The medical chart may be produced after care and must record details such as complaints of the pregnant mother, internal examination, ultrasonography, fetal heart rate monitoring, transfer of the mother, and the performance of a cesarean section.

(d) System to provide emergent care

- Standardized emergency communication flow should be implemented for prompt treatment of the patient, covering the receipt of a call from a patient who complains of symptoms suggestive of placental abruption (i.e., vaginal bleeding, abdominal pain stiffness of the abdomen, decrease of fetal movement) and its prompt correspondence to medical professionals.
- Institutional standards should be created for the prompt treatment of placental abruption as to prompt forced delivery without transfer, request of maternal and/or neonatal transfer and presence of pediatrician in reference to context of the institution such as staffing for emergent surgery, care to provide the patient including blood transfusion, neonatal resuscitation, other neonatal care including hypothermia, etc.
- Procedures should be established for emergent calls for medical staff and effective communication of the level of emergency. In addition, emergency systems should be routinely improved through simulation training to provide emergent care.
- Childbirth facilities should be ready in advance to provide care for a patient who has been transferred with placental abruption or probable placental abruption. It is desirable for care plans to be deliberated upon the arrival of the patient, evaluating the well-being of the fetus and placental abruption.

For academic and professional societies:

(a) Research on the cause and early diagnosis of placental abruption is encouraged to aggregate individual cases.

(b) Public outreach is encouraged to let it be widely known that
- Placental abruption is an emergent state of disease which threatens the life of the fetus.
- Placental abruption may have profound consequences for the mother.
- Patients should consult a childbirth facility as soon as possible when they suspect they may suffer the disease.

(c) The development of guidelines for the education of pregnant mothers should be encouraged. The guidelines should outline symptoms which suggest placental abruption and actions they must take.

For central and local governments:

(a) Maternal/fetal transfer systems should be reinforced on a regional scale when they are at risk, as should regional centers for perinatal care. In particular, it is recommended to establish transfer systems beyond prefectural jurisdiction.

(b) Projects should be financed to research causes and early diagnosis of placental abruption.

Further Readings

1. Japan Council for Quality Health Care, Japan Obstetric Compensation System for Cerebral Palsy (JOCS-CP). Available from: www.sanka-hp.jcqhc.or.jp/index.html (in Japanese).
2. Ushiro S, Suzuki H, Ueda S. Japan Obstetric Compensation System for Cerebral Palsy: Strategic system of data aggregation, investigation, amelioration and no-fault compensation. J Obstet Gynaecol

Res. 2019;45(3):493–513. https://doi.org/10.1111/jog.13906.

3. The Japan Obstetric Compensation System for Cerebral Palsy patterns. Cardiotocograms of cerebral palsy cases-interpretations and considerations of FHR. Part 1 of the book: http://www.sanka-hp.jcqhc.or.jp/documents/statistics/pdf/Cardiotocograms_of_Cerebral_Palsy_Cases_No.1.pdf. Part 2 of the book: http://www.sanka-hp.jcqhc.or.jp/documents/statistics/pdf/Cardiotocograms_of_Cerebral_ Palsy_Cases_No.2.pdf. Part 3 of the book: http://www.sanka-hp.jcqhc.or.jp/documents/statistics/pdf/Cardiotocograms_of_Cerebral_Palsy_Cases_No.3.pdf. Part 4 of the book: http://www.sanka-hp.jcqhc.or.jp/documents/statistics/pdf/Cardiotocograms_of_Cerebral_Palsy_Cases_No.4.pdf.

Coping with the COVID-19 Pandemic: Roles and Responsibilities for Preparedness

34

Michela Tanzini, Elisa Romano, Aldo Bonaventura, Alessandra Vecchié, and Micaela La Regina

34.1 Introduction

The novel coronavirus disease, COVID-19, was identified in China in December 2019. The responsible agent, SARS-COV2, was first isolated in China on January 9, 2020.

Since then, thanks to a globalized world, the absolute susceptibility of the world population to a new virus and an unprecedented situation, the infection has spread worldwide, infecting until now (May 16th 2020) 462,660,327 people in 188 countries and killing 311,363 individuals [1].

Skill sets such as patient safety management and quality of care are indispensable to battling the critical issues posed by the pandemic, as they proactively and retroactively reveal weaknesses in the healthcare system. Unfortunately, in many regions where these valuable skills are present, they have not been directly applied in task forces for the management of the outbreak. Harm caused by a lack of knowledge of a new pathogen is unpredictable and in no way preventable. However, harm caused by foreseeable and preventable errors can be mitigated or avoided thanks to a systemic approach to risk management.

In this chapter, a clinical risk management perspective will be used to analyze how the world has coped with the crisis so far, highlighting measures that could have or should have been taken. The WHO pandemic plan will form the framework for the analysis. Since the pandemic is still ongoing, it should be noted that the analysis cannot be exhaustive and the solutions presented are preliminary.

M. Tanzini · E. Romano
Italian Network for Safety in Healthcare (INSH),
Florence, Italy

A. Bonaventura
Pauley Heart Center, Division of Cardiology,
Department of Internal Medicine, Virginia
Commonwealth University, Richmond, VA, USA

First Clinic of Internal Medicine, Department of
Internal Medicine, University of Genoa, Genoa, Italy

A. Vecchié
Pauley Heart Center, Division of Cardiology,
Department of Internal Medicine, Virginia
Commonwealth University, Richmond, VA, USA

M. La Regina (✉)
S.S. Risk Management, ASL5 Liguria,
La Spezia, Italy
e-mail: micaela.laregina@asl5.liguria.it

34.2 COVID-19 Summary

1. **What is COVID-19?**

   COVID-19 stands for **CO**rona**VI**rus **D**isease 20**19** and is a disease caused by a new betacoronavirus, the severe acute respiratory syndrome-associated coronavirus 2 (SARS-CoV-2).

2. **What are the symptoms of COVID-19?**

   Fever, coughing, and shortness of breath are typical symptoms in patients with COVID-

© The Author(s) 2021
L. Donaldson et al. (eds.), *Textbook of Patient Safety and Clinical Risk Management*,
https://doi.org/10.1007/978-3-030-59403-9_34

19. In the most severe cases, the infection may cause pneumonia and acute respiratory failure, the latter being potentially life-threatening. The symptoms are similar to those of the common flu or cold and for this reason a diagnostic evaluation is needed to rule out COVID-19 in patients with flu-like symptoms.

3. **How does COVID-19 spread out?**

The SARS-CoV-2 is typically transmitted via liquid droplets exhaled during speech or aerosol particles produced with coughing, breathing, and sneezing. Also, transmission may occur through direct contact with contaminated surfaces, mainly of hands which then make contact with the face, in particular the eyes, nose, and mouth. SARS-CoV-2 can survive on various surfaces (i.e. plastic, stainless steel, copper, and cardboard) for 4–72 h. However, common multi-surface cleaners are able to remove the virus.

4. **Who is at higher risk of COVID-19?**

As the virus is new, limited knowledge is available. However, initial data from cohorts of patients in China showed that elderly people with multiple comorbidities, such as hypertension, diabetes, and malignancies, are likely to be at higher risk for severe and potentially life-threatening disease. Current data have shown that children are not infected very often, and, in the case of infection, the symptoms are mild and the outcome is overall good.

5. **How do we treat COVID-19?**

To date, no approved treatments for COVID-19 are available and the management is supportive. Prompt medical assistance is essential for early treatment of the disease. A mismatch between symptoms (e.g., shortness of breath) and clinical findings (severe hypoxia) has been commonly observed and leads patients to seek medical advice only when the disease is in an advanced stage.

34.3 Magnitude of COVID-19

The pandemic has affected 188 countries and the number of deaths and affected patients worldwide is very significant. The situation still varies greatly from country to country as across the regions of Italy, probably due to the differing prevention strategies implemented.

34.4 Fundamental Aspects of the WHO Pandemic Plan

In 2005, following the outbreaks of avian influenza caused by the A/H5N1 virus, which was endemic in animals of the Far East and led to serious infections in humans, the WHO published the "WHO global influenza preparedness plan" [2] consisting of six phases, each of them including targets and specific actions that may be performed on a national or international level. The actions are divided in five different categories.

A global objective is identified for each phase. Governments are asked to adjust the plan to account for their own particular contexts and the state of the pandemic within their nation, and to provide precise recommendations for the indicated actions.

34.4.1 Phases

Interpandemic period
1. New influenza virus subtypes are detected only in animals and pose a low risk for humans.
2. New influenza virus subtypes pose a substantial risk for human disease localized to specific geographical regions.

Pandemic alert period
3. Human infection occurs with a new subtype, but human-to-human transmission is rare.
4. Small, highly localized clusters of infection form with limited human-to-human transmission. The virus is not well adapted to humans.
5. Large clusters of infection form with localized human-to-human transmission. The virus is adapted to humans and there is a real pandemic risk.

Pandemic period
6. Virus transmission in general population.

Postpandemic period
Return to Interpandemic period.

34.4.2 Framework

1. Planning and coordination.
2. Situation monitoring and assessment.
3. Prevention and containment (i.e. non-pharmaceutical public health interventions, vaccines, and antivirals).
4. Health system response.
5. Communication.

34.4.3 Overarching Goals

- **Interpandemic period, Phase 1**
  - Strengthen influenza pandemic preparedness at the global, regional, national, and sub-national levels.
- **Interpandemic period, Phase 2**
  - Minimize the risk of transmission to humans. Detect and report such transmission promptly if it occurs.
- **Pandemic alert period, Phase 3**
  - Ensure rapid characterization of the new virus subtype and early detection, notification, and response for additional cases.
- **Pandemic alert period, Phase 4**
  - Contain the new virus within limited foci or delay spread to gain time to implement preparedness measures, including vaccine development.
- **Pandemic alert period, Phase 5**
  - Maximize efforts to contain or delay spread to possibly avert a pandemic and to gain time to implement pandemic response measures.
- **Pandemic period, Phase 6**
  - Minimize the impact of the pandemic.

34.4.4 Key Actions

SURVEY	Improve virological and epidemiological surveillance
PREVENT	Implement infection prevention and control measures: • Public health interventions • Prophylaxis with antivirals • Vaccines
CURE	Coordinate patient care and assistance

KEEP	Develop plans to maintain health and essential services
TRAIN	Establish training programs
COMMUNICATE	Prepare communication strategies
CHECK	Continue monitoring • Planned actions by risk phase • Available resources • Additional resources needed • Effectiveness of interventions performed

Key actions require the implementation of specific intervention, for which actors and responsibilities must be identified.

34.5 Criticalities in the Application of the WHO Pandemic Approach During the COVID-19 Outbreak

34.5.1 Planning and Coordination

In order to adequately deal with a devastating emergency, such as the Covid-19 pandemic, it is fundamental to plan for the occurrence of similar situations even in unsuspected times.

Indeed, the pandemic plan requires WHO to coordinate member countries by taking on the role of a superior reference body [2]. A suspected underestimation of the current crisis, also by such superior reference body, had an impact mainly on the western world, which naively believed that it would be spared from what turned out to be a worldwide danger.

In particular, the most affected countries did not procure the necessary resources in the years between health crises. While countries had to develop effective mechanisms to stock up on "a global stockpile (e.g., antivirals, personal protective equipment, vaccines, laboratory diagnostics)" [2], in some countries, in particular Italy and Spain, the lack of personal protective equipment (PPE) among healthcare personnel has led to the spread of the infection in hospitals and care institutions.

During both Phase 1 and Phase 2, when the danger became more evident, effective strategies to protect health workers were not planned. In

Phases 3 and 4, strong emphasis should have been placed on ensuring proper coordination between the various actors involved in order to effectively engage the pandemic threat. The waves of the contagion could have been kept at bay by efficient identification and check of outbreaks, and the sharing of appropriate instructions, additional resources, and simple and immediate guidelines. Instead, the exchange of information between neighboring countries and the international coordination of emergency responses have happened too late. During Phase 5, which rapidly precipitated into Phase 6, attempts were made to remedy the mistakes made, learning from the most affected countries. It is precisely the lessons learnt which will allow us to prevent such a worldwide tragedy from happening again in the future.

34.5.2 Situation Monitoring and Assessment

Monitoring must be continuous and adopt a transversal approach, integrating and analyzing information systems data, in order to make an effective assessment.

The lack of information on the epidemiological and virological monitoring from China in the early stages of the disease and the subsequent delay in taking appropriate actions to assess the risk of a pandemic will certainly be analyzed worldwide at the end of the emergency. The various levels of responsibility, with subsequently difficult international solutions, will be also identified. The Western countries did not prepare themselves adequately because they did not have on hand, especially in the early stages, reliable and accurate information on the new viral strain and on the epidemiological trend of the disease. Yet the national and international objectives and actions of the aforementioned framework stated precisely what to do and how to do it. Unfortunately, the wasted time has resulted in tens of thousands of deaths. Thankfully, after a period of recovery, scientific communities across the globe have been quick to share data on new viral strains, develop a

diagnosis, experiment with new therapeutic protocols, and work towards the production of a vaccine.

34.5.3 Prevention and Containment

Prevention and containment measures include actions aimed to avoid or slow down the spreading of infection, such as non-pharmaceutical Public Health Measures (PHM), vaccines, and antivirals [2].

PHMs include individual protective measures for the target community [3], such as:

- Hand-hygiene.
- Face masks.
- Respiratory etiquette.
- Environmental measures.
- Surface and object disinfection.
- Travel restrictions such as border closure, tourism restrictions, entry and exit screening at airports and ports.
- Social distancing to reduce crowding and potential restrictions on nonessential activities; for example, in many workplaces and schools, "key-workers" may continue to work with extra precautions, while other employees should work from home wherever possible.
- Contact tracing, self-isolation of exposed individuals, and quarantine of those infected. The length of time suggested for quarantine and self-isolation will depend on the estimated period of infectivity of the pathogen.

These measures aim to delay and reduce the size of the "peak" of an infection trend and to slow transmission, so that the impact of the pandemic is mitigated and hospitals are not overwhelmed. Cultural, socioeconomic, regulatory, and political factors can affect or limit the application of PHMs with serious, preventable consequences for the entire population.

First of all, updated national guidance on PHMs should be available in the interpandemic period (Phases 1 and 2). Included interventions must be planned and shared with decision-makers from sectors other than healthcare (e.g., transportation) to avoid subsequent conflict that can delay implementation. Necessary resources and legal authority should be addressed in advance. Proposed interventions should be tested in simulations and improved. During the pandemic period (Phases 3–6), contingency measures should be assessed and improved in affected countries and prepared in those not yet affected [2].

During the Covid-19 pandemic, given the lack of effective vaccines or treatments [4] the only tool currently available to reduce SARS-CoV-2 transmission has been to identify and isolate contagious individuals.

Each country has implemented different strategies of prevention and control with varying results. For example, poorer nations have tended to introduce stricter measures than richer countries, relative to the severity of their outbreaks; their abundance of caution maybe be due to the fact that their healthcare systems are generally less developed. Europe, Sweden, the United Kingdom, and the Netherlands were relatively slow to take action. In the early stages of their epidemics, all three implemented "herd immunity" strategies, which involved few measures or relied on voluntary compliance. Later, however, the United Kingdom and the Netherlands switched to more aggressive responses, including country-wide lockdown. Meanwhile, Germany and Austria adopted aggressive control strategies early on, as compared to Italy, France, and Spain, which implemented similar measures, including lockdown, but later in their epidemics. So far, Germany and Austria have seen fewer deaths per capita attributed to COVID-19 than the other countries mentioned. A transmission model built on contact survey data for Wuhan and Shangai before and during the outbreak and on contact tracing information from Hunan Province has allowed the impact of social distancing and school closure on transmission to be studied and has shown that social distancing alone, as implemented in China, is sufficient to control COVID-19. Meanwhile, proactive school closures can reduce peak incidence by 40–60% and delay the epidemic.

It is also becoming increasingly clear that testing is a relevant contributing factor in controlling the epidemic. At present, countries such as South Korea and Singapore, and Italian regions like Veneto that have implemented aggressive contact tracing, broader case definitions, and/or intensive testing (i.e., case findings), in conjunction with isolation, have achieved better results [5]. Emerging evidence shows an inverse correlation between the number of tests per million inhabitants and rates of active infections, new cases, and deaths [6].

34.5.4 Healthcare System Response

This category includes interventions aimed to plan (interpandemic phase 1 and 2) and to deliver (pandemic phases 3–5) a timely, appropriate, safe, and coordinated response of healthcare facilities to pandemic. So, in the interpandemic phases 1 and 2, any healthcare organization should

- Provide itself with contingency plans with clear indications of authorities, responsibilities, and pathways.
- Set priorities and produce guidance about triage systems, surge capacity, specimen handling, diagnostic test deployment, human and material resource management.
- Share protocols or algorithm for case-finding, treatment and management, infection control guidelines.
- Increase awareness and skills of healthcare workers on pandemics.
- Assess pharmaceuticals and PPE inventory to secure supply [2].

Phases 3 and 4 include:

- The activation of emergency coordinating committees (at national, regional, and local levels).

- The start of a pre-established coordination between the healthcare sector and its partners for avoiding nosocomial transmission and laboratory infections, and ensuring biosafety.
- The review of contingency plans (especially surge capacity).
- The test of decision-making process and command chain [2].

Phases 5 and 6 focus is on the full implementation of contingency plans. The objective is to ensure that healthcare systems are able to scale up their response and implement changes in triage or treatment priorities for the efficient use of healthcare facilities. At the end of the pandemic or between waves, it must be ensured that healthcare staff have due rest, inventory is taken of supplies, plans are revised in anticipation of subsequent waves, and essential services are reinforced [2].

Apart from the inevitable issues arising from facing an unknown pathogen and the continuous acquisitions of knowledge determining continuous adjustments of strategies and protocols, the most common dysfunctions observed in terms of healthcare system responses during Covid-19 are listed below:

1. **Poorly coordinated application of the national pandemic plan and frequent derailing of systemic measures taken within a hierarchical decision-making process**. During the initial phase, patients tended to be treated in hospitals, disregarding primary care services. Later, in Italy, the best performing regions in mitigating the propagation of the pandemic were those with an early involvement and more robust organization of primary care services, such as Toscana and Veneto.

2. **Conflicting indications about essential issues**. The WHO's recommendation to "wear a mask if you are coughing or sneezing" [7] did not consider asymptomatic patients. Furthermore, if masks protect people besides the wearer, the prescription of wearing a mask should have been extended to everyone to ensure a more healthy environment. National authorities have followed the international policies to alleviate their responsibility and/or liability, but forgetting that global measures usually express minimum standards.

3. **Global shortage of Personal Protective Equipment (PPE)**. If not adequately protected, healthcare workers representing the first line of defense against the virus can infect colleagues and patients and be quarantined, leading to the depletion of the healthcare workforce. The WHO has estimated that

nearly 89 million masks per month are required to face the Covid-19 pandemic, along with 76 million examination gloves and 1.6 million medical goggles. The supply of PPE, antivirals, and vaccines is an essential component of the healthcare system response to the pandemic. The determinants of the shortage seen include the off-shoring of PPE production to low-cost manufacturers, the abrupt disruption of production in the People's Republic of China, the first country hit by Covid-19, trade restrictions, and export bans [8].

4. **Global shortage of diagnostic test reagents**. This shortage is caused by the same reasons as the PPE shortage and it represents a serious problem in infection controls, considering the increasing value of intensive testing strategies. In any case, reagent production is not the only bottleneck: the lack of qualified technicians and labs running the tests has caused a cascade of dysfunctions, including laboratory congestion and staff overload, elevated need for specimen transportation, and manual order entry and reporting for outsourced tests leading to losses of information, identification errors, and delays in analyzing and communicating results. In addition, the diagnostic performance has been hampered by over-restrictive testing criteria and lack of swab technique standardization (increased number of false negative).

5. **Failure to learn from previous and current experiences**. There are several causes for this failure:
   (a) Confirmation bias, the tendency to focus on information that confirms our preferred position or initial hypothesis. Threats such as pandemics that evolve in a nonlinear fashion (i.e., via exponential growth) are especially tricky to confront because of the challenge to rapidly interpret events occurring in real time. It is most effective to take strong action extremely early, when the threat appears to be small or potentially even before there are any confirmed cases. However, if the intervention actually works, those

same actions will likely be considered an overreaction in retrospect.

(b) Over-reliance on "gut feeling" or the opinions of one's inner circle. In a time of uncertainty, it is essential to resist this temptation and instead take the time to collect partial knowledge dispersed across different fields of expertise.

(c) Dependence on incomplete solutions instead of a systematic approach. An effective response to the virus needs to be orchestrated as a coherent system of actions taken simultaneously. The results of the approaches taken in China and South Korea underscore this point.

(d) Individualization and politicization of emergency management.

(e) Inadequate collection and dissemination of data.

(f) Sunk cost bias and premature closure, two cognitive biases that obstruct the revision of previously made decisions.

6. **Structural limitations of emergency departments and/or wards** have negatively affected safety, hindering the isolation of suspect cases.

7. **Reduced staffing of public health units**, which have been responsible for the administration of vaccines for decades, has prevented aggressive contact tracing.

8. **The lack of primary care resources** has initially compromised the home management of patients, before the forced reorganization.

9. **Delayed or insufficient treatment of non-Covid-19 patients**. For example, during the week of the 12th of March when the maximum daily infection rate was reached in Italy, the number of admissions to hospitals for heart attacks was half that of the same week in 2019, while the mortality more than tripled. The two figures are not contradictory, but suggest that many people suffering from a heart attack did not go to the hospital and those who did arrived late in more critical condition. The time between the onset of symptoms and the angioplasty increased by over 39.2%, so that, in absolute terms, the number of deaths from heart failure almost doubled in hospitals

within the period considered, despite the fact that far fewer patients were treated [9].

34.5.5 Communication

Clear, consistent, and timely communication is crucial for managing disaster and emergency response efforts. Without proper communication, misinformation and misinterpretation can flourish and result in injury or fatalities. A communications manager should be identified and involved in the task force to support communications strategies at all levels, international, national, regional, and local. Proper communication management during a health pandemic must also include both operational messages addressed to health workers and public safety announcements. In any case, there are general criteria for effective communication regardless of the target audience.

34.5.5.1 Make the Message Clear
Information must be presented with simplicity and clarity so that everyone understands the context and the instructions to follow. The aim is to outline the situation, highlighting the necessary background information, as well as the actions that need to be taken or will be taken soon.

34.5.5.2 Keep the Message Consistent
As important as clarity, the consistency of a message helps ensure that everyone is on the same page. There may be more than one authority sharing information so all messages must be in agreement. When information is presented, it needs to be with one voice; this is particularly important for avoiding misinformation and miscommunication.

It can also help to repeat the same message so there is less room for confusion. People become disoriented during emergencies and may need to hear the same message multiple times before it sinks in.

34.5.5.3 Timeliness
Being open and sharing information as soon as possible are important communication techniques

during a pandemic to promote trust and reliability. The risk of miscommunication and incorrect assumptions increases when time goes by without any novel information or updates. Even when there is nothing new to report, reassure others with a repeating message as well as a rough timeline for when new information will be available.

Messages should be timely, consistent, and clear across all communication platforms. While these platforms often include TV and radio, there is another resource that is being used more and more for immediate information: social media.

34.5.5.4 Monitor Social Media

Social media has become a major information source for many people. According to the Global Digital Report released in 2019, the number of social media users worldwide had risen to nearly 3.5 billion in early 2019, with 288 million new users in the previous 12 months, bringing global usage to 45%.

Due to its widespread use and ability to update instantaneously, social media platforms need to be utilized and monitored. In an effort to keep the messages clear and consistent, communication managers must address any misinformation and provide the correct information before it gets out of control.

34.5.5.5 Select the Most Appropriate Method of Communication

The right methods of communication can reach all people affected by a crisis, and can be reliable even with limited accessibility. Integrated strategies with municipalities and voluntary associations must also be development so that messages are distributed as widely as possible.

Furthermore, it is necessary to clarify the roles and responsibilities of relevant parties when sharing purely operational messages related to diagnosis, treatment, etc. Situation awareness—that is, taking the right steps at the right times—should be integral to collaborative efforts.

During the current pandemic, on the other hand, we have witnessed a phenomenon of "overcommunication" in which the following critical issues were encountered: *ambiguous messages*, such as incomplete or distorted information regarding the use of PPE for both healthcare professionals and citizens; *inconsistent messages*, as a result of too

many experts expressing their own point of view; and *unclear messages*, such as recommendations that are called into question, retracted, and possibly reaffirmed in quick succession.

34.6 Improvement Actions Based on Lessons Learned

In the context of clinical risk management (CRM), the analysis of an incident report ends with recommendations in order to share the lessons learned with others and thereby avoid re-occurrence of the incident. Here, we present a series of suggestions that have been developed with reference to documents and papers published by Italian national institutions (such as Istituto Superiore di Sanità, I.S.S.) and international scientific societies and journals, based on reports and questions forwarded to the clinical risk managers of the Italian Network for Health Safety (INSH) from physicians working on the front line during the Covid-19 epidemic outbreak [10]. Recommendations are available in 5 languages at: https://isqua.org/blog/covid-19/covid19-resources/patient-safety-recommendations-for-covid19-epidemic-outbreak.html.

To ensure effective collaboration and communication, it is essential to promptly activate an emergency task force with a clear chain of command, roles, and responsibilities, equipped with reliable information-sharing tools. The task force should adopt a proactive approach, providing the front line with clear and continuously updated information, maintaining a streamlined reporting and learning system, and collecting and disseminating good practices. CRM units can play a relevant role in this setting. In addition, key human factors messages to help under pressure [11] should be implemented: (1) short but inclusive briefing and de-briefing, (2) open and inclusive leadership, (3) clarity of roles, (4) clear language protocols, (5) to ask questions—open questions—before acting, (6) to focus on what not on who, (7) to help staff unfamiliar with the work, (8) to use checklists, (9) to encourage staff to speak up and collect staff concern, (10) to take a pause before thinking what to do, (11) to recognize performance limiting factors each other, as anyone is not good at recognizing them him/herself.

Healthcare organizations should provide early and appropriate instructions for environment disinfection (e.g. regarding detergents, duration, and frequency) to prevent in-hospital infection spread, arrange germicide galenic preparations to avoid insufficient supply, and designate a hospital or building for infected patients rather than separate clean/dirty pathways in the same block. Hospital contamination can be further reduced by screening patients admitted for any reason (e.g. surgery, coronary angioplasty, labor and delivery), by restricting access and establishing mandatory precautionary measures for visitors (i.e. surgical masks and 1 m of separation between waiting room seats), and by limiting or suspending nonurgent hospital admissions, routine outpatient appointments, and postponable surgical procedures.

Early educational training and refresher courses are useful to enhance staff awareness and skills regarding infection transmission and management, medical and protective devices, and pandemic-related patient safety practices such as hand hygiene, the SEPSIS bundle, and the bundle for the prevention of ventilator-associated pneumonia or central venous catheter infections. A preliminary evaluation of surge capacity is highly recommended to aid in the creation of a competence-based strategy for staff re-allocation during the emergency. Expert doctors and nurses should be supported early-on by young colleagues or colleagues from other specialties, who should receive proper training in preparation of the event that they may be called upon to take over.

Shortages of PPE must be prevented by taking continual stock of supplies and establishing policies for limited reuse or extended use, for secure, centralized storage and distribution, and for distribution priorities. Every effort should be made to ensure that medical devices (i.e., haemogas-analyzers, pulsi-oximeter, mechanical ventilators, suction pumps, and oxygen therapy) are available in care areas and are well-functioning.

34.6.1 General Guidelines

The development of reliable clinical pathways to reduce preventable harm requires the identification of high-risk steps in the diagnosis and treatment of infection, in care transitions (i.e., hospital discharge), and in special settings or categories of patients (e.g., surgery, obstetrics, pediatric care, oncologic or immunosuppressed patients). The following points should be addressed for safe diagnosis and treatment:

- With regard to diagnostic tests
  - Availability of diagnostic tests.
  - Reliability and timeliness of the diagnostic process.
  - Clear and updated criteria.
  - Standardization and quality validation.
  - Knowledge of uncommon presentations.
- With regard to treatment
  - Possible complications and prognostic factors.
  - Criteria for severity stratification for safe discharge or in-hospital allocation.
  - Parameters to monitor and to be alarmed for.
  - Criteria for setting upgrade.
  - Recall on drug-drug or drug-disease interactions.
  - Eventual not recommended drugs or other treatment precautions (i.e. in COVID-19 patients nebulizers are not recommended for the potential spread of virus; non-invasive ventilation is suggested only in selected patients for no more than 1–2 h in case of unresponsiveness).

During discharge, information transferred must be clear and structured: it is important to address follow-ups and social or work-related restrictions, such as whether the patient is cured or only clinically cured, whether the patient needs home isolation, and any precautions to be observed in case of home isolation.

34.6.2 Guidelines for Obstetrics and Pediatrics

In obstetrics, pandemic-related risk management is focused on the prevention of maternal and newborn contagion. To minimize the exposure of the mother, prenatal care may be limited, cases screened, and quarantine protocols implemented. To protect the newborn, water birth may be avoided, extra precautions may be taken during breastfeeding (e.g. use of a breast pump), and the mother and newborn may be separated. It should be noted that Covid-19 is not a criterion for pre-term delivery or cesarean section.

To prevent unnecessary risks for children, changes in clinical presentation, laboratorial or instrumental examinations, and management must be highlighted for parents.

34.6.3 Guidelines for Caring for Immunocompromised Patients

For oncologic and other immunocompromised patients, good practices ensure the safety of required procedures and adequate infection pre-vention. To this end, the postponement of anti-neoplastic treatment should be evaluated on a case-by-case basis; in any case, immunosuppres-sant drugs must not be suspended, but dose increases should be postponed and a route of administration suitable for home treatment should be considered. Steroids can be continued with cautions. To minimize the risk of infection, indi-vidual protective measures must be thoroughly applied, and limitations should be put in place for visitation in therapy rooms or hospital wards.

34.6.4 Guidelines for Special Contexts

In special contexts such as surgery or autopsy, particular attention must be payed to the environ-ment and operator safety to avoid infection spreading. Preventive measures may include the use of negative pressure environments, appropri-ate PPE, mindfulness of aerosol-generating pro-cedures, granting access to the operating theater only to essential staff, and reliably reporting cases of infection.

34.6.5 Guidelines for General Practitioners

It is helpful to create special continuity units that visit people at home to prevent infection spread-ing and patient harm. In addition, general practi-tioners are strongly recommended to

- Educate patients about infection transmission and prevention.
- Inform patients about designated pathways for suspected/affected subjects.
- Reduce office contamination by avoiding overcrowding, preventing suspected patients access, appropriate cleaning, and utilizing PPE.
- Use tools for the early identification of cases and for the classification of the severity.
- Use checklists to avoid missing information and to ensure regulatory compliance.
- Strictly follow-up on home-managed cases.

34.6.6 Guidelines for Long-Term Care Facilities

In long-term care facilities and nursing homes, as well as in residential psychiatric facilities, risks can be reduced by

- Appropriate cleaning.
- The limitation of external visits and contact with the hospital.
- Restrictions on physical contact and careful, clinical monitoring of residents.
- Daily screening and measurement of body temperature for healthcare workers.
- Prompt isolation of suspected cases among residents or healthcare workers.
- Possible accommodation within the facility for healthcare workers.
- Provision of appropriate PPE.
- The creation of a filter area for new or return-ing residents.
- The creation of an isolation area for affected not requiring hospitalization.

34.6.7 Guidelines for Hemodialysis Patients

Recommended interventions include:

- Separate paths for affected/suspected cases.
- Screening and measurement of body temperature upon any access for patients and healthcare workers.
- Prompt referral to assessment and eventual isolation of suspected cases among patients and healthcare workers.
- Preference for home dialysis if feasible.
- Wide staggering of appointments and prohibition of carer access to waiting room.
- Use of private means of transportation or organization of individual medical transportation.
- Periodic screening with serologic tests or swabs of patients and healthcare workers according to local epidemiological trends.

Last, but not least, every effort must be made to ensure safe and appropriate care for noninfected patients. The rapid conversion of many hospitals to Covid-19 treatment centers should not hamper emergency care. Explicit priority criteria and dedicated, clean paths should be identified, taking into account pandemic status, hospital resources, and the need to avoid harmful delays in patient treatment, especially for oncologic patients.

34.7 Conclusions

Pandemic is a complex problem and the range of action must take into account the geographical area involved, international and national regulations, production autonomies and commercial exchanges, lifestyle, culture and ethical values of the affected population, available technology, characteristics of care facilities, organization of the doctor-patient unit, and safety of staff, patients, and uninfected citizens.

Only a careful "*a posteriori*" analysis will allow to understand if the suspected delayed alarm by China and lack of awareness of the epidemic spread in other countries was due to lightness, incompetence, negligence, or guiltiness. The global involvement and the self-defense carried on by the countries involved will not help to fully clarify the responsibilities. However, we must learn from this tragedy that no event, albeit improbable, should be considered impossible.

China may have thought it have done everything possible to contain the contagion in a defined area, but forgot that probably the virus had already arrived in the rest of the world. The difference for other countries was the ability of national organizations to react in terms of resilience (Box 34.1) [12].

Box 34.1 The Four Essential Abilities of Resilience

- **The ability to respond**. Knowing what to do, or being able to respond to regular and irregular changes, disturbances, and opportunities by activating prepared actions or by adjusting current mode of functioning.
- **The ability to monitor**. Knowing what to look for, or being able to monitor that which is or could seriously affect the system's performance in the near term—positively or negatively. The monitoring must cover the system's own performance as well as what happens in the environment.
- **The ability to learn**. Knowing what has happened, or being able to learn from experience, in particular to learn the right lessons from the right experience.
- **The ability to anticipate**. Knowing what to expect, or being able to anticipate developments further into the future, such as potential disruptions, novel demands or constraints, new opportunities, or changing operating conditions.

All four abilities are necessary.

To **respond** to a critical event effectively, the organization **learn** what and how to do it, identifying who does it and with what resources.

Monitoring requires learning from experiences; thus, it will allow you to effectively **anticipate** dangerous situations [13].

Asia, Europe, Africa, the USA, Canada, South America, Australia, the entire planet has suffered an epochal arrest, paying a very high price in terms of life, economic recession, and political credibility. Yet everything was predictable, it was enough to think that it could happen.

References

1. COVID-19 Dashboard by the Center for Systems Science and Engineering (CSSE) at Johns Hopkins University (JHU). https://coronavirus.jhu.edu/map. html. Accessed 16 May 2020.
2. WHO global influenza preparedness plan. The role of WHO and recommendations for national measures before and during pandemics. https://www.who.int/csr/resources/publications/influenza/WHO_CDS_CSR_GIP_2005_5.pdf. Accessed 16 May 2020.
3. World Health Organization. Non-pharmaceutical public health measures for mitigating the risk and impact of epidemic and pandemic influenza: annex: report of systematic literature reviews. Contract No.: WHO/WHE/IHM/GIP/2019.1. Geneva: World Health Organization; 2019.
4. Cheng MP, Lee TC, Tan DHS, Murthy S. Generating randomized trial evidence to optimize treatment in the COVID-19 pandemic. CMAJ. 2020;192(15):E405–7.
5. Cheng MP, Papenburg J, Desjardins M, Kanjilal S, Quach C, Libman M, et al. Diagnostic testing for severe acute respiratory syndrome-related coronavirus-2: a narrative review. Ann Intern Med. 2020;172(11):726–34.
6. Ghosal S, Sinha B, Sengupta S, Majumder M. Frequency of testing for COVID 19 infection and the presence of higher number of available beds per country predict outcomes with the infection, not the GDP of the country - a descriptive statistical analysis. medRxiv. 2020:2020.04.01.20047373.
7. Coronavirus disease (COVID-19) advice for the public: when and how to use masks. https://www.who.int/emergencies/diseases/novel-coronavirus-2019/advice-for-public/when-and-how-to-use-masks. Accessed 17 May 2020.
8. Global shortage of Personal Protective Equipment amid Covid-19: supply chains, bottlenecks and policy implications, ADB brief, No. 130. 2020. https://www.adb.org/sites/default/files/publication/579121/ppe-covid-19-supply-chains-bottlenecks-policy.pdf. Accessed 18 May 2020.
9. De Rosa S, Spaccarotella C, Basso C, et al. Reduction of hospitalizations for myocardial infarction in Italy in the COVID-19 era. Eur Heart J. 2020;41(22):2083–8.
10. ISQUA/INSH. Patient safety recommendations for COVID-19 epidemic outbreak. https://www.isqua.org/images/COVID19/PATIENT_SAFETY_RECOMMENDATIONS_V2.0_04052020.pdf. Accessed 18 May 2020.
11. Clinical Human factors group, Key Human Factors messages when under pressure. https://chfg.org.
12. Hollnagel E. How resilient is your organisation? An introduction to the Resilience Analysis Grid (RAG). Sustainable transformation: building a resilient organization, Toronto, Canada. 2010:hal-00613986. https://hal-mines-paristech.archives-ouvertes.fr/hal-00613986/document. Accessed 18 May 2020.
13. Hollnagel E, Pariès J, Woods DD, Wreathall J. Resilience engineering in practice. a guidebook. Ashgate: Farnham, UK; 2011.

Printed in the United States
by Baker & Taylor Publisher Services